W9-CHU-175

The Fundamentals

A Testimony to the Truth

"To the Law and to the Testimony"
Isaiah 8:20

Edited by R. A. Torrey, A. C. Dixon and Others

VOLUME I

Baker Books

A Division of Baker Book House Co
Grand Rapids, Michigan 49516

Reprinted from the original
four-volume edition issued by
the Bible Institute of Los Angeles in 1917.

Reprinted 2003 by Baker Books
a division of Baker Book House Company
P.O. Box 6287, Grand Rapids, MI 49516-6287

ISBN: 0-8010-1264-3
Two Volume Set

Printed in the United States of America

For information about academic books,
resources for Christian leaders, and all new
releases available from Baker Book House,
visit our web site:
http://www.bakerbooks.com/

CONTENTS

VOLUME I

(The Fundamental set contains four volumes)

CONTENTS

PREFACE

In 1909 God moved two Christian laymen to set aside a large sum of money for issuing twelve volumes that would set forth the fundamentals of the Christian faith, and which were to be sent free to ministers of the gospel, missionaries, Sunday School superintendents, and others engaged in aggressive Christian work throughout the English speaking world. A committee of men who were known to be sound in the faith was chosen to have the oversight of the publication of these volumes. Rev. Dr. A. C. Dixon was the first Executive Secretary of the Committee, and upon his departure for England Rev. Dr. Louis Meyer was appointed to take his place. Upon the death of Dr. Meyer the work of the Executive Secretary devolved upon me. We were able to bring out these twelve volumes according to the original plan. Some of the volumes were sent to 300,000 ministers and missionaries and other workers in different parts of the world. On the completion of the twelve volumes as originally planned the work was continued through The King's Business, published at 536 South Hope St., Los Angeles, California. Although a larger number of volumes were issued than there were names on our mailing list, at last the stock became exhausted, but appeals for them kept coming in from different parts of the world. As the fund was no longer available for this purpose, the Bible Institute of Los Angeles, to whom the plates were turned over when the Committee closed its work, have decided to bring out the various articles that appeared in The Fundamentals in four volumes at the cheapest price possible. All the articles that appeared in The Fundamentals, with the exception of a very few that did not seem to be in exact keeping with the original purpose of The Fundamentals, will be published in this series.

R. A. TORREY

DEDICATION

To the two laymen whose generosity made it possible to send several millions of volumes of "The Fundamentals" to ministers and missionaries in all parts of the world, for their confirmation and upbuilding in the faith, these volumes are dedicated.

THE FUNDAMENTALS

CHAPTER I

THE HISTORY OF THE HIGHER CRITICISM.

BY CANON DYSON HAGUE, M. A.,

RECTOR OF THE MEMORIAL CHURCH, LONDON, ONTARIO.

LECTURER IN LITURGICS AND ECCLESIOLOGY, WYCLIFFE COL-
LEGE, TORONTO, CANADA.

EXAMINING CHAPLAIN TO THE BISHOP OF HURON.

*What is the meaning of the Higher Criticism? Why is
it called higher? Higher than what?*

At the outset it must be explained that the word "Higher"
is an academic term, used in this connection in a purely special
or technical sense. It is not used in the popular sense of the
word at all, and may convey a wrong impression to the ordinary man. Nor is it meant to convey the idea of superiority.
It is simply a term of contrast. It is used in contrast to the
phrase, "Lower Criticism."

One of the most important branches of theology is called
the science of Biblical criticism, which has for its object the
study of the history and contents, and origins and purposes,
of the various books of the Bible. In the early stages of the
science Biblical criticism was devoted to two great branches,
the Lower, and the Higher. The Lower Criticism was employed to designate the study of the text of the Scripture, and
included the investigation of the manuscripts, and the different readings in the various versions and codices and manuscripts in order that we may be sure we have the original
words as they were written by the Divinely inspired writers.
(See Briggs, Hex., page 1.) The term generally used now-a-
days is Textual Criticism. If the phrase were used in the
twentieth century sense, Beza, Erasmus, Bengel, Griesbach,
Lachmann, Tregelles, Tischendorff, Scrivener, Westcott, and

Hort would be called Lower Critics. But the term is not now-a-days used as a rule. The Higher Criticism, on the contrary, was employed to designate the study of the historic origins, the dates, and authorship of the various books of the Bible, and that great branch of study which in the technical language of modern theology is known as Introduction. It is a very valuable branch of Biblical science, and is of the highest importance as an auxiliary in the interpretation of the Word of God. By its researches floods of light may be thrown on the Scriptures.

The term Higher Criticism, then, means nothing more than the study of the literary structure of the various books of the Bible, and more especially of the Old Testament. Now this in itself is most laudable. It is indispensable. It is just such work as every minister or Sunday School teacher does when he takes up his Peloubet's Notes, or his Stalker's St. Paul, or Geikie's Hours with the Bible, to find out all he can with regard to the portion of the Bible he is studying; the author, the date, the circumstances, and purpose of its writing.

WHY IS HIGHER CRITICISM IDENTIFIED WITH UNBELIEF?

How is it, then, that the Higher Criticism has become identified in the popular mind with attacks upon the Bible and the supernatural character of the Holy Scriptures?

The reason is this. No study perhaps requires so devout a spirit and so exalted a faith in the supernatural as the pursuit of the Higher Criticism. It demands at once the ability of the scholar, and the simplicity of the believing child of God. For without faith no one can explain the Holy Scriptures, and without scholarship no one can investigate historic origins.

There is a Higher Criticism that is at once reverent in tone and scholarly in work. Hengstenberg, the German, and Horne, the Englishman, may be taken as examples. Perhaps the greatest work in English on the Higher Criticism is Horne's

Introduction to the Critical Study and Knowledge of the Holy Scripture. It is a work that is simply massive in its scholarship, and invaluable in its vast reach of information for the study of the Holy Scriptures. But Horne's Introduction is too large a work. It is too cumbrous for use in this hurrying age. (Carter's edition in two volumes contains 1,149 pages, and in ordinary book form would contain over 4,000 pages, i. e., about ten volumes of 400 pages each.) Latterly, however, it has been edited by Dr. Samuel Davidson, who practically adopted the views of Hupfield and Halle and interpolated not a few of the modern German theories. But Horne's work from first to last is the work of a Christian believer; constructive, not destructive; fortifying faith in the Bible, not rationalistic. But the work of the Higher Critic has not always been pursued in a reverent spirit nor in the spirit of scientific and Christian scholarship.

SUBJECTIVE CONCLUSIONS.

In the first place, the critics who were the leaders, the men who have given name and force to the whole movement, have been men who have based their theories largely upon their own subjective conclusions. They have based their conclusions largely upon the very dubious basis of the author's style and supposed literary qualifications. Everybody knows that style is a very unsafe basis for the determination of a literary product. The greater the writer the more versatile his power of expression; and anybody can understand that the Bible is the last book in the world to be studied as a mere classic by mere human scholarship without any regard to the spirit of sympathy and reverence on the part of the student. The Bible, as has been said, has no revelation to make to un-Biblical minds. It does not even follow that because a man is a philological expert he is able to understand the integrity or credibility of a passage of Holy Scripture any more than the beauty and spirit of it.

The qualification for the perception of Biblical truth is neither philosophic nor philological knowledge, but spiritual insight. The primary qualification of the musician is that he be musical; of the artist, that he have the spirit of art. So the merely technical and mechanical and scientific mind is disqualified for the recognition of the spiritual and infinite. Any thoughtful man must honestly admit that the Bible is to be treated as unique in literature, and, therefore, that the ordinary rules of critical interpretation must fail to interpret it aright.

GERMAN FANCIES.

In the second place, some of the most powerful exponents of the modern Higher Critical theories have been Germans, and it is notorious to what length the German fancy can go in the direction of the subjective and of the conjectural. For hypothesis-weaving and speculation, the German theological professor is unsurpassed. One of the foremost thinkers used to lay it down as a fundamental truth in philosophical and scientific enquiries that no regard whatever should be paid to the conjectures or hypotheses of thinkers, and quoted as an axiom the great Newton himself and his famous words, "Non fingo hypotheses": I do not frame hypotheses. It is notorious that some of the most learned German thinkers are men who lack in a singular degree the faculty of common sense and knowledge of human nature. Like many physical scientists, they are so preoccupied with a theory that their conclusions seem to the average mind curiously warped. In fact, a learned man in a letter to Descartes once made an observation which, with slight verbal alteration, might be applied to some of the German critics: "When men sitting in their closet and consulting only their books attempt disquisitions into the Bible, they may indeed tell how they would have made the Book if God had given them that commission. That is, they may describe chimeras which correspond to the fatuity of their own minds, but without an understanding truly Divine they can never form such an idea to themselves as the Deity had in creating it." "If," says Matthew Arnold, "you shut a number of men up to make study and learning the business of their lives, how many of them, from want of some discipline or other, seem to lose all balance of judgment, all common sense."

The learned professor of Assyriology at Oxford said that the investigation of the literary source of history has been a peculiarly German pastime. It deals with the writers and readers of the ancient Orient as if they were modern German professors, and the attempt to transform the ancient Israelites into somewhat inferior German compilers, proves a strange want of familiarity with Oriental modes of thought. (Sayce, "Early History of the Hebrews," pages 108-112.)

ANTI-SUPERNATURALISTS.

In the third place, the dominant men of the movement were men with a strong bias against the supernatural. This is not an ex-parte statement at all. It is simply a matter of fact, as we shall presently show. Some of the men who have been most distinguished as the leaders of the Higher Critical movement in Germany and Holland have been men who have no faith in the God of the Bible, and no faith in either the necessity or the possibility of a personal supernatural revelation. The men who have been the voices of the movement, of whom the great majority, less widely known and less influential, have been mere echoes; the men who manufactured the articles the others distributed, have been notoriously opposed to the miraculous.

We must not be misunderstood. We distinctly repudiate the idea that all the Higher Critics were or are anti-supernaturalists. Not so. The British-American School embraces within its ranks many earnest believers. What we do say, as we will presently show, is that the dominant minds which have led and swayed the movement, who made the theories that the others circulated, were strongly unbelieving.

Then the higher critical movement has not followed its true and original purposes in investigating the Scriptures for the purposes of confirming faith and of helping believers to understand the beauties, and appreciate the circumstances of the origin of the various books, and so understand more completely the Bible?

No. It has not; unquestionably it has not. It has been deflected from that, largely owing to the character of the men whose ability and forcefulness have given predominance to their views. It has become identified with a system of criticism which is based on hypotheses and suppositions which have for their object the repudiation of the traditional theory, and has investigated the origins and forms and styles and contents, apparently not to confirm the authenticity and credibility and reliability of the Scriptures, but to discredit in most cases their genuineness, to discover discrepancies, and throw doubt upon their authority.

THE ORIGIN OF THE MOVEMENT.

Who, then, were the men whose views have moulded the views of the leading teachers and writers of the Higher Critical school of today?

We will answer this as briefly as possible.

It is not easy to say who is the first so-called Higher Critic, or when the movement began. But it is not modern by any means. Broadly speaking, it has passed through three great stages:

1. The French-Dutch.
2. The German.
3. The British-American.

In its origin it was Franco-Dutch, and speculative, if not skeptical. The views which are now accepted as axiomatic by the Continental and British-American schools of Higher

Criticism seem to have been first hinted at by Carlstadt in 1521 in his work on the Canon of Scripture, and by Andreas Masius, a Belgian scholar, who published a commentary on Joshua in 1574, and a Roman Catholic priest, called Peyrere or Pererius, in his Systematic Theology, 1660. (LIV. Cap. i.)

But it may really be said to have originated with Spinoza, the rationalist Dutch philosopher. In his Tractatus Theologico-Politicus (Cap. vii-viii), 1670, Spinoza came out boldly and impugned the traditional date and Mosaic authorship of the Pentateuch and ascribed the origin of the Pentateuch to Ezra or to some other late compiler.

Spinoza was really the fountain-head of the movement, and his line was taken in England by the British philosopher Hobbes. He went deeper than Spinoza, as an outspoken antagonist of the necessity and possibility of a personal revelation, and also denied the Mosaic authorship of the Pentateuch. A few years later a French priest, called Richard Simon of Dieppe, pointed out the supposed varieties of style as indications of various authors in his Historical Criticism of the Old Testament, "an epoch-making work." Then another Dutchman, named Clericus (or Le Clerk), in 1685, advocated still more radical views, suggesting an Exilian and priestly authorship for the Pentateuch, and that the Pentateuch was composed by the priest sent from Babylon (2 Kings, 17), about 678, B. C., and also a kind of later editor or redactor theory. Clericus is said to have been the first critic who set forth the theory that Christ and his Apostles did not come into the world to teach the Jews criticism, and that it is only to be expected that their language would be in accordance with the views of the day.

In 1753 a Frenchman named Astruc, a medical man, and reputedly a free-thinker of profligate life, propounded for the first time the Jehovistic and Elohistic divisive hypothesis, and opened a new era. (Briggs' Higher Criticism of the

Pentateuch, page 46.) Astruc said that the use of the two names, Jehovah and Elohim, shewed the book was composed of different documents. (The idea of the Holy Ghost employing two words, or one here and another there, or both together as He wills, never seems to enter the thought of the Higher Critic!) His work was called "Conjectures Regarding the Original Memoirs in the Book of Genesis," and was published in Brussels.

Astruc may be called the father of the documentary theories. He asserted there are traces of no less than ten or twelve different memoirs in the book of Genesis. He denied its Divine authority, and considered the book to be disfigured by useless repetitions, disorder, and contradiction. (Hirschfelder, page 66.) For fifty years Astruc's theory was unnoticed. The rationalism of Germany was as yet undeveloped, so that the body was not yet prepared to receive the germ, or the soil the weed.

THE GERMAN CRITICS.

The next stage was largely German. Eichhorn is the greatest name in this period, the eminent Oriental professor at Gottingen who published his work on the Old Testament introduction in 1780. He put into different shape the documentary hypothesis of the Frenchman, and did his work so ably that his views were generally adopted by the most distinguished scholars. Eichhorn's formative influence has been incalculably great. Few scholars refused to do honor to the new sun. It is through him that the name Higher Criticism has become identified with the movement. He was followed by Vater and later by Hartmann with their fragment theory which practically undermined the Mosaic authorship, made the Pentateuch a heap of fragments, carelessly joined by one editor, and paved the way for the most radical of all divisive hypotheses.

In 1806 De Wette, Professor of Philosophy and Theology

at Heidelberg, published a work which ran through six editions in four decades. His contribution to the introduction of the Old Testament instilled the same general principles as Eichhorn, and in the supplemental hypotheses assumed that Deuteronomy was composed in the age of Josiah (2 Kings 22:8). Not long after, Vatke and Leopold George (both Hegelians) unreservedly declared the post-Mosaic and post-prophetic origin of the first four books of the Bible. Then came Bleek, who advocated the idea of the Grundschift or original document and the redactor theory; and then Ewald, the father of the Crystallization theory; and then Hupfield (1853), who held that the original document was an independent compilation; and Graf, who wrote a book on the historical books of the Old Testament in 1866 and advocated the theory that the Jehovistic and Elohistic documents were written hundreds of years after Moses' time. Graf was a pupil of Reuss, the redactor of the Ezra hypothesis of Spinoza.

Then came a most influential writer, Professor Kuenen of Leyden in Holland, whose work on the Hexateuch was edited by Colenso in 1865, and his "Religion of Israel and Prophecy in Israel," published in England in 1874-1877. Kuenen was one of the most advanced exponents of the rationalistic school. Last, but not least, of the continental Higher Critics is Julius Wellhausen, who at one time was a theological professor in Germany, who published in 1878 the first volume of his history of Israel, and won by his scholarship the attention if not the allegiance of a number of leading theologians. (See Higher Criticism of the Pentateuch, Green, pages 59-88.)

It will be observed that nearly all these authors were Germans, and most of them professors of philosophy or theology.

THE BRITISH-AMERICAN CRITICS.

The third stage of the movement is the British-American. The best known names are those of Dr. Samuel Davidson, whose "Introduction to the Old Testament," published in 1862, was largely based on the fallacies of the German rationalists. The supplementary hypothesis passed over into England through him and with strange incongruity, he borrowed frequently from Baur. Dr. Robertson Smith, the Scotchman, recast the German theories in an English form in his works on the Pentateuch, the Prophets of Israel, and the Old Testament in the Jewish Church, first published in 1881, and followed the German school, according to Briggs, with great boldness and thoroughness. A man of deep piety and high spirituality, he combined with a sincere regard for the Word of God a critical radicalism that was strangely inconsistent, as did also his namesake, George Adam Smith, the most influential of the present-day leaders, a man of great insight and scriptural acumen, who in his works on Isaiah, and the twelve prophets, adopted some of the most radical and least demonstrable of the German theories, and in his later work, "Modern Criticism and the Teaching of the Old Testament," has gone still farther in the rationalistic direction.

Another well-known Higher Critic is Dr. S. R. Driver, the Regius professor of Hebrew at Oxford, who, in his "Introduction to the Literature of the Old Testament," published ten years later, and his work on the Book of Genesis, has elaborated with remarkable skill and great detail of analysis the theories and views of the continental school. Driver's work is able, very able, but it lacks originality and English independence. The hand is the hand of Driver, but the voice is the voice of Kuenen or Wellhausen.

The third well-known name is that of Dr. C. A. Briggs, for some time Professor of Biblical Theology in the Union Theological Seminary of New York. An equally earnest advocate of the German theories, he published in 1883 his "Biblical Study"; in 1886, his "Messianic Prophecy," and a little later his "Higher Criticism of the Hexateuch." Briggs studied the Pentateuch, as he confesses, under the guidance chiefly of Ewald. (Hexateuch, page 63.)

Of course, this list is a very partial one, but it gives most of the names that have become famous in connection with the movement, and the reader who desires more will find a complete summary of the literature of the Higher Criticism in Professor Bissell's work on the Pentateuch (Scribner's, 1892). Briggs, in his "Higher Criticism of the Hexateuch" (Scribner's, 1897), gives an historical summary also.

We must now investigate another question, and that is the religious views of the men most influential in this movement. In making the statement that we are about to make, we desire to deprecate entirely the idea of there being anything uncharitable, unfair, or unkind, in stating what is simply a matter of fact.

THE VIEWS OF THE CONTINENTAL CRITICS.

Regarding the views of the Continental Critics, three things can be confidently asserted of nearly all, if not all, of the real leaders.

1. They were men who denied the validity of miracle, and the validity of any miraculous narrative. What Christians consider to be miraculous they considered legendary or mythical; "legendary exaggeration of events that are entirely explicable from natural causes."

2. They were men who denied the reality of prophecy and the validity of any prophetical statement. What Christians have been accustomed to consider prophetical, they called dexterous conjectures, coincidences, fiction, or imposture.

3. They were men who denied the reality of revelation, in the sense in which it has ever been held by the universal Christian Church. They were avowed unbelievers of the supernatural. Their theories were excogitated on pure grounds of human reasoning. Their hypotheses were constructed on the assumption of the falsity of Scripture. As to the inspira-

tion of the Bible, as to the Holy Scriptures from Genesis to Revelation being the Word of God, they had no such belief. We may take them one by one. Spinoza repudiated absolutely a supernatural revelation. And Spinoza was one of their greatest. Eichhorn discarded the miraculous, and considered that the so-called supernatural element was an Oriental exaggeration; and Eichhorn has been called the father of Higher Criticism, and was the first man to use the term. De Wette's views as to inspiration were entirely infidel. Vatke and Leopold George were Hegelian rationalists, and regarded the first four books of the Old Testament as entirely mythical. Kuenen, says Professor Sanday, wrote in the interests of an almost avowed Naturalism. That is, he was a freethinker, an agnostic; a man who did not believe in the Revelation of the one true and living God. (Brampton Lectures, 1893, page 117.) He wrote from an avowedly naturalistic standpoint, says Driver (page 205). According to Wellhausen the religion of Israel was a naturalistic evolution from heathendom, an emanation from an imperfectly monotheistic kind of semi-pagan idolatry. It was simply a human religion.

THE LEADERS WERE RATIONALISTS.

In one word, the formative forces of the Higher Critical movement were rationalistic forces, and the men who were its chief authors and expositors, who "on account of purely philological criticism have acquired an appalling authority," were men who had discarded belief in God and Jesus Christ Whom He had sent. The Bible, in their view, was a mere human product. It was a stage in the literary evolution of a religious people. If it was not the resultant of a fortuitous concourse of Oriental myths and legendary accretions, and its Jahveh or Jahweh, the excogitation of a Sinaitic clan, it certainly was not given by the inspiration of God, and is not the Word of the living God. "Holy men of God spake as they were moved by the Holy Ghost," said Peter. "God, who at sundry times and in diverse manners spake by the prophets," said Paul. Not so, said Kuenen; the prophets were not moved to speak by God. Their utterances were all their own. (Sanday, page 117.)

These then were their views and these were the views that have so dominated modern Christianity and permeated modern ministerial thought in the two great languages of the modern world. We cannot say that they were men whose rationalism was the result of their conclusions in the study of the Bible. Nor can we say their conclusions with regard to the Bible were wholly the result of their rationalism. But we can say, on the one hand, that inasmuch as they refused to recognize the Bible as a direct revelation from God, they were free to form hypotheses ad libitum. And, on the other hand, as they denied the supernatural, the animus that animated them in the construction of the hypotheses was the desire to construct a theory that would explain away the supernatural. Unbelief was the antecedent, not the consequent, of their criticism.

Now there is nothing unkind in this. There is nothing that is uncharitable, or unfair. It is simply a statement of fact which modern authorities most freely admit.

THE SCHOOL OF COMPROMISE.

When we come to the English-writing Higher Critics, we approach a much more difficult subject. The *British-American Higher Critics* represent a school of compromise. On the one hand they practically accept the premises of the Continental school with regard to the antiquity, authorship, authenticity, and origins of the.Old Testament books. On the other hand, they refuse to go with the German rationalists in altogether denying their inspiration. They still claim to accept the Scriptures as containing a Revelation from God. But may they not hold their own peculiar views with regard to the origin and date and literary structure of the Bible without endangering either their own faith or the faith of Chris-

tians? This is the very heart of the question, and, in order
that the reader may see the seriousness of the adoption of the
conclusions of the critics, as brief a resumé as possible of
the matter will be given.

THE POINT IN A NUTSHELL.

According to the faith of the universal church, the Pentateuch, that is, the first five books of the Bible, is one consistent, coherent, authentic and genuine composition, inspired
by God, and, according to the testimony of the Jews, the statements of the books themselves, the reiterated corroborations of
the rest of the Old Testament, and the explicit statement of
the Lord Jesus (Luke 24:44, John 5:46-47) was written by
Moses (with the exception, of course, of Deut. 34, possibly
written by Joshua, as the Talmud states, or probably by Ezra)
at a period of about fourteen centuries before the advent of
Christ, and 800 years or so before Jeremiah. It is, moreover,
a portion of the Bible that is of paramount importance, for it
is the basic substratum of the whole revelation of God, and
of paramount value, not because it is merely the literature of
an ancient nation, but because it is the introductory section
of the Word of God, bearing His authority and given by
inspiration through His servant Moses. That is the faith of
the Church.

THE CRITICS' THEORY.

But according to the Higher Critics:

1. The Pentateuch consists of four completely diverse documents. These completely different documents were the primary sources of the composition which they call the Hexateuch: (a) The Yahwist or Jahwist, (b) the Elohist, (c) the
Deuteronomist, and (d) the Priestly Code, the Grundschift,
the work of the first Elohist (Sayce Hist. Heb., 103), now
generally known as J. E. D. P., and for convenience designated by these symbols.

2. These different works were composed at various peri-

ods of time, not in the fifteenth century, B. C., but in the ninth, seventh, sixth and fifth centuries; J. and E. being referred approximately to about 800 to 700 B. C.; D to about 650 to 625 B. C., and P. to about 525 to 425 B. C. According to the Graf theory, accepted by Kuenen, the Elohist documents were post-exilian, that is, they were written only five centuries or so before Christ. Genesis and Exodus as well as the Priestly Code, that is, Leviticus and part of Exodus and Numbers were also post-exilic.

3. These different works, moreover, represent different traditions of the national life of the Hebrews, and are at variance in most important particulars.

4. And, further. They conjecture that these four suppositive documents were not compiled and written by Moses, but were probably constructed somewhat after this fashion: For some reason, and at some time, and in some way, some one, no one knows who, or why, or when, or where, wrote J. Then someone else, no one knows who, or why, or when, or where, wrote another document, which is now called E. And then at a later time, the critics only know who, or why, or when, or where, an anonymous personage, whom we may call Redactor I, took in hand the reconstruction of these documents, introduced new material, harmonized the real and apparent discrepancies, and divided the inconsistent accounts of one event into two separate transactions. Then some time after this, perhaps one hundred years or more, no one knows who, or why, or when, or where, some anonymous personage wrote another document, which they style D. And after a while another anonymous author, no one knows who, or why, or when, or where, whom we will call Redactor II, took this in hand, compared it with J. E., revised J. E., with considerable freedom, and in addition introduced quite a body of new material. Then someone else, no one knows who, or why, or when, or where, probably, however, about 525, or

perhaps 425, wrote P.; and then another anonymous Hebrew, whom we may call Redactor III, undertook to incorporate this with the triplicated composite J. E. D., with what they call redactional additions and insertions. (Green, page 88, cf. Sayce, Early History of the Hebrews, pages 100-105.)

It may be well to state at this point that this is not an exaggerated statement of the Higher Critical position. On the contrary, we have given here what has been described as a position "established by proofs, valid and cumulative" and "representing the most sober scholarship." The more advanced continental Higher Critics, Green says, distinguish the writers of the primary sources according to the supposed elements as J1 and J2, E1 and E2, P1, P2 and P3, and D1 and D2, nine different originals in all. The different Redactors, technically described by the symbol R., are Rj., who combined J. and E.; Rd., who added D. to J. E., and Rh., who completed the Hexateuch by combining P. with J. E. D. (H. C. of the Pentateuch, page 88.)

A DISCREDITED PENTATEUCH.

5. These four suppositive documents are, moreover, alleged to be internally inconsistent and undoubtedly incomplete. How far they are incomplete they do not agree. How much is missing and when, where, how and by whom it was removed; whether it was some thief who stole, or copyist who tampered, or editor who falsified, they do not declare.

6. In this redactory process no limit apparently is assigned by the critic to the work of the redactors. With an utter irresponsibility of freedom it is declared that they inserted misleading statements with the purpose of reconciling incompatible traditions; that they amalgamated what should have been distinguished, and sundered that which should have amalgamated. In one word, it is an axiomatic principle of the divisive hypothesizers that the redactors "have not only misapprehended, but misrepresented the originals" (Green,

page 170). They were animated by "egotistical motives." They confused varying accounts, and erroneously ascribed them to different occasions. They not only gave false and colored impressions; they destroyed valuable elements of the suppositive documents and tampered with the dismantled remnant.

7. And worst of all. The Higher Critics are unanimous in the conclusion that these documents contain three species of material:

(a) The probably true.
(b) The certainly doubtful.
(c) The positively spurious.

"The narratives of the Pentateuch are usually trustworthy, though partly mythical and legendary. The miracles recorded were the exaggerations of a later age." (Davidson, Introduction, page 131.) The framework of the first eleven chapters of Genesis, says George Adam Smith in his "Modern Criticism and the Preaching of the Old Testament," is woven from the raw material of myth and legend. He denies their historical character, and says that he can find no proof in archæology for the personal existence of characters of the Patriarchs themselves. Later on, however, in a fit of apologetic repentance he makes the condescending admission that it is extremely probable that the stories of the Patriarchs have at the heart of them historical elements. (Pages 90-106.)

Such is the view of the Pentateuch that is accepted as conclusive by "the sober scholarship" of a number of the leading theological writers and professors of the day. It is to this the Higher Criticism reduces what the Lord Jesus called the writings of Moses.

A DISCREDITED OLD TESTAMENT.

As to the rest of the Old Testament, it may be briefly said that they have dealt with it with an equally confusing hand.

The time-honored traditions of the Catholic Church are set at
naught, and its thesis of the relation of inspiration and genuineness and authenticity derided. As to the Psalms, the harp
that was once believed to be the harp of David was not
handled by the sweet Psalmist of Israel, but generally by some
anonymous post-exilist; and Psalms that are ascribed to David
by the omnicient Lord Himself are daringly attributed to some
anonymous Maccabean. Ecclesiastes, written, nobody knows
when, where, and by whom, possesses just a possible grade
of inspiration, though one of the critics "of cautious and well-
balanced judgment" denies that it contains any at all. "Of
course," says another, "it is not really the work of Solomon."
(Driver, Introduction, page 470.) The Song of Songs is an
idyl of human love, and nothing more. There is no inspiration in it; it contributes nothing to the sum of revelation.
(Sanday, page 211.) Esther, too, adds nothing to the sum of
revelation, and is not historical (page 213). Isaiah was, of
course, written by a number of authors. The first part,
chapters 1 to 40, by Isaiah; the second by a Deutero-Isaiah
and a number of anonymous authors. As to Daniel, it was
a purely pseudonymous work, written probably in the second
century B. C.

With regard to the New Testament: The English writing school have hitherto confined themselves mainly to the
Old Testament, but if Professor Sanday, who passes as a
most conservative and moderate representative of the ·critical
school, can be taken as a sample, the historical books are "yet
in the first instance strictly histories, put together by ordinary historical methods, or, in so far as the methods on
which they are composed, are not ordinary, due rather to the
peculiar circumstances of the case, and not to influences, which
need be specially described as supernatural" (page 399). The
Second Epistle of Peter is pseudonymous, its name counterfeit, and, therefore, a forgery, just as large parts of Isaiah,

Zachariah and Jonah, and Proverbs were supposititious and quasi-fraudulent documents. This is a straightforward statement of the position taken by what is called the moderate school of Higher Criticism. It is their own admitted position, according to their own writings.

The difficulty, therefore, that presents itself to the average man of today is this: How can these critics still claim to believe in the Bible as the Christian Church has ever believed it?

A DISCREDITED BIBLE.

There can be no doubt that Christ and His Apostles accepted the whole of the Old Testament as inspired in every portion of every part; from the first chapter of Genesis to the last chapter of Malachi, all was implicitly believed to be the very Word of God Himself. And ever since their day the view of the Universal Christian Church has been that the Bible is the Word of God; as the twentieth article of the Anglican Church terms it, it is God's Word written. The Bible as a whole is inspired. "All that is written is God-inspired." That is, the Bible does not merely *contain* the Word of God; it *is* the Word of God. It contains a revelation. "All is not revealed, but all is inspired." This is the conservative and, up to the present day, the almost universal view of the question. There are, it is well known, many theories of inspiration. But whatever view or theory of inspiration men may hold, plenary, verbal, dynamical, mechanical, superintendent, or governmental, they refer either to the inspiration of the men who wrote, or to the inspiration of what is written. In one word, they imply throughout the work of God the Holy Ghost, and are bound up with the concomitant ideas of authority, veracity, reliability, and truth divine. (The two strongest works on the subject from this standpoint are by Gaussen and Lee. Gaussen on the Theopneustia is published in an American edition by Hitchcock & Walden, of

Cincinnati; and Lee on the Inspiration of Holy Scripture is published by Rivingtons. Bishop Wordsworth, on the "Inspiration of the Bible," is also very scholarly and strong. Rivingtons, 1875.)

The Bible can no longer, according to the critics, be viewed in this light. It *is* not the Word in the old sense of that term. It is not the Word of God in the sense that all of it is given by the inspiration of God. It simply *contains* the Word of God. In many of its parts it is just as uncertain as any other human book. It is not even reliable history. Its records of what it does narrate as ordinary history are full of falsifications and blunders. The origin of Deuteronomy, e. g., was "a consciously refined falsification." (See Möller, page 207.)

THE REAL DIFFICULTY.

But do they still claim to believe that the Bible is inspired? Yes. That is, in a measure. As Dr. Driver says in his preface, "Criticism in the hands of Christian scholars does not banish or destroy the inspiration of the Old Testament; it pre-supposes it." That is perfectly true. Criticism in the hands of Christian scholars is safe. But the preponderating scholarship in Old Testament criticism has admittedly *not* been in the hands of men who could be described as Christian scholars. It has been in the hands of men who disavow belief in God and Jesus Christ Whom He sent. Criticism in the hands of Horne and Hengstenberg does not banish or destroy the inspiration of the Old Testament. But, in the hands of Spinoza, and Graf, and Wellhausen, and Kuenen, inspiration is neither pre-supposed nor possible. Dr. Briggs and Dr. Smith may avow earnest avowals of belief in the Divine character of the Bible, and Dr. Driver may assert that critical conclusions do not touch either the authority or the inspiration of the Scriptures of the Old Testament, but from first to last, they treat God's Word with an indifference almost equal to that of the Germans. They certainly handle the Old Testament as if it were ordinary literature. And in all their theories they seem like plastic wax in the hands of the rationalistic moulders. But they still claim to believe in Biblical inspiration.

A REVOLUTIONARY THEORY.

Their theory of inspiration must be, then, a very different one from that held by the average Christian.

In the Bampton Lectures for 1903, Professor Sanday of Oxford, as the exponent of the later and more conservative school of Higher Criticism, came out with a theory which he termed the inductive theory. It is not easy to describe what is fully meant by this, but it appears to mean the presence of what they call "a divine element" in certain parts of the Bible. What that really is he does not accurately declare. The language always vapours off into the vague and indefinite, whenever he speaks of it. In what books it is he does not say. "It is present in different books and parts of books in different degrees." "In some the Divine element is at the maximum; in others at the minimum." He is not always sure. He is sure it is not in Esther, in Ecclesiastes, in Daniel. If it is in the historical books, it is there as conveying a religious lesson rather than as a guarantee of historic veracity, rather as interpreting than as narrating. At the same time, if the histories as far as textual construction was concerned were "natural processes carried out naturally," it is difficult to see where the Divine or supernatural element comes in. It is an inspiration which seems to have been devised as a hypothesis of compromise. In fact, it is a tenuous, equivocal, and indeterminate something, the amount of which is as indefinite as its quality. (Sanday, pages 100-398; cf. Driver, Preface, ix.)

But its most serious feature is this: It is a theory of inspiration that completely overturns the old-fashioned ideas of the Bible and its unquestioned standard of authority and truth. For whatever this so-called Divine element is, it appears to be quite consistent with defective argument, incorrect interpretation, if not what the average man would call forgery or falsification.

It is, in fact, revolutionary. To accept it the Christian will have to completely readjust his ideas of honor and honesty, of falsehood and misrepresentation. Men used to think that forgery was a crime, and falsification a sin. Pusey, in his great work on Daniel, said that "to write a book under the name of another and to give it out to be his is in any case a forgery, dishonest in itself and destructive of all trustworthiness." (Pusey, Lectures on Daniel, page 1.) But according to the Higher Critical position, all sorts of pseudonymous material, and not a little of it believed to be true by the Lord Jesus Christ Himself, is to be found in the Bible, and no antecedent objection ought to be taken to it.

Men used to think that inaccuracy would affect reliability and that proven inconsistencies would imperil credibility. But now it appears that there may not only be mistakes and errors on the part of copyists, but forgeries, intentional omissions, and misinterpretations on the part of authors, and yet, marvelous to say, faith is not to be destroyed, but to be placed on a firmer foundation. (Sanday, page 122.) They have, according to Briggs, enthroned the Bible in a higher position than ever before. (Briggs, "The Bible, Church and Reason," page 149.) Sanday admits that there is an element in the Pentateuch derived from Moses himself. An element! But he adds, "However much we may believe that there is a genuine Mosaic foundation in the Pentateuch, it is difficult to lay the finger upon it, and to say with confidence, here Moses himself is speaking." "The strictly Mosaic element in the Pentateuch must be indeterminate." "We ought not, perhaps, to use them (the visions of Ex. 3 and 33) without reserve for Moses himself" (pages 172-174-176). The ordinary Christian, however, will say: Surely if we deny the Mosaic authorship and the unity of the Pentateuch we must undermine its credibility. The Pentateuch claims to be Mosaic. It was the universal tradition of the Jews. It is expressly stated in nearly all the subsequent books of the Old Testament. The Lord Jesus said so most explicitly. (John 5:46-47.)

IF NOT MOSES, WHO?

For this thought must surely follow to the thoughtful man: If Moses did not write the Books of Moses, who did?

If there were three or four, or six, or nine authorized original writers, why not fourteen, or sixteen, or nineteen? And then another and more serious thought must follow that. Who were these original writers, and who originated them? If there were manifest evidences of alterations, manipulations, inconsistencies and omissions by an indeterminate number of unknown and unknowable and undateable redactors, then the question arises, who were these redactors, and how far had they authority to redact, and who gave them this authority? If the redactor was the writer, was he an inspired writer, and if he was inspired, what was the degree of his inspiration; was it partial, plenary, inductive or indeterminate? This is a question of questions: What is the guarantee of the inspiration of the redactor, and who is its guarantor? Moses we know, and Samuel we know, and Daniel we know, but ye anonymous and pseudonymous, who are ye? The Pentateuch, with Mosaic authorship, as Scriptural, divinely accredited, is upheld by Catholic tradition and scholarship, and appeals to reason. But a mutilated cento or scrap-book of anonymous compilations, with its pre- and post-exilic redactors and redactions, is confusion worse confounded.

At least that is the way it appears to the average Christian. He may not be an expert in philosophy or theology, but his common sense must surely be allowed its rights. And that is the way it appears, too, to such an illustrious scholar and critic as Dr. Emil Reich. (Contemporary Review, April, 1905, page 515.)

It is not possible then to accept the Kuenen-Wellhausen theory of the structure of the Old Testament and the Sanday-Driver theory of its inspiration without undermining faith in the Bible as the Word of God. For the Bible is either the Word of God, or it is not. The children of Israel were the children of the Only Living and True God, or they were not. If their Jehovah was a mere tribal deity, and their religion a human evolution; if their sacred literature was natural with mythical and pseudonymous admixtures; then the Bible is dethroned from its throne as the exclusive, authoritative, Divinely inspired Word of God. It simply ranks as one of the sacred books of the ancients with similar claims of inspiration and revelation. Its inspiration is an indeterminate quantity and any man has a right to subject it to the judgment of his own critical insight, and to receive just as much of it as inspired as he or some other person believes to be inspired. When the contents have passed through the sieve of his judgment the inspired residuum may be large, or the inspired residuum may be small. If he is a conservative critic it may be fairly large, a maximum; if he is a more advanced critic it may be fairly small, a minimum. It is simply the ancient literature of a religious people containing somewhere the Word of God; "a revelation of no one knows what, made no one knows how, and lying no one knows where, except that it is to be somewhere between Genesis and Revelation, but probably to the exclusion of both." (Pusey, Daniel, xxviii.)

NO FINAL AUTHORITY.

Another serious consequence of the Higher Critical movement is that it threatens the Christian system of doctrine and the whole fabric of systematic theology. For up to the present time any text from any part of the Bible was accepted as a proof-text for the establishment of any truth of Christian teaching, and a statement from the Bible was considered an end of controversy. The doctrinal systems of the Anglican, the Presbyterian, the Methodist and other Churches are all based upon the view that the Bible contains the truth, the whole truth, and nothing but the truth. (See 39 Articles Church of England, vi, ix, xx, etc.) They accept as an axiom that the Old and New Testaments in part, and as a whole, have been given and sealed by God the Father, God the Son, and God the Holy Ghost. All the doctrines of the Church of Christ, from the greatest to the least, are based on this. All the proofs of the doctrines are based also on this. No text was questioned; no book was doubted; all Scripture was received by the great builders of our theological systems with that unassailable belief in the inspiration of its texts, which was the position of Christ and His apostles.

But now the Higher Critics think they have changed all that.

They claim that the science of criticism has dispossessed the science of systematic theology. Canon Henson tells us that the day has gone by for proof-texts and harmonies. It is not enough now for a theologian to turn to a book in the Bible, and bring out a text in order to establish a doctrine. It might be in a book, or in a portion of the Book that the German critics have proved to be a forgery, or an anachronism. It might be in Deuteronomy, or in Jonah, or in Daniel, and in that case, of course, it would be out of the question to accept it. The Christian system, therefore, will have to be re-adjusted if not revolutionized, every text and chapter and book will have to be inspected and analyzed in the light of its date, and origin, and circumstances, and authorship, and so on, and only after it has passed the examining board of the modern Franco-Dutch-German criticism will it be allowed to stand as a proof-text for the establishment of any Christian doctrine.

But the most serious consequence of this theory of the structure and inspiration of the Old Testament is that it overturns the juridic authority of our Lord Jesus Christ.

WHAT OF CHRIST'S AUTHORITY?

The attitude of Christ to the Old Testament Scriptures must determine ours. He is God. He is truth. His is the final voice. He is the Supreme Judge. There is no appeal from that court. Christ Jesus the Lord believed and affirmed the historic veracity of the whole of the Old Testament writings implicitly (Luke 24:44). And the Canon, or collection of Books of the Old Testament, was precisely the same in Christ's time as it is today. And further. Christ Jesus our Lord believed and emphatically affirmed the Mosaic authorsip of the Pentateuch (Matt. 5:17-18; Mark 12:26-36; Luke 16:31; John 5:46-47). That is true, the critics say. But, then, neither Christ nor His Apostles were critical scholars! Perhaps not in the twentieth century sense of the term. But, as a German scholar said, if they were not critici doctores, they were doctores veritatis who did not come into the world to fortify popular errors by their authority. But then they say, Christ's knowledge as man was limited. He grew in knowledge (Luke 2:52). Surely that implies His ignorance. And if His ignorance, why not His ignorance with regard to the science of historical criticism? (Gore, Lux Mundi, page 360; Briggs, H. C. of Hexateuch, page 28.) Or even if He did know more than His age, He probably spoke as He did in accommodation with the ideas of His contemporaries! (Briggs, page 29.)

In fact, what they mean is practically that Jesus did know perfectly well that Moses did not write the Pentateuch, but allowed His disciples to believe that Moses did, and taught His disciples that Moses did, simply because He did not want to upset their simple faith in the whole of the Old Testament as the actual and authoritative and Divinely revealed Word of God. (See Driver, page 12.) Or else, that Jesus imagined, like any other Jew of His day, that Moses wrote the books that bear his name, and believed, with the childlike Jewish belief of His day, the literal inspiration, Divine authority and historic veracity of the Old Testament, and yet was completely mistaken, ignorant of the simplest facts, and wholly in error. In other words, He could not tell a forgery from an original, or a pious fiction from a genuine document. (The analogy of Jesus speaking of the sun rising as an instance of the theory of accommodation is a very different thing.)

This, then, is their position: Christ knew the views He taught were false, and yet taught them as truth. Or else, Christ didn't know they were false and believed them to be true when they were not true. In either case the Blessed One is dethroned as True God and True Man. If He did not know the books to be spurious when they were spurious and the fables and myths to be mythical and fabulous; if He accepted legendary tales as trustworthy facts, then He was not and is not omniscient. He was not only intellectually fallible, He was morally fallible; for He was not true enough "to miss the ring of truth" in Deuteronomy and Daniel.

And further. If Jesus did know certain of the books to be lacking in genuineness, if not spurious and pseudonymous; if He did know the stories of the Fall and Lot and Abraham and Jonah and Daniel to be allegorical and imaginary, if not unverifiable and mythical, then He was neither trustworthy nor good. "If it were not so, I would have told you." We feel, those of us who love and trust Him, that if these stories were not true, if these books were a mass of historical unveracities, if Abraham was an eponymous hero, if Joseph was an astral myth, that He would have told us so. It is a matter that concerned His honor as a Teacher as well as His knowledge as our God. As Canon Liddon has conclusively pointed out, if our Lord was unreliable in these historic and documentary matters of inferior value, how can He be followed as the teacher of doctrinal truth and the revealer of God? (John 3:12.) (Liddon, Divinity of Our Lord, pages 475-480.)

AFTER THE KENOSIS.

Men say in this connection that part of the humiliation of Christ was His being touched with the infirmities of our human ignorance and fallibilities. They dwell upon the so-called doctrine of the Kenosis, or the emptying, as explaining satisfactorily His limitations. But Christ spoke of the Old Testament Scriptures after His resurrection. He affirmed after His glorious resurrection that "all things must be fulfilled which were written in the law of Moses, and in the prophets, and in the Psalms concerning Me" (Luke 24:44). This was not a statement made during the time of the Kenosis, when Christ was a mere boy, or a youth, or a mere Jew after the flesh (1 Cor. 13:11). It is the statement of Him Who has been declared the Son of God with power. It is the Voice that is final and overwhelming. The limitations of the Kenosis are all abandoned now, and yet the Risen Lord not only does not give a shadow of a hint that any statement in the Old Testament is inaccurate or that any portion thereof needed revision or correction, not only most solemnly declared that those books which we receive as the product of Moses were indeed the books of Moses, but authorized with His Divine imprimatur the whole of the Old Testament Scriptures from beginning to end.

There are, however, two or three questions that must be raised, as they will have to be faced by every student of present day problems. The first is this: Is not refusal of the higher critical conclusions mere opposition to light and progress and the position of ignorant alarmists and obscurantists?

NOT OBSCURANTISTS.

It is very necessary to have our minds made perfectly clear on this point, and to remove not a little dust of misunderstanding.

The desire to receive all the light that the most fearless search for truth by the highest scholarship can yield is the desire of every true believer in the Bible. No really healthy Christian mind can advocate obscurantism. The obscurant who opposes the investigation of scholarship, and would throttle the investigators, has not the spirit of Christ. In heart and attitude he is a Mediævalist. To use Bushnell's famous apologue, he would try to stop the dawning of the day by wringing the neck of the crowing cock. No one wants to put the Bible in a glass case. But it is the duty of every Christian who belongs to the noble army of truth-lovers to test all things and to hold fast that which is good. He also has rights even though he is, technically speaking, unlearned, and to accept any view that contradicts his spiritual judgment simply because it is that of a so-called scholar, is to abdicate his franchise as a Christian and his birthright as a man. (See that excellent little work by Professor Kennedy, "Old Testament Criticism and the Rights of the Unlearned," F. H. Revell.) And in his right of private judgment he is aware that while the privilege of investigation is conceded to all, the conclusions of an avowedly prejudiced scholarship must be subjected to a peculiarly searching analysis. The most ordinary Bible reader is learned enough to know that the investigation of the Book that claims to be supernatural by those who are avowed enemies of all that is supernatural, and the study of subjects that can be understood only by men of humble and contrite heart by men who are admittedly irreverent in spirit, must certainly be received with caution. (See Parker's striking work, "None Like It," F. H. Revell, and his last address.)

THE SCHOLARSHIP ARGUMENT.

The second question is also serious: Are we not bound to receive these views when they are advanced, not by rationalists, but by Christians, and not by ordinary Christians, but by men of superior and unchallengeable scholarship?

There is a widespread idea among younger men that the so-called Higher Critics must be followed because their scholarship settles the questions. This is a great mistake. No expert scholarship can settle questions that require a humble heart, a believing mind and a reverent spirit, as well as a knowledge of Hebrew and philology; and no scholarship can be relied upon as expert which is manifestly characterized by a biased judgment, a curious lack of knowledge of human nature, and a still more curious deference to the views of men with a prejudice against the supernatural. No one can read such a suggestive and sometimes even such an inspiring writer as George Adam Smith without a feeling of sorrow that he has allowed this German bias of mind to lead him into such an assumption of infallibility in many of his positions and statements. It is the same with Driver. With a kind of sic volo sic jubeo airy ease he introduces assertions and propositions that would really require chapter after chapter, if not even volume after volume, to substantiate. On page after page his "must be," and "could not possibly be," and "could certainly not," extort from the average reader the natural exclamation: "But why?" "Why not?" "Wherefore?" "On what grounds?" "For what reason?" "Where are the proofs?" But of proofs or reason there is not a trace. The reader must be content with the writer's assertions. It reminds one, in fact, of the "we may well suppose," and "perhaps" of the Darwinian who offers as the sole proof of the origination of a different species his random supposition! ("Modern Ideas of Evolution," Dawson, pages 53-55.)

A GREAT MISTAKE.

There is a widespread idea also among the younger students that because Graf and Wellhausen and Driver and Cheyne are experts in Hebrew that, therefore, their deductions as experts in language must be received. This, too, is a mistake. There is no such difference in the Hebrew of the so-called original sources of the Hexateuch as some suppose. The argument from language, says Professor Bissell ("Introduction to Genesis in Colors," page vii), requires extreme care for obvious reasons. There is no visible cleavage line among the supposed sources. Any man of ordinary intelligence can see at once the vast difference between the English of Tennyson and Shakespeare, and Chaucer and Sir John de Mandeville. But no scholar in the world ever has or ever will be able to tell the dates of each and every book in the Bible by the style of the Hebrew. (See Sayce, "Early History of the Hebrews," page 109.) The unchanging Orient knows nothing of the swift lingual variations of the Occident. Pusey, with his masterly scholarship, has shown how even the Book of Daniel, from the standpoint of philology, cannot possibly be a product of the time of the Maccabees. ("On Daniel," pages 23-59.) The late Professor of Hebrew in the University of Toronto, Professor Hirschfelder, in his very learned work on Genesis, says: "We would search in vain for any peculiarity either in the language or the sense that woud indicate a two-fold authorship." As far as the language of the original goes, "the most fastidious critic could not possibly detect the slightest peculiarity that would indicate it to be derived from two sources" (page 72). Dr. Emil Reich also, in his "Bankruptcy of the Higher Criticism," in the Contemporary Review, April, 1905, says the same thing.

NOT ALL ON ONE SIDE.

A third objection remains, a most serious one. It is that all the scholarship is on one side.. The old-fashioned conservative views are no longer maintained by men with pretension to scholarship. The only people who oppose the Higher Critical views are the ignorant, the prejudiced, and the illiterate. (Briggs' "Bible, Church and Reason," pages 240-247.)

This, too, is a matter that needs a little clearing up. In the first place it is not fair to assert that the upholders of what are called the old-fashioned or traditional views of the Bible are opposed to the pursuit of scientific Biblical investigation. It is equally unfair to imagine that their opposition to the views of the Continental school is based upon ignorance and prejudice.

What the Conservative school oppose is not Biblical criticism, but Biblical criticism by rationalists. They do not oppose the conclusions of Wellhausen and Kuenen because they are experts and scholars; they oppose them because the Biblical criticism of rationalists and unbelievers can be neither expert nor scientific. A criticism that is characterized by the most arbitrary conclusions from the most spurious assumptions has no right to the word scientific. And further. Their adhesion to the traditional views is not only conscientious but intelligent. They believe that the old-fashioned views are as scholarly as they are Scriptural. It is the fashion in some quarters to cite the imposing list of scholars on the side of the German school, and to sneeringly assert that there is not a scholar to stand up for the old views of the Bible.

This is not the case. Hengstenberg of Basle and Berlin, was as profound a scholar as Eichhorn, Vater or De Wette; and Keil or Kurtz, and Zahn and Rupprecht were competent to compete with Reuss and Kuenen. Wilhelm Möller, who confesses that he was once "immovably convinced of the irrefutable correctness of the Graf-Wellhausen hypothesis," has revised his former radical conclusions on the ground of reason and deeper research as a Higher Critic; and Professor Winckler, who has of late overturned the assured and settled results of the Higher Critics from the foundations, is, according to Orr, the leading Orientalist in Germany, and a man of enormous learning.

Sayce, the Professor of Assyriology at Oxford, has a right to rank as an expert and scholar with Cheyne, the Oriel Professor of Scripture Interpretation. Margoliouth, the Laudian Professor of Arabic at Oxford, as far as learning is concerned, is in the same rank with Driver, the Regius Professor of Hebrew, and the conclusion of this great scholar with regard to one of the widely vaunted theories of the radical school, is almost amusing in its terseness.

"Is there then nothing in the splitting theories," he says in summarizing a long line of defense of the unity of the book of Isaiah; "is there then nothing in the splitting theories? To my mind, *nothing at all!*" ("Lines of Defense," page 136.)

Green and Bissell are as able, if not abler, scholars than Robertson Smith and Professor Briggs, and both of these men, as a result of the widest and deepest research, have come to the conclusion that the theories of the Germans are unscientific, unhistorical, and unscholarly. The last words of Professor Green in his very able work on the "Higher Criticism of the Pentateuch" are most suggestive. "Would it not be wiser for them to revise their own ill-judged alliance with the enemies of evangelical truth, and inquire whether Christ's view of the Old Testament may not, after all, be the true view?"

Yes. That, after all, is the great and final question. We trust we are not ignorant. We feel sure we are not malignant. We desire to treat no man unfairly, or set down aught in malice.

But we desire to stand with Christ and His Church. If we have any prejudice, we would rather be prejudiced against rationalism. If we have any bias, it must be against a teaching which unsteadies heart and unsettles faith. Even at the expense of being thought behind the times, we prefer to stand with our Lord and Saviour Jesus Christ in receiving the Scriptures as the Word of God, without objection and without a doubt. A little learning, and a little listening to rationalistic theorizers and sympathizers may incline us to uncertainty; but deeper study and deeper research will incline us as it inclined Hengstenberg and Möller, to the profoundest conviction of the authority and authenticity of the Holy Scriptures, and to cry, "Thy word is very pure; therefore. Thy servant loveth it."

CHAPTER II

THE MOSAIC AUTHORSHIP OF THE PENTATEUCH

BY PROFESSOR GEORGE FREDERICK WRIGHT, D. D., LL. D.,

OBERLIN COLLEGE, OBERLIN, OHIO

During the last quarter of a century an influential school of critics has deluged the world with articles and volumes attempting to prove that the Pentateuch did not originate during the time of Moses, and that most of the laws attributed to him did not come into existence until several centuries after his death, and many of them not till the time of Ezekiel. By these critics the patriarchs are relegated to the realm of myth or dim legend and the history of the Pentateuch generally is discredited. In answering these destructive contentions and defending the history which they discredit we can do no better than to give a brief summary of the arguments of Mr. Harold M. Wiener, a young orthodox Jew, who is both a well established barrister in London, and a scholar of the widest attainments. What he has written upon the subject during the last ten years would fill a thousand octavo pages; while our condensation must be limited to less than twenty. In approaching the subject it comes in place to consider

I. THE BURDEN OF PROOF

The Mosaic authorship of the Pentateuch has until very recent times been accepted without question by both Jews and Christians. Such acceptance, coming down to us in unbroken line from the earliest times of which we have any information, gives it the support of what is called general consent, which, while perhaps not absolutely conclusive, compels those who would discredit it to produce incontrovertible opposing evidence. But the evidence which the critics produce in this case is wholly circumstantial, consisting of inferences derived from a literary analysis of the documents and from the application of a discredited evolutionary theory concerning the development of human institutions.

II. FAILURE OF THE ARGUMENT FROM LITERARY ANALYSIS

(a) *Evidence of Textual Criticism.*

It is an instructive commentary upon the scholarly pretensions of this whole school of critics that, without adequate examination of the facts, they have based their analysis of the Pentateuch upon the text which is found in our ordinary Hebrew Bibles. While the students of the New Testament have expended an immense amount of effort in the comparison of manuscripts, and versions, and quotations to determine the original text, these Old Testament critics have done scarcely anything in that direction. This is certainly a most unscholarly proceeding, yet it is admitted to be the fact by a higher critic of no less eminence than Principal J. Skinner of Cambridge, England, who has been compelled to write: "I do not happen to know of any work which deals exhaustively with the subject, the determination of the original Hebrew texts from the critical standpoints."

Now the fact is that while the current Hebrew text, known as the Massoretic, was not established until about the seventh century A. D., we have abundant material with which to compare it and carry us back to that current a thousand years nearer the time of the original composition of the books. (1) The Greek translation known as the Septuagint was made from Hebrew manuscripts current two or three centuries before the Christian era. It is from this version that most of the quotations in the New Testament are made. Of the 350 quotations from the Old Testament in the New, 300, while differing more or less from the Massoretic text, do not differ materially from the Septuagint. (2) The

Samaritans early broke away from the Jews and began the transmission of a Hebrew text of the Pentateuch on an independent line which has continued down to the present day. (3) Besides this three other Greek versions were made long before the establishment of the Massoretic text. The most important of these was one by Aquila, who was so punctilious that he transliterated the word Jehovah in the old Hebrew characters, instead of translating it by the Greek word meaning Lord as was done in the Septuagint. (4) Early Syriac material often provides much information concerning the original Hebrew text. (5) The translation into Latin known as the Vulgate preceded the Massoretic text by some centuries, and was made by Jerome, who was noted as a Hebrew scholar. But Augustine thought it sacrilegious not to be content with the Septuagint.

All this material furnishes ample ground for correcting in minor particulars the current Hebrew text; and this can be done on well established scientific principles which largely eliminate conjectural emendations. This argument has been elaborated by a number of scholars, notably by Dahse, one of the most brilliant of Germany's younger scholars, first in the *"Archiv fuer Religions-Wissenschaft"* for 1903, pp. 305-319, and again in an article which will appear in the *"Neue Kirchliche Zeitschrift"* for this year; and he is following up his attack on the critical theories with an important book entitled, *"Textkritische Materialien zur Hexateuchfrage,"* which will shortly be published in Germany. Although so long a time has elapsed since the publication of his first article on the subject, and in spite of the fact that it attracted world-wide attention and has often been referred to since, no German critic has yet produced an answer to it. In England and America Dr. Redpath and Mr. Wiener have driven home the argument. (See Wiener's "Essays in Pentateuchal Criticism", and "Origin of the Pentateuch.")

On bringing the light of this evidence to bear upon the

subject some remarkable results are brought out, the most important of which relate to the very foundation upon which the theories concerning the fragmentary character of the Pentateuch are based. The most prominent clue to the documentary division is derived from the supposed use by different writers of the two words, "Jehovah" and "Elohim," to designate the deity. Jehovah was translated in the Septuagint by a word meaning "Lord", which appears in our authorized version in capitalized form, "LORD." The revisers of 1880, however, have simply transliterated the word, so that "Jehovah" usually appears in the revision wherever "LORD" appeared in the authorized version. Elohim is everywhere translated by the general word for deity, "God."

Now the original critical division into documents was made on the supposition that several hundred years later than Moses there arose two schools of writers, one of which, in Judah, used the word "Jehovah" when they spoke of the deity, and the other, in the Northern Kingdom, "Elohim." And so the critics came to designate one set of passages as belonging to the J document and the other to the E document. These they supposed had been cut up and pieced together by a later editor so as to make the existing continuous narrative. But when, as frequently occurred, one of these words is found in passages where it is thought the other word should have been used, it is supposed, wholly on theoretical grounds, that a mistake had been made by the editor, or, as they call him, the "redactor," and so with no further ceremony the objection is arbitrarily removed without consulting the direct textual evidence.

But upon comparing the early texts, versions, and quotations it appears that the words, "Jehovah" and "Elohim," were so nearly synonymous that there was originally little uniformity in their use. Jehovah is the Jewish *name* of the deity, and Elohim the *title*. The use of the words is precisely like that of the English in referring to their king or the

Americans to their president. In ordinary usage, "George V.", "the king," and "King George" are synonymous in their meaning. Similarly "Taft," "the president," and "President Taft" are used by Americans during his term of office to indicate an identical concept. So it was with the Hebrews. "Jehovah" was the name, "Elohim" the title, and "Jehovah Elohim"—Lord God—signified nothing more. Now on consulting the evidence it appears that while in Genesis and the first three chapters of Exodus (where this clue was supposed to be most decisive) Jehovah occurs in the Hebrew text 148 times, in 118 of these places other texts have either Elohim or Jehovah Elohim. In the same section, while Elohim alone occurs 179 times in the Hebrew, in 49 of the passages one or the other designation takes its place; and in the second and third chapters of Genesis where the Hebrew text has Jehovah Elohim (LORD God) 23 times, there is only one passage in which all the texts are unanimous on this point.

These facts, which are now amply verified, utterly destroy the value of the clue which the higher critics have all along ostentatiously put forward to justify their division of the Pentateuch into conflicting E and J documents, and this the critics themselves are now compelled to admit. The only answer which they are able to give is in Dr. Skinner's words that the analysis is correct even if the clue which led to it be false, adding "even if it were proved to be so altogether fallacious, it would not be the first time that a wrong clue has led to true results."

On further examination, in the light of present knowledge (as Wiener and Dahse abundantly show), legitimate criticism removes a large number of the alleged difficulties which are put forward by higher critics and renders of no value many of the supposed clues to the various documents. We have space to notice but one or two of these. In the Massoretic text of Ex. 18:6 we read that Jethro says to Moses, "I thy father-in-law Jethro am come," while in the seventh verse it is said that Moses goes out to meet his father-in-law and that they exchange greetings and then come into the tent. But how could Jethro speak to Moses before they had had a meeting? The critics say that this confusion arises from the bungling patchwork of an editor who put two discordant accounts together without attempting to cover up the discrepancy. But scientific textual criticism completely removes the difficulty. The Septuagint, the old Syriac version, and a copy of the Samaritan Pentateuch, instead of "I thy father-in-law Jethro am come", read, "And one said unto Moses, *behold* thy father-in-law Jethro" comes. Here the corruption of a single letter in the Hebrew gives us "behold" in place of "I". When this is observed the objection disappears entirely.

Again, in Gen. 39:20-22 Joseph is said to have been put into the prison "where the king's prisoners were bound. . . . And the *keeper of the prison*" promoted him. But in chapter 40:2-4, 7 it is said that he was "in ward of the house of the *captain of the guard* . . . and the captain of the guard" promoted Joseph. But this discrepancy disappears as soon as an effort is made to determine the original text. In Hebrew, "keeper of the prison" and "captain of the guard" both begin with the same word and in the passages where the "captain of the guard" causes trouble by its appearance, the Septuagint either omitted the phrase or read "keeper of the prison," in one case being supported also by the Vulgate.

In many other instances also, attention to the original text removes the difficulties which have been manufactured from apparent discrepancies in the narrative.

(b) Delusions of Literary Analysis.

But even on the assumption of the practical inerrancy of the Massoretic text the arguments against the Mosaic authorship of the Pentateuch drawn from the literary analysis are seen to be the result of misdirected scholarship, and to be utterly fallacious. The long lists of words adduced as characteristic of the writers to whom the various parts of the Pentateuch are assigned are readily seen to be occasioned by the different objects aimed at in the portions from which the lists are made.

Here, however, it is necessary to add that besides the E and J documents the critics suppose that Deuteronomy, which they designate "D", is an independent literary production written in the time of Josiah. Furthermore, the critics pretend to have discovered by their analysis another document which they call the Priestly Code and designate as "P". This provides the groundwork of most of the narrative, and comprises the entire ceremonial portion of the law. This document, which, according to these critics did not come into existence till the time of Ezekiel, largely consists of special instructions to priests telling them how they were to perform the sacrifices and public ceremonials, and how they were to determine the character of contagious diseases and unsanitary conditions. Such instructions are necessarily made up largely of technical language such as is found in the libraries of lawyers and physicians, and it is easy enough to select from such literature a long list of words which are not to be found in contemporary literature dealing with the ordinary affairs of life and aiming directly at elevating the tone of morality and stimulating devotion to higher spiritual ends. Furthermore, an exhaustive examination (made by Chancellor Lias) of the entire list of words found in this P document attributed to the time of Ezekiel shows absolutely no indication of their belonging to an age later than that of Moses.

The absurdity of the claims of the higher critics to having established the existence of different documents in the Pentateuch by a literary analysis has been shown by a variety of examples. The late Professor C. M. Mead, the most influential of the American revisers of the translation of the Old Testament, in order to exhibit the fallacy of their procedure, took the Book of Romans and arbitrarily divided it into three parts, according as the words "Christ Jesus," "Jesus," or "God" were used; and then by analysis showed that the lists of peculiar words characteristic of these three passages were even more remarkable than those drawn up by the destructive critics of the Pentateuch from the three leading fragments into which they had divided it. The argument from literary analysis after the methods of these critics would prove the composite character of the Epistle to the Romans as fully as that of the critics would prove the composite character of the Pentateuch. A distinguished scholar, Dr. Hayman, formerly head-master of Rugby, by a similar analysis demonstrated the composite character of Robert Burns' little poem addressed to a mouse, half of which is in the purest English and the other half in the broadest Scotch dialect. By the same process it would be easy to prove three Macaulays and three Miltons by selecting lists of words from the documents prepared by them when holding high political offices and from their various prose and poetical writings.

III. MISUNDERSTANDING LEGAL FORMS AND THE SACRIFICIAL SYSTEM

Another source of fallacious reasoning into which these critics have fallen arises from a misunderstanding of the sacrificial system of the Mosaic law. The destructive critics assert that there was no central sanctuary in Palestine until several centuries after its occupation under Joshua, and that at a later period all sacrifices by the people were forbidden except at the central place when offered by the priests, unless it was where there had been a special theophany. But these statements evince an entire misunderstanding or misrepresentation of the facts. In what the critics reckon as the oldest documents (J and E) the people were required three times a year to present themselves with sacrifices and offerings *"at the house of the Lord"* (Ex. 34:26; 23:19). Before the building of the temple this "house of the Lord was at Shiloh"

(Josh. 18:1; Judges 18:31; 1 Sam. 2:24). The truth is that the destructive critics upon this point make a most humiliating mistake in repeatedly substituting "sanctuaries" for "altars," assuming that since there was a plurality of altars in the time of the Judges there was therefore a plurality of sanctuaries. They have completely misunderstood the permission given in Ex. 20:24: "An altar of earth thou shalt make unto Me and shalt sacrifice thereon thy burnt offerings, and thy peace offerings, thy sheep, and thine oxen; in all places, A. V.; [in every place, R. V.], where I record My name I will come unto thee and I will bless thee. And if thou make Me an altar of stone, thou shalt not build it of hewn stones." In reading this passage we are likely to be misled by the erroneous translation. Where the revisers read in "every place" and the authorized version in "all places" the correct translation is "in all the place" or "in the whole place." The word is in the singular number and has a definite article before it. The whole place referred to is Palestine, the Holy Land, where sacrifices such as the patriarchs had offered were always permitted to laymen, provided they made use only of an altar of earth or unhewn stones which was kept free from the adornments and accessories characteristic of heathen altars. These lay sacrifices were recognized in Deuteronomy as well as in Exodus. (Deut. 16:21.) But altars of earth or unhewn stone, often used for the nonce only and having no connection with a temple of any sort, are not houses of God and will not become such on being called sanctuaries by critics several thousand years after they have fallen out of use.

In accordance with this command and permission the Jews have always limited their sacrifices to the land of Palestine. When exiled to foreign lands the Jews to this day have ceased to offer sacrifices. It is true that an experiment was made of setting up a sacrificial system in Egypt for a time by a certain portion of the exiles; but this was soon abandoned. Ultimately a synagogue system was established and worship outside of Palestine was limited to prayer and the reading of Scriptures.

But besides the lay sacrifices which were continued from the patriarchal times and guarded against perversion, there were two other classes of offerings established by statute; namely, those individual offerings which were brought to the "house of God" at the central place of worship and offered with priestly assistance, and the national offerings described in Numbers 28ff. which were brought on behalf of the whole people and not of an individual. A failure to distinguish clearly between these three classes of sacrifices has led the critics into endless confusion, and error has arisen from their inability to understand legal terms and principles. The Pentateuch is not mere literature, but it contains a legal code. It is a product of statesmanship consisting of three distinct elements which have always been recognized by lawgivers; namely, the civil, the moral, and the ceremonial, or what Wiener calls the "jural laws," the "moral code" and "procedure." The jural laws are those the infractions of which can be brought before a court, such as "Thou shalt not remove thy neighbor's landmark." But "Thou shalt love thy neighbor as thyself" can be enforced only by public sentiment and Divine sanctions. The Book of Deuteronomy is largely occupied with the presentation of exhortations and motives, aiming to secure obedience to a higher moral code, and is in this largely followed by the prophets of the Old Dispensation and the preachers of the present day. The moral law supplements the civil law. The ceremonial law consists of directions to the priests for performing the various technical duties, and were of as little interest to the mass of people as are the legal and medical books of the present time. All these strata of the law were naturally and necessarily in existence at the same time. In putting them as successive strata, with the ceremonial law last, the critics have made an egregious and misleading blunder.

IV. THE POSITIVE EVIDENCE

Before proceeding to give in conclusion a brief summary of the circumstantial evidence supporting the ordinary belief in the Mosaic authorship of the Pentateuch it is important to define the term. By it we do not mean that Moses wrote *all* the Pentateuch with his own hand, or that there were *no* editorial additions made after his death. Moses was the author of the Pentateuchal Code, as Napoleon was of the code which goes under his name. Apparently the Book of Genesis is largely made up from existing documents, of which the history of the expedition of Amraphel in chapter 14 is a noted specimen; while the account of Moses' death, and a few other passages are evidently later editorial additions. But these are not enough to affect the general proposition. The Mosaic authorship of the Pentateuch is supported by the following, among other weighty considerations:

1. The Mosaic era was a literary epoch in the world's history when such codes were common. It would have been strange if such a leader had not produced a code of laws. The Tel-el-Amarna tablets and the Code of Hammurabi testify to the literary habits of the time.

2. The Pentateuch so perfectly reflects the conditions in Egypt at the period assigned to it that it is difficult to believe that it was a literary product of a later age.

3. Its representation of life in the wilderness is so perfect and so many of its laws are adapted only to that life that it is incredible that literary men a thousand years later should have imagined it.

4. The laws themselves bear indubitable marks of adaptation to the stage of national development to which they are ascribed. It was the study of Maine's works on ancient law that set Mr. Wiener out upon his re-investigation of the subject.

5. The little use that is made of the sanctions of a future

life is, as Bishop Warburton ably argued, evidence of an early date and of a peculiar Divine effort to guard the Israelites against the contamination of Egyptian ideas upon the subject.

6. The omission of the hen from the lists of clean and unclean birds is incredible if these lists were made late in the nation's history after that domestic fowl had been introduced from India.

7. As Rev. A. C. Robinson showed in Volume VII of this series it is incredible that there should have been no intimation in the Pentateuch of the existence of Jerusalem, or of the use of music in the liturgy, nor any use of the phrase, "Lord of Hosts," unless the compilation had been completed before the time of David.

8. The subordination of the miraculous elements in the Pentateuch to the critical junctures in the nation's development is such as could be obtained only in genuine history.

9. The whole representation conforms to the true law of historical development. Nations do not rise by virtue of inherent resident forces, but through the struggles of great leaders enlightened directly from on high or by contact with others who have already been enlightened.

The defender of the Mosaic authorship of the Pentateuch has no occasion to quail in presence of the critics who deny that authorship and discredit its history. He may boldly challenge their scholarship, deny their conclusions, resent their arrogance, and hold on to his confidence in the well authenticated historical evidence which sufficed for those who first accepted it. Those who now at second hand are popularizing in periodicals, Sunday School lessons, and volumes of greater or less pretentions the errors of these critics must answer to their consciences as best they can, but they should be made to feel that they assume a heavy responsibility in putting themselves forward as leaders of the blind when they themselves are not able to see.

FALLACIES OF THE HIGHER CRITICISM.

BY FRANKLIN JOHNSON, D. D., LL. D.

The errors of the higher criticism of which I shall write pertain to its very substance. Those of a secondary character the limits of my space forbid me to consider. My discussion might be greatly expanded by additional masses of illustrative material, and hence I close it with a list of books which I recommend to persons who may wish to pursue the subject further.

DEFINITION OF "THE HIGHER CRITICISM."

As an introduction to the fundamental fallacies of the higher criticism, let me state what the higher criticism is, and then what the higher critics tell us they have achieved.

The name "the higher criticism" was coined by Eichhorn, who lived from 1752 to 1827. Zenos,* after careful consideration, adopts the definition of the name given by its author: "The discovery and verification of the facts regarding the origin, form and value of literary productions upon the basis of their internal characters." The higher critics are not blind to some other sources of argument. They refer to history where they can gain any polemic advantage by doing so. The background of the entire picture which they bring to us is the assumption that the hypothesis of evolution is true. But after all their chief appeal is to the supposed evidence of the documents themselves.

Other names for the movement have been sought. It has been called the "historic view," on the assumption that it represents the real history of the Hebrew people as it must have unfolded itself by the orderly processes of human evolution.

*"The Elements of the Higher Criticism."

But, as the higher critics contradict the testimony of all the
Hebrew historic documents which profess to be early, their
theory might better be called the "unhistoric view." The higher criticism has sometimes been called the "documentary hypothesis." But as all schools of criticism and all doctrines of
inspiration are equally hospitable to the supposition that the
biblical writers may have consulted documents, and may have
quoted them, the higher criticism has no special right to this
title. We must fall back, therefore, upon the name "the higher criticism" as the very best at our disposal, and upon the
definition of it as chiefly an inspection of literary productions
in order to ascertain their dates, their authors, and their value,
as they themselves, interpreted in the light of the hypothesis
of evolution, may yield the evidence.

"ASSURED RESULTS" OF THE HIGHER CRITICISM.

I turn now to ask what the higher critics profess to have
found out by this method of study. The "assured results" on
which they congratulate themselves are stated variously. In
this country and England they commonly assume a form less
radical than that given them in Germany, though sufficiently
startling and destructive to arouse vigorous protest and a vigorous demand for the evidences, which, as we shall see, have
not been produced and cannot be produced. The less startling
form of the "assured results" usually announced in England
and America may be owing to the brighter light of Christianity in these countries. Yet it should be noticed that there are
higher critics in this country and England who go beyond the
principal German representatives of the school in their zeal
for the dethronement of the Old Testament and the New, in so
far as these holy books are presented to the world as the very
Word of God, as a special revelation from heaven.

The following statement from Zenos* may serve to introduce us to the more moderate form of the "assured results"

*Page 205.

reached by the higher critics. It is concerning the analysis of the Pentateuch, or rather of the Hexateuch, the Book of Joshua being included in the survey. "The Hexateuch is a composite work whose origin and history may be traced in four distinct stages: (1) A writer designated as J. Jahvist, or Jehovist, or Judean prophetic historian, composed a history of the people of Israel about 800 B. C. (2) A writer designated as E. Elohist, or Ephraemite prophetic historian, wrote a similar work some fifty years later, or about 750 B. C. These two were used separately for a time, but were fused together into JE by a redactor [an editor], at the end of the seventh century. (3) A writer of different character wrote a book constituting the main portion of our present Deuteronomy during the reign of Josiah, or a short time before 621 B. C. This writer is designated as D. To his work were added an introduction and an appendix, and with these accretions it was united with JE by a second redactor, constituting JED. (4) Contemporaneously with Ezekiel the ritual law began to be reduced to writing. It first appeared in three parallel forms. These were codified by Ezra not very much earlier than 444 B. C., and between that date and 280 B. C. it was joined with JED by a final redactor. Thus no less than nine or ten men were engaged in the production of the Hexateuch in its present form, and each one can be distinguished from the rest by his vocabulary and style and his religious point of view."

Such is the analysis of the Pentateuch as usually stated in this country. But in Germany and Holland its chief representatives carry the division of labor much further. Wellhausen distributes the total task among twenty-two writers, and Kuenen among eighteen. Many others resolve each individual writer into a school of writers, and thus multiply the numbers enormously. There is no agreement among the higher critics concerning this analysis, and therefore the cautious learner may well wait till those who represent the theory tell him just what it is they desire him to learn.

While some of the "assured results" are thus in doubt, certain things are matters of general agreement. Moses wrote little or nothing, if he ever existed. A large part of the Hexateuch consists of unhistorical legends. We may grant that Abraham, Isaac, Jacob, Ishmael and Esau existed, or we may deny this. In either case, what is recorded of them is chiefly myth. These denials of the truth of the written records follow as matters of course from the late dating of the books, and the assumption that the writers could set down only the national tradition. They may have worked in part as collectors of written stories to be found here and there; but, if so, these written stories were not ancient, and they were diluted by stories transmitted orally. These fragments, whether written or oral, must have followed the general law of national traditions, and have presented a mixture of legendary chaff, with here and there a grain of historic truth to be sifted out by careful winnowing.

Thus far of the Hexateuch.

The Psalms are so full of references to the Hexateuch that they must have been written after it, and hence after the captivity, perhaps beginning about 400 B. C. David may possibly have written one or two of them, but probably he wrote none, and the strong conviction of the Hebrew people that he was their greatest hymn-writer was a total mistake.

These revolutionary processes are carried into the New Testament, and that also is found to be largely untrustworthy as history, as doctrine, and as ethics, though a very good book, since it gives expression to high ideals, and thus ministers to the spiritual life. It may well have influence, but it can have no divine authority. The Christian reader should consider carefully this invasion of the New Testament by the higher criticism. So long as the movement was confined to the Old Testament many good men looked on with indifference, not reflecting that the Bible, though containing "many parts" by many writers, and though recording a progressive revelation, is, after all, one book. But the limits of the Old Testament have long since been overpassed by the higher critics, and it is demanded of us that we abandon the immemorial teaching of the church concerning the entire volume. The picture of Christ which the New Testament sets before us is in many respects mistaken. The doctrines of primitive Christianity which it states and defends were well enough for the time, but have no value for us today except as they commend themselves to our independent judgment. Its moral precepts are fallible, and we should accept them or reject them freely, in accordance with the greater light of the twentieth century. Even Christ could err concerning ethical questions, and neither His commandments nor His example need constrain us.

The foregoing may serve as an introductory sketch, all too brief, of the higher criticism, and as a basis of the discussion of its fallacies, now immediately to follow.

FIRST FALLACY: THE ANALYSIS OF THE PENTATEUCH.

I. The first fallacy that I shall bring forward is its analysis of the Pentateuch.

1. We cannot fail to observe that these various documents and their various authors and editors are only imagined. As Green* has said, "There is no evidence of the existence of these documents and redactors, and no pretense of any, apart from the critical tests which have determined the analysis. All tradition and all historical testimony as to the origin of the Pentateuch are against them. The burden of proof is wholly upon the critics. And this proof should be clear and convincing in proportion to the gravity and the revolutionary character of the consequences which it is proposed to base upon it."

2. Moreover, we know what can be done, or rather what cannot be done, in the analysis of composite literary productions. Some of the plays of Shakespeare are called his "mixed plays," because it is known that he collaborated with another

*"Moses and His Recent Critics," pages 104, 105.

author in their production. The very keenest critics have sought to separate his part in these plays from the rest, but they confess that the result is uncertainty and dissatisfaction. Coleridge professed to distinguish the passages contributed by Shakespeare by a process of feeling, but Macaulay pronounced this claim to be nonsense, and the entire effort, whether made by the analysis of phraseology and style, or by esthetic perceptions, is an admitted failure. And this in spite of the fact that the style of Shakespeare is one of the most peculiar and inimitable. The Anglican Prayer Book is another composite production which the higher critics have often been invited to analyze and distribute to its various sources. Some of the authors of these sources lived centuries apart. They are now well known from the studies of historians. But the Prayer Book itself does not reveal one of them, though its various vocabularies and styles have been carefully interrogated. Now if the analysis of the Pentateuch can lead to such certainties, why should not the analysis of Shakespeare and the Prayer Book do as much? How can men accomplish in a foreign language what they cannot accomplish in their own? How can they accomplish in a dead language what they cannot accomplish in a living language? How can they distinguish ten or eighteen or twenty-two collaborators in a small literary production, when they cannot distinguish two? These questions have been asked many times, but the higher critics have given no answer whatever, preferring the safety of a learned silence;
"The oracles are dumb."

3. Much has been made of differences of vocabulary in the Pentateuch, and elaborate lists of words have been assigned to each of the supposed authors. But these distinctions fade away when subjected to careful scrutiny, and Driver admits that "the phraseological criteria * * * are slight." Orr,* who quotes this testimony, adds, "They are slight, in fact, to a degree of tenuity that often makes the recital of them appear like trifling."

---
*"The Problem of the Old Testament," page 230.

SECOND FALLACY: THE THEORY OF EVOLUTION AP-
PLIED TO LITERATURE AND RELIGION.

II.　A second fundamental fallacy of the higher criticism is
its dependence on the theory of evolution as the explanation
of the history of literature and of religion.　The progress of
the higher criticism towards its present state has been rapid
and assured since Vatke[1] discovered in the Hegelian philosophy
of evolution a means of biblical criticism.　The Spencerian
philosophy of evolution, aided and reinforced by Darwinism, has added greatly to the confidence of the higher critics.
As Vatke, one of the earlier members of the school, made the
hypothesis of evolution the guiding presupposition of his critical work, so today does Professor Jordan,[2] the very latest representative of the higher criticism.　"The nineteenth century,"
he declares, "has applied to the history of the documents of
the Hebrew people its own magic word, evolution.　The
thought represented by that popular word has been found to
have a real meaning in our investigations regarding the religious life and the theological beliefs of Israel."　Thus, were
there no hypothesis of evolution, there would be no higher
criticism.　The "assured results" of the higher criticism have
been gained, after all, not by an inductive study of the biblical
books to ascertain if they present a great variety of styles and
vocabularies and religious points of view.　They have been
attained by assuming that the hypothesis of evolution is true,
and that the religion of Israel must have unfolded itself by
a process of natural evolution.　They have been attained by
an interested cross-examination of the biblical books to constrain them to admit the hypothesis of evolution.　The imagination has played a large part in the process, and the so-called
evidences upon which the "assured results" rest are largely
imaginary.

　But the hypothesis of evolution, when applied to the his-

[1]"Die Biblische Theologie Wissenschaftlich Dargestellt."

[2]"Biblical Criticism and Modern Thought," T. and T. Clark, 1909.

tory of literature, is a fallacy, leaving us utterly unable to
account for Homer, or Dante, or Shakespeare, the greatest
poets of the world, yet all of them writing in the dawn of the
great literatures of the world. It is a fallacy when applied to
the history of religion, leaving us utterly unable to account for
Abraham and Moses and Christ, and requiring us to deny that
they could have been such men as the Bible declares them to
have been. The hypothesis is a fallacy when applied to the
history of the human race in general. Our race has made progress under the influence of supernatural revelation; but progress under the influence of supernatural revelation is one thing,
and evolution is another. Buckle* undertook to account for
history by a thorough-going application of the hypothesis of
evolution to its problems; but no historian today believes that
he succeeded in his effort, and his work is universally regarded
as a brilliant curiosity. The types of evolution advocated by
different higher critics are widely different from one another,
varying from the pure naturalism of Wellhausen to the recognition of some feeble rays of supernatural revelation; but the
hypothesis of evolution in any form, when applied to human
history, blinds us and renders us incapable of beholding the
glory of God in its more signal manifestations.

THIRD FALLACY: THE BIBLE A NATURAL BOOK.

III. A third fallacy of the higher critics is the doctrine
concerning the Scriptures which they teach. If a consistent
hypothesis of evolution is made the basis of our religious
thinking, the Bible will be regarded as only a product of human
nature working in the field of religious literature. It will be
merely a natural book. If there are higher critics who recoil
from this application of the hypothesis of evolution and who
seek to modify it by recognizing some special evidences of the
divine in the Bible, the inspiration of which they speak rises
but little higher than the providential guidance of the writers.

*"History of Civilization in England."

The church doctrine of the full inspiration of the Bible is almost never held by the higher critics of any class, even of the more believing. Here and there we may discover one and another who try to save some fragments of the church doctrine, but they are few and far between, and the salvage to which they cling is so small and poor that it is scarcely worth while. Throughout their ranks the storm of opposition to the supernatural in all its forms is so fierce as to leave little place for the faith of the church that the Bible is the very Word of God to man. But the fallacy of this denial is evident to every believer who reads the Bible with an open mind. He knows by an immediate consciousness that it is the product of the Holy Spirit. As the sheep know the voice of the shepherd, so the mature Christian knows that the Bible speaks with a divine voice. On this ground every Christian can test the value of the higher criticism for himself. The Bible manifests itself to the spiritual perception of the Christian as in the fullest sense human, and in the fullest sense divine. This is true of the Old Testament, as well as of the New.

FOURTH FALLACY: THE MIRACLES DENIED.

IV. Yet another fallacy of the higher critics is found in their teachings concerning the biblical miracles. If the hypothesis of evolution is applied to the Scriptures consistently, it will lead us to deny all the miracles which they record. But if applied timidly and waveringly, as it is by some of the English and American higher critics, it will lead us to deny a large part of the miracles, and to inject as much of the natural as is any way possible into the rest. We shall strain out as much of the gnat of the supernatural as we can, and swallow as much of the camel of evolution as we can. We shall probably reject all the miracles of the Old Testament, explaining some of them as popular legends, and others as coincidences. In the New Testament we shall pick and choose, and no two of us will agree concerning those to be rejected and those to be accepted. If the higher criticism shall be adopted as the doctrine of the church, believers will be left in a distressing state of doubt and uncertainty concerning the narratives of the four Gospels, and unbelievers will scoff and mock. A theory which leads to such wanderings of thought regarding the supernatural in the Scriptures must be fallacious. God is not a God of confusion.

Among the higher critics who accept some of the miracles there is a notable desire to discredit the virgin birth of our Lord, and their treatment of this event presents a good example of the fallacies of reasoning by means of which they would abolish many of the other miracles. One feature of their argument may suffice as an exhibition of all. It is the search for parallels in the pagan mythologies. There are many instances in the pagan stories of the birth of men from human mothers and divine fathers, and the higher critics would create the impression that the writers who record the birth of Christ were influenced by these fables to emulate them, and thus to secure for Him the honor of a celestial paternity. It turns out, however, that these pagan fables do not in any case present to us a virgin mother; the child is always the product of commerce with a god who assumes a human form for the purpose. The despair of the higher critics in this hunt for events of the same kind is well illustrated by Cheyne,* who cites the record of the Babylonian king Sargon, about 3,800 B. C. This monarch represents himself as having "been born of a poor mother in secret, and as not knowing his father." There have been many millions of such instances, but we do not think of the mothers as virgins. Nor does the Babylonian story affirm that the mother of Sargon was a virgin, or even that his father was a god. It is plain that Sargon did not intend to claim a supernatural origin, for, after saying that he "did not know his father," he adds that "the brother of his father lived in the mountains." It was a case

*"Bible Problems," page 86.

like multitudes of others in which children, early orphaned, have not known their fathers, but have known the relations of their fathers. This statement of Sargon I quote from a translation of it made by Cheyne himself in the "Encyclopedia Biblica." He continues, "There is reason to suspect that something similar was originally said by the Israelites of Moses." To substantiate this he adds, "See Encyclopedia Biblica, 'Moses,' section 3 with note 4." On turning to this reference the reader finds that the article was written by Cheyne himself, and that it contains no evidence whatever.

FIFTH FALLACY: THE TESTIMONY OF ARCHAEOLOGY DENIED.

V. The limitation of the field of research as far as possible to the biblical books as literary productions has rendered many of the higher critics reluctant to admit the new light derived from archaeology. This is granted by Cheyne.* "I have no wish to deny," he says, "that the so-called 'higher critics' in the past were as a rule suspicious of Assyriology as a young, and, as they thought, too self-assertive science, and that many of those who now recognize its contributions to knowledge are somewhat too mechanical in the use of it, and too skeptical as to the influence of Babylonian culture in relatively early times in Syria, Palestine and even Arabia." This grudging recognition of the testimony of archaeology may be observed in several details.

1. It was said that the Hexateuch must have been formed chiefly by the gathering up of oral traditions, because it is not to be supposed that the early Hebrews possessed the art of writing and of keeping records. But the entire progress of archaeological study refutes this. In particular the discovery of the Tel el-Amarna tablets has shown that writing in cuneiform characters and in the Assyrio-Babylonian language was common to the entire biblical world long before the exodus.

*"Bible Problems," page 142.

The discovery was made by Egyptian peasants in 1887. There are more than three hundred tablets, which came from various lands, including Babylonia and Palestine. Other finds have added their testimony to the fact that writing and the preservation of records were the peculiar passions of the ancient civilized world. Under the constraint of the overwhelming evidences, Professor Jordan writes as follows: "The question as to the age of writing never played a great part in the discussion." He falls back on the supposition that the nomadic life of the early Hebrews would prevent them from acquiring the art of writing. He treats us to such reasoning as the following: "If the fact that writing is very old is such a powerful argument when taken alone, it might enable you to prove that Alfred the Great wrote Shakespeare's plays."

2. It was easy to treat Abraham as a mythical figure when the early records of Babylonia were but little known. The entire coloring of those chapters of Genesis which refer to Mesopotamia could be regarded as the product of the imagination. This is no longer the case. Thus Clay,* writing of Genesis 14, says: "The theory of the late origin of all the Hebrew Scriptures prompted the critics to declare this narrative to be a pure invention of a later Hebrew writer. * * * The patriarchs were relegated to the region of myth and legend. Abraham was made a fictitious father of the Hebrews. * * * Even the political situation was declared to be inconsistent with fact. * * * Weighing carefully the position taken by the critics in the light of what has been revealed through the decipherment of the cuneiform inscriptions, we find that the very foundations upon which their theories rest, with reference to the points that could be tested, totally disappear. The truth is, that wherever any light has been thrown upon the subject through excavations, their hypotheses have invariably been found wanting." But the higher critics are

*"Light on the Old Testament from Babel." 1907. Clay is Assistant Professor and Assistant Curator of the Babylonian Section, Department of Archaeology, in the University of Pennsylvania.

still reluctant to admit this new light. Thus Kent[1] says, "The primary value of these stories is didactic and religious, rather than historical."

3. The books of Joshua and Judges have been regarded by the higher critics as unhistorical on the ground that their portraiture of the political, religious, and social condition of Palestine in the thirteenth century B. C. is incredible. This cannot be said any longer, for the recent excavations in Palestine have shown us a land exactly like that of these books. The portraiture is so precise, and is drawn out in so many minute lineaments, that it cannot be the product of oral tradition floating down through a thousand years. In what details the accuracy of the biblical picture of early Palestine is exhibited may be seen perhaps best in the excavations by Macalister[2] at Gezer. Here again there are absolutely no discrepancies between the Land and the Book, for the Land lifts up a thousand voices to testify that the Book is history and not legend.

4. It was held by the higher critics that the legislation which we call Mosaic could not have been produced by Moses, since his age was too early for such codes. This reasoning was completely negatived by the discovery of the code of Hammurabi, the Amraphel[3] of Genesis 14. This code is very different from that of Moses; it is more systematic; and it is at least seven hundred years earlier than the Mosaic legislation.

In short, from the origin of the higher criticism till this present time the discoveries in the field of archaeology have given it a succession of serious blows. The higher critics were shocked when the passion of the ancient world for writing and the preservation of documents was discovered. They were shocked when primitive Babylonia appeared as the land of Abraham. They were shocked when early Palestine appeared as the land of Joshua and the Judges. They were shocked when

[1]Biblical World, Dec., 1906.
[2]"Bible Side-Lights from the Mound of Gezer."
[3]On this matter see any dictionary of the Bible, art. "Amraphel."

Amraphel came back from the grave as a real historical character, bearing his code of laws. They were shocked when the stele
of the Pharaoh of the exodus was read, and it was proved that
he knew a people called Israel, that they had no settled place
of abode, that they were "without grain" for food, and that
in these particulars they were quite as they are represented by
the Scriptures to have been when they had fled from Egypt
into the wilderness.*   The embarrassment created by these
discoveries is manifest in many of the recent writings of the
higher critics, in which, however, they still cling heroically to
their analysis and their late dating of the Pentateuch and their
confidence in the hypothesis of evolution as the key of all
history.

SIXTH FALLACY: THE PSALMS WRITTEN AFTER THE
EXILE.

VI.   The Psalms are usually dated by the higher critics
after the exile.   The great majority of the higher critics are
agreed here, and tell us that these varied and touching and
magnificent lyrics of religious experience all come to us from
a period later than 450 B. C.   A few of the critics admit an
earlier origin of three or four of them, but they do this waveringly, grudgingly, and against the general consensus of opinion among their fellows.   In the Bible a very large number
of the Psalms are ascribed to David, and these, with a few
insignificant and doubtful exceptions, are denied to him and
brought down, like the rest, to the age of the second temple.
This leads me to the following observations:

---

*The higher critics usually slur over this remarkable inscription,
and give us neither an accurate translation nor a natural interpretation of it. I have, therefore, special pleasure in quoting the following from Driver, "Authority and Archaeology," page 61: "Whereas
the other places named in the inscription all have the determinative
for 'country,' Ysiraal has the determinative for 'men': it follows that
the reference is not to the land of Israel, but to Israel as a tribe or
people, whether migratory, or on the march." Thus this distinguished
higher critic sanctions the view of the record which I have adopted.
He represents Maspero and Naville as doing the same.

1. Who wrote the Psalms? Here the higher critics have no answer. Of the period from 400 to 175 B. C. we are in almost total ignorance. Josephus knows almost nothing about it, nor has any other writer told us more. Yet, according to the theory, it was precisely in these centuries of silence, when the Jews had no great writers, that they produced this magnificent outburst of sacred song.

2. This is the more remarkable when we consider the well known men to whom the theory denies the authorship of any of the Psalms. The list includes such names as Moses, David, Samuel, Nathan, Solomon, Isaiah, Jeremiah, and the long list of preëxilic prophets. We are asked to believe that these men composed no Psalms, and that the entire collection was contributed by men so obscure that they have left no single name by which we can identify them with their work.

3. This will appear still more extraordinary if we consider the times in which, it is said, no Psalms were produced, and contrast them with the times in which all of them were produced. The times in which none were produced were the great times, the times of growth, of mental ferment, of conquest, of imperial expansion, of disaster, and of recovery. The times in which none were produced were the times of the splendid temple of Solomon, with its splendid worship. The times in which none were produced were the heroic times of Elijah and Elisha, when the people of Jehovah struggled for their existence against the abominations of the pagan gods. On the other hand, the times which actually produced them were the times of growing legalism, of obscurity, and of inferior abilities. All this is incredible. We could believe it only if we first came to believe that the Psalms are works of slight literary and religious value. This is actually done by Wellhausen, who says,* "They certainly are to the smallest extent original, and are for the most part imitations which illustrate the saying about much writing." The Psalms are not all of an

*Quoted by Orr, "The Problem of the Old Testament," page 435.

equally high degree of excellence, and there are a few of them which might give some faint color of justice to this depreciation of the entire collection. But as a whole they are exactly the reverse of this picture. Furthermore, they contain absolutely no legalism, but are as free from it as are the Sermon on the Mount and the Pauline epistles. Yet further, the writers stand out as personalities, and they must have left a deep impression upon their fellows. Finally, they were full of the fire of genius kindled by the Holy Spirit. It is impossible for us to attribute the Psalms to the unknown mediocrities of the period which followed the restoration.

4. Very many of the Psalms plainly appear to be ancient. They sing of early events, and have no trace of allusion to the age which is said to have produced them.

5. The large number of Psalms attributed to David have attracted the special attention of the higher critics. They are denied to him on various grounds. He was a wicked man, and hence incapable of writing these praises to the God of righteousness. He was an iron warrior and statesman, and hence not gifted with the emotions found in these productions. He was so busy with the cares of conquest and administration that he had no leisure for literary work. Finall y, his conception of God was utterly different from that which moved the psalmists.

The larger part of this catalogue of inabilities is manifestly erroneous. David, with some glaring faults, and with a single enormous crime, for which he was profoundly penitent, was one of the noblest of men. He was indeed an iron warrior and statesman, but also one of the most emotional of all great historic characters. He was busy, but busy men not seldom find relief in literary occupations, as Washington, during the Revolutionary War, poured forth a continual tide of letters, and as Cæsar, Marcus Aurelius, and Gladstone, while burdened with the cares of empire, composed immortal books. The conception of God with which David began his career was indeed narrow (I. Sam. 26:19). But did he learn nothing in all his later experiences, and his associations with holy priests and prophets? He was certainly teachable: did God fail to make use of him in further revealing Himself to His people? To deny these Psalms to David on the ground of his limited views of God in his early life, is this not to deny that God made successive revelations of Himself wherever He found suitable channels? If, further, we consider the unquestioned skill of David in the music of his nation and his age (I. Sam. 16:14-25), this will constitute a presupposition in favor of his interest in sacred song. If, finally, we consider his personal career of danger and deliverance, this will appear as the natural means of awakening in him the spirit of varied religious poetry. His times were much like the Elizabethan period, which ministered unexampled stimulus to the English mind.

From all this we may turn to the singular verdict of Professor Jordan: "If a man says he cannot see why David could not have written Psalms 51 and 139, you are compelled to reply as politely as possible that if he did write them then any man can write anything." So also we may say, "as politely as possible," that if Shakespeare, with his "small Latin and less Greek," did write his incomparable dramas, "then any man can write anything"; that if Dickens, with his mere elementary education, did write his great novels, "then any man can write anything"; and that if Lincoln, who had no early schooling, did write his Gettysburg address, "then any man can write anything."

SEVENTH FALLACY: DEUTERONOMY NOT WRITTEN BY MOSES.

VII. One of the fixed points of the higher criticism is its theory of the origin of Deuteronomy. In I. Kings 22 we have the history of the finding of the book of the law in the temple, which was being repaired. Now the higher critics present this finding, not as the discovery of an ancient document, but as the finding of an entirely new document, which had been concealed in the temple in order that it might be found, might be accepted as the production of Moses, and might produce an effect by its assumed authorship. It is not supposed for a moment that the writer innocently chose the fictitious dress of Mosaic authorship for merely literary purposes. On the contrary, it is steadfastly maintained that he intended to deceive, and that others were with him in the plot to deceive. This statement of the case leads me to the following reflections:

1. According to the theory, this was an instance of pious fraud. And the fraud must have been prepared deliberately. The manuscript must have been soiled and frayed by special care, for it was at once admitted to be ancient. This supposition of deceit must always repel the Christian believer.

2. Our Lord draws from the Book of Deuteronomy all the three texts with which He foils the tempter, Matt. 4:1-11, Luke 4:1-14. It must always shock the devout student that his Saviour should select His weapons from an armory founded on deceit.

3. This may be called an appeal to ignorant piety, rather than to scholarly criticism. But surely the moral argument should have some weight in scholarly criticism. In the sphere of religion moral impossibilities are as insuperable as physical and mental.

4. If we turn to consideration of a literary kind, it is to be observed that the higher criticism runs counter here to the statement of the book itself that Moses was its author.

5. It runs counter to the narrative of the finding of the book, and turns the finding of an ancient book into the forgery of a new book.

6. It runs counter to the judgment of all the intelligent men of the time who learned of the discovery. They judged the book to have come down from the Mosaic age, and to be from the pen of Moses. We hear of no dissent whatever.

7. It seeks support in a variety of reasons, such as style, historical discrepancies, and legal contradictions, all of which prove of little substance when examined fairly.

EIGHTH FALLACY: THE PRIESTLY LEGISLATION NOT ENACTED UNTIL THE EXILE.

VIII. Another case of forgery is found in the origin of the priestly legislation, if we are to believe the higher critics. This legislation is contained in a large number of passages scattered through Exodus, Leviticus, and Numbers. It has to do chiefly with the tabernacle and its worship, with the duties of the priests and Levites, and with the relations of the people to the institutions of religion. It is attributed to Moses in scores of places. It has a strong coloring of the Mosaic age and of the wilderness life. It affirms the existence of the tabernacle, with an orderly administration of the ritual services. But this is all imagined, for the legislation is a late production. Before the exile there were temple services and a priesthood, with certain regulations concerning them, either oral or written, and use was made of this tradition; but as a whole the legislation was enacted by such men as Ezekiel and Ezra during and immediately after the exile, or about 444 B. C. The name of Moses, the fiction of a tabernacle, and the general coloring of the Mosaic age, were given it in order to render it authoritative and to secure the ready obedience of the nation. But now:

1. The moral objection here is insuperable. The supposition of forgery, and of forgery so cunning, so elaborate, and so minute, is abhorrent. If the forgery had been invented and executed by wicked men to promote some scheme of selfishness, it would have been less odious. But when it is presented to us as the expedient of holy men, for the advancement of the religion of the God of righteousness, which afterwards blossomed out into Christianity, we must revolt.

2. The theory gives us a portraiture of such men as

Ezekiel and Ezra which is utterly alien from all that we know of them. The expedient might be worthy of the prophets of Baal or of Chemosh; it was certainly not worthy of the prophets of Jehovah, and we dishonor them when we attribute it to them and place them upon a low plane of craft and cunning of which the records concerning them are utterly ignorant.

3. The people who returned from the exile were among the most intelligent and enterprising of the nation, else they would not have returned, and they would not have been deceived by the sudden appearance of Mosaic laws forged for the occasion and never before heard of.

4. Many of the regulations of this legislation are drastic. It subjected the priests and Levites to a rule which must have been irksome in the extreme, and it would not have been lightly accepted. We may be certain that if it had been a new thing fraudulently ascribed to Moses, these men would have detected the deceit, and would have refused to be bound by it. But we do not hear of any revolt, or even of any criticism.

Such are some of the fundamental fallacies of the higher criticism. They constitute an array of impossibilities. I have stated them in their more moderate forms, that they may be seen and weighed without the remarkable extravagances which some of their advocates indulge. In the very mildest interpretation which can be given them, they are repugnant to the Christian faith.

NO MIDDLE GROUND.

But might we not accept a part of this system of thought without going to any hurtful extreme? Many today are seeking to do this. They present to us two diverse results.

1. Some, who stand at the beginning of the tide, find themselves in a position of doubt. If they are laymen, they know not what to believe. If they are ministers, they know not what to believe or to teach. In either case, they have no firm footing, and no Gospel, except a few platitudes which do little harm and little good.

2. The majority of those who struggle to stand here find it impossible to do so, and give themselves up to the current. There is intellectual consistency in the lofty church doctrine of inspiration. There may be intellectual consistency in the doctrine that all things have had a natural origin and history, under the general providence of God, as distinguished from His supernatural revelation of Himself through holy men, and especially through His co-equal Son, so that the Bible is as little supernatural as the "Imitation of Christ" or the "Pilgrim's Progress." But there is no position of intellectual consistency between these two, and the great mass of those who try to pause at various points along the descent are swept down with the current. The natural view of the Scriptures is a sea which has been rising higher for three-quarters of a century. Many Christians bid it welcome to pour lightly over the walls which the faith of the church has always set up against it, in the expectation that it will prove a healthful and helpful stream. It is already a cataract, uprooting, destroying, and slaying.

CHAPTER IV

THE BIBLE AND MODERN CRITICISM

BY F. BETTEX, D. D.,
PROFESSOR EMERITUS, STUTTGART, GERMANY

TRANSLATED FROM THE ORIGINAL GERMAN
BY DAVID HEAGLE, D. D.

It is undeniable that the universe, including ourselves, exists. Whence comes it all? For any clear-thinking mind there are only three possibilities. Either the universe has existed always, it produced itself, or it was created by a Divine, a Supreme Being.

THE UNIVERSE NOT ETERNAL

The eternity of the universe is most clearly disproved by its evolution. From a scientific point of view that hypothesis is now discredited and virtually abandoned. Astronomers, physicists, biologists, philosophers, are beginning to recognize more and more, and men like Secchi, Dubois-Reymond, Lord Kelvin, Dr. Klein and others, unanimously affirm that creation has had a beginning. It always tends towards an entropy, that is, toward a perfect equilibrium of its forces, a complete standstill; and the fact that it has not yet reached such a condition is proof that it has not always existed. Should creation, however, ever come to a standstill, it could never again put itself in motion. It has had a beginning, and it will have an end. That is demonstrated most clearly by its still unfinished evolution. Should anyone say to us, of a growing tree or of a young child, that either of these forms of life has existed forever, we would at once reply, Why has it not then long ago, in the past eternity, grown up so as to reach the heaven of heavens? In like manner, reasons that great astronomer, William Herschel, with regard to the Milky-Way, that just as its breaking up into different parts shows that it cannot always endure, so we have. in this same fact, proof that it has not eternally existed.

GOD THE AUTHOR OF ALL THINGS

There remains, therefore, only this alternative: either the world produced itself, or it was created. That all things came into existence spontaneously, and therefore that we must suppose an origination of immeasurably great effects without any cause, or believe that at some time a nothing, without either willing or knowing it, and without the use of means, became a something—this is the most unreasonable assumption that could possibly be attributed to a human being. How could anything act before it existed? or a thing not yet created produce something? There is nothing more unreasonable than the creed of the unbeliever, notwithstanding all his prating about the excellence of reason.

But if this world did not produce itself, then it must have been created by some Higher Power, some Cause of all causes, such as was that First Principle upon which the dying Cicero called. Or, to use the words of Dr. Klein, that originating cause must have been a "Supreme Intelligence that has at its command unlimited creative power" (*Kosmologische Briefe,* p. 27). Hence what that Intelligence does is both illimitable and unfathomable, and it can at any time either change this world or make a new one. It is therefore *prima facie* silly for us, with our prodigiously narrow experience, to set any kind of bounds to the Supreme Being; and a God who works no miracles and is the slave of his own laws implanted in nature, such a God as the New Theology preaches, is as much lacking in being a true Divinity as is the unconscious, but all-wise "cosmic ether" of Spiller, or the "eternal stuff" of other materialists.

We conclude, then, that the universe was created, or that God is the author of all things.

REVELATION IN NATURE

But now the question arises whether God, who is both the Creator of all things and the Father of spirits, has revealed Himself to his creatures, or to His own children, the work of His hands. Such a question might surely provoke one's laughter. For what is the entire universe? what is this created nature of which we form a part? what is air? and water? and fire? what are all organized beings, my body with its many parts put together in such a highly artistic and inscrutable fashion; my soul with its infinite capabilities so little understood by myself? What are all these matters but a progressive revelation of God, given to us, as it were, in a series of concentric circles rising one above another toward their Source? For this purpose it was that God created the visible, so that through it we might perceive the invisible, and for this purpose the whole creation was made, so that through it might be manifested the invisible things of God, even his eternal power and godhead (Rom. 1:20). Creation is only the language of "the Word that was in the beginning, and was with God, and was God, and by Whom all things were made" (John 1:1-3). What does this Word declare? What else but the great infinite name of God the Father, the primal source of all things, the name that must be hallowed? There was a time, however, even before the world was, when there existed nothing but God and his name. All the different works of creation are only letters in this great name.

REVELATION IN THE BIBLE

But there is another revelation which God has given of Himself to men—a more definite and personal one. Thus, e. g., he declared Himself to Adam, and through Enoch and Noah to the antediluvians, and again after the flood to other generations through Noah and his sons. But because at the building of the tower of Babel men turned stubbornly away from God, He gave them up to the thoughts of their own heart, and selected one man, Abraham, to go out from his friends and kindred, so that in his seed all the nations of the world might be blessed. Then, first, out of Abraham came the people of Israel, to whom were committed the oracles of God; and from this period began the history of the written Word. Moses narrates the beginning of things, also records the law, and holy men of God speak and write as they are moved by the Holy Spirit. That is inspiration—a divine *in-breathing.*

But here a distinction must be made. The Bible reports matters of history, and in doing so includes many genealogies which were composed, first of all, not for us, but for those most immediately concerned, and for the angels (1 Cor. 4:9). Also it reports many sins and shameful deeds; for just as the sun first illuminates himself and then sheds his radiance upon the ocean and the puddle, the eagle and the worm, so the Bible undertakes to represent to us not only God, but also man just as he is. In giving us these narratives it may be said, moreover, that God, who numbers the very hairs of our head, exercised a providential control, so that what was reported by His chosen men should be the real facts, and nothing else. To what extent He inspired those men with the very words used by them, it is not for us to know, but probably more fully than we suspect.

But when God, after having communicated the law to Moses on Mount Sinai and in the Tabernacle, communes with him as a friend with friend, and Moses writes "all the words of this law in a book" (Deut. 28:58; 31:24), then Moses really becomes the pen of God. When God speaks to the prophets, "Behold, I put my words in thy mouth," and "all the words that thou hearest thou shalt say to this people," then these prophets become the very mouth of God. When Christ appears to John on Patmos, and says, "To the angel of the church write these things," this is an instance of verbal dictation.

But just here we are amused at those weak-minded critics who, with hackneyed phrases, talk so glibly about "mechanical instruments" and "mere verbal dictation." Does then a self-revelation of the Almighty and a making known of His counsels, a gracious act which exalts the human agent to be a co-worker with Jehovah, annihilate personal freedom? Or does it not rather enlarge that freedom, and lift it up to a higher and more joyous activity? Am I then a "mechanical instrument" when with deep devotion and with enthusiasm I repeat after Christ, word for word, the prayer which He taught his disciples? The Bible is, consequently, a book which originated according to the will and with the co-operation of God; and as such it is our guide to eternity, conducting man, seemingly without a plan and yet with absolute certainty, all the way from the first creation and from Paradise on to the second or higher creation and to the New Jerusalem (Comp. Gen. 2:8-10 with Rev. 21:1, 2).

PROOF OF THE BIBLE'S INSPIRATION

How does the Bible prove itself to be a divinely inspired, heaven-given book, a communication from a Father to His children, and thus a revelation?

First, by the fact that, as does no other sacred book in the world, it condemns man and all his works. It does not praise either his wisdom, his reason, his art, or any progress that he has made; but it represents him as being in the sight of God, a miserable sinner, incapable of doing anything good, and deserving only death and endless perdition. Truly, a book which is able thus to speak, and in consequence causes millions of men, troubled in conscience, to prostrate themselves in the dust, crying, "God be merciful to me a sinner," must contain more than mere ordinary truth.

Secondly, the Bible exalts itself far above all merely human books by its announcement of the great incomprehensible mystery that, "God so loved the world that He gave His only begotten Son; that whosover believeth in Him should not perish, but have everlasting life" (John 3:16). Where is there a god among all the heathen nations, be he Osiris, Brahma, Baal, Jupiter or Odin, that would have promised those people that, by taking upon himself the sin of the world and suffering its punishment, he would thus become a savior and redeemer to them?

Thirdly, the Bible sets the seal of its divine origin upon itself by means of the prophecies. Very appropriately does God inquire, through the prophet Isaiah, "Who, as I, shall call, and shall declare it, and set it in order for Me since I established the ancient people? and the things that are coming and shall come to pass, let them declare" (Ch. 44:7). Or says again, "I am God, declaring the end from the beginning, and from ancient times, things not yet done, saying, My counsel shall stand, and I will do all My pleasure; calling a ravenous bird from the east, and the man of My counsel from a far country. Yea, I have spoken, I will also bring it to pass; I have purposed, I will also do it" (Ch. 46:10, 11). Or, addressing Pharaoh, "Where are thy wise men, and let them tell thee, and let them know what the Lord of Hosts hath purposed upon Egypt" (Ch. 19:12). Again we say, where is there a god, or gods, a founder of religion, such as Confucius, Buddha, or Mohammed, who could, with such certainty, have predicted the future of even his own people? Or where is there a statesman who in these times can foretell what will be the condition of things in Europe one hundred or even ten years from now? Nevertheless the prophecies of Moses and his threatened judgments upon the Israelites have been literally fulfilled. Literally also have been fulfilled, (although who at the time would have believed it?) the prophecies respecting the destruction of those great ancient cities,

Babylon, Nineveh and Memphis. Who in these times would believe a like prophecy respecting London, Paris, or New York? Moreover, in a literal way has been fulfilled what the prophets David and Isaiah foresaw concerning the last sufferings of Christ—His death on the cross, His drinking of vinegar, and the casting of lots for His garments. And there are other prophecies which will still be most literally fulfilled, such as the promises made to Israel, the final judgment, and the end of the world. "For," as Habakkuk says, "the vision is yet for an appointed time, and will not lie. Though it tarry, wait for it; it will surely come" (Ch. 2:3).

Furthermore, the Bible has demonstrated its peculiar power by its influence with the martyrs. Think of the hundreds of thousands who, at different times and among different peoples, have sacrificed their all, their wives, their children, all their possessions, and finally life itself, on account of this book. Think of how they have, on the rack and at the stake, confessed the truth of the Bible, and borne testimony to its power. However, O ye critics and despisers of God's Word, if you will only write such a book and then die for it, we will believe you.

Lastly, the Bible shows itself every day to be a divinely given book by its beneficent influence among all kinds of people. It converts to a better life the ignorant and the learned, the beggar on the street and the king upon his throne, yonder poor woman dwelling in an attic, the greatest poet and the profoundest thinker, civilized Europeans and uncultured savages. Despite all the scoffing and derision of its enemies, it has been translated into hundreds of languages, and has been preached by thousands of missionaries to millions of people. It makes the proud humble and the dissolute virtuous; it consoles the unfortunate, and teaches man how to live patiently and die triumphantly. No other book or collection of books accomplishes for man the exceeding great benefits accomplished by this book of truth.

MODERN CRITICISM AND ITS RATIONALISTIC METHOD

In these times there has appeared a criticism which, constantly growing bolder in its attacks upon this sacred book, now decrees, with all self-assurance and confidence, that it is simply a human production. Besides other faults found with it, it is declared to be full of errors, many of its books to be spurious, written by unknown men at later dates than those assigned, etc., etc. But we ask, upon what fundamental principle, what axiom, is this verdict of the critics based? It is upon the idea that, as Renan expressed it, reason is capable of judging all things, but is itself judged by nothing. That is surely a proud dictum, but an empty one if its character is really noticed. To be sure, God has given reason to man, so that, in his customary way of planting and building, buying and selling, he may make a practical use of created nature by which he is surrounded. But is reason, even as respects matters of this life, in accord with itself? By no means. For, if that were so, whence comes all the strife and contention of men at home and abroad, in their places of business and their public assemblies, in art and science, in legislation, religion and philosophy? Does it not all proceed from the conflicts of reason? The entire history of our race is the history of millions of men gifted with reason who have been in perpetual conflict one with another. Is it with such reason, then, that sentence is to be pronounced upon a divinely given book? A purely rational revelation would certainly be a contradiction of terms; besides, it would be wholly superfluous. But when reason undertakes to speak of things entirely supernatural, invisible and eternal, it talks as a blind man does about colors, discoursing of matters concerning which it neither knows nor can know anything; and thus it makes itself ridiculous. It has not ascended up to heaven, neither has it descended into the deep; and therefore a purely rational religion is no religion at all.

INCOMPETENCY OF REASON FOR SPIRITUAL TRUTH

Reason alone has never inspired men with great sublime conceptions of spiritual truth, whether in the way of discovery or invention; but usually it has at first rejected and ridiculed such matters. And just so it is with these rationalistic critics, they have no appreciation or understanding of the high and sublime in God's Word. They understand neither the majesty of Isaiah, the pathos of David's repentance, the audacity of Moses' prayers, the philosophic depth of Ecclesiastes, nor the wisdom of Solomon which "uttereth her voice in the streets." According to them ambitious priests, at a later date than is commonly assigned, compiled all those books to which we have alluded; also they wrote the Sinaitic law, and invented the whole story of Moses' life. ("A magnificent fiction"—so one of the critics calls that story.) But if all this is so, then we must believe that cunning falsifiers, who were, however, so the critics say, devout men, genuine products of their day (although it calls for notice that the age in which those *devout men* lived, should, as was done to Christ, have persecuted and killed them, when usually an age loves its own children); that is to say, we must believe not only that shallow-minded men have uncovered for us eternal truths and the most distant future, but also that vulgar, interested liars, have declared to us the inexorable righteousness of a holy God! Of course, all that is nonsense; no one can believe it.

But if these critics discourse, as sometimes they do, with great self-assurance upon topics such as the history of Israel, the peculiar work of the prophets, revelation, inspiration, the essence of Christianity, the difference between the teachings of Christ and those of Paul, anyone who intelligently reads what they say is impressed with the idea that, although they display much ingenuity in their efforts, after all they do not really understand the matters concerning which they speak. In like manner they talk with much ingenuity and show of learning about men with whom they have only a far-off acquaintance; and they discuss events in the realm of the Spirit where they have had no personal experience. Thus they both illustrate and prove the truth of the Scripture teaching that "the natural man receiveth not the things of the Spirit of God." These critics say that God, not being a man, cannot speak; consequently there is no word of God! Also, God cannot manifest Himself in visible form; therefore all the accounts of such epiphanies are mythical tales! Inspiration, they tell us, is unthinkable; hence all representations of such acts are diseased imagination! Of prophecy there is none; what purports to be such was written after the events! Miracles are impossible; therefore all the reports of them, as given in the Bible, are mere fictions! Men always seek, thus it is explained, their own advantage and personal glory, and just so it was with those "prophets of Israel."

Such is what they call "impartial science," "unprejudiced research," "objective demonstration."

NOTHING NEW IN THESE "NEW" VIEWS

Moreover, these critics claim for their peculiar views that they are "new theology," and the "latest investigation." But that also is untrue. Even in the times of Christ the famous rabbi Hillel and his disciple Gamaliel substituted for the Mosaic law all manner of "traditions" (Matt. 15:2-9; 23:16-22). Since then other learned rabbis, such as Ben Akiba, Maimonides and others, have engaged in Bible criticism; not only casting doubts upon the genuineness of various books of the Old Testament, but also denying the miracles and talking learnedly about "myths." Even eighteen hundred years ago Celsus brought forward the same objections as those now raised by modern criticism; and in his weak and bungling production, the "Life of Jesus," David Strauss has in part repeated them. Also there have been other noted heretics, such as Arius (317 A. D.), who denied the divinity of Christ, and Pelagius in the fifth century, who rejected the doctrine of original sin. Indeed this exceedingly new theology adopts even the unbelief of those old Sadducees who said "there is no resurrection, neither angel nor spirit" (Acts 23:8), and whom Christ reproved with the words, "Ye do err, not knowing the Scriptures nor the power of God" (Matt. 22:29). It certainly does not argue for the spiritual progress of our race, that such a threadbare and outworn unbelieving kind of science should again, in these days, deceive and even stultify thousands of people.

NO AGREEMENT AMONG THE CRITICS

Do these critics then, to ask the least of them, agree with one another? Far from it. To be sure, they unanimously deny the inspiration of the Bible, the divinity of Christ and of the Holy Spirit, the fall of man and the forgiveness of sins through Christ; also prophecy and miracles, the resurrection of the dead, the final judgment, heaven and hell. But when it comes to their pretendedly sure results, not any two of them affirm the same things; and their numerous publications create a flood of disputable, self-contradictory and mutually destructive hypotheses. For example, the Jehovah of the Old Testament is made to be some heathen god, either a nomadic or steppe god, the weather-god Jahu, or the god of West-Semitism. It was David who first introduced this divinity; and according to some authors the peculiar worship of this god was, with its human sacrifices (!), only a continuation of the Baal-Moloch worship! Of Abraham it is sometimes affirmed that he never existed, but at other times that he was a Canaanite chief, dwelling at Hebron. No! he is the myth of the Aurora; and Sarah, or Scharratu, is the wife of the moon-god Sin, and so on. The twelve sons of Jacob are very probably the twelve months of the year. As to Moses, some teach there never was such a man, also that the ten commandments were composed in the time of Manasseh. No! the more moderate writers say that Moses is a historical character. It was in Midian that he learned about Jah, the tribal god of the Kenites; and he determined with this divinity to liberate his people. Elijah is simply a myth; or he was some unfortunate prophet who had perhaps been struck by lightning. And so, too, this modern criticism knows for sure that it was not Solomon, but a wholly unknown king, living after the time of Ezra, who wrote Ecclesiastes; also that there never was a Daniel, but that again some unknown author wrote the book bearing that name. Moreover, Kautsch tells us that this book first made its appearance in January, 164 B. C., while other critics are positive that it was in 165. Query: Why could not that unknown author have been named Daniel?

So also Wellhausen knows of twenty-two different authors—all of them, to be sure, unknown—for the books of Moses, while Kuenen is satisfied with sixteen. The noted English critic, Canon Cheyne, is said to have taken great pains to tear the book of Isaiah's prophecies into one hundred and sixty pieces, all by unknown writers; which pieces were scattered through ten different epochs including four and a half centuries ("Modern Puritan," 1907, p. 400). Likewise this critic knows that the first chapter of 1 Samuel originated with an unknown writer living some five hundred years after the time of that prophet; also that Hannah's glory-song, as found in 2 Kings, was written by some other "unknown." That Eli ruled over Israel for forty years is, "in all likelihood," the unauthentic statement of a later day (Hastings' Bible Dictionary). Why so? we may ask.—The book of Deuteronomy was written, we are told, in 561 B. C., and Ecclesiastes in 264 B. C.; and a German critic, Budde, is certain that the book of Job has somehow lost its last chapter, and that fifty-nine verses of this book should be wholly expunged.

Such are a few illustrations of the way in which Holy Scripture is treated by the criticism we are considering.

But, surely, it would not require much sagacity and intelligence for one, by applying such peculiar methods, say, to Goethe's works, to demonstrate critically that a good share of those productions, such as Erlkönig, Iphigenia, Götz von Berlichingen, the Wahlverwandschaften, Faust (Parts I. and II.), belong, if judged of by their style of composition and their historical and philosophical views, to wholly different epochs, and that they originated with many different authors. Moreover, it could easily be shown that none of those authors lived in the times when Napoleon Bonaparte revolutionized Europe, since his name is not mentioned in any of the productions specified.

CRITICISM AS APPLIED TO THE NEW TESTAMENT

Of course this modern criticism does not stop short of the New Testament. This part of the Bible, Harnack says, narrates for us incredible stories respecting the birth and childhood of Christ. "Nevermore," he goes on to assert, "shall we believe that he walked upon the sea and commanded the storm." It stands to reason that He did not rise from the dead. The Fourth Gospel is spurious, and so also is (according to late critical authority) the Epistle to the Romans. The Book of Revelation is only the occasion for derisive laughter on the part of these skeptical critics; and because it is so, the curse mentioned in its last chapter is made applicable to them (vs. 18, 19). Nevertheless, these men sin most seriously against Christ. In their view the very Son of God, the Word that was in the beginning with God, and that was God, and without Whom nothing exists, is only a fanatical young rabbi; entangled in the peculiar views and superstitions of his people; and he died upon the cross only because he misconceived of the character of his own mission and the nature of his times. Jesus "is not indispensable to the Gospel," so writes Harnack.

Now all this is what is denominated Biblical criticism. It is a jumble of mere hypotheses, imaginings and assertions, brought forward often without even the shadow of proof, and with no real certainty. Still, in these times it represents itself to thousands of nominal Christians and to hundreds of miserably deceived theological students who are to become preachers of God's word, as being the "assured results of the latest scientific research." May God have mercy, if such is the case!

WHAT ARE THE FRUITS OF THIS CRITICISM?

Now, if these people were of the truth, and if they would only believe Him who says, "I am the way, the truth and the life," they would not be under the necessity of tediously working their way through the numerous publications (statistics show that there appear in Europe and America annually some eight hundred of these works) ; but they would find in His teaching a simple and sure means for testing the character of these critical doctrines. "Ye shall know them by their fruits," is what Christ says of the false teachers who came in His name. "Do men gather grapes of thorns, or figs of thistles?" (Matt. 7:16). Are the fruits of modern criticism good? Where are the grapes or figs that grow on this thorn-bush? Has not this criticism already robbed, and perhaps forever, thousands of people of their first love, their undoubting faith, and their joyous hope? Has it not sowed dissension, fostered pride and self-conceit, and injured before all the world the authority of both the church and its ministers? Has it not offended Christ's "little ones?" (Matt. 18:6, 7). And does it not every day furnish the enemies of God with opportunities for deriding and scorning the truth? Where are the souls that it has led to God—comforting, strengthening, purifying and sanctifying them? Where are the individuals who even in the hour of death have continued to rejoice in the benefits of this criticism?

In the study-room it ensnares, in lecture-halls it makes great pretenses, for mere popular lectures it is still serviceable; but when the thunders of God's power break in upon the soul, when despair at the loss of all one has loved takes possession of the mind, when remembrance of a miserable lost life or of past misdeeds is felt and realized, when one is on a sick-bed and death approaches, and the soul, appreciating that it is now on the brink of eternity, calls for a Savior—just at this time when its help is most needed, this modern religion utterly fails. In the year 1864, in Geneva, one of those modern theologians was summoned to prepare for execution a young man who had committed murder and robbery. But he candidly exclaimed, "Call some one else, I have nothing to say to him." This incompetent criticism did not know of any consolation for the sin-burdened soul; therefore an orthodox clergyman was obtained, and the wretched man, murderer though he was, died reconciled to God through the blood of Christ.

But suppose that all the teachings of this criticism were true, what would it avail us? It would put us in a sad condition indeed. For then, sitting beside ruined temples and broken-down altars, with no joy as respects the hereafter, no hope of everlasting life, no God to help us, no forgiveness of sins, feeling miserable, all desolate in our hearts and chaotic in our minds, we should be utterly unable either to know or believe anything more. Can such a view of the world, such a religion, which, as was said of Professor Harnack's lectures in America, only destroys, removes and tears down, be true? No! If this modern criticism is true, then away with all so-called Christianity, which only deceives us with idle tales! Away with a religion which has nothing to offer us but the commonplace teachings of morality! Away with faith! Away with hope! Let us eat and drink, for tomorrow we die!

THESE TEACHINGS IN THE LIGHT OF SCRIPTURE

But let us hear what God's word has to say regarding this topic:

2 Pet. 1:21.—"For no prophecy ever came by the will of man; but holy men of God spake as they were moved by the Holy Ghost."

2 Tim. 3:16, 17.—"All Scripture given by inspiration of God is profitable for doctrine, for reproof, for correction, for instruction in righteousness; that the man of God may be perfect, thoroughly furnished unto all good works."

Gal. 1:11, 12.—"I certify you, brethren, that the Gospel which was preached by me is not after man, neither was I taught it, but by the revelation of Jesus Christ."

Rom. 1:16.—"I am not ashamed of the Gospel of Christ; for it is the power of God unto salvation to every one that believeth."

Acts 20:30.—But "of your own selves shall men arise, speaking perverse things, to draw away disciples after them."

2 Pet. 2:1.—"There were false prophets also among the people, * * * who privily shall bring in damnable heresies, even denying the Lord that bought them."

1 Cor. 1:20, 21.—"Where is the wise? where is the scribe? where is the disputer of this world? Hath not God made foolish the wisdom of this world? For after that in the wisdom of God the world by wisdom knew not God, it pleased God by the foolishness of preaching to save them that believe."

Col. 2:4-8.—"This I say, lest any man should beguile you with enticing words," or "spoil you through philosophy and vain deceit, after the rudiments of the world, and not after Christ."

1 Cor. 3:19.—"For the wisdom of this world is foolishness with God."

1 Cor. 2:5.—"That your faith should not stand in the wisdom of men, but in the power of God."

1 Cor. 2:4.—"And my speech and my preaching was not with enticing words of man's wisdom, but in demonstration of the Spirit and of power."

1 Cor. 2:12, 13.—"Now we have received, not the spirit of the world, but the spirit which is of God, that we might know the things that are freely given to us of God. Which things also we speak, not in the words which man's wisdom teacheth, but which the Holy Ghost teacheth; comparing spiritual things with spiritual."

Col. 1:21 and 2 Cor. 10:5.—Therefore "you that were sometime alienated and enemies in your minds by wicked works," now "bring into captivity every thought to the obedience of Christ."

Gal. 1:9.—"As we said before, so say I now again, If any man preach any other gospel unto you than that ye have received, let him be accursed."

1 Cor. 15:17.—"Whosoever says that Christ is not risen, his faith is vain, he is yet in his sins."

2 John, vs. 7, 9, 10, 11.—"For many deceivers are entered into the world, who confess not that Jesus Christ is come in the flesh. This is a deceiver and an antichrist. * * * Whosoever transgresseth and abideth not in the doctrine of Christ, hath not God. He that abideth in the doctrine of Christ, he hath both the Father and the Son. If there come any unto you, and bring not this doctrine, receive him not into your house, neither bid him God speed; for he that biddeth him God speed is partaker of his evil deeds."

Luke 11:52.—"Woe unto you lawyers! for ye have taken away the key of knowledge; ye entered not in yourselves, and them that were entering in ye hindered."

CONCLUSION

Let us then, by repudiating this modern criticism, show our condemnation of it. What does it offer us? Nothing. What does it take away? Everything. Do we have any use for it? No! It neither helps us in life nor comforts us in death; it will not judge us in the world to come. For our Biblical faith we do not need either the encomiums of men, nor the approbation of a few poor sinners. We will not attempt to improve the Scriptures and adapt them to our liking, but we will believe them. We will not criticize them, but we will ourselves be directed by them. We will not exercise authority over them, but we will obey them. We will trust Him who is the way, the truth, and the life. His word shall make us free.

Respice finem, "consider the end"—that is what even the old Romans said. True rationalism adjudges all things from the standpoint of eternity; and it asks of every religion, What can you do for me with regard to the great beyond? What does this Biblical criticism offer us here? Only fog and mist, or, at best, an endless state of indecision, something impersonal and inactive, just like its god, whose very nature is inconceivable. "Eternal life," writes one of these modernists, "is only the infinitely weak vestige of the present life." (!) Here also the maxim proves itself true, "By their fruits ye shall know them." Just as for our present life this criticism offers us no consolation, no forgiveness of sins, no deliverance from "the fear of death, through which we are all our lifetime subject to bondage," so also it knows nothing respecting the great beyond—nothing with regard to that new heaven and new earth wherein righteousness shall dwell, nothing with regard to that golden city which shines with eternal light, nothing with regard to a God who wipes away all tears from our eyes. It is utterly ignorant of the glory of God, and on that account it stands condemned.

"Lord, to whom shall we go? Thou hast the words of eternal life. And we believe and are sure that Thou art that Christ, the Son of the living God" (John 6:68, 69). And He answered, "Behold, I come quickly: hold that fast which thou hast; that no man take thy crown" (Rev. 3:11).

CHAPTER V

HOLY SCRIPTURE AND MODERN NEGATIONS

BY PROFESSOR JAMES ORR, D. D.,
UNITED FREE CHURCH COLLEGE, GLASGOW, SCOTLAND

Is there today in the midst of criticism and unsettlement a tenable doctrine of Holy Scripture for the Christian Church and for the world; and if there is, what is that doctrine? That is unquestionably a very pressing question at the present time. "Is there a book which we can regard as the repository of a true revelation of God and an infallible guide in the way of life, and as to our duties to God and man?" is a question of immense importance to us all. Fifty years ago, perhaps less than that, the question hardly needed to be asked among Christian people. It was universally conceded, taken for granted, that there is such a book, the book which we call the Bible. Here, it was believed, is a volume which is an inspired record of the whole will of God for man's salvation; accept as true and inspired the teaching of that book, follow its guidance, and you cannot stumble, you cannot err in attaining the supreme end of existence, in finding salvation, in grasping the prize of a glorious immortality.

Now, a change has come. There is no disguising the fact that we live in an age when, even within the Church, there is much uneasy and distrustful feeling about the Holy Scriptures—a hesitancy to lean upon them as an authority and to use them as the weapons of precision they once were; with a corresponding anxiety to find some surer basis in external Church authority, or with others, in Christ Himself, or again in a Christian consciousness, as it is named,—a surer basis for Christian belief and life. We often hear in these days reference to the substitution, in Protestantism, of an "INFAL-

LIBLE BIBLE FOR AN INFALLIBLE CHURCH", and
the implication is that the one idea is just as baseless as the
other. Sometimes the idea is taken up, quite commonly perhaps, that the thought of an authority external to ourselves—
to our own reason or conscience or spiritual nature—must be
wholly given up; that only that can be accepted which carries
its authority within itself by the appeal it makes to reason or
to our spiritual being, and therein lies the judge for us of what
is true and what is false.

That proposition has an element of truth in it; it may be
true or may be false according as we interpret it. However,
as it is frequently interpreted it leaves the Scriptures—but
more than that, it leaves Jesus Christ Himself—without any
authority for us save that with which our own minds see fit
to clothe Him. But in regard to the INFALLIBLE BIBLE
AND THE INFALLIBLE CHURCH, it is proper to point
out that there is a considerable difference between these two
things—between the idea of an authoritative Scripture and the
idea of an infallible Church or an infallible Pope, in the
Roman sense of that word. It may be a clever antithesis
to say that Protestantism substituted the idea of an infallible
Book for the older Romish dogma of an infallible Church;
but the antithesis, the contrast, unfortunately has one fatal inaccuracy about it. The idea of the authority of Scripture is
not younger, but older than Romanism. It is not a late invention of Protestantism. It is not something that Protestants
invented and substituted for the Roman conception of the infallible Church; but *it is the original conception that lies in
the Scriptures themselves.* There is a great difference there.
It is a belief—this belief in the Holy Scripture—which was
accepted and acted upon by the Church of Christ from the
first. The Bible itself claims to be an authoritative Book,
and an infallible guide to the true knowledge of God and of
the way of salvation. This view is implied in every reference

made to it, so far as it then existed, by Christ and His Apostles. That the New Testament, the work of the Apostles and of apostolic men, does not stand on a lower level of inspiration and authority than the Old Testament, is, I think, hardly worth arguing. And in that sense, as a body of writings of Divine authority, the books of the Old and the New Testament were accepted by the Apostles and by the Church of the post-apostolic age.

Take the writings of any of the early Church fathers—I have waded through them wearily as teacher of Church History—take Tertullian or Origen, or others, and you will find their words saturated with references to Scripture. You will find the Scriptures treated in precisely the same way as they are used in the Biblical literature of today; namely, as the ultimate authority on the matters of which they speak. I really do the fathers an injustice in this comparison, for I find things said and written about the Holy Scriptures by teachers of the Church today which those early fathers would never have permitted themselves to utter. It has now become fashionable among a class of religious teachers to speak disparagingly of or belittle the Holy Scriptures as an authoritative rule of faith for the Church. The leading cause of this has undoubtedly been the trend which the criticism of the Holy Scriptures has assumed during the last half century or more.

By all means, let criticism have its rights. Let purely literary questions about the Bible receive full and fair discussion. Let the structure of books be impartially examined. If a reverent science has light to throw on the composition or authority or age of these books, let its voice be heard. If this thing is of God we cannot overthrow it; if it be of man, or so far as it is of man, or so far as it comes in conflict with the reality of things in the Bible, it will come to naught— as in my opinion a great deal of it is fast coming today through its own excesses. No fright, therefore, need be taken at the mere word, "Criticism."

On the other hand, we are not bound to accept every wild critical theory that any critic may choose to put forward and assert, as the final word on this matter. We are entitled, nay, we are bound, to look at the presuppositions on which each criticism proceeds, and to ask, How far is the criticism controlled by those presuppositions? We are bound to look at the evidence by which the theory is supported, and to ask, Is it really borne out by that evidence? And when theories are put forward with every confidence as fixed results, and we find them, as we observe them, still in constant process of evolution and change, constantly becoming more complicated, more extreme, more fanciful, we are entitled to inquire, Is this the certainty that it was alleged to be? *Now that is my complaint against much of the current criticism of the Bible* —not that it is criticism, but that it starts from the wrong basis, that it proceeds by arbitrary methods, and that it arrives at results which I think are demonstrably false results. That is a great deal to say, no doubt, but perhaps I shall have some justification to offer for it before I am done.

I am not going to enter into any general tirade against criticism; but it is useless to deny that a great deal of what is called criticism is responsible for the uncertainty and unsettlement of feeling existing at the present time about the Holy Scriptures. I do not speak especially of those whose philosophical standpoint compels them to take up an attitude of negation to supernatural revelation, or to books which profess to convey such a revelation. Criticism of this kind, criticism that starts from the basis of the denial of the supernatural, has of course, to be reckoned with. In its hands everything is engineered from that basis. There is the denial to begin with, that God ever has entered into human history, in word and deed, in any supernatural way. The necessary result is that whatever in the Bible affirms or flows from such interposition of God is expounded or explained away. *The Scriptures on this showing, instead of being the living ora-*

cles of God, become simply the fragmentary remains of an
ancient Hebrew literature, the chief value of which would
seem to be the employment it affords to the critic to dissect
it into its various parts, to overthrow the tradition of the
past in regard to it, and to frame ever new, ever changing, ever
more wonderful theories of the origin of the books and the
so-called legends they contain.* Leaving, however, such futile,
rationalistic criticism out of account—because that is not the
kind of criticism with which we as Christian people have
chiefly to deal in our own circles—there is certainly an immense change of attitude on the part of many who still sincerely hold faith in the supernatural revelation of God.   I
find it difficult to describe this tendency, for I am desirous not
to describe it in any way which would do injustice to any
Christian thinker, and it is attended by so many signs of an
ambiguous character.   Jesus is recognized by the majority
of those who represent it as "the Incarnate Son of God,"
though with shadings off into more or less indefinite assertions even on that fundamental article, which make it sometimes doubtful where the writers exactly stand.   The process of thought in regard to Scripture is easily traced.   First,
there is an ostentatious throwing overboard, joined with some
expression of contempt, of what is called the verbal inspiration of Scripture—a very much abused term.   Jesus is still
spoken of as the highest revealer, and it is allowed that His
words, if only we could get at them—and on the whole it is
thought we can—furnish the highest rule of guidance for
time and for eternity.   But even criticism, we are told, must
have its rights.   Even in the New Testament the Gospels
go into the crucible, and in the name of synoptical criticism,
historical criticism, they are subject to wonderful processes,
in the course of which much of the history gets melted out
or is peeled off as Christian characteristics.   Jesus, we are reminded, was still a man of His generation, liable to error in
His human knowledge, and allowance must be made for the

limitations in His conceptions and judgments. **Paul is alleged** to be still largely dominated by his inheritance of **Rabbinical** and Pharisaic ideas. He had been brought up **a** Pharisee, brought up with the rabbis, and when he **became** a Christian, he carried a great deal of that into his Christian thought, and we have to strip off that thought when we come to the study of his Epistles. He is therefore a teacher not to be followed further than our own judgment of Christian truth leads us. That gets rid of a great deal that is inconvenient about Paul's teaching.

THE OLD TESTAMENT AND THE CRITICS

If these things are done in the "green tree" of the New Testament, it is easy to see what will be done in the "dry tree" of the Old. The conclusions of the more advanced school of critics are here generally accepted as once for all settled, with the result—in my judgment, at any rate—that the Old Testament is immeasurably lowered from the place it once held in our reverence. Its earlier history, down to about the age of the kings, is largely resolved into myths and legends and fictions. It is ruled out of the category of history proper. No doubt we are told that the legends are just as good as the history, and perhaps a little better, and that the ideas which they convey to us are just as good, coming in the form of legends, as if they came in the form of fact.

But behold, its laws, when we come to deal with them in this manner, lack Divine authority. They are the products of human minds at various ages. Its prophecies are the utterances of men who possessed indeed the Spirit of God, which is only in fuller degree what other good men, religious teachers in all countries, have possessed—not a spirit qualifying, for example, to give real predictions, or to bear authoritative messages of the truth to men. And so, in this whirl and confusion of theories—you will find them in our magazines, you will find them in our encyclopedias, you will find them in our re-

views, you will find them in many books which have appeared
to annihilate the conservative believers—in this whirl and
confusion of theories, is it any wonder that many should be
disquieted and unsettled, and feel as if the ground on which
they have been wont to rest was giving way beneath their feet?
And so the question comes back with fresh urgency. What is
to be said of the place and value of Holy Scripture?

IS THERE A TENABLE DOCTRINE FOR THE CHRISTIAN CHURCH OF TODAY?

One of the urgent needs of our time, and a prime need
of the Church, is just a replacement of Holy Scripture, with
due regard, I grant, to any really ascertained facts in regard
to its literary history, in the faith and lives of men, as the
truly inspired and divinely sealed record of God's revealed
will for men in great things of the soul. But then, is such a
position tenable? In the fierce light of criticism that beats
upon the documents and upon the revelation of God's grace
they profess to contain, can this position be maintained? I
venture to think, indeed, I am very sure, it can. Let me try
to indicate—for I can do hardly any more—the lines along
which I would answer the question, Have we or can we
have a tenable doctrine of Holy Scripture?

For a satisfactory doctrine of Holy Scripture—and by
that I mean a doctrine which is satisfactory for the needs
of the Christian Church, a doctrine which answers to the
claim the Scripture makes for itself, to the place it holds
in Christian life and Christian experience, to the needs of
the Christian Church for edification and evangelization, and
in other ways—I say, for a satisfactory doctrine of Holy
Scripture it seems to me that three things are indispensably
necessary. There is necessary, *first,* a more positive view of
the structure of the Bible than at present obtains in many
circles. There is necessary, *second,* the acknowledgment of

a true supernatural revelation of God in the history and religion of the Bible. There is necessary, *third,* the recognition of a true supernatural inspiration in the record of that revelation. These three things, to my mind, go together—a more positive view of the structure of the Bible; the recognition of the supernatural revelation embodied in the Bible; and a recognition in accordance with the Bible's own claim of a supernatural inspiration in the record of the Bible. Can we affirm these three things? Will they bear the test? I think they will.

THE STRUCTURE OF THE BIBLE

First as to the structure of the Bible, there is needed a more positive idea of that structure than is at present prevalent. You take much of the criticism and you find the Bible being disintegrated in many ways, and everything like structure falling away from it. You are told, for example, that these books—say the Books of Moses—are made up of many documents, which are very late in origin and cannot claim historical value. You are told that the laws they contain are also, for the most part, of tolerably late origin, and the Levitical laws especially are of post-exilian construction; they were not given by Moses; they were unknown when the Children of Israel were carried into captivity. Their temple usage perhaps is embodied in the Levitical law, but most of the contents of that Levitical law were wholly unknown. They were the construction—the invention, to use a term lately employed—of priests and scribes in the post-exilian period. They were put into shape, brought before the Jewish community returned from Babylon, and accepted by it as the law of life. Thus you have the history of the Bible turned pretty much upside down, and things take on a new aspect altogether.

Must I then, in deference to criticism, accept these theories, and give up the structure which the Bible presents? Taking the Bible as it stands, I find—and you will find if you look there also, without any particular critical learning you will find it—what seems to be evidence of a very definite internal structure, part fitting into part and leading on to part, making up a unity of the whole in that Bible. The Bible has undeniably a structure as it stands. It is distinguished from all other books of the kind, from all sacred books in the world, from Koran and Buddhist scriptures and Indian scriptures and every other kind of religious books. It is distinguished just by this fact, that it is the embodiment of a great plan or scheme or purpose of Divine grace extending from the beginning of time through successive ages and dispensations down to its culmination in Jesus Christ and the Pentecostal outpourings of the Spirit. The *history* of the Bible is the history of that development of God's redemptive purpose. The *promises* of the Bible mark the stages of its progress and its hope. The *covenants* of the Bible stand before us in the order of its unfolding. You begin with Genesis. Genesis lays the foundation and leads up to the Book of Exodus; and the Book of Exodus, with its introduction of the law-giving, leads up to what follows. Deuteronomy looks back upon the history of the rebellions and the laws given to the people, and leads up to the conquest. I need not follow the later developments, coming away down through the monarchy and the prophecy and the rest, but you find it all gathered up and fulfilled in the New Testament. The Bible, as we have it, closes in Gospel and Epistle and Apocalypse, fulfilling all the ideas of the Old Testament. There the circle completes itself with the new heaven and the new earth wherein dwelleth righteousness. Here is a structure; here is the fact; here is a structure, a connected story, a unity of purpose extending through this Book and binding all its parts together. Is that structure an illusion? Do we only, and many with us, dream that it is there? Do our eyes deceive us when we think we see it? Or has somebody of a later date invented it, and put it all, inwrought it all, in these earlier records, legends and stories, or whatever you like to call it—skilfully woven into the story until it presents there the appearance of naturalness and truth? I would like to find the mind capable of inventing it, and then the mind capable of putting it in and working it into a history once they got the idea itself. But if not invented, it belongs to the reality and the substance of the history; it belongs to the facts; and therefore to the Book that records the facts. And there are internal attestations in that structure of the Bible to the genuineness of its contents that protest against the efforts that are so often made to reduce it to fragments and shiver up that unity and turn it upside down. "Walk about Zion . . . tell the towers thereof; mark ye well her bulwarks;" you will find there's something there which the art of man will not avail to overthrow.

"Now, that is all very well," I hear some one say, "but there are facts on the other side; there are those manifold proofs which our critical friends adduce that the Bible is really a collection of fragments and documents of much later date, and that the history is really quite a different thing from what the Bible represents it to be." Well, are we to sit down and accept their dictum on that subject without evidence? When I turn to the evidence I do not find them to have that convincing power which our critical friends assign to them.

I am not rejecting this kind of critical theory because it goes against my prejudices or traditions; I reject it simply because it seems to me the evidence does not sustain it, and that the stronger evidence is against it. I cannot go into details; but take just the one point that I have mentioned—this post-exilian origin of the Levitical law. I have stated what is said about that matter—that those laws and institutions that you find in the middle of the Books of the Pentateuch—those laws and institutions about priests and Levites and sacrifices and all that—had really no existence, had no authoritative form, and to a large extent had not existence of any kind until after the Jews returned from Babylon, and then they were given out as a code of laws which the Jews accepted. That is the theory which is stated once and again. But let the reader put himself in the position of that returned community, and see what the thing means. These exiles had returned from Babylon. They had been organized into a new community. They had rebuilt their Temple, and then long years after that, when things had got into confusion, those two great men, Ezra and Nehemiah, came among them, and by and by Ezra produced and publicly proclaimed this law of Moses—what he called the law of Moses, the law of God by the hand of Moses—which he had brought from Babylon. A full description of what happened is given in the eighth chapter of the Book of Nehemiah. Ezra reads that law from his pulpit of wood day after day to the people, and the interpreter gives the sense. Now, mind you, most of the things in this law, in this book that he is reading to the people, had never been heard of before—never had existed, in fact; priests and Levites such as are there described had never existed. The law itself was long and complicated and burdensome, but the marvelous thing is that the people meekly accept it all as true—meekly accept it as law, at any rate—and submit to it, and take upon themselves its burdens without a murmur of dissent.

That is a very remarkable thing to start with. But remember, further, what that community was. It was not a community with oneness of mind, but it was a community keenly divided in itself. If you read the narrative you will find that there were strong opposing factions in that community; there were parties strongly opposed to Ezra and

Nehemiah and their reforms; there were many, as you see in the Book of Malachi, who were religiously faithless in that community. But marvelous to say, they all join in accepting this new and burdensome and hitherto unheard of law as the law of Moses, the law coming down to them from hoary antiquity. There were priests and Levites in that community who knew something about their own origin; they had genealogies and knew something about their own past. According to the new theory, these Levites were quite a new order; they had never existed at all before the time of the exile, and they had come into existence through the sentence of degradation that the prophet Ezekiel had passed upon them in the 44th chapter of his book. History is quite silent about this degradation. If anyone asks who carried out the degradation, or why was it carried out, or when was it done, and how came the priests to submit to the degradation, there is no answer to be given at all. But it came about somehow, so we are told.

And so these priests and Levites are there, and they stand and listen without astonishment as they learn from Ezra how the Levites had been set apart long centuries before in the wilderness by the hand of God, and had an ample tithe provision made for their support, and cities, and what not, set apart for them to live in. People know a little about their past. These cities never had existed except on paper; but they took it all in. They are told about these cities, which they must have known had never existed as Levitical cities. They not only hear but they accept the heavy tithe burdens without a word of remonstrance, and they make a covenant with God pledging themselves to faithful obedience to all those commands. Those tithes laws, as we discover, had no actual relation to their situation at all. They were drawn up for a totally different case. They were drawn up for a state of things in which there were few priests and many Levites. The priests were only to get the tithe of a tenth, but in this restored community there were a great many priests and few Levites. The tithe laws did not apply at all, but they accepted these as laws of Moses.

And so I might go over the provisions of the law one by one—tabernacle and priests and ritual and sacrifices and Day of Atonement—these things, in their post-exilian form, had never existed; they were spun out of the inventive brains of scribes; and yet the people accepted them all as the genuine handiwork of the ancient law-giver. Was ever such a thing heard of before? Try it in any city. Try to get the people to take upon themselves a series of heavy burdens of taxation or tithes or whatever you like, on the ground that it had been handed down from the middle ages to the present time. Try to get them to believe it; try to get them to obey it, and you will find the difficulty. Is it credible to anyone who leaves books and theories in the study and takes a broad view of human nature with open eyes? I aver that for me, at any rate, it is not; and it will be a marvel to me as long as I am spared to live, how such a theory has ever gained the acceptance it has done among unquestionably able and sound-minded men. I am convinced that the structure of the Bible vindicates itself, and that these counter theories break down.

A SUPERNATURAL REVELATION

I think it is an essential element in a tenable doctrine of Scripture, in fact the core of the matter, that it contains a record of a true supernatural revelation; and that is what the Bible claims to be—not a development of man's thoughts about God, and not what this man and that one came to think about God, how they came to have the ideas of a Jehovah or Yahveh, who was originally the storm-god of Sinai, and how they manufactured out of this the great universal God of the prophets—but a supernatural revelation of what God revealed Himself in word and deed to men in history. And if that claim to a supernatural revelation from God falls, the Bible falls, because it is bound up with it from beginning to end. Now, it is just here that a great deal of our modern thought parts company with the Bible. I am quite well aware that many of our friends who accept these newer critical theories, claim to be just as firm believers in Divine revelation as I am myself, and in Jesus Christ and all that concerns Him. I rejoice in the fact, and I believe that they are warranted in saying that there is that in the religion of Israel which you cannot expunge, or explain on any other hypothesis but Divine revelation.

But what I maintain is that this theory of the religion of the Bible which has been evolved, which has peculiarly come to be known as the critical view, had a very different origin—in men who did not believe in the supernatural revelation of God in the Bible. This school as a whole, as a widespread school, holds the fundamental position—the position which its adherents call that of the modern mind—that miracles did not happen and cannot happen. It takes the ground that they are impossible; therefore its followers have to rule everything of that kind out of the Bible record.

I have never been able to see how that position is tenable to a believer in a living personal God who really loves His creatures and has a sincere desire to bless them. Who dare to venture to assert that the power and will of such a Being as we must believe God to be—the God and Father of our Lord Jesus Christ—is exhausted in the natural creation? That there are no higher things to be attained in God's providence than can be attained through the medium of natural law? That there is in such a Being no capability of revealing Himself in words and deeds beyond nature? If there is a dogmatism in the world, it is that of the man who claims to limit the Author of the universe by this finite bound. We are told sometimes that it is a far higher thing to see God in the natural than to see Him in something that transcends the natural; a far higher thing to see God in the orderly regular working of nature than to suppose that there has ever been anything transcending that ordinary natural working. I think we all do see God, and try to see Him more and more, in the ordinary and regular working of nature. I hope all try every day to see God there. But the question is, Has this natural working not its limits? Is there not something that nature and natural workings cannot reach, cannot do for men, that we need to have done for us? And are we so to bind God that He cannot enter into communion with man in a supernatural economy of grace, an economy of revelation, an economy of salvation? Are we to deny that He has done so? That is really the dividing line both in Old Testament and New between the different theories. *Revelation,* surely, all must admit if man is to attain the clear knowledge of God that is needed; and the question is one of fact, Has God so revealed Himself? And I believe that it is an essential part of the answer, the true doctrine of Scripture, to say, "Yes, God has so revealed Himself, and the Bible is the record of that revelation, and that revelation shines in its light from the beginning to the end of it." And unless there is a wholehearted acceptance of the fact that God has entered, in word and deed, into human history for man's salvation, for man's renovation, for the deliverance of this world, a revelation culminating in the great Revealer Himself—unless we accept that, we do not get the foundation for the true doctrine of Holy Scripture.

THE INSPIRED BOOK

Now, just a word in closing, on Inspiration. I do not think that anyone will weigh the evidence of the Bible itself very carefully without saying that at least it claims to be in a peculiar and especial manner an *inspired book*. There is hardly anyone, I think, who will doubt that Jesus Christ treats the Old Testament in that way. Christ treats it as an imperfect stage of revelation, no doubt. Christ, as the Son of Man, takes up a lordly, discretionary attitude towards that revelation, and He supersedes very much what is in it by something higher, but Christ recognizes that there was true Divine revelation there, that He was the goal of it all; He came to fulfil the law and the prophets. The Scriptures are the last word with Him—*"Have ye not read?" "Ye do err, not knowing the Scriptures."* And it is just as certain that the Apostles treated the Old Testament in that way, and that they claimed in a peculiar sense the Spirit of God themselves. They claimed that in them and in their word was laid "the foundation on which the Church was built," Jesus Christ Himself, as the substance of their testimony, being the chief corner-stone; "built upon the foundation of the Apostles and Prophets." And if you say, "Well, are these New Testament Apostles and Prophets?" That is in Ephesians, 2nd chapter. You go to the fifth verse of the third chapter and you find this mystery of Christ which God had revealed to His holy Apostles and Prophets by His Spirit; and it is on that the Church was built. And when you come to Timothy (2 Tim. 3:14-17) to that classical passage, you find the marks there by which inspired Scripture is distinguished.

Take the book of Scripture and ask just this question: Does it answer to the claim of this inspired volume? How are we to test this? I do not enter here into the question that has divided good men as to theories of inspiration—questions about inerrancy in detail, and other matters. I want to get away from these things at the circumference to the center. But take the broader test.

THE BIBLE'S OWN TEST OF INSPIRATION

What does the Bible itself give us as the test of its inspiration? What does the Bible itself name as the qualities that inspiration imparts to it? Paul speaks in Timothy of the

Sacred Writings that were able to make wise unto salvation through faith which is in Christ Jesus. He goes on to tell us that *ALL Scripture is given by inspiration of God and is profitable for doctrine, for reproof, for correction, for instruction in righteousness, in order that the man of God may be perfect, throughly furnished unto all good works.* When you go back to the Old Testament and its praise of the Word of God you will find the qualities of inspiration are just the same. "The law of the Lord is perfect", etc. Those are the qualities which the inspired Book is alleged to sustain— qualities which only a true inspiration of God's Spirit could give; qualities beyond which we surely do not need anything more.

Does anyone doubt that the Bible possesses these qualities? Look at its structure; look at its completeness; look at it in the clearness and fullness and holiness of its teachings; look at it in its sufficiency to guide every soul that truly seeks light unto the saving knowledge of God. Take the Book as a whole, in its whole purpose, its whole spirit, its whole aim and tendency, and the whole setting of it, and ask, Is there not manifest the power which you can only trace back, as it traces back itself, to God's Holy Spirit really in the men who wrote it?

CHAPTER VI

CHRIST AND CRITICISM.

BY SIR ROBERT ANDERSON, K. C. B., LL. D.

AUTHOR OF "THE BIBLE AND MODERN CRITICISM," ETC., ETC., LONDON, ENGLAND.

In his "Founders of Old Testament Criticism" Professor Cheyne of Oxford gives the foremost place to Eichhorn. He hails him, in fact, as *the* founder of the cult. And according to this same authority, what led Eichhorn to enter on his task was "his hope to contribute to the winning back of the educated classes to religion." The rationalism of Germany at the close of the eighteenth century would accept the Bible only on the terms of bringing it down to the level of a human book, and the problem which had to be solved was to get rid of the element of miracle which pervades it. Working on the labors of his predecessors, Eichhorn achieved this to his own satisfaction by appealing to the oriental habit of thought, which seizes upon ultimate causes and ignores intermediate processes. This commended itself on two grounds. It had an undoubted element of truth, and it was consistent with reverence for Holy Scripture. For of the founder of the "Higher Criticism" it was said, what cannot be said of any of his successors, that "faith in that which is holy, even in the miracles of the Bible, was never shattered by Eichhorn in any youthful mind."

In the view of his successors, however, Eichhorn's hypothesis was open to the fatal objection that it was altogether inadequate. So the next generation of critics adopted the more drastic theory that the Mosaic books were "mosaic" in the sense that they were literary forgeries of a late date, composed of materials supplied by ancient documents and the myths and legends of the Hebrew race. And though this theory has been

111

modified from time to time during the last century, it remains substantially the "critical" view of the Pentateuch. But it is open to two main objections, either of which would be fatal. It is inconsistent with the evidence. And it directly challenges the authority of the Lord Jesus Christ as a teacher; for one of the few undisputed facts in this controversy is that our Lord accredited the books of Moses as having divine authority.

THE TRUE AND THE COUNTERFEIT.

It may be well to deal first with the least important of these objections. And here we must distinguish between the true Higher Criticism and its counterfeit. The rationalistic "Higher Criticism," when putting the Pentateuch upon its trial, began with the verdict and then cast about to find the evidence; whereas, true criticism enters upon its inquiries with an open mind and pursues them without prejudice. The difference may be aptly illustrated by the position assumed by a typical French judge and by an ideal English judge in a criminal trial. The one aims at convicting the accused, the other at elucidating the truth. "The proper function of the Higher Criticism is to determine the origin, date, and literary structure of an ancient writing." This is Professor Driver's description of *true* criticism. But the aim of the counterfeit is to disprove the genuineness of the ancient writings. The justice of this statement is established by the fact that Hebraists and theologians of the highest eminence, whose investigation of the Pentateuch problem has convinced them of the genuineness of the books, are not recognized at all.

In Britain, at least—and I am not competent to speak of Germany or America—no theologian of the first rank has adopted their "assured results." But the judgment of such men as Pusey, Lightfoot and Salmon, not to speak of men who are still with us, they contemptuously ignore; for the rationalistic Higher Critic is not one who investigates the evidence, but one who accepts the verdict.

THE PHILOLOGICAL INQUIRY.

If, as its apostles sometimes urge, the Higher Criticism is a purely philological inquiry, two obvious conclusions follow. The first is that its verdict must be in favor of the Mosaic books; for each of the books contains peculiar words suited to the time and circumstances to which it is traditionally assigned. This is admitted, and the critics attribute the presence of such words to the Jesuitical skill of the priestly forgers. But this only lends weight to the further conclusion that Higher Criticism is wholly incompetent to deal with the main issue on which it claims to adjudicate. For the genuineness of the Pentateuch must be decided on the same principles on which the genuineness of ancient documents is dealt with in our courts of justice. And the language of the documents is only one part of the needed evidence, and not the most important part. And fitness for dealing with evidence depends upon qualities to which Hebraists, as such, have no special claim. Indeed, their writings afford signal proofs of their unfitness for inquiries which they insist on regarding as their special preserve.

Take, for example, Professor Driver's grave assertion that the presence of two Greek words in Daniel (they are the names of musical instruments) *demand* a date for the book subsequent to the Greek conquest. It has been established by Professor Sayce and others that the intercourse between Babylon and Greece in, and before, the days of Nebuchadnezzar would amply account for the presence in the Chaldean capital of musical instruments with Greek names. And Colonel Conder, moreover,—a very high authority—considers the words to be Akkadian, and not Greek at all! But apart from all this, we can imagine the reception that would be given to such a statement by any competent tribunal. The story bears repeating—it is a record of facts—that at a church bazaar in Lincoln some years ago, the alarm was raised that pickpockets were at work, and two ladies had lost their purses. The empty purses were afterwards found in the pocket of the Bishop of the Diocese! On the evidence of the two purses the Bishop should be convicted as a thief, and on the evidence of the two words the book of Daniel should be convicted as a forgery!

HISTORICAL BLUNDER.

Here is another typical item in the Critics' indictment of Daniel. The book opens by recording Nebuchadnezzar's siege of Jerusalem in the third year of Jehoiakim, a statement the correctness of which is confirmed by history, sacred and secular. Berosus, the Chaldean historian, tells us that during this expedition Nebuchadnezzar received tidings of his father's death, and that, committing to others the care of his army and of his Jewish and other prisoners, "he himself hastened home across the desert." But the German skeptics, having decided that Daniel was a forgery, had to find evidence to support their verdict. And so they made the brilliant discovery that Berosus was here referring to the expedition of the following year, when Nebuchadnezzar won the battle of Carchemish against the army of the king of Egypt, and that he had not at that time invaded Judea at all. But Carchemish is on the Euphrates, and the idea of "hastening home" from there to Babylon across the desert is worthy of a schoolboy's essay! That he crossed the desert is proof that he set out from Judea; and his Jewish captives were, of course, Daniel and his companion princes. His invasion of Judea took place before his accession, in Jehoiakam's *third* year, whereas the battle of Carchemish was fought after his accession, in the king of Judah's *fourth* year, as the biblical books record. But this grotesque blunder of Bertholdt's "Book of Daniel" in the beginning of the nineteenth century is gravely reproduced in Professor Driver's "Book of Daniel" at the beginning of the twentieth century.

CRITICAL PROFANITY.

But to return to Moses.   According to "the critical hypothesis," the books of the Pentateuch are literary forgeries of the Exilic Era, the work of the Jerusalem priests of those evil days.   From the Book of Jeremiah we know that those men were profane apostates; and if "the critical hypothesis" be true, they were infinitely worse than even the prophet's inspired denunciations of them indicate.   For no eighteenth century atheist ever sank to a lower depth of profanity than is displayed by their use of the Sacred Name.   In the preface to his "Darkness and Dawn," Dean Farrar claims that he "never touches the early preachers of Christianity with the finger of fiction." When his story makes Apostles speak, he has "confined their words to the words of a revelation."   But *ex. hyp.*, the authors of the Pentateuch "touched with the finger of fiction" not only the holy men of the ancient days, but their Jehovah God.   "Jehovah spake unto Moses, saying."   This and kindred formulas are repeated times without number in the Mosaic books.   If this be romance, a lower type of profanity is inconceivable, unless it be that of the man who fails to be shocked and revolted by it.

But no; facts prove that this judgment is unjust.   For men of unfeigned piety and deep reverence for divine things can be so blinded by the superstitions of "religion" that the *imprimatur* of the church enables them to regard these discredited books as Holy Scripture.   As critics they brand the Pentateuch as a tissue of myth and legend and fraud, but as religionists they assure us that this "implies no denial of its inspiration or disparagement of its contents."*

ERRORS REFUTED BY FACTS.

In controversy it is of the greatest importance to allow opponents to state their position in their own words; and here

*"The Higher Criticism: Three Papers," by Professors Driver and Kirkpatrick.

is Professor Driver's statement of the case against the Books of Moses:

"We can only argue on grounds of probability derived from our view of the progress of the art of writing, or of literary composition, or of the rise and growth of the prophetic tone and feeling in ancient Israel, or of the period at which the traditions contained in the narratives might have taken shape, or of the probability that they would have been written down before the impetus given to culture by the monarchy had taken effect, and similar considerations, for estimating most of which, though plausible arguments on one side or the other may be advanced, a standard on which we can confidently rely scarcely admits of being fixed." ("Introduction," 6th ed., page 123.)

This modest reference to "literary composition" and "the art of writing" is characteristic. It is intended to gloss over the abandonment of one of the chief points in the original attack. Had "Driver's Introduction" appeared twenty years earlier, the assumption that such a literature as the Pentateuch could belong to the age of Moses would doubtless have been branded as an anachronism. For one of the main grounds on which the books were assigned to the latter days of the monarchy was that the Hebrews of six centuries earlier were an illiterate people. And after that error had been refuted by archaelogical discoveries, it was still maintained that a code of laws so advanced, and so elaborate, as that of Moses could not have originated in such an age. This figment, however, was in its turn exploded, when the spade of the explorer brought to light the now famous Code of Khammurabi, the Amraphel of Genesis, who was king of Babylon in the time of Abraham.

Instead, however, of donning the white sheet when confronted by this new witness, the critics, with great effrontery, pointed to the newly-found Code as the original of the laws of Sinai. Such a conclusion is natural on the part of men who treat the Pentateuch as merely human. But the critics cannot have it both ways. The Moses who copied Khammurabi must have been the real Moses of the Exodus, and not the mythical Moses of the Exile, who wrote long centuries after Khammurabi had been forgotten!

AN INCREDIBLE THEORY.

The evidence of the Khammurabi Code refutes an important count in the critics' indictment of the Pentateuch; but we can call another witness whose testimony demolishes their whole case. The Pentateuch, as we all know, and the Pentateuch alone, constitutes the Bible of the Samaritans. Who, then, were the Samaritans? And how and when did they obtain the Pentateuch? Here again the critics shall speak for themselves. Among the distinguished men who have championed their crusade in Britain there has been none more esteemed, none more scholarly, than the late Professor Robertson Smith; and here is an extract from his "Samaritans" article in the "Encyclopedia Britannica":

"They (the Samaritans) regard themselves as Israelites, descendants of the ten tribes, and claim to possess the orthodox religion of Moses * * * The priestly law, which is throughout based on the practice of the priests in Jerusalem before the Captivity, was reduced to form after the Exile, and was published by Ezra as the law of the rebuilt temple of Zion. The Samaritans must, therefore, have derived their Pentateuch from the Jews after Ezra's reforms." And in the same paragraph he says that, according to the contention of the Samaritans, "not only the temple of Zion, but the earlier temple of Shiloh and the priesthood of Eli, were schismatical." And yet, as he goes on to say, "the Samaritan religion was built on the Pentateuch alone."

Now mark what this implies. We know something of racial bitterness. We know more, unfortunately, of the fierce bitterness of religious strife. And both these elements combined to alienate the Samaritans from the Jews. But more than this, in the post-exilic period distrust and dislike were turned to intense hatred—"abhorrence" is Robertson Smith's word—by the sternness and contempt with which the Jews spurned their proffered help in the work of reconstruction at Jerusalem, and refused to acknowledge them in any way. And yet we are asked to believe that, at this very time and in these very circumstances, the Samaritans, while hating the Jews much as Orangemen hate the Jesuits, and denouncing the whole Jewish cult as schismatical, not only accepted these Jewish books relating to that cult as the "service books" of their own ritual, but adopted them as their "Bible," to the exclusion even of the writings of their own Israelite prophets, and the venerated and sacred books which record the history of their kings. In the whole range of controversy, religious or secular, was there ever propounded a theory more utterly incredible and preposterous!

ANOTHER PREPOSTEROUS POSITION.

No less preposterous are the grounds on which this conclusion is commended to us. Here is a statement of them, quoted from the standard textbook of the cult, Hasting's "Bible Dictionary":

"There is at least one valid ground for the conclusion that the Pentateuch was first accepted by the Samaritans after the Exile. Why was their request to be allowed to take part in the building of the second temple refused by the heads of the Jerusalem community? Very probably because the Jews were aware that the Samaritans did not as yet possess the Law-Book. It is hard to suppose that otherwise they would have met with this refusal. Further, anyone who, like the present writer, regards the modern criticism of the Pentateuch as essentially correct, has a second decisive reason for adopting the above view." (Professor König's article, "Samaritan Pentateuch," page 68.)

Here are two "decisive reasons" for holding that "the Pentateuch was first accepted by the Samaritans after the Exile." First, because "very probably" it was because they had not those forged books that the Jews spurned their help; and so they went home and adopted the forged books as their Bible! And, secondly, because criticism has proved that the books were not in existence till then. To characterize the writings of these scholars as they deserve is not a grateful task but the time has come to throw off reserve, when such drivel as this is gravely put forward to induce us to tear from our Bible the Holy Scriptures on which our Divine Lord based His claims to Messiahship.

THE IDEA OF SACRIFICE A REVELATION.

The refutation of the Higher Criticism does not prove that the Pentateuch is inspired of God. The writer who would set himself to establish such a thesis as that within the limits of a Review Article might well be admired for his enthusiasm and daring, but certainly not for his modesty or discretion. Neither does it decide questions which lie within the legitimate province of the true Higher Criticism, as *ex. gr.,* the authorship of Genesis. It is incredible that for the thousands of years that elapsed before the days of Moses, God left His people on earth without a revelation. It is plain, moreover, that many of the ordinances divinely entrusted to Moses were but a renewal of an earlier revelation. The religion of Babylon is clear evidence of such a primeval revelation. How else can the universality of sacrifice be accounted for? Could such a practice have originated in a human brain?

If some demented creature conceived the idea that killing a beast before his enemy's door would propitiate him, his neighbors would no doubt have suppressed him. And if he evolved the belief that his god would be appeased by such an offensive practice, he must have supposed his god to be as mad as himself. The fact that sacrifice prevailed among all races can be explained only by a primeval revelation. And the Bible student will recognize that God thus sought to impress on men that death was the penalty of sin, and to lead them to look forward to a great blood shedding that would bring life and blessing to mankind. But Babylon was to the ancient world what Rome has been to Christendom. It corrupted every divine ordinance and truth, and perpetuated them as thus corrupted. And in the Pentateuch we have the divine re-issue of the true cult. The figment that the debased and corrupt version was the original may satisfy some professors of Hebrew, but no one who has any practical knowledge of human nature would entertain it.

INSUFFICIENT EVIDENCE.

At this stage, however, what concerns us is not the divine authority of the books, but the human error and folly of the critical attack upon them. The only historical basis of that attack is the fact that in the revival under Josiah, "the book of the law" was found in the temple by Hilkiah, the high priest, to whom the young king entrusted the duty of cleansing and renovating the long neglected shrine. A most natural discovery it was, seeing that Moses had in express terms commanded that it should be kept there (2 Kings 22:8; Deut. 31:26). But according to the critics, the whole business was a detestable trick of the priests. For they it was who forged the books and invented the command, and then hid the product of their infamous work where they knew it would be found.

And apart from this, the only foundation for "the assured results of modern criticism," as they themselves acknowledge, consists of "grounds of probability" and "plausible arguments"! In no civilized country would an habitual criminal be convicted of petty larceny on such evidence as this; and yet it is on these grounds that we are called upon to give up the sacred books which our Divine Lord accredited as "the Word of God" and made the basis of His doctrinal teaching.

CHRIST OR CRITICISM?

And this brings us to the second, and incomparably the

graver, objection to "the assured results of modern criticism." That the Lord Jesus Christ identified Himself with the Hebrew Scriptures, and in a very special way with the Book of Moses, no one disputes. And this being so, we must make choice between Christ and Criticism. For if "the critical hypothesis" of the Pentateuch be sustained, the conclusion is seemingly inevitable, either that He was not divine, or that the records of His teaching are untrustworthy.

Which alternative shall we adopt? If the second, then every claim to inspiration must be abandoned, and agnosticism must supplant faith in the case of every fearless thinker. Inspiration is far too great a question for incidental treatment here; but two remarks with respect to it may not be inopportune. Behind the frauds of Spiritualism there lies the fact, attested by men of high character, some of whom are eminent as scientists and scholars, that definite communications are received in precise words from the world of spirits.* And this being so, to deny that the Spirit of God could thus communicate truth to men, or, in other words, to reject verbal inspiration on *a priori* grounds, betrays the stupidity of systematized unbelief. And, secondly, it is amazing that any one who regards the coming of Christ as God's supreme revelation of Himself can imagine that (to put it on no higher ground than "Providence") the Divine Spirit could fail to ensure that mankind should have a trustworthy and true record of His mission and His teaching.

A MORE HOPELESS DILEMMA.

But if the Gospel narrative be authentic, we are driven back upon the alternative that He of whom they speak could not be divine. "Not so," the critics protest, "for did He not Himself confess His ignorance? And is not this explained by the Apostle's statement that in His humiliation He emptied Himself of His Deity?" And the inference drawn from this (to

---

*The fact that, as the Christian believes, these spirits are demons who personate the dead, does not affect the argument.

quote the standard text-book of the cult) is that the Lord of Glory "held the current Jewish notions respecting the divine authority and revelation of the Old Testament." But even if this conclusion—as portentous as it is profane—could be established, instead of affording an escape from the dilemma in which the Higher Criticism involves its votaries, it would only serve to make that dilemma more hopeless and more terrible. For what chiefly concerns us is not that, *ex. hyp.,* the Lord's doctrinal teaching was false, but that in unequivocal terms, and with extreme solemnity, He declared again and again that His teaching was not His own but His Father's, and that the very words in which He conveyed it were God-given.

A few years ago the devout were distressed by the proceedings of a certain Chicago "prophet," who claimed divine authority for his lucubrations. Kindly disposed people, rejecting a severer estimate of the man and his platform utterances, regarded him merely as a profane fool. Shall the critics betray us into forming a similarly indulgent estimate of —— My pen refuses to complete the sentence!

And will it be believed that the only scriptural basis offered us for this astounding position is a verse in one of the Gospels and a word in one of the Epistles! Passing strange it is that men who handle Holy Scripture with such freedom when it conflicts with their "assured results" should attach such enormous importance to an isolated verse or a single word, when it can be misused to support them. The verse is Mark 13:32, where the Lord says, with reference to His coming again: "Of that day and hour knoweth no one; no, not the angels which are in heaven, neither the Son, but the Father." But this follows immediately upon the words: "Heaven and earth shall pass away, but My words shall not pass away."

THE WORDS OF GOD.

The Lord's words were not "inspired"; they were the words of God in a still higher sense. "The people were astonished at His teaching," we are told, "for He taught them as one having *exousia.*" The word occurs again in Acts 1:7, where He says that times and seasons "the Father hath put in His own *exousia.*" And this is explained by Phil. 2:6, 7: "He counted it not a prize (or a thing to be grasped) to be on an equality with God, but *emptied* Himself"—the word on which the *kenosis* theory of the critics depends. And He not only stripped Himself of His glory as God; He gave up His liberty as a man. For He never spoke His own words, but only the words which the Father gave Him to speak. And this was the limitation of His "authority"; so that, beyond what the Father gave Him to speak, He knew nothing and was silent.

But when He spoke, "He taught them as one who had authority, and not as their scribes." From their scribes they were used to receive definite teaching, but it was teaching based on "the law and the prophets." But here was One who stood apart and taught them from a wholly different plane. "For," He declared, "I spake not·from Myself; but the Father which sent Me, He hath given Me a commandment what I should say and what I should speak. * * * The things, therefore, which I speak, even as the Father hath said unto Me, so I speak" (John 12:49, 50, R. V.).

And let us not forget that it was not merely the substance of His teaching that was divine, but the very language in which it was conveyed. So that in His prayer on the night of the betrayal He could say, not only "I have given them Thy word," but "I have given them *the words* which Thou gavest Me."* His words, therefore, about Moses and the Hebrew Scriptures were not, as the critics, with such daring and seeming profanity, maintain, the lucubrations of a superstitious and ignorant Jew; they were the words of God, and conveyed truth that was divine and eternal.

When in the dark days of the Exile, God needed a prophet

*Both the λόγος and the ρήματα John 17:8, 14; as again in Chap. 14:10, 24.

who would speak only as He gave him words, He struck Ezekiel dumb.   Two judgments already rested on that people—
the seventy years' Servitude to Babylon, and then the Captivity
—and they were warned that continued impenitence would
bring on them the still more terrible judgment of the seventy
years' desolations.   And till that last judgment fell, Ezekiel
remained dumb (Ezek. 3:26; 24:27; 33:22).   But the Lord
Jesus Christ needed no such discipline.   He came to do the
Father's will, and no words ever passed His lips save the
words given Him to speak.

In this connection, moreover, two facts which are strangely
overlooked claim prominent notice.   The first is that in Mark
13 the antithesis is not at all between man and God, but between the Son of God and the Father.   And the second is
that He had been re-invested with all that, according to Phil.
2, He laid aside in coming into the world.   "All things
have been delivered unto Me of My Father," He declared; and
this at a time when the proofs that "He was despised and rejected of men" were pressing on Him.   His reassuming the
glory awaited His return to heaven, but here on earth the all
things were already His (Matt. 11:27).

AFTER THE KENOSIS.

The foregoing is surely an adequate reply to the *kenosis*
figment of the critics; but if any should still doubt or cavil,
there is another answer which is complete and crushing.
Whatever may have been the limitations under which He rested
during His ministry on earth, He was released from them when
He rose from the dead.   And it was in His post-resurrection
teaching that He gave the fullest and clearest testimony to the
Hebrew Scriptures.   Then it was that, *"beginning at Moses,*
and all the prophets, He expounded unto them in all the Scriptures the things concerning Himself."   And again, confirming
all His previous teaching about those Scriptures, "He said unto
them, These are the words which I spake unto you while I was

yet with you, that all things must be fulfilled which were written in the law of Moses, and in the prophets, and in the psalms, concerning Me."

And the record adds: "Then opened He their mind that they might understand the Scriptures." And the rest of the New Testament is the fruit of that ministry, enlarged and unfolded by the Holy Spirit given to lead them into all truth. And in every part of the New Testament the Divine authority of the Hebrew Scriptures, and especially of the Books of Moses, is either taught or assumed.

THE VITAL ISSUE.

Certain it is, then, that the vital issue in this controversy is not the value of the Pentateuch, but the Deity of Christ. And yet the present article does not pretend to deal with the truth of the Deity. Its humble aim is not even to establish the authority of the Scriptures, but merely to discredit the critical attack upon them by exposing its real character and its utter feebleness. The writer's method, therefore, has been mainly destructive criticism, the critics' favorite weapon being thus turned against themselves.

A DEMAND FOR CORRECT STATEMENT.

One cannot but feel distress at having to accord such treatment to certain distinguished men whose reverence for divine things is beyond reproach. A like distress is felt at times by those who have experience in dealing with sedition, or in suppressing riots. But when men who are entitled to consideration and respect thrust themselves into "the line of fire," they must take the consequences. These distinguished men will not fail to receive to the full the deference to which they are entitled, if only they will dissociate themselves from the dishonest claptrap of this crusade ("the assured results of modern criticism"; "all scholars are with us"; and so on—bluster and falsehood by which the weak and ignorant are browbeaten or deceived) and acknowledge that their "assured results" are mere hypotheses, repudiated by Hebraists and theologians as competent and eminent as themselves.

The effects of this "Higher Criticism" are extremely grave. For it has dethroned the Bible in the home, and the good, old practice of "family worship" is rapidly dying out. And great national interests also are involved. For who can doubt that the prosperity and power of the Protestant nations of the world are due to the influence of the Bible upon character and conduct? Races of men who for generations have been taught to think for themselves in matters of the highest moment will naturally excel in every sphere of effort or of enterprise. And more than this, no one who is trained in the fear of God will fail in his duty to his neighbor, but will prove himself a good citizen. But the dethronement of the Bible leads practically to the dethronement of God; and in Germany and America, and now in England, the effects of this are declaring themselves in ways, and to an extent, well fitted to cause anxiety for the future.

CHRIST SUPREME.

If a personal word may be pardoned in conclusion, the writer would appeal to every book he has written in proof that he is no champion of a rigid, traditional "orthodoxy." With a single limitation, he would advocate full and free criticism of Holy Scripture. And that one limitation is that the words of the Lord Jesus Christ shall be deemed a bar to criticism and "an end of controversy" on every subject expressly dealt with in His teaching. "The Son of God is come"; and by Him came both grace and TRUTH. And from His hand it is that we have received the Scriptures of the Old Testament.

CHAPTER VII

OLD TESTAMENT CRITICISM AND NEW TESTA-MENT CHRISTIANITY

BY PROFESSOR W. H. GRIFFITH THOMAS, D. D.,
WYCLIFFE COLLEGE, TORONTO, CANADA

A large number of Christians feel compelled to demur to the present attitude of many scholars to the Scriptures of the Old Testament. It is now being taught that the patriarchs of Jewish history are not historic persons; that the records connected with Moses and the giving of the law on Sinai are unhistorical; that the story of the tabernacle in the wilderness is a fabricated history of the time of the Exile; that the prophets cannot be relied on in their references to the ancient history of their own people, or in their predictions of the future; that the writers of the New Testament, who assuredly believed in the records of the Old Testament, were mistaken in the historical value they assigned to those records; that our Lord Himself, in His repeated references to the Scriptures of His own nation, and in His assumption of the Divine authority of those Scriptures, and of the reality of the great names they record, was only thinking and speaking as an ordinary Jew of His day, and was as liable to error in matters of history and of criticism as any of them were.

The present paper is intended to give expression to some of the questions that have arisen in the course of personal study, in connection with collegiate work and also during several years of ordinary pastoral ministry. It is often urged that problems of Old Testament criticism are for experts alone, and can only be decided by them. We venture to question the correctness of this view, especially when it is remembered that to many people "experts" means experts in Hebrew philology only. By all means let us have all possible expert knowledge; but, as Biblical questions are complex, and involve several considerations, we need expert knowledge in archaeology, history, theology, and even spiritual experience, as well as in philology. Every available factor must be taken into account, and the object of the present paper is to emphasize certain elements which appear liable to be overlooked, or at least insufficiently considered.

We do not question for an instant the right of Biblical criticism considered in itself. On the contrary, it is a necessity for all who use the Bible to be "critics" in the sense of constantly using their "judgment" on what is before them. What is called "higher" criticism is not only a legitimate but a necessary method for all Christians, for by its use we are able to discover the facts and the form of the Old Testament Scriptures. Our hesitation, consequently, is not intended to apply to the method, but to what is believed to be an illegitimate, unscientific, and unhistorical use of it. In fact, we base our objections to much modern criticism of the Old Testament on what we regard as a proper use of a true higher criticism.

1. IS THE TESTIMONY OF NINETEEN CENTURIES OF CHRISTIAN
    HISTORY AND EXPERIENCE OF NO ACCOUNT
    IN THIS QUESTION?

For nearly eighteen centuries these modern views of the Old Testament were not heard of. Yet this is not to be accounted for by the absence of intellectual power and scholarship in the Church. Men like Origen, Jerome, Augustine, Thomas Aquinas, Erasmus, Calvin, Luther, Melancthon, to say nothing of the English Puritans and other divines of the seventeenth century, were not intellectually weak or inert, nor were they wholly void of critical acumen with reference to Holy Scripture. Yet they, and the whole Church with them, never hesitated to accept the view of the Old Testament which had come down to them, not only as a heritage from Judaism, but as endorsed by the apostles. Omitting all reference to our Lord, it is not open to question that the views of St. Paul and St. Peter and St. John about the Old Testament were the views of the whole Christian Church until the end of the eighteenth century. And, making every possible allowance for the lack of historical spirit and of modern critical methods, are we to suppose that the whole Church for centuries never exercised its mind on such subjects as the contents, history, and authority of the Old Testament?

Besides, this is a matter which cannot be decided by intellectual criticism alone. Scripture appeals to conscience, heart and will, as well as to mind; and the Christian consciousness, the accumulated spiritual experience of the body of Christ, is not to be lightly regarded, much less set aside, unless it is proved to be unwarranted by fact. While we do not say that "what is new is not true," the novelty of these modern critical views should give us pause before we virtually set aside the spiritual instinct of centuries of Christian experience.

2. DOES THE NEW CRITICISM READILY AGREE WITH THE HISTORICAL POSITION OF THE JEWISH NATION?

The Jewish nation is a fact in history, and its record is given to us in the Old Testament. There is no contemporary literature to check the account there given, and archaeology affords us assistance on points of detail only, not for any long or continuous period. This record of Jewish history can be proved to have remained the same for many centuries. Yet much of modern criticism is compelled to reconstruct the history of the Jews on several important points. It involves, for instance, a very different idea of the character of the earliest form of Jewish religion from that seen in the Old Testament as it now stands; its views of the patriarchs are largely different from the conceptions found on the face of the Old Testament narrative; its views of Moses and David are essentially altered from what we have before us in the Old Testament.

Now what is there in Jewish history to support all this reconstruction? Absolutely nothing. We see through the centuries the great outstanding objective fact of the Jewish nation, and the Old Testament is at once the means and the record of their national life. It rose with them, grew with them, and it is to the Jews alone we can look for the earliest testimony to the Old Testament canon.

In face of these facts, it is bare truth to say that the fundamental positions of modern Old Testament criticism are utterly incompatible with the historic growth and position of the Jewish people. Are we not right, therefore, to pause before we accept this subjective reconstruction of history? Let anyone read Wellhausen's article on "Israel" in the Encyclopaedia Britannica, and then ask himself whether he recognizes at all therein the story as given in the Old Testament.

3. ARE THE RESULTS OF THE MODERN VIEW OF THE OLD TESTAMENT REALLY ESTABLISHED?

It is sometimes said that modern criticism is no longer a matter of hypothesis; it has entered the domain of facts. Principal George Adam Smith has gone so far as to say that "modern criticism has won its war against the traditional theories. It only remains to fix the amount of the indemnity." But is this really so? Can we assert that the results of modern criticism are established facts? Indeed Dr. Smith has himself admitted, since writing the above words, that there are questions still open which were supposed to be settled and closed twenty years ago.

In the first place, is the excessive literary analysis of the Pentateuch at all probable or even thinkable on literary grounds? Let anyone work through a section of Genesis as given by Dr. Driver in his "Introduction", and see whether such a complex combination of authors is at all likely, or whether, even if likely, the various authors can now be distinguished? Is not the whole method far too purely subjective to be probable and reliable?

Further, the critics are not agreed as to the number of documents, or as to the portions to be assigned to each author. A simple instance of this may be given. It is not so many years ago when criticism was content to say that Isa. 40-66, though not by Isaiah, was the work of one author, an unknown prophet of the Exile. But the most recent writers like Duhm, Macfadyen and Wade consider these chapters to be the work of two writers, and that the whole Book of Isaiah (from three authors) did not receive its present form until long after the return from the Exile.

Then, these differences in literary analysis involve differences of interpretation and differences of date, character, and meaning of particular parts of the Old Testament. To prove this, we ask attention to the following extracts from a review of a work on Genesis by Professor Gunkel of Berlin. The review is by Professor Andrew Harper of Melbourne, and appeared in the "Critical Review" for January, 1902. Professor Harper's own position would, we imagine, be rightly characterized as generally favorable to the moderate position of the critical movement. His comments on Gunkel's book are, therefore, all the more noteworthy and significant.

"It will change the whole direction of the conflict as to the early books of the Pentateuch and lead it into more fruitful directions, for it has raised the fundamental question whether the narratives in Genesis are not far older than the authors of the documents marked J. E. P., and whether they are not faithful witnesses to the religion of Israel before prophetic times." "His conclusion will, in many respects, be welcome to those who have felt how incredible some of the assumptions of the Kuenen-Wellhausen school of critics are."

"It will be obvious at a glance what an upsetting of current conceptions in regard to the history of religion must follow if it be accepted."

"They are sufficient, if made good, to upset the whole of the current reconstructions of the religion of Israel. To most readers it will be seen that he has in large part made them good."

"There can be no doubt that his book most skillfully begins a healthy and much-needed reaction. It should, therefore, be read and welcomed by all students of the Old Testament whose minds are open."

In view of Gunkel's position thus endorsed by Professor Harper, is it fair to claim victory for the modern critical theories of the Old Testament? When an able scholar like Professor Harper can speak of a new work as "sufficient to upset the whole of the current reconstructions of the religion of Israel," it is surely premature to speak even in a moment of rhetorical enthusiasm, as Dr. George Adam Smith does, of "victory" and "indemnity." Dr. Smith himself now admits that Gunkel has overturned the Wellhausen theory of the patriarchal narratives. And the same scholar has told us that distinction in the use of the name for God is "too precarious" as the basis of arguments for distinctions of sources. For ourselves we heartily endorse the words of an American scholar when he says:

"We are certain that there will be no final settlement of Biblical questions on the basis of the higher criticism that is now commonly called by that name. Many specific teachings of the system will doubtless abide. But so far forth as it goes upon the assumption that statements of fact in the Scriptures are pretty generally false, so far forth it is incapable of establishing genuinely permanent results."* Sir W. Robertson

*Dr. G. A. Smith, "Modern Criticism and the Preaching of the Old Testament", p. 35. Dr. Willis J. Beecher, in "The Bible Student and Teacher", January, 1904.

Nicoll, editor of the "British Weekly," remarked quite recently that the "assured results" seem to be vanishing, that no one really knows what they are.

4. IS THE POSITION OF MODERN CRITICISM REALLY COMPATIBLE WITH A BELIEF IN THE OLD TESTAMENT AS A DIVINE REVELATION?

The problem before us is not merely literary, nor only historical; it is essentially religious, and the whole matter resolves itself into one question: Is the Old Testament the record of a Divine revelation? This is the ultimate problem. It is admitted by both sides to be almost impossible to minimize the differences between the traditional and the modern views of the Old Testament. As a reviewer of Dr. George Adam Smith's book, "Modern Criticism and the Preaching of the Old Testament", rightly says:

"The difference is immense; they involve different conceptions of the relation of God to the world; different views as to the course of Israel's history, the process of revelation, and the nature of inspiration. We cannot be lifted from the old to the new position by the influence of a charming literary style, or by the force of the most enthusiastic eloquence."*

In view of this fundamental difference, the question of the trustworthiness of the Old Testament becomes acute and pressing. In order to test this fairly and thoroughly, let us examine some of the statements made on behalf of the modern view.

We may consider first the rise and progress of religion in Israel. Dr. G. A. Smith says: "It is plain, then, that to whatever heights the religion of Israel afterwards rose, it remained before the age of the great prophets not only similar to, but in all respects above-mentioned identical with, the general Semitic religion; which was not a monotheism, but a polytheism with an opportunity for monotheism at the heart of it, each tribe

---

*"American Journal of Theology", Vol. VI., p. 114.

being attached to one god, as to their particular Lord and Father."*

Consider what is meant by the phrase, "in all respects above-mentioned identical with the general Semitic religion," as applied to the religion of Israel previous to the eighth century B. C. Can this view be fairly deduced from the Old Testament as we now have it? Still more, is such a view conceivable in the light of the several preceding centuries of God's special dealings with Israel? Wherein, on this assumption, consisted the uniqueness of Israel from the time of Abraham to the eighth century B. C.?

We may next take the character of the narratives of Genesis. The real question at issue is the historical character. Modern criticism regards the account in Genesis as largely mythical and legendary. Yet it is certain that the Jews of the later centuries accepted these patriarchs as veritable personages, and the incidents associated with them as genuine history. St. Paul and the other New Testament writers assuredly held the same view. If, then, they are not historical, surely the truths emphasized by prophets and apostles from the patriarchal stories are so far weakened in their supports?

Take, again, the legislation which in the Pentateuch is associated with Moses, and almost invariably introduced by the phrase, "The Lord spake unto Moses." Modern criticism regards this legislation as unknown until the Exile, or a thousand years after the time of Moses. Is it really possible to accept this as satisfactory? Are we to suppose that "The Lord spake to Moses" is only a well-known literary device intended to invest the utterance with greater importance and more solemn sanction? This position, together with the generally accepted view of modern criticism about the invention of Deuteronomy in the days of Josiah, cannot be regarded as in accordance with historial fact or ethical principle.

Canon Driver and Dr. G. A. Smith, it is true, strongly assert

*"Modern Criticism", p. 130.

the compatibility of the new views with a belief in the Divine authority of the Old Testament, and so far as they themselves are concerned we of course accept their statements *ex animo.* But we wish they would give us more clearly and definitely than they have yet done, the grounds on which this compatibility may be said to rest. To deny historicity, to correct dates by hundreds of years, to reverse judgments on which a nation has rested for centuries, to traverse views which have been the spiritual sustenance of millions, and then to say that all this is consistent with the Old Testament being regarded as a Divine revelation, is at least puzzling, and does not afford mental or moral satisfaction to many who do not dream of questioning the *bona fides* of scholars who hold the views now criticized. The extremes to which Dr. Cheyne has gone seem to many the logical outcome of the principles with which modern criticism, even of a moderate type, starts. *Facilis descensus Averno,* and we should like to be shown the solid and logical halting-place where those who refuse to go with Cheyne think that they and we can stand.

Sir W. Robertson Nicoll, commenting March 12, 1903, on a speech delivered by the then Prime Minister of Great Britain (Mr. Balfour) in connection with the Bible Society's Centenary, made the following significant remarks: "The immediate results of criticism are in a high degree disturbing. So far they have scarcely been understood by the average Christian. But the plain man who has been used to receive everything in the Bible as a veritable Word of God cannot fail to be perplexed, and deeply perplexed, when he is told that much of the Old Testament and the New is unhistorical, and when he is asked to accept the statement that God reveals Himself by myth and legend as well as by the truth, of fact. Mr. Balfour must surely know that many of the higher critics have ceased to be believers. More than twenty years ago the present writer, walking with Julius Wellhausen in the quaint streets of Greifswald, ventured to ask him whether, if his views were accepted, the Bible could retain its place in the estimation of the common people. 'I cannot see how that is possible,' was the sad reply."

It is no mere question of how we may use the Old Testament for preaching, or how much is left for use after the critical views are accepted. But even our preaching will lack a great deal of the note of certitude. If we are to regard certain biographies as unhistorical, it will not be easy to draw lessons for conduct, and if the history is largely legendary, our deductions about God's government and providence must be essentially weakened. But the one point to be faced is the historic credibility of those parts of the Old Testament questioned by modern criticism, and the historical and religious value of the documents of the Pentateuch. Meanwhile, we ask to have clear proof of the compatibility of the modern views with the acceptance of the Old Testament as the record of a Divine revelation.

5   IS MODERN CRITICISM BASED ON A SOUND PHILOSOPHY SUCH
AS CHRISTIANS CAN ACCEPT?

At the foundation of much modern thought is the philosophy known as Idealism, which, as often interpreted, involves a theory of the universe that finds no room for supernatural interpositions of any kind. The great law of the universe, including the physical, mental, and moral realms, is said to be evolution, and though this doubtless presupposes an original Creator, it does not, on the theory now before us, permit of any subsequent direct intervention of God during the process of development. This general philosophical principle applied to history has assuredly influenced, if it has not almost moulded, a great deal of modern criticism of the Old Testament. It is not urged that all who accept even the position of a moderate criticism, go the full length of the extreme evolutionary theory; but there can be no reasonable doubt that most of the criticism of the Old Testament is materially affected by an evolutionary theory of all history which tends to minimize Divine intervention in the affairs of the people of Israel. It is certainly correct to say that the presupposition of much present-day critical reasoning is a denial of the supernatural, and especially of the predictive element in prophecy.

As to the theory of evolution regarded as a process of uninterrupted differentiation of existences, under purely natural laws, and without any Divine intervention, it will suffice to say that it is "not proven" in the sphere of natural science, while in the realms of history and literature it is palpably false. The records of history and of literature reveal from time to time the great fact and factor of personality, the reality of personal power, and this determinative element has a peculiar way of setting at naught all idealistic theories of a purely natural and uniform progress in history and letters. The literature of today is not necessarily higher than that produced in the past; the history of the last century is not in every way and always superior to that of its predecessors. Even a "naturalistic" writer like Professor Percy Gardner testifies to the fact and force of personality in the following remarkable terms:

"There is, in fact, a great force in history which is not, so far as we can judge, evolutional, and the law of which is very hard to trace—the force of personality and character." And quite apart from such instances of personality as have arisen from time to time through the centuries, there is one Personality who has not yet been accounted for by any theory of evolution—the Person of Jesus of Nazareth.

There are sufficient data in current Old Testament criticism to warrant the statement that it proceeds from presuppositions concerning the origins of history, religion, and the Bible, which, in their essence, are subversive of belief in a Divine revelation. And such being the case, we naturally look with grave suspicion on results derived from so unsound a philosophical basis.

6. CAN PURELY NATURALISTIC PREMISES BE ACCEPTED WITH-
OUT COMING TO PURELY NATURALISTIC CONCLUSIONS?

Kuenen and Wellhausen are admittedly accepted as masters by our leading Old Testament "higher critics" in England, Scotland, and America, and the results of their literary analysis of the Pentateuch are generally regarded as conclusive by their followers. On the basis of this literary dissection, certain conclusions are formed as to the character and growth of Old Testament religion, and, as a result, the history of the Jews is reconstructed. The Book of Deuteronomy is said to be mainly, if not entirely, a product of the reign of Josiah, the accounts of the tabernacle and worship are of exilic date; monotheism in Israel was of late date, and was the outcome of a growth from polytheism; and the present Book of Genesis reflects the thoughts of the time of its composition or compilation in or near the date of the Exile.

Now it is known that Kuenen and Wellhausen deny the supernatural element in the Old Testament. This is the "presupposition" of their entire position. Will anyone say that it does not materially affect their conclusions? And is there any safe or logical halting-ground for those who accept so many of their premises? The extreme subjectivity of Canon Cheyne ought not to be a surprise to any who accept the main principles of modern higher criticism; it is part of the logical outcome of the general position. We gladly distinguish between the extremists and the other scholars who see no incompatibility between the acceptance of many of the literary and historical principles of Kuenen and Wellhausen and a belief in the Divine source and authority of the Old Testament. But we are bound to add that the unsatisfying element in the writings of moderate men like Canon Driver and Principal George Adam Smith is that, while accepting so much of the "naturalism" of the German school, they do not give us any clear assurance of the strength of the foundation on which they rest and ask us to rest. The tendency of their position is certainly towards a minimizing of the supernatural in the Old Testament.

Take, as one instance, the Messianic element. In spite of the universal belief of Jews and Christians in a personal Messiah, a belief derived in the first place solely from the Old Testament, and supported for Christians by the New, modern criticism will not allow much clear and undoubted prediction of Him. Insight into existing conditions is readily granted to the prophets, but they are not allowed to have had much foresight into future conditions connected with the Messiah. Yet Isaiah's glowing words remain, and demand a fair, full exegesis such as they do not get from many modern scholars. Dr. James Wells, of Glasgow, wrote in the "British Weekly" some time ago of the new criticism on this point:

"The fear of prediction in the proper sense of the term is ever before its eyes. It gladly enlarges on fore-shadowings, a moral historical growth which reaches its culmination in Christ; and anticipations of the Spirit of Christ; but its tendency is always to minimize the prophetic element in the Old Testament."

Another example of the tendency of modern criticism to minimize and explain away the supernatural element may be given from a book entitled, "The Theology and Ethics of the Hebrews," by Dr. Archibald Duff, Professor in the Yorkshire College, Bradford. This is his account of Moses at the burning bush:

"He was shepherding his sheep among the red granite mountains. . . . The man sat at dawn by the stream, and watched the fiery rocks. Yonder gleamed the level sunlight across the low growth. Each spine glistened against the rising sun. The man was a poet, one fit for inspiration. He felt that the dreams of his soul were the whisperings of his God, the place His sanctuary. He bowed and worshipped,"

(p. 6.) This, at least, is not the prima facie impression derived from the account given in Exodus.

One more illustration may be given of modern critical methods of dealing with narratives of the Old Testament which were evidently intended to be regarded as historical. In the "International Critical Commentary" on Numbers, Dr. G. B. Gray, of Mansfield College, Oxford, thus writes on what he terms "the priestly section of the book":

"For the history of the Mosaic age the whole section is valueless." "The historical impression given by (P) of the Mosaic age is altogether unhistorical, and much of the detail . . . can . . . be demonstrated to be entirely unreal, or at least untrue of the age in question." "This history is fictitious."

These statements at once set aside the history contained in more than three-quarters of the whole Book of Numbers, while as to the rest Dr. Gray's verdict is by no means reassuring, and he clearly does not possess much confidence in even the small quantity that escapes his condemnation. The brazen serpent is said to be an invention on the part of some "who had come under the higher prophetic teaching" before Hezekiah, and is meant "to controvert the popular belief" in the healing power of the serpent by ascribing it to Jehovah. As to the story of Balaam, Dr. Gray wrotes:

"It may, indeed, contain other historical features, such as the name of Balak, who may have been an actual king of Moab; but no means at present exist for distinguishing any further between the historical or legendary elements and those which are supplied by the creative faculty and the religious feeling of the writers."

What is any ordinary earnest Christian to make of all these statements? The writer of the Book of Numbers evidently composed what professes to be history, and what he meant to be read as history, and yet according to Dr. Gray all this has no historical foundation. We can only say that the Christian Church will require very much more convincing proofs before they can accept the critical position, and it does not facilitate our acceptance of this wholesale process of invention to be told that it is due to "the creative faculty and the religious feeling of the writers."

As to the fact that so many of our British and American "higher critics" are firm believers in the Divine authority of the Old Testament, and of a Divine revelation embodied in it, we cannot but feel the force of the words of the late Dr. W. H. Green, of Princeton: "They who have themselves been thoroughly grounded in the Christian faith may, by a happy inconsistency, hold fast their old convictions, while admitting principles, methods, and conclusions that are logically at war with them. But who can be surprised if others shall with stricter logic carry what has been thus commended to them to its legitimate conclusions?"

7. CAN WE OVERLOOK THE EVIDENCE OF ARCHAEOLOGY?

It is well known that during the last sixty years a vast number of archaeological discoveries have been made in Egypt, Palestine, Babylonia, and Assyria. Many of these have shed remarkable light on the historical features of the Old Testament. A number of persons and periods have been illuminated by these discoveries and are now seen with a clearness which was before impossible.

Now it is a simple and yet striking fact that not one of these discoveries during the whole of this time has given any support to the distinctive features and principles of the higher critical position, while, on the other hand, many of them have afforded abundant confirmation of the traditional and conservative view of the Old Testament.

Let us consider a few of these discoveries. Only a little over forty years ago the conservative "Speaker's Commentary" actually had to take into consideration the critical arguments then so prevalent in favor of the late invention of writing. This is an argument which is never heard now in critical circles. The change of attack is most striking. While forty or fifty years ago it was argued that Moses could not possibly have had sufficient learning to write the Pentateuch, now it is argued as the result of these modern discoveries that he would have been altogether behind his contemporaries if he had not been able to write. Again, the Babylonian story of the flood agrees in long sections with the account in Genesis, and it is known that the Babylonian version was in existence for ages before the dates assigned to the Genesis narrative by the critical school. Professor Sayce rightly calls this a crucial test of the critical position. The historicity of the kings mentioned in Genesis 14 was once seriously questioned by criticism, but this is impossible today, for their historical character has been proved beyond all question, and, in particular, it is now known that the Amraphel of that chapter is the Hammurabi of the Monuments and a contemporary with Abraham. The puzzling story of Sarah and Hagar is also now seen to be in exact agreement with Babylonian custom. Then again, the Egypt of Joseph and Moses is true to the smallest details of the life of the Egypt of that day and is altogether different from the very different Egypt of later ages. Sargon, who for centuries was only known from the one reference to him in Isa. 20:1, is now seen to have been one of the most important kings of Assyria. And the Aramaic language of Daniel and Ezra, which has so often been accused of lateness, is proved to be in exact accord with the Aramaic of that age, as shown by the Papyri discovered at Elephantinè in Egypt.

Now these, and others like them, are tangible proofs which can be verified by ordinary people. Hebrew philology is beyond most of us and is too subjective for any convincing argument to be based upon it, but archaeology offers an objective method of putting historical theories to the test.

Not the least important feature of the archaeological argument is that a number of leading archaeologists who were formerly in hearty agreement with the critical school, have now abandoned this view and oppose it. As Sir William Robertson Nicoll has forcibly said: "The significant fact is that the great first-hand archaeologists as a rule do not trust the higher criticism. This means a great deal more than can be put on paper to account for their doubt. It means that they are living in an atmosphere where arguments that flourish outside do not thrive."

Professor Flinders Petrie, the great Egyptologist, uttered these words not long ago: "I have come to the conclusion that there is a far more solid basis than seems to be supposed by many critics. . . . I have not the slightest doubt that contemporary documents give a truly solid foundation for the records contained in the Pentateuch. . . . The essential point is that some of these critical people support from an *a priori* basis instead of writing upon ascertained facts. We should remember that writing at the time of the Exodus was as familiar as it is now. . . . The fact is that it is hopeless for these people by means merely of verbal criticism to succeed in solving all difficulties that arise."

8. ARE THE VIEWS OF MODERN CRITICISM CONSISTENT WITH THE WITNESS OF OUR LORD TO THE OLD TESTAMENT?

The Christian Church approaches the Old Testament mainly and predominantly from the standpoint of the resurrection of Christ. We naturally inquire what our Master thought of the Old Testament, for if it comes to us with His authority, and we can discover His view of it, we ought to be satisfied.

In the days of our Lord's life on earth one pressing question was, "What think ye of the Christ?" Another was, "What is written in the Law? How readest thou?" These questions are still being raised in one form or another, and today, as of old, the two great problems—two "storm-centers", as they have well been called—are Christ and the Bible.

The two problems really resolve themslves into one, for Christ and the Bible are inseparable. If we follow Christ, He will teach us of the Bible; and if we study our Bible, it will point us to Christ. Each is called the Word of God.

Let us, first of all, be quite clear as to our meaning of our Lord as "The Word of God." "In the beginning was the Word." A word is an oral or visible expression of an invisible thought. The thought needs the word for its expression, and the word is intended to represent the thought accurately, even if not completely. We cannot in any degree be sure of the thought unless we can be sure of the word. Our Lord as the Word, therefore, is the personal and visible expression of the invisible God. (John 14; Heb. 1:3.) We believe that He is an accurate "expression" of God, and that as the Word He reveals God and conveys God's will to us in such a way as to be inerrant and infallible. As the Incarnate Word He is infallible.

He came, among other things, to bear witness to the truth (John 18:37), and it is a necessary outcome of this purpose that He should bear infallible witness. He came to reveal God and God's will, and this implies and requires special knowledge. It demands that every assertion of His be true. The Divine knowledge did not, because it could not, undergo any change by the Incarnation. He continued to subsist in the form of God even while He existed in the form of man. (Phil. 2:6. See Dr. Gifford's "The Incarnation.")

In view of this position, we believe that, as Bishop Ellicott says ("Christus Comprobator") we have a right to make this appeal to the testimony of Christ to the Old Testament. The place it occupied in His life and ministry is sufficient warrant for referring to His use of it. It is well known that, as far as the Old Testament canon is concerned, our highest authority is that of our Lord Himself; and what is true of the Old Testament as a whole, is surely true of these parts to which our Lord specifically referred.

Let us be clear, however, as to what we mean in making this appeal. We do not for an instant intend thereby to close all possible criticism of the Old Testament. There are numbers of questions quite untouched by anything our Lord said, and there is consequently ample scope for sober, necessary, and valuable criticism. But what we do say is, that anything in the Old Testament stated by our Lord as a fact, or implied as a fact, is, or ought to be, thereby closed for those who hold Christ to be infallible. Criticism can do anything that is not incompatible with the statements of our Lord; but where Christ has spoken, surely "the matter is closed."

What, then, is our Lord's general view of the Old Testament? There is no doubt that His Old Testament was practically, if not actually, the same as ours, and that He regarded it as of Divine authority, as the final court of appeal for all questions connected with it. The way in which He quotes it shows this. To the Lord Jesus the Old Testament was authoritative and final, because Divine.

No one can go through the Gospels without being impressed with the deep reverence of our Lord for the Old Testament, and with His constant use of it in all matters of religious thought and life. His question, "Have ye never read?" His assertion, "It is written," His testimony, "Ye search the Scriptures" (R. V), are plainly indicative of His view of the Divine authority of the Old Testament as we have it. He sets His seal to its historicity and its revelation of God. He supplements, but never supplants it. He amplifies and modifies, but never nullifies it. He fulfills, i. e. fills full, but never makes void.

This general view is confirmed by His detailed references to the Old Testament. Consider His testimonies to the persons, and to the facts of the old covenant.

There is scarcely a historical book, from Genesis to 2 Chronicles, to which our Lord does not refer; while it is perhaps significant that His testimony includes references to every book of the Pentateuch, to Isaiah, to Jonah, to Daniel, and to miracles—the very parts most called in question today.

Above all, it is surely of the deepest moment that at His temptation He should use three times as the Word of God the book about which there has, perhaps, been most controversy of all.

Again, therefore, we say that everything to which Christ can be said, on any honest interpretation, to have referred, or which He used as a fact, is thereby sanctioned and sealed by the authority of our Infallible Lord. "Dominus locutus est; causa finita est."

Nor can this position be turned by the statement that Christ simply adopted the beliefs of His day without necessarily sanctioning them as correct. Of this there is not the slightest proof, but very much to the contrary. On some of the most important subjects of His day He went directly against prevailing opinion. His teaching about God, about righteousness, about the Messiah, about tradition, about the Sabbath, about the Samaritans, about women, about divorce, about the baptism of John, were diametrically opposed to that of the time. And this opposition was deliberately grounded on the Old Testament which our Lord charged them with misinterpreting. The one and only question of difference between Him and the Jews as to the Old Testament was that of interpretation. Not a vestige of proof can be adduced that He and they differed at all in their general view of its historical character or Divine authority. If the current Jewish views were wrong, can we think our Lord would have been silent on a matter of such moment, about a book which He cites or alludes to over four hundred times, and which He made His constant topic in teaching concerning Himself? If the Jews were wrong, Jesus either knew it, or He did not. If He knew it, why did He not correct them as in so many other and detailed instances? If He did not know it—but I will not finish.

Nor can this witness to the Old Testament be met by asserting that the limitation of our Lord's earthly life kept Him within current views of the Old Testament which need not have been true views. This statement ignores the essential force of His personal claim to be "the Word."

On more than one occasion our Lord claimed to speak from God, and that everything He said had the Divine warrant. Let us notice carefully what this involves. It is sometimes said that our Lord's knowledge was limited, and that He lived here as man, not as God. Suppose we grant this for argument's sake. Very well; as man He lived in God and on God, and He claimed that everything He said and did was from God and through God. If, then, the limitations were from God, so *also were the utterances;* and, as God's warrant was claimed for every one of these, they are therefore Divine and infallible. (John 5:19; 5:30; 7:13; 8:26; 12:49; 14:24; 17:8.) Even though we grant to the full a theory that will compel us to accept a temporary disuse or non-use of the functions of Deity in the Person of our Lord, yet the words actually uttered as man are claimed to be from God, and therefore we hold them to be infallible. We rest, therefore, upon our Lord's personal claim to say all and do all by the Father, from the Father, for the Father.

There is, of course, no question of partial knowledge after the resurrection, when our Lord was manifestly free from all limitations of earthly conditions. Yet it was after His resurrection also that He set His seal to the Old Testament. (Luke 24:44.)

We conclude that our Lord's positive statements on the subject of the Old Testament are not to be rejected without charging Him with error. If, on these points, on which we can test and verify Him, we find that He is not reliable, what real comfort can we have in accepting His higher teaching, where verification is impossible? We believe we are on absolutely safe ground when we say that what the Old Testament was to our Lord, it must be and shall be to us.

CONCLUSION

We ask a careful consideration of these eight inquiries. Taken separately, they carry weight, but taken together they have a cumulative effect, and should be seriously pondered by all who are seeking to know the truth on this momentous subject.

We may be perfectly sure that no criticism of the Old Testament will ever be accepted by the Christian Church as a whole, which does not fully satisfy the following conditions:

1. It must admit in all its assumptions, and take fully into consideration, the supernatural element which differentiates the Bible from all other books.

2. It must be in keeping with the enlightened spiritual experience of the saints of God in all ages, and make an effectual appeal to the piety and spiritual perception of those who know by personal experience the power of the Holy Ghost.

3. It must be historically in line with the general tradition of Jewish history and the unique position of the Hebrew nation through the centuries.

4. It must be in unison with that apostolic conception of the authority and inspiration of the Old Testament, which is so manifest in the New Testament.

5. Above all, it must be in accordance with the universal belief of the Christian Church in our Lord's infallibility as a Teacher, and as "the Word made flesh."

If and when modern higher criticism can satisfy these requirements, it will not merely be accepted, but will command the universal, loyal, and even enthusiastic adhesion of all Christians. Until then, we wait, and also maintain our position that "the old is better."

CHAPTER VIII

THE TABERNACLE IN THE WILDERNESS: DID IT EXIST?

A QUESTION INVOLVING THE TRUTH OR FALSITY OF THE ENTIRE HIGHER-CRITIC THEORY

BY DAVID HEAGLE, PH. D., D. D.,

PROFESSOR OF THEOLOGY AND ETHICS, EWING COLLEGE; TRANS-
LATOR "BREMEN LECTURES"; AUTHOR OF "MORAL
EDUCATION," "THAT BLESSED HOPE," ETC.

INTRODUCTORY

The question as to whether or not the old Mosaic Tabernacle ever existed is one of far greater consequence than most people imagine. It is so, particularly because of the very intimate connection existing between it and the truth or falsity of the higher-critic theory in general. If that theory is all that the critics claim for it, then of course the Tabernacle had no existence; and this is the view held by at least most of the critics. But if, on the other hand, the old Mosaic Tabernacle did really exist, and the story of it as given in the Bible is not, as the critics assert, merely a fiction, then the higher-critic scheme cannot be true.

The question, therefore, to be discussed in the following pages, viz., whether the Mosaic Tabernacle really did or did not exist, is certainly one of great and wide-reaching significance; which significance will become more and more apparent as the discussion goes forward. With this brief introduction we take up the subject; merely premising further, that this article was originally prepared as a booklet, in which shape it contained a considerable amount of matter not appearing here.

THE DISCUSSION

One peculiarity of the higher criticism is what may be called its unbounded audacity in attacking and attempting to destroy many of the most solidly established facts of the Bible. No matter with what amount of evidence any particular Scripture fact may be capable of demonstration, if it happens to oppose any of the more fundamental notions of the critical hypothesis, away it must go as unworthy of acceptance by so-called "science," or at all events, the entire array of critical doubts and imaginings is brought to bear, in order to cast suspicion upon it, or to get rid of it in some way.

I. THE BIBLE SIDE OF THE QUESTION

A striking illustration of such procedure is furnished by the peculiar treatment accorded by the critics to that old religious structure which, being built by Moses near Mt. Sinai, is usually named the Tabernacle, or the Tabernacle in the Wilderness. That such a structure not only existed, but was for some five hundred years a very conspicuous object in ancient Israelitish history, is a fact to which the Bible itself lends no small amount of evidence. For example, there are found in the book of Exodus alone some thirteen chapters devoted to a minute description of the plan and construction of that building. Then, as explanatory of the Tabernacle's services, its dedication, means of transportation, the work of the priests and Levites to some extent, and various other matters connected with the structure, the entire book of Leviticus with some ten chapters in Numbers may be cited. Besides, scattered all through both the Old and New Testaments there are many allusions and notices—some of them merely incidental, but others more historical in nature—all of which go toward establishing the Tabernacle's historicity. And finally—

which is perhaps the most convincing testimony of all—we have given us in the New Testament one whole book, the Epistle to the Hebrews, which concerns, especially explaining from a Christian point of view, the typology and religious significance of that old building.

II. THE HIGHER-CRITIC VIEW

With so much evidence, therefore, to be adduced, even from the Scriptures, in support of the Tabernacle's historicity, one would think that it requires at least some literary bravery, not to say presumptuous audacity, for any individual or class of men to assail, with the expectation of overthrowing, a fact so solidly established as would seem to be that of the Tabernacle's real existence. Nevertheless, difficult as such task may appear, the critics have not hesitated most vigorously to undertake it. According to their notion the whole story of the Tabernacle, as recorded in the Bible, is simply a fiction, or, more properly speaking, a literary forgery—a concoction gotten up perhaps by some of those priestly scribes who returned with Ezra from the Babylonian exile; their special purpose in devising such a story being to help in the introduction of a new temple ritual at Jerusalem, or perhaps it was also to glorify the distant past in the history of the Israelites.*

III. THE QUESTION MORE FULLY STATED

Thus we have presented to us two widely different and opposing views respecting the Tabernacle's existence. One of them, which is the view of at least most higher critics, is that this old structure never existed at all; while, on the other hand, the orthodox and Biblical conception is that not only in the days of Moses but long afterwards this fabric had a most interesting and important history. Which, then, of these two so widely different doctrines are we pleased to accept?

---

*As explained by Nödelke, another purpose of this forgery was "to give pre-existence to the temple and to the unity of worship." But this is virtually included in the two purposes above named.

IV. IMPORTANCE OF THIS DISCUSSION

1. Whichever one is accepted by us, certain it is that an earnest discussion, such as we hope to effect, of the question above stated, is a matter of no little consequence. Such a discussion is important, first of all, because of the light which it will throw upon all the history of God's first chosen people—the Israelites. It will at least tell us something about the kind of civilization this ancient people must have had; and more particularly will it tell us whether that civilization was, as the higher critics represent, one low down on the scale, or whether these Israelites had already made a good degree of progress in all the arts, disciplines, and branches of knowledge which usually belong to a moderately high state of civilization. Surely, then, there is at least some benefit to be derived from the study before us.

2. But another advantage which will come from this same study is that it will help us to a solution of a somewhat curious, but yet important, historical problem; viz., whether as a matter of history the Temple preceded the Tabernacle, as the higher critics claim, and, therefore, that the Tabernacle must be regarded as only "a diminutive copy" of the Temple; or vice versa, whether, as is taught by the Bible, the Tabernacle went first, and hence that the Temple was in its construction patterned after the Tabernacle. To be sure, at first sight this does not appear to be a very important question; yet when the historical, literary and other connections involved in it are considered, it does after all become a question of no little significance.

3. But the most determinative and therefore the most significant interest we have in a discussion of the question as proposed, is the bearing which it has upon the truth or falsity of the higher criticism. As is known to persons conversant with that peculiar method of Bible study, one of its main contentions is that the whole Levitical or ceremonial law—

that is, the law of worship as recorded especially in Exodus, Leviticus and Numbers—did not originate, or at all events did not make its appearance, until somewhere near the close of the Babylonian exile, or about the time when Ezra first appears in Jewish history. By thus removing all that part of the Pentateuch down the centuries, from the time of Moses to the time of Ezra, the critics are able not only to deny the Mosaic authorship of this Pentateuchal literature, but also to construct a scheme of their own by which all the separate "documents" into which they are accustomed to divide the Pentateuch can be put together in a kind of whole; each particular document being singled out and designated according to its date, authorship, and other peculiarities, such as the critics suppose belong to it. Moreover, in this way the Pentateuch is all torn to pieces, and instead of its being really a connected, organic whole, such as the orthodox world has always conceived it to be, it is by this peculiar higher-critic method transformed into a mere patch-work, a disjointed affair, having no more divine authority or inspiration connected with it than any other piece of human literature that has come into being through the law of evolution.

Such, however, is exactly what the critics would make of the Pentateuch, and indeed of much else in the Bible, if they could have their way.

But now suppose that after all the old Mosaic Tabernacle did really exist, what effect would that have upon the success of the critical hypothesis? It would absolutely frustrate all attempts to carry this hypothesis successfully through. Such would necessarily be the result, because, first of all, if that portion of the Pentateuch which contains the ceremonial or Levitical law is transferred down to Ezra's time, the old Tabernacle, for the services of which this law was designed, must necessarily come with it. But then, in the second place, a really existing Tabernacle so far down the centuries, or long after the Temple at Jerusalem had been built and was regarded by the Jews as their great central place of worship, would have been not only an architectural curiosity, but an anachronism such as even the critical imagination could scarcely be accused either of devising or accepting.

The only way, therefore, open for the critics, if they are still to hold fast their theory, is for them to do precisely what they have undertaken; namely, to blot out or destroy the Tabernacle as a real existence, and then to reconstruct the entire story of it, as given in the Bible, in the form of a fiction. This they have really attempted.

But by so doing the critics must, after all, confess that the foundation upon which they build is very insecure, because it is simply an assumption. If, therefore, in opposition to such assumption, this article shall be able to demonstrate that the old Mosaic Tabernacle actually existed, then the underpinning of the critical hypothesis is at once removed, and the entire edifice with all of its many stories must collapse. And if all this is true, then it is not too much to say, as is affirmed in the sub-title of this article, that the whole truth or falsity of the critical scheme depends upon what may be proven true respecting the Tabernacle's non-existence or existence.

And thus, moreover, is made to appear the exceeding importance of the discussion we have undertaken.

V. QUOTATIONS FROM THE HIGHER CRITICS

But what do the higher critics themselves say with regard to this matter of the Tabernacle's real existence? To quote from only a few of them, Wellhausen, e. g., who is the great coryphæus of the higher-critic doctrine, writes as follows: "The Temple, which in reality was not built until Solomon's time, is by this document [the so-called Priestly Code] regarded as so indispensable, even for the troubled days of the wilderness before the settlement, that it is made portable, and in the form of a tabernacle set up in the very beginning of things. For the truth is that the Tabernacle is a copy, not the prototype, of the temple at Jerusalem" (Proleg., Eng. trans., p. 37). So also Graf, who preceded Wellhausen in higher-critic work, affirms that the Tabernacle is only "a diminutive copy of the Temple," and that "all that is said about this structure in the middle books of the Pentateuch is merely post-exilic accretion." Once more, to hear from a more recent authority, Dr. A. R. S. Kennedy, in Hastings' *Dictionary of the Bible,* has these words: "The attitude of modern Old Testament scholarship to the priestly legislation as now formulated in the Pentateuch, and in particular to those sections of it which deal with the sanctuary and its worship, is opposed to the historicity of P's [that is, the old Mosaic] Tabernacle." The same or a similar representation is given by Benzinger in the *Encyclopaedia Biblica;* and in fact this is, and must necessarily be, the attitude of all consistent higher critics toward the matter under consideration. For it would never do for the adherents of the critic theory to admit that away back in the old Mosaic times the Tabernacle, with all its elaborate ritual, and with the lofty moral and spiritual ideas embodied in it, could have existed; because that would be equivalent to admitting the falsity of their own doctrine. Accordingly with one voice the critics all, or nearly all, stoutly proclaim that no historicity whatever must be allowed to Moses' Tabernacle.

VI. CERTAIN GREAT PRESUMPTIONS

To come then to the actual discussion of our subject, it might be said, in the first place, that there are certain great presumptions which lie in the way of our accepting the higher-critic theory as true.

1. One of these presumptions is, that this whole critic hypothesis goes on the assumption that what the Bible tells us regarding the real existence of the Tabernacle is not true, or, in other words, that in a large part of its teachings the Bible speaks falsely. Can we believe that? Most assuredly

not, so long as we have any real appreciation of the lofty system of moral truth which is taught in this wonderful book—a book which, more than any other ever produced, has taught the entire world common honesty, whether in literary work or other acts. Therefore we say, regarding this whole matter of the Bible's speaking falsely, *Judaeus Apella credat, non ego!* Let the higher critics believe that if they will, but surely not we!

Robert Burns has a poem, in which he says of lying in general:

> "Some books are lies frae end to end,
> And some great lies were never penned;
> E'en ministers, they hae been kenned,
> In holy rapture,
> A rousing whid at times to vend,
> An' nail it wi' Scripture."

Surely, the higher critics would not undertake to reduce our Christian Scriptures to the level of a book that has in it no truth from beginning to end; and yet it must be confessed that one serious tendency of their theory is greatly to lessen the general credibility of this sacred volume.

2. But another presumption lying against the truthfulness of this higher criticism is, that it makes all the civilized ages from Ezra down to the present time to be so utterly lacking both in historic knowledge and literary sagacity, that, excepting a few higher critics, no one ever supposed the whole world was being deceived by this untrue story of the Tabernacle's real existence; when, if the facts were told, all these numerous ages have not only been themselves deceived, but have been also instrumental, one after another, in propagating that same old falsehood down the centuries! Again we say: *Judaeus Apella credat, non ego!* The higher-critic pretensions to having a greater wisdom and knowledge than is possessed by all the rest of the world, are very well known; but

this illustration of that peculiarity seems to us rather to cap the climax.

3. And here, if we choose to go farther, it might be shown that, if this peculiar doctrine is true, then the Savior and all of his Apostles were mistaken. For certainly Christ (see Matt. 12:3, 4) and perhaps all the Apostles without exception, did believe in the Tabernacle as a real existence; and one of the Apostles, or at least an apostolic writer, went so far, in the Book of Hebrews, as to compose what may be termed an extensive and inspired commentary on that sacred structure—on its apartments, furniture, priesthood and services; bringing out particularly, from a Christian point of view, the rich typical significance of all those matters. Now that all these inspired men and the Savior Himself should either have been themselves deceived or should try to deceive others with regard to an important matter of Old Testament history is surely incredible.

VII. EXTERNAL EVIDENCE

1. Just here, however, we desire to introduce some considerations of a different nature. There exists, even outside of the Bible, a small amount of evidence in support of the Tabernacle's existence, and although we have already alluded to a part of this testimony, under the head of favoring presumptions, yet it will bear repetition or rather a fuller consideration. Now, as we conceive of this evidence, it consists, in the first place, of various notices or even of full descriptions of the Tabernacle as a real existence, which are found in very ancient writings, some of these writings being quite different from our Christian Scriptures. To be sure, a large part of this literature is copied in one way and another from the Bible, and none of it dates anything like so far back in time as do at least the earlier books of the Old Testament; and yet, as we shall see, some of it is very old, sufficiently so to give it a kind of confirmatory force in support of what the Bible has to say concerning the matter in hand.

The first testimony, then, of this sort to which we allude, is a full description of the Tabernacle in all its parts, services, priesthood and history, very nearly the same as that which is given in our modern Bibles, which can be found in the earliest translation ever made of the Old Testament—that is, the Septuagint. This translation appeared some two or three centuries before the time of Christ, and therefore it ought to be pretty good evidence of at least what its contemporaries, or those far-off times, held to be true with regard to the matter under consideration. Then another testimony of like character comes from the Greek Apocrypha to the Old Testament, a work which appeared, or at least most of it, before the time of Christ; in which production there are found various allusions to the Tabernacle, and all of them to it as a real existence; as, e. g., in Jud. 9:8; Wis. of Sol. 9:8; Eccl. 24:10, 15; and 2 Mac. 2:5. Moreover, in his *Antiquities,* Josephus, who wrote toward the end of the first century, gives another full description of that old structure in its every part, including also something of its history. (See Antiq., Bk. III., Chs. VI. to XII.; also Bk. V., Ch. I., Sec. 19; Ch. II., Sec. 9; Ch. X., Sec. 2; Bk. VIII., Ch. IV., Sec. 1.) And finally, in that vast collection of ancient Jewish traditions, comments, laws, speculations, etc., which goes under the name of the Talmud, there are not infrequent references made to this same old structure; and one of the treatises (part of the Bereitha)* in that collection is devoted exclusively to a consideration of this building.

With so much literature, therefore, of one kind and another, all telling us something about the Tabernacle, and all or at least most of it going back for its origin to very near the time when at least the last part of the Old Testament was

---

*The Bereitha (or Baraitha) is an apocryphal part of the Talmud; but it is very old, and embodies about the same quality of tradition in general as does the compilation made by Jehudah ha-Nasi, which is usually considered the genuine Mishna, or basis of the Talmud.

written, we have in these various sources, considered as a whole, if not an independent or direct testimony to the Tabernacle's existence, certainly something that points clearly in that direction. Or, in other words, inasmuch as these old writings, containing the various notices and descriptions which we have mentioned, existed away back so near to Old Testament times, these must have been acquainted with the best traditions of their day regarding what is taught in that part of our Bible; and, therefore, they must have known more about the truth of things as connected with the Tabernacle and its real existence than any authorities existing in these late times of ours possibly could. Or, at all events, they knew more about those matters than any of the mere guesswork speculations of modern higher critics possibly can, or are in a condition to know.*

2. But there is another kind of evidence, of this external nature. which is more direct and independent, and therefore more significant with regard to the Tabernacle's existence. That evidence is what may be called the archæological contribution to our argument. Part of it will be given later;† but here we will simply call attention, first, to the fact that in all the region of Mt. Sinai there are to be seen at least some evidences of the possible presence there, even as is recorded

---

*The value of this evidence is of course only that which belongs to tradition; still it should be remembered that this tradition is a written one, dating away back to near the times of the Old Testament. Moreover, it could be shown that this same kind of written tradition reaches back through the later books of the Old Testament, at least in a negative way, even to the time of Ezra; who surely ought to know whether, as the critics say, the story of the Tabernacle as a fact of history was invented in his own day and generation. But inasmuch as Ezra does not tell us anything about that matter, it stands to reason, that as has since been reported by this long line of tradition, most of it being of a positive nature, no such invention ever took place, but that this story is simply a narrative of actual fact. At all events, as said in the text, it is far more likely that this old and long-continued tradition is correct in what it asserts, than is any of the denials of the higher critics.

†See pp. 183-85.

in the Bible, of the Israelites, at the time when they built the Tabernacle.* Moreover, there have recently been made some discoveries in the Holy Land connected with the different places where the Bible locates the Tabernacle during the long period of its history in that country, which, to say the least, are not contradictory, but rather confirmatory of Biblical statements. One such discovery, as we will call it, is connected with a fuller exploration recently made of that old site where for some 365 years, according to Jewish tradition, the old Mosaic Tabernacle stood, and where it underwent the most interesting of its experiences in the Holy Land. That site was, as is well known, the little city of Shiloh, located near the main thoroughfare leading up from Bethel to Shechem. In the year 1873 the English Palestine Exploration Fund, through some of its agents, made a thorough examination of this old site, and among other of its very interesting ruins was found a place which Colonel Charles Wilson thinks is the *very spot* where, once and for so long a time, the Tabernacle stood. That particular place is at the north of a rather low "tell," or mound, upon which the ruins are located; and, to copy from Colonel Wilson's description, this tell "slopes down to a broad shoulder, across which a sort of local court, 77 feet wide and 412 feet long, has been cut out. The rock is in places scarped to a height of five feet, and along the sides are several excavations and a few small cisterns." This is the locality where, as Colonel Wilson thinks, the Mosaic Tabernacle once really stood; and as confirmatory of his conclusion he farther says that this spot is the only one connected with the ruins which is large enough to receive a building of the dimensions of the Tabernacle. Therefore his judgment is that it is "not improbable" that this place was originally "prepared" as a site for that structure.

*See Page 187.

Now whether the general judgment of men either at present or in the future will coincide with Colonel Wilson as to the matter in hand we do not know; but we will simply repeat Colonel Wilson's words, and say that it is *not improbable* that this site, as indicated, is a real discovery as to the place where the old Tabernacle once stood. We need not dwell longer here on the matter, but will only observe that if the very ruins of the old Tabernacle, so far as its site is concerned, can still be seen, that surely ought to be pretty good evidence that this building once existed.

VIII. POSITIVE BIBLICAL EVIDENCES

But to come now to the more positive and conclusive evidences regarding the matter under consideration, we may observe that these consist particularly of various historical notices scattered throughout the Old Testament; and so numerous and clear in their testimony are these notices that they would seem to prove, beyond all possibility of doubt, that the old Mosaic Tabernacle really existed.* However, the critics claim here that it is only the earlier historical books of the Old Testament that can be legitimately used for proving a matter so far in the past as was this structure.

1. TESTIMONY OF FIRST KINGS

Complying then with that requirement, at least in part, we begin our investigation with the First Book of Kings. This is a piece of literature against the antiquity and general credibility of which the critics can raise no valid objection; hence it should be considered particularly good evidence. Moreover, it might be said of this book, that having probably been constructed out of early court-records as they were kept

---

*According to Bishop Hervey, in his Lectures on Chronicles (p. 171), mention is made of the Tabernacle some eighteen times in the historical books following the Pentateuch—that is, in Joshua, Judges, 1 and 2 Samuel, 1 and 2 Kings, and 1 and 2 Chronicles; and in the Pentateuch itself, which the higher critics have by no means proven to be unhistorical, that structure is mentioned over eighty times.

by the different kings of Judah and Israel, those original documents, or at least some of them, take us away back to the very times of Solomon and David, or to the period when, as we shall soon see, the Mosaic Tabernacle was still standing at Gibeon. This was also, it may be observed, the general period during which the Tabernacle, having been taken down, was removed from Gibeon and stored away in Solomon's temple at Jerusalem; and it is to the account of this transference that our attention is now, first of all, directed. In 1 Kings, Chap. 8, v. 4, we read: "And they brought up the ark of Jehovah, and the tent of meeting, and all the holy vessels that were in the tent; even these did the priests and Levites bring up." A mere cursory reading of these words gives one the impression that the "tent of meeting," which was brought up from somewhere by the priests and Levites, was nothing else than the old Mosaic Tabernacle; and as to the place from which it was brought, that is not told us in the Scriptures; but a comparison of texts (see 2 Chron. 1:3; 1 Kings, 3:1, 4) would seem to indicate that the Tabernacle was first transported from Gibeon to Mt. Zion, where the ark of the covenant was at this time, and then afterwards it was, with other sacred matters, carried up to Mt. Moriah, where it was put away in the temple.

All this seems to be sufficiently clear; only now the question arises whether, after all, this was really the old Mosaic structure or some other tent, as, e. g., the one built by David in Jerusalem, and which seems, at this time, to have been still in existence.* Most of the critics, including even Wellhausen, are agreed that the words, "tent of meeting" *(ohel moed),* as used in this and various other texts of· Scripture, do really signify the old Mosaic structure; and one reason for their so holding is that those words form a kind of technical expression by which that old structure was commonly,

---

*See 2 Sam. 6:17 and 7:2; 1 Chron. 15:1 and 16:1. Cf. 1 Kings 1:29.

or at least often, denoted in the Bible.* Only one other term is used as frequently as this is to indicate that structure; this other term being, in Hebrew, *mishkan,* which is usually translated, in our English versions, "tabernacle," and means "dwelling-place." Now if this rendering of those words is correct, we would seem to have already reached the goal of our endeavor. That is to say, we have actually found the Tabernacle in existence. It existed, as an undeniable reality in the times of David and Solomon, or at least in those of Solomon; and a positive proof of that matter are these words we have just quoted from 1 Kings 8:4.

But the higher critics, or especially Wellhausen, are not so easily to be caught with an admission as to an interpretation of words; for even though Wellhausen does concede that the words "tent of meeting" signify as we have stated; nevertheless he undertakes to get rid of their real force by asserting that in this passage they are an interpolation, or that they do not belong to the original Hebrew text. However, neither he nor any other higher critic has ever yet been able to give any textual authority for such an assertion; they only try to argue the matter from internal evidence. But internal evidence alone, and especially such slim evidence of that kind as the critics have been able to adduce in this connection, is insufficient to establish the end desired. Besides, those words, "tent of meeting," are certainly found in our present Hebrew text, as also in the Septuagint version; both of which items being so, it is not at all likely that Wellhausen's *ipse dixit* will have the effect of changing them. Such being the case, we may conclude that the structure

*The words *ohel moed* seem to have been used first to designate the smaller tent (see p. 37 with footnote) which Moses used as a place of communion between Jehovah and his people; hence it was called the "tent of meeting." But afterwards, when the regular tabernacle became such a place, the words were applied also to that structure.

which was carried by the priests and Levites up to Mt. Moriah and stored away in the temple, was really the old Mosaic Tabernacle.

We quote only one other passage from this First Book of Kings. It is a part of the account of Solomon's going to Gibeon, and of his offering sacrifice there. The words are found in v. 4, Chap. 3, and read as follows: "And the king went to Gibeon, to sacrifice there; for that was the great high place." Then in the second verse of this same chapter the king's conduct in thus going to Gibeon is farther explained by the statement that the people sacrificed in the high places, because "there was no house built for the name of Jehovah until those days." The "days" here indicated are, as is explained by the preceding verse, those in which "Solomon made an end of building his own house and the house of Jehovah;" and the entire passage then would signify that at least one reason why Solomon offered sacrifice in Gibeon was because this was the customary way among the people. They offered sacrifices in the high places before the temple at Jerusalem was built, but not ordinarily, or legitimately, afterwards. Then there is another reason indicated why Solomon went particularly to Gibeon—because this was the *"great* high place." Why it was so called, must have been because of some special fact or circumstance connected with it; and among the explanations given none appears so natural or to accord so well with other teachings of Scripture as the suggestion that this distinction was applied to Gibeon because the old Mosaic Tabernacle, with the brazen altar, was still there. That would certainly be a sufficient reason for accrediting peculiar eminence to this one of all the many high places which at that time seem to have existed in the Holy Land. Accordingly, Solomon went over to Gibeon, and offered sacrifice there; and then we read that, in the night following this devotional act, the king had a dream in which Jehovah appeared unto him and made to him very extraordinary promises. Now this epiphany of Jehovah at Gibeon is really another reason for one's believing that the Tabernacle was located at this place. For it is not to be supposed that any Jewish author, writing after the temple was built (when this account of Solomon's dream was written), would allow it to be said that the great and idolatry-hating God of the Israelites had made a gracious and extraordinary revelation of himself at any of the common high places in the Holy Land, half-heathenish and largely devoted to the service of idols, as these places generally were.

But if it must be admitted that the Tabernacle was really located at Gibeon, then all becomes clear, both why Solomon went there to offer sacrifice, and why Jehovah made at this place a gracious revelation of himself; also why this, of all the high places in the Holy Land, was called emphatically *"great."* Then, moreover, it might be said that we have surely demonstrated the existence of the Tabernacle, not only as taught by this passage from First Kings, but also by the other one which we have noticed.

2. TESTIMONY OF CHRONICLES

But now turning over to the two books of Chronicles, we find here quite a number of passages which teach in the clearest and most positive manner that the Tabernacle existed at Gibeon not only in the time of Solomon, but also before. These two books of Chronicles, it should be remembered, are really a kind of commentary, or an extension made, upon Samuel and Kings. Such is the opinion of many competent scholars; and one reason for their so holding, is that very evidently the books of Samuel and Kings were among the principal sources from which the author of Chronicles drew his information; although it must be acknowledged also that he used still other sources besides those named. Writing then at a somewhat distant date, say one or two hundred years from the time of the final composition, or redaction, of

Kings and Samuel,* and doubtless having at his command a considerable amount of tradition, besides his written sources, the Chronicler must have been in very good condition to write what may be considered a kind of interpretive commentary upon not only the books of Samuel, but also upon the First Book of Kings, two passages from which we have just noticed. If that was so, and the two books of Chronicles are to be understood then as giving us some additional information as to what is found in Kings, then the historical notices in First Kings which we have examined become as it were illuminated and made stronger and more positive in their nature than when considered alone. For instance, in First Kings we were told that Solomon went to Gibeon and offered sacrifice there, because "that was the great high place:" but now in 1 Chron. 1:3 we have it all explained, both how Gibeon came to be so called, and what was Solomon's special reason for going there to offer sacrifice. It was, as is taught very plainly here in Chornicles, because *"the tent of meeting of God which Moses the servant of Jehovah had made in the wilderness"* was at that time in Gibeon. Thus the rather uncertain mention of matters at Gibeon which is given in First Kings is made clear and positive by what is said in Chronicles. So also in 1 Chron. 21:29, which is a part of the account given of David's offering sacrifice on the threshing-floor of Ornan, we have again stronger language used than is found in Kings, telling us of the existence of the old Mosaic Tabernacle. For in explaining David's conduct the Chronicler says as follows: "For the *tabernacle of Jehovah*

---

*It is claimed by the critics that all the historical books of the Old Testament underwent a revision during the exile; and according to the best authorities, Chronicles was composed shortly after the Persian rule, or about 330 B. C. Selecting, then, about the middle of the exilic period (586 to 444 B. C.) as the date for the final revision of Kings and Samuel, this would make the composition of Chronicles fall near 200 years after that revision. But of course Samuel and Kings were originally composed, or compiled, at a much earlier date; the former appearing probably about 900, and the latter about 600 B. C.

*which Moses made in the wilderness and the altar of burnt
offering were at that time in the high place at Gibeon."* Whatever of uncertainty, therefore, or lack of positive indication,
may exist as connected with the passages we have quoted
from Kings, there is no such uncertainty or lack of positive-
ness here in Chronicles. On the contrary, these two books,
which give us quite an amount of information respecting the
Tabernacle, are always, or at least generally, very clear and
positive; and on this account, it might be added, the statements made in Chronicles have sometimes been taken as a
kind of guide to the study of the Tabernacle history in general.

But here again the critics make their appearance, and are
"all up in arms" against any use to be made of these two
books of Chronicles for determining a matter of ancient
history. Of all the untrustworthy historical literature to be
found in the Old Testament there is nothing quite so bad, so
the critics tell us, as is in general Chronicles; and Wellhausen
goes so far as to say that one special purpose served by these
two books is that they show how an author may use his
original sources with such freedom as to make them say
about what he pleases, or anything according to his own
ideas. (See Proleg., Eng. trans., p. 49.) So also Graf,
DeWette, and others, have very energetically attacked the
credibility of these two books. But over against all that is
said by the critics as to the Chronicler's lack of veracity and
his violent dealing with his sources, we will simply, or first,
put the testimony of one of the higher critics themselves.
It is what Dillman, who in point of learning and reliability
is acknowledged to be among the very foremost of all the
critics, says with regard to this very matter in hand: "It is
now recognized," affirms that eminent critic, "that the Chronicler has worked according to sources, and there can be no
talk, with regard to him, of fabrications or misrepresentations
of the history." So also Dr. Orr observes that there is no
reason for doubting "the perfect good faith" of the author of

Chronicles; and Prof. James Robertson, of Glasgow University, farther adds that all such matters as the critics have urged against the Chronicler's veracity or misuse and even invention of sources, are "superficial and unjust;" and that "there is no reason to doubt the honesty of the author in the use of such materials as he has command of, nor is there any to question the existence of the writings to which he refers."

We take it, therefore, that these two books of Chronicles embody not only the best historical knowledge, but also the best traditions still in existence at their date; and such being the case, it is clearly incontrovertible that, as is so unmistakably taught in these books, the old Mosaic Tabernacle must have existed. And so long as the critics are unable to impeach the testimony of these books, which would seem to be impossible, that testimony must stand.*

3. TESTIMONY OF SAMUEL

Now, however, let us give attention to the books of Samuel. Here is certainly another piece of literature against the general credibility of which the critics can have but little to say. And what do these books tell us respecting the Taber-

---

*It is claimed by the critics, and especially by Wellhausen, that during the exile the Jewish notions respecting the past of their national and tribal history underwent a radical change, so much so that nearly all the religious features of that history were conceived of as having been very different from what they really were. Or in other words, the Jewish writers of the exilic period were, so the critics tell us, accustomed to project religious and priestly matters belonging to their history in a much later period away back to the earliest times. Consequently the general ideas of the temple and of the temple service were thus projected back even to the days of Moses; and in this way, it is explained, the notion of a Mosaic Tabernacle with an elaborate ritualistic service came into being. But really there is no evidence in all the Old Testament writings, or at all events no evidence that the Jews knew anything about, that such a change ever took place. Hence the critics are decidedly wrong when they represent that the author of Chronicles was only influenced by the spirit of his age when he undertook to misrepresent, as it is claimed he did, numerous matters connected with the past history of this people. The truth is that the Chronicler was either a base falsifier, or what he tells us in his history must be received as genuine facts.

nacle's history? Very much, indeed; far more than we shall have space here fully to examine. In the first place, these books tell us that during at least part of the times which they in general describe, the Mosaic Tabernacle was located at Shiloh, up in the Ephraimite district. Then next we learn that at least one of the great festivals connected with the Tabernacle services—the "yearly sacrifice" it is called—was still being observed. Also we learn that this is the place where Samuel's parents, Elkanah and Hannah, went up every year, in order to take part in that sacrifice. Moreover, it was in the sanctuary at Shiloh, or in some one of its apartments, that Samuel slept at the time when he had those extraordinary revelations of Jehovah talking with him, and where also he came into such intimate and important relations with the aged Eli and his house.

And among still other items reported in those books there is one that invites our special attention. In 1 Sam., Chap. 2, v. 22, mention is made of certain "women that did service at the door of the tent meeting." And it was with these women, as we farther learn, that Eli's two sons, Hophni and Phinehas, committed at least a part of their wickedness, for which they were so severely condemned, and afterward punished by Jehovah. Now whatever else this passage may signify, it certainly intends to teach, by its use of the words "tent of meeting," that in the time of Samuel the old Mosaic Tabernacle was in existence at Shiloh. For, as we have already seen, those words, "tent of meeting," formed a characteristic expression by which in Old Testament times the Tabernacle was, quite often at least, designated and known. This much, as we have already noticed, even Wellhausen is willing to admit.

However, the critics raise here two objections. One of them is that the sanctuary at Shiloh was not really a tent or tabernacle, but rather a solid structure, built perhaps out of stone, wood, or some other material; and the special reason given by the critics for this view is that, in Samuel's account of the structure at Shiloh, there are "posts," "doors," and some other matters usually indicative of a solid structure mentioned. But this difficulty can be very easily explained from a statement made in the Jewish Mishna,* which is that the lower part of the sanctuary at Shiloh "was of stone," but that above this there was a tent. Or a more decisive answer to this objection is that in various Scriptures (such as 2 Sam. 7:6; Psa. 78:60; 1 Kings 8:4; Josh. 18:1, and still others) the structure under consideration is positively called "a tent" and "a tabernacle."

Then the other objection raised by the critics is that these words, "tent of meeting," as found in 1 Sam. 2:22, are an interpolation, or that the whole passage containing those words is spurious. The reason which they give for such an assertion is that this passage is not found in the Septuagint. But in reply to such objection it may be said, first, that this is not the only passage in the Bible in which mention is made of these women "at the door of the tent of meeting." In Ex. 38:8, like mention is made; and, as Dr. Orr has observed, it is inconceivable even on the supposition, which he does not accept, of a post-exilic origin of the last indicated passage, that just this one mention of the matter alluded to should occur, unless there was behind this matter some old and well-established tradition; or, in other words, the genuineness of the text in Exodus argues for the genuineness of the text in Samuel. Besides, as Dr. Orr has again suggested, there may have been some special reason of delicacy or of regard for the good moral reputation of the Israelites, on the account of which the makers of the Septuagint version threw out this item respecting the wickedness of Hophni and Phinehas as connected with these women. Then, moreover, as an offset to the Septuagint's authority—which, owing to the known

---

*See Conder's "Tent Work in Palestine," Vol. 2, p. 84.

faultiness of its present text and its general inexactness as a translation, is surely not great—it can be urged that the entire clause containing the words "tent of meeting" is found alike in the old Syriac or Peshito version, in the Vulgate, and in the only extant Targum (that of Jonathan Ben Uzziel) on this particular passage; all of which very ancient authorities* render it as certain as anything of a textual nature could well be made, that the old original text in 1 Sam. 2:22 was exactly as it is now in our present-day Hebrew Bible.

And, finally, as perhaps the crowning feature of this array of evidence for the genuineness of the text under consideration, it can be affirmed that, for English readers at least, there exists one authority, easy to be consulted, which would seem to put beyond all reasonable doubt the genuineness of this text. That authority is our Revised English Version of the Scriptures—a literary work that in point of scholarship and general reliability stands perhaps second to none produced in recent years. And now, if anybody will take the trouble to consult this Revised Version, he will see that this entire disputed passage is retained, or that the many eminent scholars, both English and American, who wrought on this translation are agreed that the words, "tent of meeting," or *ohel moed,* as in Hebrew, are genuine, and properly belong to this passage.

Such being the case, the critics are put in a bad plight; and anyway it does not argue much to the credit of their hypothesis when, in order to carry it through, it becomes necessary so often to make the claim of interpolation. Of course, anyone can make what he pleases of any passage of Scripture, provided he only has the privilege of doctoring it

---

*The Targum on Samuel, which is attributed to Jonathan Ben Uzziel, is commonly believed to have been produced some time during the first century; the Peshito version of the Scriptures is thought to have been made somewhat later, probably in the second century; while the Latin Vulgate, by Jerome, was completed between the years 390 and 405 A. D.

sufficiently beforehand. And with regard to this particulaɪ passage it may be said that neither Wellhausen nor any other higher critic can do anything to alter it; because so long as those words *ohel moed,* or "tent of meeting," remain in the various textual authorities which we have quoted, so long it will be impossible to expunge them from our present Hebrew Bible; and no matter what authorities the critics may be able to quote as omitting these words, the preponderance of authority, as matters now stand, will always be in favor of their retention. We claim then a real victory here, in being able to substantiate so conclusively, as we think we have done, the genuineness of this text in Samuel.

But what now is the general result of our examinations with regard to the testimony which Samuel gives us? If our conclusion with regard to the passage just examined is correct, and we are fully persuaded that it is, then we surely have demonstrated in the clearest way that not only in the days of Samuel, but probably long before, the Tabernacle did exist, and was located at Shiloh.

4. TESTIMONY OF JEREMIAH AND PSALM 78

And here, if we care to go still further in this investigation of passages, we might find some very interesting testimony to the Tabernacle's historicity in Psalm 78 and in the prophecy of Jeremiah. But since we wish to be as brief as possible, while not neglecting the real strength of our argument, we will simply indicate, or quote, the Scriptures referred to, and leave the discussion or interpretation of them to the reader himself. One of these passages is found, as said, in Psa. 78, vs. 59, 60, and reads as follows: "When God heard this he was wroth, and greatly abhorred Israel; so that he forsook the *tabernacle of Shiloh, the tent* which he placed among men." Another passage, from Jer. 7:12-14, reads thus: "But go ye now unto *my place which was in Shiloh, where I caused my name to dwell at the first,* and see what I did to it for the wickedness of my people Israel. Therefore will I do unto the house which is called by my name, wherein ye trust [the temple at Jerusalem], and unto the place which I gave to you and to your fathers, as I have done to Shiloh." Still another passage may be found in Jer. 26:6, and reads: "Then will I make this house like Shiloh, and will make this city [Jerusalem] a curse to all nations of the earth."*

All these passages, it should be observed, compare the Temple at Jerusalem with the Tabernacle at Shiloh; and they express the threat, that, unless the Israelites repented, God would destroy the Temple at Jerusalem as he had long before destroyed, or removed, the Tabernacle at Shiloh.

5. TESTIMONY OF JUDGES AND JOSHUA

Yet once more, in order to make our story of the Tabernacle complete, it is necessary for us to go back somewhat in history; and so we now quote from the books of Judges and Joshua. In Josh. 18:1 we read: "And the whole congregation of the children of Israel assembled themselves together at Shiloh and set up the *tent of meeting* there." Then, turning over to Judg. 18:31, we again read, about the idolatrous images set up in Dan, that these continued there "all the time that the *house of God* was at Shiloh." From these two passages we learn not only how the "house of God" came to be located at Shiloh—because the children of Israel, probably under the leadership of Joshua, set it up there— but we learn also that the two descriptive terms, "tent of meeting" and "house of God," signify the same thing; for it

*These passages in Jeremiah are very important as evidence in favor of the Tabernacle's real existence, since even the higher critics must admit that the chapters containing them were written a considerable time before the exile; and therefore these passages could not, except upon the violent theory of redaction, have been affected by writings appearing either during or after the exile. And as to Psalm 78, which is even more explicit about the structure at Shiloh's being the old Mosaic Tabernacle, it is much easier to say, as the critics do, that this Psalm is post-exilic, than it is to prove such assertion.

is hardly possible that the "tent of meeting" erected at Shiloh in the days of Joshua had been replaced in the time of the Judges by another structure, different in kind, and now called the "house of God."

6. ARGUMENT FROM HISTORY OF THE SACRED ARK

But now yet, before we give the entire story of the Tabernacle, we desire to notice another kind of argument, which is drawn from the history of the sacred ark. There does not seem to be any notice of the Tabernacle as a structure by itself in the book of Deuteronomy; but in the tenth chapter of this book, verses 1 to 5, there is given an account of the construction, not of the Tabernacle, but of what must be considered as its most important piece of furniture, that is, the Ark of the Covenant, as it is usually called, or as the critics prefer to term it, the Ark of Jahweh (Jehovah). Now, although the critics take a very different view regarding the date and authority of Deuteronomy from that which has always been accepted by orthodox scholars, yet especially upon the ground of the passage referred to, they are willing to admit that at least some kind of a sacred ark was constructed even in the days of Moses. Moreover, if consistent with the facts as recorded in the Bible, the critics cannot deny that this same sacred ark, whatever was its form or purpose, was not only carried by the Israelites on all their journeys through the wilderness, but was also finally located by them at Shiloh; whence, after undergoing various fortunes, it was deposited in the holy of holies of Solomon's Temple. This the critics in general admit; and they are compelled to do so by their own accepted documents of "J," "E," etc.

Now, that being the case, it follows that if the history of the sacred ark can be traced all the way through, or rather all the way back from the days of Solomon's Temple to the days of Moses, somewhat the same thing can be done also with the Tabernacle. For the Tabernacle, as is very evident from what the critics call the Priestly Document, was built, among other purposes, for the housing of this sacred ark; and the same documentary evidence which establishes that fact establishes also the farther fact that for a long period such was really the case. That is to say, the sacred ark and the old Mosaic Tabernacle went together, according to Biblical history, down to the times of Shiloh; and they were, after some period of separation, even brought together again at the dedicatory services of Solomon's Temple. To be sure, not all of this is admitted by the critics; but they cannot deny that the same old ark, which, according to Deut. 10:1-5, was built by Moses, was finally deposited in Solomon's Temple.* With this much conceded, all the rest that we have claimed must necessarily follow; or, in other words, the admitted history of the Ark of Jehovah establishes also the historicity of the Mosaic Tabernacle, or at least helps to do so.

IX. ENTIRE STORY OF THE TABERNACLE

Now then we are prepared to give the entire story of that old structure which was built at Mt. Sinai; only one item being still lacking. This we can learn from 1 Sam., Chaps. 21 and 22; and it is, that for a brief period the Tabernacle seems to have been located at Nob, some distance south of Shiloh. With this item then supplied, our story may go forward. As vouched for by the different historic notices we have been considering, it is as follows:

Built by the Israelites near Mt. Sinai, it was afterward carried by that people all through the wilderness. Then, having crossed the Jordan with them, and being set up at Shiloh, it seems for a long time to have remained in that

---

*Wellhausen positively states that according to the Law, that is, the Priestly Document, the Tabernacle is "the inseparable companion of the ark," and that "The two things necessarily belong to each other." He also admits, on the ground of other Biblical evidence, that toward the end of the period of Judges there are distinct traces of the ark as existing; moreover, that this same "ark of Jehovah" was finally deposited in Solomon's Temple. (See Proleg., Eng. Trans., pp. 41, 42.)

place. Next, for a brief period, it would appear to have been located at Nob, down in the Benjaminite country; and from this point being carried a little to the north and west, it was set up at Gibeon, where it seems to have remained for many years. And finally upon the erection of the temple in Jerusalem, it was transferred to that place, and stored away there for safe-keeping; and this is the last notice which the Bible gives of it as a matter of history. It had served its purpose, and the time came now for it to be laid aside as a memorial, or to give place for another and a more imposing structure.

X. INTIMATE CONNECTION OF THIS STORY WITH OTHER BIBLICAL HISTORY

Speaking somewhere of the extraordinary influence exerted by Christianity in our world, Renan says that any attempt to separate this religion from the history of humanity would be like "tearing up the tree of civilization by its roots." Very much like that, it seems to us, is the intimacy of relation existing between the history of the Tabernacle and all the rest of the history recorded in the Old Testament. Any attempt, therefore, such as that which is made by the critics, to remove the Tabernacle as a matter of fact from Old Testament history, or to turn it into a mere fiction, would necessarily result in failure. It would do so because the effect of it would be really to destroy all the surrounding and connected history given in the Old Testament; which is, of course, impossible. The very extravagance, therefore, of this higher-critic theory, or the vastness of its undertaking, is a sure proof of its inherent falsity. Dr. Valpy French, considering only the peculiar construction of this Tabernacle story, how wide-reaching it is, and how it is made to conform so accurately with many details of archæology and topography, pronounces it, if viewed as a mere fiction, "a literary impossibility;" and he suggests that a simpler method to be employed by the critics, in getting rid of this troublesome story, would be for them "to credit the last redactor with the authorship of the whole Old Testament Scriptures." So also Professor Sayce affirms that, regarded as an invention, the Tabernacle story is "too elaborate, too detailed to be conceivable."

XI. OBJECTIONS OF THE HIGHER CRITICS

It remains for us yet, in order to render our discussion really complete, to notice a few of the many objections which the higher critics have brought forward against the Tabernacle's historicity. These objections, however, are, for the most part, so very frivolous in character, or so utterly lacking in support either from fact or reason, that they do not really deserve an answer. Nevertheless, to furnish the reader with some notion of their real character, we will undertake to give them a cursory examination.

They may all be divided into four classes. The first class embraces all those objections which are based upon the idea that the account given in the Bible of the Tabernacle's construction and services, is very unrealistic or impractical in its nature.

A second class proceeds on the notion that the Mosaic Tabernacle is altogether too costly, highly artistic, and ponderous an affair, to have been produced by the Israelites at Mt. Sinai, and afterward carried by them all through the wilderness.

Another of these classes—which is really only one objection—represents that in the very oldest sources out of which the Pentateuch was, according to the critic notion, constructed, there is mention made of another tent, much smaller than was the Mosaic Tabernacle, and different from that structure also in other respects; and that, therefore, this second tabernacle, as it may be called, being better substantiated by literary documents than is the Mosaic structure, it is not consistent with an acceptance of all the facts in the case to allow that the larger or Mosaic tent really existed.

And finally, there is still one class, or a single objection, which makes bold to affirm that in all the earlier historic books of the Old Testament, even from Judges to 2 Kings, there is no sure mention made of the Tabernacle as a real existence.

Now, if we were to try to answer all these objections, it might be said of the last one, that it is already answered. We have answered that objection by showing not only that there is mention made in those earlier historic books of the Old Testament of the Tabernacle as a real existence, but also that this mention is both sure and abundant. The many historical notices which we have examined, all telling about the Tabernacle's construction and history, is positive proof to that effect.

Then, furthermore, with regard to the alleged fact that in the earliest sources, out of which according to the critic theory the Pentateuch was constructed, there is mention made of another or second tent, different from the Mosaic structure, we have to say with respect to this objection, first of all, that it is far from being proven that there are in the Pentateuch any such oldest sources as the critics allege. That item is only a part of the still unproven theory of the higher critics, in their interpretation of the Old Testament.* And then, secondly, we might say, respecting this objection, that it is a difficulty which orthodox scholars have often noticed and which they have explained in various ways. Perhaps the best explanation is to allow the reality of the difficulty and to attribute it to some obscurity or even seeming contradiction existing in the Pentateuchal notices.   But

---

*The fact of the higher-critic theory being as yet in an unproven state might be urged as one important consideration in favor of the Tabernacle's real existence; and especially could such an argument be legitimately made, inasmuch as the proof of the correctness of that theory does not all come from an assured non-existence of the Mosaic structure.   But since an argument of that kind would be, to some extent at least, "reasoning in a circle," we do not make use of it.

whatever the real difficulty may be, it certainly is not insuperable; and a very good explanation of it is that there were really two tents, but one of them, that is, the smaller tent, was only a kind of provisional structure, perhaps the dwelling-place of Moses, which was used also for religious purposes, while the larger or Sinaitic Tabernacle was being prepared.* With some allowance for one or two statements made in the Pentateuch which seem not fully to accord with this view, it will answer all the real exigencies of the case. Or, at all events, nearly any explanation which preserves the integrity of the Pentateuchal literature, and tries to reconcile its seeming differences of statement, on the ground that this literature deals with facts, and is not in large share pure fiction, is vastly preferable to any of the theories which the critics have thus far advanced with regard to this matter.

There remain then only two classes of objections which need still to be answered. And with regard to one of these classes, that is, the first in our list, it may be stated that although the objections put forward under this head are quite numerous, yet a single illustration of them will show how utterly lacking in substantial character or reasonableness

*Notices of such smaller tent seem to be made in Ex. 33:7-11; Num. 11:16; 12:4, 5, and Deut. 31:14, 15; and from these various passages the critics claim that they can discover at least three points of difference existing between this smaller tent and the larger or Levitical one. These differences are as follows: (1) The smaller tent was always pitched outside the camp; but according to the priestly or Levitical history the larger tent was located within the camp. (2) The smaller tent was only a place of Jehovah's revelation, or of his communing with his people; but the larger or priestly structure was, besides, a place of most elaborate worship. (3) In the Levitical or larger tent the priests and Levites regularly served, but in the smaller structure it was only Joshua, the "servant" of Moses, who had charge of the building.

All these differences, however, are easily explained by the theory, given above, of there having been really two tents. Besides, it should be observed that after Moses' death no further mention is made in the Scriptures of this smaller structure; which fact would seem to be a strong proof that the smaller one of the two tents was, primarily at least, a private structure used by Moses.

each and all of them really are. The illustration of which
we will make use is taken from Bishop Colenso's famous
attack upon the truthfulness of the Pentateuch and the Book
of Joshua. In that attack he puts forward the singular
objection that the Tabernacle was, in its dimensions, far too
small to accommodate all the vast host of the Israelites standing before its door, as the Scriptures seem to indicate was the
case with them on a few occasions.* That vast host must
have numbered, according to the data given in the Pentateuch,
as many at least as some two millions of people; and now
Colenso makes the objection that this great host, standing
in ranks, as he would make it, of nine, one rank behind
another, in front of the Tabernacle door, would have formed
a procession some *sixty miles long;* which, surely, would have
been not only a practical impossibility so far as their gathering at the door of the Tabernacle was concerned, but
would have been also a complete demonstration of the un-
truthfulness or unreliability of this Pentateuchal record.

But there is one thing connected with this record which
Bishop Colenso seems not to have understood. It is that
when the author of it was speaking of the whole congregation
of Israel as standing, or gathered, in front of the Tabernacle
door, he was speaking only in general terms. His language
then would imply, not that every individual belonging to the
vast Israelitish host stood at the place mentioned, but only
that a large and representative multitude of these people
was thus gathered. Or the words might signify that even
the whole congregation of the Israelites was, on a few occasions, gathered about the Tabernacle, as it had been gathered
around Mt. Sinai when the law was given—not all the people
near the Tabernacle door, but only the leaders, while the
great body of the congregation stood behind them, or around

*Vid. Lev. 8:35; Num. 10:3, and 27:18-22. Also comp. Num.
16:16-19.

the structure, like a great sea of human beings stretching away in the distance.

Either of these explanations would meet all the demands of the language used; and, as Dr. Orr has remarked, some least particle of common sense must be allowed to the writer of this Pentateuchal record; otherwise, with the "crude absurdities" attributed to him by Bishop Colenso, he could never have written anything in the least degree rational, or that would bear a moment's reflection even by himself. Besides, as Dr. Orr has noticed, it is only a customary way of speaking to say that a whole town or even a large city was gathered together in mass-convention, when the place of such meeting was perhaps only some large hall or good-sized church. Before attacking, therefore, so eagerly with his arithmetical calculations the truthfulness of the Biblical account, this higher-critic bishop would have done well to have reflected a little upon the common use of language. That would have saved him from falling into a bigger blunder than he tries to fasten upon the writer of this Pentateuchal record.

XII. GREATEST OF THE OBJECTIONS

But there is still one objection raised by the critics which seems to be more serious in nature. It is an objection based upon what may be called a physical impossibility, or the incompetency of the Israelites, while at Mt. Sinai or journeying through the desert, either to construct or carry with them such a ponderous, highly artistic and costly a fabric as was the Sinaitic Tabernacle. These people in the desert and at Mt. Sinai, we are told, were the merest wandering Bedouins, having but little civilization and being "poor even to beggary;" and of course such a people possessed neither the means nor the intellectual capability necessary for the construction and transportation of the Tabernacle.

This peculiar objection, however, rests upon at least two mistakes. The first one is that the Israelites at this time were in such extreme poverty. The Bible tells us that when the children of Israel left Egypt they went out "every man armed;" and they carried with them all their herds and flocks, leaving "not a hoof behind." Moreover, by means of the many gifts, or exactions of "jewels of silver" and "jewels of gold" which they received from the Egyptians, they "utterly spoiled" that people. Such is the representation given in the Bible. And then, too, when these Israelites came to Mt. Sinai, here also, according to the reports of modern travelers and explorers, they could have found various materials necessary for constructing the Tabernacle, such as an abundance of copper existing in mines, various kinds of precious stones, as well as, growing in this region in considerable abundance, the shittim-wood or acacia tree, out of which the boards and pillars and most of the furniture of the Tabernacle were actually constructed. So far, therefore, as possessing, or being able to get, the means necessary for a construction of the Tabernacle was concerned, these people would seem to have been pretty well supplied.

And then, with regard to the other mistake made by the critics, viz., that these Israelites were intellectually incompetent to build the Tabernacle, this assertion also is not substantiated by facts. For, in the first place, it should be remembered that all these Hebrews had from their birth dwelt in Egypt, a country which, of all lands in the world, was at that time the most advanced in all kinds of mechanical, architectural and industrial art. This, e. g., was the country where the great pyramids had been produced, and where existed, at that time, at least most of the magnificent temples, tombs, obelisks, statues and palaces, the ruins of which still remain. Accordingly, when the children of Israel came out of Egypt, they must have brought with them a good amount of the architectural and mechanical wisdom peculiar to that country. Moreover, we are taught in the Bible that these people, while in Egypt, dwelt in houses; which, of course, they must have built for themselves; also that, as slaves, their lives had been made bitter by "all manner of service in the field," and by "hard service in brick and in mortar," and that they had built "store-cities," such as Pithom and Raamses. Putting, therefore, all these experiences which the Israelites had in Egypt together, it can be easily seen how they could have learned, even from the Egyptians, sufficient wisdom to construct and transport the Tabernacle.

But if we are required yet to name any one particular achievement, ever accomplished by these people, that was great enough to warrant the belief of their being able to construct and carry with them all through the wilderness the Sinaitic Tabernacle, then, both with promptness and high appreciation, we point to that very extraordinary conquest which they made of the Holy Land, and also to the almost equally extraordinarily long march made by them through the wilderness; and we wish to say that any people who could accomplish two such prodigious deeds as were these could easily have accomplished the so much easier task of building and transporting the old Mosaic "tent of meeting."

Our conclusion, therefore, is that, all teachings of the higher critics to the contrary notwithstanding, those Israelitish people were abundantly competent, both in point of intellectual ability and of material supplies, to accomplish each and all of the works which are accredited them in the Bible.

XIII. MARKS OF EGYPT AND THE DESERT

But this line of argument is one that can be pursued to a much greater extent, and it can be shown that instead of the conditions surrounding the Israelites at Mt. Sinai and while they were in the wilderness being against the truthfulness of the Biblical record appertaining to those matters, such conditions are really in favor of that record's truthfulness, as well as of the Tabernacle's real existence. For illustration, we are told in the Bible that the wood out of which a large part of the Tabernacle was constructed, was not taken from the lofty cedars growing in Lebanon, nor from the sycamores growing in the Palestinean valleys, but from the humble acacia or shittim-wood tree, which, as we have already seen, flourishes quite plentifully in the Sinaitic region; all of which particulars accord fully with the topographical facts in the case. So also, if we are to believe in the testimonies of ancient Egyptian monuments and the results of modern Egyptian explorations, there is many a resemblance which can be found to exist between matters connected with old Egyptian temples, their structure, furniture, priesthood and services, and other like matters appertaining to the Tabernacle. Indeed, some of these resemblances go so far in their minute details as to an arrangement of buildings according to the points of compass—a peculiarity which was found both in Egypt and in connection with the Tabernacle; different apartments in the structure, graded according to sanctity; the possession of a sacred ark or chest, peculiarly built and located; strange winged figures, which as existing in the Tabernacle were called "cherubim;" a gradation of the priests; priestly dress and ornaments; the breast-plate and mitre worn by the high-priest; different animals offered in sacrifice; the burning of incense, etc., that the impression left upon the mind of a person who knows about these things as existing in ancient Egypt and then reads in the Bible about similar matters connected with the Tabernacle is, that whoever wrote this Biblical account must himself have been in Egypt and have seen the old Egyptian worship and temples, in order to make his record conform in so many respects to what was found in that country.*

---

*Prof. Sayce undertakes to show that the foreign influences affecting the structure of the Tabernacle and the nature of its services came rather from Babylonia and Assyria than from Egypt, yet, so far as all the topographical items mentioned above are concerned, they can all be abundantly substantiated by facts from history and archaeology.

So also if we give attention to the peculiar experiences had by the Israelites during their march through the wilderness, we shall see from what the Bible tells us about their setting up and taking down the Tabernacle; about the wagons furnished for its transportation; about the pillar of cloud going before it or resting upon it, in connection with their long march; also about the necessity of going outside of the camp in order to perform some of the Tabernacle services,—from all these and various other indications given in the Bible, we can surely perceive that the conditions of these people were such as to warrant the belief that they did indeed, as the Bible represents, journey through a wilderness, and that they carried with them their tent of worship.

In his book, entitled "Nature and the Supernatural," Dr. Horace Bushnell tells of an important legal case that once was gained by one of the lawyers noticing, in the web of a sheet of paper which he held in his hand, certain "water-marks" which had been made in the paper during the process of its manufacture. These water-marks being indelible, they served as the best kind of proof of certain facts which it was desired to establish. And so we would characterize all those evidences coming from a correspondence of the Bible account with archæological facts, which have to do with the Israelites being in Egypt and their journeying through the Sinaitic desert, as so many water-marks left indelibly, not upon, but in the very web of the Biblical record; proving not only the undeniable truthfulness of this record, but also the real existence of the Tabernacle.

XIV. SUMMARY OF THE ARGUMENT

To sum up then the different points which we have endeavored to make in our argument, it will be remembered that, in the first place, after having outlined our general proposition, and after having from various considerations shown the importance of its discussion, we affirmed that there are certain great presumptions which lie in the way of our accepting the higher-critic theory as true. Next we introduced some archæological and other testimony external to the Bible, which we found to be helpful in proving the Tabernacle's historicity. And then, by quite an extended examination of the many historical notices respecting the Tabernacle, or respecting the sacred ark as connected with it, which are found in the Old Testament, we established, we think, as a matter beyond all reasonable doubt, the actual historicity of this structure; showing how it was built near Mt. Sinai and then was known to exist continuously for some five hundred years, or from the time of Moses unto the time of David and Solomon. And then, finally, to make our argument as complete as possible, we noticed, somewhat briefly and yet with considerable fullness, the many objections which the higher critics have raised against the Tabernacle's existence, showing that none of these objections is really valid, and turning the last one into a positive proof on our side of the question.

XV. CONCLUSION

And now, if there remains yet anything which needs to be said, it seems to us it is only the assertion that, whether the higher critics will admit it or not, the old Mosaic Tabernacle surely did exist. Or if there are persons who, in spite of all the numerous important testimonies which we have adduced from the Bible and other sources to the Tabernacle's historicity, still persist in denying such evidence, and in saying that the whole matter was only a priestly fiction, then what the Savior says, with respect perhaps to some of the skeptics living in his day, is quite applicable: "If they believe not Moses and the prophets, neither would they believe though one rose from the dead." Or, to state the case a little differently and somewhat humorously, it might be said that the fact of any person's denying the real existence of the Tabernacle, when so much positive evidence exists in favor of it, reminds one of what Lord Byron says with regard to Bishop Berkeley's philosophical denial of the existence of matter:

> "When Bishop Berkeley says it is no matter.
> Then 'tis no matter what he says."

But if the Tabernacle in the wilderness did really exist, then what becomes of the peculiar theory of the higher critics? That necessarily falls to the ground, or is proven to be untrue; for, as was shown in the early part of this discussion, the entire critic hypothesis rests upon, or has for one of its main pillars, the assumed non-existence of the Tabernacle, or what amounts to the same thing, the alleged late origin of the Mosaic ritualistic law. Both of these premises being now demonstrated to be unsound, the Tabernacle "which Moses made in the wilderness" will very likely remain where the Bible puts it—among the great undeniable facts of the world's history, and not, as the critics would have it, among fictions or forgeries.

ADDENDA

VARIOUS FACTS RESPECTING PLACES WHERE THE TABERNACLE WAS BUILT OR LOCATED

I. MOUNT SINAI

ITS LOCATION AND PRESENT APPEARANCE

Dr. J. W. Dawson, in his "Modern Science in Bible Lands," gives the following facts with regard to the location and present appearance of the mountain near which the Tabernacle was built.

"The actual position of Mount Sinai has been a subject of keen controversy, which may be reduced to two questions: 1st, Was Mount Sinai in the peninsula of that name or elsewhere? 2d, Which of the mountains of the peninsula was the Mount of the Law? As to the first of these questions, the claims of the peninsula are supported by an overwhelming mass of tradition and of authority, ancient and modern.

"If this question be considered as settled, then it remains to inquire which of the mountain summits of that group of hills in the southern end of the peninsula, which seems to be designated in the Bible by the general name of Horeb, should be regarded as the veritable 'Mount of the Law?' Five of the mountain summits of this region have laid claim to this distinction; and their relative merits the explorers [those of the English Ordnance Survey] test by seven criteria which must be fulfilled by the actual mountain. These are: (1) A mountain overlooking a plain on which the millions of Israel could be assembled. (2) Space for the people to 'remove and stand afar off' when the voice of the Lord was heard, and yet to hear that voice. (3) A defined peak distinctly visible from the plain. (4) A mountain so precipitous that the people might be said to stand under it and to touch its base. (5) A mountain capable of being isolated by boundaries. (6) A mountain with springs and streams of water in its vicinity. (7) Pasturage to maintain the flocks of the people for a year.

"By these criteria the surveyors reject two of the mountains, Jebel el Ejmeh and Jebel Ummalawi, as destitute of sufficient water and pasturage. Jebel Katharina, whose claims arise from a statement of Josephus that Sinai was the highest mountain of the district, which this peak actually is, with the exception of a neighboring summit twenty-five feet higher, they reject because of the fact that it is not visible from any plain suitable for the encampment of the Israelites. Mount Serbal has in modern times had some advocates; but the surveyors allege in opposition to these that they do not find, as has been stated, the Sinaitic inscriptions more plentiful there than elsewhere, that the traces of early Christian occupancy do not point to it any more than early tradition, and that it does not meet the topographical requirements in presenting a defined peak, convenient camping-ground, or a sufficient amount of pasturage.

"There only remains the long-established and venerated Jebel Musa—the orthodox Sinai; and this, in a remarkable and conspicuous manner, fulfils the required conditions, and, besides, illustrates the narrative itself in unexpected ways. This mountain has, however, two dominant peaks, that of Jebel Musa proper, 7,363 feet in height, and that of Ras Sufsafeh, 6,937 feet high; and of these the explorers do not hesitate at once to prefer the latter. This peak or ridge is described as almost isolated, as descending precipitously to the great plain of the district, Er Rahah, which is capable of accommodating two millions of persons in full view of the peak, and has ample camping ground for the whole host in its tributary valleys. Further, it is so completely separated from the neighboring mountains that a short and quite intelligible description would define its limits, which could be easily marked out.

"Another remarkable feature is, that we have here the brook descending out of the mount referred to in Exodus (Ch. 32:20), and, besides this, five other perennial streams in addition to many good springs. The country is by no means desert, but supplies much pasturage; and when irrigated and attended to, forms good gardens, and is indeed one of the best and most fertile spots of the whole peninsula. The explorers show that the statements of some hasty travelers who have given a different view are quite incorrect, and also that there is reason to believe that there was greater rainfall and more verdure in ancient times than at present in this part of the country. They further indicate the Wady Shreick, in which is the stream descending from the mount, as the probable place of the making and destruction of the golden calf, and a hill known as Jebel Moneijeh, the mount of conference, as the probable site of the Tabernacle. They think it not improbable that while Ras Sufsafeh was the Mount of the Law, the retirement of Moses during his sojourn on the mount may have been behind the peak, in the recesses of Jebel Musa, which thus might properly bear his name."

II. SHILOH

ITS RUINS AS RECENTLY INVESTIGATED

Colonel Sir Charles Wilson thus describes the present ruins of Shiloh, in "Exploration Fund Quarterly Statement" for 1873, pp. 37, 38:

"The ruins of Seilûn (Shiloh) cover the surface of a 'tell,' or mound, on a spur which lies between two valleys, that unite about a quarter of a mile above Khan Lubban, and thence run to the sea. The existing remains are those of a *fellahin* village, with few earlier foundations, possibly of the date of the Crusades. The walls are built with old materials, but none of the fragments of columns mentioned by some travelers can now be seen. On the summit are a few heavy foundations, perhaps those of a keep, and on the southern side is a building with a heavy sloping buttress. The rock is exposed over nearly the whole surface, so that little can be expected from excavation. Northwards, the 'tell' slopes down to a broad shoulder across which a sort of level court, 77 feet wide and 412 feet long, has been cut out. The rock is in places scarped to a height of five feet, and along the sides are several excavations and a few small cisterns. The level portion of the rock is covered by a few inches of soil. It is not improbable that the place was thus prepared to receive the Tabernacle, which, according to Rabbinical traditions, was a structure of low stone walls, with the tent stretched over the top. At any rate, there is no other level space on the 'tell' sufficiently large to receive a tent of the dimensions of the Tabernacle.

"The spring of Seilûn is in a small valley which joins the main one a short distance northeast of the ruins. The supply, which is small, after running a few yards through a subterranean channel, was formerly led into a rock-hewn reservoir, but now runs to waste."

To the above items Major Claude R. Conder, R. E., in his "Tent Life in Palestine," Vol I, pp. 81, 82, adds as follows:

"There is no site in the country fixed with greater certainty than that of Shiloh. The modern name Seilûn preserves the most archaic form, which is found in the Bible in the ethnic Shilonite (1 Kings 11:29). The position of the ruins agrees exactly with the very definite description given in the Old Testament of the position of Shiloh, as 'on the north side of Bethel (now Beitin), on the east side of the highway that goeth up from Bethel to Shechem, and on the south of Lebonah' (Lubbin) (Judg. 21:19). It is just here that Shiloh still stands in ruins. The scenery of the wild mountains is finer than that in Judea; the red color of the cliffs, which are of great height, is far more picturesque than the shapeless chalk mountains near Jerusalem; the fig gardens and olive groves are more luxuriant, but the crops are poor compared with the plain and round Bethlehem. A deep valley runs behind the town on the north, and in its sides are many rock-cut sepulchers.

"The vineyards of Shiloh have disappeared, though very possibly once surrounding the spring, and perhaps extending down the valley westwards, where water is also found. With the destruction of the village, desolation has spread over the barren hills around."

III. NOB

SITE OF THE VILLAGE IDENTIFIED

So thinks Rev. W. Shaw Caldecott. See his treatise on "The Tabernacle, Its History and Structure," pp. 53, 54:

"Four miles to the north of Jerusalem, and at the distance of a quarter of a mile to the east of the main road, is a curiously knobbed and double-topped hill, named by the Arabs *Tell* (or Tuleil) *el-Full*. The crown of this hill is thirty feet higher than Mount Zion, and Jerusalem can be plainly seen from it. On its top is a large pyramidal mound of unhewn stones, which Robinson supposes to have been originally a square tower of 40 or 50 feet, and to have been violently thrown down. No other foundations are to be seen. At the foot of the hill are ancient substructions, built of large unhewn stones in low, massive walls. These are on the south side, and adjoin the great road.

"If we take the Scriptural indications as to the site of Nob (height), this hill and these ruins fulfill all the conditions of the case.

"(a) Nob was so far regarded as belonging to Jerusalem, as one of its villages (thus involving its proximity), that David's bringing Goliath's head and sword to the Tabernacle at Nob was regarded as bringing them to Jerusalem (1 Sam. 17:54).

"(b) A clearer indication as to its situation is, however, gained by the record of the restoration towns and villages in which Nob is mentioned, the name occurring between those of Anathoth and Ananiah (Neh. 11:32). These two places still bear practically the same names, and their sites are well known. In the narrow space between Anata and Hanina stands the hill Tell el-Full, which we take to be ancient Nob.

"(c) Another indication is contained in Isaiah's account of Sennacherib's march on Jerusalem, the picturesque climax of which is, 'This very day shall he halt at Nob; he shaketh his hand at the mount of the daughter of Zion, the hill of Jerusalem' (Isa. 10:28-32). There are only two hills on the north from which the city can be seen, so as to give reality to the poet's words. One of these is *Neby Samwil*, and the other is *Tell el-Full*."

IV. GIBEON

IDENTITY OF ANCIENT CITY WITH EL-JIB, ALSO THE "GREAT HIGH PLACE," OF 1 KINGS 3:4, INDICATED

In Hastings' *Dictionary of the Bible*, Art. Gibeon, J. F. Stenning says as follows:

"The identity of Gibeon with the village of El-Jib, which lies some six or seven miles northwest of Jerusalem, is practically beyond dispute. The modern village still preserves the first part of the older name, while its situation agrees in every respect with the requirements of the history of the Old Testament. Just beyond Tell el-Full (Gibeah), the main road north from Jerusalem to Beitin (Bethel) is joined by a branch road leading up from the coast. The latter forms the continuation of the most southerly of three routes which connect the Jordan valley with the Maritime Plains. * * * Now just before this road (coming up from the Jordan valley) leaves the higher ground and descends to the Shepheleh, it divides into two, the one branch leading down to the Wady Suleiman, the other running in a more southerly direction by way of the Bethhorons. Here, on this fertile, open plateau, slightly to the south of the main road, rises the hill on which the modern village of El-Jib is built, right on the frontier line which traverses the central range to the south of Bethel. It was the natural pass across Palestine, which in early times served as the political border between North and South Israel, and it was owing to its position that Gibeon acquired so much prominence in the reigns of David and Solomon. A short distance to the east of the village, at the foot of the hill, there is, further, a stone tank o. reservoir of considerable size, supplied by a spring which rises in a cave higher up."

This spring, the explorers tell us, was probably the ancient "pool of Gibeon" mentioned in 2 Sam. 2:13.

Also, respecting the "great high place," Smith's *Dictionary* has the following:

"The most natural position for the high place of Gibeon is the twin mountain immediately south of El-Jib, so close as to be all but a part of the town, and yet quite separate and distinct. The testimony of Epiphanius, viz., that the 'Mount of Gibeon' was the highest round Jerusalem, by which Dean Stanley supports his conjecture (that the present Neby Samwil was the great high place), should be received with caution, standing, as it does, quite alone and belonging to an age which, though early, was marked by ignorance and by the most improbable conclusions."

Some additional facts, as given by Rev. W. Shaw Caldecott (ibid. pp. 60-62), are as follows:

"El-Jib is built upon an isolated oblong hill standing in a plain or basin of great fertility. The northern end of the hill is covered over with old massive ruins, which have fallen down in every direction, and in which the villagers now live. Across the plain to the south is the lofty range of Neby Samwil. * * * Gibeon was one of the four towns in the division of Benjamin given as residences for the sons of Aaron (Josh. 21:17). It was thus already inhabited by priests, and this, added to its other advantages, made it, humanly speaking, a not unsuitable place for the capital of the new kingdom. No remains of (very ancient) buildings have been discovered, such as those of er-Ramah and Tell el-Full."

CHAPTER IX

THE INTERNAL EVIDENCE
OF THE FOURTH GOSPEL

BY CANON G. OSBORNE TROOP, M. A.,
MONTREAL, CANADA

The whole Bible is stamped with the Divine "Hall-Mark"; but the Gospel according to St. John is *primus inter pares.* Through it, as through a transparency, we gaze entranced into the very holy of holies, where shines in unearthly glory "the great vision of the face of Christ". Yet man's perversity has made it the "storm center" of New Testament criticism, doubtless for the very reason that it bears such unwavering testimony both to the deity of our Lord and Saviour, Jesus Christ, and to His perfect humanity. The Christ of the Fourth Gospel is no unhistoric, idealized vision of the later, dreaming church, but is, as it practically claims to be, the picture drawn by "the disciple whom Jesus loved", an eye-witness of the blood and water that flowed from His pierced side. These may appear to be mere unsupported statements, and as such will at once be dismissed by a scientific reader. Nevertheless the appeal of this article is to the instinct of the "one flock" of the "one Shepherd". "They know His voice" . . . "a stranger will they not follow."

1. There is one passage in this Gospel that flashes like lightning—it dazzles our eyes by its very glory. To the broken-hearted Martha the Lord Jesus says with startling suddenness, "*I am* the resurrection and the life; he that believeth on Me, though he die, yet shall he live; and whosoever liveth and believeth in Me, shall never die."

It is humbly but confidently submitted that these words are utterly beyond the reach of human invention. It could

193

never have entered the heart of man to say, "*I am* the resurrection and the life." "There is a resurrection and a life," would have been a great and notable saying, but *this Speaker* identifies *Himself* with the resurrection and with life eternal. The words can only be born from above, and He who utters them is worthy of the utmost adoration of the surrendered soul.

In an earlier chapter John records a certain question addressed to and answered by our Lord in a manner which has no counterpart in the world's literature. "What shall we do," the eager people cry; "What shall we do that we might work the works of God?" "This is the work of God", our Lord replies, "that ye believe on Him whom He hath sent" (John 6:28, 29). I venture to say that such an answer to such a question has no parallel. This is the work of God that ye accept ME. I am the Root of the tree which bears the only fruit pleasing to God. Our Lord states the converse of this in chapter 16, when He says that the Holy Spirit will "convict the world of sin . . . because they believe not on ME." The root of all evil is unbelief in Christ. The condemning sin of the world lies in the rejection of the Redeemer. Here we have the root of righteousness and the root of sin in the acceptance or rejection of His wondrous personality. This is unique, and proclaims the Speaker to be "separate from sinners" though "the Lord hath laid on Him the iniquity of us all." Truly,

> "He is His own best evidence,
> His witness is within."

2. Pass on to the fourteenth chapter, so loved of all Christians. Listen to that Voice, which is as the voice of many waters, as it sounds in the ears of the troubled disciples: "Let not your heart be troubled; ye believe in God, believe *also* in *ME*. In My Father's house are many mansions: *if it were not so, I would have told you.* I go to prepare a place

for you. And if I go and prepare a place for you, I will come again, and receive you unto Myself; that where I am, there ye may be also."

Who is he who dares to say: "Ye believe in *God,* believe *also* in Me"? He ventures thus to speak because He is the Father's Son. Man's son is man: can God's Son be anything less than God? Elsewhere in this Gospel He says: "I and the Father are one". The fourteenth chapter reveals the Lord Jesus as completely at home in the heavenly company. He speaks of His Father and of the Holy Spirit as Himself being one of the utterly holy Family. He knows all about His Father's house with its many mansions. He was familiar with it before the world was. Mark well, too, the exquisite touch of transparent truthfulness: "If it were not so, I would have told you." An *ear*-witness alone could have caught and preserved that touching parenthesis, and who more likely than the disciple whom Jesus loved?

As we leave this famous chapter let us not forget to note the wondrous words in verse 23: "If a man love Me, he will keep My words; and My Father will love him, and *WE* will come unto him and make our abode with him."

This saying can only be characterized as blasphemous, if it be not the true utterance of one equal with God. On the other hand, does any reasonable man seriously think that such words originated in the mind of a forger? "Every one that is of the truth heareth My voice", and surely that voice is here.

3. When we come to chapter 17 we pass indeed into the very inner chamber of the King of kings. It records the high-priestly prayer of our Lord, when He "lifted up His eyes to heaven and said, Father, the hour is come, glorify Thy Son that Thy Son may also glorify Thee." Let any man propose to himself the awful task of forging such a prayer, and putting it into the mouth of an imaginary Christ. The brain reels at the very thought of it. It is, however, per-

fectly natural that St. John should record it. It must have fallen upon the ears of himself and his fellow-disciples amidst an awe-stricken silence in which they could hear the very throbbing of their listening hearts. For their very hearts were listening through their ears as the Son poured out His soul unto the Father. It is a rare privilege, and one from which most men would sensitively shrink, to listen even to a fellow-man alone with God. Yet the Lord Jesus in the midst of His disciples laid bare His very soul before His Father, as really as if He had been alone with Him. He prayed with the cross and its awful death full in view, but in the prayer there is no slightest hint of failure or regret, and there is no trace of confession of sin or need of forgiveness. These are all indelible marks of genuineness. It would have been impossible for a sinful man to conceive such a prayer. But all is consistent with the character of Him who "spake as never man spake", and could challenge the world to convict Him of sin.

With such thoughts in mind let us now look more closely into the words of the prayer itself.

"Father, the hour is come; glorify Thy Son, that Thy Son also may glorify Thee: As Thou hast given Him power over all flesh, that He should give eternal life to as many as Thou hast given Him. And this is life eternal, that they might know Thee, the only true God, and *Jesus Christ whom Thou hast sent.*"

Here we have again the calm placing of Himself on a level with the Father in connection with eternal life. And it is not out of place to recall the consistency of this utterance with that often-called "Johannine" saying recorded in St. Matthew and St. Luke: "All things are delivered unto Me of My Father: and no man knoweth the Son, but the Father; neither knoweth any man the Father, save the Son, and he to whomsoever the Son willeth to reveal Him."

We read also in St. John 14:6: "No man cometh unto

the Father but by Me". And as we reverently proceed further in the prayer we find Him saying: "And now, O Father, glorify Thou Me with Thine own self, with the glory which I had with Thee *before the world was.*"

These words are natural to the Father's Son as we know and worship Him, but they are beyond the reach of an uninspired man, and who can imagine a forger inspired of the Holy Ghost? Such words would, however, be graven upon the very heart of an ear-witness such as the disciple whom Jesus loved.

We have in this prayer also the fuller revelation of the "one flock" and "one Shepherd" pictured in chapter ten: "Neither pray I for these alone, but for them also which shall believe on Me through their word; that they all may be one; *as Thou, Father, art in Me, and I in Thee, that they also may be one in us:* That *the world* may believe that Thou hast sent Me. And the glory which Thou gavest Me I have given them; that they may be one, even as we are one: I in them, and Thou in Me, that they may be perfected into one; and that the world may know that Thou hast sent Me, and *hast loved them, as Thou hast loved Me.*"

In these holy words there breathes a cry for such a unity as never entered into the heart of mortal man to dream of. It is no cold and formal ecclesiastical unity, such as that suggested by the curious and unhappy mistranslation of "one fold" for "one flock" in St. John 10:16. It is the living unity of the living flock with the living Shepherd of the living God. It is actually the same as the unity subsisting between the Father and the Son. And according to St. Paul in Rom. 8:19, the creation is waiting for its revelation. The one Shepherd has from the beginning had His one flock in answer to His prayer, but the world has not yet seen it, and is therefore still unconvinced that our Jesus is indeed the Sent of God. The world has seen the Catholic Church and the Roman Catholic Church, but the Holy Catholic Church no eye as yet has seen but God's. For the Holy Catholic Church and the Shepherd's one flock are one and the same, and the world will not see either "till He come." The *Holy* Catholic Church is an object of faith and not of sight, and so is the one flock. In spite of all attempts at elimination and organization wheat and tares together grow, and sheep and wolves-in-sheep's-clothing are found together in the earthly pasture grounds. But when the Good Shepherd returns He will bring His beautiful flock with Him, and eventually the world will see and believe. "O the depth of the riches both of the wisdom and knowledge of God! How unsearchable are His judgments, and His ways past finding out!"

The mystery of this spiritual unity lies hidden in the high-priestly prayer, but we may feel sure that no forger could ever discover it, for many of those who profess and call themselves Christians are blind to it even yet.

4. The "Christ before Pilate" of St. John is also stamped with every mark of sincerity and truth. What mere human imagination could evolve the noble words: "My kingdom is not of this world; if My kingdom were of this world, then would My servants fight, that I should not be delivered to the Jews: but now is My kingdom not from hence . . . To this end was I born, and for this cause came I into the world, that I should bear witness unto the truth. Every one that is of the truth heareth My voice"?

The whole wondrous story of the betrayal, the denial, the trial, the condemnation and crucifixion of the Lord Jesus, as given through St. John, breathes with the living sympathy of an eye-witness. The account, moreover, is as wonderful in the delicacy of its reserve as in the simplicity of its recital. It is entirely free from sensationalism and every form of exaggeration. It is calm and judicial in the highest degree. If it is written by the inspired disciple whom Jesus loved, all is natural and easily "understanded of the people"; while on any other supposition, it is fraught with difficulties that cannot be explained away. "I am not credulous enough to be an unbeliever," is a wise saying in this as in many similar connections.

5. The Gospel opens and closes with surpassing grandeur. With Divine dignity it links itself with the opening words of Genesis: *"In the beginning* was the Word, and the Word was with God, and the Word was *God.* . . . And the Word became flesh, and dwelt among us, and we beheld His glory, the glory as of the Only Begotten of the Father, full of grace and truth." What a lifelike contrast with this sublime description is found in the introduction of John the Baptist: "There came *a man* sent from God whose name was John". In the incarnation Christ did not become *a* man but *man.* Moreover in this St. Paul and St. John are in entire agreement.

"There is one God", says St. Paul to Timothy; "one Mediator also between God and man—*Himself Man*—Christ Jesus." The reality of the Divine Redeemer's human nature is beautifully manifested in the touching interview between the weary Saviour and the guilty Samaritan woman at the well; as also in His perfect human friendship with Mary and Martha and their brother Lazarus, culminating in the priceless words, "Jesus wept".

And so by the bitter way of the Cross the grandeur of the incarnation passes into the glory of the resurrection. The last two chapters are alive with thrilling incident. If any one wishes to form a true conception of what those brief chapters contain, let him read "Jesus and the Resurrection," by the saintly Bishop of Durham (Dr. Handley Moule) and his cup of holy joy will fill to overflowing. At the empty tomb we breathe the air of the unseen kingdom, and presently we gaze enraptured on the face of the Crucified but risen and everliving King. Mary Magdalene, standing in her broken-hearted despair, is all unconscious of the wondrous fact that holy angels are right in front of her and standing behind her is her living Lord and Master. Slowly but surely the glad story spreads from lip to lip and heart to heart, until even the honest but stubborn Thomas is brought to his knees, crying in a burst of remorseful, adoring joy, "My Lord and my God!"

Then comes the lovely story of the fruitless all-night toil of the seven fishermen, the appearance at dawn of the Stranger on the beach, the miraculous draught of fishes, the glad cry of recognition, "It is the Lord!" the never-to-be-forgotten breakfast with the risen Saviour, and His searching interview with Peter, passing into the mystery of St. John's old age.

In all these swiftly-drawn outlines we feel ourselves instinctively in the presence of the truth. We are crowned with the Saviour's beatitude: "Blessed are they that have not seen, and yet have believed," and we are ready to yield a glad assent to the statement which closes chapter twenty: "Many other signs truly did Jesus in the presence of His disciples, which are not written in this book; but these are written that ye might believe that Jesus is the Christ, the Son of God; and that believing ye might have life in His Name."

CHAPTER X

THE TESTIMONY OF CHRIST TO THE OLD TESTAMENT

BY WILLIAM CAVEN, D. D., LL. D.,
LATE PRINCIPAL OF KNOX COLLEGE, TORONTO, CANADA

Both Jews and Christians receive the Old Testament as containing a revelation from God, while the latter regard it as standing in close and vital relationship to the New Testament. Everything connected with the Old Testament has, of recent years, been subjected to the closest scrutiny—the authorship of its several books, the time when they were written, their style, their historical value, their religious and ethical teachings. Apart from the veneration with which we regard the Old Testament writings on their own account, the intimate connection which they have with the Christian Scriptures necessarily gives us the deepest interest in the conclusions which may be reached by Old Testament criticism. For us the New Testament Dispensation presupposes and grows out of the Mosaic, so the books of the New Testament touch those of the Old at every point: *In vetere testamento novum latet, et in novo vetus patet.* (In the Old Testament the New is concealed, and in the New the Old is revealed.)

We propose to take a summary view of the testimony of our Lord to the Old Testament, as it is recorded by the Evangelists. The New Testament writers themselves largely quote and refer to the Old Testament, and the views which they express regarding the old economy and its writings are in harmony with the statements of their Master; but, for various reasons, we here confine ourselves to what is related of the Lord Himself.

Let us refer, first, to what is contained or necessarily implied in the Lord's testimony to the Old Testament Scriptures, and, secondly, to the critical value of His testimony.

I. THE LORD'S TESTIMONY TO THE OLD TESTAMENT

Our Lord's authority—though this is rather the *argumentum silentio*—may be cited in favor of the Old Testament canon as accepted by the Jews in His day. He never charges them with adding to or taking from the Scriptures, or in any way tampering with the text. Had they been guilty of so great a sin it is hardly possible that among the charges brought against them, this matter should not even be alluded to. The Lord reproaches His countrymen with ignorance of the Scriptures, and with making the law void through their traditions, but He never hints that they have foisted any book into the canon, or rejected any which deserved a place in it.

Now, the Old Testament canon of the first century is the same as our own. The evidence for this is complete, and the fact is hardly questioned. The New Testament contains, indeed, no catalogue of the Old Testament books, but the testimony of Josephus, of Melito of Sardis, of Origen, of Jerome, of the Talmud, decisively shows that the Old Testament canon, once fixed, has remained unaltered. Whether the steady Jewish tradition that the canon was finally determined by Ezra and the Great Synagogue is altogether correct or not, it is certain that the Septuagint agrees with the Hebrew as to the canon, thus showing that the subject was not in dispute two centuries before Christ. Nor is the testimony of the Septuagint weakened by the fact that the common Old Testament Apocrypha are appended to the canonical books; for "of no one among the Apocryphal books is it so much as hinted, either by the author, or by any other Jewish writer, that it was worthy of a place among the sacred books" (Kitto's Cyclo., art. "Canon"). The Lord, it is observed, never quotes any of the aprocryphal books, nor refers to them.

If our Lord does not name the writers of the books of the Old Testament in detail, it may at least be said that no word of His calls in question the genuineness of any book, and that he distinctly assigns several parts of Scripture to the writers whose names they pass under. The Law is ascribed to Moses; David's name is connected with the Psalms; the prophecies of Isaiah are attributed to Isaiah, and the prophecies of Daniel to Daniel. We shall afterward inquire whether these references are merely by way of accommodation, or whether more importance should be attached to them; in the meantime, we note that the Lord does not, in any instance, express dissent from the common opinion, and that, as to several parts of Scripture, He distinctly endorses it.

The references to Moses as legislator and writer are such as these: To the cleansed leper He says, "Go thy way, shew thyself to the priest, and offer the gift that Moses commanded" (Matt. 8:4). "He saith unto them, Moses because of the hardness of your hearts suffered you to put away your wives" (Matt. 19:8). "If they hear not Moses and the prophets, neither will they be persuaded, though one rose from the dead" (Luke 16:31). " For Moses said, Honor thy father and thy mother; and, Whoso curseth father or mother, let him die the death" (Mark 7:10). "And beginning at Moses and all the prophets, he expounded unto them in all the Scriptures the things concerning himself" (Luke 24:27). "All things must be fulfilled which were written in the law of Moses, and in the prophets, and in the psalms, concerning me" (Luke 24:44). "There is one that accuseth you, even Moses, in whom ye trust. For had ye believed Moses, ye would have believed Me: For he wrote of Me. But if ye believed not his writings, how shall ye believe My words?" (John 5:45-47). "Did not Moses give you the law, and yet none of you keepeth the law?" (John 7:19). "Moses therefore gave unto you circumcision. * * * If a man on the Sabbath day receive circumcision, that the law of Moses should not be broken," etc. (John 7:22, 23). The omitted parenthetical words—"not because it is of Moses, but of the fathers"—seem clearly to show, it may be remarked in passing, that the Lord is not unobservant of historical exactness.

The Psalms are quoted by our Lord more than once, but only once is a writer named. The 110th Psalm is ascribed to David; and the vadidity of the Lord's argument depends on its being Davidic. The reference, therefore, so far as it goes, confirms the inscriptions of the Psalms in relation to authorship.

Isa. 6:9 is quoted thus: "In them is fulfilled the prophecy of Esaias, which saith, By hearing ye shall hear, and shall not understand" (Matt. 13:14, 15). Again, chapter 29:13 of Isaiah's prophecy is cited: "Well hath Esaias prophesied of you hypocrites. * * * This people honoreth me with their lips, but their heart is far from me" (Mark 7:6). When, in the beginning of His ministry, the Lord came to Nazareth, there was delivered unto Him in the synagogue "the book of the prophet Esaias. And when he had opened the book, he found the place where it was written, The Spirit of the Lord is upon me, because He hath anointed me to preach the Gospel to the poor," etc. (Luke 4:17, 18). The passage read by our Lord is from the 61st chapter of Isaiah, which belongs to the section of the book very often, at present, ascribed to the second, or pseudo, Isaiah; but we do not press this point, as it may be said that the Evangelist, rather than Christ, ascribes the words to Isaiah.

In His great prophecy respecting the downfall of the Jewish state the Lord refers to "the abomination of desolation, spoken of by Daniel the prophet:" As in Dan. 9:27, we read that "For the overspreading of abominations he shall make it desolate," and in chapter 12:11, that "the abomination that maketh desolate (shall) be set up."

NARRATIVES AND RECORDS AUTHENTIC

When Christ makes reference to Old Testament narratives and records, He accepts them as authentic, as historically true. He does not give or suggest in any case a mythical or allegorical interpretation. The accounts of the creation, of the flood, of the overthrow of Sodom and Gomorrah, as well as many incidents and events of later occurrence, are taken as authentic. It may, of course, be alleged that the Lord's references to the creation of man and woman, the flood, the cities of the plain, etc., equally serve His purpose of illustration whether He regards them as historical or not. But on weighing His words it will be seen that they lose much of their force and appropriateness unless the events alluded to had a historical character.

Let us refer more particularly to this matter. When the Pharisees ask Christ whether it is lawful for a man to put away his wife for every cause, He answers them: "Have ye not read, that He which made them in the beginning made them male and female, and said, For this cause shall a man leave father and mother, and shall cleave to his wife: and they twain shall be one flesh?" (Matt. 19:4, 5). Again: "As the days of Noe were, so shall also the coming of the Son of Man be. For as in the days that were before the flood, they were eating and drinking, marrying and giving in marriage, until the day that Noe entered into the ark, and knew not, until the flood came, and took them all away; so shall also the coming of the Son of Man be" (Matt. 24:37, 39). Again: "And thou, Capernaum, which art exalted unto heaven, shalt be brought down to hell: for if the mighty works, which have been done in thee, had been done in Sodom, it would have remained until this day. But I say unto you, That it shall be more tolerable for the land of Sodom in the day of judgment, than for thee" (Matt. 11:23, 24). These utterances, every one feels, lose their weight and solemnity, if there was no flood such as is described in Genesis, and if the destruction of wicked Sodom may be only a myth. Illustrations and parallels may, for certain purposes, be adduced from fictitious literature, but when the Lord would awaken the conscience of men and alarm their fears by reference to the certainty of divine judgment, He will not confirm His teaching by instances of punishment which are only fabulous. His argument that the Holy and Just God will do as He has done—will make bare His arm as in the days of old—is robbed, in this case, of all validity.

A view frequently urged in the present day is that, as with other nations, so with the Jews, the mythical period precedes the historical, and thus the earlier narratives of the Old Testament must be taken according to their true character. In later periods of the Old Testament we have records which, on the whole, are historical; but in the very earliest times we must not look for authentic history at all. An adequate examination of this theory (which has, of course, momentous exegetical consequences) cannot here be attempted. We merely remark that our Lord's brief references to early Old Testament narrative would not suggest the distinction so often made between earlier and later Old Testament records on the score of trustworthiness.

THE OLD TESTAMENT FROM GOD

We advance to say that Christ accepts the Old Dispensation and its Scriptures as, in a special sense, from God; as having special, divine authority. Many who recognize no peculiar sacredness or authority in the religion of the Jews above other religions of the world, would readily admit that it is from God. But their contention is that all religions (especially what they are pleased to call the *great religions*) have elements of truth in them, that they all furnish *media* through which devout souls have fellowship with the Power which rules the universe, but that none of them should exalt its pretensions much above the others, far less claim exclusive divine sanction; all of them being the product of man's spiritual nature, as molded by his history and environment, in different nations and ages. This is the view under which the study of comparative religion is prosecuted by many eminent scholars. A large and generous study of religions— their characteristics and history—tends, it is held, to bring them into closer fellowship with each other; and only ignorance or prejudice (say these unbiased thinkers) can isolate the religion of the Old Testament or of the New, and refuse to acknowledge in other religions the divine elements which entitle them to take rank with Judaism or Christianity.

The utterances of Jesus Christ on this question of the divinity of the Old Testament religion and cults are unmistakable; and not less clear and decided is His language respecting the writings in which this religion is delivered. God is the source in the directest sense, of both the religion and the records of it. No man can claim Christ's authority for classing Judaism with Confucianism, Hinduism, Buddhism, and Parseeism. There is nothing, indeed, in the Lord's teaching which forbids us to recognize anything that is good in ethnic religions—any of those elements of spiritual truth which become the common property of the race and which were not completely lost in the night of heathenism; but, on the other hand, it is abundantly evident that the Jewish faith is, to our Lord, the one true faith, and that the Jewish Scriptures have a place of their own—a place which cannot be shared with the sacred books of other peoples. Samaritanism, even though it had appropriated so largely from the religion of Israel, He will not recognize. "For salvation is of the Jews."

Almost any reference of our Lord to the Old Testament will support the statement that He regards the Dispensation and its Scriptures as from God. He shows, e. g., that Old Testament prophecy is fulfilled in Himself, or He vindicates

His teaching and His claims by Scripture, or He enjoins obedience to the law (as in the case of the cleansed lepers), or He asserts the inviolability of the law till its complete fulfillment, or He accuses a blinded and self-righteous generation of superseding and vacating a law which they were bound to observe. A few instances of explicit recognition of the Old Testament Scriptures as proceeding from God and having divine authority, may be here adduced. In His Sermon on the Mount the Lord makes this strong and comprehensive statement: "Verily, I say unto you, Till heaven and earth pass, one jot or one tittle shall in no wise pass from the law, till all be fulfilled" (Matt. 5:18).

In the context the law is distinguished from the prophets and designates, therefore, the Pentateuch; and surely the divine origin of this part of Scripture is unquestionably implied. No such inviolability could be claimed for any merely human institution or production. When the hypocritical and heartless son pretended to devote to God what should have gone to support his indigent parents, he "made the commandment of God of none effect," "for God commanded, saying, Honor thy father and mother" (Matt. 15:4). In purging the temple the Lord justifies His action in these words: "It is written, My house shall be called the house of prayer" (Matt. 21:13). Again: "As touching the resurrection of the dead, have ye not read that which was spoken unto you by God, saying, I am the God of Abraham, and the God of Isaac, and the God of Jacob?" (Matt. 22:32). Again: "Laying aside the commandment of God, ye hold the tradition of men, as the washing of pots and cups: and many other such like things ye do" (Mark 7:8). So many passages of the Old Testament are quoted or alluded to by the Lord as having received, or as awaiting fulfillment, that it is scarcely necessary to make citations of this class. These all most certainly imply the divinity of Scripture; for no man, no creature, can tell what is hidden in the remote future.

We are not forgetting that the Lord fully recognizes the imperfect and provisional character of the Mosaic law and of the Old Dispensation. Were the Old faultless, no place would have been found for the New. Had grace and truth come by Moses, the advent of Jesus Christ would have been unnecessary. So when the Pharisees put the question to Christ why Moses commanded to give to a wife who has found no favor with her husband a writing of divorcement and to put her away, He replied: "Moses, because of the hardness of your hearts suffered you to put away your wives: but from the beginning it was not so" (Matt. 19:8). The Mosaic legislation was not in every part absolutely the best that could be given, but it was such as the divine wisdom saw best for the time being and under the special circumstances of the Hebrew people. Not only did the Old Testament set forth a typical economy, which must give place to another, but it embodied ethical elements of a provisional kind which must pass away when the incarnate Son had fully revealed the Father. The Old Testament is conscious of its own imperfections, for Jeremiah thus writes: "Behold the days come, saith the Lord, that I will make a new covenant with the house of Israel, and with the house of Judah: not according to the covenant that I made with their fathers, in the day that I took them by the hand to bring them out of the land of Egypt." But in all this there is nothing to modify the proposition which we are illustrating, viz., that our Lord accepts the Old Testament economy and its Scriptures as from God, as stamped with divine authority, and as truly making known the divine mind and will.

Marcion and the Gnostics did not receive any part of the Old Testament Scriptures, and the Old Dispensation itself they held to be of evil origin. So decided were they against the Old Testament that they would not admit into their New Testament canon the books which especially bear witness to the Old. But the Christian Church has followed its Master in regarding the Old Testament as the Word of God, as the Bible of the ages before the Advent, and as still part of the Bible for the Christian Church. Not until the days of developed rationalism was this position called in question, except among unbelievers. But it is obvious that the style of criticism which, in our own time, is frequently applied to the Old Testament (not to say anything about the New), touching its histories, its laws, its morality, is quite inconsistent with the recognition of any special divine characteristics or authority as belonging to it. The very maxim so often repeated, that criticism must deal with these writings precisely as it deals with other writings is a refusal to Scripture, *in limine,* of the peculiar character which it claims, and which the Church has ever recognized in it. If a special divine authority can be vindicated for these books, or for any of them, this fact, it is clear, ought to be taken into account by the linguistic and historical critic. Logically, we should begin our study of them by investigating their title to such authority, and, should their claim prove well founded, it should never be forgotten in the subsequent critical processes. The establishment of this high claim will imply in these writings moral characteristics (not to mention others) which should exempt them from a *certain suspicion* which the critic may not unwarrantably allow to be present when he begins to examine documents of an ordinary kind. It is not, therefore, correct to say that criticism, in commencing its inquiries, should know nothing of the alleged divine origin or sacred character of a book. If the book has no good vouchers for its claims to possess a sacred character, criticism must proceed unhindered; but correct conceptions of critical methods demand that every important fact already ascertained as to any writings should be kept faithfully before the mind in the examination of them. Science must here unite with reverential feeling in requiring right treatment of a book which claims special divine sanction, and is willing to have its claims duly investigated. The examination of a witness of established veracity and rectitude would not be conducted in precisely the same manner as that of a witness whose character is unknown or under suspicion. Wellhausen's style of treating the history of Israel can have no justification unless he should first show that the claim so often advanced in "Thus saith the Lord" is entirely baseless. So far from admitting the validity of the axiom referred to, we distinctly hold that it is unscientific. A just and true criticism must have respect to everything already known and settled regarding the productions to which it is applied, and assuredly so momentous a claim as that of divine authority demands careful preliminary examination.

But criticism, it may be urged, is the very instrument by which we must test the pretensions of these writings to a special divine origin and character, and, hence, it cannot stand aside till this question has been considered. In requiring criticism to be silent till the verdict has been rendered, we are putting it under restrictions inconsistent with its functions and prerogatives. The reply, however, is that the principal external and internal evidences for the divine origin of the Scriptures can be weighed with sufficient accuracy to determine the general character and authority of these writings before criticism, either higher or lower, requires to apply its hand. "The heavenliness of the matter, the efficacy of the doctrine, the majesty of the style, the consent of all the parts, the scope of the whole (which is to give glory to God), the full discovery it makes of the only way of man's salvation, the many other incomparable excellences, and the entire perfection thereof, are arguments whereby it doth abundantly evince itself to be the word of God" (Conf. of Faith I:5). But all of these considerations can, in all that is material, be weighed and estimated before technical criticism begins its labors, as they have been estimated to the entire conviction of the divinity of Scripture on the part of thousands who had no acquaintance with criticism. Should the fair application of criticism, when its proper time comes, tend to beget doubt as to the general conclusion already reached regarding the Bible, it will doubtless be right to review carefully the evidence on which our conclusion depends; but the substantive and direct proofs of the Scriptures being from God should first be handled, and the decision arrived at should be kept in mind, while criticism is occupied with its proper task. This seems to us the true order of the procedure.

GOD SPEAKS

Our Lord certainly attributes to the Old Testament a far higher character than many have supposed. God speaks in it throughout; and while He will more perfectly reveal Himself in His Son, not anything contained in the older revelation shall fail of its end or be convicted of error. Christ does not use the term "inspiration" in speaking of the Old Testament, but when we have adduced His words regarding the origin and authority of these writings, it will be evident that to Him they are God-given in every part. It will be seen that His testimony falls not behind that of His Apostles who say: "Every Scripture inspired of God" (2 Tim. 3:16), and "The prophecy came not in old time by the will of man; but holy men of God spake as they were moved by the Holy Ghost" (2 Pet. 1:21).

WORDS AND COMMANDS OF GOD

In speaking of Christ as teaching that the Old Testament is from God we have referred to passages in which He says that its words and commands are the words and commands of God; e. g., "God commanded, saying, Honor thy father and thy mother: and He that curseth father or mother, let him die the death" (Matt. 15:4). Again: "Have ye not read that which was spoken unto you by God, saying, I am the God of Abraham, the God of Isaac, and the God of Jacob?"

In a comprehensive way the laws of the Pentateuch, or of the Old Testament, are called "the commandments of God." "In vain do they worship me, teaching for doctrines the commandments of men. For laying aside the commandment of God, ye hold the tradition of men. * * * Full well ye reject the commandment of God, that ye may keep your own tradition" (Mark 7:8, 9) ; and in the context of this last quotation the commandment of God is identified with what "Moses spake," showing that the words of Moses are also the words of God.

Passages like these do more than prove that the Old Testament Scriptures express *on the whole* the mind of God, and, therefore, possess very high authority. If it can certainly be said that God spake certain words, or that certain words and commandments are the words and commandments of God, we have more than a general endorsement; as when, e. g., the editor of a periodical states that he is responsible for the general character and tendency of articles which he admits, but not for every sentiment or expression of opinion contained in them.

It needs, of course, no proof that the words quoted in the New Testament as spoken by God are not the only parts of the Old which have direct divine authority. The same thing might evidently be said of other parts of the book. The impression left, we think, on every unprejudiced mind is that such quotations as the Lord made are only specimens of a book in which God speaks throughout. There is not encouragement certainly to attempt any analysis of Scripture into its divine and its human parts or elements—to apportion the authorship between God and the human penman, for, as we have seen, the same words are ascribed to God and to His servant Moses. The whole is spoken by God and by Moses also. All is divine and at the same time all is human. The divine and the human are so related that separation is impossible.

ABSOLUTE INFALLIBILITY OF SCRIPTURE

Attention may be specially called to three passages in which the Lord refers to the origin and the absolute infallibility of Scripture. Jesus asked the Pharisees, "What think ye of Christ? Whose Son is He? They say unto Him, The Son of David. He saith unto them, How then doth David *in spirit* call Him Lord?" The reference is to Psalm 110, which the Lord says David spake or wrote "in spirit;" i. e., David was completely under the Spirit's influence in the production of the Psalm, so that when he calls the Messiah his "Lord" the word has absolute authority. Such is clearly the Lord's meaning, and the Pharisees have no reply to His argument. The Lord does not say that the entire Old Testament was written "in the Spirit," nor even that all the Psalms were so produced; He makes no direct statement of this nature; yet the plain reader would certainly regard this as implied. His hearers understood their Scriptures to have been all written by immediate inspiration of God, and to be the word of God; and He merely refers to Psalm 110 as having the character which belonged to Scripture at large.

In John 10:34-36 Christ vindicates Himself from the charge of blasphemy in claiming to be the Son of God: "Jesus answered them, Is it not written in your law, I said, Ye are gods. If he called them gods unto whom the word of God came, and the Scripture cannot be broken; say ye of Him whom the Father hath sanctified, and sent into the world, Thou blasphemest; because I said, I am the Son of God?" The Scripture cannot be broken—*ou dunatai luthēnai*. The verb signifies to loose, unbind, dissolve, and as applied to Scripture means to subvert or deprive of authority. The authority of Scripture is then so complete—so pervasive— as to extend to its individual terms. *"Gods"* is the proper word because it is used to designate the Jewish rulers. If this is not verbal inspiration, it comes very near it. One may, of course, allege that the Lord's statement of inerrancy implies only that the principal words of Scripture must be taken precisely as they are, but that He does not claim the like authority for all its words. Without arguing this point, we merely say that it is not certain or obvious that the way is left open for this distinction. In face of Christ's utterances it devolves on those who hold that inspiration extends to the thought of Scripture only, but not to the words, or to the leading words but not to the words in general, to adduce very cogent arguments in support of their position. The *onus probandi,* it seems to us, is here made to rest on them. The theory that inspiration may be affirmed only of the main views or positions of Scripture, but neither of the words nor of the development of the thoughts, cannot, it seems clear, be harmonized with the Lord's teaching. Before adverting to a third text we may be allowed to set down these words of Augustine in writing to Jerome: "For I acknowledge with high esteem for thee, I have learned to ascribe such reverence and honor to those books of the Scriptures alone, which are now called canonical, that I believe most firmly that not one of their authors has made a mistake in writing them. And should I light upon anything in those writings, which may seem opposed to truth, I shall contend for nothing else, than either that the manuscript was full of errors, or that the translator had not comprehended what was said, or that I had not understood it in the least degree."

In His sermon on the Mount our Lord thus refers to His own relation to the Old Testament economy and its Scriptures: "Think not that I am come to destroy the law, or the prophets: I am not come to destroy but to fulfil. For verily I say unto you, Till heaven and earth pass, one jot or one tittle shall in no wise pass from the law, till all be fulfilled" (Matt. 5:17, 18). No stronger words could be employed to affirm the divine authority of every part of the Old Testament; for the law and the prophets mean the entire Old

Testament Scriptures. If this declaration contemplates the *moral* element of these Scriptures, it means that no part of them shall be set aside by the New Dispensation, but "fulfilled"—i. e., filled up and completed by Jesus Christ as a sketch is filled up and completed by the painter. If, as others naturally interpret, the *typical* features of the Old Testament are included in the statement, the term "fulfilled," as regards this element, will be taken in the more usual meaning. In either case the inviolability and, by implication, the divine origin of the Old Testament could not be more impressively declared. Mark how comprehensive and absolute the words are: "One jot or one tittle." "Jot" (iōta) is *yod,* the smallest letter of the Hebrew alphabet; "tittle," literally little horn or apex, designates the little lines or projections by which Hebrew letters, similar in other respects, differ from each other. We have here, one might say, the inspiration of *letters* of the Old Testament. Everything contained in it has divine authority, and must, therefore, be divine in origin; for it is unnecessary to show that no such authority could be ascribed to writings merely human, or to writings in which the divine and the human interests could be separated analytically.

Should it be said that the "law," every jot and tittle of which must be fulfilled, means here the economy itself, the ordinances of Judaism, but not the record of them in writing, the reply is that we know nothing of these ordinances except through the record, so that what is affirmed must apply to the Scriptures as well as to the Dispensation.

The only questions which can be well raised are, first, whether the "law and the prophets" designate the entire Scriptures or two great divisions of them only; and, secondly, whether the words of Jesus can be taken at their full meaning, or, for some reason or other, must be discounted. The first question it is hardly worth while to discuss, for, if neither jot nor tittle of the "law and the prophets" shall fail, it will hardly be contended that the Psalms, or whatever parts of the Old Testament are not included, have a less stable character. The latter question, of momentous import, we shall consider presently.

FULFILMENT OF PROPHECY

The inspiration of the Old Testament Scriptures is clearly implied in the many declarations of our Lord respecting the fulfilment of prophecies contained in them. It is God's prerogative to know, and to make known, the future. Human presage cannot go beyond what is foreshadowed in events which have transpired, or is wrapped up in causes which we plainly see in operation. If, therefore, the Old Testament reveals, hundreds of years in advance, what is coming to pass, omniscience must have directed the pen of the writer; i. e., these Scriptures, or at least their predictive parts, must be inspired.

The passage already quoted from the Sermon on the Mount may be noticed as regards its bearing on prophecy: "I am not come to destroy the law or the prophets, but to fulfil." While *plērōsai,* as referring to the *law,* has the special meaning above pointed out; as referring to the *prophets,* it has its more common import. We have here, then, a general statement as to the Old Testament containing prophecies which were fulfilled by Christ and in Him. Here are examples. The rejection of Messiah by the Jewish authorities, as well as the ultimate triumph of His cause, is announced in the 118th Psalm, in words which Christ applies to Himself: "The stone which the builders rejected is become the head of the corner." The desertion of Jesus by His disciples when He was apprehended fulfils the prediction of Zechariah: "I will smite the shepherd, and the sheep shall all be scattered" (Matt. 26:31). Should angelic intervention rescue Jesus from death, "how then should the Scriptures be fulfilled, that thus it must be?" All that related to His betrayal, apprehension, and death took place, "that the Scriptures of the prophets might be fulfilled" (Matt. 26:56). "Had ye believed Moses," said our Lord, "ye would have believed Me, for he wrote of Me" (John 5:46). The 41st Psalm preannounces the treachery of Judas in these words: "He that eateth bread with Me hath lifted up his heel against Me;" and the defection of the son of perdition takes place, "that the Scriptures may be fulfilled" (John 17:12). The persistent and malignant opposition of His enemies fulfils that which is written: "They hated Me without a cause" (John 15:25). Finally, in discoursing to the two disciples on the way to Emmaus, the Lord, "beginning at Moses and all the prophets, expounded unto them in all the Scriptures the things concerning Himself. "And He said unto them: These are the words which I spake unto you, while I was yet with you, that all things must be fulfilled which were written in the law of Moses, and in the prophets, and in the Psalms, concerning Me. Then opened He their understanding that they might understand the Scriptures, and said unto them: "Thus it is written, and thus it behooved Christ to suffer and to rise from the dead the third day" (Luke 24:44-46).

It is not denied that in some instances the word "fulfil" is used in the New Testament merely as signifying that some event or condition of things corresponds with or realizes something that is written in the Old Testament; as when the words in Isaiah, "By hearing ye shall hear and shall not understand," are said to be fulfilled in the blind obduracy of the Pharisees. Nor, again, is it denied that "fulfil" has the meaning of filling, or expanding, or completing. But clearly our Lord, in the passages here cited, employs the term in another acceptation. He means nothing less than this: that the Scriptures which He says were "fulfilled" were intended by the Spirit of God to have the very application which He makes of them; they were predictions in the sense ordinarily meant by that term. If the Messiah of the Old Testament were merely an ideal personage, there would be little force in saying that the Lord "opened the understanding" of the disciples that they might see His death and resurrection to be set forth in the prophecies. But to teach that the Old Testament contains authentic predictions is, as we have said, to teach that it is inspired. The challenge to heathen deities is, "Show the things that are to come hereafter, that we may know that ye are gods" (Isa. 41:23).

We thus find that our Lord recognizes the same Old Testament canon as we have, that so far as He makes reference to particular books of the canon He ascribes them to the writers whose names they bear, that He regards the Jewish religion and its sacred books as in a special sense—a sense not to be affirmed of any other religion—from God, that the writers of Scripture, in His view, spake in the Spirit, that their words are so properly chosen that an argument may rest on the exactness of a term, that no part of Scripture shall fail of its end or be convicted of error, and that the predictions of Scripture are genuine predictions, which must all in their time receive fulfilment.

We cannot here discuss the doctrine of inspiration; but on the ground of the Lord's testimony to the Old Testament, as above summarized, we may surely affirm that He claims for it throughout all that is meant by inspiration when we use that term in the most definite sense. No higher authority could well be ascribed to apostolic teaching, or to any part of the New Testament Scriptures, than the Lord attributes to the more ancient Scriptures when He declares that "jot or tittle shall not pass from them till all be fulfilled," and that if men "hear not Moses and the prophets, neither will they be persuaded though one rose from the dead" (Luke 16:31).

II. THE VALUE OF CHRIST'S TESTIMONY

It remains that we should briefly advert to the value, for the scientific student of the Bible, of Christ's testimony to the Old Testament. The very announcement of such a topic may not be heard without pain, but in view of theories with which Biblical students are familiar, it becomes necessary to look into the question. Can we, then, accept the utterances of Christ on the matters referred to as having value— as of authority—in relation to the Biblical scholarship? Can we take them at their face value, or must they be discounted? Or again, are these words of Jesus valid for criticism on some questions, but not on others?

There are two ways in which it is sought to invalidate Christ's testimony to the Old Testament.

1. IGNORANCE OF JESUS ALLEGED

It is alleged that Jesus had no knowledge beyond that of His contemporaries as to the origin and literary characteristics of the Scriptures. The Jews believed that Moses wrote the Pentateuch, that the narratives of the Old Testament are all authentic history, and that the words of Scripture are all inspired. Christ shared the opinions of His countrymen on these topics, even when they were in error. To hold this view, it is maintained, does not detract from the Lord's qualifications for His proper work, which was religious and spiritual, not literary; for in relation to the religious value of the Old Testament and its spiritual uses and applications He may confidently be accepted as our guide. His knowledge was adequate to the delivery of the doctrines of His kingdom, but did not necessarily extend to questions of scholarship and criticism. Of these He speaks as any other man; and to seek to arrest, or direct, criticism by appeal to His authority, is procedure which can only recoil upon those who adopt it. This view is advanced, not only by critics who reject the divinity of Christ, but by many who profess to believe that doctrine. In the preface to his first volume on the Pentateuch and Joshua, Colenso thus writes: "It is perfectly consistent with the most entire and sincere belief in our

Lord's divinity to hold, as many do, that when He vouchsafed to become a 'Son of man' He took our nature fully, and voluntarily entered into all the conditions of humanity, and, among others, into that which makes our growth in all ordinary knowledge gradual and limited. * * * It is not supposed that, in His human nature, He was acquainted more than any Jew of His age with the mysteries of all modern sciences, nor * * * can it be seriously maintained that, as an infant or young child, He possessed a knowledge surpassing that of the most pious and learned adults of His nation, upon the subject of the authorship and age of the different portions of the Pentateuch. At what period, then, of His life on earth, is it to be supposed that He had granted to Him as the Son of man, supernaturally, full and accurate information on these points?" etc. (vol. i., p. 32). "It should also be observed," says Dr. S. Davidson, "that historical and critical questions could only belong to His human culture, a culture stamped with the characteristics of His age and country."

The doctrine of the Kenosis is invoked to explain the imperfection of our Lord's knowledge on critical questions, as evidenced by the way in which He speaks of the Pentateuch and of various Old Testament problems. The general subject of the limitation of Christ's knowledge during His life on earth is, of course, a very difficult one, but we do not need here to consider it. The Gospel of Mark does speak of the day and hour when the heaven and earth shall pass away as being known to the Father only, and not to the Son; but without venturing any opinion on a subject so mysterious, we may, at least, affirm that the Lord's knowledge was entirely adequate to the perfect discharge of His prophetical office. To impute imperfection to Him as the Teacher of the Church were indeed impious. Now the case stands thus: By a certain class of critics we are assured that, in the interests of truth, in order to an apologetic such as the present time absolutely requires, the traditional opinions regarding the authorship of the Old Testament books and the degree of authority which attaches to several, if not all of them, must be revised. In order to save the ship, we must throw overboard this cumbrous and antiquated tackling. Much more, we are assured, than points of scholarship are involved; for intelligent and truth-loving men cannot retain their confidence in the Bible and its religion, unless we discard the opinions which have prevailed as to the Old Testament, even though these opinions can apparently plead in their favor the authority of Jesus Christ.

Now mark the position in which the Lord, as our Teacher, is thus placed. We have followed Him in holding opinions which turn out to be unscientific, untrue; and so necessary is it to relinquish these opinions that neither the Jewish nor the Christian faith can be satisfactorily defended if we cling to them. Is it not, therefore, quite clear that the Lord's teaching is, in something material, found in error—that His prophetical office is assailed? For the allegation is that, in holding fast to what He is freely allowed to have taught, we are imperiling the interests of religion. The critics whom we have in view must admit either that the points in question are of no importance, or that the Lord was imperfectly qualified for His prophetical work. Those who have reverence for the Bible will not admit either position. For why should scholarship so magnify the necessity to apologetics of correcting the traditional opinion as to the age and authorship of the Pentateuch, and other questions of Old Testament criticism, unless it means to show that the Old Testament requires more exact, more enlightened, handling than the Lord gave it? Should it be replied that the Lord, had He been on earth *now,* would have spoken otherwise on the topics concerned, the obvious answer is, that the Lord's teaching is for all ages, and that His word "cannot be broken."

2. THEORY OF ACCOMMODATION

The theory of accommodation is brought forward in explanation of those references of Christ to the Old Testament which endorse what are regarded as inaccuracies or popular errors. He spake, it is said, regarding the Old Testament, after the current opinion or belief. This belief would be sometimes right and sometimes wrong; but where no interest of religion or morality was affected—where spiritual truth was not involved—He allowed Himself, even where the common belief was erroneous, to speak in accordance with it. Some extend the principle of accommodation to the *interpretation* of the Old Testament as well as to questions of canon and authorship; and in following it the Lord is declared to have acted prudently, for no good end could have been served, it is alleged, by crossing the vulgar opinion upon matters of little importance, and thus awakening or strengthening suspicion as to His teaching in general.

As to the accommodation thus supposed to have been practiced by our Lord, we observe that if it implies, as the propriety of the term requires, a more accurate knowledge on His part than His language reveals, it becomes difficult, in many instances, to vindicate His perfect integrity. In some cases where accommodation is alleged, it might, indeed, be innocent enough, but in others it would be inconsistent with due regard to truth; and most of the statements of the Lord touching the Old Testament to which attention has been directed in this discussion seem to be of this latter kind. Davidson himself says: "Agreeing as we do in the sentiment that our Savior and His Apostles accommodated their mode of reasoning to the habitual notions of the Jews, no authority can be attributed to that reasoning *except when it takes the form of an independent declaration or statement,* and so rests on the speaker's credit." Now the statements of Christ respecting the Old Testament Scriptures to which we desire specially to direct attention are precisely of this nature. Are not these "independent declarations"? "One jot or one tittle shall not pass," etc.; "The Scripture cannot be broken;" "David in spirit calls him Lord;" "All things must be fulfilled which are written in the Law of Moses, and in the prophets, and in the psalms concerning Me."

Further, we may say as before, that if our Lord's statements—His *obiter dicta,* if you will—about the authorship of parts of Scripture give a measure of countenance to opinions which are standing in the way of both genuine scholarship and of faith, it is hard to see how they can be regarded as instances of a justifiable accommodation. It seems to us (may we reverently use the words) that in this case you cannot vindicate the Lord's absolute truthfulness except by imputing to Him a degree of ignorance which would unfit Him for His office as permanent Teacher of the Church. Here is the dilemma for the radical critic—either he is agitating the Church about trifles, or, if his views have the apologetical importance which he usually attributes to them, he is censuring the Lord's discharge of His prophetic office; for the allegation is that Christ's words prove perplexing and misleading in regard to weighty issues which the progress of knowledge has obliged us to face. Surely we should be apprehensive of danger if we discover that views which claim our adhesion, on any grounds whatever, tend to depreciate the wisdom of Him whom we call "Lord and Master," upon whom the Spirit was bestowed "without measure," and who "spake as never man spake." It is a great thing in this controversy to have the Lord on our side.

Are, then, the Lord's references to Moses and the law to be regarded as evidence that He believed the Pentateuch to be written by Moses, or should they be classed as instances of accommodation? When we take *in cumulo* all the passages in which the legislation of the Pentateuch and the writing of it are connected with Moses, a very strong case is made out against mere accommodation. The obvious accuracy of speech observed in some of these references cannot be overlooked; e. g., "Moses, therefore, gave you circumcision *(not because it is of Moses, but of the fathers)."* Again, "There is one that accuseth you, even Moses in whom ye trust; for had ye believed Moses ye would have believed Me, for he wrote of Me; but if ye believe not his writings, how shall ye believe My words?" This is not the style of one who does not wish his words to be taken strictly!

TWO POSITIONS CLEAR

Two positions may, I think, be affirmed: 1. The legislation of the Pentateuch is actually ascribed to Moses by the Lord. If this legislation is, in the main, long subsequent to Moses, and a good deal of it later than the exile, the Lord's language is positively misleading, and endorses an error which vitiates the entire construction of Old Testament history and the development of religion in Israel. 2. Moses is to such extent the writer of the law that it may, with propriety, be spoken of as "his writings." All admit that there are passages in the Books of Moses which were written by another hand or other hands, and should even additions other than certain brief explanatory interpolations and the last chapter of Deuteronomy have to be recognized (which has not yet been demonstrated) the Pentateuch would remain Mosaic. Should Moses have dictated much of his writings, as Paul did, they would, it is unnecessary to say, be not the less his. The words of Jesus we consider as evidence that He regarded Moses as, substantially, the writer of the books which bear his name. Less than this robs several of our Lord's statements of their point and propriety.

It is hardly necessary to say that we have no desire to see a true and reverent criticism of the Old Testament, and of the New as well, arrested in its progress, or in the least hin-

dered. Criticism must accomplish its task, and every lover
of truth is more than willing that it should do so. Reluctance
to see truth fully investigated, fully ascertained and established, in any department of thought and inquiry, and most
of all in those departments which are highest, is lamentable
evidence of moral weakness, of imperfect confidence in Him
who is the God of truth. But criticism must proceed by
legitimate methods and in a true spirit. It must steadfastly
keep before it all the facts essential to be taken into account.
In the case of its application to the Bible and religion, it is
most reasonable to demand that full weight should be allowed
to all the teachings, all the words of Him who only knows
the Father, and who came to reveal Him to the world, and
who is Himself the Truth. If all Scripture bears testimony
to Christ, we cannot refuse to hear Him when He speaks of
its characteristics. It is folly, it is unutterable impiety, to decide differently from the Lord any question regarding the Bible
on which we have His verdict; nor does it improve the case
to say that we shall listen to Him when He speaks of spiritual
truth, but shall count ourselves free when the question is one
of scholarship. Alas for our scholarship when it brings us
into controversy with Him who is the Prophet, as He is the
Priest and King of the Church, and by whose Spirit both
Prophets and Apostles spake!

Nothing has been said in this paper respecting the proper
method of *interpreting* the different books and parts of the
Old Testament, nor the way of dealing with specific difficulties.

Our object has been to show that the Lord regards the
entire book, or collection of books, as divine, authoritative,
infallible. But in the wide variety of these writings there are
many forms of composition, and every part, it is obvious
to say, must be understood and explained in accordance with
the rules of interpretation which apply to literature of its
kind. We have not been trying in advance to bind up the
interpreter to an unintelligent literalism in exegesis, which

should take no account of what is peculiar to different species of writing, treating poetry and prose, history and allegory, the symbolical and the literal, as if all were the same. The consideration of this most important subject of interpretation with which apologetical interests are, indeed, closely connected, has not been before us. But nothing which we could be called upon to advance regarding the interpretation of the Old Testament could modify the results here reached in relation to the subject of which we have spoken. Our Lord's testimony to the character of the Old Testament must remain unimpaired.

CHAPTER XI

THE EARLY NARRATIVES OF GENESIS

BY PROFESSOR JAMES ORR, D. D.,

UNITED FREE CHURCH COLLEGE, GLASGOW, SCOTLAND

By the early narratives of Genesis are to be understood the first eleven chapters of the book—those which precede the times of Abraham. These chapters present peculiarities of their own, and I confine attention to them, although the critical treatment applied to them is not confined to these chapters, but extends throughout the whole Book of Genesis, the Book of Exodus, and the later history with much the same result in reducing them to legend.

We may begin by looking at the matter covered by these eleven chapters with which we have to deal. See what they contain. First, we have the sublime proëm to the Book of Genesis, and to the Bible as a whole, in the account of the Creation in Gen. 1. However it got there, this chapter manifestly stands in its fit place as the introduction to all that follows. Where is there anything like it in all literature? There is nothing anywhere, in Babylonian legend or anywhere else. You ask perhaps what interest has religious faith in the doctrine of creation—in any theory or speculation on how the world came to be? I answer, it has the very deepest interest. The interest of religion in the doctrine of creation is that this doctrine is our guarantee for the dependence of all things on God—the ground of our assurance that everything in nature and Providence is at His disposal. "My help cometh from the Lord which made heaven and earth." Suppose there was anything in the universe that was not created by God—that existed independently of Him—how could we be sure that that element might not thwart, defeat, destroy the fulfillment of God's purposes? The Biblical doctrine of creation forever excludes that supposition.

Following on this primary account of creation is a second narrative in a different style—from chapter 2 to 4—but closely connected with the first by the words, "In the day that the Lord God made earth and heaven." This is sometimes spoken of as a second narrative of creation, and is often said to contradict the first. But this is a mistake. As the critic Dillmann points out, this second narrative is not a history of creation in the sense of the first at all. It has nothing to say of the creation of either heaven or earth, of the heavenly bodies, of the general world of vegetation. It deals simply with man and God's dealings with man when first created, and everything in the narrative is regarded and grouped from this point of view. The heart of the narrative is the story of the temptation and the fall of man. It is sometimes said that the Fall is not alluded to in later Old Testament Scripture, and therefore cannot be regarded as an essential part of revelation. It would be truer to say that the story of the Fall, standing there at the commencement of the Bible, furnishes the key to all that follows. What is the picture given in the whole Bible—Old Testament and New? Is it not that of a world turned aside from God—living in rebellion and defiance to Him—disobedient to His calls and resisting His grace? What is the explanation of this universal apostasy and transgression if it is not that man has fallen from his first estate? For certainly this is not the state in which God made man, or wishes him to be. The truth is, if this story of the Fall were not there at the beginning of the Bible, we would require to put it there for ourselves in order to explain the moral state of the world as the Bible pictures it to us, and as we know it to be. In chapter 4, as an appendage to these narratives, there follows the story of Cain and Abel, with brief notices of the beginning of civilization in the line of Cain, and of the start of a holier line in Seth.

Next, returning to the style of Gen. 1—what is called the "Elohistic" style—we have the genealogical line of Seth extending from Adam to Noah. You are struck with the longevity ascribed to those patriarchal figures in the dawn of time, but not less with the constant mournful refrain which ends each notice, Enoch's alone excepted, "and he died." This chapter connects directly with the account of creation in Genesis 1, but presupposes equally the narrative of the Fall in the intervening chapters. We often read in critical books assertions to the contrary of this. The "priestly writer," we are told, "knows nothing" of a Fall. But that is not so. Wellhausen, that master-critic, is on my side here. Speaking of the so-called "priestly" sections in the story of the flood, he says, "The flood is well led up to; in Q. [that is his name for the priestly writing] we should be inclined to ask in surprise how the earth has come all at once to be so corrupted after being in the best of order. Did we not know it from J. E.? [that is, the Fall Narrative]." Another leading critical authority, Dr. Carpenter, writes in the same strain.

Then you come to the flood story in Gen. 6:9, in which two narratives are held to be interblended. There are two writers here, criticism says—the Elohistic and the Jehovistic,—yet criticism must own that these two stories fit wonderfully into one another, and the one is incomplete without the other. If one, for instance, gives the command to Noah and his house to enter the Ark, it is the other that narrates the building of the Ark. If one tells of Noah's "house," it is the other that gives the names of Noah's sons. What is still more striking, when you compare these Bible stories with the Babylonian story of the deluge, you find that it takes both of these so-called "narratives" in Genesis to make up the one complete story of the tablets. Then, following on the flood and the covenant with Noah, the race of mankind spreads out again as depicted in the table of nations in chapter 10. In verse 25 it is noted that in the

days of **Peleg** was the earth divided; then in chapter 11 you
have the story of the divine judgment at Babel confusing
human speech, and this is followed by a new genealogy
extending to Abraham.

Such is a brief survey of the material, and on the face of
it it must be acknowledged that this is a wonderfully well-
knit piece of history of its own kind which we have before
us, not in the least resembling the loose, incoherent, confused
mythologies of other nations. There is nothing resembling
it in any other history or religious book, and when we come
to speak of the great ideas which pervade it, and give it its
unity, our wonder is still increased.

Ah, yes, our critical friends will tell us, the great ideas
are there, but they were not originally there. They were
put in later by the prophets. The prophets took the old
legends and put these grand ideas into them, and made
them religiously profitable. If that was the way in which
God chose to give us His revelation, we would be bound
gratefully to accept it, but I must be pardoned if I prefer to
believe that the great ideas did not need to be put into these
narratives; that they were there in the things themselves
from the very first.

The truth is, a great deal here depends on your method of
approach to these old narratives. There is a saying, "Everything can be laid hold of by two handles," and that is true
of these ancient stories. Approach them in one way and
you make them out to be a bundle of fables, legends, myths,
without historical basis of any kind. Then wonderful feats
can be performed in the handling of the myths. Prof. Gunkel, for example, that very capable Old Testament scholar,
is not content with the analysis of books and chapters and
verses, but adds to it the analysis of personalities. He will
show you, for instance, that Cain is composed originally
out of three distinct figures, blended together, Noah out of
another three, and so on. I have ventured to describe Gun-

kel's theory as the explanation of the patriarchal history on the ancient principle of a fortuitous concourse of atoms. Only that does not quite answer to the kind of history we have in these narratives, which stand in such organic connection with the rest of revelation. Approach these narratives in another way and they are the oldest and most precious traditions of our race; worthy in their intrinsic merit of standing where they do at the commencement of the Word of God, and capable of vindicating their right to be there; not merely vehicles of great ideas, but presenting in their own archaic way—for archaic they are in form—the memory of great historic truths. The story of the Fall, for example, is not a myth, but enshrines the shuddering memory of an actual moral catastrophe in the beginning of our race, which brought death into the world and all our woe.

Coming now to deal a little more closely with these narratives, I suppose I ought to say something on the critical aspect of the question. But this I must pass over briefly, for I want to get to more important matters. In two points only I would desire to indicate my decided break with current critical theory. The one is the carrying down of the whole Levitical system and history connected with it to the post-exilian age. That, I believe, is not a sound result of criticism, but one which in a very short time will have to be abandoned, as indeed it is already being abandoned or greatly modified in influential quarters. This applies specially to the date of Gen. 1. Professor Delitzsh, a commentator often cited as having come round practically to the newer critical view, takes a firm stand here. In his new commentary on Gen. 1, he tells us: "The essential matters in the account of the creation are among the most ancient foundations of the religion of Israel—there are no marks of style which constrain us to relegate the Elohistic account of the creation to the exile—it is in any case a tradition reaching back to the Mosaic period."

The other point on which I dissent is the idea that the Israelites began their religious history without the idea of the one true God, Maker of heaven and earth; that they began with a tribal god, the storm god of Sinai or some other local deity, and gradually clothed him from their own minds with the attributes which belong to Jehovah. This, which is the product of the evolutionary theory of religion, and not a fair deduction from any evidence we possess, I entirely disbelieve, and I am glad to say that this view also is being greatly modified or parted with. It is this theory, however, which lies behind a great deal of the criticism of these early narratives of Genesis. Those things, it is said, could not be; those great ideas could not be there; for man at that early stage could not have evolved them. Even God, it appears, could not have given them to him. Our "could be's," however, will have to be ruled by facts, and my contention is that the facts are adverse to the theory as currently set forth.

I come now to the question, Is there any external corroboration or confirmation of these early narratives in Genesis? Here let me say a little of the relation of these narratives to Babylonia. Everyone has heard something of the wonderful discoveries in Babylonia, and it would be difficult to exaggerate the brillance and importance of these marvelous discoveries. The point which concerns us chiefly is the extraordinary light thrown on the high culture of early Babylonia. Here, long before the time of Abraham, we find ourselves in the midst of cities, arts, letters, books, libraries, and Abraham's own age—that of Hammurabi—was the bloomtime of this civilization. Instead of Israel being a people just emerging from the dim dawn of barbarism, we find in the light of these discoveries that it was a people on whom from its own standpoint the ends of the earth had come—heir to the riches of a civilization extending millenniums into the past. If you say this creates a difficulty in representing the chronology

(I may touch on this later), I answer that it gives much greater help by showing how the knowledge of very ancient things could be safely handed down. For us the chief interest of these discoveries is the help they give us in answering the question, How far do these narratives in Genesis embody for us the oldest traditions of our race? There are two reasons which lead us to look with some confidence to Babylonia for the answer to this question. For one thing, in early Babylonia we are already far back into the times to which many of these traditions relate; for another, the Bible itself points to Babylonia as the original city of those traditions. Eden was in Babylonia, as shown by its rivers, the Euphrates and Tigris. It was in Babylonia the Ark was built; and on a mountain in the neighborhood of Babylonia the Ark rested. It was from the plain of Shinar, in Babylonia, that the new distribution of the race took place. To Babylonia, therefore, if anywhere, we are entitled to look for light on these ancient traditions, and do we not find it? I read sometimes with astonishment of the statement that Babylonian discovery has done little or nothing for the confirmation of these old parts of Genesis—has rather proved that they belong to the region of the mythical.

Take only one or two examples. I leave over meanwhile the Babylonian story of the creation and the flood, and take that old tenth chapter of Genesis, the "Table of Nations." Professor Kautzsch, of Halle, a critic of note, says of that old table, "The so-called Table of Nations remains, according to all results of monumental exploration, an ethnographic original document of the first rank which nothing can replace." In this tenth chapter of Genesis, verses 8-10, we have certain statements about the origin of Babylonian civilization. We learn (1) that Babylonia is the oldest of civilizations; (2) that Assyrian civilization was derived from Babylonia; and (3) strangest of all, that the founders of Babylonian civilization were not Semites, but Hamites—descendants of

Cush. Each of these statements was in contradition to old classical notices and to what was currently believed till recently about those ancient people. Yet it will not be disputed that exploration has justified the Bible on each of these points. Assyria, undoubtedly, was younger than Babylonia; it derived its civilization, arts, religion, institutions, all that it had, from Babylonia. Strangest of all, the originators of Babylonia civilization, the Accadians, or Sumerians, were a people not of Semitic, but apparently of Turanian or what the Bible would call Hamitic stock. Take another instance; in verse 22 Elam appears as the son of Shem, but here was a difficulty. The Elamites of history were not a Semitic, but an Aryan people, and their language was Aryan. Even Professor Hommel, in defending the ancient Hebrew tradition, thought he had to admit an error here. But was there? A French expedition went out to excavate Susa, the capital of Elam, and below the ruins of the historical Elam discovered bricks and other remains of an older civilization, with Babylonian inscriptions showing the people to be of Semitic stock; so Elam was, after all, the son of Shem. In the story of the Tower of Babel in chapter 11, again is it not interesting to find the Bible deriving all the streams of mankind from the Plain of Shinar, and to find archaeology bringing corroborative proof that probably all the greater streams of civilization do take their origin from this region? For that is the view to which the opinions of scholars now tend.

Glance now at the stories of Creation, of Paradise, and of the Deluge. The story of Paradise and the Fall we may dismiss in this connection, for except in the case of the picture on an ancient seal which does bear some relation to the story of the temptation in Eden, there has yet been no proper parallel to the Bible story of the fall. On the other hand, from the ruins of Assyrian libraries have been disinterred fragments of an account of creation, and the Babylonian version of the story of the deluge, both of which have been brought into comparison with the narratives of the Bible. Little need be said of the Babylonian creation story. It is a debased, polytheistic, long-drawn-out, mythical affair, without order, only here and there suggesting analogies to the divine works in Genesis. The flood story has much more resemblance, but it too is debased and mythical, and lacks wholly in the higher ideas which give its character to the Biblical account. Yet this is the quarry from which our critical friends would have us derive the narratives in the Bible. The Israelites borrowed them, it is thought, and purified these confused polytheistic legends and made them the vehicles of nobler teaching. We need not discuss the time and manner of this borrowing, for I cannot see my way to accept this version of events at all. There is not only no proof that these stories were borrowed in their crude form from the Babylonians, but the contrast in spirit and character between the Babylonians' products and the Bible's seems to me to forbid any such derivation. The debased form may conceivably arise from corruption of the higher, but not vice versa. Much rather may we hold with scholars like Delitzsch and Kittel, that the relation is one of cognateness, not of derivation. These traditions came down from a much older source, and are preserved by the Hebrews in their purer form. This appears to me to explain the phenomena as no theory of derivation can do, and it is in accordance with the Bible's own representation of the line of revelation from the beginning along which the sacred tradition can be transmitted.

Leaving Babylonia, I must now say a few words on the scientific and historical aspects of these narratives. Science is invoked to prove that the narratives of creation in Genesis 1, the story of man's origin and fall in chapters 2 and 3, the account of patriarchal longevity in chapters 5 and 11, the story of the deluge, and other matters, must all be rejected because in patent contradiction to the facts of modern knowledge. I would ask you, however, to suspend judgment until we have looked at the relation in which these two things, science and the Bible, stand to each other. When science is said to contradict the Bible, I should like to ask first, What is meant by contradiction here? The Bible was never given us in order to anticipate or forestall the discoveries of modern twentieth century science. The Bible, as every sensible interpreter of Scripture has always held, takes the world as it is, not as it is seen through the eyes of twentieth century specialists, but as it lies spread out before the eyes of original men, and uses the popular every-day language appropriate to this standpoint. As Calvin in his commentary on Genesis 1 says: "Moses wrote in the popular style, which, without instruction, all ordinary persons endowed with common sense are able to understand. * * * He does not call us up to heaven; he only proposes things that lie open before our eyes."

It does not follow that because the Bible does not teach modern science, we are justified in saying that it contradicts it. What I see in these narratives of Genesis is that, so true is the standpoint of the author, so divine the illumination with which he is endowed, so unerring his insight into the order of nature, there is little in his description that even yet, with our advanced knowledge, we need to change. You say there is the "six days" and the question whether those days are meant to be measured by the twenty-four hours of the sun's revolution around the earth—I speak of these things popularly. It is difficult to see how they should be so measured when the sun that is to measure them is not introduced until the fourth day. Do not think that this larger reading of the days is a new speculation. You find Augustine in early times declaring that it is hard or altogether impossible to say of what fashion these days are, and Thomas Aquinas, in the middle ages, leaves the matter an open question. To my mind these narratives in Genesis stand out as a marvel, not for its discordance with science, but for *its agreement with it.*

Time does not permit me to enter into the details of the story of man's origin in Genesis, but I have already indicated the general point of view from which I think this narrative is to be regarded. It would be well if those who speak of disagreement with science would look to the great truths embedded in these narratives which science may be called upon to confirm. There is, for example:

(1) The truth that man is the last of God's created works —the crown and summit of God's creation. Does science contradict that?

(2) There is the great truth of the unity of the human race. No ancient people that I know of believed in such unity of the race, and even science until recently cast doubts upon it. How strange to find this great truth of the unity of the mankind confirmed in the pages of the Bible from the very beginning. This truth holds in it already the doctrine of monotheism, for if God is the Creator of the beings from whom the whole race sprang, He is the God of the whole race that sprang from them.

(3) There is the declaration that man was made in God's image—that God breathed into man a spirit akin to His own —does the science of man's nature contradict that, or does it not rather show that in his personal, spiritual nature man stands alone as bearing the image of God on earth, and founds a new kingdom in the world which can only be carried back in its origin to the divine creative cause.

(4) I might cite even the region of man's origin, for I think science increasingly points to this very region in Babylonia as the seat of man's origin. Is it then the picture of the condition in which man was created, pure and unfallen, and the idea that man, when introduced into the world, was not left as an orphaned being—the divine care was about him—that God spake with him and made known His will to him in such forms as he was able to apprehend—is it this that is in contradiction with history? It lies outside the

sphere of science to contradict this. Personally, I do not know of any worthier conception than that which supposes God to have placed Himself in communication with man, in living relations with His moral creatures, from the very first. Certainly there would be contradiction if Darwinian theory had its way and we had to conceive of man as a slow, gradual ascent from the bestial stage, but I am convinced, and have elsewhere sought to show, that genuine science teaches no such doctrine. Evolution is not to be identified offhand with Darwinianism. Later evolutionary theory may rather be described as a revolt against Darwinianism, and leaves the story open to a conception of man quite in harmony with that of the Bible. Of the fall, I have already said that if the story of it were not in the Bible we should require to put it there for ourselves in order to explain the condition of the world as it is.

On the question of patriarchial longevity, I would only say that there is here on the one hand the question of interpretation, for, as the most conservative theologians have come gradually to see, the names in these genealogies are not necessarily to be construed as only individuals. But I would add that I am not disposed to question the tradition of the extraordinary longevity in those olden times. Death, as I understand it, is not a necessary part of man's lot at all. Had man not sinned, he would never have died. Death—the separation of soul and body, the two integral parts of his nature—is something for him abnormal, unnatural. It is not strange, then, that in the earliest period life should have been much longer than it became afterward. Even a physiologist like Weissmann tells us that the problem for science today is—not why organisms live so long, but why they ever die.

I have referred to Babylonian story of the flood, and can only add a word on the alleged contradiction of science on this subject. Very confident statements are often made as to the impossibility of such a submergence of the inhabited world, and destruction of human and animal life as the Bible represents. It would be well if those who speak thus confidently would study the accumulated evidence which distinguished scientific men have brought forward, that such a catastrophe as Genesis describes is not only possible, but has actually taken place since the advent of man. My attention was first drawn to this subject by an interesting lecture by the late Duke of Argyle given in Glasgow, and the same view has been advocated by other eminent geological specialists on glacial and post-glacial times, as Prestwich, Dawson, Howorth, Dr. Wright, etc. The universal terms employed need not be read as extending beyond the regions inhabited by man. There seems to be no substantial reason for doubting that in the flood of Noah we have an actual historical occurrence of which traditions appear to have survived in most regions of the world.

In conclusion, it is clear that the narratives of Creation, the Fall, the Flood, are not myths, but narratives enshrining the knowledge or memory of real transactions. The creation of the world was certainly not a myth, but a fact, and the representation of the stages of creation dealt likewise with facts. The language used was not that of modern science, but, under divine guidance, the sacred writer gives a broad, general picture which conveys a true idea of the order of the divine working in creation. Man's fall was likewise a tremendous fact, with universal consequences in sin and death to the race. Man's origin can only be explained through an exercise of direct creative activity, whatever subordinate factors evolution may have contributed. The flood was an historical fact, and the preservation of Noah and his family is one of the best and most widely attested of human traditions. In these narratives in Genesis and the facts which they embody are really laid the foundation of all else in the Bible. The unity of revelation binds them up with the Christian Gospel.

CHAPTER XII

ONE ISAIAH

BY PROFESSOR GEORGE L. ROBINSON, D. D.,
MCCORMICK THEOLOGICAL SEMINARY, CHICAGO, ILLINOIS

"For about twenty-five centuries no one dreamt of doubting that Isaiah the son of Amoz was the author of every part of the book that goes under his name; and those who still maintain the unity of authorship are accustomed to point, with satisfaction, to the unanimity of the Christian Church on the matter, till a few German scholars arose, about a century ago, and called in question the unity of this book." Thus wrote the late Dr. A. B. Davidson, Professor of Hebrew in New College, Edinburgh, (*Old Testament Prophecy,* p. 244, 1903).

THE HISTORY OF CRITICISM

The critical disintegration of the Book of Isaiah began with Koppe, who in 1780 first doubted the genuineness of chapter 50. Nine years later Doederlein suspected the whole of chapters 40-66. He was followed by Rosenmueller, who was the first to deny to Isaiah the prophecy against Babylon in chapters 13:1-14:23. Eichhorn, at the beginning of the last century, further eliminated the oracle against Tyre in chapter 23, and, with Gesenius and Ewald, also denied the Isaianic origin of chapters 24-27. Gesenius also ascribed to some unknown prophet chapters 15 and 16. Rosenmueller went further, and pronounced against chapters 34 and 35; and not long afterwards (1840), Ewald questioned chapters 12 and 33. Thus by the middle of the nineteenth century some thirty-seven or thirty-eight chapters were rejected as no part of Isaiah's actual writings.

In 1879-80, the celebrated Leipzig professor, Franz

Delitzsch, who for years previous had defended the genuineness of the entire book, finally yielded to the modern critical position, and in the new edition of his commentary published in 1889, interpreted chapters 40-66, though with considerable hesitation, as coming from the close of the period of Babylonian exile. About the same time (1888-90), Canon Driver and Dr. George Adam Smith gave popular impetus to similar views in Great Britain.

Since 1890, the criticism of Isaiah has been even more trenchant and microscopic than before. Duhm, Stade, Guthe, Hackmann, Cornill and Marti on the Continent, and Cheyne, Whitehouse, Box, Glazebrook, Kennett and others in Great Britain and America, have questioned portions which hitherto were supposed to be genuine.

THE DISINTEGRATION OF "DEUTERO-ISAIAH"

Even the unity of chapters 40-66, which were supposed to be the work of the Second, or "Deutero-Isaiah," is given up. What prior to 1890 was supposed to be the unique product of some celebrated but anonymous sage who lived in Babylonia (about 550 B. C.), is now commonly divided and subdivided and in large part distributed among various writers from Cyrus to Simon.

At first it was thought sufficient to separate chapters 63-66 as a later addition to "Deutero-Isaiah's" prophecies; but more recently it has become the fashion to distinguish between chapters 40-55, which are alleged to have been written in Babylonia about 549-538 B. C., and chapters 56-66, which are now claimed to have been composed about 460-445 B. C. Some carry disintegration farther even than this, especially in the case of chapters 56-66, which are subdivided into various fragments and said to be the product of a school of writers rather than of a single pen. Opinions also conflict as to the place of their composition, whether in Babylonia, Palestine, Phoenicia, or Egypt.

Among the latest to investigate the problem is the Rev. Robert H. Kennett, D. D., Regius Professor of Hebrew and Fellow of Queen's College, Cambridge, whose Schweich Lectures (1909) have recently been published for the British Academy by the Oxford University Press, 1910. The volume is entitled, "The Composition of the Book of Isaiah in the Light of History and Archaeology", and is a professed "attempt to tell in a simple way the story of the book of Isaiah." The results of his investigations he sums up as follows (pp. 84-85): (1) All of chapters 3, 5, 6, 7, 20 and 31, and portions of chapters 1, 2, 4, 8, 9, 10, 14, 17, 22 and 23, may be assigned to Isaiah the son of Amoz. (2) All of chapters 13, 40 and 47, and portions of chapters 14, 21, 41, 43, 44, 45, 46 and 48, may be assigned to the time of Cyrus. (3) All of chapters 15, 36, 37 and 39, and portions of chapters 16 and 38, may be assigned to the period between Nebuchadnezzar and Alexander the Great, but cannot be dated precisely. (4) Chapter 23:1-14 may be assigned to the time of Alexander the Great (332 B. C.). (5) All of chapters 11, 12, 19, 24-27, 29, 30, 32-35, 42, 49-66, and portions of chapters 1, 2, 4, 8, 9, 10, 16, 17, 18, 23, 41, 44, 45 and 48, may be assigned to the second century B. C. Dr. Kennett thus assigns more than one-half of the book of Isaiah to the Maccabean Age.

Prof. C. F. Kent, also, in his "Sermons, Epistles and Apocalypses of Israel's Prophets," 1910, makes the following noteworthy observations on the prophecies of the so-called "Deutero-Isaiah." He says: "The prophecies of Haggai and Zechariah. . . . afford by far the best approach for the study of the difficult problems presented by Isaiah 40-66. . . . Chapters 56-66 are generally recognized as post-exilic. . . . In Isaiah 56 and the following chapters there are repeated references to the temple and its service, indicating that it had already been restored. Moreover, these references are not confined to the latter part of the book. . . . . The fact, on the one hand, that there are few, if any, allusions to contemporary events in these chapters, and, on the other hand, that little or nothing is known of the condition and hopes of the Jews during this period (the closing years of the Babylonian exile) makes the dating of these prophecies possible although far from certain. . . . Also the assumption that the author of these chapters lived in the Babylonian exile is not supported by a close examination of the prophecies themselves. Possibly their author was one of the few who, like Zerubbabel, had been born in Babylon and later returned to Palestine. He was also dealing with such broad and universal problems that he gives few indications of his date and place of abode; but all the evidence that is found points to Jerusalem as the place where he lived and wrote. . . The prophet's interest and point of view center throughout in Jerusalem, and he shows himself far more familiar with conditions in Palestine than in distant Babylon. Most of his illustrations are drawn from the agricultural life of Palestine. His vocabulary is also that of a man dwelling in Palestine, and in this respect is in marked contrast with the synonyms employed by Ezekiel, the prophet of the Babylonian exile" (pp. 27, 28).

That is to say, the two most recent investigators of the Book of Isaiah reach conclusions quite at variance with the opinions advocated in 1890, when Delitzsch so reluctantly allowed that chapters 40-66 may have sprung from the period of Babylonian exile. These last twenty-seven chapters are now found to have been written most probably in Palestine rather than in Babylonia, and are no longer claimed to speak primarily to the suffering exiles in captivity as was formerly supposed.

THE PRESENT STATE OF THE QUESTION

The present state of the Isaiah question is, to say the least, complex, if not chaotic. Those who deny the integrity of the book may be divided into two groups which we may call moderates and radicals. Among the moderates may be included Drs. Driver, G. A. Smith, Skinner, Kirkpatrick, Koenig, A. B. Davidson and Whitehouse. These all practically agree that the following chapters and verses are *not Isaiah's*: 11:10-16; 12:1-6; 13:1-14:23; 15:1-16:12; 21:1-10; 24-27; 34-66. That is to say, some forty-four chapters out of the whole number, sixty-six, were not written by Isaiah; or, approximately 800 out of 1,292 verses are not genuine.

Among the radicals are Drs. Cheyne, Duhm, Hackmann, Guthe, Marti and Kennett. These all reject approximately 1,030 verses out of the total 1,292, retaining the following only as *the genuine product of Isaiah and his age:* 1:2-26, 29-31; 2:6-19; 3:1, 5, 8, 9, 12-17, 24; 4:1; 5:1-14, 17-29; 6:1-13; 7:1-8:22; 9:8-10:9; 10:13, 14, 27-32; 14:24-32; 17:1-14; 18:1-6; 20:1-6; 22:1-22; 28:1-4, 7-22; 29:1-6, 9, 10, 13-15; 30:1-17; 31:1-4. That is, only about 262 verses out of the total, 1,292, are allowed to be genuine.

This is, we believe, a fair statement of the Isaiah question as it exists today.

On the other hand, there are those who still defend the unity of Isaiah's book, e. g., Strachey (1874), Naegelsbach (1877), Bredenkamp (1887), Douglas (1895), W. H. Cobb (1883-1908), W. H. Green (1892), Vos (1898-99), Thirtle (1907) and Margoliouth (1910)*.

THE PRIME REASON FOR DISSECTING ISAIAH

The fundamental axiom of criticism is the dictum that a prophet always spoke out of a definite historical situation to the present needs of the people among whom he lived, and that a definite historical situation shall be pointed out for each prophecy. This fundamental postulate underlies all modern criticism of Old Testament prophecy.

---

*Compare also the writer's "The Book of Isaiah," Y. M. C. A. Press, N. Y., 1910.

This principle on the whole is sound, but it can easily be overworked. Certain cautions are necessary, for example:

(1) It is impossible to trace each separate section of prophecy, independently of its context, to a definite historical situation. Besides, the prophets often speak in poetry, and poetry ought not as a rule to be taken literally.

(2) It is not necessarily the greatest event in a nation's history or the event about which we happen to know the most, that may actually have given birth, humanly speaking, to a particular prophecy. Israel's history is full of crises and events, any one of which may easily be claimed to furnish an appropriate, or at least a possible, background for a given prophecy.

(3) The prophets usually spoke directly to the needs of their own generation, but they spoke also to the generations yet to come. Isaiah, for example, commanded, "Bind thou up the testimony, *seal the law among My disciples*" (8:16); that is, preserve My teachings for the future. Again in 30:8, he says, "Now go, write it before them on a tablet, and inscribe it in a book, *that it may be for the time to come forever and ever.*" And also in 42:23, "Who is there among you that will give ear to this? *that will hearken and hear for the time to come?*"

ALLEGED EXTERNAL EVIDENCE AGAINST UNITY

Recently certain writers have appealed to the author of 2 Chronicles to prove that chapters 40-66 existed as a separate collection in his age. Whitehouse in the New Century Bible ("Isaiah", Vol. I, p. 70), says: "This is clear from 2 Chron. 36:22 ff, in which the passage Isa. 44:28 (that Cyrus would cause the temple to be built) is treated as the word of Jeremiah. The so-called 'Deutero-Isaiah' (chs. 40-66) must at that time (c. 300 B. C.) have been regarded as a body of literature standing quite apart from the Isaianic collection or collections which then existed." But the evidence obtained from this source is so doubtful that it is well-nigh valueless.

For it is not the prediction concerning Cyrus to which the chronicler points as "the word of Jehovah by the mouth of Jeremiah," but "the three-score-and-ten years" spoken of in verse 21 of the same context which Jeremiah did predict. Cf. 2 Chron. 36:21. On the other hand, the *order* of the prophets among the Jews of antiquity was (1) Jeremiah, (2) Ezekiel, (3) Isaiah, and (4) The Twelve; accordingly, any portion of any of these prophecies might be cited as belonging to Jeremiah, because his book stood first.

In any case, to seek for external evidence in behalf of the dissection of the book is indicative!

THE LITERARY HISTORY OF THE BOOK

When or how the Book of Isaiah was edited and brought into its present form is unknown. Jesus ben-Sirach, the author of Ecclesiasticus, writing c. 180 B. C., cites Isaiah as one of the notable worthies of Hebrew antiquity, in whose days, "the sun went backward and he added life to the king" (Ecclus. 48:20-25; cf. Isa. 38:4-8) ; and he adds, who "saw by an excellent spirit that which should come to pass at the last, and comforted them that mourned in Zion." Evidently, therefore, at the beginning of the second century B. C., at the latest, the Book of Isaiah had reached its present form, and the last twenty-seven chapters were already ascribed to the son of Amoz.

Furthermore, there is absolutely no proof that chapters 1-39, or any other considerable section of Isaiah's prophecies ever existed by themselves as an independent collection; nor is there any ground for thinking that the promissory and Messianic portions have been systematically interpolated by editors long subsequent to Isaiah's own time. It is quite arbitrary to suppose that the earlier prophets only threatened.

CERTAIN FALSE PRESUPPOSITIONS

Certain false presuppositions govern critics in their disintegration of the Book of Isaiah. Only a few examples need be given by way of illustration.

(1) To one, "the conversion of the heathen" lay quite beyond the horizon of any eighth-century prophet, and consequently Isa. 2:2-4 and all similar passages should be relegated to a subsequent age.

(2) To another, "the picture of universal peace" in Isa. 11:1-9 is a symptom of late date, and therefore this section and kindred ones must be deleted.

(3) To another, the thought of "universal judgment" upon "the whole earth" in chapter 14:26 quite transcends Isaiah's range of thought.

(4) To still another, the apocalyptic character of chapters 24-27 represents a phase of Hebrew thought which prevailed in Israel only after Ezekiel.

(5) Even to those who are considered moderates the poetic character of a passage like chapter 12 and the references to a *return* from captivity as in 11:11-16, and the promises and consolations such as are found in chapter 33, are cited as grounds for assigning these and kindred passages to a much later age. Radicals deny *in toto* the existence of Messianic passages among Isaiah's own predictions.

But, to deny to Isaiah of the eighth century all catholicity of grace, all universalism of salvation or judgment, every highly developed Messianic ideal, every rich note of promise and comfort, all sublime faith in the sacrosanct character of Zion, as some do, is unwarrantably to create a new Isaiah of greatly reduced proportions, a mere preacher of righteousness, a statesman of not very optimistic vein, and the exponent of a cold ethical religion without the warmth and glow of the messages which are actually ascribed to the prophet of the eighth century.

THE WRITER'S PERSONAL ATTITUDE

More and more the writer is persuaded that the fundamental postulates of much criticism are unsound, and that broad facts must decide the unity or collective character of Isaiah's book. To determine the exact historical background of each individual section is simply impossible, as the history of criticism plainly shows. Verbal exegesis may do more harm than good. Greater regard must be paid to the *structure* of the book. When treated as an organic whole, the book is a grand masterpiece. One great purpose dominates the author throughout, which, as he proceeds, is brought to a climax in a picture of Israel's redemption and the glorification of Zion. Failure to recognize this unity incapacitates a man to do it exegetical justice. The prophecies of the Book of Isaiah simply can not be properly understood without some comprehension of the author's scheme of thought as a whole. There is an obvious, though it may be to some extent an editorial, unity to Isaiah's prophecies. But there is as true a unity in the Book of Isaiah as is usually found *in a volume of sermons*. To regard them as a heterogeneous mass of miscellaneous prophecies which were written at widely separated times and under varied circumstances from Isaiah's own period down to the Maccabean age, and freely interpolated throughout the intervening centuries, is to lose sight of the great historic realities and perspective of the prophet. In short the whole problem of how much or how little Isaiah wrote would become immensely simplified if critics would only divest themselves of a mass of unwarranted presuppositions and arbitrary restrictions which fix hard and fast what each century can think and say.

Accordingly, the writer's attitude is that of those who, while welcoming all ascertained results of investigation, decline to accept any mere conjectures or theories as final conclusions. And while he acknowledges his very great debt to critics of all latitudes, he nevertheless believes that the Book of Isaiah, practically as we have it, may have been, and probably was, all written by Isaiah, the son of Amoz, in the latter half of the eighth century B. C.

ARGUMENTS FOR ONE ISAIAH

It is as unreasonable to expect to be able to prove the unity of Isaiah as to suppose that it has been disproven. Internal evidence is indecisive in either case. There are arguments, however, which corroborate a belief that there was but one Isaiah. Here are some of those which might be mentioned:

1. *The Circle of Ideas* is st: 'kingly the same throughout. For example, take the name for God which is almost peculiar to the Book of Isaiah, "the Holy One of Israel". This title for Jehovah occurs in the Book of Isaiah a total of twenty-five times and only six times elsewhere in the Old Testament (one of which is in a parallel passage). It interlocks all the various portions with one another and stamps them with the personal imprimatur of him who saw the vision of the majestic God seated upon His throne, high and lifted up, and heard the angelic choirs singing: "Holy, Holy, Holy is Jehovah of hosts: the whole earth is full of Thy glory" (Chapter 6). The presence of this Divine name in all the different sections of the book is of more value in identifying Isaiah as the author of all these prophecies than though his name had been inscribed at the beginning of every chapter, for the reason that his theology is woven into the very fiber and texture of the whole book.

The title occurs twelve times in chapters 1-39, and thirteen times in chapters 40-66; and it is simply unscientific to say that the various alleged authors of the disputed portions all employed the same title through imitation. (Isa. 1:4; 5:19, 24; 10:20; 12:6; 17:7; 29:19; 30:11, 12, 15; 31:1; 37:23. Also, 41:14, 16, 20; 43:3, 14; 45:11; 47:4; 48:17; 49:7; 54:5; 55:5; 60:9, 14. Compare 2 Kings 19:22; Psa. 71:22; 78:41; 89:18; Jer. 50:29; 51:5.)

Another unique idea which occurs with considerable repetition in the Book of Isaiah is the thought of a "highway". Cf. 11:16; 35:8; 40:3; 43:19; 49:11; 57:14; 62:10.

Another is the idea of a "remnant". Cf. 1:9; 6:13; 10:20, 21, 22; 11:11, 12, 16; 14:22, 30; 15:9; 16:14; 17:3, 6; 21:17; 28:5; 37:31; 46:3; 65:8, 9.

Another is the position occupied by "Zion" in the prophet's thoughts. Cf. 2:3; 4:5; 18:7; 24:23; 27:13; 28:16; 29:8; 30:19; 31:9; 33:5, 20; 34:8; 46:13; 49:14; 51:3, 11; 52:1; 57:13; 59:20; 60:14; 62:1, 11; 65:11, 25; 66:8.

Still another is the expression, "pangs of a woman in travail." Cf. 13:8; 21:3; 26:17, 18; 42:14;54:1; 66:7.

All these, and many others which are less distinctive, stamp psychologically the book with an individuality which it is difficult to account for if it be broken up into various sections and distributed, as some do, over the centuries.

2. *Literary Style.*

As negative evidence, literary style is not a very safe argument, for as Professor McCurdy says, "In the case of a writer of Isaiah's endowments, st··le is not a sure criterion of authorship" ("History, Prophecy and the Monuments," II, p. 317 n.). Yet it is remarkable that the clause, "for the mouth of Jehovah hath spoken it", should be found three times in the Book of Isaiah, and nowhere else in the Old Testament. Cf. 1:20; 40:5; 58:14.

It is also singular that the Divine title, "the Mighty One of Israel," should occur three times in Isaiah and nowhere else in the Old Testament. Cf. 1:24; 49:26; 60:16.

And it is noteworthy that the phrase, "streams of water," should occur twice in Isaiah and nowhere else. Cf. 30:25; 44:4.

And most peculiar is the tendency on the part of the author to emphatic reduplication. Cf. 2:7, 8; 6:3; 8:9; 24:16, 19; 40:1; 43:11, 25; 48:15; 51:12; 57:19; 62:10.

Isaiah's style differs widely from that of every other Old Testament prophet and is as far removed as possible from that of Ezekiel and the post-exilic prophets.

3. *Historical References.*

Take for example, first, the prophet's constant reference to Judah and Jerusalem, 1:7-9; 3:8; 5:13; 24:19; 25:2; 40:2, 9; 62:4. Also, to the temple and its ritual of worship and sacrifice. In chapter 1:11-15, when all was prosperous, the prophet complained that the people are profuse and formal in their ceremonies and sacrifices; in chapter 43:23, 24, on the contrary, when the country had been overrun by the Assyrians and Sennacherib had beseiged the city, the prophet complains that they had not brought to Jehovah the sheep of their burnt offerings, nor honored Him with their sacrifices. In chapter 66:1-3, 6, 20, not only is the existence of the temple and the observance of the temple ritual presupposed, but those are sentenced who place their trust in the material temple, and the outward ceremonials of temple worship.

As for the "exile", the prophet's attitude to it throughout is that of both anticipation and realization. Thus in chapter 57:1, judgment is only threatened, not yet inflicted: "The righteous is taken away *from the evil to come.*" That is to say, the exile is described as still future. On the other hand, in chapter 3:8, "Jerusalem is ruined, and Judah is fallen"; while in chapter 11:11, 12, "the Lord will set His hand again the second time to recover the remnant . . . from the four corners of the earth." To interpret such statements literally without regard to Isaiah's manifest attitude to the exile, leads only to confusion. No prophet realized so keenly or described so vividly the destiny of the Hebrews.

4. *The Predictive Element.*

This is the strongest proof of the unity of the Book of Isaiah. Prediction is the very essence of prophecy. Isaiah was pre-eminently a *prophet of the future.* With unparalleled suddenness he repeatedly leaps from despair to hope, from threat to promise, from the actual to the ideal. What Kent says of "Deutero-Isaiah" may with equal justice be said of Isaiah himself: "While in touch with his own age, the great unknown prophet lives in the atmosphere of the past and the future" (Cf. "Sermons, Epistles and Apocalypses of Israel's Prophets", p. 28).

Isaiah spoke to his own age, but he also addressed himself to the ages to come. His verb tenses are characteristically futures and prophetic perfects. Of him A. B. Davidson's words are particularly true: "If any prophetic book be examined . . . it will appear that the ethical and religious teaching is always secondary, and that the essential thing in the book or discourse is the prophet's outlook into the future" (Hastings' Dictionary of the Bible, article, "Prophecy and Prophets").

Isaiah was exceptionally given to predicting: thus,

(1) *Before the Syro-Ephraimitic war (734 B. C.),* he predicted that within sixty-five years Ephraim should be broken in pieces (7:8); and that before the child Maher-shalal-hash-baz should have knowledge to cry, "My father" or "My mother", the riches of Damascus and the spoil of Samaria should be carried away (8:4; cf. 7:16). There are numerous other predictions among his earlier prophecies. (Cf. 1:27, 28; 2:2-4; 6:13; 10:20-23; 11:6-16; 17:14.)

(2) *Shortly before the downfall of Samaria in 722 B. C.* Isaiah predicted that Tyre shall be forgotten seventy years, and that after the end of seventy years her merchandise shall be holiness of Jehovah. (Cf. Isa. 23:15.)

(3) *Likewise prior to the siege of Ashdod in 711 B. C.,* he proclaimed that within three years Moab should be brought into contempt (Isa. 16:14), and that within a year all the glory of Kedar should fail (Isa. 21:16).

(4) *And not long prior to the siege of Jerusalem by Sennacherib in 701 B. C.,* he predicted that in an instant, suddenly, a multitude of Jerusalem's foes should be as dust (Isa. 29:5); that yet a very little while and Lebanon should be turned into a fruitful field (Isa. 29:17); that Assyria should be dismayed and fall by the sword but not of men (Isa. 30:17, 31; 31:8). Furthermore, that for days beyond a year, the careless women

of Jerusalem should be troubled (Isa. 32:10, 16-20); and that the righteous in Zion should see Jerusalem a quiet habitation, and return and come with singing (Isa. 33:17-24; 35:4, 10); but that Sennacherib on the contrary should hear tidings and return without shooting an arrow into the city (Isa. 37:7, 26-29, 33-35).

In like manner *after* the siege of Jerusalem by Sennacherib, 701 B. C., the prophet continued to predict; and, in order to demonstrate to the suffering remnant about him the deity of Jehovah and the folly of idolatry, pointed to the predictions which he had already made in the earlier years of his ministry, and to the fact that they had been fulfilled. For example, he says:

In chapter 41:21-23, 26 ff.: "Who hath declared it from the beginning that we may know, and beforetime that we may say, He is right?"

In chapter 42:9, 23: "Behold the former things are come to pass and new things do I declare; before they spring forth I tell you of them."

In chapter 43:9, 12: "Who among them can declare this and show us former things? [i. e., things to come in the immediate future.] I have declared, and I have saved and I have showed."

In chapter 44:7, 8, 27, 28: "Who, as I, shall call, and shall declare it? . . . The things that are coming and that shall come to pass, let them [the idols] declare. Have not I declared unto thee of old and showed it? And ye are My witnesses. . . . That saith of Cyrus, He is My shepherd, and shall perform all My pleasure, even saying of Jerusalem, she shall be built; and of the temple, thy foundation shall be laid."

In chapter 45:1-4, 11, 21: "It is I Jehovah, who call thee by thy name, even the God of Israel. . . . I have called thee by thy name: I have surnamed thee though thou hast not known Me. . . . Ask of Me the things that are to come.

. . . I have raised him [Cyrus] up in righteousness, and he shall build My city, and he shall let My exiles go free."

In chapter 46:10, 11: "Declaring the end from the beginning, and from ancient times things that are not yet done; . . . calling a ravenous bird [Cyrus] from the east, the man of My counsel. . . . Yea, I have spoken, I will also bring it to pass."

In chapter 48:3, 5: "I have declared the former things from of old, . . . and I showed them, suddenly I did them, and they came to pass. . . . I have declared it to thee from of old; before it came to pass I showed it thee; lest thou shouldest say, Mine idol hath done them."

And again in chapter 48:6-8, 14-16: "I have showed thee new things from this time, even hidden things; . . . before this day thou heardest them not, . . . yea, from of old thine ear was not opened, . . . Who, among them hath declared these things? . . . I even I have spoken; yea, I have called him; from the beginning I have not spoken in secret." To which long list of predictions the prophet adds by way of lamentation: "Oh, that thou hadst hearkened to my commandments [including predictions]! then had thy peace been like a river, and thy righteousness as the waves of the sea" (48:18).

CYRUS A SUBJECT OF PREDICTION

From all these numerous explicit and oft-repeated predictions one thing is obvious, namely, that great emphasis is laid on prediction throughout the Book of Isaiah. "Cyrus" must be considered as predicted from any point of view. The only question is, Does the prophet emphasize the fact that he is himself predicting the coming of Cyrus? or, that former predictions concerning Cyrus are now in his time coming to pass?

Canon Cheyne's remark upon this point is apropos. He says: "The editor, who doubtless held the later Jewish theory of prophecy, may have inferred from a number of passages, especially 41:26; 48:3, 6, 14, that the first appearance of Cyrus had been predicted by an ancient prophet, and observing certain Isaianic elements in the phraseology of these chapters may have identified the prophet with Isaiah" ("Introduction to the Book of Isaiah," p. 238). Why not regard "the editor's" inference legitimate?

Dr. George Adam Smith likewise allows that Cyrus is the fulfillment of *former predictions*. He says: "Nor is it possible to argue as some have tried to do, that the prophet is predicting these things as if they had already happened. For as part of an argument for the unique divinity of the God of Israel, Cyrus, alive and irresistible, and already accredited with success, is pointed out as the unmistakable proof that *former* prophecies of a deliverance for Israel are already coming to pass. Cyrus, in short, is not presented as a prediction but as a proof *that a prediction is being fulfilled*" (Hastings' Dictionary of the Bible, art. "Isaiah", p. 493). Further, he says: "The chief claim, therefore, which chapters 40 ff. make for the God of Jehovah is His power to direct the history of the world in conformity to a long predicted and faithfully followed purpose. This claim starts from the proof *that Jehovah has long before predicted events now happening* or about to happen, with Cyrus as their center" (Idem, p. 496).*

Hence in any case it must be allowed that Cyrus is the subject of prediction. It really makes little difference at which end of history one stands, whether in the eighth century B. C. or in the sixth, *Cyrus, to the author of chapters 40-48, is the subject of prediction.* Whether, indeed, he is really predicting Cyrus in advance of all fulfillment, or whether Cyrus to him is the fulfillment of some ancient prediction does not alter the fact that Cyrus was the subject of prediction on the part of somebody. As was stated above, the whole question is, which does the prophet emphasize, (1) the fact that he is predict-

---
*The italics are ours.

ing? or, (2) that former predictions are now before his eyes coming to pass? The truth is, the prophet seems to live in the atmosphere of both the past and the future. This is true of Isaiah, who in his inaugural vision (ch. 6) paints a scene which Delitzsch describes as "like a prediction in the process of being fulfilled". The same is presumably true of chapters 24-27. There the prophet repeatedly projects himself into the future, and speaks from the standpoint of the fulfillment of his prediction. This was an outstanding characteristic of Isaiah. At one time he emphasizes the fact that he is predicting, and a little later he seems to emphasize that his predictions are coming to pass. Accordingly, if a decision must be made as to when Cyrus was actually predicted, it is obviously necessary to assume that he was predicted *long before his actual appearance.*

This is in keeping with the Deuteronomic test of prophecy, which says: "When a prophet speaketh in the name of Jehovah, if the thing follow not, nor come to pass, that is the thing which Jehovah hath not spoken; the prophet hath spoken it presumptuously, thou shalt not be afraid of him" (Deut. 18:22).

There is a similar prediction in the Old Testament: King Josiah was predicted by name two centuries before he came. (1 Kings 13:2; cf. 2 Kings 23:15, 16.)

Dr. W. H. Cobb, in the "Journal of Biblical Literature and Exegesis", 1901 (p. 79), pleads for a "shrinkage of Cyrus", because Cyrus figures only in chapters 40-48, and is then dismissed. Dr. Thirtle in his volume entitled, "Old Testament Problems" (pp. 244-264), argues that the name "Cyrus" is a mere appellative, being originally not *Koresh* (Cyrus), but *Horesh* (workman, artificer, image-breaker), and that chapter 44:27, 28 is therefore a gloss. But in opposition to these views the present writer prefers to write Cyrus large, and to allow frankly that he is the subject of prediction; for, the very point of the author's argument is, that he is predicting events which Jehovah alone is capable of foretelling or bringing to pass; in other words, that prescience is the proof of Jehovah's deity.

Isaiah lived in an age when prediction was needed; cf. Amos 3:9. Political events were kaleidoscopic and there was every incentive to predict. But Jehovah's predictions alone were trustworthy.

That Isaiah's prophecies contain wonderful predictions is attested both by Jesus ben-Sirach in Ecclus. 48-20-25, which was written about 180 B. C., and by Josephus in his "Antiquities" XI, I, 1, 2, dating from about 100 A. D.

Why should men object to prediction on so large a scale? Unless there is definiteness about any given prediction, unless it transcends ordinary prognostication there is no especial value in it. The only possible objection is that prediction of so minute a character is "abhorrent to reason". But the answer to such an objection is already at hand; it may be abhorrent to reason, but it is certainly a handmaid to faith. Faith has to do with the future even as prediction has to do with the future; and the Old Testament is pre-eminently a book which encourages faith.

The one outstanding differentiating characteristic of Israel's religion is predictive prophecy. Only the Hebrews ever predicted the coming of the Messiah of the kingdom of God. Accordingly, to predict the coming of a Cyrus as the *human* agent of Israel's salvation is but the reverse side of the same prophet's picture of the *Divine* agent, the obedient, suffering Servant of Jehovah, who would redeem Israel from their sin.

Deny to Isaiah the son of Amoz the predictions concerning Cyrus, and the prophecy is robbed of its essential character and unique perspective; emasculate these latter chapters of Isaiah of their predictive feature, and they are reduced to a mere *vaticinium ex eventu,* and their religious value is largely lost.

CHAPTER XIII

THE BOOK OF DANIEL

BY PROFESSOR JOSEPH D. WILSON, D. D.,
THEOLOGICAL SEMINARY OF THE REFORMED EPISCOPAL CHURCH,
PHILADELPHIA, PENNSYLVANIA,
AUTHOR OF "DID DANIEL WRITE DANIEL?"

Modern objections to the Book of Daniel were started by German scholars who were prejudiced against the supernatural. Daniel foretells events which have occurred in history. Therefore, argue these scholars, the alleged predictions must have been written after the events.

But the supernatural is not impossible, nor is it improbable, if sufficient reason for it exists. It is not impossible, for instance, that an event so marvellous as the coming of the Divine into humanity in the person of Jesus Christ should be predicted. So far from being impossible, it seems to common sense exceedingly probable; and furthermore, it seems not unreasonable that a prophet predicting a great and far distant event, like that indicated above, should give some evidence to his contemporaries or immediate successors that he was a true prophet. Jeremiah foretold the seventy years captivity. Could his hearers be warranted in believing that? Certainly. For he also foretold that all those lands would be subjected to the king of Babylon. A few years showed this latter prophecy to be true, and reasonable men believed the prediction about the seventy years.

But the attacks of the German scholars would have been innocuous had it not been for their copyists. The German scholars—even theological professors—are not necessarily Christians. Religion is with them an interesting psychological phenomenon. Their performances are not taken too seriously by their compeers. But outside of their learned circles a considerable number of writers and professors in schools, anxious to be in the forefront, have taken the German theories for proven facts, and by saying "all scholars are agreed," etc., have spread an opinion that the Book of Daniel is a pious fraud.

There is another class of impugners of Daniel—good men, who do not deny the ability of God to interpose in human affairs and foretell to His servants what shall be hereafter. These men, accepting as true what they hear asserted as the judgment of "all scholars" and regretfully supposing that Daniel is a fiction, have endeavored to save something from the wreck of a book which has been the stay of suffering saints through the ages, by expatiating on its moral and religious teaching. It is probable that these apologists—victims themselves of a delusion which they did not create but which they have hastily and foolishly accepted—have done more harm than the mistaken scholars or the hasty copyists, for they have fostered the notion that a fraud may be used for holy ends, and that a forger is a proper teacher of religious truth, and that the Son of God approved a lie.

The scholars find that in chapter 8 of Daniel, under the figure of a very little horn, Antiochus Epiphanes is predicted as doing much hurt to the Jews. The vision is of the ram and he-goat which represent Persia and Greece, so specified by name. A notable horn of the he-goat, Alexander the Great, was broken, and in its place came four horns, the four kingdoms into which the Greek empire was divided. From one of these four sprang the little horn. That this refers primarily to Antiochus Epiphanes there is no doubt. He died about 163 B. C. The theory of the rationalistic critics is that some "pious and learned Jew" wrote the Book of Daniel at that time to encourage the Maccabees in their revolt against this bad king; that the book pretends to have been written in Babylon, 370 years before, in order to make it pass current as a revelation from God. This theory has been supported by numerous arguments, mostly conjectural, all worthless and, in a recent publication, a few designedly delusive.

The imaginary Jew is termed "pious" because lofty religious ideas mark the book, and "learned" because he exhibits so intimate an acquaintance with the conditions and environments of the Babylonian court four centuries before his date. But as no man, however learned, can write an extended history out of his own imagination without some inaccuracies, the critics have searched diligently for mistakes. The chief of these supposed mistakes will be considered below.

We meet a difficulty at the threshold of the critics' hypothesis. Dan. 9:26 predicts the destruction of Jerusalem and the temple; a calamity so frightful to the Jewish mind that the Septuagint shrank from translating the Hebrew. What sort of encouragement was this? The hypothesis limps at the threshold.

Having Antiochus Epiphanes in chapter 8 the rationalistic critics try to force him into chapter 7. They find a little horn in chapter 7, and struggle to identify him with the "very little horn" of chapter 8. There is no resemblance between them. The words translated "little horn" are different in the different chapters. The little horn of chapter 7 springs up as an eleventh horn among *ten* kings. He is diverse from other kings. He continues till the Son of Man comes in the clouds of heaven and the kingdom which shall never be destroyed is set up. Antiochus Epiphanes, the little horn of chapter 8, comes out of one of the *four* horns into which Alexander's kingdom resolved itself. He was not diverse from other kings, but was like scores of other bad monarchs, and he did not continue till the Son of Man.

These divergencies render the attempted identification absurd, but an examination of the two sets of prophecies in their entirety shows this clearly. Chapters 2 and 7 are a prophecy of the world's history to the end. Chapters 8 and 11 refer to a crisis in Jewish history, a crisis now long past.

Chapter 2, the Image with its head of gold, breast of silver, belly of brass, legs of iron, feet and toes of mingled iron and clay, tells of four world-kingdoms, to be succeeded by a number of sovereignties, some strong, some weak, which would continue till the God of heaven should set up a kingdom never to be destroyed. Chapter 7, the Four Beasts, is parallel to the Image. The same four world-empires are described; the fourth beast, strong and terrible, to be succeeded by ten kings, who should continue till the coming of the Son of Man, who should set up an everlasting kingdom.

These four world-empires were Babylon, Persia, Greece and Rome. There have been no other world-empires since. Efforts have been made to unite the divided sovereignties of Europe by royal intermarriages and by conquest, but the iron and clay would not cleave together. The rapidity of the Greek conquest is symbolized by the swift leopard with four wings; its division by four heads. The Roman empire is diverse from the others—it was a republic and its iron strength is dissipated among the nations which followed it and which exist today, still iron and clay.

These prophecies which are illustrated in every particular by history to the present moment stand in the way of the unbelieving theory. The Roman empire, the greatest of all, must be eliminated to get rid of prediction, and any shift promising that end has been welcomed. One set of critics makes the kingdom of the Seleucidae, which was one of the parts of the Greek empire, the fourth world-kingdom, but it never was a world-kingdom. It was part of the Greek empire—one of the four heads upon the leopard. Another set creates an imaginary Median empire between Babylon and Persia. There· was no such empire. The Medo-Persian empire was one. Cyrus, the Persian, conquered Babylon. All history says so and the excavations prove it.

Among the nations which were to take the place of the fallen Roman empire, another power was to rise—"a little horn," shrewd and arrogant. It was to wear out the saints of the Most High, to be diverse from the other ten sovereignties, to have the other sovereignties given into its hand, and to keep its dominion till the coming of the Son of Man.

Whatever this dread power is, or is to be, it was to follow the fall of the Roman empire and to rise among the nations which, ever since, in some form or other have existed where Rome once held sway. Whether that power, differing from civil governments and holding dominance over them, exists now and has existed for more than a thousand years, or is to be developed in the future, it was to arise in the Christian era. The words are so descriptive, that no reader would ever have doubted were it not that the prophecy involves prediction.

The attempt of the "very little horn" of chapter 8, Antiochus Epiphanes, to extirpate true religion from the earth, failed. Yet it was well-nigh successful. The majority of the nation were brought to abandon Jehovah and to serve Diana. The high priest in Jerusalem sent the treasurers of the temple to Antioch as an offering to Hercules. Jews out-bade each other in their subservience to Antiochus. His cruelties were great but his blandishments were more effective for his purpose; "by peace he destroyed many". Idolatrous sacrifices were offered throughout Judea. Judaism was all but dead, and with its death the worship of the one God would have found no place in all the earth.

This prophecy encouraged the few faithful ones to resist the Greek and their own faithless fellow countrymen. God foresaw and forewarned. The warning was unheeded by the mass of the Jews. Sadduceeism then did not believe in the supernatural and it has repeated its disbelief. Fortunately there was a believing remnant and true religion was saved from extinction.

The Seventy Weeks. (Dan. 9:24-27.) "Weeks" in this prophecy are not weeks of days but "sevens," probably years, but whether astronomical years of 365¼ days or prophetic years of 360 days does not appear. Our Lord's saying when referring to the prophecy of Daniel (Matt. 24:15), "Let him that readeth understand," seems to indicate a peculiarity about the period foretold.

From the issuance of a commandment to restore and rebuild Jerusalem unto Messiah there would be sixty-nine sevens, i. e., 483 years. Messiah would be cut off and have nothing, and the people of a prince would destroy Jerusalem and the temple.

It came to pass in the procuratorship of Pontius Pilate. Messiah appeared; He was cut off; He had nothing, no place to lay His head, nothing except a cross. And before the generation which crucified Him passed away, the soldiers of the Roman emperor destroyed the city and sanctuary, slew all the priests and ended Jewish church and nation.

Unto Messiah the Prince there were to be 483 years from an edict to rebuild Jerusalem. That edict was issued in the twentieth year of Artaxerxes Longimanus. Somewhere between 454 B. C. and 444 B. C. is the date, with the preponderance of opinion in favor of the later date. Four hundred and eighty-three years brings us to 29—39 A. D. Or, if prophetic years are meant, the *terminus ad quem* is 22—32 A. D. Pontius Pilate was procurator of Judea from 26 A. D. to 36 A. D.

All this is plain enough, and if the words of Daniel had been written after the death of our Saviour and the fall of Jerusalem, no one could fail to see that Jesus Christ is indicated. But if written in the exile this would be supernatural prediction, and hence the struggles of the critics to evade somehow the implications of the passage. To find some prominent person who was "cut off" prior to 163 B. C. was the first desideratum. The high priest Onias, who was murdered through the intrigues of rival candidates for his office, was the most suitable person. He was in no respect the Messiah, but having been anointed he might be made to serve. He died 171 B. C. The next step was to find an edict to restore and rebuild Jerusalem, 483 years before 171 B. C. That date was 654 B. C., during the reign of Manasseh, son of Hezekiah. No edict could be looked for there. But by deducting 49 years, the date was brought to 605 B. C., and as in that year Jeremiah had foretold (Jer. 25:9) the destruction of Jerusalem, perhaps this would do.

There were two objections to this hypothesis; one, that a prophecy of desolation and ruin to a city and sanctuary then in existence was not a commandment to restore and rebuild, and the other objection was that this also was a supernatural prediction, and as such, offensive to the critical mind. Accordingly, recourse was had to the decree of Cyrus (Ezra 1:1-4) made in 536 B. C. But the decree of Cyrus authorized, not the building of Jerusalem, but the building of the temple. It is argued that forts and other defences, including a city wall must have been intended by Cyrus, and this would be rebuilding Jerusalem; but the terms of the edict are given and no such defences are mentioned. Nor is it likely that a wise man like Cyrus would have intended or permitted a fortified city to be built in a remote corner of his empire close to his enemy, Egypt, with which enemy the Jews had frequently coquetted in previous years. At all events, the city was not restored until the twentieth year of Artaxerxes, as appears from Neh. 2:3, 8, 13, etc., where Nehemiah laments the defenceless condition of Jerusalem. Permission to build could safely be given then, for Egypt had been conquered and the loyalty of the Jews to Persia had been tested. Moreover, the date of Cyrus' decree does not meet the conditions. From 536 B. C. to 171 B. C. is 365 years and not 483. A "learned and pious Jew" would not have made such a blunder in arithmetic in foisting a forgery upon his countrymen.

There were four decrees concerning Jerusalem issued by the Persian court. The first under Cyrus, alluded to above, the second under Darius Hystaspis. (Ezra 6.) The third in the seventh year of Artaxerxes. (Ezra 7:12-26.) All of these concern the temple. The fourth in the twentieth year of Artaxerxes was the only one to restore and rebuild a walled town.

The Book of Daniel was translated into Greek about 123 B. C., forty years after the death of Antiochus Epiphanes. This prophecy of the Seventy Weeks troubled the Jewish translators. It foretold disaster to Jerusalem. City and sanctuary would be destroyed. They had been destroyed 464 years before by Nebuchadnezzar. Would they be destroyed again? The translators were unwilling to believe that such a calamity would occur again. Could they not make out that the words referred to the troubles under Antiochus? It was true that he had destroyed neither city nor temple, but he had polluted the temple. Perhaps that was equivalent to destruction. At all events they did not dare to say that another destruction of Jerusalem lay in the future.

But there stood the words. From the going forth of commandment to restore Jerusalem unto Messiah the Prince would be seven weeks and three score and two weeks, 483 years. They could do nothing with those words. They left them out, and mangled the rest of the passage to give obscurely the impression that the disasters there foretold were a thing of the past.

This mistranslation of a Divine oracle to make it say what they wished it to say was a high-handed proceeding, but it did not prevent its fulfillment. At the time appointed Messiah came and was crucified and Jerusalem fell. The critics' efforts to force some meaning, other than a prediction of Christ, into this prophecy is thus seen to be not without precedent.

SUPPOSED INACCURACIES

But the rationalistic interpretations of the forementioned great prophecies are so unnatural, so evidently forced in order to sustain a preconceived theory, that they would have deceived none except those predisposed to be deceived. Accordingly attempts have been made to discredit the Book of Daniel; to show that it could not have been written in Babylon; to expose historical inaccuracies and so forth. The scholars discovered some supposed inaccuracies, and, the fashion having been set, the imitation scholars eagerly sought for more and with the help of imagination have compiled a considerable number. They are in every case instances of the inaccuracy of the critics.

(1) First, may be mentioned, as the only one ever having had any weight, *the fact that no historian mentions Belshazzar*. It was therefore assumed that "the learned and pious Jew", whom the critics imagined, had invented the name. Since 1854 this "inaccuracy" has disappeared from the rationalistic dictionaries and other productions. The excavations have answered that.

(2) Disappointed at the discovery of the truth, the critics now find fault with *the title "king" which Daniel gives to Belshazzar* and assert that *no tablets have been found dated in his reign*. It is not probable that any such tablets will be found, for his father outlived him and even though Belshazzar were co-king, his father's name would be in the dates. The tablets, however, show that Belshazzar was the commander of the troops, that he was the man of action— his father being a studious recluse—that he was the darling of the people and that the actual administration was in his hands. He was the heir to the throne and even if not formally invested, was the virtual king in the eyes of the people.

(3) It is objected next that *Belshazzar was not the son of Nebuchadnezzar as the queen mother says in Dan. 5:11*. If he were the grandson through his mother the same language would be used, and the undisturbed reign of Nabonidus in turbulent Babylon is accounted for in this way.

(4) The quibble that *the monuments do not say that*

Belshazzar was slain at the taking of Babylon is unworthy of the scholar who makes it. It is admitted that Belshazzar was a prominent figure before the city was captured, that "the son of the king died" and that he then "disappeared from history". He was heir to the kingdom. He was a soldier. His dynasty was overthrown. He disappeared from history. Common sense can make its inference.

(5) It is hard, however, for the impugners of Daniel to let the Belshazzar argument go. To have him appear prominently in the inscriptions, after criticism had decided that he never existed, is awkward. Accordingly, we have a long dissertation ("Sayce's Higher Crit. and Monuments," 497-531) showing that *the claim of Cyrus to have captured Babylon without fighting* is inconsistent with the accounts of the secular historians, which dwell upon the long siege, the desperate fighting, the turning of the river, the surprise at night, etc. Very well, the two accounts are inconsistent. But what has this to do with Daniel? His account is as follows:

"In that night was Belshazzar the Chaldean king slain, and Darius the Mede received the kingdom" (Dan. 5:31). Not a word about a siege, etc. An account entirely consistent with the inscription of Cyrus. And yet the critic has the audacity to say that "the monumental evidence has here pronounced against the historical accuracy of the Scripture narrative"! ("H. C. & M.", 531). This is not criticism; it is misrepresentation.

(6) *Daniel mentions the "Chaldeans" as a guild of wise men.* This has been made a ground of attack. "In the time of the exile", they tell us, "the Chaldeans were an imperial nation. Four centuries afterward the term signified a guild; therefore, Daniel was written four centuries afterward". It is strange that none of the critics consulted Herodotus, the historian nearest to Daniel in time. He visited Babylon in the same century with Daniel and uses the word in the same sense as Daniel and in no other. (Herod. 1:181, 185.)

(7) *The Book of Daniel spells Nebuchadnezzar with an "n" in the penultimate instead of an "r"*; therefore, the critics argue, it must have been written 370 years later. But Ezra spells it with an "n". So do 2 Kings, 1 & 2 Chronicles, and so does Jeremiah seven times out of sixteen. Jeremiah preceded Daniel and if either Kings or Chronicles was written in Babylon we have the same spelling in the same country and about the same time.

(8) As to *the Greek words in Daniel,* relied on by Driver to prove a late date: when we discover that these are the names of musical instruments and that the Babylonians knew the Greeks in commerce and in war and realize that musical instruments carry their native names with them, this argument vanishes like the rest.

(9) But, it is urged, *Daniel gives the beginning of the captivity* (1:1) *in the third year of Jehoiakim, 606 B. C., whereas Jerusalem was not destroyed till 587 B. C.,* therefore, etc.

Daniel dates the captivity from the time that he and the other youths were carried away. A glance at the history will suggest when that was. Pharaoh Necho came out of Egypt against Babylon in 609 B. C. He met and defeated Josiah at Megiddo. He then marched on northward. In three months he marched back to Egypt, having accomplished nothing against Babylon. The interval, 609 to 605 B. C., was the opportunity for Nebuchadnezzar. He secured as allies or as subjects the various tribes in Palestine, as appears from Berosus. Among the rest "Jehoiakim (2 Kings 24:1) became his servant three years". During that time he took as guests or as hostages the noble youths. At the end of the three years, in 605, Necho re-appeared on his way to fatal Carchemish. Jehoiakim renounced Nebuchadnezzar, and sided with Necho. A merciful Providence counted the seventy years captivity from the very first deportation and Daniel tells us when that was. The captivity ended in 536 B. C.

(10) *The Aramaic.* One critic said Aramaic was not spoken in Babylon. Others, not so self-confident, said the Aramaic in Babylon was different from Daniel's Aramaic. None of them knew what Aramaic was spoken in Babylon. There was Ezra's Aramaic. It was like Daniel's and Ezra was a native of Babylon. To save their argument they then post-dated Ezra too.

In 1906 and 1908, there were unearthed papyrus rolls in Aramaic written in the fifth century, B. C. It is impossible to suggest redactors and other imaginary persons in this case, and so the Aramaic argument goes the way of all the rest. Before these recent finds the Aramaic weapon had begun to lose its potency. The clay tablets, thousands of which have been found in Babylonia, are legal documents and are written in Babylonian. Upon the backs of some of them were Aramaic filing marks stating in brief the contents. These filings were for ready reference and evidently in the common language of the people, the same language which the frightened Chaldeans used when the angry monarch threatened them. (Dan. 2:4.)

There are some other alleged inaccuracies more frivolous than the above. Lack of space forbids their consideration here.

Two new objections to the genuineness of Daniel appear in a dictionary of the Bible, edited by three American clergymen. The article on Daniel states that "the BABA BATHRA* ascribes the writing not to Daniel but along with that of some other books to the men of the Great Synagogue".* THIS STATEMENT IS CORRECT IN WORDS, BUT BY CONCEALMENT CONVEYS A FALSE IMPRESSION. The trick lies in the phrase, "some other books". What are those other books? They are Ezekiel, Hosea, Amos—all the minor prophets—and Esther. The

---

*The passage is found in the Talmud Babylon, Tract Baba Bathra, fol. 15a., and reads, "The men of the Great Synagogue have written Ezekiel, the Twelve Minor Prophets, Daniel and Esther."—Editor.

statement itself is nonsensical, like many .other things in the Talmud, but whatever its meaning, it places Daniel on the same footing as Ezekiel and the rest.

The other objection is as follows: "Chapter 11 [of Daniel] with its four world-kingdoms is wonderfully cleared when viewed from this standpoint [i. e. as a Maccabean production]. The third of these kingdoms is explicitly named as the Persian. (11:2.) The fourth to follow is evidently the Greek".

Every phrase in this is false. The chapter says nothing about four world-kingdoms. Nor does 11:2 say explicitly, or any other way, that the Persian was the third; nor that the Greek was the fourth.

No explanation or modification of these astonishing statements is offered. How could the writer expect to escape detection? True, the Baba Bathra is inaccessible to most people, but Daniel 11 is in everybody's hands.

Daniel was a wise and well-known man in the time of Ezekiel, else all point in the irony of Ezek. 28:3 is lost. He was also eminent for goodness and must have been esteemed an especial recipient of God's favor and to have had intercourse with the Most High like Noah and Job. Ezek. 14:15, 20: "When the land sinneth, though Noah, Daniel and Job were in it, they shall deliver but their own souls". A striking collocation: Noah the second father of the race, Job the Gentile and Daniel the Jew.

Daniel is better attested than any other book of the Old Testament. Ezekiel mentions the man. Zechariah appears to have read the book. The bungling attempt of the Septuagint to alter a prediction of disaster to one of promise; our Saviour's recognition of Daniel as a prophet; these are attestations. Compare Ezekiel; there is not a word in the Bible to show that he ever existed, but as he does not plainly predict the Saviour no voice is raised or pen wagged against him.

CHAPTER XIV

THE DOCTRINAL VALUE
OF THE FIRST CHAPTERS OF GENESIS

BY THE REV. DYSON HAGUE, M. A.,
VICAR OF THE CHURCH OF THE EPIPHANY; PROFESSOR OF LIT-
URGICS, WYCLIFFE COLLEGE, TORONTO, ONTARIO, CANADA

The Book of Genesis is in many respects the most important book in the Bible. It is of the first importance because it answers, not exhaustively, but sufficiently, the fundamental questions of the human mind. It contains the first
authoritative information given to the race concerning these
questions of everlasting interest: the Being of God; the
origin of the universe; the creation of man; the origin of
the soul; the fact of revelation; the introduction of sin; the
promise of salvation; the primitive division of the human
race; the purpose of the elected people; the preliminary part
in the program of Christianity. In one word, in this inspired
volume of beginnings, we have the satisfactory explanation of
all the sin and misery and contradiction now in this world, and
the reason of the scheme of redemption.

Or, to put it in another way. The Book of Genesis is
the seed in which the plant of God's Word is enfolded. It
is the starting point of God's gradually-unfolded plan of
the ages. Genesis is the plinth of the pillar of the Divine
revelation. It is the root of the tree of the inspired Scriptures. It is the source of the stream of the holy writings
of the Bible. If the base of the pillar is removed, the pillar
falls. If the root of the tree is cut out, the tree will wither
and die. If the fountain head of the stream is cut off, the
stream will dry up. The Bible as a whole is like a chain
hanging upon two staples. The Book of Genesis is the one
staple; the Book of Revelation is the other. Take away

either staple, the chain falls in confusion. If the first chapters of Genesis are unreliable, the revelation of the beginning of the universe, the origin of the race, and the reason of its redemption are gone. If the last chapters of Revelation are displaced the consummation of all things is unknown. If you take away Genesis, you have lost the explanation of the first heaven, the first earth, the first Adam, and the fall. If you take away Revelation you have lost the completed truth of the new heaven, and the new earth, man redeemed, and the second Adam in Paradise regained.

Further: in the first chapters of the Book of Genesis, you have the strong and sufficient foundation of the subsequent developments of the kingdom of God; the root-germ of all Anthropology, Soteriology, Christology, Satanology, to say nothing of the ancient and modern problems of the mystery and culpability of sin, the Divine ordinance of the Lord's Day, the unity of the race, and God's establishment of matrimony and the family life.

We assume from the start the historicity of Genesis and its Mosaic authorship. It was evidently accepted by Christ the Infallible, our Lord and God, as historical, as one single composition, and as the work of Moses. It was accepted by Paul the inspired. It was accepted universally by the divinely inspired leaders of God's chosen people. (See Green's "Higher Criticism of the Pentateuch.") It has validated itself to the universal Church throughout the ages by its realism and consistency, and by what has been finely termed its subjective truthfulness. We postulate especially the historicity of the first chapters. These are not only valuable, they are vital. They are the essence of Genesis. The Book of Genesis is neither the work of a theorist or a tribal annalist. It is still less the product of some anonymous compiler or compilers in some unknowable era, of a series of myths, historic in form but unhistoric in fact. Its opening is an apocalypse, a direct revelation from the God of all truth. Whether it was given in a vision or otherwise, it would be impossible to say. But it is possible, if not probable, that the same Lord God, who revealed to His servant as he was in the Spirit on the Lord's Day the apocalypse of the humanly unknown and unknowable events of man's history which will transpire when this heaven and this earth have passed away, would also have revealed to His servant, being in the Spirit, the apocalypse of the humanly unknowable and unknown events which transpired before this earth's history began. It has been asserted that the beginning and the end of things are both absolutely hidden from science. Science has to do with phenomena. It is where science must confess its impotence that revelation steps in, and, with the authority of God, reveals those things that are above it. The beginning of Genesis, therefore, is a divinely inspired narrative of the events deemed necessary by God to establish the foundations for the Divine Law in the sphere of human life, and to set forth the relation between the omnipotent Creator and the man who fell, and the race that was to be redeemed by the incarnation of His Son.

The German rationalistic idea, which has passed over into thousands of more or less orthodox Christian minds, is that these earliest chapters embody ancient traditions of the Semitic-oriental mind. Others go farther, and not only deny them to be the product of the reverent and religious mind of the Hebrew, but assert they were simply oriental legends, not born from above and of God, but born in the East, and probably in pagan Babylonia.

We would therefore postulate the following propositions:

1. The Book of Genesis has no doctrinal value if it is not authoritative.

2. The Book of Genesis is not authoritative if it is not true. For if it is not history, it is not reliable; and if it is not revelation, it is not authoritative.

3. The Book of Genesis is not true if it is not from God. For if it is not from God, it is not inspired; and if it

is not inspired, it possesses to us no doctrinal value whatever.

4. The Book of Genesis is not direct from God if it is a heterogeneous compilation of mythological folklore by unknowable writers.

5. If the Book of Genesis is a legendary narrative, anonymous, indefinitely erroneous, and the persons it described the mere mythical personifications of tribal genius, it is of course not only non-authentic, because non-authenticated, but an insufficient basis for doctrine. The residuum of dubious truth, which might with varying degrees of consent be extracted therefrom, could never be accepted as a foundation for the superstructure of eternally trustworthy doctrine, for it is an axiom that that only is of doctrinal value which is God's Word. Mythical and legendary fiction, and still more, erroneous and misleading tradition, are incompatible not only with the character of the God of all truth, but with the truthfulness, trustworthiness, and absolute authority of the Word of God. We have not taken for our credentials cleverly invented myths. The primary documents, if there were such, were collated and revised and re-written by Moses by inspiration of God.

A sentence in Margoliouth's "Lines of Defence" deserves an attentive consideration today. We should have some opportunity, said the Oxford professor, of gauging the skill of those on whose faith the old-fashioned belief in the authenticity of Scripture has been abandoned. (p. 293.) One would perhaps prefer to put the idea in this way. Our modern Christians should have more opportunity not only of appraising the skill, but of gauging also the spiritual qualifications of a critical school that has been characterized notoriously by an enthusiasm against the miraculous, and a precipitate adoption of any conclusion from a rationalistic source which militates against the historicity of Genesis.

Christians are conceding too much nowadays to the agnostic scientist, and the rationalistic Hebraist, and are often to blame if they allow them to go out of their specific provinces without protest. Their assumptions ought to be watched with the utmost vigilance and jealousy. (See Gladstone, "The Impregnable Rock of Holy Scripture," pp. 62-83.)

But to resume. The Book of Genesis is the foundation on which the superstructure of the Scriptures rests. The foundation of the foundation is the first three chapters, which form in themselves a complete monograph of revelation. And of this final substructure the first three verses of the first chapter are the foundation.

In the first verse of Genesis in words of supernatural grandeur, we have a revelation of God as the first cause, the Creator of the universe, the world and man. The glorious Being of God comes forth without explanation, and without apology. It is a revelation of the one, personal, living, God. There is in the ancient philosophic cosmogony no trace of the idea of such a Being, still less of such a Creator, for all other systems began and ended with pantheistic, materialistic, or hylozoistic conceptions. The Divine Word stands unique in declaring the absolute idea of the living God, without attempt at demonstration. The spirituality, infinity, omnipotence, sanctity of the Divine Being, all in germ lie here. Nay more. The later and more fully revealed doctrine of the unity of God in the Trinity may be said to lie here in germ also, and the last and deepest revelation to be involved in first and foremost. The fact of God in the first of Genesis is not given as a deduction of reason or a philosophic generalization. It is a revelation. It is a revelation of that primary truth which is received by the universal human mind as a truth that needs no proof, and is incapable of it, but which being received, is verified to the intelligent mind by an irresistible force not only with ontological and cosmological, but with teleological and moral arguments. Here we have in this first verse of Genesis, not only a postulate apart from Revelation, but three great truths which have constituted the glory of our religion.

(1)   The Unity of God; in contradiction to all the polytheisms and dualisms of ancient and modern pagan philosophy.

(2)   The Personality of God; in contradiction to that pantheism whether materialistic or idealistic, which recognizes God's immanence in the world, but denies His transcendence. For in all its multitudinous developments, pantheism has this peculiarity, that it denies the personality of God, and excludes from the realm of life the need of a Mediator, a Sin-Bearer, and a personal Saviour.

(3)   The Omnipotence of God; in contradiction, not only to those debasing conceptions of the anthropomorphic deities of the ancient world, but to all those man-made idols which the millions of heathenism today adore.   God made these stars and suns, which man in his infatuation fain would worship. Thus in contradiction to all human conceptions and human evolutions, there stands forth no mere deistic abstraction, but the one, true, living and only God.   He is named by the name Elohim, the name of Divine Majesty, the Adorable One, our Creator and Governor; the same God who in a few verses later is revealed as Jehovah-Elohim, Jehovah being the Covenant name, the God of revelation and grace, the Ever-Existent Lord, the God and Father of us all.   (Green, "Unity of Genesis," pp. 31, 32; "Fausset's Bib. Ency.," p. 258.)

One of the theories of modernism is that the law of evolution can be traced through the Bible in the development of the idea of God. The development of the idea of God? Is there in the Scriptures any real trace of the development of the idea of God?   There is an expansive, and richer, and fuller revelation of the attributes and dealings and ways and workings of God; but not of the idea of God.   The God of Gen. 1:1 is the God of Psa. 90; of Isa. 40:28; of Heb. 1:1; and Rev. 4:11.

"In the beginning God created the heaven and the earth." Here in a sublime revelation is the doctrinal foundation of the creation of the universe, and the contradiction of the ancient and modern conceptions of the eternity of matter. God only is eternal.

One can well believe the story of a Japanese thinker who took up a strange book, and with wonderment read the first sentence: "In the beginning God created the heaven and the earth." It struck him that there was more philosophy of a theological character, and satisfying to the mind and soul, in that one sentence than in all the sacred books of the orient.

That single sentence separates the Scriptures from the rest of human productions. The wisest philosophy of the ancients, Platonic-Aristotelian or Gnostic, never reached the point that the world was created by God in the sense of absolute creation. In no cosmogony outside of the Bible is there a record of the idea that God created the heaven and the earth, as an effort of His will, and the fiat of His eternal, self-existent Personality. *Ex nihilo nihil fit.* The highest point reached by their philosophical speculations was a kind of atomic theory; of cosmic atoms and germs and eggs possessed of some inexplicable forces of development, out of which the present cosmos was through long ages evolved. Matter was almost universally believed to have existed from eternity. The Bible teaches that the universe was not *causa sui* or a mere passive evolution of His nature, nor a mere transition from one form of being to another, from non-being to being, but that it was a direct creation of the personal, living, working God, who created all things out of nothing, but the fiat of His will, and the instrumentality of the eternal Logos. In glorious contrast to agnostic science with its lamentable creed, "I believe that behind and above and around the phenomena of matter and force remains the unsolved mystery of the universe," the Christian holds forth his triumphant solution, "I believe that in the beginning God created the heaven and the earth." (John 1; 1-3; Heb. 1:1; Col. 1:16.) The first verse of the Bible is a proof that the Book is of God.

And so with regard to the subsequent verses. Genesis is admittedly not a scientific history. It is a narrative for mankind to show that this world was made by God for the habitation of man, and was gradually being fitted for God's children. So in a series of successive creative developments from the formless chaos, containing in embryonic condition all elemental constituents, chemical and mechanical, air, earth, fire, and water, the sublime process is recorded, according to the Genesis narrative in the following order:

1. The creation by direct Divine act of matter in its gaseous, aqueous, terrestrial and mineral condition successively. (Gen. 1:1-10; cf. Col. 1:16; Heb. 11:3.)

2. The emergence by Divine creative power of the lowest forms of sea and land life. (Gen. 1:11-13.)

3. The creation by direct Divine act of larger forms of life, aquatic and terrestrial; the great sea monsters and gigantic reptiles (the sheretjim and tanninim). (Dawson, "Origin of the World," p. 213; Gen. 1:20-21.)

4. The emergence by Divine creative power of land animals of higher organization, herbivora and smaller mammals and carnivora. (Gen. 1:24-25.)

5. And finally the creation by direct Divine act of man. (Gen. 1:26, 27.) Not first but last. The last for which the first was made, as Browning so finely puts it. Herein is the compatability of Genesis and science, for this sublime order is just the order that some of the foremost of the nineteenth and twentieth century scientists have proclaimed. It is remarkable, too, that the word for absolutely new creation is only used in connection with the introduction of life. (Gen. 1:1, 2, 27.) These three points where the idea of absolute creation is introduced are the three main points at which modern champions of evolution find it impossible to make their connection.

Next we have in this sublime revelation the doctrinal foundation for the beginning of mankind.

Man was created, not evolved. That is, he did not come from protoplasmic mud-mass, or sea ooze bathybian, or by descent from fish or frog, or horse, or ape; but at once, direct, full made, did man come forth from God. When you read what some writers, professedly religious, say about man and his bestial origin your shoulders unconsciously droop; your head hangs down; your heart feels sick. Your self-respect has received a blow. When you read Genesis, your shoulders straighten, your chest emerges. You feel proud to be that thing that is called man. Up goes your heart, and up goes your head. The Bible stands openly against the evolutionary development of man, and his gradual ascent through indefinite aeons from the animal. Not against the idea of the development of the plans of the Creator in nature, or a variation of species by means of environment and processes of time. That is seen in Genesis, and throughout the Bible, and in this world. But the Bible does stand plainly against that garish theory that all species, vegetable and animal, have originated through evolution from lower forms through long natural processes. The materialistic form of this theory to the Christian is most offensive. It practically substitutes an all-engendering protoplasmic call for the only and true God. But even the theistic-supernaturalistic theory is opposed to the Bible and to Science for these reasons.

1. There is no such universal law of development. On the contrary, scientific evidence is now standing for deterioration. The flora and the fauna of the latest period show no trace of improvement, and even man, proud man, from the biological and physiological standpoint has gained nothing to speak of from the dawn of history. The earliest archæological remains of Egypt, Assyria, Babylonia, show no trace of slow emergence from barbarism. That species can be artificially improved is true, but that is not transmutation of species. (Dawson, "Origin of the World," pp. 227-277.)

2. No new type has ever been discovered. Science is

universally proclaiming the truth of Gen. 1:11, 12, 21, 24, 25 "after his kind," "after their kind"; that is, species by species. Geology with its five hundred or so species of ganoids proclaims the fact of the non-transmutation of species. If, as they say, the strata tell the story of countless aeons, it is strange that during those countless aeons the trilobite never produced anything but a trilobite, nor has the ammonite ever produced anything but an ammonite. The elaborately artificial exceptions of modern science only confirm the rule. (See Townsend, "Collapse of Evolution.")

3. Nor is there any trace of transmutation of species. Man develops from a single cell, and the cell of a monkey is said to be indistinguishable from that of a man. But the fact that a man cell develops into a man and the monkey cell develops into a monkey, shows there is an immeasurable difference between them. And the development from a cell into a man has nothing whatever to do with the evolution of one species into another. "To science, species are practically unchangeable units" ("Origin of the World," p. 227). Man is the sole species of his genus, and the sole representative of his species. The abandonment of any original type is said to be soon followed by the complete extinction of the family.

4. Nor has the missing link been found. The late Robert Etheridge of the British Museum, head of the geological department, and one of the ablest of British paleontologists, has said: "In all that great museum there is not a particle of evidence of transmutation of species. Nine-tenths of the talk of evolutionists is not founded on observation, and is wholly unsupported by facts." And Professor Virchow is said to have declared with vehemence regarding evolution: "It's all nonsense. You are as far as ever you were from establishing any connection between man and the ape." A great gulf is fixed between the theory of evolution and the sublime statement of Gen. 1:26, 27. These verses give man his true place in the universe as the consummation of creation. Made out of the

dust of the ground, and created on the same day with the highest group of animals, man has physiological affinities with the animal creation. But he was made in the image of God, and therefore transcendently superior to any animal. "Man is a walker, the monkey is a climber," said the great French scientist, De Quatrefages, years ago. A man does a thousand things every day that a monkey could not do if he tried ten thousand years. Man has the designing, controlling, ordering, constructive, and governing faculties. Man has personality, understanding, will, conscience. Man is fitted for apprehending God, and for worshipping God. The Genesis account of man is the only possible basis of revelation. The revelation of fatherhood; of the beautiful, the true, the good; of purity, of peace; is unthinkable to a horse, a dog, or a monkey. The most civilized simian could have no affinity with such ideas. There is no possibility of his conceiving such conceptions, or of receiving them if revealed. It is, moreover, the only rational basis for the doctrine of regeneration in opposition to the idea of the evolution of the human character, and of the great doctrine of the incarnation. Man once made in the image of God, by the regenerating power of the Holy Ghost is born again and made in the image of God the Son.

Further, we have in this sublime revelation of Genesis the doctrinal foundation of—

1. The unity of the human race.
2. The fall of man.
3. The plan of redemption.

1. With regard to the first, Sir William Dawson has said that the Bible knows but one Adam. Adam was not a myth, or an ethnic name. He was a veritable man, made by God; not an evolutionary development from some hairy anthropoid in some imaginary continent of Lemuria. The Bible knows but one species of man, one primitive pair. This is confirmed by the Lord Jesus Christ in Matt. 19:4. It is re-affirmed

by Paul in Acts 17:26, whichever reading may be taken, and in Rom. 5:12; 1 Cor. 15:21, 47, 49. Nor is there any ground for supposing that the word Adam is used in a collective sense, and thus leave room for the hypotheses of the evolutionary development of a large number of human pairs. All things in both physiology and ethnology, as well as in the sciences, which bear on the subject, confirm the idea of the unity of the human race. (Saphir, p. 206.)

2. With regard to the fall of man. The foundation of all Hamartology and Anthropology lies in the first three chapters of Genesis. It teaches us that man was originally created for communion with God, and that whether his personality was dichotomistic or trichotomistic, he was entirely fitted for personal, intelligent fellowship with his Maker, and was united with Him in the bonds of love and knowledge. Every element of the Bible story recommends itself as a historic narrative. Placed in Eden by his God, with a work to do, and a trial-command, man was potentially perfect, but with the possibility of fall. Man fell, though it was God's will that man should rise from that human *posse non peccari* as a free agent into the Divine *non posse peccari*. (Augustine, "De Civitate Dei", Book 22, Chap. 30.) Man fell by disobedience, and through the power of a supernatural deceiver called that old serpent, the devil and Satan, who from Gen. 3 to Rev. 19 appears as the implacable enemy of the human race, and the head of that fallen angel-band which abandoned through the sin of pride their first principality.

This story is incomprehensible if only a myth. The great Dutch theologian, Van Oosterzee says, "The narrative presents itself plainly as history. Such an historico-fantastic clothing of a pure philosophic idea accords little with the genuine spirit of Jewish antiquity." (Dog. ii, p. 403.)

Still more incomprehensible is it, if it is merely an allegory which refers fruit, serpent, woman, tree, eating, etc., to entirely different things from those mentioned in the Bible. It is history. It is treated as such by our Lord Jesus Christ, who surely would not mistake a myth for history, and by St. Paul, who hardly built Rom. 5, and 1 Cor. 15, on cleverly composed fables. It is the only satisfactory explanation of the corruption of the race. From Adam's time death has reigned.

This story of the fall stands, moreover, as a barrier against all Manicheism, and against that Pelagianism which declares that man is not so bad after all, and derides the doctrine of original sin which in all our Church confessions distinctly declares the possession by every one from birth of this sinful nature. (See, e. g., Art. IX of "Anglican Church.") The penalty and horror of sin, the corruption of our human nature, and the hopelessness of our sinful estate are things definitely set forth in the Holy Scripture, and are St. Paul's divinely-inspired deductions from this fact of the incoming of sin and death through the disobedience and fall of Adam, the original head of the human race. The race is in a sinful condition. (Rom. 5:12.) Mankind is a solidarity. As the root of a tree lives in stem, branch, leaf and fruit; so in Adam, as Anselm says, a person made nature sinful, in his posterity nature made persons sinful. Or, as Pascal finely puts it, original sin is folly in the sight of man, but this folly is wiser than all the wisdom of man. For without it, who could have said what man is. His whole condition depends upon this imperceptible point. ("Thoughts," ch. xiii-11.) This Genesis story further is the foundation of the Scripture doctrine of all human responsiblity, and accountability to God. A lowered anthropology always means a lowered theology, for if man was not a direct creation of God, if he was a mere indirect development, through slow and painful process, of no one knows what, or how, or why, or when, or where, the main spring of moral accountability is gone. The fatalistic conception of man's personal and moral life is the deadly gift of naturalistic evolution to our age, said Prof. D. A. Curtis recently.

3. With regard to our redemption, the third chapter of Genesis is the basis of all Soteriology. If there was no fall, there was no condemnation, no separation and no need of reconciliation. If there was no need of reconciliation, there was no need of redemption; and if there was no need of redemption, the Incarnation was a superfluity, and the crucifixion folly. (Gal. 3:21.) So closely does the apostle link the fall of Adam and the death of Christ, that without Adam's fall the science of theology is evacuated of its most salient feature, the atonement. If the first Adam was not made a living soul and fell, there was no reason for the work of the Second Man, the Lord from heaven. The rejection of the Genesis story as a myth, tends to the rejection of the Gospel of salvation. One of the chief corner stones of the Christian doctrine is removed, if the historical reality of Adam and Eve is abandoned, for the fall will ever remain as the starting point of special revelation, of salvation by grace, and of the need of personal regeneration. In it lies the germ of the entire apostolic Gospel.

Finally, we have in Gen. 2 the doctrinal foundation of those great fundamentals, the necessity of labor, the Lord's Day of rest, the Divine ordinance of matrimony, and the home life of mankind. The weekly day of rest was provided for man by his God, and is planted in the very forefront of revelation as a Divine ordinance, and so also is marriage and the home. Our Lord Jesus Christ endorses the Mosaic story of the creation of Adam and Eve, refers to it as the explanation of the Divine will regarding divorce, and sanctions by His infallible *imprimatur* that most momentous of ethical questions, monogamy. Thus the great elements of life as God intended it, the three universal factors of happy, healthy, helpful life, law, labor, love, are laid down in the beginning of God's Book.

Three other remarkable features in the first chapters of Genesis deserve a brief reference.

The first is the assertion of the original unity of the language of the human race. (Gen. 11:1.) Max Muller, a foremost ethnologist and philologist, declares that all our languages, in spite of their diversities, must have originated in one common source. (See Saphir, "Divine Unity," p. 206; Dawson, "Origin of the World," p. 286; Guinness, "Divine Programme," p. 75.)

The second is that miracle of ethnological prophecy by Noah in Gen. 9:26, 27, in which we have foretold in a sublime epitome the three great divisions of the human race, and their ultimate historic destinies. The three great divisions, Hamitic, Shemitic, and Japhetic, are the three ethnic groups into which modern science has divided the human race. The facts of history have fulfilled what was foretold in Genesis four thousand years ago. The Hamitic nations, including the Chaldean, Babylonic, and Egyptian, have been degraded, profane, and sensual. The Shemitic have been the religious with the line of the coming Messiah. The Japhetic have been the enlarging, and the dominant races, including all the great world monarchies, both of the ancient and modern times, the Grecian, Roman, Gothic, Celtic, Teutonic, British and American, and by recent investigation and discovery, the races of India, China, and Japan. Thus Ham lost all empire centuries ago; Shem and his race acquired it ethically and spiritually through the Prophet, Priest and King, the Messiah; while Japheth, in world-embracing enlargement and imperial supremacy, has stood for industrial, commercial, and political dominion.

The third is the glorious promise given to Abraham, the man to whom the God of glory appeared and in whose seed, personal and incarnate, the whole world was to be blessed. Abraham's personality is the explanation of the monotheism of the three greatest religions in the world. He stands out in majestic proportion, as Max Muller says, as a figure, second only to One in the whole world's history. Apart from that promise the miraculous history of the Hebrew race is inexplicable. In him centers, and on him hangs, the central fact of the whole of the Old Testament, the promise of the Saviour and His glorious salvation. (Gen. 11:3; 22:18; Gal. 3:8-16.)

In an age, therefore, when the critics are waxing bold in claiming settledness for the assured results of their hypothetic eccentricities, Christians should wax bolder in contending earnestly for the assured results of the revelation in the opening chapters of Genesis.

The attempt of modernism to save the supernatural in the second part of the Bible by mythicalizing the supernatural in the first part, is as unwise as it is fatal. Instead of lowering the dominant of faith amidst the chorus of doubt, and admitting that a chapter is doubtful because some *doctrinaire* has questioned it, or a doctrine is less authentic because somebody has floated an unverifiable hypothesis, it would be better to take our stand with such men as Romanes, Lord Kelvin, Virchow, and Liebig, in their ideas of a Creative Power, and to side with Cuvier, the eminent French scientist, who said that Moses, while brought up in all the science of Egypt, was superior to his age, and has left us a cosmogony, the exactitude of which verifies itself every day in a reasonable manner; with Sir William Dawson, the eminent Canadian scientist, who declared that Scripture in all its details contradicts no received result of science, but anticipates many of its discoveries; with Professor Dana, the eminent American scientist, who said, after examining the first chapters of Genesis as a geologist, "I find it to be in perfect accord with known science"; or, best of all, with Him who said, "Had you believed Moses, you would have believed Me, for he wrote of Me. But if you believe not his writings, how shall you believe My words?" (John 5:45, 46.)

THREE PECULIARITIES OF THE PENTATEUCH WHICH ARE INCOMPATIBLE WITH THE GRAF-WELLHAUSEN THEORIES OF ITS COMPOSITION

BY ANDREW CRAIG ROBINSON, M. A.,
BALLINEEN, COUNTY CORK, IRELAND,
AUTHOR OF "WHAT ABOUT THE OLD TESTAMENT?"

There are—amongst others—three very remarkable peculiarities in the Pentateuch which seem to be incompatible with modern theories of its composition, and to call for some explanation from the critics.

The first of these peculiarities is:

THE ABSENCE OF THE NAME "JERUSALEM" FROM THE ENTATEUCH

The first occurrence of the name "Jerusalem" in the Bible is in the Book of Joshua (10:1): "Now it came to pass when Adonizedek, King of Jerusalem", etc. In the Pentateuch the city is only once named (Gen. 14) and then it is called "Salem" —an abbreviation of its cuneiform name "Uru-salem". Now on the traditional view of the Pentateuch the absence of the name Jerusalem presents no difficulty; the fact that Bethel, Hebron, and other shrines are named, whilst Jerusalem is not, would merely mean that at these other shrines the patriarchs had built their altars, whilst at Jerusalem they had not.

But from the point of view of modern critics who hold that the Pentateuch was in great part composed to glorify the priesthood at Jerusalem, and that the Book of Deuteronomy in particular was produced to establish Jerusalem as the central and only acceptable shrine for the worship of

Israel—this omission to name the great city, then of his-toric and sacred fame, which they wished to exalt and glorify, seems very strange indeed. According to the theories of the critics the composers of the Pentateuch had a very free hand to write whatsoever they wished, and they are held to have freely exercised it. It seems strange then to find the "Yahvist," supposed to have been written in the Southern Kingdom, and to have been imbued with all its prejudices, consecrating Bethel by a notable theophany (Gen. 28:16, 19), whilst in all that he is supposed to have written in the Pentateuch he never once even names his own Jerusalem. And so the "priestly writer" also, to whom a shrine like Bethel ought to be anathema, is found nevertheless conse-crating Bethel with another theophany: "Jacob called the name of the place where God spoke with him Bethel" (Gen. 35:14, 15), and he never even names Jerusalem.

What is the explanation of all this? What is the inner meaning of this absence of the name Jerusalem from the Pentateuch? Is it not this: that at the time the Pentateuch was written, Jerusalem, with all her sacred glories, *had not entered yet into the life of Israel.*

The second remarkable peculiarity to which attention is called is:

THE ABSENCE OF ANY MENTION OF SACRED SONG FROM THE
RITUAL OF THE PENTATEUCH

This is in glaring contrast to the ritual of the second temple, in which timbrels, harps, and Levite singers bore a conspicuous part. Yet it was just in the very time of the second temple that the critics allege that a great portion of the Pentateuch was composed. How is it then that none of these things occur in the Mosaic ritual? It might have been ex-pected that the priests in post-exilic times would have sought to establish the highest possible sanction for this musical ritual, by representing it as having been ordained by Moses.

But no such ordinance in point of fact occurs, and the Pentateuch stands in its primitive simplicity, destitute of any ordinance of music in connection with the ritual, except those passages in which the blowing of the trumpets is enjoined at the
Feast of Trumpets, the blowing of the trumpet throughout
the land in the year of Jubilee, and the command, contained
in a single passage (Num. 10:10), that in the day of gladness, and in the beginnings of the months, over the burnt
offerings and over the sacrifices of the peace offerings the
silver trumpets were to sound. No mention in connection
with the ritual of cymbals, harps, timbrels, or psalteries; no
mention of sacred song, or Levite singers. No music proper
entered into the ritual, only the crude and warlike blare of
trumpets. No ordinance of sacred song, no band of Levite
singers. The duties of the Levites, in the Book of Numbers,
are specially defined. The sons of Gershom were to bear
the tabernacle and its hangings on the march; the sons of
Kohath bore the altars and the sacred vessels; the sons of
Merari were to bear the boards and bands and pillars of the
sanctuary. No mention whatsoever of any ministry of sacred
song. A strange omission this would be, if the "Priestly
Code" (so-called) which thus defines the duties of the Levites,
had been composed in post-exilic times, when Levite singers—
sons of Asaph—cymbals, harp, and song of praise formed
leading features in the ritual. Does it not seem that the
Mosaic Code, enjoining no music but the simple sounding
of the trumpet-blast, *stands far behind* these niceties of music
and of song, *seeming to know nothing of them all?*

*The third remarkable peculiarity to which attention is
called is:*

THE ABSENCE OF THE DIVINE TITLE "LORD OF HOSTS" FROM THE PENTATEUCH

The first occurrence of this Divine title in the Bible is in
1 Sam. 1:3: "And this man went out of his city yearly to

worship and to sacrifice unto the Lord of hosts in Shiloh."
After this it occurs in a number of the remaining books of the
Bible, and with increasing frequency. The pre-Samuelitic
period of the history of Israel is thus differentiated from the
post-Samuelitic period by this circumstance, that in connection
with the former period this title is never used, whilst in connection with the latter it is used, and with growing frequency—at all stages of the history, even down to the end of
the Book of Malachi; occurring altogether 281 times.

Now the theory of the criticism of the present day is
that the Pentateuch was composed, edited, and manipulated,
during a period of more than four hundred years, by motley
groups and series of writers, of differing views, and various
tendencies. One writer composed one part, and one composed
another; these parts were united by a different hand; and then
another composed a further part; and this by yet another was
united to the two that went before; and after this another portion was composed by yet another scribe, and afterwards was
joined on to the three. Matter was absorbed, interpolated,
harmonized, smoothed over, colored, edited from various points
of view, and with different—not to say opposing—motives.
And yet when the completed product—the Pentateuch—coming
out of this curious literary seething pot is examined, it is found
to have this remarkable characteristic, that not one of the
manifold manipulators—neither "J", nor "E", nor "JE", nor
"D", nor "RD", nor "P", nor "P2", nor "P3", nor "P4", nor
any one of the "Redactors of P", who were innumerable—
would appear to have allowed himself to be betrayed even
by accident into using this title, "Lord of hosts", so much in
vogue in the days in which he is supposed to have written;
and the Pentateuch, devoid as it is of this expression, shows
an unmistakable mark that it could not possibly have been
composed in the way asserted by the criticism, because it
would have been a literary impossibility for such a number
of writers, extending over hundreds of years, to have one

and all, never even by accident, slipped into the use of this Divine title for Jehovah, "Lord of hosts", so much in vogue during those centuries.

In point of fact the Pentateuch *was written before the title was invented.*

These three peculiarities of the Pentateuch to which attention is here drawn, are points absolutely undeniable. No one can say that the name "Jerusalem" *does* occur in the Pentateuch; no one can say that any mention of sacred song *does* occur in the ritual of the Pentateuch; and no one can say that the Divine title "Lord of hosts" *does* occur in the Pentateuch.

CHAPTER XVI

THE TESTIMONY OF THE MONUMENTS TO THE TRUTH OF THE SCRIPTURES.

BY PROF. GEORGE FREDERICK WRIGHT, D. D., LL. D.,
OBERLIN COLLEGE.

All history is fragmentary. Each particular fact is the center of an infinite complex of circumstances. No man has intelligence enough to insert a supposititious fact into circumstances not belonging to it and make it exactly fit. This only infinite intelligence could do. A successful forgery, therefore, is impossible if only we have a sufficient number of the original circumstances with which to compare it. It is this principle which gives such importance to the cross-examination of witnesses. If the witness is truthful, the more he is questioned the more perfectly will his testimony be seen to accord with the framework of circumstances into which it is fitted. If false, the more will his falsehood become apparent.

Remarkable opportunities for cross-examining the Old Testament Scriptures have been afforded by the recent uncovering of long-buried monuments in Bible lands and by deciphering the inscriptions upon them. It is the object of this essay to give the results of a sufficient portion of this cross-examination to afford a reasonable test of the competence and honesty of the historians of the Old Testament, and of the faithfulness with which their record has been transmitted to us. But the prescribed limits will not permit the half to be told; while room is left for an entire essay on the discoveries of the last five years to be treated by another hand, specially competent for the task.

Passing by the monumental evidence which has removed objections to the historical statements of the New Testament, as less needing support, attention will be given first to one of the Old Testament narratives, which is nearest to us in time, and against which the harshest judgments of modern critics have been hurled. We refer to the statements in the Book of Daniel concerning the personality and fate of Belshazzar.

THE IDENTIFICATION OF BELSHAZZAR.

In the fifth chaper of Daniel Belshazzar is called the "son of Nebuchadnezzar," and is said to have been "king" of Babylon and to have been slain on the night in which the city was taken. But according to the other historians he was the son of Nabonidus, who was then king, and who is known to have been out of the city when it was captured, and to have lived some time afterwards.

Here, certainly, there is about as glaring an apparent discrepancy as could be imagined. Indeed, there would seem to be a flat contradiction between profane and sacred historians. But in 1854 Sir Henry Rawlinson found, while excavating in the ruins of Mugheir (identified as the site of the city of Ur, from which Abraham emigrated), inscriptions which stated that when Nabonidus was near the end of his reign he associated with him on the throne his eldest son, Bil-shar-uzzur, and allowed him the royal title, thus making it perfectly credible that Belshazzar should have been in Babylon, as he is said to have been in the Bible, and that he should have been called king, and that he should have perished in the city while Nabonidus survived outside. That he should have been called king while his father was still living is no more strange than that Jehoram should have been appointed by his father, Jehoshaphat, king of Judah, seven years before his father's death (see 2 Kings 1:17 and 8:16), or that Jotham should have been made king before his father, Uzziah, died of leprosy, though Uzziah is still called king in some of the references to him.

That Belshazzar should have been called son of Nebuchadnezzar is readily accounted for on the supposition that he was his grandson, and there are many things to indicate that Nabonidus married Nebuchadnezzar's daughter, while there is nothing known to the contrary. But if this theory is rejected, there is the natural supposition that in the loose use of terms of relationship common among Oriental people "son" might be applied to one who was simply a successor. In the inscriptions on the monuments of Shalmaneser II., referred to below, Jehu, the *extirpator* of the house of Omri, is called the "son of Omri."

The status of Belshazzar implied in this explanation is confirmed incidentally by the fact that Daniel is promised in verse 6 the "third" place in the kingdom, and in verse 29 is given that place, all of which implies that Belshazzar was second only.

Thus, what was formerly thought to be an insuperable objection to the historical accuracy of the Book of Daniel proves to be, in all reasonable probability, a mark of accuracy. The coincidences are all the more remarkable for being so evidently undesigned.

THE BLACK OBELISK OF SHALMANESER.

From various inscriptions in widely separated places we are now able to trace the movements of Shalmaneser II. through nearly all of his career. In B. C. 842 he crossed the Euphrates for the sixteenth time and carried his conquests to the shores of the Mediterranean. Being opposed by Hazael of Damascus, he overthrew the Syrian army, and pursued it to the royal city and shut it up there, while he devastated the territory surrounding. But while there is no mention of his fighting with the Tyrians, Sidonians, and Israelites, he is said to have received tribute from them and "from Jehu, the son of Omri." This inscription occurs on the celebrated Black Obelisk discovered many years ago by Sir Henry Rawlinson in the ruins of Nimroud. On it are represented strings of captives with evident Jewish features, in the act of bringing their tribute to the Assyrian king. Now, though there is no mention in the sacred records of any defeat of Jehu by the Assyrians, nor of the paying of tribute by him, it is most natural that tribute should have been paid under the circumstances; for in the period subsequent to the battle of Karkar, Damascus had turned against Israel, so that Israel's most likely method of getting even with Hazael would have been to make terms with his enemy, and pay tribute, as she is said to have done, to Shalmaneser.

THE MOABITE STONE.

One of the most important discoveries, giving reality to Old Testament history, is that of the Moabite Stone, discovered at Dibon, east of the Jordan, in 1868, which was set up by King Mesha (about 850 B. C.) to signalize his deliverance from the yoke of Omri, king of Israel. The inscription is valuable, among other things, for its witness to the civilized condition of the Moabites at that time and to the close similarity of their language to that of the Hebrews. From this inscription we learn that Omri, king of Israel, was compelled by the rebellion of Mesha to resubjugate Moab; and that after doing so, he and his son occupied the cities of Moab for a period of forty years, but that, after a series of battles, it was restored to Moab in the days of Mesha. Whereupon the cities and fortresses retaken were strengthened, and the country repopulated, while the methods of warfare were similar to those practiced by Israel. On comparing this with 2 Kings 3:4-27, we find a parallel account which dovetails in with this in a most remarkable manner, though naturally the biblical narrative treats lightly of the reconquest by Mesha, simply stating that, on account of the horror created by the idolatrous sacrifice of his eldest son upon the walls before them, the Israelites departed from the land and returned to their own country.

THE EXPEDITION OF SHISHAK.

In the fourteenth chapter of 1 Kings we have a brief account of an expedition of Shishak, king of Egypt, against Jerusalem in the fifth year of Rehoboam. To the humiliation of Judah, it is told that Shishak succeeded in taking away the treasures of the house of Jehovah and of the king's house, among them the shields of gold which Solomon had made; so that Rehoboam made shields of brass in their stead. To this simple, unadorned account there is given a wonderful air of reality as one gazes on the southern wall of the court of the temple of Amen at Karnak and beholds the great expanse of sculptures and hieroglyphics which are there inscribed to represent this campaign of Shishak. One hundred and fifty-six places are enumerated among those which were captured, the northernmost being Megiddo. Among the places are Gaza, Adullam, Beth-Horon, Aijalon, Gibeon, and Juda-Malech, in which Dr. Birch is probably correct in recognizing the sacred city of Jerusalem,—*Malech* being the word for royalty.

ISRAEL IN EGYPT.

The city of Tahpanhes, in Egypt, mentioned by Jeremiah as the place to which the refugees fled to escape from Nebuchadnezzar, was discovered in 1886 in the mound known as Tel Defenneh, in the northeastern portion of the delta, where Mr. Flinders Petrie found not only evidences of the destruction of the palace caused by Nebuchadnezzar, but apparently the very "brick work or pavement" spoken of in Jer. 43:8: "Then came the word of the Lord unto Jeremiah in Tahpanhes, saying, Take great stones in thine hand, and hide them in mortar in the brickwork, which is at the entry of Pharaoh's house in Tahpanhes, in the sight of the men of Judah," adding that

Nebuchadnezzar would "set his throne upon these stones," and "spread his royal pavilion over them."

A brick platform in partial ruins, corresponding to this description, was found by Mr. Petrie adjoining the fort "upon the northwest." In every respect the arrangement corresponded to that indicated in the Book of Jeremiah.

Farther to the north, not a great way from Tahpanhes, on the Tanitic branch of the Nile, at the modern village of San, excavations revealed the ancient Egyptian capital Tanis, which went under the earlier name of Zoan, where the Pharaoh of the oppression frequently made his headquarters. According to the Psalmist, it was in the field of "Zoan" that Moses and Aaron wrought their wonders before Pharaoh; and, according to the Book of Numbers, "Hebron" was built only seven years before Zoan. As Hebron was a place of importance before Abraham's time, it is a matter of much significance that Zoan appears to have been an ancient city which was a favorite dwelling-place of the Hyksos, or Shepherd Kings, who preceded the period of the Exodus, and were likely to be friendly to the Hebrews, thus giving greater credibility to the precise statements made in Numbers, and to the whole narrative of the reception of the patriarchs in Egypt.

The Pharaoh of the Oppression, "who knew not Joseph," is generally supposed to be Rameses II., the third king of the nineteenth dynasty, known among the Greeks as Sesostris, one of the greatest of the Egyptian monarchs. Among his most important expeditions was one directed against the tribes of Palestine and Syria, where, at the battle of Kadesh, east of the Lebanon Mountains, he encountered the Hittites. The encounter ended practically in a drawn battle, after which a treaty of peace was made. But the whole state of things revealed by this campaign and subsequent events shows that Palestine was in substantially the same condition of affairs which was found by the children of Israel when they occupied it shortly after, thus confirming the Scripture account.

This Rameses during his reign of sixty-seven years was among the greatest builders of the Egyptian monarchs. It is estimated that nearly half of the extant temples were built in his reign, among which are those at Karnak, Luxor, Abydos, Memphis, and Bubastis. The great Rameseum at Thebes is also his work, and his name is found carved on almost every monument in Egypt. His oppression of the children of Israel was but an incident in his remarkable career. While engaged in his Asiatic campaigns he naturally made his headquarters at Bubastis, in the land of Goshen, near where the old canal and the present railroad turn off from the delta toward the Bitter Lakes and the Gulf of Suez. Here the ruins of the temple referred to are of immense extent and include the fragments of innumerable statues and monuments which bear the impress of the great oppressor. At length, also, his mummy has been identified; so that now we have a photograph of it which illustrates in all its lineaments the strong features of his character.

THE STORE CITIES OF PITHOM AND RAMESES.

But most interesting of all, in 1883, there were uncovered, a short distance east of Bubastis, the remains of vast vaults, which had evidently served as receptacles for storing grain preparatory to supplying military and other expeditions setting out for Palestine and the far East. Unwittingly, the engineers of the railroad had named the station Rameses. But from the inscriptions that were found it is seen that its original name was Pithom, and its founder was none other than Rameses II., and it proves to be the very place where it is said in the Bible that the children of Israel "built for Pharaoh store-cities, Pithom and Raamses" (Ex. 1:11), when the Egyptians "made their lives bitter with hard bondage, in mortar and in brick." It was in connection with the building of these cities that the oppression of the children of Israel reached its climax, when they were compelled (after the straw with which the brick were held together failed) to gather for themselves stubble which should serve the purpose of straw, and finally, when even the stubble failed, to make brick without straw (Ex. 5).

Now, as these store pits at Pithom were uncovered by Mr. Petrie, they were found (unlike anything else in Egypt) to be built with *mortar*. Moreover, the lower layers were built of brick which contained straw, while the middle layers were made of brick in which stubble, instead of straw, had been used in their formation, and the upper layers were of brick made without straw. A more perfect circumstantial confirmation of the Bible account could not be imagined. Every point in the confirmation consists of unexpected discoveries. The use of mortar is elsewhere unknown in Ancient Egypt, as is the peculiar succession in the quality of the brick used in the construction of the walls.

Thus have all Egyptian explorations shown that the writer of the Pentateuch had such familiarity with the country, the civilization, and the history of Egypt as could have been obtained only by intimate, personal experience. The leaf which is here given is in its right place. It could not have been inserted except by a participant in the events, or by direct Divine revelation.

THE HITTITES.

In Joshua 1:4, the country between Lebanon and the Euphrates is called the land of the Hittites. In 2 Sam. 24:6, according to the reading of the Septuagint, the limit of Joab's conquests was that of "the Hittites of Kadesh," which is in Coele Syria, some distance north of the present Baalbeck. Solomon is also said to have imported horses from "the kings of the Hittites"; and when the Syrians were besieging Samaria, according to 2 Kings 7:6, they were alarmed from fear that the king of Israel had hired against them "the kings of the Hittites." These references imply the existence of a strong nation widely spread over the northern part of Syria and the regions beyond. At the same time frequent mention is made of Hittite families in Palestine itself. It was of a Hittite (Gen. 23:10) that Abraham bought his burying-place at Hebron. Bathsheba, the mother of Solomon, had been the wife of Uriah the Hittite, and Esau had two Hittite wives. Hittites are also mentioned as dwelling with the Jebusites and Amorites in the mountain region of Canaan.

Until the decipherment of the inscriptions on the monuments of Egypt and Assyria, the numerous references in the Bible to this mysterious people were unconfirmed by any other historical authorities, so that many regarded the biblical statements as mythical, and an indication of the general untrustworthiness of biblical history. A prominent English biblical critic declared not many years ago that an alliance between Egypt and the Hittites was as improbable as would be one at the present time between England and the Choctaws. But, alas for the over-confident critic, recent investigations have shown, not only that such an alliance was natural, but that it actually occurred.

From the monuments of Egypt we learn that Thothmes III. of the eighteenth dynasty, in 1470 B. C., marched to the banks of the Euphrates and received tribute from "the Greater Hittites" to the amount of 3,200 pounds of silver and a "great piece of crystal." Seven years later tribute was again sent from "the king of the Greater Hittite land." Later, Amenophis III. and IV. are said, in the Tel el-Amarna tablets, to have been constantly called upon to aid in repelling the attacks of the Hittite king, who came down from the north and intrigued with the disaffected Canaanitish tribes in Palestine; while in B. C. 1343, Rameses the Great attempted to capture the Hittite capital at Kadesh, but was unsuccessful, and came near losing his life in the attempt, extricating himself from an ambuscade only by most heroic deeds of valor. Four years later a treaty of peace was signed between the Hittites and the Egyptians, and a daughter of the Hittite king was given in marriage to Rameses.

The Assyrian monuments also bear abundant testimony to the prominence of the Hittites north and west of the Euphrates, of which the most prominent state was that with its capital at Carchemish, in the time of Tiglath-pileser I., about 1100 B. C. In 854 B. C. Shalmaneser II. included the kings of Israel, of Ammon, and of the Arabs, among the "Hittite" princes whom he had subdued, thus bearing most emphatic testimony to the prominence which they assumed in his estimation.

The cuneiform inscriptions of Armenia also speak of numerous wars with the Hittites, and describe "the land of the Hittites" as extending far westward from the banks of the Euphrates.

Hittite sculptures and inscriptions are now traced in abundance from Kadesh, in Coele Syria, westward to Lydia, in Asia Minor, and northward to the Black Sea beyond Marsovan. Indeed, the extensive ruins of Boghaz-Keui, seventy-five miles southwest of Marsovan, seem to mark the principal capital of the Hittites. Here partial excavations have already revealed sculptures of high artistic order, representing deities, warriors and amazons, together with many hieroglyphs which have not yet been translated. The inscriptions are written in both directions, from left to right, and then below back from right to left. Similar inscriptions are found in numerous other places. No clue to their meaning has yet been found, and even the class of languages to which they belong has not been discovered. But enough is known to show that the Hittites exerted considerable influence upon the later civilization which sprung up in Greece and on the western coasts of Asia Minor. It was through them that the emblem of the winged horse made its way into Europe. The mural crown carved upon the head of some of the goddesses at Boghaz-Keui also passed into Grecian sculpture; while the remarkable lions sculptured over the gate at Mycenae are thought to represent Hittite, rather than Babylonian art.

It is impossible to overestimate the value of this testimony in confirmation of the correctness of biblical history. It shows conclusively that the silence of profane historians regarding facts stated by the biblical writers is of small account, in face of direct statements made by the biblical historians. All the doubts entertained in former times concerning the accuracy of the numerous biblical statements concerning the Hittites is now seen to be due to our ignorance. It was pure ignorance, not superior knowledge, which led so many to discredit these representations. When shall we learn the inconclusiveness of negative testimony?

THE TEL EL-AMARNA TABLETS.

In 1887 some Arabs discovered a wonderful collection of tablets at Tel el-Amarna, an obscure settlement on the east bank of the Nile, about two hundred miles above Cairo and about as far below Thebes. These tablets were of clay, which had been written over with cuneiform inscriptions, such as are found in Babylonia, and then burnt, so as to be indestructible. When at length the inscriptions were deciphered, it appeared that they were a collection of official letters, which had been sent shortly before 1300 B. C. to the last kings of the eighteenth dynasty.

There were in all about three hundred letters, most of which were from officers of the Egyptian army scattered over Palestine to maintain the Egyptian rule which had been established by the preceding kings, most prominent of whom was Tahutimes III., who flourished about one hundred years earlier. But many of the letters were from the kings and princes of Babylonia. What surprised the world most, however, was that this correspondence was carried on, not in the hieroglyphic script of Egypt, but in the cuneiform script of Babylonia.

All this was partly explained when more became known about the character of the Egyptian king to whom the letters were addressed. His original title was Amenhotep IV., indicating that he was a priest of the sun god who is worshiped at Thebes. But in his anxiety to introduce a religious reform he changed his name to Aken-Aten,—Aten being the name of the deity worshiped at Heliopolis, near Cairo, where Joseph got his wife. The efforts of Aken-Aten to transform the religious worship of Egypt were prodigious. The more perfectly to accomplish it, he removed his capital from Thebes to Tel el-Amarna, and there collected literary men and artists and architects in great numbers and erected temples and palaces, which, after being buried in the sand with all their treasures for more than three thousand years, were discovered by some wandering Arabs twenty-two years ago.

A number of the longest and most interesting of the letters are those which passed between the courts of Egypt and those of Babylonia. It appears that not only did Aken-Aten marry a daughter of the Babylonian king, but his mother and grandmother were members of the royal family in Babylonia, and also that one of the daughters of the king of Egypt had been sent to Babylonia to become the wife of the king. All this comes out in the letters that passed back and forth relating to the dowry to be bestowed upon these daughters and relating to their health and welfare.

From these letters we learn that, although the king of Babylon had sent his sister to be the wife of the king of Egypt, that was not sufficient. The king of Egypt requested also the daughter of the king of Babylon. This led the king of Babylon to say that he did not know how his sister was treated; in fact, he did not know whether she was alive, for he could not tell whether or not to believe the evidence which came to him. In response, the king of Egypt wrote: "Why don't you send some one who knows your sister, and whom you can trust?" Whereupon the royal correspondents break off into discussions concerning the gifts which are to pass between the two in consideration of their friendship and intimate relations.

Syria and Palestine were at this time also, as at the present day, infested by robbers, and the messengers passing between these royal houses were occasionally waylaid. Where-upon the one who suffered loss would claim damages from the other if it was in his territory, because he had not properly protected the road. An interesting thing in connection with one of these robberies is that it took place at "Hannathon," one of the border towns mentioned in Josh. 19:14, but of which nothing else was ever known until it appeared in this unexpected manner.

Most of the Tel el-Amarna letters, however, consist of those which were addressed to the king of Egypt (Amenhotep IV.) by his officers who were attempting to hold the Egyptian fortresses in Syria and Palestine against various enemies who were pressing hard upon them. Among these were the Hittites, of whom we hear so much in later times, and who, coming down from the far north, were gradually extending their colonies into Palestine and usurping control over the northern part of the country.

About sixty of the letters are from an officer named Rib-addi, who is most profuse in his expressions of humility and loyalty, addressing the king as "his lord" and "sun," and calling himself the "footstool of the king's feet," and saying that he "prostrates himself seven times seven times at his feet." He complains, however, that he is not properly supported in his efforts to defend the provinces of the king, and is constantly wanting more soldiers, more cavalry, more money, more provisions, more everything. So frequent are his importunities that the king finally tells him that if he will write less and fight more he would be better pleased, and that there would be more hopes of his maintaining his power. But Rib-addi says that he is being betrayed by the "curs" that are surrounding him, who represent the other countries that pretend to be friendly to Egypt, but are not.

From this correspondence, and from letters from the south of Palestine, it is made plain that the Egyptian power was fast losing its hold of the country, thus preparing the way for the condition of things which prevailed a century or two later, when Joshua took possession of the promised land, and found no resistance except from a number of disorganized tribes then in possession.

In this varied correspondence a large number of places are mentioned with which we are familiar in Bible history, among them Damascus, Sidon, Lachish, Ashkelon, Gaza, Joppa, and Jerusalem. Indeed, several of the letters are written from Jerusalem by one Abd-hiba, who complains that some one is slandering him to the king, charging that he was in revolt against his lord. This, he says, the king ought to know is absurd, from the fact that "neither my father nor my mother appointed me to this place. The strong arm of the king inaugurated me in my father's territory. Why should I commit an offense against my lord, the king?" The argument being that, as his office is not hereditary, but one which is held by the king's favor and appointment, his loyalty should be above question.

A single one of these Jerusalem letters may suffice for an illustration:

"To My Lord the King:—Abd-hiba, your servant. At the feet of my lord the king, seven and seven times I fall. Behold the deed which Milki-il and Suardata have done against the land of my lord the king—they have hired the soldiers of Gazri, of Gimti and of Kilti, and have taken the territory of Rubuti. The territory of the king is lost to Habiri. And now, indeed, a city of the territory of Jerusalem, called Bit-Ninib, one of the cities of the king, has been lost to the people of Kilti. Let the king listen to Abd-hiba, his servant, and send troops that I may bring back the king's land to the king. For if there are no troops, the land of the king will be lost to the Habiri. This is the deed of Suardata and Milki-il * * * [defective], and let the king take care of his land."

The discovery of these Tel el-Amarna letters came like a flash of lightning upon the scholarly world. In this case the overturning of a few spadefuls of earth let in a flood of light upon the darkest portion of ancient history, and in every way confirmed the Bible story.

As an official letter-writer, Rib-addi has had few equals, and he wrote on material which the more it was burned the longer it lasted. Those who think that a history of Israel could not have been written in Moses' time, and that, if written, it could not have been preserved, are reasoning without due knowledge of the facts. Considering the habits of the time, it would have been well nigh a miracle if Moses and his band of associates coming out of Egypt had not left upon imperishable clay tablets a record of the striking events through which they passed.

ACCURACY OF GEOGRAPHICAL DETAILS.

Many persons doubtless wonder why it is that the Bible so abounds in "uninteresting" lists of names both of persons and places which seem to have no relation to modern times or current events. Such, however, will cease to wonder when they come to see the relation which these lists sustain to our confidence in the trustworthiness of the records containing them. They are like the water-marks in paper, which bear indelible evidence of the time and place of manufacture. If, furthermore, one should contemplate personal explorations in Egypt, Canaan, or Babylonia, he would find that for his purposes the most interesting and important portions of the Bible would be these very lists of the names of persons and places which seemed to encumber the historical books of the Old Testament.

One of the most striking peculiarities of the Bible is the "long look" toward the permanent wants of mankind which is everywhere manifested in its preparation; so that it circulates best in its entirety. No man knows enough to abridge the Bible without impairing its usefulness. The parts which the reviser would cut out as superfluous are sure, very soon, to be found to be "the more necessary." If we find that we have not any use for any portion of the Bible, the reason doubtless

is that we have not lived long enough, or have not had sufficiently wide experience to test its merits in all particulars.

Gezer was an important place in Joshua's time, but it afterward became a heap of ruins, and its location was unknown
until 1870, when M. Clermont-Ganneau discovered the site in
Tel Jezer, and, on excavating it, found three inscriptions, which
on interpretation read "Boundary of Gezer."

Among the places conquered by Joshua one of the most important and difficult to capture was Lachish (Josh. 10:31).
This has but recently been identified in Tel el-Hesy, about
eighteen miles northeast of Gaza. Extensive excavations, first
in 1890 by Dr. Flinders Petrie, and finally by Dr. Bliss, found
a succession of ruins, one below the other, the lower foundations of which extended back to about 1700 B. C., some time before the period of conquest, showing at that time a walled
city of great strength. In the debris somewhat higher than
this there was found a tablet with cuneiform inscriptions corresponding to the Tel el-Amarna tablets, which are known to
have been sent to Egypt from this region about 1400 B. C. At
a later period, in the time of Sennacherib, Lachish was as-
saulted and taken by the Assyrian army, and the account of
the siege forms one of the most conspicuous scenes on the
walls of Sennacherib's palace in Nineveh. These sculptures
are now in the British Museum.

Among the places mentioned in the Tel el-Amarna correspondence from which letters were sent to Egypt about 1400
B. C., are Gebal, Beirut, Tyre, Accho (Acre), Hazor, Joppha,
Ashkelon, Makkadah, Lachish, Gezer, Jerusalem; while mention is also made of Rabbah, Sarepta, Ashtaroth, Gaza, Gath,
Bethshemesh, all of which are familiar names, showing that the
Palestine of Joshua is the Palestine known to Egypt in the
preceding century. Two hundred years before this (about
1600 B. C.) also, Thothmes III. conquered Palestine, and gives
in an inscription the names of more than fifty towns which
can be confidently identified with those in the Book of Joshua.

Finally, the forty-two stations named in Num. 33 as camping places for the children of Israel on their way to Palestine, while they cannot all of them be identified, can be determined in sufficient numbers to show that it is not a fictitious list, nor a mere pilgrim's diary, since the scenes of greatest interest, like the region immediately about Mount Sinai, are specially adapted to the great transactions which are recorded as taking place. Besides, it is incredible that a writer of fiction should have encumbered his pages with such a barren catalogue of places. But as part of the great historical movement they are perfectly appropriate.

This conformity of newly discovered facts to the narrative of Sacred Scripture confirms our confidence in the main testimony; just as the consistency of a witness in a cross-examination upon minor and incidental points establishes confidence in his general testimony. The late Sir Walter Besant, in addition to his other literary and philanthropic labors, was for many years secretary of the Palestine Exploration Fund. In reply to the inquiry whether the work of the survey under his direction sustained the historical character of the Old Testament, he says: "To my mind, absolute truth in local details, a thing which cannot possibly be invented, when it is spread over a history covering many centuries, is proof almost absolute as to the truth of the things related." Such proof we have for every part of the Bible.

THE FOURTEENTH OF GENESIS.

The fourteenth chapter of Genesis relates that "In the days of Amraphel, king of Shinar, Arioch, king of Ellasar, Chedorlaomer, king of Elam, and Tidal, king of Goiim (nations), they made war with Bera, king of Sodom, and with Bersha, king of Gomorrah, and Shinab, king of Admah, and Shemeber, king of Zeboim, and the king of Bela (the same is Zoar)." The Babylonian kings were successful and the region about the Dead Sea was subject to them for twelve years, when a rebellion was instigated and in the following year Chedorlaomer and the kings that were with him appeared on the scene and, after capturing numerous surrounding cities, joined battle with the rebellious allies in the vale of Siddim, which was full of slime pits. The victory of Chedorlaomer was complete, and after capturing Lot and his goods in Sodom he started homeward by way of Damascus, near which place Abraham overtook him, and by a successful stratagem scattered his forces by night and recovered Lot and his goods. This story, told with so many details that its refutation would be easy if it were not true to the facts and if there were contemporary records with which to compare it, has been a special butt for the ridicule of the Higher Critics of the Wellhausen school, Professor Nöldeke confidently declaring as late as 1869 that criticism had forever disproved its claim to be historical. But here again the inscriptions on the monuments of Babylonia have come to the rescue of the sacred historian, if, indeed, he were in need of rescue. (For where general ignorance was so profound as it was respecting that period forty years ago, true modesty should have suggested caution in the expression of positive opinions in contradiction to such a detailed historical statement as this is.)

From the inscriptions already discovered and deciphered in the Valley of the Euphrates, it is now shown beyond reasonable doubt that the four kings mentioned in the Bible as joining in this expedition are not, as was freely said, "etymological inventions," but real historical persons. Amraphel is identified as the Hammurabi whose marvelous code of laws was so recently discovered by De Morgan at Susa. The "H" in the latter word simply expresses the rough breathing so well known in Hebrew. The "p" in the biblical name has taken the place of "b" by a well-recognized law of phonetic change. "Amrap" is equivalent to "Hamrab." The addition of "il" in the biblical name is probably the suffix of the divine name, like "el" in Israel.

Hammurabi is now known to have had his capital at Babylon at the time of Abraham. Until recently this chronolgy was disputed, so that the editors and contributors of the New Schaff-Herzog Cyclopedia dogmatically asserted that as Abraham lived nearly 300 years later than Hammurabi, the biblical story must be unhistorical. Hardly had these statements been printed, however, when Dr. King of the British Museum discovered indisputable evidence that two of the dynasties which formerly had been reckoned as consecutive were, in fact, contemporaneous, thus making it easy to bring Hammurabi's time down exactly to that of Abraham.

Chedorlaomer is pretty certainly identified as Kudur-Lagamar (servant of Lagamar, one of the principal Elamite gods). Kudur-Lagamar was king of Elam, and was either the father or the brother of Kudur-Mabug, whose son, Eri-Aku (Arioch), reigned over Larsa and Ur, and other cities of southern Babylonia. He speaks of Kudur-Mabug "as the father of the land of the Amorites," *i. e.*, of Palestine and Syria.

Tidal, "king of nations," was supposed by Dr. Pinches to be referred to on a late tablet in connection with Chedorlaomer and Arioch under the name Tudghula, who are said, together, to have "attacked and spoiled Babylon."

However much doubt there may be about the identification of some of these names, the main points are established, revealing a condition of things just such as is implied by the biblical narrative. Arioch styles himself king of Shumer and Accad, which embraced Babylon, where Amraphel (Hammurabi) was in his early years subject to him. This furnishes a reason for the association of Chedorlaomer and Amraphel in a campaign against the rebellious subjects in Palestine. Again, Kudur-Mabug, the father of Arioch, styles himself "Prince of the land of Amurru," *i. e.*, of Palestine and Syria. Moreover, for a long period before, kings from Babylonia had claimed possession of the whole eastern shore of the Mediterranean, including the Sinaitic Peninsula.

In light of these well-attested facts, one reads with astonishment the following words of Wellhausen, written no longer ago than 1889: "That four kings from the Persian Gulf should, 'in the time of Abraham,' have made an incursion into the Sinaitic Peninsula, that they should on this occasion have attacked five kinglets on the Dead Sea Littoral and have carried them off prisoners, and finally that Abraham should have set out in pursuit of the retreating victors, accompanied by 318 men servants, and have forced them to disgorge their prey,—all these incidents are sheer impossibilities which gain nothing in credibility from the fact that they are placed in a world which had passed away."

And we can have little respect for the logic of a later scholar (George Adam Smith), who can write the following: "We must admit that while archæology has richly illustrated the possibility of the main outlines of the Book of Genesis from Abraham to Joseph, it has not one whit of proof to offer for the personal existence or the characters of the patriarchs themselves. This is the whole change archæology has wrought; it has given us a background and an atmosphere for the stories of Genesis; it is unable to recall or certify their heroes."

But the name Abraham does appear in tablets of the age of Hammurabi. (See Professor George Barton in Journal of Biblical Literature, Vol. 28, 1909, page 153.) It is true that this evidently is not the Abraham of the Bible, but that of a small farmer who had rented land of a well-to-do land owner. The preservation of his name is due to the fact that the most of the tablets preserved contain contracts relating to the business of the times. There is little reason to expect that we should find a definite reference to the Abraham who in early life migrated from his native land. But it is of a good deal of significance that his name appears to have been a common one in the time and place of his nativity.

In considering the arguments in the case, it is important to keep in mind that where so few facts are known, and general ignorance is so great, negative evidence is of small account, while every scrap of positive evidence has great weight. The burden of proof in such cases falls upon those who dispute the positive evidence. For example, in the article above referred to, Professor Barton argues that it is not "quite certain" that Arioch (Eri-Agu) was a real Babylonian king. But he admits that our ignorance is such that we must admit its "possibility." Dr. Barton further argues that "we have as yet no evidence from the inscriptions that Arad-Sin, even if he were called Iri-Agu, ever had anything to do with Hammurabi." But, he adds, "Of course, it is possible that he may have had, as their reigns must have overlapped, but that remains to be proved."

All such reasoning (and there is any amount of it in the critics of the prevalent school) reveals a lamentable lack in their logical training. When we have a reputable document containing positive historical statements which are shown by circumstantial evidence to be possible, that is all we need to accept them as true. When, further, we find a great amount of circumstantial evidence positively showing that the statements conform to the conditions of time and place, so far as we know them, this adds immensely to the weight of the testimony. We never can fill in all the background of any historical fact. But if the statement of it fits into the background so far as we can fill it in, we should accept the fact until positive contrary evidence is produced. No supposition can be more extravagant than that which Professor Barton seems to accept (which is that of the German critic, Meyer) that a Jew, more than 1,000 years after the event, obtained in Babylon the amount of exact information concerning the conditions in Babylonia in Abraham's time, found in the fourteenth chapter of Genesis, and interpolated the story of Chedorlaomer's expedition into the background thus furnished. To entertain such a supposition discredits the prevalent critical scholarship, rather than the Sacred Scriptures.

But present space forbids further enumeration of particulars. It is sufficient to say that while many more positive confirmations of the seemingly improbable statements of the sacred historians can be adduced, there have been no discoveries which necessarily contravene their statements. The cases already here enumerated relate to such widely separated times and places, and furnish explanations so unexpected, yet natural, to difficulties that have been thought insuperable, that their testimony cannot be ignored or rejected. That this history should be confirmed in so many cases and in such a remarkable manner by monuments uncovered 3,000 years after their erection, can be nothing else than providential. Surely, God has seen to it that the failing faith of these later days should not be left to grope in darkness. When the faith of many was waning and many heralds of truth were tempted to speak with uncertain sound, the very stones have cried out with a voice that only the deaf could fail to hear. Both in the writing and in the preservation of the Bible we behold the handiwork of God.

CHAPTER XVII

THE RECENT TESTIMONY OF ARCHAEOLOGY TO THE SCRIPTURES.

BY M. G. KYLE, D. D., LL. D.,

EGYPTOLOGIST.

PROFESSOR OF BIBLICAL ARCHAEOLOGY, XENIA THEOLOGICAL SEMINARY.

CONSULTING EDITOR OF THE RECORDS OF THE PAST, WASHINGTON, D. C.

(The numbers in parentheses throughout this article refer to the notes at the end of the article.)

INTRODUCTION.

"Recent" is a dangerously capacious word to intrust to an archaeologist. Anything this side of the Day of Pentecost is "recent" in biblical archaeology. For this review, however, anything since 1904 is accepted to be, in a general way, the meaning of the word "recent."

"Recent testimony of archaeology" may be either the testimony of recent discoveries or recent testimony of former discoveries. A new interpretation, if it be established to be a true interpretation, is a discovery. For to uncover is not always to discover; indeed, the real value of a discovery is not its emergence, but its significance, and the discovery of its real significance is the real discovery.

The most important testimony to the Scriptures of this five-year archaeological period admits of some classification:

I. THE HISTORICAL SETTING OF THE PATRIARCHAL RECEPTION IN EGYPT.

The reception in Egypt accorded to Abraham and to Jacob and his sons[1] and the elevation of Joseph there[2] per-

315

emptorily demand either the acknowledgment of a mythical
element in the stories, or the belief in a suitable historical setting therefor.   Obscure, insignificant, private citizens are not
accorded such recognition at a foreign and unfriendly court.
While some have been conceding a mythical element in the
stories[3], archaeology has uncovered to view such appropriate
historical setting that the patriarchs are seen not to have
been obscure, insignificant, private citizens, nor Zoan a foreign
and unfriendly court.

The presence of the Semitic tongue in Hyksos' territory
has long been known[4]; from still earlier than patriarchal
times until much later, the Phoenicians, first cousins of the Hebrews, did the foreign business of the Egyptians[5], as the
English, the Germans, and the French do the foreign business
of the Chinese of today; and some familiarity, even sympathy, with Semitic religion has been strongly suspected from
the interview of the Hyksos kings with the patriarchs[6];
but the discovery in 1906[7], by Petrie, of the great fortified
camp at Tel-el-Yehudiyeh set at rest, in the main, the biblical
question of the relation between the patriarchs and the Hyksos.
The abundance of Hyksos scarabs and the almost total absence of all others mark the camp as certainly a Hyksos
camp[8]; the original character of the fortifications, before
the Hyksos learned the builders' craft from the Egyptians,
shows them to have depended upon the bow for defense[9];
and, finally, the name Hyksos, in the Egyptian Haq Shashu[10]
"Bedouin princes," brings out, sharp and clear, the harmonious
picture of which we have had glimpses for a long time, of the
Hyksos as wandering tribes of the desert, of "Upper and
Lower Ruthen"[11]; *i. e.,* Syria and Palestine, northern and
western Arabia, "Bow people"[12], as the Egyptians called
them, their traditional enemies as far back as pyramid
times[13].

Why, then, should not the patriarchs have had a royal reception in Egypt?   They were themselves also the heads of

wandering tribes of "Upper and Lower Ruthen," in the tongue of the Egyptians, Haq Shashu, "Bedouin princes"; and among princes, a prince is a prince, however small his principality. So Abraham, the Bedouin prince, was accorded princely consideration at the Bedouin court in Egypt; Joseph, the Bedouin slave, became again the Bedouin prince when the wisdom of God with him and his rank by birth became known. And Jacob and his other sons were welcome, with all their followers and their wealth, as a valuable acquisition to the court party, always harassed by the restive and rebellious native Egyptians. This does not prove racial identity between the Hyksos and the patriarchs, but very close tribal relationship. And thus every suspicion of a mythical element in the narrative of the reception accorded the patriarchs in Egypt disappears when archaeology has testified to the true historical setting.

II. THE HITTITE VINDICATION.

A second recent testimony of archaeology gives us the great Hittite vindication. The Hittites have been, in one respect, the Trojans of Bible history; indeed, the inhabitants of old Troy were scarcely more in need of a Schliemann to vindicate their claim to reality than the Hittites of a Winckler.

In 1904 one of the foremost archaeologists of Europe said to me: "I do not believe there ever were such people as the Hittites, and I do not believe 'Kheta' in the Egyptian inscriptions was meant for the name Hittites." We will allow that archaeologist to be nameless now. But the ruins of Troy vindicated the right of her people to a place in real history, and the ruins of Boghatz-Köi bid fair to afford a more striking vindication of the Bible representation of the Hittites.

Only the preliminary announcement of Winckler's great treasury of documents from Boghatz-Köi has yet been made[14]. The complete unfolding of a long-eclipsed great national history is still awaited impatiently. But enough has been published to redeem this people completely from their half-mythical plight, and give them a firm place in sober history greater than imagination had ever fancied for them under the stimulus of any hint contained in the Bible.

There has been brought to light a Hittite empire[15] in Asia Minor, with central power and vassal dependencies round about and with treaty rights on equal terms with the greatest nations of antiquity, thus making the Hittite power a third great power with Babylonia and Egypt, as was, indeed, foreshadowed in the great treaty of the Hittites with Rameses II., inscribed on the projecting wing of the south wall of the Temple of Amon at Karnak[16], though Rameses tried so hard to obscure the fact. The ruins at the village of Boghatz-Köi are shown also to mark the location of the Hittite capital[17], and the unknown language on the cuneiform tablets recovered there to be the Hittite tongue[18], while the cuneiform method of writing, as already upon the Amarna tablets[19], so still more clearly here, is seen to have been the diplomatic script, and in good measure the Babylonian to have been the diplomatic language of the Orient in that age[20]. And the large admixture of Babylonian words and forms in these Hittite inscriptions opens the way for the real decipherment of the Hittite language[21], and imagination can scarcely promise too much to our hopes for the light which such a decipherment will throw upon the historical and cultural background of the Bible.

Only one important point remains to be cleared up, the relation between the Hittite language of these cuneiform tablets and the language of the Hittite hieroglyphic inscription[22]. That these were identical is probable; that the hieroglyphic inscriptions represent an older form of the language, a kind of "Hieratic," is possible; that it was essentially different from the language of these tablets is improbable. There has been the Hittite vindication; the complete illumination of Hittite history is not likely to be long delayed.

III. THE PALESTINIAN CIVILIZATION.

Other recent testimony of archaeology brings before us the Palestinian civilization of the conquest period. Palestinian explorations within the last few years have yielded a startling array of "finds" illustrating things mentioned in the Bible, finds of the same things, finds of like things, and finds in harmony with things[23]. Individual mention of them all is here neither possible nor desirable. Of incomparably greater importance than these individually interesting relics of Canaanite antiquity is the answer afforded by recent research to two questions:

1. First in order, Does the Canaanite culture as revealed by the excavations accord with the story of Israel at the conquest as related in the Bible? How much of a break in culture is required by the Bible account, and how much is revealed by the excavations? For answer, we must find a standpoint somewhere between that of the dilettante traveler in the land of the microscopic scientist thousands of miles away. The careful excavator in the field occupies that sane and safe middle point of view. Petrie[24], Bliss[25], Macalister[26], Schumacker[27] and Sellin[28]—these are the men with whom to stand. And for light on the early civilization of Palestine, the great work of Macalister at Gezer stands easily first.

HISTORICAL VALUE OF POTTERY.

In determining this question of culture, too much importance has been allowed to that estimate of time and chronological order which is gained exclusively from the study of pottery. The pottery remains are not to be undervalued, and neither are they to be overvalued. Time is only one thing that shows itself in similarity or dissimilarity in pottery. Different stages of civilization at different places at the same time, and adaptation to an end either at the same time or at widely different times, show themselves in pottery, and render very uncertain any chronological deduction. And, still more,

available material may result in the production of similar pottery in two very different civilizations arising one thousand
years or more apart. This civilization of pots, as a deciding
criterion, is not quite adequate, and is safe as a criterion at
all only when carefully compared with the testimony of location, intertribal relations, governmental domination, and literary attainments.

These are the things, in addition to the pots, which help
to determine—indeed, which do determine—how much of a
break in culture is required by the Bible account of the Conquest, and how much is shown by excavations. Since the
Israelites occupied the cities and towns and vineyards and
olive orchards of the Canaanites, and their "houses full of all
good things"[29], had the same materials and in the main
the same purposes for pottery and would adopt methods of
cooking suited to the country, spoke the "language of Canaan"[30], and were of the same race as many of the people
of Canaan, intermarried, though against their law[31], with
the people of the land, and were continually chided for lapses
into the idolatry and superstitious practices of the Canaanites[32], and, in short, were greatly different from them only in
religion, it is evident that the only marked, immediate change
to be expected at the Conquest is a change in religion, and
that any other break in culture occasioned by the devastation
of war will be only a break in continuance of the same kind
of culture, evidence of demolition, spoliation, and reconstruction. Exactly such change in religion and interruption in culture at the Conquest period excavations show.

RELIGION AND CULTURE.

(a) The rubbish at Gezer shows history in distinct layers,
and the layers themselves are in distinct groups[33]. At the
bottom are layers Canaanite, not Semitic; above these, layers
Semitic, Amorite giving place to Jewish; and higher still, layers of Jewish culture of the monarchy and later times.

(b) The closing up of the great tunnel to the spring within the fortifications at Gezer is placed by the layers of history in the rubbish heaps at the period of the Conquest[34]. But when a great fortification is so ruined and the power it represents so destroyed that it loses sight of its water-supply, surely the culture of the time has had an interruption, though it be not much changed. Then this tunnel, as a great engineering feat, is remarkable testimony to the advanced state of civilization at the time of its construction; but the more remarkable the civilization it represents, the more terrible must have been the disturbance of the culture which caused it to be lost and forgotten[35].

(c) Again, there is apparent an enlargement of the populated area of the city of Gezer by encroaching upon the Temple area at the period of the Conquest[36], showing at once the crowding into the city of the Israelites without the destruction of the Canaanites, as stated in the Bible, and a corresponding decline in reverence for the sacred inclosure of the High Place. While, at a time corresponding to the early period of the Monarchy[37], there is a sudden decrease of the populated area corresponding to the destruction of the Canaanites in the city by the father of Solomon's Egyptian wife[38].

(d) Of startling significance, the hypothetical Musri Egypt in North Arabia, concerning which it has been said[39] the patriarchs descended thereto, the Israelites escaped therefrom, and a princess thereof Solomon married, has been finally and definitely discredited. For Gezer was a marriage dower of that princess whom Solomon married[40], a portion of her father's dominion, and so a part of the supposed Musri, if it ever existed, and if so, at Gezer, then, we should find some evidence of this people and their civilization. Of such there is not a trace. But, instead, we find from very early times, but especially at this time, Egyptian remains in great abundance[41].

(e) Indeed, even Egyptian refinement and luxuries were

not incongruous in the Palestine of the Conquest period. The great rock-hewn, and rock-built cisterns at Taannek[42], the remarkable engineering on the tunnel at Gezer[43], the great forty-foot city wall in an Egyptian picture of Canaanite war[44], the list of richest Canaanite booty given by Thothmes III.[45], the fine ceramic and bronze utensils and weapons recovered from nearly every Palestinian excavation[46], and the literary revelations of the Amarna tablets[47], together with the reign of law seen by a comparison of the scriptural account with the Code of Hammurabi, show[48] Canaanite civilization of that period to be fully equal to that of Egypt.

(f)	Then the Bible glimpses of Canaanite practices and the products of Canaanite religion now uncovered exactly agree. The mystery of the High Place of the Bible narrative, with its sacred caves, lies bare at Gezer and Taannek. The sacrifice of infants, probably first-born, and the foundation and other sacrifices of children, either infant or partly grown, appear in all their ghastliness in various places at Gezer and "practically all over the hill" at Taannek[49].

(g)	But the most remarkable testimony of archaeology of this period is to the Scripture representations of the spiritual monotheism of Israel in its conflict with the horrible idolatrous polytheism of the Canaanites, the final overthrow of the latter and the ultimate triumph of the former. The history of that conflict is as plainly written at Gezer in the gradual decline of the High Place and giving way of the revolting sacrifice of children to the bowl and lamp deposit as it is in the inspired account of Joshua, Judges and Samuel. And the line that marks off the territory of divine revelation in religion from the impinging heathenism round about is as distinct as that line off the coast of Newfoundland where the cold waters of the North beat against the warm life-giving flow of the Gulf Stream. The revelation of the spade in Palestine is making to stand out every day more clearly the revelation that God made. There is no evidence of a purer religion growing up out of that vile culture, but rather of a purer religion coming down and overwhelming it.

2. Another and still more important question concerning Palestine civilization is, What was the source and course of the dominant civilization and especially the religious culture reflected in the Bible account of the millennium preceding and the millennium succeeding the birth of Abraham? Was it from without toward Canaan or from Canaan outward? Did Palestine in her civilization and culture of those days, in much or in all, but reflect Babylonia, or was she a luminary?

PALESTINE AND BABYLONIA.

The revision of views concerning Palestinian civilization forced by recent excavations at once puts a bold interrogation point to the opinion long accepted by many of the source and course of religious influence during this formative period of patriarchal history, and the time of the working out of the principles of Israel's religion into the practices of Israel's life. If the Palestinian civilization during this period was equal to that of Egypt, and so certainly not inferior to that of Babylonia, then the opinion that the flow of religious influence was then from Babylonia to Palestine must stand for its defense. Here arises the newest problem of biblical archaeology.

And one of the most expert cuneiform scholars of the day, Albert T. Clay[50], has essayed this problem and announces a revolutionary solution of it by a new interpretation of well-known material as well as the interpretation of newly acquired material. The solution is nothing less, indeed, than that instead of the source of religious influence being Babylonia, and its early course from Babylonia into Palestine, exactly the reverse is true. "That the Semitic Babylonian religion is an importation from Syria and Palestine (Amurru), that the creation, deluge, ante-diluvian patriarchs, etc., of the Babylonian came from Amurru, instead of the Hebraic stories having come from Babylonia, as held by nearly all Semitic scholars."

This is startling and far reaching in its consequences. Clay's work must be put to the test; and so it will be, before it can be finally accepted. It has, however, this initial advantage, that it is in accord with the apparent self-consciousness of the Scripture writers and, as we have seen, exactly in the direction in which recent discoveries in Palestinian civilization point.

IV. PALESTINE AND EGYPT.

Again archaeology has of late furnished illumination of certain special questions of both Old and New Testament criticism.

1. "Light from Babylonia" by L. W. King[51] of the British Museum on the chronology of the first three dynasties helps to determine the date of Hammurabi, and so of Abraham's call and of the Exodus, and, indeed, has introduced a corrective element into the chronology of all subsequent history down to the time of David and exerts a far-reaching influence upon many critical questions in which the chronological element is vital.

SACRIFICE IN EGYPT.

2. The entire absence from the offerings of old Egyptian religion of any of the great Pentateuchal ideas of sacrifice, substitution, atonement, dedication, fellowship, and, indeed, of almost every essential idea of real sacrifice, as clearly established by recent very exhaustive examination of the offering scenes[52], makes for the element of revelation in the Mosaic system by delimiting the field of rationalistic speculation on the Egyptian side. Egypt gave nothing to that system, for she had nothing to give.

THE FUTURE LIFE IN THE PENTATEUCH.

3. Then the grossly materialistic character of the Egyptian conception of the other world and of the future life, and the fact, every day becoming clearer, that the so-called and

so-much-talked-about resurrection in the belief of the Egyptians was not a resurrection at all, but a resuscitation to the same old life on "oxen, geese, bread, wine, beer, and all good things," is furnishing a most complete solution of the problem of the obscurity of the idea of the resurrection in the Pentateuchal documents. For, whether they came from Moses when he had just come from Egypt or are by some later author attributed to Moses, when he had just come from Egypt, the problem is the same: Why is the idea of the resurrection so obscure in the Pentateuch? Now to have put forth in revelation the idea of the resurrection at that time, before the growth of spiritual ideas of God and of worship here, of the other world and the future life there, and before the people under the influence of these new ideas had outgrown their Egyptian training, would have carried over into Israel's religious thinking all the low, degrading materialism of Egyptian belief on this subject. The Mosaic system made no use of Egyptian belief concerning the future life because it was not by it usable, and it kept away from open presentation of the subject altogether, because that was the only way to get the people away from Egypt's conception of the subject.

WELLHAUSEN'S MISTAKE.

4. The discovery of the Aramaic papyri at Syene[53] made possible a new chapter in Old Testament criticism, raised to a high pitch hopes for contemporary testimony on Old Testament history which hitherto hardly dared raise their heads, and contributed positive evidence on a number of important points. Tolerable, though not perfect, identifications are made out for Bagoas, Governor of the Jews; of Josephus and Diodorus; Sanballat, of Nehemiah and Josephus; and Jochanan, of Nehemiah and Josephus. But more important than all these identifications is the information that the Jews had, at that period, built a temple and offered sacrifice far from Jerusalem. Wellhausen[54] lays down the first stone

of the foundation of his Pentateuchal criticism in these words: "The returning exiles were thoroughly imbued with the ideas of Josiah's reformation and had no thought of worshiping except in Jerusalem. It cost them no sacrifice of their feelings to leave the ruined High Places unbuilt. From this date, all Jews understood, as a matter of course, that the one God had only one sanctuary." So much Wellhausen. But here is this petition of the Jews at Syene in the year 407 B. C. after Nehemiah's return declaring that they had built a temple there and established a system of worship and of sacrifices, and evidencing also that they expected the approval of the Jews at Jerusalem in rebuilding that temple and re-establishing that sacrificial worship, and, what is more, received from the governor of the Jews permission so to do, a thing which, had it been opposed by the Jews at Jerusalem was utterly inconsistent with the Jewish policy of the Persian Empire in the days of Nehemiah.

NEW TESTAMENT GREEK.

5. Then the redating of the Hermetic writings[55] whereby they are thrown back from the Christian era to 500-300 B. C. opens up a completely new source of critical material for tracing the rise and progress of theological terms in the Alexandrian Greek of the New Testament. In a recent letter from Petrie, who has written a little book on the subject, he sums up the whole case, as he sees it, in these words: "My position simply is that the current religious phrases and ideas of the B. C. age must be grasped in order to understand the usages of religious language in which the New Testament is written. And we can never know the real motive of New Testament writings until we know how much is new thought and how much is current theology in terms of which the *Eu-angelos* is expressed." Whether or not all the new dates for the writings shall be permitted to stand, and Petrie's point of view be justified, a discussion of the dates and a criti-

cal examination of the Hermetic writings from the standpoint of their corrected dates alone can determine; but it is certain that the products of the examination cannot but be far-reaching in their influence and in the illumination of the teachings of Christ and the Apostles.

V. IDENTIFICATIONS.

Last and more generally, of recent testimony from archaeology to Scripture we must consider the identification of places, peoples, and events of the Bible narrative.

For many years archaeologists looked up helplessly at the pinholes in the pediment of the Parthenon, vainly speculating about what might have been the important announcement in bronze once fastened at those pinholes. At last an ingenious young American student carefully copied the pinholes, and from a study of the collocation divined at last the whole imperial Roman decree once fastened there. So, isolated identification of peoples, places, and events in the Bible may not mean so much; however startling their character, they may be, after all, only pinholes in the mosaic of Bible history, but the collocation of these identifications, when many of them have been found, indicates at last the whole pattern of the mosaic.

Now the progress of important identifications has of late been very rapid. It will suffice only to mention those which we have already studied for their intrinsic importance together with the long list of others within recent years. In 1874, Clermont-Ganneau discovered one of the boundary stones of Gezer[56], at which place now for six years Mr. R. A. Stewart Macalister has been uncovering the treasures of history of that Levitical city[57]; in 1906, Winckler discovered the Hittites at their capital city; in 1904-5, Schumacker explored Megiddo; in 1900-02, Sellin, Taannek; Jericho has now been accurately located by Sellin and the foundations of her walls laid bare; the Edomites, long denied existence in patriarchal times, have been given historical place in the time of Meremptah by the papyrus Anastasia[58]; Moab, for some time past in dispute, I identified beyond further controversy at Luxor in 1908, in an inscription of Rameses II., before the time of the Exodus[59]; while Hilprecht at Nippur[60], Glaser in Arabia[61], Petrie at Maghereh and along the route of the Exodus[62], and Reisner at Samaria have been adding a multitude of geographical, ethnographical and historical identifications.

The completion of the whole list of identifications is rapidly approaching, and the collocation of these identifications has given us anew, from entirely independent testimony of archaeology, the whole outline of the biblical narrative and its surroundings, at once the necessary material for the historical imagination and the surest foundation of apologetics. Fancy for a moment that the peoples, places and events of the wanderings of Ulysses should be identified: all the strange route of travel followed; the remarkable lands visited and described, the curious creatures, half human and half monstrous, and even unmistakable traces of strange events, found, all just as the poet imagined, what a transformation in our views of Homer's great epic must take place! Henceforth that romance would be history. Let us reverse the process and fancy that the peoples, places, and events of the Bible story were as little known from independent sources as the wanderings of Ulysses; the intellectual temper of this age would unhesitatingly put the Bible story in the same mythical category in which have always been the romances of Homer. If it were possible to blot out biblical geography, biblical ethnology, and biblical history from the realm of exact knowledge, so would we put out the eyes of faith, henceforth our religion would be blind, stone blind.

Thus the value of the rapid progress of identifications appears. It is the identifications which differentiate history from myth, geography from the "land of nowhere," the record of events from tales of "never was," Scripture from folklore, and the Gospel of the Saviour of the world from the delusions of hope. Every identification limits by so much the field of historical criticism. When the progress of identification shall reach completion, the work of historical criticism will be finished.

CONCLUSION.

The present status of the testimony from archaeology to Scripture, as these latest discoveries make it to be, may be pointed out in a few words.

NOT EVOLUTION.

1. The history of civilization as everywhere illuminated is found to be only partially that of the evolutionary theory of early Israelite history, but very exactly that of the biblical narrative; that is to say, this history, like all history sacred or profane, shows at times, for even a century or two, steady progress, but the regular, orderly progress from the most primitive state of society toward the highest degree of civilization, which the evolutionary theory imperatively demands, if it fulfill its intended mission, fails utterly. The best ancient work at Taannek is the earliest. From the cave dwellers to the city builders at Gezer is no long, gentle evolution; the early Amorite civilization leaps with rapid strides to the great engineering feats on the defenses and the water-works. Wherever it has been possible to institute comparison between Palestine and Egypt, the Canaanite civilization in handicraft, art, engineering, architecture, and education has been found to suffer only by that which climate, materials and location impose; in genius and in practical execution it is equal to that of Egypt, and only eclipsed, before Graeco-Roman times, by the brief glory of the Solomonic period.

HARMONY WITH SCRIPTURE.

2. When we come to look more narrowly at the details of archaeological testimony, the historical setting thus afforded for the events of the Bible narrative is seen to be exactly in

harmony with the narrative. This is very significant of the
final outcome of research in early Bible history. Because
views of Scripture must finally square with the results of
archaeology; that is to say, with contemporaneous history, and
the archaeological testimony of these past five years well indicates the present trend toward the final conclusion. The
Bible narrative plainly interpreted at its face value is everywhere being sustained, while, of the great critical theories pro-
posing to take Scripture recording events of that age at other
than the face value, as the illiteracy of early Western Semitic
people, the rude nomadic barbarity of Palestine and the Desert
in the patriarchal age, the patriarchs not individuals but personifications, the Desert "Egypt," the gradual invasion of Palestine, the naturalistic origin of Israel's religion, the incon-
sequence of Moses as a law-giver, the late authorship of the
Pentateuch, and a dozen others, not a single one is being definitely supported by the results of archaeological research. Indeed, reconstructing criticism hardly finds it worth while, for
the most part, to look to archaeology for support.

The recent testimony of archaeology to Scripture, like all
such testimony that has gone before, is definitely and uniformly favorable to the Scriptures at their face value, and not to the
Scriptures as reconstructed by criticism.

AUTHORITIES REFERRED TO ABOVE.

ABBREVIATIONS USED IN REFERENCES.

O. L. Z.=Orientalistischen Litteratur-Zeitung.

Q. S.=Quarterly Statement of the Palestine Exploration Society.

REFERENCES.

(1)   Gen. 12:10-20; 13:1; 47:1-12.
(2)   Gen. 41:14-46.
(3)   Orr, "The Problem of the Old Testament," pp. 57-58,
      quoting Schultz, Wellhausen, Kuenen, W. R. Smith,
      G. B. Gray, H. P. Smith, F. H. Woods.

(4)   Brugsch, "Egypt under the Pharaohs," Broderick edition, Chap. VI.
(5)   Ibid.
(6)   Gen. 41:25-39.
(7)   Petrie, "Hyksos and Israelite Cities."
(8)   Ibid, pp. 3 and 10, Plate IX.
(9)   Ibid, pp. 5-9.   Plates II, III, IV.
(10) Budge, "History of Egypt," Vol. III, pp. 137-138.
(11) Kyle, Recueil de Travaux, Vol. XXX, "Geographic and Ethnic Lists of Rameses II."
(12) Müller, "Asien und Europa."   2tes Kapitel.
(13) Ibid.
(14) Winckler, O. L. Z., December 15, 1906.
(15) Ibid.
(16) Bouriant, Recueil de Travaux, Vol. XIII, pp. 15 ff.; Budge, "History of Egypt," Vol. V, pp. 48 ff.; Goodwin, "Records of the Past," 1st Series, Vol. IV, pp. 25 ff.
(17) Mitteilungen der Vorderasiatischen Gesselschaft: 1902, p. 5.   Müller, Recueil de Travaux, Vol. VIII, 126 ff. Budge, "History of Egypt," V, 30 ff.
(18) Winckler, O. L. Z., December 15, 1906.   (Sonderabzug, p. 15.)
(19) Ibid.   (Sonderabzug, p. 22.)
(20) Conder.   "Tel Amarna Tablets."   Budge, "History of Egypt," Vol. IV, pp. 184-241.
(21) Winckler, O. L. Z., December 15, 1906.   Sonderabzug.
(22) Messersmidt, Mitteilungen der Vorderasiatischen Gesselchaft; Corpus, Unscrip. Het.—1902.
(23) Vincent, "Canaan."
(24) Petrie, "Lachish."
(25) Bliss, "A Mound of Many Cities."
(26) Macalister, "Bible Side Lights from the Mound of Gezer."
(27) Schumacker, "Excavations at Megiddo."

(28) Sellin, Tel-Taannek, "Denkschriften der Kaiserlichen Akademie in Wien."

(29) Deut. 6:10-11; Josh. 24:13; Neh. 9:25.

(30) Isa. 19:18.

(31) Ezek. 16:44-46; Deut. 7:3.

(32) Judges 2:11-15; 3:7; 8:33-35; 18:30-31.

(33) Macalister, Q. S., 1903, pp. 8-9, 49.

(34) Macalister, Q. S., 1908, p. 17.

(35) Vincent, in Q. S., 1908, p. 228.

(36) Macalister, Q. S., 1903, p. 49.

(37) Ibid.

(38) I. Kings 9:16.

(39) Winckler, Orientalistische Forschungen, Series I, pp. 24-41.

(40) I. Kings 9:16.

(41) Macalister, Q. S., 1903, p. 309.

(42) Sellin, "Tel-Taannek," p. 92.

(43) Macalister, Q. S., 1908, Jan.-Apr.

(44) Petrie, "Deshasha," Plate IV.

(45) Birch, "Records of the Past," 1st Series, Vol. II, pp. 35-52, "Battle of Megiddo." Also Lepsius, "Denk-mäler." Abth. III. Bl. 32, 31st, 30th, 30B, "Auswahl," XII, L. 42-45.

(46) Macalister-Vincent, Q. S., 1898-08.

(47) Budge, "History of Egypt," Vol. IV, pp. 184-241.

(48) Gen. 21-38. King, "Code of Hammurabi."

(49) Macalister, Q. S., 1903, ff., and "Bible Side Lights," Chap. III. Also Sellin, "Tel-Taannek," pp. 96-97.

(50) Clay, "Amurru, The Home of the Northern Semites."

(51) King, "Chronology of the First Three Babylonian Dynasties."

(52) Kyle, Recueil de Travaux. "Egyptian Sacrifices." Vol. XXVII, "Further Observations," Vol. XXXI. Bibliotheca Sacra, Apr., 1905, pp. 323-336.

(53) Margoliouth, "Expository Times," December, 1907. Jo-

sephus, "Antiquities," 11:7; Deadorus Siculus: Sec. 3; 17-35. Neh. 13:28; 12:22; 2 Esdras 5:14.

(54) Wellhausen, Ency. Brit., Vol. 18, p. 509.
(55) Petrie, "Personal Religion in Egypt Before Christianity."
(56) Clermont-Ganneau in "Bible Side Lights," p. 22.
(57) Macalister, "Bible Side Lights." Also Q. S., 1902-09.
(58) Müller, "Asien und Europa."
(59) Kyle, Recueil de Travaux, Vol. XXX. "Ethnic and Geographical Lists of Rameses II."
(60) Hilprecht, "Explorations in Babylonia."
(61) Weber, Forschungsreisen—Edouard Glaser; also "Studien zur Südarabischen Altertumskunde," Weber.
(62) Petrie, "Researches in Sinai."

CHAPTER XVIII

SCIENCE AND CHRISTIAN FAITH

BY REV. PROF. JAMES ORR, D. D.,

UNITED FREE CHURCH COLLEGE, GLASGOW, SCOTLAND

In many quarters the belief is industriously circulated that the advance of "science," meaning by this chiefly the physical sciences — astronomy, geology, biology, and the like — has proved damaging, if not destructive, to the claims of the Bible, and the truth of Christianity. Science and Christianity are pitted against each other. Their interests are held to be antagonistic. Books are written, like Draper's "Conflict Between Religion and Science," White's "Warfare of Science with Theology in Christendom," and Foster's "Finality of the Christian Religion," to show that this warfare between science and religion has ever been going on, and can never in the nature of things cease till theology is destroyed, and science holds sole sway in men's minds.

This was not the attitude of the older investigators of science. Most of these were devout Christian men. Naville, in his book, "Modern Physics," has shown that the great discoverers in science in past times were nearly always devout men. This was true of Galileo, Kepler, Bacon, and Newton; it was true of men like Faraday, Brewster, Kelvin, and a host of others in more recent times. The late Professor Tait, of Edinburgh, writing in "The International Review," said: "The assumed incompatibility of religion and science has been so often and confidently asserted in recent times that it has come * * * to be taken for granted by the writers of leading articles, etc., and it is, of course, perpetually thrust before their too trusting readers. But the whole thing is a mistake, and a mistake so grave that no truly scientific man * * * runs, in Britain, at least, the smallest risk of making it. * * * With a few, and these very singular exceptions, the truly scientific men and true theologians of the present day have not found themselves under the necessity of quarrelling." The late Professor G. J. Romanes has, in his "Thoughts on Religion," left the testimony that one thing which largely influenced him in his return to faith was the fact that in his own university of Cambridge nearly all the men of most eminent scientific attainments were avowed Christians. "The curious thing," he says, "is that all the most illustrious names were ranged on the side of orthodoxy. Sir W. Manson, Sir George Stokes, Professors Tait, Adams, Clerk Maxwell, and Bayley—not to mention a number of lesser lights, such as Routte, Todhunter, Ferrers, etc.,—were all avowed Christians" (page 137). It may be held that things are now changed. To some extent this is perhaps true, but anyone who knows the opinions of our leading scientific men is aware that to accuse the majority of being men of unchristian or unbelieving sentiment is to utter a gross libel.

If by a conflict of science and religion is meant that grievous mistakes have often been made, and unhappy misunderstandings have arisen, on one side and the other, in the course of the progress of science,—that new theories and discoveries, as in astronomy and geology, have been looked on with distrust by those who thought that the truth of the Bible was being affected by them,—that in some cases the dominant church sought to stifle the advance of truth by persecution,—this is not to be denied. It is an unhappy illustration of how the best of men can at times err in matters which they imperfectly understand, or where their prejudices and traditional ideas are affected. But it proves nothing against the value of the discoveries themselves, or the deeper insight into the ways of God of the men who made them, or of real contradiction between the new truth and the essential teaching of the Scriptures. On the contrary, as a minority generally perceived from the first, the supposed disharmony with the truths of the Bible was an unreal one, early giving way to better understanding on both sides, and finally opening up new vistas in the contemplation of the Creator's power, wisdom, and majesty. It is never to be forgotten, also, that the error was seldom all on one side; that science, too, has in numberless cases put forth its hasty and unwarrantable theories and has often had to retract even its truer speculations within limits which brought them into more perfect harmony with revealed truth. If theology has resisted novelties of science, it has often had good reason for so doing.

It is well in any case that this alleged conflict of Christianity with science should be carefully probed, and that it should be seen where exactly the truth lies in regard to it.

I. SCIENCE AND LAW—MIRACLE

It is perhaps more in its *general outlook* on the world than in its specific results that science is alleged to be in conflict with the Bible and Christianity. The Bible is a record of revelation. Christianity is a supernatural system. Miracle, in the sense of a direct entrance of God in word and deed into human history for gracious ends, is of the essence of it. On the other hand, the advance of science has done much to deepen the impression of the universal reign of *natural law*. The effect has been to lead multitudes whose faith is not grounded in direct spiritual experience to look askance on the whole idea of the supernatural. God, it is assumed, has His own mode of working, and that is by means of secondary agencies operating in absolutely uniform ways; miracles, therefore, cannot be admitted. And, since miracles are found in Scripture,—since the entire Book rests on the idea of a supernatural economy of grace,—the whole must be dismissed as in conflict with the modern mind. Professor G. B. Foster goes so far as to declare that a man can hardly be intellectually honest who in these days professes to believe in the miracles of the Bible.

It is overstating the case to speak of this *repugnance to miracle*, and rejection of it in the Bible, as if it were really new. It is as old as rationalism itself. You find it in Spinoza, in Reimarus, in Strauss, in numberless others. DeWette and Vatke, among earlier Old Testament critics, manifested it as strongly as their followers do now, and made it a pivot of their criticism. It governed the attacks on Christianity made in the age of the deists. David Hume wrote an essay against miracles which he thought had settled the question forever. But, seriously considered, can this attack on the idea of miracle, derived from our experience of the uniformity of nature's laws, be defended? Does it not in itself involve a huge assumption, and run counter to experience and common sense? The question is one well worth asking.

First, what *is* a miracle? Various definitions might be given, but it will be enough to speak of it here as *any effect in nature, or deviation from its ordinary course, due to the interposition of a supernatural cause.* It is no necessary part, it should be observed, of the Biblical idea of miracle, that natural agencies should not be employed as far as they will go. If the drying of the Red Sea to let the Israelites pass over was due in part to a great wind that blew, this was none the less of God's ordering, and did not detract from the supernatural character of the event as a whole. It was still at God's command that the waters were parted, and that a way was made at that particular time and place for the people to go through. These are what theologians call "providential" miracles, in which, so far as one can see, natural agencies, under divine direction, suffice to produce the result. There is, however, another and more conspicuous class, the instantaneous cleansing of the leper, e. g., or the raising of the dead, in which natural agencies are obviously altogether transcended.

It is this class about which the chief discussion goes on. They are miracles in the stricter sense of a complete transcendence of nature's laws.

What, in the next place, is meant by the *uniformity of nature?* There are, of course, laws of nature—no one disputes that. It is quite a mistake to suppose that the Bible, though not written in the twentieth century, knows nothing of a regular order and system of nature. The world is God's world; it is established by His decree; He has given to every creature its nature, its bounds, its limits; all things continue according to His ordinances (Psa. 119:91). Only, law in the Bible is never viewed as having an independent existence. It is always regarded as an expression of the power or wisdom of God. And this gives the right point of view for considering the relation of law to miracle. What, to begin with, do we mean by a "law" of nature? It is, as science will concede, only our registered observation of the order in which we find causes and events linked together in our experience. That they are so linked no one questions. If they were not, we should have no world in which we could live at all. But then, next, what do we mean by "uniformity" in this connection? We mean no more than this—that, given like causes, operating under like conditions, like effects will follow. Quite true; no one denies this either.

But then, as J. S. Mill, in his *Logic*, pointed out long ago, a miracle in the strict sense is not a denial of either of these truths. A miracle is not the assertion that, the same causes operating, a different result is produced. It is, on the contrary, the assertion that a *new* cause has intervened, and this a cause which the theists cannot deny to be a *vera causa*—the will and power of God. Just as, when I lift my arm, or throw a stone high in the air, I do not abolish the law of gravitation but counteract or overrule its purely natural action by the introduction of a new spiritual force; so, but in an infinitely higher way, is a miracle due to the interposition of the First Cause of all, God Himself. What the scientific man needs to prove to establish his objection to miracle is, not simply that natural causes operate uniformly, but that no other than natural causes exist; that natural causes exhaust all the causation in the universe. And that, we hold, he can never do.

It is obvious from what has now been said that the real question at issue in miracle is not natural law, but *Theism*. It is to be recognized at once that miracle can only profitably be discussed on the basis of a theistic view of the universe. It is not disputed that there are views of the universe which exclude miracle. The atheist cannot admit miracle, for he has no God to work miracles. The pantheist cannot admit miracle, for to him God and nature are one. The deist cannot admit miracle, for he has separated God and the universe so far that he can never bring them together again. The question is not, Is miracle possible on an atheistic, a materialistic, a pantheistic, view of the world, but, Is it possible on a theistic view—on the view of God as at once immanent in His world, and in infinite ways transcending it? I say nothing of intellectual "honesty," but I do marvel, as I have often said, at the *assurance* of any one who presumes to say that, for the highest and holiest ends in His personal relations with His creatures, God can work only within the limits which nature imposes; that He cannot act without and above nature's order if it pleases Him to do so. Miracles stand or fall by their evidence, but the attempt to rule them out by any *a priori* dictum as to the uniformity of natural law must inevitably fail. The same applies to the denial of providence or of answers to prayer on the ground of the uniformity of natural law. Here no breach of nature's order is affirmed, but only a governance or direction of nature of which man's own use of natural laws, without breach of them, for special ends, affords daily examples.

II. SCRIPTURE AND THE SPECIAL SCIENCES

Approaching more nearly the alleged conflict of the Bible or Christianity with the special sciences, a first question of importance is, What is the *general relation* of the Bible to science? How does it claim to relate itself to the advances of natural knowledge? Here, it is to be feared, mistakes are often made on both sides—on the side of science in affirming contrariety of the Bible with scientific results where none really exists; on the side of believers in demanding that the Bible be taken as a text-book of the newest scientific discoveries, and trying by forced methods to read these into them. The truth on this point lies really on the surface. The Bible clearly does not profess to anticipate the scientific discoveries of the nineteenth and twentieth centuries. Its design is very different; namely, to reveal God and His will and His purposes of grace to men, and, as involved in this, His general relation to the creative world, its dependence in all its parts on Him, and His orderly government of it in Providence for His wise and good ends. Natural things are taken as they are given, and spoken of in simple, popular language, as we ourselves every day speak of them. The world it describes is the world men know and live in, and it is described as it appears, not as, in its recondite researches, science reveals its inner constitution to us. Wise expositors of the Scriptures, older and younger, have always recognized this, and have not attempted to force its language further. To take only one example, John Calvin, who wrote before the Copernican system of astronomy had obtained common acceptance, in his commentary on the first chapter of Genesis penned these wise words: "He who would learn astronomy and other recondite arts," he said, "let him go elsewhere. Moses wrote in a popular style things which, without instruction, all ordinary persons indued with common sense are able to understand. * * * He does not call us up to heaven, he only proposes things that lie open before our eyes." To this hour, with all the light of modern science around us, we speak of sun, moon and stars "rising" and "setting," and nobody misunderstands or affirms contradiction with science. There is no doubt another side to this, for it is just as true that in depicting natural things, the Bible, through the Spirit of revelation that animates it, seizes things in so just a light—still with reference to its own purposes—that the mind is prevented from being led astray from the great truths intended to be conveyed.

It will serve to illustrate these positions as to the relation of the Bible to science if we look at them briefly in their application to the two sciences of *astronomy* and *geology,* in regard to which conflict has often been alleged.

1. The change from the *Ptolemaic* to the *Copernican* system of *astronomy*—from the view which regarded the earth as the center of the universe to the modern and undoubtedly true view of the earth as moving round the sun, itself, with its planets, but one of innumerable orbs in the starry heavens— of necessity created great searchings of heart among those who thought that the language of the Bible committed them to the older system. For a time there was strong opposition on the part of many theologians, as well as of students of science, to the new discoveries of the telescope. Galileo was imprisoned by the church. But truth prevailed, and it was soon perceived that the Bible, using the language of appearances, was no more committed to the literal moving of the sun round the earth than are our modern almanacs, which employ the same forms of speech. One would have to travel far in these days to find a Christian who feels his faith in the least affected by the discovery of the true doctrine of the solar system. He rejoices that he understands nature better, and reads his Bible without the slightest sense of contradiction. Yet Strauss was confident that the Copernican system had given its death-blow to Christianity; as Voltaire

before him had affirmed that Christianity would be overthrown by the discovery of the law of gravitation and would not survive a century. Newton, the humble-minded Christian discoverer of the law of gravitation, had no such fear, and time has shown that it was he, not Voltaire, who was right. These are specimens of the "conflicts" of Christianity with science.

The so-called "astronomical objection" to Christianity more specially takes the form of enlarging on the *illimitableness* of the universe disclosed by science in contrast with the *peculiar interest* of God in man displayed in the Christian Gospel. "What is man that thou art mindful of him?" (Psa. 8:4). Is it credible that this small speck in an infinity of worlds should be singled out as the scene of so tremendous an exhibition of God's love and grace as is implied in the Incarnation of the Son of God, the Sacrifice of the Cross, the Redemption of Man? The day is well-nigh past when even this objection is felt to carry much weight. Apart from the strange fact that up to this hour no evidence seems to exist of other worlds inhabited by rational intelligences like man—no planets, no known systems (on this point A. R. Wallace's "Man and the Universe" may be consulted)— thoughtful people have come to realize that quantitative bigness is no measure of God's love and care; that the value of a soul is not to be estimated in terms of stars and planets; that sin is not less awful a fact even if it were proved that this is the only spot in the universe in which it has emerged. It is of the essence of God's infinity that He cares for the little as well as for the great; not a blade of grass could wave, or the insect of a day live its brief life upon the wing, if God were not actually present, and minutely careful of it. Man's position in the universe remains, by consent, or rather by proof, of science, an altogether peculiar one. Link between the material and the spiritual, he is the one being that seems fitted, as Scripture affirms he is, to be the bond of unity **in** the creation (Heb. 2:6-9). This is the hope held out to us in Christ (Eph. 1:10). One should reflect also that, while the expanse of the *physical* universe is a modern thought, there has never been a time in the Christian Church when God—Himself infinite—was not conceived of as adored and served by *countless hosts* of ministering spirits. Man was never thought of as the only intelligence in creation. The mystery of the divine love to our world was in reality as great before as after the stellar expanses were discovered. The sense of "conflict," therefore, though not the sense of wonder, awakened by the "exceeding riches" of God's grace to man in Christ Jesus, vanishes with increasing realization of the depths and heights of God's love "which passeth knowledge" (Eph. 3:19). Astronomy's splendid demonstration of the majesty of God's wisdom and power is undiminished by any feeling of disharmony with the Gospel.

2. As it is with astronomy, so it has been with the revelations of *geology* of the age and gradual formation of the earth. Here also doubt and suspicion were—naturally enough in the circumstances—at first awakened. The gentle Cowper could write in his "Task" of those

> "* * * who drill and bore
> The solid earth and from the strata there
> Extract a register, by which we learn
> That He who made it, and revealed its date
> To Moses, was mistaken in its age."

If the intention of the first chapter of Genesis was really to give us the "date" of the creation of the earth and heavens, the objection would be unanswerable. But things, as in the case of astronomy, are now better understood, and few are disquieted in reading their Bibles because it is made certain that the world is immensely older than the 6,000 years which the older chronology gave it. Geology is felt only to have expanded our ideas of the vastness and marvel of the Creator's operations through the æons of time during which the world, with its teeming populations of fishes, birds, reptiles, mammals, was preparing for man's abode—when the mountains were being upheaved, the valleys being scooped out, and veins of precious metals being inlaid into the crust of the earth.

Does science, then, really, contradict Genesis I.? Not surely if what has been above said of the essentially popular character of the allusions to natural things in the Bible be remembered. Here certainly is no detailed description of the process of the formation of the earth in terms anticipative of modern science—terms which would have been unintelligible to the original readers—but a sublime picture, true to the order of nature, as it is to the broad facts even of geological succession. If it tells how God called heaven and earth into being, separated light from darkness, sea from land, clothed the world with vegetation, gave sun and moon their appointed rule of day and night, made fowl to fly, and sea-monsters to plow the deep, created the cattle and beasts of the field, and finally made man, male and female, in His own image, and established him as ruler over all God's creation, this orderly rise of created forms, man crowning the whole, these deep ideas of the narrative, setting the world at the very beginning in its right relation to God, and laying the foundations of an enduring philosophy of religion, are truths which science does nothing to subvert, but in myriad ways confirms. The "six days" may remain as a difficulty to some, but, if this is not part of the symbolic setting of the picture—a great divine "week" of work—one may well ask, as was done by Augustine long before geology was thought of, what kind of "days" these were which rolled their course before the sun, with its twenty-four hours of diurnal measurement, was appointed to that end? There is no violence done to the narrative in substituting in thought "æonic" days—vast cosmic periods—for "days" on our narrower, sun-measured scale. Then the last trace of apparent "conflict" disappears.

III. EVOLUTION AND MAN

In recent years the point in which "conflict" between Scripture and science is most frequently urged is the apparent contrariety of the theory of *evolution* to the Bible story of the direct *creation* of the animals and man. This might be met, and often is, as happened in the previous cases, by denying the reality of any evolutionary process in nature. Here also, however, while it must be conceded that evolution is not yet *proved,* there seems a growing appreciation of the strength of the evidence for the fact of some form of evolutionary origin of species—that is, of some genetic connection of higher with lower forms. Together with this, at the same time, there is manifest an increasing disposition to limit the scope of evolution, and to modify the theory in very essential points—those very points in which an apparent conflict with Scripture arose.

Much of the difficulty on this subject has arisen from the unwarrantable confusion or identification of evolution with *Darwinism.* Darwinism is a theory of the process of evolution, and both on account of the skill with which it was presented, and of the singular eminence of its propounder, obtained for a time a very remarkable prestige. In these later days, as may be seen by consulting a book like R. Otto's "Naturalism and Religion," published in "The Crown Library," that prestige has greatly declined. A newer evolution has arisen which breaks with Darwin on the three points most essential to his theory: 1. The *fortuitous character of the variations* on which "natural selection" works. Variations are now felt to be along definite lines, and to be guided to definite ends. 2. The *insufficiency of "natural selection"* (on which Darwin almost wholly relied) to accomplish the tasks Darwin assigned to it. 3. *The slow and insensible rate of the changes* by which new species were supposed to be produced. Instead of this the newer tendency is to seek the origin of new species in rapid and sudden changes, the causes of which lie within the organism—in "mutations," as they are coming to be called—so that the process may be as brief as formerly it was supposed to be long. "Evolution," in short, is coming to be recognized as but a new name for "creation," only that the creative power now works from *within,* instead of, as in the old conception, in an *external,* plastic fashion. It is, however, creation none the less.

In truth, no conception of evolution can be formed, compatible with all the facts of science, which does not take account, at least at certain great critical points, of the entrance of *new factors* into the process we call creation. 1. One such point is the transition from inorganic to organic existence—the entrance of the new power of *life.* It is hopeless to seek to account for life by purely mechanical and chemical agencies, and science has well-nigh given up the attempt. 2. A second point is in the transition from purely organic development to *consciousness.* A sensation is a mental fact different in kind from any merely organic change, and inexplicable by it. Here, accordingly, is a new rise, revealing previously unknown spiritual powers. 3. The third point is in the transition to *rationality, personality,* and *moral life* in man. This, as man's capacity for self-conscious, self-directed, progressive life evinces, is something different from the purely animal consciousness, and marks the beginning of a new kingdom. Here, again, the Bible and science are felt to be in harmony. Man is the last of God's created works—the crown and explanation of the whole—and he is made in God's image. To account for him, a special act of the Creator, constituting him what he is, must be presupposed. This creative act does not relate to the soul only, for higher spiritual powers could not be put into a merely animal brain. There must be a rise on the physical side as well, corresponding with the mental advance. In body, as in spirit, man comes from his Creator's hand.

If this new evolutionary conception is accepted, most of

the difficulties which beset the Darwinian theory fall away. 1. For one thing, man need no longer be thought of as a *slow development* from the animal stage—an ascent through brutishness and savagery from an ape-like form. His origin may be as sudden as Genesis represents. 2. The need for assuming an enormous *antiquity* of man to allow for the slow development is no longer felt. And (3), the need of assuming man's *original condition* to have been one of brutal passion and subjection to natural impulse disappears. Man may have come from his Creator's hand in as morally pure a state, and as capable of sinless development, as Genesis and Paul affirm. This also is the most worthy view to take of man's origin. It is a view borne out by the absence of all reliable evidence of those ape-like intermediate forms which, on the other hypothesis, must have intervened between the animal-progenitors and the finished human being. It is a view not contradicted by the alleged evidences of man's very great antiquity—100,000, 200,000, or 500,000 years—frequently relied on; for most of these and the extravagant measurements of time connected with them, are precarious in the extreme. The writer's book, "God's Image in Man and Its Defacement," may be consulted on these points.

The conclusion from the whole is, that, up to the present hour, science and the Biblical views of God, man, and the world, do not stand in any real relation of conflict. Each book of God's writing reflects light upon the pages of the other, but neither contradicts the other's essential testimony. Science itself seems now disposed to take a less materialistic view of the origin and nature of things than it did a decade or two ago, and to interpret the creation more in the light of the spiritual. The experience of the Christian believer, with the work of missions in heathen lands, furnishes a testimony that cannot be disregarded to the reality of this spiritual world, and of the regenerating, transforming forces proceeding from it. To God be all the glory!

CHAPTER XIX

MY PERSONAL EXPERIENCE WITH THE HIGHER CRITICISM

BY PROF. J. J. REEVE, SOUTHWESTERN BAPTIST THEOLOGICAL SEMINARY, FORT WORTH, TEXAS, U. S. A.

The purpose of this article is to state in a very brief way the influences which led me to accept certain of the views of the Higher Criticism, and after further consideration, to reject them. Necessarily the reasons for rejecting will be given at greater length than those for accepting. Space will not permit me to mention names of persons, books, articles and various other influences which combined to produce these results. I shall confine myself to an outline of the mental processes which resulted from my contact with the Critical Movement.

In outlining this change of view, I shall deal with—

I. THE PRESUPPOSITIONS OF THE HIGHER CRITICISM

These presuppositions and assumptions are the determining elements in the entire movement. Once they are understood, it is not difficult to understand the higher critics. It is their philosophy or world-view that is responsible for all their speculations and theories. Their mental attitude towards the world and its phenomena is the same as their attitude toward the Bible and the religion therein revealed. These presuppositions appealed to me very strongly. Having spent some time at one of the great American universities, thus coming in contact with some of the leading minds of the country, the critical view was presented to me very ably and attractively. Though resisted for a time, the forcefulness of the teaching and influence of the university atmosphere largely won my assent. The critics seemed to have the logic of things on their side. The results at which they had arrived seemed inevitable. But upon closer thinking I saw that the whole movement with its conclusions was the result of the adoption of the hypothesis of evolution. My professors had accepted this view, and were thoroughly convinced of its correctness as a working hypothesis. Thus I was made to feel the power of this hypothesis and to adopt it. This world-view is wonderfully fascinating and almost compelling. The vision of a cosmos developing from the lowest types and stages upward through beast and man to higher and better man is enchanting and almost overwhelming. That there is a grain of truth in all this most thinkers will concede. One can hardly refuse to believe that through the ages "An increasing purpose runs," that there is "One God, one law, one element, and one far-off divine event to which the whole creation moves." This world-view had to me at first a charm and witchery that was almost intoxicating. It created more of a *revolution* than an *evolution* in my thinking. But more careful consideration convinced me that the little truth in it served to sugar-coat and give plausibility to some deadly errors that lurked within. I saw that the hypothesis did not apply to a great part of the world's phenomena.

That this theory of evolution underlies and is the inspiration of the Higher Criticism goes without saying. That there is a grain of truth in it we may admit or not, as we see fit, but the whole question is, what kind of evolution is it that has given rise to this criticism. There are many varieties of the theory. There is the Idealism of Hegel, and the Materialism of Haeckel; a theistic evolution and an antitheistic; the view that it is God's only method, and the view that it is only one of God's methods; the theory that includes a Creator, and the theory that excludes Him; the deistic evolution, which starts the world with God, who then withdraws and leaves it a closed system of cause and effect, antecedent and consequent, which admits of no break or change in the natural process. There is also the theory that on the whole there is progress, but allowance must be made for retrogression and degeneration. This admits of the direct action of God in arresting the downward process and reversing the current; that is, there is an evolution through revelation, etc., rather than a revelation by evolution. On examining the evolution of the leaders of the Critical School, I found that it was of a naturalistic or practically deistic kind. All natural and mental phenomena are in a closed system of cause and effect, and the hypothesis applies universally, to religion and revelation, as well as to mechanisms.

This type of evolution may not be accepted by all adherents of the Critical School, but it is substantially the view of the leaders, Reuss, Graf, Vatke, Kuenen and Wellhausen. To them all nature and history are a product of forces within and in process of development. There has not been and could not be any direct action of God upon man, there could be no break in the chain of cause and effect, of antecedent and consequent. Hence there can be no miracle or anything of what is known as the supernatural. There could be no "interference" in any way with the natural course of events, there could be no "injection" of any power into the cosmic process from without, God is shut up to the one method of bringing things to pass. He is thus little more than a prisoner in His own cosmos. Thus I discovered that the Critical Movement was essentially and fundamentally anti-supernatural and anti-miraculous. According to it all religious movements are human developments along natural and materialistic lines. The religion of Israel and the Bible is no exception, as there can be no exception to this principle. The revelation contained in the Bible is, strictly speaking, no *revelation;* it is a natural development with God in the cosmic process behind it, but yet a steady, straight-lined, mechanical development such as can be traced step by step as a flight of stairs may be measured by a foot-rule. There could have been no epoch-making revelation, no revivals and lapses, no marvelous exhibitions of divine power, no real redemption. With these foregone conclusions fixed in their minds, the entire question is practically settled beforehand. As it is transparently clear that the Bible on the face of it does not correspond to this view, it must be rearranged so as to correspond to it. To do this, they must deny point-blank the claims and statements of most of the Bible writers. Now, if the Bible claims to be anything, it claims to be a revelation from God, a miraculous or supernatural book, recording the numerous direct acts of God in nature and history, and His interference with the natural course of events. Are the writers of the Bible correct, or are the critics? It is impossible that both should be right.

Reasoning thus, it became perfectly clear to me that the presuppositions and beliefs of the Bible writers and of the critics were absolutely contradictory. To maintain that the modern view is a development and advance upon the Biblical view, is absurd. No presupposition can develop a presupposition which contradicts and nullifies it. To say that the critical position and the Biblical position, or the traditional evangelical view which is the same as the Biblical, are reconcilable, is the most fatuous folly and delusion. Kuenen and others have recognized this contradiction and have acknowledged it, not hesitating to set aside the Biblical view. Many of their disciples have failed to see as clearly as their masters. They think the two can be combined. I was of the same opinion myself, but further reflection showed this to be an impossibility. I thought it possible to accept the results of the Higher Criticism without accepting its presuppositions. This is saying that one can accept as valid and true the results of a process and at the same time deny the validity of the process itself. But does not this involve an inner contradiction and absurdity? If I accept the results of the Kuenen-Wellhausen hypothesis as correct, then I accept as correct the methods and processes which led to these results, and if I accept these methods, I also accept the presuppositions which give rise to these methods. If the "assured results" of which the critics are so fond of boasting are true, then the naturalistic evolution hypothesis which produced these results is correct. Then it is impossible to accept the miraculous or supernatural, the Bible as an authoritative record of supernatural revelation is completely upset and its claims regarding itself are false and misleading. I can see no way of escaping these conclusions. There is no possible middle ground as I once fondly imagined there was. Thus I was compelled to conclude that although there is some truth in the evolutionary view of the world, yet as an explanation of history and revelation it is utterly inadequate, so inadequate as to be erroneous and false. A world-view must be broad enough to admit of all the facts of history and experience. Even then it is only a human point of view and necessarily imperfect. Will any one dare to say that the evolutionary hypothesis is divine? Then we would have a Bible and a philosophy both claiming to be divine and absolutely contradicting each other. To attempt to eliminate the miraculous and supernatural from the Bible and accept the remainder as divine is impossible, for they are all one and inextricably woven together. In either case the Book is robbed of its claims to authority. Some critics do not hesitate to deny its authority and thus cut themselves loose from historical Christianity.

In spite, however, of the serious faults of the Higher Criticism, it has given rise to what is known as the Scientific and Historical method in the study of the Old Testament. This method is destined to stay and render invaluable aid. To the scholarly mind its appeal is irresistible. Only in the light of the historical occasion upon which it was produced, can the Old Testament be properly understood. A flood of light has already been poured in upon these writings. The scientific spirit which gave rise to it is one of the noblest instincts in the intellectual life of man. It is a thirst for the real and the true, that will be satisfied with nothing else. But, noble as is this scientific spirit, and invaluable as is the historical method, there are subtle dangers in connection with them. Everything depends upon the presuppositions with which we use the method. A certain mental attitude there must be. What shall it be? A materialistic evolution such as Kuenen and his confreres, or a theistic evolution which admits the supernatural? Investigating in the mental attitude of the first of these, the scholar will inevitably arrive at or accept the results of the critics. Another, working at the same problem with Christian presuppositions, will arrive at very different conclusions. Which shall we have, the point of view of the Christian or the critic? I found that the critics' claim to possess the only really scientific method was slightly true but largely false. His results were scientific because they fitted his hypothesis. The Christan scholar with his broader presuppositions was peremptorily ruled out of court. Anything savoring of the miraculous, etc., could not be scientific to the critic, and hence it could not be true, therefore, it must be discarded or branded as Myth, Legend, Poesy, Saga, etc. Such narrowness of view is scarcely credible on the part of scholars who claim to be so broad and liberal.

Another question confronted me. How can so many Christian scholars and preachers accept the views of the critics and still adhere to evangelical Christianity with intense devotion? As we have seen, to accept the results of Criticism is to accept the methods and presuppositions which produced these results. To accept their assumptions is to accept a naturalistic evolution which is fundamentally contradictory to the Biblical and Christian point of view. It is therefore essentially contradictory to Christianity, for what is the latter if it is not a supernaturally revealed knowledge of the plan of salvation, with supernatural power to effectuate that salvation? All who have experienced the power of Christianity will in the main assent to this definition. How then can Christians who are Higher Critics escape endorsing the presuppositions of the Critics? There is an inner contradiction between the assumptions of their scientific reason and the assumptions of their religious faith. A careful study of the attitude of these mediating critics, as they are called, has revealed a sense of contradiction somewhere of which they are vaguely conscious. They maintain their attitude by an inconsistency. Thus it is they have many difficulties which they cannot explain. This inner contradiction runs through much of their exegesis and they wonder that evangelical Christians do not accept their views. Already many of them are not quite so sure of their "assured results" as they were. Many evangelical Christians do not accept these views because they can "see through" them.

The second line of thinking which led me to reject the Critics' view was a consideration of

II. THEIR METHODS

At first I was enthusiastic over the method. Now at last we have the correct method that will in time solve all difficulties. Let it be readily granted that the historical method has settled many difficulties and will continue to do so, yet the whole question lies in the attitude of mind a man brings to the task. Among the critics their hypothesis is absolute and dominates every attempt to understand the record, shapes every conclusion, arranges and rearranges the facts in its own order, discards what does not fit or reshapes it to fit. The critics may deny this but their treatment of the Old Testament is too well known to need any proof of it. The use of the Redactor is a case in point. This purely imaginary being, unhistorical and unscientific, is brought into requisition at almost every difficulty. It is acknowledged that at times he acts in a manner wholly inexplicable. To assume such a person interpolating names of God, changing names and making explanations to suit the purposes of their hypothesis and imagination is the very negation of science, notwithstanding their boast of a scientific method. Their minds seem to be in abject slavery to their theory. No reason is more impervious to facts than one preoccupied with a theory which does not agree with these facts. Their mental attitude being biased and partial, their methods are partial and the results very one-sided and untrustworthy. They give more credence to the guesses of some so-called scholar, a clay tablet, a heathen king's boast, or a rude drawing in stone, than to the Scripture record. They feel instinctively that to accept the Bible statements would be the ruin of their hypothesis, and what they call their hard-won historical method. In this their instinct is true. The Bible and their hypothesis are irreconcilable. As their theory must not be interfered with, since it is identical with the truth itself, the Bible must stand aside in the interests of truth.

For this reason they deny all historicity to Genesis 1-11, the stories of Creation, the Fall, the Flood, etc. No theory of naturalistic evolution can possibly admit the truth of these chapters. Likewise, there is but a substratum of truth in the stories of Abraham, Isaac, Jacob, Joseph and Moses. Nearly all legislation is denied to the latter, because it represents too rapid an advance, or a stage too advanced. But is such the case? Centuries before Moses, laws, government, civilization, culture, art, education, religion, temples, ritual and priesthood had flourished in Babylonia and Egypt and were a chief factor in the education of Moses. With all this previous development upon which to build, what objections to ascribing these laws to Moses, who, during the forty years under divine guidance, selected, purified, heightened, and adopted such laws as best served the needs of the people. The development of external laws and customs had preceded Moses, and there is no need to suppose a development afterward in the history of the people. That history records the fitful attempts at the assimilation of these laws. To maintain that they were at first put in the exact form in which they have come down to us is wholly unnecessary and contrary to certain facts in the records themselves. But to my mind one of the greatest weaknesses of the critical position is, that because there is little or no mention of the laws in the history that follows the death of Moses, therefore these laws could not have existed. To the critic this is one of the strongest arguments in his favor. Now he has found out how to make the history and the laws correspond. But does the non-mention or non-observance of a law prove its non-existence? All history shows that such is not the case. Moreover, the books of Joshua, Judges and Samuel make no pretence at giving a complete detailed history. If non-mention or non-observance were proof of non-existence, then the Book of the Covenant and Deuteronomy could not have existed until the return from Exile; for the laws against idolatry were not carried out until then. Apply this same method of reasoning to laws in general and the most absurd results will follow. The Decalogue could never have existed, for all of its laws are constantly being broken. No New Testament could have existed through the Dark Ages, for almost every precept in it was violated during that period. The facts of life plainly show that men with the law of God in their hands will continually violate them. But why did not Joshua and those succeeding him for several centuries carry out the law of Moses? The answer is obvious. The circumstances did not permit of it, and no one, not even Moses, had any idea of the law being fully observed at once. He looked forward to a time when they should be settled and should have a capital and central sanctuary. Moreover, a large portion of the laws was intended for the priest alone and may have been observed. The laws were flexible and to be fulfilled as the circumstances permitted. If the Book of Deuteronomy could not be observed, the Book of the Covenant could be followed. Changes and modifications were purposely made by Moses to meet the demands of the changing circumstances. If the non-fulfillment of these laws proved their non-existence, then the Book of the Covenant and Deuteronomy were not in existence in the time of Jehoiakim, for idolatry was then rampant.

By its arbitrary methods, Modern Criticism does wholesale violence to the record of the discovery of the Law Book as recorded in 2 Kings 22:8-20. It denies any real discovery, distinctly implies fraud upon the part of the writers, assumes a far too easy deception of the king, the prophetess, the king's counsellors, Jeremiah and the people. It implies a marvelous success in perpetrating this forged document on the people. The writers did evil that good might come, and God seems to have been behind it all and endorsed it. Such a transaction is utterly incredible. "The people would not hear Moses and the prophet, yet they were easily persuaded by a forged Mosaic document." The critics disagree among themselves regarding the authorship of the Book of Deuteronomy. Some maintain it was by the priestly class and some by the prophetic class, but there are insuperable objections to each. They have failed to show why there were so many laws incorporated in it which absolutely contradict a later date and why the Mosaic dress succeeded so well although contradictory to some of the genuinely Mosaic laws.

According to the critics also, Ezra perpetrated a tremendous fraud when he palmed off his completed Code as of Mosaic origin. That the people should accept it as genuinely Mosaic, although it increased their burdens and contradicted many laws previously known as Mosaic, is incredible. That such a people at such a time and under such circumstances could be so easily imposed upon and deceived, and that such a man as Ezra could perform such a colossal fraud and have it all succeed so well, seems inconceivable except by a person whose moral consciousness is dulled or benumbed by some philosophical theory. According to the critics, the authors of Deuteronomy and the Levitical Code not only produced such intensely religious books and laws, but were at the same time deliberate inventors and falsifiers of history as well as deceivers of the people. What such views imply regarding the character of God who is behind it all we shall consider later.

Space does not permit me to more than refer to the J. E. P. analysis. That certain documents existed and were ultimately combined to make up the five books of Moses no one need doubt. It in no way detracts from their inspiration or authenticity to do so, nor does it in any way deny the essentially Mosaic origin of the legislation. But the J. E. P. analysis on the basis of the different names for God I found to require such an arbitrary handling and artificial manipulation of the text, to need the help of so many Redactors whose methods and motives are wholly inexplicable, with a multitude of exceptions to account for, that I was convinced the analysis could not be maintained. Astruc's clue in Exodus 6:3, which was the starting point for the analysis, cannot be made to decide the time of the use of the names of God, for the text is not perfectly certain. There is considerable difference between the two readings, "was known," "made myself known." Even if God had not previously revealed Himself by the name Jahveh, that does not prove the name unknown or that God was not known by that name. And even if he had so revealed Himself, the earlier record would not be less authentic, for they were either written or rewritten and edited after the revelation to Moses in the light of a fuller revelation. Thus it was made perfectly clear that El, Elohim, El-Elyon, El-Shaddai, were identical with Jahveh.

The methods of the critics in regarding the earlier histories as little more than fiction and invention, to palm off certain laws as genuinely Mosaic, found some lodgment in my mind for a time. But the more I considered it, the more I was convinced that it was the critics who were the inventors and falsifiers. They were the ones who had such a facile imagination, they could "manufacture" history at their "green tables" to suit their theories and were doing so fast and loose. They could create nations and empires out of a desert, and like the alchemists of the Middle Ages with their magic wand, transform all things into their own special and favorite metal. To charge the Scripture writers with this invention and falsification is grossly to malign them and slander the God that wrought through them. The quality of their products does not lend countenance to such a view, and it is abhorrent to the Christian consciousness. Such a conception cannot be long held by any whose moral and religious natures have not been dulled by their philosophical presuppositions. The habit of discarding the Books of Chronicles, because they give no history of Northern Israel, lay considerable emphasis upon the temple and priesthood, pass over the faults and sins of the kings, etc., and are therefore a biased and untrustworthy history, has appeared to me an aberration from common sense, and is scarcely credible among men of such intelligence. When the compiler of Chronicles covers the same history of Kings, he agrees with these histories substantially, though varying in some minor details. If he is reliable in this material, why not in the other material, not found in Kings? The real reason is that he records many facts about the temple and its services which do not fit in with the critics' hypothesis, and therefore something must be done to discredit the Chronicler and get rid of his testimony.

But my third reason for rejecting the critical standpoint is

III. THE SPIRIT OF THE MOVEMENT

Grant that there is a genuine scientific interest underlying it all, the real question is, what is the standpoint of the scientific mind which investigates. What is authoritative with him? His philosophical theory and working hypothesis, or his religious faith? In other words, does his *religion* or *philosophy* control his thinking? Is it reason or faith that is supreme? Is his authority human or divine? There is no question here of having one without the other, that is, having faith without reason, for that is impossible. The question is, which is supreme? For some time I thought one could hold these views of the Old Testament and still retain his faith in evangelical Christianity. I found, however, that this could be done only by holding my philosophy in check and within certain limits. It could not be rigorously applied to all things. Two supreme things could not exist in the mind at the same time. If my theories were supreme, then I was following human reason, not faith, and was a rationalist to that extent. If the presuppositions of my religious faith were supreme and in accordance with the Biblical presuppositions and beliefs, then my philosophy must be held in abeyance. The fundamentals of our religious faith, as known in the Bible and history, are a belief in divine revelation, the miraculous birth, the life and resurrection of Jesus Christ, the God-Man. Inseparable from these there is also the fact of a supernatural power in regeneration. The philosophy of the critics cannot consistently make room for these. Thus the real question becomes one of authority, viz.: shall the scientific hypothesis be supreme in my thinking, or the presuppositions of the Christian faith? If I make my philosophical viewpoint supreme, then I am compelled to construe the Bible and Christianity through my theory and everything which may not fit into that theory must be rejected. This is the actual standpoint of the critic. His is a philosophical rather than a religious spirit. Such was Gnosticism in the early centuries. It construed Christ and Christianity through the categories of a Graeco-Oriental philosophy and thus was compelled to reject some of the essentials of Christianity. Such was the Scholasticism of the Middle Ages, which construed Christianity through the categories of the Aristotelian Logic and the Neo-platonic Philosophy. Such is the Higher Criticism which construes everything through the hypothesis of evolution. The spirit of the movement is thus essentially scholastic and rationalistic.

It became more and more obvious to me that the movement was entirely intellectual, an attempt in reality to intellectualize all religious phenomena. I saw also that it was a partial and one-sided intellectualism, with a strong bias against the fundamental tenets of Biblical Christianity. Such a movement does not produce that intellectual humility which belongs to the Christian mind. On the contrary, it is responsible for a vast amount of intellectual pride, an aristocracy of intellect with all the snobbery which usually accompanies that term. Do they not exactly correspond to Paul's word, "vainly puffed up in his fleshly mind and not holding fast the head, etc.?" They have a splendid scorn for all opinions which do not agree with theirs. Under the spell of this sublime contempt they think they can ignore anything that does not square with their evolutionary hypothesis. The center of gravity of their thinking is in the theoretical not in the religious, in reason, not in faith. Supremely satisfied with its self-constituted authority, the mind thinks itself competent to criticise the Bible, the thinking of all the centuries, and even Jesus Christ Himself. The followers of this cult have their full share of the frailties of human nature. Rarely, if ever, can a thoroughgoing critic be an evangelist, or even evangelistic; he is educational. How is it possible for a preacher to be a power for God, whose source of authority is his own reason and convictions? The Bible can scarcely contain more than good advice for such a man.

I was much impressed with their boast of having all scholarship on their side. It is very gratifying to feel oneself abreast with the times, up to date, and in the front rank of thought. But some investigation and consideration led me to see that the boast of scholarship is tremendously overdone. Many leading scholars are with them, but a majority of the most reverent and judicious scholars are not. The arrogant boasts of these people would be very amusing, if they were not so influential. Certainly most of the books put forth of late by

Old Testament scholars are on their side, but there is a formidable list on the other side and it is growing larger every day. Conservative scholarship is rapidly awakening, and, while it will retain the legitimate use of the invaluable historical method, will sweep from the field most of the speculations of the critics. A striking characteristic of these people is a persistent ignoring of what is written on the other side. They think to kill their antagonist by either ignoring or despising him. They treat their opponents something as Goliath treated David, and in the end the result will be similar. They have made no attempt to answer Robertson's "The Early Religion of Israel;" Orr's "The Problem of the Old Testament;" Wiener's "Studies in Biblical Law" and "Studies in Pentateuchical Criticism," etc. They still treat these books which have undermined the very foundations of their theories with the same magnificent scorn. There is a nemesis in such an attitude.

But the spirit of the critical movement manifests some very doubtful aspects in its practical working out among the pastors and churches. Adherents of this movement accept the spiritual oversight of churches which hold fast to the Biblical view of the Bible, while they know that their own views will undermine many of the most cherished beliefs of the churches. Many try to be critics and conservative at the same time. They would "run with the hare and hunt with the hounds," professing to be in full sympathy with evangelical Christianity while abiding their opportunity to inculcate their own views, which, as we have seen, is really to forsake the Christian standpoint. The morality of such conduct is, to say the least, very doubtful. It has led to much mischief among the churches and injury to the work. A preacher who has thoroughly imbibed these beliefs has no proper place in an evangelical Christian pulpit. Such a spirit is not according to the spirit of the religion they profess to believe.

But another weighty reason for rejecting the Higher Criticism is

IV. A CONSIDERATION OF ITS RESULTS

Ten or twenty years ago these scholars believed their views would immensely advance the cause of Christianity and true religion. They are by no means so sure of that now. It is not meeting with the universal acceptance they anticipated. Making a mere hypothesis the supreme thing in our thinking, we are forced to construe everything accordingly. Thus the Bible, the Christ and the religious experiences of men are subjected to the same scientific analysis. Carry this out to its logical conclusion and what would be the result? There would be all science and no religion. In the array of scientific facts all religion would be evaporated. God, Christ, the Bible, and all else would be reduced to a mathematical or chemical formula. This is the ideal and goal of the evolutionary hypothesis. The rationalist would rejoice at it, but the Christian mind shrinks with horror from it. The Christian consciousness perceives that an hypothesis which leads to such results is one of its deadliest foes.

Another danger also arises here. When one makes his philosophy his authority, it is not a long step until he makes himself his own god. His own reason becomes supreme in his thinking and this reason becomes his lord. This is the inevitable logic of the hypothesis mentioned, and some adherents of the school have taken this step. They recognize no authority but their own moral instincts and philosophical reason. Now, as the evolution theory makes all things exist only in a state of change, of flux, or of becoming, God is therefore changing and developing, the Bible and Christ will be outgrown, Christianity itself will be left behind. Hence, there is no *absolute* truth, nothing in the moral religious world is fixed or certain. All truth is in solution; there is no precipitate upon which we can rely. There is no *absolute* standard of Ethics, no *authority* in religion, every one is practically his own god. Jesus Christ is politely thanked for His services in the past, gallantly conducted to the confines of His world and bowed out as He is no longer needed and His presence might be very troublesome to some people. Such a religion is the very negation of Christianity, is a distinct reversion to heathenism. It may be a cultured and refined heathenism with a Christian veneer, but yet a genuine heathenism.

I am far from saying that all adherents of this school go to such lengths, but why do they not? Most of them had an early training under the best conservative influences which inculcated a wholesome reverence for the Bible as an authority in religion and morals. This training they can never fully outgrow. Many of them are of a good, sturdy religious ancestry, of rigid, conservative training and genuine religious experience. Under these influences they have acquired a strong hold upon Christianity and can never be removed from it. They hold a theoretical standpoint and a religious experience together, failing, as I believe, to see the fundamental contradiction between them. Slowly the Christian consciousness and Christian scholarship are asserting themselves. Men are beginning to see how irreconcilable the two positions are and there will be the inevitable cleavage in the future. Churches are none too soon or too seriously alarmed. Christianity is beginning to see that its very existence is at stake in this subtle attempt to do away with the supernatural. I have seen the Unitarian, the Jew, the free thinker, and the Christian who has imbibed critical views, in thorough agreement on the Old Testament and its teachings. They can readily hobnob together, for the religious element becomes a lost quantity; the Bible itself becomes a plaything for the intellect, a merry-go-round for the mind partially intoxicated with its theory.

As has been already intimated, one of the results of the critical processes has been to rearrange the Bible according to its own point of view. This means that it has to a large extent set it aside as an authority. Such a result is serious enough, but a much more serious result follows. This is the reflection such a Bible casts upon the character and methods of God in His revelation of Himself to men. It will scarcely be doubted by even a radical critic, that the Bible is the most uplifting book in the world, that its religious teachings are the best the world has known. If such be the case, it must reflect more of God's character and methods than any other book. The writers themselves must exemplify many of the traits of the God they write about. What then must be the methods of a holy and loving God? If He teaches men truth by parable or history or illustration, the one essential thing about these parables or histories is that they be true to life or history or nature. Can a God who is absolutely just and holy teach men truths about Himself by means of that which is false? Men may have taught truth by means of falsehoods and other instruments and perhaps succeeded, but God can hardly be legitimately conceived of as using any such means. Jesus Christ taught the greatest of truths by means of parables, illustrations, etc., but every one was true to life or nature or history. The Christian consciousness, which is the highest expression of the religious life of mankind, can never conceive of Jesus as using that which was in itself untrue, as a vehicle to convey that which is true. In like manner if God had anything to do with the Old Testament, would He make use of mere myths, legends, sagas, invented and falsified history, which have no foundation in fact and are neither true to nature, history nor life? Will God seek to uplift mankind by means of falsehood? Will He sanction the use of such dishonest means and pious frauds, such as a large part of the Pentateuch is, if the critics are right? Could He make use of such means for such a holy purpose and let His people feed on falsehood for centuries and centuries and deceive them into righteousness? Falsehood will not do God's will; only truth can do that. Is there nothing in the story of creation, of the fall, the flood, the call and promise to Abraham, the life of Jacob and Joseph and the great work of Moses? If all these things are not true to fact or to life, then God has been an arch-deceiver and acts on the Jesuit maxim, "The end justifies the means." This would apply to the finding of the Law in Josiah's time, and the giving of the law under Ezra. That such a lot of spurious history, deceptive inventions and falsifying history should achieve such a success is most astonishing. Is it possible that a holy God should be behind all this and promote righteousness thereby? This surely is conniving at evil and using methods unworthy of the name of God. To say that God was shut up to such a method is preposterous. Such a conception of God as is implied in the critical position is abhorrent to one who believes in a God of truth.

Perhaps the Book of Daniel at the hands of the critic best illustrates this point. No one can deny the religious quality of the book. It has sublime heights and depths and has had a mighty influence in the world. No one can read the book carefully and reverently without feeling its power. Yet according to the modern view the first six or seven chapters have but a grain of truth in them. They picture in a wonderfully vivid manner the supernatural help of God in giving Daniel power to interpret dreams, in delivering from the fiery furnace, in saving from the lion's mouth, smiting King Nebuchadnezzar, etc. All this is high religious teaching, has had a great influence for good and was intended for a message from God to encourage faith. Yet, according to the critics these events had no foundation in fact, the supernatural did not take place, the supposed facts upon which these sublime religious lessons are based could never have occurred. Yet the God of truth has used such a book with such teaching to do great good in the world. He thus made abundant use of fiction and falsehood. According to this view He has also been deceiving the best people of the world for millenniums, using the false and palming it off as true. Such a God may be believed in by a critic, but the Christian consciousness revolts at it. It is worthy of a Zeus, or perhaps the Demiurge of Marcion, but He is not the God of Israel, not the God and Father of Jesus Christ. "But," says the critic, "the religious lessons are great and good." Are they? Can a story or illustration or parable teach good religious lessons when it is in itself essentially untrue to nature, history and life? To assert such a thing would seem to imply a moral and religious blindness that is scarcely credible. It is true there are many grave difficulties in the book of Daniel, but are they as great as the moral difficulty implied in the critical view?

The foregoing embody my chief reasons for rejecting the position of the Critical School with which I was once in sympathy. Their positions are not merely vagaries, they are essentially attempts to undermine revelation, the Bible and evangelical Christianity. If these views should ultimately prevail, Christianity will be set aside for what is known as the New Religion, which is no religion, but a philosophy. All critics believe that traditional Christianity will largely, if not altogether, give place to the modern view, as it is called. But we maintain that traditional Christianity has the right of way. It must and will be somewhat modified by the conception of a developing revelation and the application of the historical method, but must prevail in all its essential features. It has a noble ancestry and a glorious history. The Bible writers are all on its side; the bulk of Jewish scholars of the past are in the procession; it has Jesus, the Son of God, in its ranks, with the apostles, prophets, the martyrs, the reformers, the theologians, the missionaries and the great preachers and evangelists. The great mass of God's people are with it. I prefer to belong to that goodly company rather than with the heathen Porphyry, the pantheistic Spinoza, the immoral Astruc, the rationalistic Reuss, Vatke, Graf, Kuenen and Wellhausen, with a multitude of their disciples of all grades. Theirs is a new traditionalism begun by those men and handed down to others in England and America. Most of these disciples owe their religious life and training almost entirely to the traditional view. The movement has quickened study of the Old Testament, has given a valuable method, a great many facts, a fresh point of view, but its extravagancies, its vagaries, its false assumptions and immoralities will in time be sloughed by the Christian consciousness as in the past it has sloughed off Gnosticism, Pantheism, Scholasticism and a host of other philosophical or scientific fads and fancies.

The Fundamentals

A Testimony to the Truth

"To the Law and to the Testimony"
Isaiah 8:20

Edited by R. A. Torrey, A. C. Dixon and Others

VOLUME II

Baker Books

A Division of Baker Book House Co
Grand Rapids, Michigan 49516

Reprinted from the original
four-volume edition issued by
the Bible Institute of Los Angeles in 1917.

Reprinted 2003 by Baker Books
a division of Baker Book House Company
P.O. Box 6287, Grand Rapids, MI 49516-6287

ISBN: 0-8010-1264-3
Two Volume Set

Printed in the United States of America

For information about academic books,
resources for Christian leaders, and all new
releases available from Baker Book House,
visit our web site:
http://www.bakerbooks.com/

CONTENTS

VOLUME II

CONTENTS

PREFACE

In 1909 God moved two Christian laymen to set aside a large sum of money for issuing twelve volumes that would set forth the fundamentals of the Christian faith, and which were to be sent free to ministers of the gospel, missionaries, Sunday School superintendents, and others engaged in aggressive Christian work throughout the English speaking world. A committee of men who were known to be sound in the faith was chosen to have the oversight of the publication of these volumes. Rev. Dr. A. C. Dixon was the first Executive Secretary of the Committee, and upon his departure for England Rev. Dr. Louis Meyer was appointed to take his place. Upon the death of Dr. Meyer the work of the Executive Secretary devolved upon me. We were able to bring out these twelve volumes according to the original plan. Some of the volumes were sent to 300,000 ministers and missionaries and other workers in different parts of the world. On the completion of the twelve volumes as originally planned the work was continued through The King's Business, published at 536 South Hope St., Los Angeles, California. Although a larger number of volumes were issued than there were names on our mailing list, at last the stock became exhausted, but appeals for them kept coming in from different parts of the world. As the fund was no longer available for this purpose, the Bible Institute of Los Angeles, to whom the plates were turned over when the Committee closed its work, have decided to bring out the various articles that appeared in The Fundamentals in four volumes at the cheapest price possible. All the articles that appeared in The Fundamentals, with the exception of a very few that did not seem to be in exact keeping with the original purpose of The Fundamentals, will be published in this series.

R. A. TORREY

DEDICATION

To the two laymen whose generosity made it possible to send several millions of volumes of "The Fundamentals" to ministers and missionaries in all parts of the world, for their confirmation and upbuilding in the faith, these volumes are dedicated.

THE FUNDAMENTALS

VOLUME II

CHAPTER I

THE INSPIRATION OF THE BIBLE—DEFINITION, EXTENT AND PROOF

BY REV. JAMES M. GRAY, D. D.,
DEAN OF MOODY BIBLE INSTITUTE, CHICAGO, ILL.

In this paper the authenticity and credibility of the Bible are assumed, by which is meant (1), that its books were written by the authors to whom they are ascribed, and that their contents are in all material points as when they came from their hands; and (2), that those contents are worthy of entire acceptance as to their statements of fact. Were there need to prove these assumptions, the evidence is abundant, and abler pens have dealt with it.

Let it not be supposed, however, that because these things are assumed their relative importance is undervalued. On the contrary, they underlie inspiration, and, as President Patton says, come in on the ground floor. They have to do with the historicity of the Bible, which for us just now is the basis of its authority. Nothing can be settled until this is settled, but admitting its settlement which, all things considered, we now may be permitted to do, what can be of deeper interest than the question as to how far that authority extends?

This is the inspiration question, and while so many have taken in hand to discuss the others, may not one be at liberty to discuss this? It is an old question, so old, indeed, as again in the usual recurrence of thought to have become new. Our fathers discussed it, it was the great question once upon a time, it was sifted to the bottom, and a great storehouse of fact, and argument, and illustration has been left for us to draw upon in a day of need.

For a long while the enemy's attack has directed our energies to another part of the field, but victory there will drive us back here again. The other questions are outside of the Bible itself, this is inside. They lead men away from the contents of the book to consider how they came, this brings us back to consider what they are. Happy the day when the inquiry returns here, and happy the generation which has not forgotten how to meet it.

I. DEFINITION OF INSPIRATION

1. *Inspiration is not revelation.* As Dr. Charles Hodge expressed it, revelation is the act of communicating divine knowledge to the mind, but inspiration is the act of the same Spirit controlling those who make that knowledge known to others. In Chalmer's happy phrase, the one is the influx, the other the efflux. Abraham received the influx, he was granted a revelation; but Moses was endued with the efflux, being inspired to record it for our learning. In the one case there was a flowing in and in the other a flowing out. Sometimes both of these experiences met in the same person, indeed Moses himself is an illustration of it, having received a revelation at another time and also the inspiration to make it known, but it is of importance to distinguish between the two.

2. *Inspiration is not illumination.* Every regenerated Christian is illuminated in the simple fact that he is indwelt by the Holy Spirit, but every such an one is not also inspired, but only the writers of the Old and New Testaments. Spiritual illumination is subject to degrees, some Chrisitans possessing more of it than others, but, as we understand it, inspiration is not subject to degrees, being in every case the breath of God, expressing itself through a human personality.

3. *Inspiration is not human genius.* The latter is simply a natural qualification, however exalted it may be in some cases, but inspiration in the sense now spoken of is supernatural throughout. It is an enduement coming upon the writers of the Old and New Testaments directing and enabling them to write those books, and on no other men, and at no other time, and for no other purpose. No human genius of whom we ever heard introduced his writings with the formula, "Thus saith the Lord," or words to that effect, and yet such is the common utterance of the Bible authors. No human genius ever yet agreed with any other human genius as to the things it most concerns men to know, and, therefore, however exalted his equipment, it differs not merely in degree but in kind from the inspiration of the Scriptures.

In its mode the divine agency is inscrutable, though its effects are knowable. We do not undertake to say just how the Holy Spirit operated on the minds of these authors to produce these books any more than we undertake to say how He operates on the human heart to produce conversion, but we accept the one as we do the other on the testimony that appeals to faith.

4. When we speak of the Holy Spirit coming upon the men in order to the composition of the books, it should be further understood that *the object is not the inspiration of the men but the books*—not the writers but the *writings*. It terminates upon the record, in other words, and not upon the human instrument who made it.

To illustrate: Moses, David, Paul, John, were not always and everywhere inspired, for then always and everywhere they would have been infallible and inerrant, which was not the case. They sometimes made mistakes in thought and erred in conduct. But however fallible and errant they may have been as men compassed with infirmity like ourselves, such fallibility or errancy was never under any circumstances communicated to their sacred writings.

Ecclesiastes is a case in point, which on the supposition of its Solomonic authorship, is giving us a history of his search for happiness "under the sun." Some statements in that book are only partially true while others are altogether false, therefore it cannot mean that Solomon was inspired as he tried this or that experiment to find what no man has been able to find outside of God. But it means that his language is inspired as he records the various feelings and opinions which possessed him in the pursuit.

This disposes of a large class of objections sometimes brought against the doctrine of inspiration—those, for example, associated with the question as to whether the Bible is the Word of God or only contains that Word. If by the former be meant that God spake every word in the Bible, and hence that every word is true, the answer must be *no;* but if it be meant that God caused every word in the Bible, true or false, to be recorded, the answer should be *yes.* There are words of Satan in the Bible, words of false prophets, words of the enemies of Christ, and yet they are God's words, not in the sense that He uttered them, but that He caused them to be recorded, infallibly and inerrantly recorded, for our profit. In this sense the Bible does not merely contain the Word of God, it *is* the Word of God.

Of any merely human author it is the same. This paper is the writer's word throughout, and yet he may quote what other people say to commend them or dispute them. What they say he records, and in doing so he makes the record his in the sense that he is responsible for its accuracy.

5. Let it be stated further in this definitional connection, that *the record for whose inspiration we contend is the original record*—the autographs or parchments of Moses, David, Daniel, Matthew, Paul or Peter, as the case may be, and not any particular translation or translations of them whatever. There is no translation absolutely without error, nor could there be, considering the infirmities of human copyists, unless

God were pleased to perform a perpetual miracle to secure it.

But does this make nugatory our contention? Some would say it does, and they would argue speciously that to insist on the inerrancy of a parchment no living being has ever seen is an academic question merely, and without value. But do they not fail to see that the character and perfection of the God-head are involved in that inerrancy?

Some years ago a "liberal" theologian, deprecating this discussion as not worth while, remarked that it was a matter of small consequence whether a pair of trousers were originally perfect if they were now rent. To which the valiant and witty David James Burrell replied, that it might be a matter of small consequence to the wearer of the trousers, but the tailor who made them would prefer to have it understood that they did not leave his shop that way. And then he added, that if the Most High must train among knights of the shears He might at least be regarded as the best of the guild, and One who drops no stitches and sends out no imperfect work.

Is it not with the written Word as with the incarnate Word? Is Jesus Christ to be regarded as imperfect because His character has never been perfectly reproduced before us? Can He be the incarnate Word unless He were absolutely without sin? And by the same token, can the scriptures be the written Word unless they were inerrant?

But if this question be so purely speculative and valueless, what becomes of the science of Biblical criticism by which properly we set such store today? Do builders drive piles into the soft earth if they never expect to touch bottom? Do scholars dispute about the scripture text and minutely examine the history and meaning of single words, "the delicate coloring of mood, tense and accent," if at the end there is no approximation to an absolute? As Dr. George H. Bishop says, does not our concordance, every time we take it up, speak loudly to us of a once inerrant parchment? Why do we not possess concordances for the very words of other books?

Nor is that original parchment so remote a thing as some suppose. Do not the number and variety of manuscripts and versions extant render it comparatively easy to arrive at a knowledge of its text, and does not competent scholarship today affirm that as to the New Testament at least, we have in 999 cases out of every thousand the very word of that original text? Let candid consideration be given to these things and it will be seen that we are not pursuing a phantom in contending for an inspired autograph of the Bible.

II. EXTENT OF INSPIRATION

1. *The inspiration of scripture includes the whole and every part of it.* There are some who deny this and limit it to only the prophetic portions, the words of Jesus Christ, and, say, the profounder spiritual teachings of the epistles. The historical books in their judgment, and as an example, do not require inspiration because their data were obtainable from natural sources.

The Bible itself, however, knows of no limitations, as we shall see: "*All* scripture is given by inspiration of God." The historical data, most of it at least, might have been obtained from natural sources, but what about the supernatural guidance required in their selection and narration? Compare, for answer, the records of creation, the fall, the deluge, etc., found in Genesis with those recently discovered by excavations in Bible lands. Do not the results of the pick-axe and the spade point to the same original as the Bible, and yet do not their childishness and grotesqueness often bear evidence of the human and sinful mould through which they ran? Do they not show the need of some power other than man himself to lead him out of the labyrinth of error into the open ground of truth?

Furthermore, are not the historical books in some respects the most important in the Bible? Are they not the bases of its doctrine? Does not the doctrine of sin need for its starting point the record of the fall? Could we so satisfactorily understand justification did we not have the story of God's dealings with Abraham? And what of the priesthood of Christ? Dismiss Leviticus and what can be made of Hebrews? Is not the Acts of the Apostles historical, but can we afford to lose its inspiration?

And then, too, the historical books are, in many cases, prophetical as well as historical. Do not the types and symbols in them show forth the Saviour in all the varying aspects of His grace? Has not the story of Israel the closest relation as type and anti-type to our spiritual redemption? Does not Paul teach this in 1 Cor., 10:6-11? And if these things were thus written for our learning, does not this imply their inspiration?

Indeed, the historical books have the strongest testimony borne to their importance in other parts of the Bible. This will appear more particularly as we proceed, but take, in passing, Christ's use of Deuteronomy in His conflict with the tempter. Thrice does He overcome him by a citation from that historical book without note or comment. Is it not difficult to believe that neither He nor Satan considered it inspired?

Thus without going further, we may say, with Dr. DeWitt of Princeton, that it is impossible to secure the *religious* infalliability of the Bible—which is all the objector regards as necessary—if we exclude Bible history from the sphere of its inspiration. But if we include Bible history at all, we must include the whole of it, for who is competent to separate its parts?

2. *The inspiration includes not only all the books of the Bible in general but in detail, the form as well as the substance, the word as well as the thought.* This is sometimes called the *verbal* theory of inspiration and is vehemently spoken against in some quarters. It is too mechanical, it degrades the writers to the level of machines, it has a tendency to make skeptics, and all that.

This last remark, however, is not so alarming as it sounds.

The doctrine of the eternal retribution of the wicked is said to make skeptics, and also that of a vicarious atonement, not to mention other revelations of Holy Writ. The natural mind takes to none of these things. But if we are not prepared to yield the point in one case for such a reason, why should we be asked to do it in another?

And as to degrading the writers to the level of machines, even if it were true, as it is not, why should fault be found when one considers the result? Which is the more important, the free agency of a score or two of mortals, or the divinity of their message? The whole argument is just a spark from the anvil on which the race is ever trying to hammer out the deification of itself.

But we are insisting upon no theory—not even the verbal theory—if it altogether excludes the human element in the transmission of the sacred word. As Dr. Henry B. Smith says, "God speaks through the personality as well as the lips of His messengers," and we may pour into that word "personality" everything that goes to make it—the age in which the person lived, his environment, his degree of culture, his temperament and all the rest. As Wayland Hoyt expressed it, "Inspiration is not a mechanical, crass, bald compulsion of the sacred writers, but rather a dynamic, divine influence over their freely-acting faculties" in order that the latter in relation to the subject-matter then in hand may be kept inerrant, *i. e.,* without mistake or fault. It is limiting the Holy One of Israel to say that He is unable to do this without turning a human being into an automaton. Has He who created man as a free agent left himself no opportunity to mould his thoughts into forms of speech inerrantly expressive of His will, without destroying that which He has made?

And, indeed, wherein resides man's free agency, in his mind or in his mouth? Shall we say he is free while God controls his thought, but that he becomes a mere machine when that control extends to the *expression* of his thought?

But returning to the argument, if the divine influence upon the writers did not extend to the form as well as the substance of their writings; if, in other words, God gave them only the thought, permitting them to express it in their own words, what guarantee have we that they have done so?

An illustration the writer has frequently used will help to make this clear. A stenographer in a mercantile house was asked by his employer to write as follows:

"Gentlemen: We misunderstood your letter and will now fill your order."

Imagine the employer's surprise, however, when a little later this was set before him for his signature:

"Gentlemen: We misunderstood your letter and will *not* fill your order."

The mistake was only of a single letter, but it was entirely subversive of his meaning. And yet the thought was given clearly to the stenographer, and the words, too, for that matter. Moreover, the latter was capable and faithful, but he was human, and it is human to err. Had not his employer controlled his expression down to the very letter, the thought intended to be conveyed would have failed of utterance.

In the same way the human authors of the Bible were men of like passions with ourselves. Their motives were pure, their intentions good, but even if their subject-matter were the commonplaces of men, to say nothing of the mysterious and transcendent revelation of a holy God, how could it be an absolute transcript of the mind from which it came in the absence of miraculous control?

In the last analysis, it is the Bible itself, of course, which must settle the question of its inspiration and the extent of it, and to this we come in the consideration of the proof, but we may be allowed a final question. Can even God Himself give a thought to man without the words that clothe it? Are not the two inseparable, as much so "as a sum and its figures, or a tune and its notes?" Has any case been known in human history where a healthy mind has been able to create ideas without expressing them to its own perception? In other words, as Dr. A. J. Gordon once observed: "To deny that the Holy Spirit speaks in scripture is an intelligible proposition, but to admit that He speaks, it is impossible to know what He says except as we have His Words."

III. PROOF OF INSPIRATION

1. *The inspiration of the Bible is proven by the philosophy, or what may be called the nature of the case.*

The proposition may be stated thus: The Bible is the history of the redemption of the race, or from the side of the individual, a supernatural revelation of the will of God to men for their salvation. But it was given to certain men of one age to be conveyed in writing to other men in different ages. Now all men experience difficulty in giving faithful reflections of their thoughts to others because of sin, ignorance, defective memory and the inaccuracy always incident to the use of language.

Therefore it may be easily deduced that if the revelation is to be communicated precisely as originally received, the same supernatural power is required in the one case as in the other. This has been sufficiently elaborated in the foregoing and need not be dwelt upon again.

2. *It may be proven by the history and character of the Bible, i. e.,* by all that has been assumed as to its authenticity and credibility. All that goes to prove these things goes to prove its inspiration.

To borrow in part, the language of the Westminster Confession, "the heavenliness of its matter, the efficacy of its doctrine, the unity of its various parts, the majesty of its style and the scope and completeness of its design" all indicate the divinity of its origin.

The more we think upon it the more we must be convinced that men unaided by the Spirit of God could neither have conceived, nor put together, nor preserved in its integrity that precious deposit known as the Sacred Oracles.

3. *But the strongest proof is the declarations of the Bible itself* and the inferences to be drawn from them. Nor is this reasoning in a circle as some might think. In the case of a man as to whose veracity there is no doubt, no hesitancy is felt in accepting what he says about himself; and since the Bible is demonstrated to be true in its statements of fact by unassailable evidence, may we not accept its witness in its own behalf?

Take the argument from Jesus Christ as an illustration. He was content to be tested by the prophecies that went before on Him, and the result of that ordeal was the establishment of His claims to be the Messiah beyond a peradventure. That complex system of prophecies, rendering collusion or counterfeit impossible, is the incontestable proof that He was what He claimed to be. But of course, He in whose birth, and life, and death, and resurrection such marvelous prophecies met their fulfilment, became, from the hour in which His claims were established, a witness to the divine authority and infallible truth of the sacred records in which these prophecies are found.—(The New Apologetic, by Professor Robert Watts, D. D.)

It is so with the Bible. The character of its contents, the unity of its parts, the fulfilment of its prophecies, the miracles wrought in its attestation, the effects it has accomplished in the lives of nations and of men, all these go to show that it is divine, and if so, that it may be believed in what it says about itself.

A. ARGUMENT FOR THE OLD TESTAMENT

To begin with the Old Testament, (*a*) consider how the writers speak of the origin of their messages. Dr. James H. Brookes is authority for saying that the phrase, "Thus saith the Lord" or its equivalent is used by them 2,000 times. Suppose we eliminate this phrase and its necessary context from the Old Testament in every instance, one wonders how much of the Old Testament would remain.

(*b*) Consider how the utterances of the Old Testament writers are introduced into the New. Take Matthew 1:22 as an illustration, "Now all this was done that it might be fulfilled which was spoken by the Lord through the prophet." It was not the prophet who spake, but the Lord who spake through the prophet.

(*c*) Consider how Christ and His apostles regard the Old Testament. He came "not to destroy but to fulfill the law and the prophets." Matt. 5:17. "The Scripture cannot be broken." John 10:35. He sometimes used single words as the bases of important doctrines, twice in Matthew 22, at verses 31, 32 and 42-45. The apostles do the same. See Galatians 3:16, Hebrews 2:8, 11 and 12:26, 27.

(*d*) Consider what the apostles directly teach upon the subject. Peter tells us that "No prophecy ever came by the will of man, but men spake from God, being moved by the Holy Spirit" (2 Peter 1:21, R. V.). "Prophecy" here applies to the word written as is indicated in the preceding verse, and means not merely the foretelling of events, but the utterances of any word of God without reference as to time past, present or to come. As a matter of fact, what Peter declares is that the will of man had nothing to do with any part of the Old Testament, but that the whole of it, from Genesis to Malachi, was inspired by God.

Of course Paul says the same, in language even plainer, in 2 Timothy 3:16, "All scripture is given by inspiration of God, and is profitable." The phrase "inspiration of God" means literally *God-breathed*. The whole of the Old Testament is God-breathed, for it is to that part of the Bible the language particularly refers, since the New Testament as such was not then generally known.

As this verse is given somewhat differently in the Revised Version we dwell upon it a moment longer. It there reads, "Every scripture inspired of God is also profitable," and the caviller is disposed to say that therefore some scripture may be inspired and some may not be, and that the profitableness extends only to the former and not the latter.

But aside from the fact that Paul would hardly be guilty of such a weak truism as that, it may be stated in reply first, that the King James rendering of the passage is not only the more consistent scripture, but the more consistent Greek. Several of the best Greek scholars of the period affirm this, including some of the revisers themselves who did not vote for the change. And secondly, even the revisers place it in the margin as of practically equal authority with their preferred translation, and to be chosen by the reader if desired. There are not a few devout Christians, however, who would be willing to retain the rendering of the Revised Version as being stronger than the King James, and who would interpolate a word in applying it to make it mean, "Every scripture (*because*) inspired of God is also profitable." We believe that both Gaussen and Wordsworth take this view, two as staunch defenders of plenary inspiration as could be named.

B. ARGUMENT FOR THE NEW TESTAMENT

We are sometimes reminded that, however strong and convincing the argument for the inspiration of the Old Testament, that for the New Testament is only indirect. "Not one of the evangelists tells us that he is inspired," says a certain theological professor, "and not one writer of an epistle, except Paul."

We shall be prepared to dispute this statement a little further, but in the meantime let us reflect that the inspiration of the Old Testament being assured as it is, why should similar evidence be required for the New? Whoever is competent to speak as a Bible authority knows that the *unity* of the Old and New Testaments is the strongest demonstration of their common source. They are seen to be not two books, but only two parts of one book.

To take then the analogy of the Old Testament. The foregoing argument proves its inspiration as a whole, although there were long periods separating the different writers, Moses and David let us say, or David and Daniel, the Pentateuch and the Psalms, or the Psalms and the Prophets. As long, or longer, than between Malachi and Matthew, or Ezra and the Gospels. If then to carry conviction for the plenary inspiration of the Old Testament as a whole, it is not necessary to prove it for every book, why, to carry conviction for the plenary inspiration of the *Bible* as a whole is it necessary to do the same?

We quote here a paragraph or two from Dr. Nathaniel West. He is referring to 2 Timothy 3:16, which he renders, "*Every* scripture is inspired of God," and adds:

"The distributive word 'Every' is used not only to particularize each individual scripture of the Canon that Timothy had studied from his youth, but also to include, along with the Old Testament the New Testament scriptures extant in Paul's day, and any others, such as those that John wrote after him.

"The Apostle Peter tells us that he was in possession, not merely of some of Paul's Epistles, but '*all* his Epistles,' and places them, canonically, in the same rank with what he calls 'the other scriptures,' *i. e.,* of equal inspiration and authority with the 'words spoken before by the Holy Prophets, and the commandment of the Lord and Savior, through the Apostles.' 2 Peter 3:2, 16.

"Paul teaches the same co-ordination of the Old and New Testaments. Having referred to the Old as a unit, in his phrase 'Holy Scriptures,' which the revisers translate 'Sacred Writings,' he proceeds to particularize. He tells Timothy that 'every scripture,' whether of Old or New Testament production, 'is inspired of God.' Let it be in the Pentateuch, the Psalms, the Prophets, the Historical Books, let it be a chapter or a verse; let it be in the Gospels, the Acts, his own or Peter's Epistles, or even John's writings, yet to be, still each part of the Sacred Collection is God-given and because of that possesses divine authority as part of the Book of God."

We read this from Dr. West twenty years ago, and rejected it as his dictum. We read it today, with deeper and fuller knowledge of the subject, and we believe it to be true.

It is somewhat as follows that Dr. Gaussen in his exhaustive "Theopneustia" gives the argument for the inspiration of the New Testament.

(*a*) The New Testament is the later, and for that reason the more important revelation of the two, and hence if the former were inspired, it certainly must be true of the latter. The opening verses of the first and second chapters of Hebrews plainly suggest this: "God, who at sundry times and in divers manners spake in time past unto the fathers by the prophets, hath in these last days spoken unto us by His Son * * * *Therefore* we ought to give the more earnest heed to the things which we have heard."

And this inference is rendered still more conclusive by the circumstance that the New Testament sometimes explains, sometimes proves, and sometimes even repeals ordinances of the Old Testament. See Matthew 1:22, 23 for an illustration of the first, Acts 13:19 to 39 for the second and Galatians 5:6 for the third. Assuredly these things would not be true if the New Testament were not of equal, and in a certain sense, even greater authority than the Old.

(*b*) The writers of the New Testament were of an equal or higher rank than those of the Old. That they were prophets is evident from such allusions as Romans 16:25-27, and Ephesians 3:4, 5. But that they were more than prophets is indicated in the fact that wherever in the New Testament prophets and apostles are both mentioned, the last-named is always mentioned first (see 1 Cor. 12:28, Ephesians 2:20,

Ephesians 4:11). It is also true that the writers of the New Testament had a higher mission than those of the Old, since they were sent forth by Christ, as he had been sent forth by the Father (John 20:21). They were to go, not to a single nation only (as Israel), but into all the world (Matthew 28:19). They received the keys of the kingdom of heaven (Matthew 16:19). And they are to be pre-eminently rewarded in the regeneration (Matthew 19:28). Such considerations and comparisons as these are not to be overlooked in estimating the authority by which they wrote.

(*c*) The writers of the New Testament were especially qualified for their work, as we see in Matthew 10:19, 20, Mark 13:11, Luke 12:2, John 14:26 and John 16:13, 14. These passages will be dwelt on more at length in a later division of our subject, but just now it may be noticed that in some of the instances, inspiration of the most absolute character was promised as to what they should *speak*—the inference being warranted that none the less would they be guided in what they wrote. Their spoken words were limited and temporary in their sphere, but their written utterances covered the whole range of revelation and were to last forever. If in the one case they were inspired, how much more in the other?

(*d*) The writers of the New Testament directly claim divine inspiration. See Acts 15:23-29, where, especially at verse 28, James is recorded as saying, "for it seemed good to the Holy Ghost and to us, to lay upon you no greater burden than these necessary things." Here it is affirmed very clearly that the Holy Ghost is the real writer of the letter in question and simply using the human instruments for his purpose. Add to this 1 Corinthians 2:13, where Paul says: "Which things also we speak, not in the words which man's wisdom teacheth, but which the Holy Ghost teacheth, comparing spiritual things with spiritual," or as the margin of the Revised Version puts it, "imparting spiritual things to spiritual men." In 1 Thessalonians 2:13 the same writer says: "For this cause also thank we God without ceasing, because when ye received the word of God which ye heard of us, ye received it not as the word of man, but as it is in truth the word of God." In 2 Peter 3:2 the apostle places his own words on a level with those of the prophets of the Old Testament, and in verses 15 and 16 of the same chapter he does the same with the writings of Paul, classifying them "with the other scriptures." Finally, in Revelation 2:7, although it is the Apostle John who is writing, he is authorized to exclaim: "He that hath an ear let him hear what the Spirit saith unto the churches," and so on throughout the epistles to the seven churches.

C. ARGUMENT FOR THE WORDS

The evidence that the inspiration includes the form as well as the substance of the Holy Scriptures, the word as well as the thought, may be gathered in this way.

1. *There were certainly some occasions when the words were given to the human agents.* Take the instance of Balaam (Numbers 22:38, 23:12, 16). It is clear that this self-seeking prophet *thought, i. e.,* desired to speak differently from what he did, but was obliged to speak the word that God put in his mouth. There are two incontrovertible witnesses to this, one being Balaam himself and the other God.

Take Saul (1 Samuel 10:10), or at a later time, his messengers (19:20-24). No one will claim that there was not an inspiration of the words here. And Caiaphas also (John 11:49-52), of whom it is expressly said that when he prophesied that one man should die for the people, "this spake he not of himself." Who believes that Caiaphas meant or really knew the significance of what he said?

And how entirely this harmonizes with Christ's promise to His disciples in Matthew 10:19, 20 and elsewhere. "When they deliver you up take no thought (be not anxious) how or what ye shall speak; for it shall be given you in that hour what ye shall speak. For it is not ye that speak but the Spirit of your Father which speaketh in you." Mark is even more emphatic: "Neither do ye *premeditate,* but whatsoever shall be given you in that hour, that speak ye, for it is not ye that speak, but the Holy Ghost."

Take the circumstance of the day of Pentecost (Acts 2:4-11), when the disciples "began to speak with other tongues as the Spirit gave them utterance." Parthians, Medes, Elamites, the dwellers in Mesopotamia, in Judea, Cappadocia, Pontus, Asia, Phrygia, Pamphylia, Egypt, in the parts of Libya about Cyrene, the strangers of Rome, Cretes and Arabians all testified, "we do here them speak in our tongues the wonderful works of God!" Did not this inspiration include the words? Did it not indeed *exclude* the thought? What clearer example could be desired?

To the same purport consider Paul's teaching in 1 Corinthians 14 about the gift of tongues. He that speaketh in an unknown tongue, in the Spirit speaketh mysteries, but no man understandeth him, therefore he is to pray that he may interpret. Under some circumstances, if no interpreter be present, he is to keep silence in the church and speak only to himself and to God.

But better still, consider the utterance of 1 Peter 1:10, 11, where he speaks of them who prophesied of the grace that should come, as "searching what, or what manner of time, the Spirit of Christ which was in them did signify when He testified beforehand the sufferings of Christ and the glory that should follow, to whom it was revealed," etc.

"Should we see a student who, having taken down the lecture of a profound philosopher, was now studying diligently to comprehend the sense of the discourse which he had written, we should understand simply that he was a pupil and not a master; that he had nothing to do with originating either the thoughts or the words of the lecture, but was rather a disciple whose province it was to understand what he had transcribed, and so be able to communicate it to others.

"And who can deny that this is the exact picture of what we have in this passage from Peter? Here were inspired writers studying the meaning of what they themselves had written. With all possible allowance for the human peculiarities of the writers, they must have been reporters of what they heard, rather than formulators of that which they had been made to understand."—A. J. Gordon in "The Ministry of the Spirit," pp. 173, 174.

2. *The Bible plainly teaches that inspiration extends to its words.* We spoke of Balaam as uttering that which God put in his mouth, but the same expression is used by God Himself with reference to His prophets. When Moses would excuse himself from service because he was not eloquent, He who made man's mouth said, "Now therefore go, and I will be with thy mouth, and teach thee what thou shalt say" (Exodus 4:10-12). And Dr. James H. Brookes' comment is very pertinent. "God did not say I will be with thy mind, and teach thee what thou shalt think; but I will be with thy mouth and teach thee what thou shalt say. This explains why, forty years afterwards, Moses said to Israel, 'Ye shall not add unto the word I command you, neither shall ye diminish ought from it.' (Deut. 4:2.)" Seven times Moses tells us that the tables of stone containing the commandments were the work of God, and the writing was the writing of God, graven upon the tables (Exodus 31:16).

Passing from the Pentateuch to the poetical books we find David saying, "The Spirit of the Lord spake by me, and His word was in my tongue" (2 Samuel 23:1, 2). He, too, does not say, God thought by me, but spake by me.

Coming to the prophets, Jeremiah confesses that, like Moses, he recoiled from the mission on which he was sent and for the same reason. He was a child and could not speak. "Then the Lord put forth His hand and touched my mouth. And the Lord said unto me, Behold I have put My word in thy mouth" (Jeremiah 1:6-9).

All of which substantiates the declaration of Peter quoted earlier, that "no prophecy ever came by the will of man, but man spake from God, being moved by the Holy Spirit." Surely, if the will of man had *nothing* to do with the prophecy, he could not have been at liberty in the selection of the words.

So much for the Old Testament, but when we reach the New, we have the same unerring and verbal accuracy guaranteed to the apostles by the Son of God, as we have seen. And we have the apostles making claim of it, as when Paul in 1 Corinthians 2:12, 13 distinguishes between the "things" or the thoughts which God gave him and the words in which he expressed them, and insisting on the divinity of both; "Which things also we speak," he says, "not in the words which man's wisdom teacheth, but which the Holy Ghost teacheth." In Galatians 3:16, following the example of His divine Master, he employs not merely a single word, but a single letter of a word as the basis of an argument for a great doctrine. The blessing of justification which Abraham received has become that of the believer in Jesus Christ. "Now to Abraham and his seed were the promises made. He saith not, And to seeds, as of many; but as of one, And to thy *seed,* which is Christ."

The writer of the epistle to the Hebrews bases a similar argument on the word "all" in chapter 1:8, on the word "one" in 1:11, and on the phrase "yet once more" in 12:26, 27.

To recur to Paul's argument in Galatians, Archdeacon Farrar in one of his writings denies that by any possibility such a Hebraist as he, and such a master of Greek usage could have argued in this way. He says Paul must have known that the plural of the Hebrew and Greek terms for "seed" is never used by Hebrew or Greek writers to designate human offspring. It means, he says, various kinds of grain.

His artlessness is amusing. We accept his estimate of Paul's knowledge of Hebrew and Greek, says Professor Watts, he was certainly a Hebrew of the Hebrews, and as to his Greek he could not only write it but speak it as we know, and quote what suited his purpose from the Greek poets. But on this supposition we feel justified in asking Dr. Farrar whether a lexicographer in searching Greek authors for the meanings they attached to *spèrmata,* the Greek for "seeds," would not be inclined to add "human offspring" on so good an authority as Paul?

Nor indeed would they be limited to his authority, since Sophocles uses it in the same way, and Aeschylus. "I was driven away from my country by my own offspring" (*spèrmata*)—literally by my own seeds, is what the former makes one of his characters say.

Dr. Farrar's rendering of *spèrmata* in Galatians 3:16 on the other hand would make nonsense if not sacrilege. "He saith not unto various kinds of grain as of many, but as of one, and to thy grain, which is Christ."

"Granting then, what we thank no man for granting, that *spèrmata* means human offspring, it is evident that despite all opinions to the contrary, this passage sustains the teaching of an inspiration of Holy Writ extending to its very words."

3. *But the most unique argument for the inspiration of the words of scripture is the relation which Jesus Christ bears to them.* In the first place, He Himself was inspired as to His words. In the earliest reference to His prophetic office (Deut. 18:18), Jehovah says, "I will put My words in His mouth, and He shall speak * * * all that I shall command Him." A limitation on His utterance which Jesus everywhere recognizes. "As My Father hath taught Me, I speak these things;" "the Father which sent Me, He gave Me a commandment what I should say, and what I should speak;" "whatsoever I speak therefore, even as the Father said unto Me, so I speak;" "I have given unto them the words which Thou gavest Me;" "the words that I speak unto you, they are spirit and they are life." (John 6:63; 8:26, 28, 40; 12:49, 50.)

The thought is still more impressive as we read of the relation of the Holy Spirit to the God-man. "The Spirit of

the Lord is upon Me because He hath annointed Me to preach
the gospel to the poor;" "He through the Holy Ghost had
given commandments unto the apostles;" "the revelation of
Jesus Christ which God gave unto Him;" "these things saith
He that holdeth the seven stars in His right hand;" "He that
hath an ear let him hear what the *Spirit* saith unto the
churches" (Luke 4:18; Acts 1:2; Rev. 1:1; 2:1, 11). If the
incarnate Word needed the unction of the Holy Ghost to give
to men the revelation He received from the Father in Whose
bosom He dwells; and if the agency of the same Spirit extended to the words He spake in preaching the gospel to the
meek or dictating an epistle, how much more must these things
be so in the case of ordinary men when engaged in the same
service? With what show of reason can one contend that any
Old or New Testament writer stood, so far as his words were
concerned, in need of no such agency."—The New Apologetic,
pp. 67, 68.

In the second place He used the scriptures as though they
were inspired as to their words. In Matthew 22:31, 32, He
substantiates the doctrine of the resurrection against the skep-
ticism of the Sadducees by emphasizing the present tense of
the verb "to be," *i. e.,* the word "am" in the language of
Jehovah to Moses at the burning bush. In verses 42-45 of the
same chapter He does the same for His own Deity by alluding to the second use of the word "Lord" in Psalm CX. "The
LORD said unto my Lord * * * If David then call him
Lord, how is he his son?" In John 10:34-36, He vindicates
Himself from the charge of blasphemy by saying, "Is it not
written in your law, I said, Ye are gods? If He called them
gods, unto whom the word of God came, and the scripture
cannot be broken; say ye of him, whom the Father hath sanctified, and sent into the world, Thou blasphemest; because I
said, I am the Son of God?"

We have already seen Him (in Matthew 4) overcoming the
tempter in the wilderness by three quotations from Deuter-

onomy without note or comment except, *"It is written."* Referring to which Adolphe Monod says, "I know of nothing in the whole history of humanity, nor even in the field of divine revelation, that proves more clearly than this the inspiration of the scriptures. What! Jesus Christ, the Lord of heaven and earth, calling to his aid in that solemn moment Moses his servant? He who speaks from heaven fortifying himself against the temptations of hell by the word of him who spake from earth? How can we explain that spiritual mystery, that wonderful reversing of the order of things, if for Jesus the words of Moses were not the words of God rather than those of men? How shall we explain it if Jesus were not fully aware that holy men of God spake as they were moved by the Holy Ghost?

"I do not forget the objections which have been raised against the inspiration of the scriptures, nor the real obscurity with which that inspiration is surrounded; if they sometimes trouble your hearts, they have troubled mine also. But at such times, in order to revive my faith, I have only to glance at Jesus glorifying the scriptures in the wilderness; and I have seen that for all who rely upon Him, the most embarrassing of problems is transformed into a historical fact, palpable and clear. Jesus no doubt was aware of the difficulties connected with the inspiration of the scriptures, but did this prevent Him from appealing to their testimony with unreserved confidence? Let that which was sufficient for Him suffice for you. Fear not that the rock which sustained the Lord in the hour of His temptation and distress will give way because you lean too heavily upon it."

In the third place, Christ teaches that the scriptures are inspired as to their words. In the Sermon on the Mount He said, "Think not that I am come to destroy the law, or the prophets: I am not come to destroy, but to fulfil. For verily I say unto you, Till heaven and earth pass, one jot or one tittle shall in no wise pass from the law, till all be fulfilled."

Here is testimony confirmed by an oath, for "verily" on the lips of the Son of Man carries such force. He affirms the indestructibility of the law, not its substance merely but its form, not the thought but the word.

"One jot or tittle shall in no wise pass from the law." The "jot" means the *yod,* the smallest letter in the Hebrew alphabet, while the "tittle" means the *horn,* a short projection in certain letters extending the base line beyond the upright one which rests upon it. A reader unaccustomed to the Hebrew needs a strong eye to see the tittle, but Christ guarantees that as a part of the sacred text neither the tittle nor the yod shall perish.

The elder Lightfoot, the Hebraist and rabbinical scholar of the Westminster Assembly time, has called attention to an interesting story of a certain letter *yod* found in the text of Deut. 32:18. It is in the word *teshi,* to forsake, translated in the King James as "unmindful." Originally it seems to have been written smaller even than usual, *i. e.,* undersized, and yet notwithstanding the almost infinite number of times in which copies have been made, that little *yod* stands there today just as it ever did. Lightfoot spoke of it in the middle of the seventeenth century and although two more centuries and a half have passed since then with all their additional copies of the book, yet it still retains its place in the sacred text. Its diminutive size is referred to in the margin, "but no hand has dared to add a hair's breadth to its length," so that we can still employ his words, and say that it is likely to remain there forever.

The same scholar speaks of the effect a slight change in the form of a Hebrew letter might produce in the substance of the thought for which it stands. He takes as an example two words, "Chalal" and "Halal," which differ from each other simply in their first radicals. The "Ch" in Hebrew is expressed by one letter the same as "H," the only distinction being a slight break or opening in the left limb of the latter. It seems too trifling to notice, but let that line be broken where it should be continuous, and "Thou shalt not *profane* the Name of thy God" in Leviticus 18:21, becomes "Thou shalt not *praise* the Name of thy God." Through that aperture, however small, the entire thought of the Divine mind oozes out, so to speak, and becomes quite antagonistic to what was designed.

This shows how truly the thought and the word expressing it are bound together, and that whatever affects the one imperils the other. As another says, "The bottles are not the wine, but if the bottles perish, the wine is sure to be spilled." It may seem like narrow-mindedness to contend for this, and an evidence of enlightenment or liberal scholarship to treat it with indifference, but we should be prepared to take our stand with Jesus Christ in the premises, and if necessary, go outside the camp bearing our reproach.

IV. DIFFICULTIES AND OBJECTIONS

That there are difficulties in the way of accepting a view of inspiration like this goes without saying. But to the finite mind there must always be difficulties connected with a revelation from the Infinite, and it can not be otherwise. This has been mentioned before. Men of faith, and it is such we are addressing, and not men of the world, do not wait to understand or resolve all the difficulties associated with other mysteries of the Bible before accepting them as divine, and why should they do so in this case?

Moreover, Archbishop Whately's dictum is generally accepted, that we are not obliged to clear away every difficulty about a doctrine in order to believe it, always provided that the facts on which it rests are true. And particularly is this the case where the rejection of such a doctrine involves greater difficulties than its belief, as it does here.

For if this view of inspiration be rejected, what have its opponents to give in its place? Do they realize that any objections to it are slight in comparison with those to any other view that can be named? And do they realize that this is true because this view has the immeasurable advantage of agreeing with the plain declarations of Scripture on the subject? In other words, as Dr. Burrell says, those who assert the inerrancy of the scripture autographs do so on the authority of God Himself, and to deny it is of a piece with the denial that they teach the forgiveness of sins or the resurrection from the dead. No amount of exegetical turning and twisting can explain away the assertions already quoted in these pages, to say nothing of the constant undertone of evidence we find in the Bible everywhere to their truth.

And speaking of this further, are we not justified in requiring of the objector two things? First, on any fair basis of scientific investigation, is he not obliged to dispose of the evidence here presented before he impugns the doctrine it substantiates? And second, after having disposed of it, is he not equally obligated to present the scriptural proof of whatever other view of inspiration he would have us accept? Has he ever done this, and if not, are we not further justified in saying that it can not be done? But let us consider some of the difficulties.

1. *There are the so-called discrepancies or contradictions between certain statements of the Bible and the facts of history or natural science.* The best way to meet these is to treat them separately as they are presented, but when you ask for them you are not infrequently met with silence. They are hard to produce, and when produced, who is able to say that they belong to the original parchments? As we are not contending for an inerrant translation, does not the burden of proof rest with the objector?

But some of these "discrepancies" are easily explained. They do not exist between statements of the Bible and facts of science, but between erroneous interpretations of the Bible and immature conclusions of science. The old story of Galileo is in point, who did not contradict the Bible in affirming that the earth moved round the sun but only the false theological assumptions about it. In this way advancing light has removed many of these discrepancies, and it is fair to presume with Dr. Charles Hodge that further light would remove all.

2. *There are the differences in the narratives themselves.* In the first place, the New Testament writers sometimes change important words in quoting from the Old Testament, which it is assumed could not be the case if in both instances the writers were inspired. But it is forgotten that in the scriptures we are dealing not so much with different human authors as with one Divine Author. It is a principle in ordinary literature that an author may quote himself as he pleases, and give a different turn to an expression here and there as a changed condition of affairs renders it necessary or desirable. Shall we deny this privilege to the Holy Spirit? May we not find, indeed, that some of these supposed misquotations show such progress of truth, such evident application of the teaching of an earlier dispensation to the circumstances of a later one, as to afford a confirmation of their divine origin rather than an argument against it?

We offered illustrations of this earlier, but to those would now add Isaiah 59:20 quoted in Romans 11:26, and Amos 9:11 quoted in Acts 15:16. And to any desiring to further examine the subject we would recommend the valuable work of Professor Franklin Johnson, of Chicago University, entitled "The Quotations in the New Testament from the Old."

Another class of differences, however, is where the *same event* is sometimes given differently by different writers. Take that most frequently used by the objectors, the inscription on the cross, recorded by all the evangelists and yet differently by each. How can such records be inspired, it is asked.

It is to be remembered in reply, that the inscription was written in three languages calling for a different arrangement of the words in each case, and that one evangelist may have translated the Hebrew, and another the Latin, while a third recorded the Greek. It is not said that any one gave the *full* inscription, nor can we affirm that there was any obligation upon them to do so. Moreover, no one contradicts any other, and no one says what is untrue.

Recalling what was said about our having to deal not with different human authors but with one Divine Author, may not the Holy Spirit here have chosen to emphasize some one particular fact, or phase of a fact of the inscription for a specific and important end? Examine the records to determine what this fact may have been. Observe that whatever else is omitted, all the narratives record the momentous circumstances that the Sufferer on the cross was THE KING OF THE JEWS.

Could there have been a cause for this? What was the charge preferred against Jesus by His accusers? Was He not rejected and crucified because He said He was the King of the Jews? Was not this the central idea Pilate was providentially guided to express in the inscription? And if so, was it not that to which the evangelists should bear witness? And should not that witness have been borne in a way to dispel the thought of collusion in the premises? And did not this involve a variety of narrative which should at the same time be in harmony with truth and fact? And do we not have this very thing in the four gospels?

These accounts supplement, but do not contradict each other. We place them before the eye in the order in which they are recorded.

This is Jesus	THE KING OF THE JEWS
	THE KING OF THE JEWS
This is	THE KING OF THE JEWS
Jesus of Nazareth	THE KING OF THE JEWS

The entire inscription evidently was "This is Jesus of Nazareth the King of the Jews," but we submit that the foregoing presents a reasonable argument for the differences in the records.

3. *There is the variety in style.* Some think that if all the writers were alike inspired and the inspiration extended to their words, they must all possess the same style—as if the Holy Spirit had but one style!

Literary style is a method of selecting words and putting sentences together which stamps an author's work with the influence of his habits, his condition in society, his education, his reasoning, his experience, his imagination and his genius. These give his mental and moral physiognomy and make up his style.

But is not God free to act with or without these fixed laws? There are no circumstances which tinge His views or reasonings, and He has no idiosyncrasies of speech, and no mother tongue through which He expresses His character, or leaves the finger mark of genius upon His literary fabrics.

It is a great fallacy then, as Dr. Thomas Armitage once said, to suppose that uniformity of verbal style must have marked God's authorship in the Bible, had He selected its words. As the author of all styles, rather does he use them all at his pleasure. He bestows all the powers of mental individuality upon His instruments for using the scriptures, and then uses their powers as He will to express His mind by them.

Indeed, the variety of style is a necessary proof of the freedom of the human writers, and it is this which among other things convinces us that, however controlled by the Holy Spirit, they were not mere machines in what they wrote.

Consider God's method in nature. In any department of vegetable life there may be but one genus, while its members are classified into a thousand species. From the bulbous root come the tulip, the hyacinth, the crocus, and the lily in every shape and shade, without any cause either of natural chemistry or culture. It is exclusively attributable to the variety of styles which the mind of God devises. And so in the sacred writings. His mind is seen in the infinite variety of expression which dictates the wording of every book. To quote Armitage again, "I cannot tell how the Holy Spirit suggested the words to the writers any more than some other man can tell how He suggested the thoughts to them. But if diversity of expression proves that He did not choose the words, the diversity of ideas proves that He did not dictate the thoughts, for the one is as varied as the other."

William Cullen Bryant was a newspaper man but a poet; Edmund Clarence Stedman was a Wall Street broker and also a poet. What a difference in style there was between their editorials and commercial letters on the one hand, and their poetry on the other! Is God more limited than a man?

4. *There are certain declarations of scripture itself.* Does not Paul say in one or two places "I speak as a man," or "After the manner of man?" Assuredly, but is he not using the arguments common among men for the sake of elucidating a point? And may he not as truly be led of the Spirit to do that, and to record it, as to do or say anything else? Of course, what he quotes from men is not of the same essential value as what he receives directly from God, but the *record* of the quotation is as truly inspired.

There are two or three other utterances of his of this character in the 7th chapter of 1 Corinthians, where he is treating of marriage. At verse 6 he says, "I speak this by permission, not of commandment," and what he means has no reference to the source of his message but the subject of it. In contradiction to the false teaching of some, he says Christians are permitted to marry, but not commanded to do so. At verse 10 he says, "Unto the married I command, yet not I, but the Lord," while at verse 12 there follows, "but to the rest speak I, not the Lord." Does he declare himself inspired in the first instance, and not in the second? By no means, but in the first he is alluding to what the Lord spake on the subject while here in the flesh, and in the second to what he, Paul, is adding thereto on the authority of the Holy Spirit speaking through him. In other words, putting his own utterances on equality with those of our Lord, he simply confirms their inspiration.

At verse 40 he uses a puzzling expression, "I think also that I have the Spirit of God." As we are contending only for an inspired record, it would seem easy to say that here he records a doubt as to whether he was inspired, and hence everywhere else in the absence of such record of doubt the inspiration is to be assumed. But this would be begging the question, and we prefer the solution of others that the answer is found in the condition of the Corinthian church at that time. His enemies had sought to counteract his teachings, claiming that they had the Spirit of God. Referring to the claim, he says with justifiable irony, "I think also that I have the Spirit of God" (R. V.). "I think" in the mouth of one having apostolic authority, says Professor Watts, may be taken as carrying the strongest assertion of the judgment in question. The passage is something akin to another in the same epistle at the 14th chapter, verse 37, where he says, "If any man think himself to be a prophet, or spiritual, let him acknowledge that the things I write unto you are the commandments of the Lord."

Time forbids further amplification on the difficulties and objections nor is it necessary, since there is not one that has not been met satisfactorily to the man of God and the child of faith again and again.

But there is an obstacle to which we would call attention before concluding—not a difficulty or objection, but a real obstacle, especially to the young and insufficiently instructed. It is the illusion that this view of inspiration is held only by the unlearned. An illusion growing out of still another as to who constitute the learned.

There is a popular impression that in the sphere of theology and religion these latter are limited for the most part to the higher critics and their relatives, and the more rationalistic and iconoclastic the critic the more learned he is esteemed to be.

But the fallacy of this is seen in that the qualities which make for a philologist, an expert in human languages, or which give one a wide acquaintance with literature of any kind, in other words the qualities of the higher critic, depend more on memory than judgment, and do not give the slightest guarantee that their possessors can draw a sound conclusion from what they know.

As the author of "Faith and Inspiration" puts it, the work of such a scholar is often like that of a quarryman to an architect. Its entire achievement, though immensely valuable in its place, is just a mass of raw and formless material until a mind gifted in a different direction, and possessing the necessary taste and balance shall reduce or put it into shape for use. The perplexities of astronomers touching Halley's comet is in point. They knew facts that common folks did not know, but when they came to generalize upon them, the man on the street knew that he should have looked in the west for the phenomenon when they bade him look in the east.

Much is said for example about an acquaintance with Hebrew and Greek, and no sensible man will underrate them for the theologian or the Bible scholar, but they are entirely unnecessary to an understanding of the doctrine of inspiration or any other doctrine of Holy Writ. The intelligent reader of the Bible in the English tongue, especially when illuminated by the Holy Spirit, is abundantly able to decide upon these questions for himself. He cannot determine how the Holy Spirit operated on the minds of the sacred penmen because that is not revealed, but he can determine on the results secured because that *is* revealed. He can determine whether the inspiration covers all the books, and whether it includes not only the substance but the form, not only the thoughts but the words.

We have spoken of scholars and of the learned, let us come to names. We suppose Dr. Sanday, of Oxford, is a scholar, and the Archbishop of Durham, and Dean Burgon, and Professor Orr, of Glasgow, and Principal Forsyth, of Hackney College, and Sir Robert Anderson, and Dr. Kuyper, of Holland, and President Patton, of Princeton, and Howard Osgood of the Old Testament Revision Committee and Matthew B. Riddle of the New, and G. Frederick Wright and Albert T. Clay, the archaeologists, and Presidents Moorehead and Mullins, and C. I. Scofield, and Luther T. Townsend, for twenty-five years professor in the Theological School of Boston University, and Arthur T. Pierson of the Missionary Review of the World, and a host of other living witnesses—Episcopalians, Presbyterians, Congregationalists, Baptists, Lutherans, Methodists, Reformed Dutch.

We had thought John Calvin a scholar, and the distinguished Bengel, and Canon Faussett, and Tregelles, and Auberlen, and Van Oosterzee, and Charles Hodge and Henry B. Smith, and so many more that it were foolishness to recall them. These men may not stand for every statement in these pages, they might not care to be quoted as holding technically the verbal theory of inspiration for reasons already named, but they will affirm the heart of the contention and testify to their belief in an inspiration of the Sacred Oracles which includes the words.

Once when the writer was challenged by the editor of a secular daily to name a single living scholar who thus believed, he presented that of a chancellor of a great university, and was told that he was not the kind of scholar that was meant! The kind of scholar not infrequently meant by such opposers is the one who is seeking to destroy faith in the Bible as the Word of God, and to substitute in its place a Bible of his own making.

The *Outlook* had an editorial recently, entitled "Whom Shall We Believe?" in which the writer reaffirmed the platitudes that living is a vital much more than an intellectual process, and that truth of the deeper kind is distilled out of experience rather than logical processes. This is the reason he said why many things are hidden from the so-called wise, who follow formal methods of exact observation, and are revealed to babes and sucklings who know nothing of these methods, but are deep in the process of living. No spectator ever yet understood a great contemporary human movement into which he did not enter.

Does this explain why the cloistered scholar is unable to accept the supernatural inspiration of the scriptures while the men on the firing line of the Lord's army believe in it even to the very words? Does it explain the faith of our missionaries in foreign lands? Is this what led J. Hudson Taylor to Inland China, and Dr. Guinness to establish the work upon the Congo, and George Müeller and William Quarrier to support the orphans at Bristol and the Bridge of Weirs? Is this—the belief in the plenary inspiration of the Bible—the secret of the evangelistic power of D. L. Moody, and Chapman, and Torrey, and Gipsy Smith, and practically every evangelist in the field, for to the extent of our acquaintance there are none of these who doubt it? Does this tell why "the best sellers on the market," at least among Christian people, have been the devotional and expository books of Andrew Murray, and Miller and Meyer, and writers of that stamp? Is this why the plain people have loved to listen to preachers like Spurgeon, and McLaren, and Campbell Morgan, and Len Broughton and A. C. Dixon and have passed by men of the other kind? It is, in a word, safe to challenge the whole Christian world for the name of a man who stands out as a winner of souls who does not believe in the inspiration of the Bible as it has been sought to be explained in these pages.

But we conclude with a kind of concrete testimony—that of the General Assembly of the Presbyterian Church of America, and of a date as recent as 1893. The writer is not a Presbyterian, and therefore with the better grace can ask his readers to consider the character and the intellect represented in such an Assembly. Here are some of our greatest merchants, our greatest jurists, our greatest educators, our greatest statesmen, as well as our greatest missionaries, evangelists and theologians. There may be seen as able and august a gathering of representatives of Christianity in other places and on other occasions, but few that can surpass it. For sobriety of thought, for depth as well as breadth of learning, for wealth of spiritual experience, for honesty of utterance, and virility of conviction, the General Assembly of the Presbyterian Church in America must command attention and respect throughout the world. And this is what it said on the subject we are now considering at its gathering in the city of Washington, the capital of the nation, at the date named:

"THE BIBLE AS WE NOW HAVE IT, IN ITS VARIOUS TRANSLATIONS AND REVISIONS, WHEN FREED FROM ALL ERRORS AND MISTAKES OF TRANSLATORS, COPYISTS AND PRINTERS, (IS) THE VERY WORD OF GOD, AND CONSEQUENTLY WHOLLY WITHOUT ERROR."

CHAPTER II

INSPIRATION

BY EVANGELIST L. W. MUNHALL, M. A., D. D.,
GERMANTOWN, PENNSYLVANIA,

AUTHOR OF "THE HIGHEST CRITICS VS. THE HIGHER CRITICS"

The Bible is inspired. It is therefore God's Word. This is fundamental to the Christian faith. "Faith cometh by hearing, and hearing by the Word of God" (Rom. 10: 17).

But, it is asked. What do you mean by inspiration? Because there are numerous theories of inspiration, this is a proper question. Also, it is well, before answering the question, to state some of these theories. First, "The thoughts of the penman were inspired." Second, "The thoughts were partially inspired." But they who hold to this view are very indefinite in their statements of the extent of this inspiration. Third, "There were different degrees of inspiration." The advocates of this view use the difference between "illumination" and inspiration to prove their theory. Fourth, "At one time the writers were inspired in the supervision of the work they did;" at another, "In the view they took of the work they were called upon to do;" and at another, "In directing the work." But in all these views the theorists are at sea, and leave all who trust to their pilotage at sea, as to the exact character and limitations of inspiration. Fifth, "Dynamic inspiration". But the efforts of those who hold to this view, to explain what they mean by the term are exceedingly vague and misty. But the popular and current theory now is that the "Concept" is inspired. But no one attempts to tell what the "Concept" is; indeed, I doubt if any one knows.

Also let this be said in this connection: Those who hold to any or all of the above named theories, in part or in whole, are

44

emphatic in declaring that the Bible is not verbally inspired. The noisy ones will say, "No scholar believes in verbal inspiration." In this they bear false witness. Another expression in common use among them is this: "Such belief drives men into infidelity." And yet no one of them ever knew of a case. This class, with as much care and evident satisfaction as an infidel, hunt out the apparent contradictions and errors in the authorized and revised versions, and exultingly declare: "Here is conclusive evidence that the Bible is not verbally inspired." Some of these gentlemen are dishonest because, First, they know that most of these apparent errors and contradictions were long ago satisfactorily answered, even to the silencing of infidel scoffers; and Second, they know that no one believes that the translations and revisions are inspired. The doctrine of verbal inspiration is simply this: The original writings, *ipsissima verba,* came through the penmen direct from God; and the critics are only throwing dust into the air when they rail against verbal inspiration and attempt to disprove it by pointing out the apparent errors and discrepancies of the authorized and revised texts.

The General Assembly of the Presbyterian Church, in 1893, by a unanimous vote made the following deliverance: "The Bible as we now have it in its various translations and revisions when freed from all errors and mistakes of translators, copyists and printers, is the very Word of God, and consequently, wholly without error."

We mean by Inspiration that the words composing the Bible are God-breathed. If they are not, then the Bible is not inspired at all, since it is composed only and solely of words.

"All Scripture is given by inspiration of God" (2 Tim. 3:16). The word rendered Scripture in this passage is *Graphe.* It means writing, anything written. The writing is composed of words. What else is this but verbal inspiration; and they wrest the "Scriptures unto their own destruction", who teach otherwise.

Prof. A. A. Hodge says: "The line can never rationally be drawn between the thoughts and words of Scripture. . . . That we have an inspired Bible, and a verbally inspired one, we have the witness of God Himself."

Prof. Gaussen says: "The theory of a Divine Revelation, in which you would have the inspiration of thoughts, without the inspiration of the language, is so inevitably irrational that it cannot be sincere, and proves false even to those who propose it."

Canon Westcott says: "The slightest consideration will show that words are as essential to intellectual processes as they are to mutual intercourse. . . . Thoughts are wedded to words as necessarily as soul to body. Without it the mysteries unveiled before the eyes of the seer would be confused shadows; with it, they are made clear lessons for human life."

Dean Burgon, a man of vast learning, says: "You cannot dissect inspiration into substance and form. As for thoughts being inspired, apart from the words which give them expression, you might as well talk of a tune without notes, or a sum without figures. No such theory of inspiration is even intelligible. It is as illogical as it is worthless, and cannot be too sternly put down."

This doctrine of the inspiration of Scripture, in all its elements and parts, has always been the doctrine of the Church. Dr. Westcott has proved this by a copious catena of quotations from Ante-Nicene Fathers in Appendix B to his "Introduction to the Study of the Gospels". He quotes Clemens Romanus as saying that the Scriptures are "the true utterances of the Holy Ghost".

Take a few quotations from the Fathers: 1. Justin, speaking of the words of Scripture, says: "We must not suppose that the language proceeds from the men that are inspired, but from the Divine Word Himself, who moves them. Their work is to announce that which the Holy Spirit proposes to teach, through them, to those who wish to learn the true religion. The Divine power acts on men just as a plectrum on a harp or lyre." "The history Moses wrote was by the Divine Inspiration." And so, of all the Bible.

2. Irenaeus. "The writers spoke as acted on by the Spirit. All who foretold the Coming of Christ (Moses, David, Isaiah, etc.), received their inspiration from the Son, for how else could Scripture 'testify' of Him alone?" "Matthew might have written, 'The generation of Jesus was on this wise,' but the Holy Spirit, foreseeing the corruption of the truth, and fortifying us against deception, says, through Matthew, 'The generation of Jesus the Messiah was on this wise.'" "The writers are beyond all falsehood" i. e., they are inerrant.

3. Clement of Alexandria. The foundations of our faith rest on no insecure basis. We have received them through God Himself through the Scripture, not one jot or tittle of which shall pass away till all is accomplished, for the mouth of the Lord, the Holy Spirit, spoke it. He ceases to be a man who spurns the tradition of the Church, and turns aside to human opinions; for the Scriptures are truly holy, since they make us holy, God-like. Of these Holy Writings or Words, the Bible is composed. Paul calls them God-breathed. (2 Tim. 3:15, 16.) The Sacred Writings consist of these holy letters or syllables, since they are "God-breathed". Again, "The Jews and Christians agree as to the inspiration of the Holy Scriptures, but differ in interpretation. By our faith, we believe that every Scripture, since it is God-breathed, is profitable. If the words of the Lord are pure words, refined silver, tried seven times, and the Holy Spirit has, with all care, dictated them accurately, it was on this account the Saviour said that not one jot or tittle of them should pass away."

4. Origen. "It is the doctrine acknowledged by all Christians, and evidently preached in the churches, that the Holy Spirit, inspired the Saints, Prophets and Apostles, and was present in those of old time, as in those He inspired at the Coming of Christ; for Christ, the Word of God, was in Moses when he wrote, and in the Prophets, and by His Spirit He did speak to them all things. The records of the Gospels are the Oracles of the Lord, pure Oracles, purified as silver seven times tried. They are without error, since they were accurately written, by the co-operation of the Holy Spirit." "It is good to adhere to the words of Paul and the Apostles, as to God and our Lord Jesus Christ. There are many writings, but only one Book; four Evangelists, but only one Gospel. All the Sacred Writings breathe the same fullness. There is nothing, in the Law, the Prophets, the Gospel, the Apostles, that did not come from the fullness of God. Whoever has received these Scriptures as inspired by the Creator of the world, must expect to find in them all the difficulties which meet those who investigate the system of the universe. But God's hand is not destroyed by our ignorance on particular points. The divinity of the Scriptures remains undisturbed by our weakness. It is a point in the teaching of the Church, that the Scriptures were written by the Spirit of God, and on this the opinion of the whole Church is one. All things that are written are true. He who is a student of God's Oracles must place himself under the teaching of God." So much for this Father of "Biblical Criticism," mighty in the Church.

5. Augustine. The view of the Holy Scriptures held by Augustine was that held by Tertullian, Cyprian and all Fathers of the North African Church. No view of verbal inspiration could be more rigid. "The Scriptures are the letters of God, the voice of God, the writings of God." "The writers record the words of God. Christ spoke by Moses, for He was the Spirit of the Creator, and all the

prophecies are the voice of the Lord. From the Spirit came the gift of tongues. All Scripture is profitable since it is inspired of God. The Scriptures, whether in History, Prophecy, Psalms or Law, are of God. They cannot stand in part and fall in part. They are from God, who spake them all." "As it was not the Apostles who spoke, but the Spirit of the Father in them, so it is the Spirit that speaks in all Scriptures". "It avails nothing what I say, what he says, but what saith the Lord".

Prof. B. B. Warfield, of Princeton Theological Seminary, said in an article, on The Westminster Doctrine of Inspiration: "Doubtless enough has been said to show that the confession teaches precisely the doctrine which is taught in the private writings of the framers, which was also the General Protestant Doctrine of the time, and not of that time only or of the Protestants only; for despite the contrary assertion that has recently become tolerably current, essentially this doctrine of inspiration (verbal) has been the doctrine of the Church of all ages and of all names."

There is nothing truer in the world than that both the Jewish Church and the Christian Church believed the doctrine, because of their conception of the Holy Scriptures as the result of the *"Creative Breath of God,"* even as matter itself, the soul of man, and the world, were created by the same *"Breath of the Almighty"*—the very conception Paul had when he said, *"Every Scripture is God-breathed!"* The pervasive evidence of verbal inspiration stares one in the face at the opening of every page of the Bible. It is not a *"few texts"*, here and there, on which it depends, but it *"stands"* rooted in the whole body of the Word of God. He who knows what the Jews understood by the expression, "the Oracles of God", a divinely oracular Book, different from every other—a Book of God's own "Testimony"—will know that no other conception of its contents could prevail than this, that it was *"divinely inspired"*, having *"God"* as its Author, and truth without error as its matter. The manner in which the *Old Testament* is quoted in the *New* is crowning demonstration of its verbal inspiration. That subjectless verb, *"saith"* (rendered, "It saith"), that nominative, the "Scripture saith", that personal subject, "He" ("He saith"), that identification of God with the "Scripture," ("the Scripture foreseeing," giving to it eyes, mouth and foreknowledge, as a living organism equal with God), that recognition of the human writer, as "Moses saith," "David saith," "Isaiah saith," is a divinely governed authorship; therefore it is all one to say, "Moses saith," "It saith," "the Scripture saith", "He saith", since in all it is *"God saith"*—all this proves the "high place," the estimate and conception which Christ, His Apostles, and the whole Jewish and Christian Church, had of the *"Scriptures"*, and that they are a God-breathed, oracular Book, created by the *Breath* of God—a verbally inspired Book, whose *"words"* were the "Words of God", infallible, authoritative, final, the court of last appeal, the very "Utterance" and "Voice" "of God," who *spoke* in time past in the Prophets, and who has spoken to us in these last days in His Son—"words" commanded to be *written* in the days of Moses and commanded to be *written* in the Apostles' days —the Spirit promised "to guide," to permit no lapse of "remembrance," and to "reveal" the future.

Such form of citation, quotation, reference, and allusion to the Old Testament came from the conception of the Scriptures as the verbally inspired Book of God. It was by means of this specific and customary formula of quotation, Christ and His Apostles made known to the Church their exalted estimate of the *"Volume of the Book."* On this ground alone arose all the high attributes ascribed to it—its Divine origin, sanctity, sublimity, infallibility, authority and sufficiency for mankind. This uniform emphasis of the Scriptures as the product of the *"Breath* of *God,"* not mere "human literature," as the critics would have it, nor a "human element" uncontrolled by the Divine, nor the miserable excuse cf "wordless thoughts", the thoughts "inspired", but the "words not"—is characteristic of the treatment the Old Testament Scriptures everywhere receive in the New Testament. On no other view than that of verbal inspiration could such a manner of quotation, whether strict or free, have arisen. It is as the *"Creation"* and the *"Oracles"* of God they are referred to. On this their authority, holiness, perfection and perpetuity rest. And as to the "authorship" of the "Books" of Scripture, the citation of different texts existing in different "Books", render the names of different human authors, as "Moses saith", "David saith", "Isaiah saith", *is* proof that the authors of the texts are the authors of the "Books" in which they are found, and which bear their name. Only "Higher Critics" could dispute this.

SOME PROOFS OF VERBAL INSPIRATION

The Bible plainly teaches that its words are inspired, and that it *is* the Word of God. Let us examine into this matter a little, by considering briefly three kinds of evidence, viz.:

First. Direct testimony.

Second. Inferential testimony.

Third. Resultant testimony.

FIRST. Let us note the Direct Testimony of the Bible to the fact of verbal inspiration.

"And Moses said unto the Lord, I am not eloquent [a man of words], neither heretofore nor since Thou hast spoken unto Thy servant: for I am slow of speech, and of a slow tongue. And the Lord said unto him, Who hath made man's mouth? . . . . Now therefore go, and I will be with thy mouth, and teach thee what thou shalt speak" (Ex. 4: 10-12). "And the Lord said unto Moses, Write thou these words: for after the tenor of these words I have made a covenant with thee, and with Israel" (Ex. 34:27). "And He said, Hear now My words: if there be a prophet among you, I the Lord will make myself known unto him in a vision, and will speak unto him in a dream. . . . With him [Moses] will I speak mouth to mouth, even apparently, and not in dark speeches; and the similitude of the Lord shall he behold" (Num. 12:6, 8). "Ye shall not add unto the word which I command you, neither shall ye diminish from it" (Deut. 4:2). "But the prophet which shall speak a word presumptuously in My name, which I have not commanded him to speak, . . . that prophet shall die" (Deut. 18:20).

In Mark 12:36, Jesus said: "David himself said in the Holy Spirit." If we turn to 2 Sam. 23:2, we will find what it was David said: "The Spirit of the Lord spake by me, and His word was upon my tongue."

Jeremiah said: "Ah! Lord God! behold I cannot speak, for I am a child. But the Lord saith unto me, Say not I am a child, for thou shalt go to all that I shall send thee, and whatsoever I command thee thou shalt speak. Be not afraid of their faces, for I am with thee to deliver thee, saith the Lord. Then the Lord put forth His hand and touched my mouth. And the Lord said unto me, Behold, I have put My words in thy mouth" (Jer. 1:6-9).

Balaam was compelled to speak against his will. He said: "Lo, I am come unto thee; have I now any power at all to say anything? the word that God putteth in my mouth, that shall I speak." He did his very utmost to curse the Israel-ites, but as often as he tried it, he blessed them. Balak at last said, "Neither curse them at all, nor bless them at all." But Balaam answered, "Told not I thee, saying, All the Lord speaketh, that must I do" (Num. 22:38; 23:26).

In the five books of Moses, in the books called historical, and books included under the general title of the Psalms, such expressions as the following occur hundreds of times: "Thus saith the Lord;" "The Lord said;" "The Lord spake;" "The Lord hath spoken;" "The saying of the Lord;" and "The word of the Lord." There is no other thought expressed in these books concerning inspiration than that the writers spoke and wrote the very words that God gave them.

Turning to the books called prophetical, we find Isaiah saying, "Hear the word of the Lord" (Isa. 1:10); and no fewer than twenty times does he explicitly declare that his writings are the "words of the Lord." Almost one hundred times does Jeremiah say, "The word of the Lord came unto me," or declare he was uttering the "words of the Lord," and the "word of the living God." Ezekiel says that his writings are the "words of God" quite sixty times. Here is a sample: "Son of man, all My words that I shall speak unto thee receive in thine heart, and hear with thine ears. And go get thee to them of the captivity, unto the children of thy people, and speak unto them, and tell them, Thus saith the Lord God" (Ezek. 3:10-11). Daniel said, "And when I heard the voice of His words" (Dan. 10:9). Hosea said, "The word of the Lord" (Hosea 1:1). "The word of the Lord that came to Joel" (Joel 1:1). Amos said, "Hear the word of the Lord" (Amos 3:1). Obadiah said, "Thus saith the Lord God" (Oba. 1:1). "The word of the Lord came unto Jonah" (Jonah 1:1). "The word of the Lord that came to Micah" (Micah 1:1). Nahum said, "Thus saith the Lord" (Nah. 1:12). Habakkuk wrote, "The Lord answered me and said" (Hab. 2:2). "The word of the Lord which came to Zephaniah" (Zeph. 1:1). "Came the word of the Lord by Haggai the prophet" (Hag. 1:1). "Came the word of the Lord unto Zechariah" (Zech. 1:1). "The word of the Lord to Israel by Malachi" (Mal. 1:1). And in this last of the Old Testament books, is it twenty-four times said, "Thus saith the Lord."

The words Jesus Himself uttered were inspired. The words He spoke were not His own, but actually put into His mouth. In the most express manner it was foretold that Christ should thus speak, just as Moses spake. "A prophet shall the Lord your God raise up, *like unto me*. To Him ye shall hearken." Twice it is said, *"like unto me."* And how like to Moses, except as the whole context shows, *"like unto"* him in *verbal inspiration?* To Moses God said: "I will be with thy mouth, and teach thee what to say. Thou shalt put words in Aaron's mouth, and I will be with thy mouth, and teach you what you shall say. And he shall be thy spokesman to the people. And he shall be to thee instead of a mouth, and thou shalt be to him instead of God" (Ex. 4:11-16). Therefore did Jesus, the Prophet, utter inspired words "like unto Moses." The very *words* He spoke God put into His mouth and on His tongue. Therefore did He say, assuring the Jews that Moses wrote of Him: "I have not spoken from Myself, but the Father who sent Me gave Me commandment what I should say and what I should speak. I speak therefore even as the Father said to Me, even so I speak" (John 12:49, 50). "I have given unto them the *words Thou gavest Me,* and they have received them" (John 17:8). "The Son can do nothing from Himself" (5:19). Since *Jesus Christ had to be divinely helped, "like unto Moses", the very words put into His mouth,* Himself *God's mouth,* and as God to the people, how should not the Evangelists and Apostles need the same Divine guidance and help to qualify them for their work, and guarantee its inerrant truthfulness and its Divine authority? If Moses and Isaiah, if Jesus Christ Himself, had to be divinely assisted, how should the narrators of New Testament history and oracles be exempted from the same Divine activity of the Spirit, all-controlling and guiding into the full truth? What are the words of Jesus to John, and to the Seven Churches of the Apocalypse, but the literal words of God dictated verbally by Jesus Christ?

Jesus said to the disciples, "And when they lead you to the judgment, and deliver you up, be not anxious beforehand what ye shall speak: but whatsoever shall be given you in that hour, that speak ye: for it is not ye that speak, but the Holy Ghost" (Mark 13:11).

This same gift included all the disciples on the day of Pentecost, for "They were all filled with the Holy Ghost, and began to speak with other tongues as the Spirit gave them utterance" (Acts 2:1, 4). The multitude that heard "marveled, saying, Behold, are not all these which speak Galileans? And how hear we every man in our own language? . . . We do hear them speaking in our tongues the mighty works of God" (Acts 2:7, 11).

Paul says: "Which things also we speak, not in words which man's wisdom teacheth, but which the Spirit teacheth" (1 Cor. 2:13). "And for this cause we also thank God without ceasing, that, when ye received from us the word of the message, *even the word* of God, ye accepted it not as the word of men, but, as it is in truth, the word of God" (1 Thess. 2:13).

And so the Bible uniformly teaches the doctrine of verbal inspiration. It *is* the Word of God. This is the invariable testimony of the Book itself. It never, in a single instance, says that the thoughts of the writers were inspired; or, that these writers had a "Concept." The Scriptures are called "The oracles of God" (Rom. 3:2); "The Word of God" (Luke 8:11); "The Word of the Lord" (Acts 13:48); "The Word of life" (Phil. 2:16); "The Word of Christ" (Col. 3:16); "The Word of truth" (Eph. 1:13); "The Word of faith" (Rom. 10:8); and, by these and similar statements, do they declare, *more than two thousand times,* that the Bible is the Word of God—that the words are God-breathed, are inspired (theopneustos).

SECOND. What of the Inferential Testimony to the fact of verbal inspiration? I mean by Inferential Testimony that which is assumed by the Bible, and the natural implication belonging to many of its statements.

The Bible assumes to be from God in that it meets man face to face with drawn sword and says: "Thou shalt!" and "Thou shalt not!" and demands immediate, unconditional and irreversible surrender to the authority of heaven, and submission to all the laws and will of God, as made known in its pages. This of itself would not signify a great deal, though unique, were it not for the striking and significant results of such submission; but, the natural inference of such assumption is, that the words of demand and command are from God.

A great many statements of the Bible plainly indicate that the words are inspired. The following are a few instances: "Forever, O Lord, Thy Word is settled in heaven" (Psa. 119:89). This is characteristic of the entire Psalm. "The words of the Lord are pure words" (Psa. 12:6). "Is not My word like as a fire? saith the Lord; and like a hammer that breaketh the rock in pieces?" (Jer. 23:29). "The Word of our God shall stand forever" (Isa. 40:8); and so on, almost *ad infinitum.* Everywhere in the sacred record you find this same suggestion of Divine authorship. Jesus and the Apostles always recognized it, and gave it prominence and emphasis. Its importance and value should not be underestimated.

THIRD. The Resultant Testimony. What of it? Paul tells us that "Every sacred writing" is "God-breathed." (*Pasa Graphe Theopneustos.*) "No prophecy ever came by the will of man; but men spake from God, being moved [*pheromenoi,* borne along] by the Holy Spirit" (2 Pet. 1:21). (This passage does not justify the so-called "mechanical theory of inspiration." Such theory is nowhere taught in the Scriptures. Indeed, the obvious fact that the individual characteristics of the writers were in no way changed or destroyed, disproves such theory.) It is said: "The Lord God formed man of the dust of the ground, and breathed into his nostrils the breath of life; and man became a living soul" (Gen. 2:7). Elihu said, "The Spirit of God hath made me, and the breath of the Almighty hath given me life" (Job 33:4). Now, then, the very same Almighty power that gave life to Adam and Elihu, and which made the "Heavens . . . and all the host of them," is, in some mysterious sense, in the words of the Sacred Record. Therefore are we told: "For the Word of God is living and active, and sharper than any two-edged sword, and piercing even to the dividing of soul and spirit, of both joints and marrow, and quick to discern the thoughts and intents of the heart" (Heb. 4:12). What results will follow believing the Word and submission to its requirements?

1. It will impart spiritual life and save the soul. "Receive with meekness the implanted Word, which is able to save your souls" (James 1:21). "Having been begotten again, not of corruptible seed, but of incorruptible, through the Word of God, which liveth and abideth" (1 Pet. 1:23). "Of His own will begat He us by the Word of truth" (James 1:18). Jesus said: "The words I have spoken unto you are spirit, and are life" (John 6:63).

As a good seed contains the germ of life, so that when cast into the soil of earth at the proper season, under the influence of sunshine and showers, it germinates and springs up to reproduce itself in kind; even so the words of the Bible, if received into the mind and heart to be believed and obeyed, germinate, and spiritual life is the result, reproducing its kind; and that believing soul is made partaker of the Divine nature. (2 Pet. 1:4.) "He is a new creature [creation]; the old things are passed away; behold, they are become new" (2 Cor. 5:17). The power and life of the Almighty lie hidden in the words of the Sacred Record; they are God-breathed; and that power and life will be manifest in the case of every one who will receive them with meekness to believe them and submit to their requirements. All the books men have written cannot do this.

2. It has cleansing power. "Wherewithal shall a young man cleanse his way? By taking heed thereto according to Thy Word" (Psa. 119:9). Jesus said: "Already ye are clean because of the Word which I have spoken unto you" (John

15:3). "That He might sanctify it, having cleansed it, by the washing of water with the Word" (Eph. 5:26).

3. By the Word we are kept from evil and the power of the evil one. The Psalmist said: "By the words of Thy lips I have kept me from the paths of the destroyer" (Psa. 17:4); and, "Thy Word have I hid in my heart, that I might not sin against Thee" (Psa. 119:11). Therefore, Jesus said: "I have given them Thy Word. . . . Sanctify them through [in] the truth. Thy Word is truth" (John 17:14, 17).

The voice said: "Cry. And he said, What shall I cry? All flesh is grass, and all the goodliness thereof is as the flower of the field. . . . The grass withereth, the flower fadeth: but the Word of our God shall stand forever" (Isa. 40:6, 8). "For we can do nothing against the truth, but for the truth" (2 Cor. 13:8).

This, then, is the sum of our contention: The Bible is made up of writings, and these are composed of words. The WORDS are inspired—God-breathed. Therefore is the Bible inspired—*is* God's Word.

This is plainly seen, first, in the uniform declaration of the Book. All the Old Testament Prophets, Jesus our Lord, and all the New Testament writers, bear the same testimony concerning this transcendentally important matter. Not a single word or thought to the contrary can anywhere be found in all their declarations. The attitude of Jesus toward the Old Testament and His utterances confirm beyond question our contention. He had the very same Old Testament we have today. He believed it to be the Word of God, and proclaimed it as such. He said, "One jot or one tittle shall in no wise pass from the laws, till all be fulfilled." In thwarting the tempter He said: "It is written! it is written! it is written!" In confounding the Jews, He said: "If ye believed Moses ye would believe Me; for he wrote of Me." He never criticised the Scriptures, but always appealed to them as His Father's words, authoritative and final.

Jesus is the life and the light of man. The same is true of the Scriptures. Jesus said: "The words that I speak unto you, they are spirit, and they are life." The Psalmist said, "Thy Word is a lamp unto my feet, and a light unto my path." In an inexplicable way Jesus is identified with the Word. "The Word was God. . . . and the Word became flesh." And when the victories of the Gospel shall have been finally accomplished, and Jesus shall assert His regal rights, His name is called, "The Word of God." (See Rev. 19:11, 13.)

Second. The Bible assumes to be God's Word by its imperious demands. Who but God has a right to require of men what the Bible does?

Third. The Bible has fulfilled all its claims and promises. The marvelous, far-reaching results of proclaiming and believing it, demonstrably prove its supernatural origin and character.

That there are difficulties, I well enough know. But many difficulties have disappeared as a result of patient, reverent, scholarly research; and without doubt others will soon go the same way. So, while I bid the scholars and reverent critics God-speed in their noble work, with the late learned Bishop Ryle I say: "Give me the plenary verbal theory with all its difficulties, rather than the doubt. I accept the difficulties, and humbly wait for their solution; but while I wait I am standing on a rock."

Let this, then, be our *attitude,* to tell it out to the wide world that the blessed Bible, the "Holy Scriptures" of both Testaments, are the product of the *"Breath of God,"* who made heaven and earth, and "breathed" into man His soul; the product of that Divine *"Breath"* that regenerates, that illuminates and sanctifies the soul; a *"God-breathed Scriptures",* whose "words" are the "words of God." Tell it to the Church in her seminaries, universities and colleges, from her pulpits, Sunday Schools and Bible classes, and sound it in every convention, conference and assembly that her conception and estimate of the Scriptures must be no lower and no less than were the high conception and estimate of the "Volume of the Book" by our Lord and His Apostles; that what they regarded as the *"Breath of God"*, she must so regard in opposition to every breath of man that dares to breathe otherwise. Say, with the immortal Athanasius, who knew how to read Greek better than the "drift of scholarly opinion" "in our time": "O my child, not only the ancient, but the new Scriptures are God-breathed, as Paul saith, 'Every Scripture is God-breathed'". Say to the rising ministry, "Speak as the Oracles of God speak"—the words that "God hath spoken," the words that Christ has written. Be at least, as decent as Balaam! "Whatsoever He saith unto you, do;" and whatsoever He saith unto you, say. Tell it to every reader and hearer of the Word, that what "Moses saith" and "David saith" and "Isaiah, Peter, Paul, John and the Scripture, saith", is what *"God saith"*. Tell it to the dying saint, when his last pulse quivers at the wrist, and friends are weeping by his bed, and "Science" has exhausted in vain all her poor resources, that God, who breathed the Scriptures, "cannot lie", that Jesus is a Rock, and that the "firm Foundation" laid in the Word for his faith can never disappoint his trust. To every question of Exegesis or of Criticism, return the answer, "What saith the Scriptures"? "How readest thou?" "It is written!" And cease to deride the most sacred, age-established, and time-honored tradition the Apostolic Church has left us. With such an *attitude* as this, the days will revisit the Church, as once they were "in the beginning", and God, honored in His Word, will no longer restrain the Spirit, but open the windows of heaven, and pour upon her a blessing so great that there will not be room to receive it. God hasten the day!

CHAPTER III

THE MORAL GLORY OF JESUS CHRIST A PROOF OF INSPIRATION

BY REV. WM. G. MOOREHEAD, D. D., PRESIDENT OF XENIA THEO-
LOGICAL SEMINARY, XENIA, OHIO, U. S. A.

The glories of the Lord Jesus Christ are threefold: Essential, official and moral. His essential glory is that which pertains to Him as the Son of God, the equal of the Father. His official glory is that which belongs to Him as the Mediator. It is the reward conferred on Him, the august promotion He received when He had brought His great work to a final and triumphant conclusion. His moral glory consists of the perfections which marked His earthly life and ministry; perfections which attached to every relation He sustained, and to every circumstance in which He was found. His essential and official glories were commonly veiled during His earthly sojourn. His moral glory could not be hid; He could not be less than perfect in everything; it belonged to Him; it was Himself. This moral glory now illumines every page of the four Gospels, as once it did every path He trod.

The thesis which we undertake to illustrate and establish is this: That the moral glory of Jesus Christ as set forth in the four Gospels cannot be the product of the unaided human intellect, that only the Spirit of God is competent to execute this matchless portrait of the Son of Man. The discussion of the theme falls into two parts: I. A brief survey of Christ's moral glory as exhibited in the Gospels. II. The application of the argument.

I. CHRIST'S MORAL GLORY
THE HUMANITY OF JESUS

1. The moral glory of Jesus appears in His development as Son of Man. The nature which He assumed was our na-

ture, sin and sinful propensities only excepted. His was a real and a true humanity, one which must pass through the various stages of growth like any other member of the race. From infancy to youth, from youth to manhood, there was steady increase both of His bodily powers and mental faculties; but the progress was orderly. "No unhealthy precocity marked the holiest of infancies." He was first a child, and afterwards a man, not a man in child's years.

As Son of Man He was compassed about with all the sinless infirmities that belong to our nature. He has needs common to all; need of food, of rest, of human sympathy and of divine assistance. He is subject to Joseph and Mary, He is a worshiper in the synagogue and the Temple; He weeps over the guilty and hardened city, and at the grave of a loved one; He expresses His dependence on God by prayer.

Nothing is more certain than that the Gospel narratives present the Lord Jesus as a true man, a veritable member of our race. But we no sooner recognize this truth than we are confronted by another which sets these records alone and unapproachable in the field of literature. This second fact is this: At every stage of His development, in every relation of life, in every part of His service He is absolutely perfect. To no part of His life does a mistake attach, over no part of it does a cloud rest, nowhere is there defect. Nothing is more striking, more unexampled, than the profound contrast between Jesus and the conflict and discord around Him, than between Him and those who stood nearest Him, the disciples, John Baptist, and the mother, Mary. All fall immeasurably below Him.

THE PATTERN MAN

2. The Gospels exalt our Lord infinitely above all other men as the representative, the ideal, the pattern man. Nothing in the judgment of historians stands out so sharply distinct as race, national character—nothing is more ineffaceable.

The very greatest men are unable to free themselves from the influences amid which they have been born and educated. Peculiarities of race and the spirit of the age leave in their characters traces that are imperishable. To the last fiber of his being Luther was German, Calvin was French, Knox was Scotch; Augustine bears the unmistakable impress of the Roman, and Chrysostom is as certainly Greek. Paul, with all his large heartedness and sympathies is a Jew, always a Jew. Jesus Christ is the only One who is justly entitled to be called the Catholic Man. Nothing local, transient, individualizing, national, or sectarian dwarfs the proportions of His wondrous character. "He rises above the parentage, the blood, the narrow horizon which bounded, as it seemed, His life; for He is the archetypal man in whose presence distinctions of race, intervals of ages, types of civilization and degrees of mental culture are as nothing" (Liddon). He belongs to all ages, He is related to all men, whether they shiver amid the snows of the arctic circle, or pant beneath the burning heat of the equator; for He is the Son of Man, the Son of mankind, the genuine offspring of the race.

UNSELFISHNESS AND DIGNITY

3. The Lord's moral glory appears in His unselfishness and personal dignity. The entire absence of selfishness in any form from the character of the Lord Jesus is another remarkable feature of the Gospels. He had frequent and fair opportunities of gratifying ambition had His nature been tainted with that passion. But "even Christ pleased not himself;" He "sought not his own glory;" He came not "to do his own will." His body and His soul with all the faculties and activities of each were devoted to the supreme aims of His mission. His self-sacrifice included the whole range of His human thought and affection and action; it lasted throughout His life; its highest expression was His ignominious death on the cross of Calvary.

The strange beauty of His unselfishness as it is displayed in the Gospel narratives appears in this, that it never seeks to draw attention to itself, it deprecates publicity. In His humility He seems as one naturally contented with obscurity; as wanting the restless desire for eminence which is common to really great men; as eager and careful that even His miracles should not add to His reputation. But amid all His self-sacrificing humility He never loses His personal dignity nor the self-respect that becomes Him. He receives ministry from the lowly and the lofty; He is sometimes hungry, yet feeds the multitudes in desert places; He has no money, yet He never begs, and He provides the coin for tribute to the government from a fish's mouth. He may ask for a cup of water at the well, but it is that He may save a soul. He never flies from enemies; He quietly withdraws or passes by unseen. Hostility neither excites nor exasperates Him. He is always calm, serene. He seems to care little for Himself, for His own ease or comfort or safety, but everything for the honor and the glory of the Father. If multitudes, eager and expectant, press upon Him, shouting, "Hosanna to the son of David," He is not elated; if all fall away, stunned by His words of power, He is not cast down. He sought not a place among men, He was calmly content to be the Lord's Servant, the obedient and the humble One. It was invariably true of Him that "He pleased not Himself."

And yet through all His amazing self-renunciation, there glances ever and anon something of the infinite majesty and supreme dignity which belong to Him because He is the Son of God. The words of Van Oosterzee are as true as they are beautiful and significant: "It is the same King's Son who today dwells in the palace of His Father, and tomorrow, out of love to His rebellious subjects in a remote corner of the Kingdom, renouncing His princely glory, comes to dwell amongst them in the form of a servant * * * and is known only by the dignity of His look, and the star of royalty on His breast, when the mean cloak is opened for a moment, apparently by accident."

SUPERIORITY TO HUMAN JUDGMENT AND INTERCESSION

4. The Gospels exhibit the Lord Jesus as superior to the judgment and the intercession of men. When challenged by the disciples and by enemies, as He often was, Jesus never apologizes, never excuses Himself, never confesses to a mistake. When the disciples, terrified by the storm on the lake, awoke Him saying, "Master, carest thou not that we perish?", He did not vindicate His sleep, nor defend His apparent indifference to their fears. Martha and Mary, each in turn, with profound grief, say, "Lord, if thou hadst been here, my brother had not died." There is not a minister of the gospel the world over who would not in similar circumstances explain or try to explain why he could not at once repair to the house of mourning when summoned thither. But Jesus does not excuse His not being there, nor His delay of two days in the place where He was when the urgent message of the sisters reached Him. In the consciousness of the perfect rectitude of His ways, He only replies, "Thy brother shall rise again." Peter once tried to admonish Him, saying, "This be far from thee, Lord; this shall not be unto thee." But Peter had to learn that it was Satan that prompted the admonition. Nor does He recall a word when the Jews rightly inferred from His language that He "being man made Himself God" (John 10:30-36). He pointed out the application of the name Elohim (God) to judges under the theocracy; and yet He irresistibly implies that His title to Divinity is higher than, and distinct in kind from, that of the Jewish magistrates. He thus arrives a second time at the assertion which had given so great offense, by announcing His identity with the Father, which involves His own proper Deity. The Jews understood Him. He did not retract what they accounted blasphemy, and they again sought His life. He is never mistaken, and never retracts.

So likewise He is superior to human intercession. He never asks even His disciples nor His nearest friends, and certainly never His mother Mary, to pray for Him. In Gethsemane He asked the three. to watch with Him, He did not ask them to pray for Him. He bade them pray that they might not enter into temptation, but He did not ask them to pray that He should not, nor that He should be delivered out of it. Paul wrote again and again, "Brethren, pray for us"— "pray for me." But such was not the language of Jesus. It is worthy of note that the Lord does not place His own people on a level with Himself in His prayers. He maintains the distance of His own personal dignity and supremacy between Himself and them. In His intercession He never uses plural personal pronouns in His petitions. He always says, "I" and "me," "these" and "them that thou hast given me;" never "we" and "us," as we speak and should speak in our prayers.

THE SINLESSNESS OF JESUS

5. The sinlessness of the Saviour witnesses to His moral glory. The Gospels present us with one solitary and unique fact of human history—an absolutely sinless Man! In His birth immaculate, in His childhood, youth and manhood, in public and private, in death and in life, He was faultless. Hear some witnesses. There is the testimony of His enemies. For three long years the Pharisees were watching their victim. As another writes, "There was the Pharisee mingling in every crowd, hiding behind every tree. They examined His disciples, they cross-questioned all around Him. They looked into His ministerial life, into His domestic privacy, into His hours of retirement. They came forward with the sole accusation they could muster—that He had shown disrespect to Caesar. The Roman judge who ought to know, pronounced it void." There was another spy—Judas. Had there been one failure in the Redeemer's career, in his awful agony Judas would have remembered it for his comfort; but the bitterness of his de-

spair, that which made his life intolerable, was, "I have betrayed the innocent blood."

There is the testimony of His friends. His disciples affirm that during their intercourse with Him His life was unsullied. Had there been a single blemish they would have detected it, and, honest historians as they were, they would have recorded it, just as they did their own shortcomings and blunders. The purest and most austere man that lived in that day, John the Baptist, shrank from baptizing the Holy One, and in conscious unworthiness he said, "I have need to be baptized of thee, and comest thou to me?" Nor is His own testimony to be overlooked. Jesus never once confesses sin. He never once asks for pardon. Yet is it not He who so sharply rebukes the self-righteousness of the Pharisees? Does He not, in His teaching, seem to ignore all human piety that is not based upon a broken heart? But yet He never lets fall a hint, He never breathes a prayer which implies the slightest trace of blameworthiness. He paints the doom of incorrigible and unrepentent sinners in the most dreadful colors found in the entire Bible, but He Himself feels no apprehension, He expresses no dread of the penal future; His peace of mind, His fellowship with Almighty God, is never disturbed nor interrupted. If He urge sorrow upon others and tears of penitence, it is for their sins; if He groan in agony, it is not for sins of His own, it is for others'. He challenges His bitterest enemies to convict Him of Sin (John 8:46). Nor is this all. "The soul," it has been said, "like the body has its pores," and the pores are always open. "Instinctively, unconsciously, and whether a man will or not, the insignificance or the greatness of the inner life always reveals itself." From its very center and essence the moral nature is ever throwing out about itself circles of influence, encompasses itself with an atmosphere of self-disclosure. In Jesus Christ this self-revelation was not involuntary, nor accidental, nor forced: it was in the highest degree deliberate. There is about Him an air of superior holiness, of aloofness from the world and its ways, a separation from evil in every form and of every grade, such as no other that has ever lived has displayed. Although descended from an impure ancestry, He brought no taint of sin into the world with Him; and though He mingled with sinful men and was assailed by fierce temptations, He contracted no guilt, He was touched by no stain. He was not merely undefiled, but He was undefilable. He was like a ray of light which parting from the fountain of light can pass through the foulest medium and still be unstained and untouched. He came down into all the circumstances of actual humanity in its sin and misery, and yet He kept the infinite purity of heaven with Him. In the annals of our race there is none next to or like Him.

ASSEMBLAGE AND CORRELATION OF VIRTUES

6. The exquisite assemblage and correlation of virtues and excellencies in the Lord Jesus form another remarkable feature of the Gospel narratives. There have been those who have displayed distinguished traits of character; those who by reason of extraordinary gifts have risen to heights which are inaccessible to the great mass of men. But who among the mightiest of men has shown himself to be evenly balanced and rightly poised in all his faculties and powers? In the very greatest and best, inequality and disproportion are encountered. Generally, the failings and vices of men are in the inverse ratio of their virtues and their powers. "The tallest bodies cast the longest shadows." In Jesus Christ there is no unevenness. In Him there is no preponderance of the imagintion over the feeling, of the intellect over the imagination, of the will over the intellect. There is in Him an uninterrupted harmony of all the powers of body and soul, in which that serves which should serve, and that rules which ought to rule, and all works together to one adorable end. In Him every grace is in its perfectness, none in excess, none out of place, and none wanting. His justice and His mercy, His

peerless love and His truth, His holiness and His freest pardon never clash; one never clouds the other. His firmness never degenerates into obstinacy, or His calmness into indifference. His gentleness never becomes weakness, nor His elevation of soul forgetfulness of others. In His best servants virtues and graces are uneven and often clash. Paul had hours of weakness and even of petulance. He seems to have regretted that he called himself a Pharisee in the Jewish Sanhedrin and appealed to that party for help, for in his address before the proconsul Felix he said, "Or let these same here say, if they found any evil doing in me, while I stood before the Council, except it be for this one voice, that I cried standing among them, Touching the resurrection of the dead I am called in question by you this day." John the Apostle of love even wished to call down fire from heaven to consume the inhospitable Samaritans. And the Virgin mother must learn that even she cannot dictate to Him as to what He shall do or not do. In Jesus there is the most perfect balance, the most amazing equipoise of every faculty and grace and duty and power. In His whole life one day's walk never contradicts another, one hour's service never clashes with another. While He shows He is master of nature's tremendous forces, and the Lord of the unseen world, He turns aside and lays His glory by to take little children in His arms and to bless them. While He must walk amid the snares His foes have privily spread for His feet, He is equal to every occasion, is in harmony with the requirements of every moment. "He never speaks where it would be better to keep silence, He never keeps silence where it would be better to speak; and He always leaves the arena of controversy a victor." His unaffected majesty, so wonderfully depicted in the Gospels, runs through His whole life, and is as manifest in the midst of poverty and scorn, at Gethsemane and Calvary, as on the Mount of Transfiguration and in the resurrection from the grave.

OMNIPOTENCE AND OMNISCIENCE

7. The evangelists do not shrink from ascribing to the Lord Jesus divine attributes, particularly Omnipotence and Omniscience. They do so as a mere matter of fact, as what might and should be expected from so exalted a personage as the Lord Jesus was. How amazing the power is which He wields when it pleases Him to do so! It extends to the forces of nature. At His word the storm is hushed into a calm, and the raging of the sea ceases. At His pleasure He walks on the water as on dry land. It extends to the world of evil spirits. At His presence demons cry out in fear and quit their hold on their victims. His power extends into the realm of disease. Every form of sickness departs at His command, and He cures the sick both when He is beside them and at a distance from them. Death likewise, that inexorable tyrant that wealth has never bribed, nor tears softened, nor human power arrested, yielded instantly his prey when the voice of the Son of God bade him.

But Jesus equally as certainly and as fully possessed a superhuman range of knowledge as well as a superhuman power. He knew men; knew them as God knows them. Thus He saw into the depths of Nathaniel's heart when he was under the fig tree; He saw into the depths of the sea, and the exact coin in the mouth of a particular fish; He read the whole past life of the woman at the well, although He had never before met with her. John tells us that "He needed not that any should testify of man: for he knew what was in man" (John ii:25). He knew the world of evil spirits. He was perfectly acquainted with the movements of Satan and of demons. He said to Peter, "Simon, Simon, behold, Satan asked to have you that he might sift you as wheat: I made supplication for thee that thy faith fail not" (Luke xxii: 31,32). He often spoke directly to the evil spirits that had control of people, ordering them to hold their peace, to come out and to enter no more into their victims. He knew the Father as no mere creature could possibly know Him. "All things are delivered unto me of my Father: and no man knoweth the Son, save the Father; neither doth any know the Father, save the Son, and he to whomsoever the Son willeth to reveal Him" (Matt. xi:27).

A difficulty will be felt when we attempt to reconcile this infinite knowledge of men, of the unseen world, and of God Himself, which the Son of God possessed, with the statement in Mark that He did not know the day nor the hour of His Second Advent. But the difficulty is no greater than that other in John, where we are told that His face was wet with human tears while the almighty voice was crying, "Lazarus, come forth." In both cases the divine and the human are seen intermingling, and yet they are perfectly distinct.

Such are some of the beams of Christ's moral glories as they shine everywhere on the pages of the Four Gospels. A very few of them are here gathered together. Nevertheless, what a stupendous picture do they form! In the annals of our race there is nothing like it. Here is One presented to us who is a true and genuine man, and yet He is the ideal, the representative, the pattern man, claiming kindred in the catholicity of His manhood with all men; sinless, yet full of tenderness and pity; higher than the highest, yet stooping to the lowest and to the most needy; perfect in all His words and ways, in His life and in His death!

Who taught the evangelists to draw this matchless portrait? The pen which traced these glories of Jesus—could it have been other than an inspired pen? This question leads us to the second part of our task, which can soon be disposed of.

II. THE APPLICATION OF THE ARGUMENT

Nothing is more obvious than the very commonplace axiom, that every effect requires an adequate cause. Given a piece of machinery, complex, delicate, exact in all its movements, we know that it must be the product of a competent mechanic. Given a work of consummate art, we know it must be the product of a consummate artist. None but a sculptor with the genius of an Angelo could carve the "Moses." None but a painter with the hand, the eye, and the brain of a Raphael could paint the "Transfiguration." None but a poet with the gifts of a Milton could write "Paradise Lost."

Here are four brief records of our Lord's earthly life. They deal almost exclusively with His public ministry; they do not profess even to relate all that He did in His official work (cf. John xxi: 25). The authors of these memorials were men whose names are as household words the world over; but beyond their names we know little more. The first was tax collector under the Roman government; the second was, it is generally believed, that John Mark who for a time served as an attendant on Paul and Barnabas, and who afterward became the companion and fellow-laborer of Peter; the third was a physician and the devoted friend and co-worker of Paul; and the fourth was a fisherman. Two of them, Matthew and John, were disciples of Jesus; whether the others, Mark and Luke, ever saw Him during His earthly sojourn cannot be determined.

These four men, unpracticed in the art of writing, unacquainted with the ideals of antiquity, write the memorials of Jesus' life. Three of them traverse substantially the same ground, record the same incidents, discourses and miracles. While they are penetrated with the profoundest admiration for their Master, they never once dilate on His great qualities. All that they do is to record His actions and His discourses with scarcely a remark. One of them indeed, John, intermingles reflective commentary with the narrative; but in doing this John carefully abstains from eulogy and panegyric. He pauses in His narrative only to explain some reference, to open some deep saying of the Lord, or to press some vital truth. Yet, despite this absence of the smallest attempt to delineate a character, these four men have accomplished what no others have done or can do—they have presented the world with the portrait of a Divine Man, a Glorious Saviour. Matthew describes Him as the promised Messiah, the glory of Israel, the Son of David, the Son of Abraham; the One in whom the covenants and the promises find their ample fulfilment; the One who accomplishes all righteousness. Mark exhibits Him as the mighty Servant of Jehovah who does man's neglected duty, and meets the need of all around. Luke depicts Him as the Friend of man, whose love is so intense and comprehensive, whose pity is so divine, that His saving power goes forth to Jew and Gentile, to the lowliest and the loftiest, to the publican, the Samaritan, the ragged prodigal, the harlot, the thief, as well as to the cultivated, the moral, the great. John presents Him as the Son of God, the Word made flesh; as Light for a dark world, as Bread for a starving world, as Life for a dead world. Matthew writes for the Jew, Mark for the Roman, Luke for the Greek, and John for the Christian; and all of them write for every kindred, and tribe, and tongue and people of the entire globe, and for all time! What the philosopher, the poet, the scholar, the artist could not do; what men of the greatest mind, the most stupendous genius have failed to do, these four unpracticed men have done—they have presented to the world the Son of Man and the Son of God in all His perfections and glories.

A FACT TO BE EXPLAINED

How comes it to pass that these unlearned and ignorant men (Acts iv:13) have so thoroughly accomplished so great a task? Let us hold fast our commonplace axiom, every effect must have an adequate cause. What explanation shall we give of this marvellous effect? Shall we ascribe their work to genius? But multitudes of men both before and since their day have possessed genius of the very highest order;

and these gifted men have labored in fields akin to this of our four evangelists. The mightiest minds of the race—men of Chaldea, of Egypt, of India, of China, and of Greece—have tried to draw a perfect character, have expended all their might to paint a god-like man. And with what result? Either he is invested with the passions and the brutalities of fallen men, or he is a pitiless and impassive spectator of the world's sorrows and woes. In either case, the character is one which may command the fear but not the love and confidence of men.

Again, we ask, How did the evangelists solve this mighty problem of humanity with such perfect originality and precision? Only two answers are rationally possible: 1. They had before them the personal and historical Christ. Men could no more invent the God-man of the Gospels than they could create a world. The almost irreverent words of Theodore Parker are grounded in absolute truth: "It would have taken a Jesus to forge a Jesus." 2. They wrote by inspiration of the Spirit of God. It cannot be otherwise. It is not enough to say that the Divine Model was before them: they must have had something more, else they never could have succeeded.

Let it be assumed that these four men, Matthew, Mark, Luke and John, were personally attendant on the ministry of Jesus—that they saw Him, heard Him, companied with Him for three years. Yet on their own showing they did not understand Him. They testify that the disciples, the Apostles among the number, got but the slenderest conceptions of His person and His mission from His very explicit teachings. They tell us of a wonderful incapacity and weakness in all their apprehensions of Him. The Sun of righteousness was shining on them and around them, and they could see only the less! He told them repeatedly of His approaching death, and of His resurrection, but they did not understand Him; they even questioned among themselves what the rising from the dead should mean (Mark ix:10)—poor men! And yet these men, once so blind and ignorant, write four little pieces about the person and the work of the Lord Jesus which the study and the research of Christendom for eighteen hundred years have not exhausted, and which the keenest and most hostile criticism has utterly failed to discredit.

But this is not all. Others have tried their hand at composing the Life and Deeds of Jesus. Compare some of these with our Four Gospels.

SPURIOUS GOSPELS

The Gospel narrative observes an almost unbroken silence as to the long abode of Jesus at Nazareth. Of the void thus left the church became early impatient. During the first four centuries many attempts were made to fill it up. Some of these apocryphal gospels are still extant, notably that which deals with the infancy and youth of the Redeemer; and it is instructive to notice how those succeeded who tried to lift the veil which covers the earlier years of Christ. Let another state the contrast between the New Testament records and the spurious gospels: "The case stands thus: our Gospels present us with a glorious picture of a mighty Saviour, the mythic gospels with that of a contemptible one. In our Gospels He exhibits a superhuman wisdom; in the mythic ones a nearly equal superhuman absurdity. In our Gospels He is arrayed in all the beauty of holiness; in the mythic ones this aspect of character is entirely wanting. In our Gospels not one stain of sinfulness defiles His character; in the mythic ones the Boy Jesus is both pettish and malicious. Our Gospels exhibit to us a sublime morality; not one ray of it shines in those of the mythologists. The miracles of the one and of the other stand contrasted on every point." (Row.)

These spurious gospels were written by men who lived not long after the apostolic age; by Christians who wished to honor the Saviour in all they said about Him; by men who had the portraiture of Him before them which the Gospels supply. And yet these men, many of them better taught than the Apostles, with the advantage of two or three centuries of Christian thought and study, could not produce a fancy sketch of the Child Jesus without violating our sense of propriety, and shocking our moral sense. The distance between the Gospels of the New Testament and the pseudo-gospels is measured by the distance between the product of the Spirit of God, and that of the fallen human mind.

UNINSPIRED "LIVES OF CHRIST"

Let us take another illustration. The nineteenth century has been very fruitful in the production of what are commonly called "Lives of Christ." Contrast with the Gospels four such "Lives," perhaps the completest and the best, taken altogether, of those written by English-speaking people—Andrews', Geikie's, Hanna's and Edersheim's. The authors of our Gospels had no models on which to frame their work. The path they trod had never before been pressed by human feet. The authors of the "Lives" have not only these incomparable narratives as their pattern and the chief source of all their material, but numberless other such "Lives" suggestive as to form and construction, and the culture and the research of eighteen centuries lying behind them. But would any one venture for a moment to set forth these "Lives" as rivals of our Gospels? Much information and helpfulness are to be derived from the labors of these Christian scholars, and others who have toiled in the same field; but how far they all fall below the New Testament record it is needless to show. Indeed, all such writings are largely antiquated and scarcely read, though they are quite young in years, so soon does man's work decay and die.

Let the contrast be noted as to size or bulk. Andrews' book contains 615 pages; Geikie's over 1,200; Hanna's over 2,100; Edersheim's, 1,500 pages. The four combined have no less than 5,490 pages, enough in these busy days to require months of reading to go but once through their contents. Bagster prints the Four Gospels in 82 pages; the Oxford, in 104; Amer. Rev., 120. In the Bagster, Matthew has but 23; Mark, 13; Luke, 25; and John, 21. Less than one hundred pages of the Four Gospels against more than five thousand four hundred of the four "Lives."

Countless volumes, great and small, in the form of commentary, exposition, notes, harmony and history are written on these brief records. How happens it that such stores of wisdom and knowledge lie garnered in these short pieces? Who taught the evangelists this superhuman power of expansion and contraction, of combination and separation, of revelation in the words and more revelation below the words? Who taught them so to describe the person and work of the Lord Jesus as that the description satisfies the most illiterate and the most learned, is adapted to minds of the most limited capacity, and to those of the widest grasp? Whence did they derive the infinite skill they display in grouping together events, discourses, and actions in such fashion that vividly before us is the deathless beauty of a perfect Life? There is but one answer to these questions, there can be no other. The Spirit of the living God filled their minds with His unerring wisdom and controlled their human speech. To that creative Spirit who has peopled the world with living organisms so minute that only the microscope can reveal their presence, it is not hard to give us in so brief a compass the sublime portrait of the Son of Man. To men it is impossible.

INSPIRATION EXTENDS THROUGHOUT THE BIBLE

Now if it be conceded that the Four Gospels are inspired, we are compelled by every rule of right reason to concede the inspiration of the rest of the New Testament. For all the later communications contained in the Acts, the Epistles, and the Revelation, are already in germ form in the Gospels, just as the Pentateuch holds in germ the rest of the Old Testament.

If the Holy Spirit is the author of the Four Gospels He is none the less the author of the entire New Testament. If He creates the germ, it is He also that must unfold it into mature fruit. If He makes the seed He must likewise give the increase. To this fundamental truth the writers of the later communications bear the most explicit testimony. Paul, John, James, Peter and Jude severally intimate that what they have to impart is from Christ by His Spirit.

Furthermore, if we admit the inspiration of the New Testament we must also admit that of the Old. For, if any one thing has been established by the devout and profound study and research of evangelical scholarship it is this, that the Scriptures of the Old Testament hold in germ the revelation contained in the New. The Latin Father spoke as profoundly as truly when he said, "The New Testament lies hid in the Old, and the Old stands revealed in the New." Ancient Judaism had one supreme voice for the chosen people, and its voice was prophetic. Its voice was the significant word, *Wait*. As if it kept reminding Israel that the Mosaic Institutions were only temporary and typical, that something infinitely better and holier was to take their place; and so it said, Wait. Wait, and the true Priest will come, the Priest greater than Aaron, greater than Melchizedek—the Priest of whom these were but thin shadows, dim pictures. Wait, and the true Prophet, like unto Moses, greater than Moses, will appear. Wait, and the real sacrifice, that of which all other offerings were but feeble images, will be made and sin be put away. If any man deny the inspiration of the Old Testament, sooner or later he will deny that of the New. For the two are inseparably bound up together. If the one fall, so will the other. Already the disastrous consequences of such a course of procedure are apparent in Christendom. For years the conflict has raged about the trustworthiness, the integrity and the authority of the Old Testament. Not long since one who is identified with the attacking party arrayed against that Scripture announced that the victory is won, and nothing now remains save to determine the amount of the indemnity. It is very noteworthy that the struggle has indeed measurably subsided as to the Old Testament, although there are no signs of weakening faith in it on the part of God's faithful children, and the fight now turns with increasing vigor on the New Testament, and pre-eminently about the Person of the Lord Jesus Christ. Men who are Christians at least in name, who occupy influential seats in great Universities and even Theological Schools, do not shrink from impeaching the New Testament record touching the Virgin Birth of the Lord Jesus, His resurrection from the dead, and His promise of one day returning to this earth in majesty and power. One cannot renounce the Scriptures of the Old Testament without relaxing his hold, sooner or later, on the New.

Christ is the center of all Scripture, as He is the center of all God's purposes and counsels. The four evangelists take up the life and the moral glory of the Son of Man, and they place it alongside of the picture of the Messiah as sketched by the prophets, the historical by the side of the prophetic, and they show how exactly the two match. So long as the Four Gospels remain unmutilated and trusted by the people of God, so long is the doctrine of the Bible's supreme authority assured.

God spoke to the fathers in the prophets: He now speaks to us in His Son whom He hath made Heir of all things. In either case, whether by the prophets or by the Son, the Speaker is God.

CHAPTER IV

THE TESTIMONY OF THE SCRIPTURES TO THEMSELVES

BY REV. GEORGE S. BISHOP, D. D.,
EAST ORANGE, NEW JERSEY

My subject is, The Testimony of the Scriptures to Themselves—their own self-evidence—the overpowering, unparticipated witness that they bring.

Permit me to expand this witness under the following heads:

1. *Immortality.*
2. *Authority.*
3. *Transcendent Doctrine.*
4. *Direct Assertion.*

1. IMMORTALITY—"I have written!" All other books die. Few old books survive, and fewer of those that survive have any influence. Most of the books we quote from have been written within the last three or even one hundred years.

But here is a Book whose antemundane voices had grown old, when voices spake in Eden. A Book which has survived not only with continued but increasing lustre, vitality, vivacity, popularity, rebound of influence. A Book which comes through all the shocks without a wrench, and all the furnaces of all the ages—like an iron safe—with every document in every pigeon-hole, without a warp upon it, or the smell of fire. Here is a Book of which it may be said, as of Immortal Christ Himself: "Thou hast the dew on Thy youth from the womb of the morning." A Book dating from days as ancient as those of the Ancient of Days, and which when all that makes up what we see and call the universe shall be dissolved, will still speak on in thunder-tones of majesty, and whisper-tones of light, and music-tones of love, for it is wrapping in itself the everlasting past, and opening and expanding from itself the everlasting future; and, like an all-irradiating sun, will still roll on, while deathless ages roll, the one unchanging, unchangeable Revelation of God.

2. Immortality is on these pages, and AUTHORITY SETS HERE HER SEAL. This is the second point. A Standard.

Useless to talk about *no* standard. Nature points to one. Conscience cries out for one—conscience which, without a law, constantly wages the internal and excruciating war of accusing or else excusing itself.

There must be a Standard and an Inspired Standard—for *Inspiration is the Essence of Authority,* and authority is in proportion to inspiration—the more inspired the greater the authority—the less, the less. Even the rationalist Rothe, a most intense opponent, has admitted that *"that* in the Bible which is not the product of direct inspiration has no binding power."

Verbal and direct inspiration is, therefore, the "Thermopylae" of Biblical and Scriptural faith. No breath, no syllable; no syllable, no word; no word, no Book; no Book, no religion.

We hold, from first to last, that there can be no possible advance in Revelation—no new light. What was written at first, the same thing stands written today, and will stand forever. The emanation of the mind of God—it is complete, perfect. "Nothing can be put to it, nor anything taken from it"; its *ipse dixit* is peremptory, final. "If any man shall add unto these things, God shall add unto him the plagues that are written in this Book; and if any man shall *take away from the words* of the Book of this prophecy, God shall take away his part out of the Book of life, and out of the Holy City. and from the things which are written in this Book."

The Bible is the Word of God, and not simply CONTAINS IT. This is clear.

Because the Bible styles itself the Word of God. "The *Word of the Lord* is right," says the Psalmist. Again, *"Thy Word* is a lamp to my feet." "Wherewithal shall a young man cleanse his way? By taking heed thereto according to *Thy Word.*" "The grass withereth," says Isaiah, "the flower thereof fadeth, but *the Word of our God* shall stand forever."

Not only is the Bible called the Word of God, but it is distinguished from all other books by that very title. It is so distinguished in the 119th Psalm, and everywhere the contrast between it and every human book is deepened and sustained.

If we will not call the Bible the Word of God, then we cannot call it anything else. If we insist upon a description rigorously exact and unexposed to shafts of wanton criticism, then the Book remains anonymous. We cannot more consistently say, "Holy Scripture," because the crimes recorded on its pages are not holy; because expressions like "Curse God and die," and others from the lips of Satan and of wicked men, are unholy. The Bible, however, is "holy" because its aim and its methods are holy. The Bible, likewise, is the Word of God, because it comes from God; because its every word was penned by God; because it is the only exponent of God; the only rule of His procedure, and the Book by which we must at last be judged.

(1) The Bible is authority because in it, from cover to cover, *God is the Speaker.* Said a leader of our so-called orthodoxy to a crowded audience but a little while ago: "The Bible is true. Any man not a fool must believe what is true. What difference does it make who wrote it?" This difference, brethren; the *solemn bearing down of God on the soul!* My friend may tell me what is true; my wife may tell me what is true; but what they say is not solemn. Solemnity comes in when God looks into my face—God! and behind Him everlasting destiny—and talks with me about my soul. In the Bible God speaks, and God is listened to, and men are

born again by God's Word. "So then faith cometh by hearing, and hearing by the Word of God." It is God's Revelation that faith hears, and it is *on God revealed* that faith rests.

(2) The Bible is the Word of God. It comes to us *announced by miracles and heralded with fire.* Take the Old Testament—Mount Sinai; take the New Testament—Pentecost. Would God Himself stretch out His hand and write on tables in the giving, and send down tongues of fire for the proclamation of a Revelation, every particle and shred of which was not His own? In other words, would He work miracles and send down tongues of fire to signalize a work merely human, or even partly human and partly Divine? How unworthy of God, how impious, how utterly impossible the supposition!

(3) The Bible comes clothed with authority in the *highhanded and exalted terms of its address.* God in the Bible speaks out of a whirlwind and with the voice of Elias. What grander proof of literal inspiration can be than in the highhanded method and imperative tone of prophets and apostles which enabled them—poor men, obscure, and without an influence; fishermen, artisans, publicans, day-laborers—to brave and boldly teach the world from Pharaoh and from Nero down? Was this due to anything less than God speaking in them—to the overpowering impulse and seizure of God? Who can believe it? Who is not struck with the power and the wisdom of God? "His words were in my bones," cries one. "I could not stay. The lion hath roared, who will not fear; the Lord hath spoken, who can but prophesy?"

(4) The Bible is the optime of authority, because it is from first to last *a glorious projection on the widest scale of the decrees of God.* The sweep of the Bible is from the creation of angels to a new heaven and new earth, across a lake of fire. What a field for events! What an expanse

beyond the sweep or even reach of human fore-thought, criticism, or co-operation! What a labyrinth upon whose least and minutest turning hangs entire redemption, since a chain is never stronger than its smallest link! Who then will dare to speak till God has spoken? "I will declare the decree!" That pushes everything aside—that makes the declaration an extension, so to say, of the Declarer. "I will declare the decree!" When we consider that the Bible is an exact projection of the decrees of God into the future, this argument is seen to lift, indeed, to a climax; and, in fact, it does reach to the very crux of controversy; for the hardest thing for us to believe about God is to believe that He exactly, absolutely knows, because He has ordained, the future. Every attribute of God is easier to grasp than that of an infallible Omniscience. "I will declare the decree," therefore, calls for direct inspiration.

(5) The Bible is the optime of authority, because *the hooks at the end of the chain prove the dictated inspiration of its every link*. Compare the fall in Genesis—one link—with the resurrection in the Apocalypse—the other. Compare the old creation in the first chapters of the Old Testament with the new creation in the last chapters of the New. "We open the first pages of the Bible," says Vallotton, "and we find there the recital of the creation of the world by the Word of God—of the fall of man, of his exile far from God, far from Paradise, and far from the tree of life. We open the last pages of the last of the 66 books dating 4,000 years later. God is still speaking. He is still creating. He creates a new heaven and a new earth. Man is found there recovered. He is restored to communion with God. He dwells again in Paradise, beneath the shadow of the tree of life. Who is not struck by the strange correspondence of this end with that beginning? Is not the one the prologue, the other the epilogue of a drama as vast as unique?"

(6) Another argument for the supreme authority of Scripture is the *character of the investigation challenged* for the Word of God. The Bible courts the closest scrutiny. Its open pages blaze the legend, "Search the Scriptures!" *Ereunao*—"Search." It is a sportsman's term, and borrowed from the chase. "Trace out," "track out"—follow the word in all its usages and windings. Scent it out to its remotest meanings, as a dog the hare. "They searched," again says St. Luke, in the Acts, of the Bereans. There it is another word, *anakrino*—"they divided up," analyzed, sifted, pulverized, as in a mortar—to the last thought.

What a solemn challenge is this! What book but a Divine Book would dare speak such a challenge? If a book has been written by man, it is at the mercy of men. Men can go through it, riddle it, sift it, and leave it behind them, worn out. But the Bible, a Book dropped from heaven, is "God-breathed." It swells, it dilates, with the bodying fullness of God. God has written it, and none can exhaust it. Apply your microscopes, apply your telescopes, to the material of Scripture. They separate, but do not fray, its threads. They broaden out its nebulae, but find them clustered stars. They do not reach the hint of poverty in Scripture. They nowhere touch on coarseness in the fabric, nor on limitations in horizon, as always is the case when tests of such a character are brought to bear on any work of man's. You put a drop of water, or a fly's wing, under a microscope. The stronger the lens, the more that drop of water will expand, till it becomes an ocean filled with sporting animalcules. The higher the power, the more exquisite, the more silken, become the tissues of the fly's wing, until it attenuates almost to the golden and gossamer threads of a seraph's. So is it with the Word of God. The more scrutiny, the more divinity; the more dissection, the more perfection. We cannot bring to it a test too penetrating, nor a light too lancinating, nor a touchstone too exacting.

The Bible is beyond all attempts at not only exhaustion, but comprehension. No human mind can, by searching, find out the fullness of God. "For what man knoweth the things of a man save the spirit of man which is in him? even so the things of God knoweth no man save the Spirit of God."

3. That leads up to the third point. The Scriptures testify to their Divine Original by their TRANSCENDENT DOCTRINE, THEIR OUTSHINING LIGHT, THEIR NATIVE RADIANCE, THE GLOW OF THE DIVINE, THE WITNESS OF THE SPIRIT.

We should expect to find a Book, that came from God, penciled with points of jasper and of sardine stone—enhaloed with a brightness from the everlasting hills. We should look for that about the Book which, flashing conviction at once, should *carry* overwhelmingly and everywhere by its bare, naked witness—by what it simply is. That, just as God, by stretching out a hand to write upon the "plaister" of a Babylonian palace, stamped, through mysterious and disjointed words, conviction of Divinity upon Belshazzar, and each one of his one thousand "lords"; so, after that same analogue— why not?—God should stretch out His hand along the unrolling palimpsests of all the ages, and write upon them *larger* words, which, to the secret recognition of each human soul, should say, not only, "This is Truth," but "This is Truth, God-spoken!"

The Bible is the Word of God, because it is the *Book of Infinites*—the revelation of what nature, without it, never could have attained, and, coming short of the knowledge of which, nature were lost.

The greatest need of the soul is salvation. It is such a knowledge of God as shall assure us of "comfort" here and hereafter. Such a knowledge, nature outside of the Bible does not contain. Everywhere groping in his darkness, man is confronted by two changeless facts. One, his guilt, which, as he looks down, sinks deeper and deeper. The other, the justice of God, which as he looks up, lifts higher and higher. Infinite against infinite—infinite here, Infinite there—no bridge between them! Nature helps to no bridge. It nowhere speaks of atonement.

Standing with Uriel in the sun, we launch the proposition that the Scriptures are Divine in their very message because they deal with *three Infinites: Infinite Guilt; Infinite Holiness; Infinite Atonement.*

A book must itself be infinite which deals with infinites; and a book must be Divine which divinely reconciles infinites.

Infinite Guilt! Has my guilt any bottom? Is Hell any deeper? Is there, in introspection, a possible lower, more bottomless nadir? Infinite guilt! That is what opens, caves away under my feet, the longer, the more carefully I plumb my own heart—my nature, my record. Infinitely guilty! That is what I am—far, Oh, how far, below the plane of self-apology, or ghastly "criticism" of the Book which testifies to this. Infinitely guilty! That is what I am. Infinitely sinking, and, below me an infinite Tophet. I know that. As soon as the Bible declares it, I know it, and with it I know that witnessing Bible Divine. I know it—I do not know how—by an instinct, by conscience, by illumination, by the power of the Spirit of God, by the Word without, and by the flashed conviction in me which accord.

And, counterpoised above me, a correlative *Infinite—God!* What can be higher? What zenith loftier? What doming of responsibility more dread or more portentous? Infinite God—above me—coming to judge me! On the way now. I must meet Him. I know that. I know it, as soon as the Bible declares it. I know it—I do not know how—by an instinct. Even the natural man must picture to himself when thus depicted, and must fear,

> "A God in grandeur, and a world on fire."

An infinitely Holy God above me, coming to judge me. That is the second Infinite.

Then the third and what completes the Triangle, and makes its sides eternally, divinely equal—*Infinite Atonement* —an Infinite Saviour—God on the cross making answer to God on the throne—my Jesus—my Refuge—my Everlasting Jehovah.

By these three Infinites—especially this last—this Infinite Atonement, for which my whole being cries out its last cry of exhaustion—by this third side of the stupendous Triangle —the side which, left to myself, I could never make out—the Bible proves itself the soul's Geometry, the one Eternal Mathematics, the true Revelation of God.

We take the ground that these three things—Guilt, God, Atonement—set thus in star-like apposition and conjunction, *speak* from the sky, more piercingly than stars do, saying: "Sinner and sufferer, this Revelation is Divine!"

We take the open ground that a single stray leaf of God's Word, found by the wayside by one who never had seen it before, would convince him at once that the strange and the wonderful words were those of his God—were Divine.

The Scriptures are their own self-evidence. We take the ground that the sun requires no critic—truth no diving-bell. When the sun shines, he *shines* the sun. When God speaks, His evidence is in the *accent* of His words.

How did the prophets of old know, when God spoke to them, that it was God? Did they subject the voice, that shook their every bone, and make their flesh dissolve upon them, to a critical test? Did they put God, so to say—as some of our moderns would seem to have done—into a crucible, into a chemist's retort, in order to certify that He was God? Did they find it necessary to hold the handwriting of God in front of the blow-pipe of anxious philosophical examination, in order to bring out and to make the invisible, visible? The very suggestion is madness.

The Scriptures are their own self-evidence. The refusal

of the Bible on its simple presentation is enough to damn any man, and, if persisted in, will damn him—for

> "A glory gilds the sacred page,
>   Majestic, like the sun;
> It gives a light to every age;
>   It gives, but borrows none."

4. Glory spreads over the face of the Scriptures, but this glory, when scrutinized closely, is seen to contain certain features and outlines—testimonies inside of itself, direct assertions, which conspire to illustrate again its high Divinity, and to *confirm* its claim.

This is our fourth point: THE SCRIPTURES SAY OF THEMSELVES THAT THEY ARE DIVINE. They not only assume it; they say it. And this, "Thus saith the Lord," is intrinsic—a witness inside of the witness, and one upon which something more than conviction—*confidence,* or Spirit-born, and *saving faith*—depends.

The argument from the self-assertion of Scripture is cumulative.

(1)   The Bible claims that, as a Book, it comes from God. In various ways it urges this claim.

One thing: *it says so.* "God in old times spake by the prophets; God now speaks by His Son." The question of Inspiration is, in its first statement, the question of Revelation itself. If the Book be Divine, then what it says of itself is Divine. The Scriptures are inspired because they say they are inspired. The question is simply one of Divine testimony, and our business is, as simply, to receive that testimony. "Inspiration is as much an assertion," says Haldane, "as is justification by faith. Both stand and equally, on the authority of Scripture, which is as much an ultimate authority upon this point as upon any other." When God speaks, and when He says, "I speak!" there is the whole of it. He is bound to be heard and obeyed.

In the Bible God speaks, and speaks not only by proxy. Leviticus is a signal example of this. Chapter after chapter of Leviticus begins: "And the Lord spake, saying;" and so it runs on through the chapter. Moses is simply a listener, a scribe. The self-announced Speaker is God.

In the Bible God Himself comes down and speaks, not in the Old Testament alone, and not alone by proxy. "The New Testament presents us," says Dean Burgon, "with the august spectacle of the Ancient of Days holding the entire volume of the Old Testament Scriptures in His hands, and interpreting it of Himself. He, the Incarnate Word, who was in the beginning with God, and who was God—that same Almighty One is set forth in the Gospels as holding the 'volume of the Book' in His hands, as opening and unfolding it, and explaining it everywhere of Himself."

Christ everywhere receives the Scripture, and speaks of the Scriptures, in their entirety—the Law, the Prophets, and the Psalms, the whole Old Testament canon—as the living Oracle of God. He accepts and He endorses everything written, and even makes most prominent those miracles which infidelity regards as most incredible. And He does all this upon the ground of the authority of God. He passes over the writer— leaves him out of account. In all His quotations from the Old Testament, He mentions but four of the writers by name. The question with Him is not a question of the *reporter,* but of the Dictator.

And this position of our Saviour which exalted Scripture as the mouthpiece of the living God was steadily maintained by the Apostles and the apostolic Church. Again and over again, in the Book of the Acts, in all the Epistles, do we find such expressions as "He saith," "God saith," "The oracles of God," "The Holy Ghost saith," "Well spake the Holy Ghost by Esaias the prophet."

The Epistle to the Hebrews furnishes a splendid illustration of this, where, setting forth the whole economy of the

Mosaic rites, the author adds, "The Holy Ghost this signifying." Further on, and quoting words of Jeremiah, he enforces them with the remark, "The Holy Ghost is witness to us also." The imperial argument on Psalm 95 he clenches with the application, "Wherefore, as the Holy Ghost saith, Today if ye will hear His voice." Throughout the entire Epistle, whoever may have been the writer quoted from, the words of the quotation are referred to God.

(2) But now let us come closer, to the very exact and categorical and unequivocal assertion. *If the Scriptures as a Book are Divine, then what they say of themselves is Divine.* What do they say?

In this inquiry, let us keep our fingers on two words, and always on two words—the apostolic keys to the whole Church position:

"Graphe"—writing, *writing,* the Writing—not somebody, something back of the Writing. The Writing. "He Graphe," *that* was inspired.

And what is meant by inspired? "Theopneustos," God-breathed.

"God breathed!" That sweeps the whole ground. God comes down as a blast on the pipes of an organ—in voice like a whirlwind, or in still whispers like Aeolian tones, and saying the Word, He seizes the hand, and makes that hand in His own the pen of a most ready writer.

Pasa Graphe Theopneustos! "All sacred writing." More exactly, "Every sacred writing," every mark on the parchment, is "God-breathed." So says St. Paul.

Pasa Graphe Theopneustos! The sacred assertion is not of the instruments, but of the Author; not of the agents, but of the product. It is the sole and *sovereign vindication of what has been left on the page when Inspiration gets through.* "What is written," says Jesus, "how readest thou?" Man can only read what is written.

Pasa Graphe Theopneustos! God inspires not men, but language. The phrase, "inspired men," is not found in the Bible. The Scripture never employs it. The Scripture says that "holy men were moved"—pheromenoi—but that their writing, their manuscript, what they put down and left on the page, was God-breathed. You breathe upon a pane of glass. Your breath congeals there; freezes there; stays there; fixes an ice-picture there. That is the notion. The writing on the page beneath the hand of Paul was just as much breathed on, breathed *into* that page, as was His soul breathed into Adam.

The chirograph was God's incarnate voice, as truly as the flesh of Jesus sleeping on the "pillow" was incarnate God.

We take the ground that *on the original parchment*—the membrane—every sentence, word, line, mark, point, pen-stroke jot, tittle was put there by God.

On the *original parchment*. There is no question of other, anterior parchments. Even were we to indulge the violent extra-Scriptural notion that Moses or Matthew transcribed from memory or from other books the things they have left us; still, in any, in every case, the selection, the expression, the shaping and turn of the phrase on the membrane was the work of an unaided God.

But what? Let us have done with extra-Scriptural, presumptuous suppositions. The burning Isaiah, the perfervid, wheel-gazing Ezekiel; the ardent, seraphic St. Paul, caught up, up, up, up into that Paradise which he himself calls the "third heaven"—were these men only "copyists," mere self-moved "redactors"? I trow not. Their pens urged, swayed, moved hither and thither by the sweep of a heavenly current, stretched their feathered tops, like that of Luke upon St. Peter's dome, into the far-off Empyrean, winged from the throne of God.

We take the ground that on the original parchment—the membrane—every sentence, word, line, mark, point, pen-stroke jot, tittle was put there by God.

On the *original parchment*. Men may destroy that parchment. Time may destroy it. To say that the membranes have suffered in the hands of men, is but to say that everything Divine must suffer, as the pattern Tabernacle suffered, when committed to our hands. To say, however, that the *writing* has suffered—the words and letters—is to say that Jehovah has failed.

The writing remains. Like that of a palimpsest, it will survive and reappear, no matter what circumstances, what changes, come in to scatter, obscure, disfigure, or blot it away. Not even one lonely THEOS* writ large by the Spirit of God on the Great Uncial "C" as, with my own eyes I have seen it— plain, vivid, glittering, outstarting from behind the pale and overlying ink of Ephraim the Syrian—can be buried. Like Banquo's ghost, it will rise; and God Himself replace it, and, with a hammer-stroke, beat down deleting hands. The parchments, the membranes, decay; the writings, the words, are eternal as God. Strip off the plaister from Belshazzar's palace, yet Mene! Mene! Tekel! Upharsin! remain. They *remain*.

Let us go through them, and from the beginning, and see what the Scriptures say of themselves.

One thing; they say that God spake, "anciently and all the way down, in the prophets." One may make if he pleases the "en" instrumental—as it is more often instrumental—i. e., "by" the prophets; but in either case, in them or by them, the Speaker was God.

Again; the Scriptures say that the laws the writers promulgated, the doctrines they taught, the stories they recorded— above all, their prophecies of Christ—were not their own; were not originated, nor conceived by them from any outside sources—were not what they had any means before of knowing, or of comprehending, but were immediately from God;

*God was manifest in the flesh (1 Tim. 3:16).

they themselves being only recipient, only concurrent with God, as God moved upon them.

Some of the speakers of the Bible, as Balaam, the Old Prophet of Bethel, Caiaphas, are seized and made to speak in spite of themselves; and, with the greatest reluctance, to utter what is farthest from their minds and hearts. Others—in fact all—are purblind to the very oracles, instructions, visions, they announce. "Searching what, or what manner of time, the Spirit of Christ which was in them did signify!" i. e., the prophets themselves did not know what they wrote. What picture can be more impressive than that of the prophet himself hanging over and contemplating in surprise, in wonder, in amazement, his own autograph—as if it had been left upon the table there—the relict of some strange and supernatural hand? How does that picture lift away the Bible from all human hands and place it back, as His original deposit, in the hands of God.

Again; it is said that "the Word of the Lord came" to such and such a writer. It is not said that the Spirit came, which is true; but that the Word itself came, the Dabar-Jehovah. And it is said: *"Hayo Haya Dabar,"* that it *substantially* came, essentially came; "essendo fuit"—so say Pagninus, Montanus, Polanus—i. e., it came germ, seed and husk and blossom—in its totality—*words* which the Holy Ghost teacheth—the "words."

Again; it is *denied,* and most emphatically, that the words are the words of the man—of the agent. "The word was in my tongue". St. Paul asserts that "Christ spake in him" (2 Cor. 13:3). "Who hath made man's mouth? Have not I, the Lord? I will put *My* words into thy mouth." That looks very much like what has been stigmatized as the "mechanical theory." It surely makes the writer a mere organ, although not an unconscious, or unwilling, unspontaneous organ. Could language more plainly assert or defend a verbal direct inspiration?

In the line with the fact, again it is said that the word came to the writers without any study—"suddenly"—as to Amos where he is taken from following the flock.

Again; when the word thus came to the prophets *they had not the power to conceal it.* It was "like a fire in their bones" which must speak or write, as Jeremiah says, or consume its human receptacle.

And to make this more clear, it is said that holy men were *pheromenoi,* "moved," or rather carried along in a supernatural ecstatic current—a *delectatio scribendi.* They were not left one instant to their wit, wisdom, fancies, memories, or judgments either to order, or arrange, or dispose, or write out. They were *only reporters,* intelligent, conscious, passive, plastic, docile, exact, and accurate reporters. They were like men who wrote with different kinds of ink. They colored their work with tints of their own personality, or rather God colored it, having made the writer as the writing, and the writer for that special writing; and because the work ran *through them* just as the same water, running through glass tubes, yellow, green, red, violet, will be yellow, violet and green, and red.

God wrote the Bible, the whole Bible, and the Bible as a whole. He wrote each word of it as truly as He wrote the Decalogue on the tables of stone.

Higher criticism tells us—the "New Departure" tells us—that Moses was inspired, but the *Decalogue* not. But Exodus and Deuteronomy seven times over declare that God stretched down the tip of His finger from heaven and left the *marks,* the gravements, the cut characters, the scratches on the stones. (Ex. 24:12.) "I will give thee tables of stone, commandments, *which I have written*" (Ex. 31:18). "And He gave unto Moses, upon Mount Sinai, two tables of testimony, tables of stone *written with the finger of God*" (Ex. 32:16). The tables were the work of God and the *writing was the writing of God,* graven upon the tables. (Deut. 4:12). "The Lord spake unto you out of the midst of the fire, and He declared unto you His covenant, even ten commandments and *He wrote them* upon two tables of stone" (Deut. 5:22). "These words the Lord spake, and *He wrote them* in two tables of stone, and delivered them unto me" (Deut. 9:10). "And the Lord delivered unto me two tables of stone *written with the finger of God"!*

Seven times, and to men to whom writing is instinct; to beings who are most of all impressed, not by vague vanishing voices, but by words arrested, fixed, set down; and who themselves cannot resist the impulse to commit their own words to some written deposit, even of stone, or of bark, if they have not the paper; seven times, to men, to whom writing is instinct and who are inclined to rely for their highest conviction on what they have styled "documentary evidence," i. e., on books; God comes in and declares, "I have written"!

The Scriptures, whether with the human instrument or without the human instrument, with Moses or without Moses, were written by God. When God had finished, Moses had nothing else to do but carry down God's autograph. That is our doctrine. The Scriptures—if ten words, then all the words —if the law, then the Gospels—the writing, the writings, *He Graphe—Hai Graphai*—expressions repeated more than fifty times in the New Testament alone—*this, these* were inspired.

Brethren, the danger of our present day—the "down grade" as it has been called, of doctrine, of conviction, of the moral sentiment—a decline more constantly patent, as it is more blatantly proclaimed—does it not find its first step in our lost hold upon the very inspiration of the Word of God?

Does not a fresh conviction here lie at the root of every remedy which we desire, as its sad lack lies at the root of every ruin we deplore?

THE TESTIMONY OF THE ORGANIC UNITY OF THE BIBLE TO ITS INSPIRATION

BY THE LATE ARTHUR T. PIERSON

The argument for the inspiration of the Bible which I am to present is that drawn from its unity. This unity may be seen in several conspicuous particulars, upon some of which it will be well to dilate.

1. THE UNITY IS STRUCTURAL. In the Book itself appears a certain archetypal, architectural plan. The two Testaments are built on the same general scheme. Each is in three parts: historic, didactic, prophetic; looking to the past, the present, and the future.

Here is a collection of books; in their style and character there is great variety and diversity; some are historical, others poetical; some contain laws, others lyrics; some are prophetic, some symbolic; in the Old Testament we have historical, poetical, and prophetical divisions; and in the New Testament we have historic narratives, then twenty-one epistles, then a symbolic apocalyptic poem in oriental imagery. And yet this is no artificial arrangement of fragments. We find "the Old Testament patent in the New; the New latent in the Old."

In such a Book, then, it is not likely that there would be unity; for all the conditions were unfavorable to a harmonious moral testimony and teaching. Here are some sixty or more separate documents, written by some forty different persons, scattered over wide intervals of space and time, strangers to each other; these documents are written in three different languages, in different lands, among different and sometimes hostile peoples, with marked diversities of literary style, and by men of all grades of culture and mental capacity, from

Moses to Malachi; and when we look into these productions, there is even in them great unlikeness, both in matter and manner of statement; and yet they all constitute one volume.

All are entirely at agreement. There is diversity in unity, and unity in diversity. It is *"e pluribus unum."* The more we study it, the more do its unity and harmony appear. Even the Law and the Gospel are not in conflict. They stand, like the cherubim, facing different ways, but their faces are toward each other. And the four Gospels, like the cherubic creatures in Ezekiel's vision, facing in four different directions, move in one. All the criticism of more than three thousand years has failed to point out one important or irreconcilable contradiction in the testimony and teachings of those who are farthest separated—there is no collision, yet there could be no collusion!

How can this be accounted for? There is no answer which can be given unless you admit the supernatural element. If God actually superintended the production of this Book, then its unity is the unity of a Divine plan and its harmony the harmony of a Supreme Intelligence.

As the baton rises and falls in the hand of the conductor of some grand orchestra, from violin and bass-viol, cornet and flute, trombone and trumpet, flageolet and clarinet, bugle and French horn, cymbals and drum, there comes one grand harmony! There is no doubt, though the conductor were screened from view, that one master mind controls all the instrumental performers. But God makes His oratorio to play for more than a thousand years; the key is never lost and never changes except by those exquisite modulations that show the master composer; and when the last strain dies away it is seen that all these glorious movements and melodies have been variations on one grand theme! Did each musician compose as he played, or was there one composer back of all the players?—"one supreme and regulating mind" in this Oratorio of the Ages? If God was the master musician planning the whole and arranging the parts, then we can understand how Moses' grand anthem of creation glided into Isaiah's oratorio of the Messiah; by and by sinks into Jeremiah's plaintive wail, swells into Ezekiel's awful chorus, changes into Daniel's rapturous lyric; and, after the quartette of the evangelists, closes with John's full choir of saints and angels!

The temple, first built upon Mount Moriah, was built of stone, made ready before it was brought thither; there was neither hammer nor ax nor any tool of iron heard in the house while it was in building. What insured symmetry in the temple when constructed, and harmony between the workmen in the quarries and the shops, and the builders on the hill? *One presiding mind planned the whole;* one intelligence built that whole structure in ideal before it was in fact. The builders built more wisely than they knew, putting together the ideas of the architect and not their own. Only so can we account for the structural unity of the Word of God. The structure was planned and wrought out in the mind of a Divine Architect, who superintended His own workmen and work. Moses laid its foundations, not knowing who should build after him, or what form the structure should assume. Workman after workman followed; he might see that there was agreement with what went before, but he could not foresee that what should come after would be only the sublime carrying out of the grand plan. During all those sixteen centuries through which the building rose toward completion, there was no sound of ax or hammer, no chipping or hacking to make one part fit its fellow. Everything is in agreement with everything else, because the whole Bible was built in the thought of God before one book was laid in order. The building rose steadily from corner-stone to cap-stone, foundations first, then story after story, pillars on pedestals, and capitals on pillars, and arches on capitals, till, like a dome flashing back the splendors of the noonday, the Apocalypse spans and crowns and completes the whole, glorious with celestial visions.

2. THE UNITY IS HISTORIC. The whole Bible is the history of the kingdom of God. Israel represents that kingdom. And two things are noticeable. All centers about the Hebrew nationality. With their origin and progress the main historical portion begins; and with their apostasy and captivity it stops. The times of the Gentiles filled the interval and have no proper history; prophecy, which is history anticipated, takes up the broken thread, and gives us the outline of the future when Israel shall again take its place among the nations.

3. THE UNITY IS DISPENSATIONAL. There are certain uniform dispensational features which distinguish every new period. Each dispensation is marked by seven features, in the following order: (a) Increased light; (b) Decline of spiritual life; (c) Union between disciples and the world; (d) A gigantic civilization worldly in type; (e) Parallel development of good and evil; (f) Apostasy on the part of God's people; (g) Concluding judgment. We are now in the seventh dispensation, and the same seven marks have been upon all alike, showing one controlling power—*Deus in Historia*.

4. THE UNITY IS PROPHETIC. Of all prophecy, there is but one center, The kingdom and the King. 1. Adam, the first king, lost his scepter by sin. His probation ended in failure and disaster. 2. The second Adam, in His probation, gained the victory, routed the tempter, and stood firm. The two comings of this King constituted the two focal centers of the prophetic ellipse. His first coming was to make possible an empire in man and over man. His second coming will be to set that empire up in glory. All prophecy moves about these two advents. It touches Israel only as related to the kingdom; and the Gentiles only as related to Israel. Hence, in the Old Testament, Nineveh, Babylon, and Egypt loom up as the main foes to the kingdom, as represented by the Hebrews; and in the New Testament, the Beast, Prophet, and Dragon are conspicuous as the gigantic adversaries of that kingdom after Israel again takes her place.

There are some six hundred and sixty-six general prophecies in the Old Testament, three hundred and thirty-three of which refer particularly to the coming Messiah, and meet only in Him.

5. THE UNITY IS THEREFORE ALSO PERSONAL:

> *"In the volume of the Book*
> *It is written of Me."*

There is but one Book, and within it but one Person. Christ is the center of the Old Testament prophecy, as He is of New Testament history. From Genesis 3 to Malachi 3, He fills out the historic and prophetic profile. Not only do the three hundred and thirty-three predictions unite in Him, but even the rites and ceremonies find in Him their only interpreter. Nay, historic characters prefigure Him, and historic events are the pictorial illustrations of His vicarious ministry. The Old Testament is a lock of which Christ is the key. The prophetic plant becomes a burning bush, as twig after twig of prediction flames with fulfillment. The crimson thread runs through the whole Bible. Beginning at any point you may preach Jesus. The profile—at first a drawing, without color, a mere outline—is filled in by successive artists, until the life tints glow on the canvas of the centuries, and the perfect portrait of the Messiah is revealed.

6. THE UNITY IS SYMBOLIC. I mean that there is a corresponding use of symbols, whether in form, color, or numbers. In form, we have the square, the cube, and the circle, throughout, and used as types of the same truths. In color, we have the white for purity, the lustrous white for glory, the red for guilt of sin and the sacrifice for sin, the blue for truth and fidelity to promise, the purple for royalty, the pale or livid hue for death, and the black for woe and disaster. In numbers there is plainly a numerical system. One seems to represent unity, two correspondence and confirmation or contradiction, three is the number of Godhead, four of the world and man. Seven, which is the sum of three and four, stands for

the combination of the Divine and human; twelve, the product of three and four, for the Divine interpenetrating the human; ten, the sum of one, two, three, and four, is the number of completeness; three and a half, the broken number, represents tribulation; six, which stops short of seven, is unrest; eight, which is beyond the number of rest, is the number of victory. All this implies one presiding mind, and it could not be man's mind.

7. THE UNITY IS DIDACTIC. In the entire range and scope of the ethical teaching of the Bible there is no inconsistency or adulteration. But we need to observe a distinction maintained throughout as to natural religion and spiritual religion. There is a natural religion. Had man remained loyal to God, the universal fatherhood of God and the universal brotherhood of man would have been the two great facts and laws of humanity; the broad, adequate basis of the natural claim of God to filial obedience, and of man to fraternal love. But man sinned. He fell from the filial relationship; he disowned God as his Father. Hence, the need of a new and spiritual relationship and religion. In Christ, God's fatherhood is restored and man's brotherhood re-established, but these are treated as universal only to the circle of believers. A new obedience is now enforced, resting its claim, not on creation and providence, but on new creation and grace. Man learns a supernatural love and life.

Upon this didactic unity we stop to expatiate.

In not one respect are these doctrinal and ethical teachings in conflict, from beginning to end; we find in them a positive oneness of doctrine which amazes us. Even where at first glance there appears to be conflict, as between Paul and James, we find, on closer examination, that instead of standing face to face, beating each other, they stand back to back, beating off common foes.

We observe, moreover, *a progressive development of revelation.* Bernhard devoted the powers of his master mind to tracing the "Progress of Doctrine in the New Testament." He shows that although the books of the New Testament are not even arranged in the order of their production, that order could not, in one instance, be changed without impairing or destroying the symmetry of the whole book; and that there is a regular progress in the unfolding of doctrine from the Gospel according to Matthew to the Revelation of St. John.

A wider examination will show the very same progress of doctrine in the whole Bible. Most wonderful of all, this moral and didactic unity could not be fully understood till the Book was completed. The progress of preparation, like a scaffolding about a building, obscured its beauty; but when John placed the cap-stone in position and declared that nothing further should be added, the scaffolding fell and a grand cathedral was revealed.

8. THE UNITY IS SCIENTIFIC. The Bible is not a scientific book, but it follows one consistent law. Like an engine on its own track, it thunders across the track of science, but is never diverted from its own.

(1). No direct teaching or anticipation of scientific truth is here found. (2). No scientific fact is ever misstated, though common, popular phraseology may be employed. (3). An elastic set of terms is used, which contain, in germ, all scientific truth as the acorn enfolds the oak.

These statements deserve a little amplification, as this has been supposed to be the weak side of the Bible. Yet, after a study of the Word on the one hand and natural science on the other, I believe we may safely challenge any living man to bring one well-established fact of science against which the Bible really and irreconcilably militates!

God led inspired men to use such language, as that without revealing scientific facts in advance, it accurately accommodates itself to them when discovered.

The language is so elastic and flexible as to contract itself to the narrowness of ignorance, and yet expand itself to the dimensions of knowledge. If the Bible may, from imperfect human language, select terms which may hold hidden truths till ages to come shall disclose the inner meaning, that would seem to be the best solution of this difficult problem. And now, when we come to compare the language of the Bible with modern science, we find just this to be the fact.

For example, we are told that the Bible term "firmament" is but an ancient blunder crystallized. Modern science says, "Ye have heard it hath been said by them of old time, there is a solid sphere above us which revolves with its starry lamps; but this is an old notion of ignorance, for there is nothing but vast space filled with ether above us, and stars have an apparent motion because the earth turns on its axis."

But this word "firmament," which has been declared "irreconcilable with modern astronomy," we find, on consulting our Hebrew lexicon, means simply an "expanse." If Moses had been Mitchell, he could not have chosen a better word to express the appearance, and yet accommodate the reality. He actually anticipated science. This is one of the "mistakes of Moses" to which the modern blasphemer does not refer!

The general correspondence between the Mosaic account of creation and the most advanced discoveries of science, proves that only He who built the world, built the Book.

As to the order of creation, Moses and geology agree. Both teach that at first there was an abyss, or watery waste, whose dense vapors shut out light. Both make life to precede light; and the life to develop beneath the abyss. Both make the atmosphere to form an expanse by lifting watery vapors into cloud, and so separating the fountains of waters above from the fountains below. Both tell us that continents next lifted themselves from beneath the great deep, and brought forth grass, herb, and tree. Both teach that the heavens became cleared of cloud, and the sun and moon and stars, which then appeared, began to serve to divide day from night, and to become signs for seasons and years. Both then represent the waters bringing forth moving and creeping creatures, and fowl flying in the expanse, followed next by the race of quadruped mammals, and, last of all, by man himself.

There is the same agreement as to the order of animal creation. Geology and comparative anatomy combine to teach that the order was from lower to higher types. First, the fish, in which the proportion of brain to spinal cord is as 2 to 1; then reptiles, in which it is as 2½ to 1; birds, 3 to 1; mammals, 4 to 1; man, 33 to 1. Now, this is exactly the order of Moses. Who told him what modern science has discovered, that fish and reptiles belong below birds? As Mr. Tullidge says: "With the advance of discovery, the opposition supposed to exist between Revelation and Geology has disappeared; and of the eighty theories which the French Institute counted in 1806 as hostile to the Bible, not one now stands."

Take an example of this scientific accuracy from astronomy. Says Jeremiah in 30:22, "The host of heaven cannot be numbered, neither the sand of the sea measured." Hipparchus about a century and a half before Christ, gave the number of stars as 1,022, and Ptolemy, in the beginning of the second century of the Christian era, could find but 1,026. We may, on a clear night, with the unaided eye, see only 1,160 or in the whole celestial sphere, about 3,000. But when the telescope began to be pointed to the heavens, less than three centuries ago, by Galileo, then men began to know that the stars are as countless as the sand on the seashore. When Lord Rosse turned his great mirror to the sky, lo! the number of visible stars increased to nearly 400,000,000! John Herschel resolves the nebulae into suns, and finds in the cloudy scarf about Orion, "a gorgeous bed of stars," and the Milky Way itself proves to be simply a grand procession of stars absolutely without number. And so, the exclamation of the prophet, 600 years before Christ, 2,200 years before Galileo, "the host of heaven cannot be numbered," proves to be not a wild, poetic exaggeration, but literal truth. Who was Jeremiah's teacher in astronomy?

Let us take an example from natural philosophy. Moses accords with modern discoveries as to the nature of light, in not representing this mystery as being made, but "called forth," commanded to shine. If light be only "a mode of motion," how appropriate such phraseology!

In Job 37: 13, 14, we read of the dayspring that it takes hold of the ends of the earth; it is turned as clay to the seal, and they stand as a garment. The ancient cylindrical seals rolled over the clay, and left an impress of artistic beauty. What was without form before, stood out in bold relief, like sculpture. So, as the earth revolves, and brings each portion of its surface successively under the sun's light and heat, what was before dull, dark, dead, discloses and develops beauty, and the clay stands like a garment, curiously wrought in bold relief and brilliant colors. Considered either as science or poetry, where, in any other book of antiquity, can you find anything equal to that? That phrase, "takes hold of the ends of the earth," conveys the idea of a bending of the rays of light, like the fingers of the hand when they lay hold. When the sunlight would touch the extremities of the earth, it is bent by the atmosphere so as to secure contact, and, but for this, vast portions, out of the direct line of the sun's rays, would be dark, cold and dead. Who taught Job, 1,500 years or more before Christ, to use terms that Longfellow or Tennyson might covet to describe refraction?

"When the morning stars sang together," Job 38:7, has been always taken to be a high flight of poetry. And when in the Psalms, 65:8, we read, "Thou makest the outgoings of the morning and evening to rejoice," the Hebrew word means to give forth a tremulous sound, or to make vibrations—to sing. In these poetic expressions, what scientific truth was wrapped up! Light comes to the eye in undulations or vibrations, as tones of sound to the ear. There is a point at which these vibrations are too rapid or delicate to be detected by our sense of hearing; then a more delicate organ, the eye, must take note of them; they appeal to the optic nerve instead of the auditory nerve, and as light and not sound. Thus, light really sings. "The lowest audible tone is made by 16.5 vibrations of air per second; the highest, by 38,000; between these extremes lie eleven octaves. Vibrations do not cease at 38,000 but our organs are not fitted to hear beyond those limitations." And so it is literally true that "the morning stars sang together." Here is Divine phraseology that has been standing there for ages uninterrupted. And now we may read it just as it stands: "Thou makest the outgoings [or light radiations] of the morning and evening to sing," i. e., to give forth sound by vibration.

"Solomon, in Eccles. 12:6, has left us a poetic description of death. How that "silver cord" describes the spinal marrow; the "golden bowl", the basin which holds the brain; the "pitcher", the lungs; and the "wheel", the heart!

The circulation of the blood was discovered twenty-six hundred years afterward by Harvey. Is it not very remarkable that the language Solomon uses exactly suits the fact—a wheel pumping up through one pipe to discharge through another?

9. Last of all, THE UNITY OF THE BIBLE IS ORGANIC. And this means it is the unity of organized being. *Organic unity implies three things: first, that all parts are necessary to a complete whole; secondly, that all are necessary to complement each other; and thirdly, that all are pervaded by one life-principle.*

Let us apply these laws to the Word of God.

(1). *All the parts of the Bible are necessary to its completeness.* Organic unity is dependent on the existence and co-operation of organs. An oratorio is not an organic unit. Any part of it may be separated from the rest, or displaced by a new composition.

But if this body of mine loses an eye, a limb, or the smallest joint of the finger, it is forever maimed; its completeness is gone.

Not one of the books of the Bible could be lost without maiming the body of truth here contained. Every book fills a place. None can be omitted.

For example, the Book of Esther has long been criticised as not necessary to the completeness of the Canon, and particularly, because "it does not even once contain the name of God." But that book is the most complete exhibition of the providence of God. It teaches a Divine Hand behind human affairs; unbiased freedom of resolution and action as consistent with God's overruling sovereignty; and all things working together to produce grand results. The book that thus exhibits God's providence does not contain the name of God; perhaps because this book is meant to teach us of the Hidden Hand that, unseen, moves and controls all things.

"Ruth" seems to be only a love-story to some; but how rich this book is in foreshadowings of Gospel truth, especially illustrating the double nature of the God-man, our Redeemer.

Boaz is a type of Christ—Lord of the Harvest, Dispenser of Bread, Giver of Rest, He is Goël—the Redeemer. Boaz, the near kinsman, buying back the lost inheritance and marrying Ruth, suggests Jesus, the God-man, our near Kinsman, yet of a higher family, the Redeemer of our lost estate, and Bridegroom of the redeemed Church.

The Epistle to Philemon seems at first only a letter to a friend about a runaway slave. But this letter is full of illustrations of grace. The sinner has run away from God, and robbed Him besides. The law allows him no right of asylum; but grace concedes him the privilege of appeal. Christ, God's Partner, intercedes. He sends him back to the Father, no more a slave but a son.

(2). *The second law of organic unity is that all parts are necessary to complement each other.*

Cuvier has framed in scientific statement this law of unity. Organized being in every case forms a whole—a complete system—all parts of which mutually correspond; none of these parts can change without the other also changing; and consequently each taken separately indicates and gives all the others. For instance, the sharp-pointed tooth of the lion requires a strong jaw; these demand a skull fitted for the attachment of powerful muscles, both for moving the jaw and raising the head; a broad, well developed shoulder-blade must accompany such a head; and there must be an arrangement of bones of the leg which admits of the leg-paw being rotated and turned upward, in order to be used as an instrument to seize and tear the prey; and of course there must be strong claws arming the paw. Hence from one tooth, the animal could be modeled though the species had perished.

Thus the Four Gospels are necessary to each other and to the whole Bible. Each presents the subject from a different point of view, and the combination gives us a Divine Person reflected, projected before us, like an object with proportions and dimensions.

Matthew wrote for the Jew, and shows Jesus as the King of the Jews, the Royal Lawgiver. Mark wrote for the Roman, and shows Him as the Power of God, the Mighty Worker. Luke wrote for the Greek, and shows Him as the Wisdom of God, the human Teacher and Friend. John, writing to supplement and complement the other Gospels, shows Him as Son of God, as well as Son of man, having and giving eternal life.

These are not Gospels of Matthew, etc., but one Gospel of Christ, according to Matthew, Mark, Luke and John. The first three present the person and work of Christ from the outward, earthly side; the last, from the inward and heavenly. In the beginning of each Gospel we find emphasized: in Matthew, Christ's genealogy, in Mark His majesty, in Luke His humanity, in John His divinity. So, in the close of each:

in Matthew His resurrection, in Mark His ascension, in Luke His parting benediction and promise of enduement, and in John the added hint of His second coming.

The Epistles are likewise all necessary to complete the whole and complément each other. There are five writers, each having his own sphere of truth. Paul's great theme is Faith, and its relations to justification, sanctificaticn, service, joy and glory. James treats of Works, their relation to faith, as its justification before man. He is the counterpart and complement of Paul. Peter deals with Hope, as the inspiration of God's pilgrim people. John's theme is Love, and its relation to the light and life of God as manifested in the believer. In his Gospel, he exhibits eternal life in Christ; in his epistles, eternal life as seen in the believer. Jude sounds the trumpet of warning against apostasy, which implies the wreck of faith, the delusion of false hope, love grown cold, and the utter decay of good works. What one of all these writers could we drop from the New Testament?

The Unity of the Bible is the unity of one organic whole. The decalogue demands the Sermon on the Mount. Isaiah's prophecy makes necessary the narrative of the Evangelists. Daniel fits into the Revelation as bone fits socket. Leviticus explains, and is explained by, the Epistle to the Hebrews. The Psalms express the highest morality and spirituality of the Old Testament; they link the Mosaic code with the Divine ethics of the Gospels and the Epistles. The passover foreshadows the Lord's supper, and the Lord's supper interprets and fulfills the passover. Even the little book of Jonah makes more complete the sublime Gospel according to John; and Ruth and Esther prophetically hint the Acts of the Apostles. Nay, when you come to the last chapters of Revelation, you find yourself mysteriously touching the first chapters of Genesis; and lo! as you survey the whole track of your thought, you find you have been following the perimeter of a golden ring; the extremities actually bend around, touch, and blend. You read in the first of Genesis of the first creation; in the last of the Revelation, of the new creation—the new heaven and the new earth; there, of the river that watered the garden; here, of the pure river of the water of life; there, of the Tree of Life in the first Eden; here, of the Tree of Life which is in the midst of the Paradise of God; there, of the God who came down to walk with and talk with man; here, we read that the Tabernacle of God is with men; there, we read of the curse that came by sin, here, we read: "And there shall be no more curse."

(3). *The third and last law of organic unity is, that one life principle must pervade the whole.* The Life of God is in His Word. That Word is "quick"—living. Is it a mirror? yes, but such a mirror as the living eye; is it a seed? yes, but a seed hiding the vitality of God; is it a sword? yes, but a sword that omnisciently discerns and omnipotently pierces the human heart. Hold it reverently; for you have a living Book in your hand. Speak to it, and it will answer you. Bend down and listen; you shall hear in it the heart-throbs of God.

This Book, thus *one,* we are to hold forth as the Word of Life and the Light of God, in the midst of a crooked and perverse generation. We shall meet opposition. Like the birds that beat themselves into insensibility against the light in the Statue of Liberty in New York Harbor, the creatures of darkness will assault this Word, and vainly seek to put out its eternal light. But they shall only fall stunned and defeated at its base, while it still rises from its rock pedestal, immovable and serene!

CHAPTER VI

FULFILLED PROPHECY A POTENT ARGUMENT FOR THE BIBLE

BY ARNO C. GAEBELEIN,
EDITOR "OUR HOPE," NEW YORK CITY.

"Produce your cause, saith the Lord; bring forth your strong reasons, saith the King of Jacob. Let them bring them forth, and show us what shall happen; let them show the former things, what they be, that we may consider them, and know the latter end of them, or declare us things to come. Show the things that are to come hereafter, that we may know, that ye are gods" (Isa. 41: 21-23). "I declare the end from the beginning, and from ancient times the things that are not yet done, saying, My counsel shall stand, and I will do all my pleasure" (Isa. 46: 10).

This is Jehovah's challenge to the idol-gods of Babylon to predict future events. He alone can do that. The Lord can declare the end from the beginning, and make known things that are not yet done. The dumb idols of the heathen know nothing concerning the future. They cannot predict what is going to happen. And man himself is powerless to know future events and cannot find out things to come.

Jehovah, who has made this challenge and declaration, has also fully demonstrated His power to do so. He has done it in His holy Word, the Bible. Other nations possess books of a religious character, called "sacred books." Not one of them contains any predictions concerning the future. If the authors of these writings had attempted to foretell the future, they would have thereby furnished the strongest evidence of their deceptions. The Bible is the *only* book in the world which contains predictions. It is pre-eminently that, which no other book could be, and none other is, a book of prophecy. These predictions are declared to be the utterances of Jehovah; they show that the Bible is a supernatural book, the revelation of God.

PROPHECY NEGLECTED AND DENIED

In view of this fact it is deplorable that the professing Church of today almost completely ignores and neglects the study of prophecy, a neglect which has for one of its results the loss of one of the most powerful weapons against infidelity. The denial of the Bible as the inspired Word of God has become widespread.

If prophecy were intelligently studied such a denial could not flourish as it does, for the fulfilled predictions of the Bible give the clearest and most conclusive evidence that the Bible is the revelation of God. To this must be added the fact that the destructive Bible criticism, which goes by the name of "Higher Criticism," denies the possibility of prophecy. The whole reasoning method of this school, which has become so popular throughout Christendom, may be reduced to the following: Prophecy is an impossibility; there is no such thing as foretelling future events. Therefore a book which contains predictions of things to come, which were later fulfilled, must have been written after the events which are predicted in the book. The methods followed by the critics, the attacks made by them upon the authenticity of the different books of the Bible, especially upon those which contain the most startling prophecies (Isaiah and Daniel), we cannot follow at this time. They deny everything which the Jewish Synagogue and the Christian Church always believed to be prophecy, a supernatural unfolding of future events.

PAST, PRESENT AND FUTURE

The prophecies of the Bible must be first of all divided into three classes. 1. Prophecies which have found already their fulfillment. 2. Prophecies which are now in process of fulfillment. Many predictions written several thousand years ago are now being accomplished before our eyes. We mention those which relate to the national and spiritual condition of the Jewish people and the predictions concerning the moral and religious condition of the present age. 3. Prophecies which are still unfulfilled. We have reference to those which predict the second, glorious and visible coming of our Lord, the re-gathering of Israel and their restoration to the land of promise, judgments which will fall upon the nations of the earth, the establishment of the Kingdom, the conversion of the world, universal peace and righteousness, the deliverance of groaning creation, and others.

These great prophecies of future things are often robbed of their literal and solemn meaning by a process of spiritualization. The visions of the prophets concerning Israel and Jerusalem, and the glories to come in a future age, are almost generally explained as having their fulfillment in the Church during the present age. However, our object is not to follow the unfulfilled prophecies, but prophecies fulfilled and in process of fulfillment. At the close of our treatise we shall point out briefly that in the light of fulfilled prophecies, the literal fulfillment of prophecies still future is perfectly assured.

FULFILLED PROPHECY A VAST THEME

Fulfilled prophecy is a vast theme of much importance. It is equally inspiring and interesting. Volumes could be written to show how hundreds of Divine predictions written in the Bible have passed into history. What God announced through His chosen instruments has come to pass. History is bearing witness to the fact that the events which transpired among nations were pre-written in the Bible, even as prophecy is nothing less than history written in advance. As much as space permits we shall call attention to the fulfilled prophecies relating to the person of Christ; to the Jewish people; and to a number of nations, whose history, whose rise and downfall, are divinely predicted in the Bible. Furthermore, we shall mention the great prophetic unfoldings as given in the Book of Daniel, and how many of these predictions have already found a most interesting fulfillment.

MESSIANIC PROPHECIES AND THEIR FULFILLMENT

The Old Testament contains a most wonderful chain of prophecies concerning the person, the life and work of our Lord. As He is the center of the whole revelation of God, the One upon whom all rests, we turn first of all to a few of the prophecies which speak of Him. This also is very necessary. The destructive criticism has gone so far as to state that there are no predictions at all concerning Christ in the Old Testament. Such a denial leads to and is linked with the denial of Christ Himself, especially the denial of His Deity and His work on the cross.

To follow the large number of prophecies concerning the coming of Christ into the world and the work He was to accomplish we cannot attempt in these pages. We point out briefly in a general way what must be familiar to most Christians who search the Scriptures. Christ is first announced in Gen. 3: 15 to be the seed of the woman, and therefore a human being. In Gen. 9:26-27 the supremacy of Shem is predicted. The full revelation of Jehovah God is connected with Shem and in due time a son of Shem, Abraham, received the promise that the predicted seed was to come from him. (Gen. 12: 8.) Messiah was to come from the seed of Abraham.

Then the fact was revealed that He was to come from Isaac and not from Ishmael, from Jacob and not from Esau. But Jacob had twelve sons. The Divine prediction pointed to Judah and later to the house of David of the tribe of Judah from which the Messiah should spring. When we come to the prophecies of Isaiah we learn that His mother is to be a virgin. (Isa. 7: 14.) But the son born of the virgin is

Immanuel, God with us. Clearly the prophetic Word in Isaiah states that the Messiah would be a child born and a Son given with the names, "Wonderful, Counsellor, Mighty God, the Everlasting Father, the Prince of Peace" (Isa. 9:6). The promised Messiah is to be the seed of a woman, of the seed of Abraham, of David, born of a virgin. He is to be Immanuel, the Son given, God manifested in the flesh.

This promised Messiah, the Son of David, should appear (according to Isa. 11:1) after the house of David had been stripped of its royal dignity and glory. And what more could we say of the prophecies which speak of His life, His poverty, the works He was to do, His rejection by His own people, the Jews. In that matchless chapter in Isaiah, the fifty-third, the rejection of Christ by His own nation is predicted. In another chapter a still more startling prophecy is recorded: "Then I said, I have labored in vain, I have spent my strength for naught and in vain." This is Messiah's lament on account of His rejection. Then follows the answer, which contains a most striking prophecy: "It is a light thing that Thou shouldest be My servant to raise up the tribes of Jacob and to restore the preserved of Israel: I also will give Thee for a light to the Gentiles, that Thou mayest be My salvation unto the ends of the earth" (Isa. 49:5, 6). Here the revelation is given that He would not alone be rejected by His own nation, but that He would also bring salvation to the Gentiles. What human mind could have ever invented such a program! The promised Messiah of Israel, the longed-for One, is predicted to be rejected by His own people and thus becomes the Saviour of the despised Gentiles. His sufferings and His death are even more minutely predicted.

In the Book of Psalms the sufferings of Christ, the deep agony of His soul, the expressions of His sorrow and His grief, are pre-written by the Spirit of God. We mention only one Psalm, the twenty-second. His death by crucifixion is prophesied. Yet death by crucifixion was in David's time an unknown mode of death. Cruel Rome invented that horrible form of death. The cry of the forsaken One is predicted in the very words which came from the lips of our Saviour out of the darkness which enshrouded the cross. So are also predicted the words of mockery by those who looked on; the piercing of His hands and feet; the parting of the garments and the casting of the lots. In the fifty-third chapter of Isaiah, the purpose of His death is so blessedly predicted. He was to die the substitute of sinners. There we find also His burial and His resurrection predicted. All this was recorded 700 years before our Lord was born. In the Psalms we find the prophecy that the rejected One would occupy a place at the right hand of God (Psalm 110:1). He was to leave the earth. David's Son and David's Lord was to have a place in the highest glory, even at the right hand of God, to wait there till His enemies are made His footstool. It is indeed a wonderful chain of prophecies concerning Christ. We could give a very few of these predictions. How they all were long ago literally fulfilled in the coming, in the life, in the death, in the resurrection and ascension of our adorable Lord, all true believers know.

THE JEWISH PEOPLE

When Frederick the Great, King of Prussia, asked the court chaplain for an argument that the Bible is an inspired book, he answered, "Your Majesty, the Jews." It was well said. To the Jews were committed the oracles of God. (Rom. 3:2.) These oracles of God, the Holy Scriptures, the Law and the Prophets, are filled with a large number of predictions relating to their own history. Their unbelief, the rejection of the Messiah, the results of that rejection, their dispersion into the corners of the earth, so that they would be scattered among all the nations, the persecutions and sorrows they were to suffer, the curses which were to come upon them, their miraculous preservation as a nation, their future great tribulation and final restoration—all these and much more were over and over announced by their own prophets. All the different epochs of the remarkable history of Israel were predicted long before they were reached. Their sojourn in Egypt and servitude, as well as the duration of that period, was announced to Abraham. The Babylonian captivity of 70 years and the return of a remnant to occupy the land once more was announced by the pre-exile prophets, who also predicted a far greater and longer exile, their present world-wide dispersion and a return which up to 1914 has not yet come. Of the deepest interest and the greatest importance in connection with the predictions of the return from Babylon is the naming of the great Persian king through whom the return was to be achieved. This great prophecy is found in the Book of Isaiah: "That saith of Cyrus, He is My shepherd, and shall perform all My pleasure: even saying of Jerusalem, She shall be built; and of the temple, Thy foundation shall be laid. Thus saith Jehovah to His anointed, to Cyrus, whose right hand I have holden, to subdue nations before him; and I will loose the loins of kings, to open the doors before him, and the gates shall not be shut" (Isa. 44:28; 45:1). This prediction was made about 200 years before Cyrus was born. A careful study of the part of Isaiah where these words are found will show that they are linked with the challenge of Jehovah and the declaration that He knows the end from the beginning; the passages we have already quoted. In naming an unborn king and showing what his work would be, Jehovah demonstrates that He knows the future. The great Jewish historian, Josephus, informs us that when Cyrus found his name in the Book of Isaiah, written about 200 years before, an earnest desire laid hold upon him to fulfill what was written. The beginning of the Book of Ezra gives the proclamation of Cyrus concerning the temple.

When the Prophet Isaiah received the message which contained the name of the Persian king, he wrote it down faithfully, though he did not know who Cyrus was. Two centuries later Cyrus appeared and then issued his proclamation which fulfilled Isaiah's prediction. Higher criticism denies the genuineness of all this. In order to disprove this prophecy as well as others, they declare that Isaiah did not write the book which bears his name. For about 2500 years no one ever thought of even suggesting that Isaiah is not the author of the book. They have invented an unknown person, whom they call Deutero-Isaiah, i. e., a second Isaiah. They claim that he wrote chapters 40-66. With this they have not stopped. They speak now of a third Isaiah, a Trito-Isaiah, as they call him. With their supposed learning they claim to have discovered that some of the chapters of Isaiah were written in Babylon and others in Palestine. However, all the arguments, advanced by the critics for a composite authorship and against one Isaiah who lived and wrote his book at the time specified in the beginning of Isaiah, are disproven by the book itself. One only needs to study this book to find out the unity of the message. One person must be the author of the Book of Isaiah.

A REMARKABLE CHAPTER

The Pentateuch contains many of the prophecies concerning the future history of the Jews. One of the most remarkable chapters is the twenty-eighth chapter in Deuteronomy.

It is one of the most solemn chapters in the Pentateuch. Orthodox Hebrews read in their synagogues each year through the entire five books of Moses. When they read this chapter, the Rabbi reads in a subdued voice. And well may they read it softly and ponder over it, for here is pre-written the sad and sorrowful history of their wonderful nation. Here thousands of years ago the Spirit of God through Moses outlined the history of the scattered nation, all their suffering and tribulation, as it has been for well nigh two millenniums and as it is still. Here are arguments for the Divine, the supernatural origin of this book which no infidel has ever been able to answer; nor will there ever be found an answer.

It would take many pages to follow the different predictions and show their literal fulfillment in the nation which turned away from Jehovah and disobeyed His Word.

Apart from such general predictions as are found in verses 64-66 and fulfilled in the dispersion of Israel, there are others which are more minute. The Roman power, which was used to break the Jews, is clearly predicted by Moses, and that in a time when no such power existed. Read verses 49-50: "The Lord shall bring a nation against thee from far, from the end of the earth, as swift as the *eagle* flieth, a nation, whose language thou shalt not understand." The eagle was the standard of the Roman armies; the Jews understood many oriental languages, but were ignorant of Latin. "Which shall not regard the person of the old, nor show favor to the young." Rome killed the old people and the children. "And he shall besiege thee in all thy gates, until thy high and fenced walls come down, wherein thou trustedst, throughout all thy land" (verse 52). Fulfilled in the siege and overthrow of Jerusalem by the Roman legions. "The tender and delicate woman among you, which would not adventure to set the sole of her foot upon the ground for delicateness and tenderness, shall eat her children, for want of all things in the siege and straitness wherewith thine enemy shall distress thee in thy gates" (54-57). Fulfilled in the dreadful sieges of Jerusalem, perhaps the most terrible events in the history of blood and tears of this poor earth. Every verse, beginning with the fifteenth, to the end of this chapter has found its oft repeated fulfillment. It does not surprise us that the enemy hates this book, which bears such a testimony, and would have it classed with legends.

Of much interest is the last verse of this great prophetic chapter. "And Jehovah will bring thee into Egypt again with ships, by the way whereof I said unto thee, Thou shalt see it no more again; and there ye shall sell yourselves unto your enemies for bondmen and bondwomen, and no man shall buy you." When Jerusalem was destroyed by the Romans, all who did not die in the awful calamity were sent to the mines of Egypt, where the slaves were constantly kept at work without being permitted to rest or sleep till they succumbed. The whip of Egypt fell once more upon them and they suffered the most terrible agonies. Others were sold as slaves. According to Josephus, about 100,000 were made slaves so that the markets were glutted and the word fulfilled, "No man shall buy you."

THEIR DISPERSION AND PRESERVATION

When Balaam beheld the camp of Israel he uttered a prophecy which is still being fulfilled. "Lo, the people shall dwell alone and shall not be reckoned among the nations" (Num. 23:9). God had separated the nation and given to them a land. And this peculiar people, living in one of the smallest countries of the earth, has been scattered throughout the world, has become a wanderer, without a home, without a land. Like Cain they wander from nation to nation. Though without a land they are still a nation. Other nations have passed away; the Jewish nation has been preserved. They are among all the nations and yet not reckoned among the nations. All this is written beforehand in the Bible. "And you will I scatter among the nations, and I will draw out the sword after you: and your land shall be a desolation and your cities shall be a waste" (Lev. 26:33). "And Jehovah will scatter you among the people, and ye shall be left few in number among the nations, whither Jehovah shall lead you away" (Deut. 4:27). "And Jehovah will scatter you among all peoples, from the one end of the earth even unto the other end of the earth; and there thou shalt serve other gods, which thou hast not known, thou nor thy fathers, even wood and stone. And among these nations shalt thou find no ease, and there shall be no rest for the sole of thy foot; but Jehovah will give thee there a trembling heart, and failing of eyes, and pining of soul. And thy life shall hang in doubt before thee; and thou shalt fear night and day, and shalt have no assurance of thy life. In the morning thou shalt say, Would it were even! and at even thou shalt say, Would it were morning! for the fear of thy heart which thou shalt fear, and for the sight of thine eyes, which thou shalt see" (Deut. 28:64-67). "And yet for all that, when they be in the land of their enemies, I will not reject them, neither will I abhor them, to destroy them utterly, and to break My covenant with them; for I am Jehovah their God" (Lev. 26:44). In many other passages the Spirit of God predicts their miraculous preservation.

"Massacred by thousands, yet springing up again from their undying stock, the Jews appear at all times and in all regions. Their perpetuity, their national immortality, is at once the most curious problem to the political inquirer; to the religious man a subject of profound and awful admiration."* Herder called the Jews "the enigma of history". What human mind could have ever foreseen that this peculiar people, dwelling in a peculiar land, was to be scattered among all nations, suffer there as no other nation ever suffered, and yet be kept and thus marked out still as the covenant people of a God, whose gifts and callings are without repentance. Here indeed is an argument for the Word of God which no infidel can answer. Jehovah has predicted the history of His earthly people. "Though I make a full end of all nations whither I have scattered thee, yet will I not make a full end of thee" (Jer. 30:11).

THE LAND AND THE CITY

Palestine, the God-given home of Israel, the land which once flowed with milk and honey, has become barren and desolate. Jerusalem, once a great city, the hallowed city of

---

*Milman: "History of the Jews."

David, is trodden down by the Gentiles. All this is more than once predicted in the Word of Prophecy. "I will make thee a wilderness, and cities which are not inhabited. And I will prepare destroyers against thee, every one with his weapons; and they shall cut down thy choice cedars, and cast them into the fire. And many nations shall pass by this city, and they shall say every man to his neighbor, Wherefore has the Lord done thus unto this great city? Then they shall answer, Because they have forsaken the covenant of the Lord their God, and worshipped other gods and served them" (Jer. 22:7-9). "And the generation to come, your children that shall rise up after you, and the foreigner that shall come from a far land shall say, when they shall see the plagues of that land . . . even all the nations shall say, Wherefore hath Jehovah done thus unto this land, what meaneth the heat of this great anger?" (Deut. 29:22-25.)

Thus it has come to pass. Their land is being visited by Gentiles from all over the world who behold the desolations. Many other passages could be added to the above—passages which prophesied the very condition of the promised land and the city of Jerusalem which are found there now, and which have existed for nearly two thousand years.

The national rejection of Israel and the fulfillment of the threatened curses have come to pass, and the land in its barren condition witnesses to it. Even the duration of all this is indicated in the prophetic Word. There is a striking passage in Hosea. "I will go and return to My place, till they acknowledge their offence and seek My face; in their affliction they will seek Me early. Come, let us return unto the Lord; for He hath torn, and He will heal us; He hath smitten and He will bind us up. After two days will He revive us; in the third day He will raise us up, and we shall live in His sight" (Hos. 5:15—6:2). According to this prophecy Jehovah is to be in their midst and is to return to His place. It refers to the manifestation of the Lord Jesus Christ among His people.

They rejected Him; He returned to His place. They are to acknowledge their offence.

Elsewhere in the Word predictions are found which speak of a future national repentance of Israel when the remnant of that nation will confess the blood-guiltiness which is upon them. According to this word in Hosea, they are going to have affliction, and when that great affliction comes they will seek His face, and confess their sins, and express their trust in Jehovah. They acknowledge that for two days they were torn and smitten by the judgments of the Lord, afflicted, as predicted by their own prophets. A third day is coming when all will be changed. These days are prophetic days. Several ancient Jewish expositors mention the fact that these days stand each for a thousand years. The two days of affliction and dispersion would therefore stand for two thousand years, and they are almost expired. The third day would mean the day of the Lord, the thousand years of the kingdom to come.

Nor must we forget that our Lord Jesus Christ, too, predicted the great dispersion of the nation, the fall of Jerusalem, and that Gentiles were to rule over that city, till the times of the Gentiles are fulfilled. (Luke 21:10-24.)

NO GOVERNMENT, NO SACRIFICE, NO HOLY PLACE

"For the children of Israel shall abide many days without a king, and without a prince, and without a sacrifice, and without an image, and without an ephod, and without teraphim" (Hos. 3:4). No further comment is needed on this striking prediction. Their political and religious condition for 1900 years corresponds to every word given through Hosea the prophet.

PROPHECIES ABOUT OTHER NATIONS

Besides the many predictions concerning the people Israel, the prophets have much to say about the nations with whom Israel came in touch and whose history is bound up with the history of the chosen people of God. Babylonia, Assyria, Egypt, Ammon, Moab, Tyre, Sidon, Idumea, and others are mentioned in the Prophetic Word. Their ultimate fate was predicted by Jehovah long before their downfall and overthrow occurred. The Prophet Ezekiel was entrusted with many of the solemn messages announcing the judgment of these nations. The reader will find these predictions in chapters 25-37. The predictions concerning Ammon, Moab, Edom and the Philistines are recorded in the twenty-fifth chapter. Tyrus and its fall is the subject of chapters 26 to 28: 19. A prophecy about Sidon is found in the concluding verses of the twenty-eighth chapter. The prophecies concerning the judgment and degradation of Egypt are given at greater length in chapters 29 and 30. Isaiah, Jeremiah, Daniel, Amos, Obadiah, Micah, Nahum and Habakkuk, all contain prophecies concerning different nations foretelling what should happen to them. A mass of evidence can be produced to show that all these predictions came true. Many of them seemed to fail, but after centuries had passed, their literal fulfillment, even to the minutest detail, had become history.

We must confine ourselves to a very few of these predictions and their fulfillment. The siege and capture of the powerful and extremely wealthy city of Tyrus by Nebuchadnezzar, king of Babylon, is predicted in Ezek. 26: 7-11. It came literally to pass. One of the proofs is to be found in a contract tablet in the British Museum dated at Tyrus in the fortieth year of the king. The overthrow predicted by Ezekiel had come to pass. The walls were broken down and the city was ruined. The noise of the song ceased and the sound of the harps was no more heard. But not all that Ezekiel predicted had been fulfilled by the Babylonian conqueror. The Divine prediction states, "They shall lay thy stones and thy timber and thy dust in the midst of the water" (verse 12). Nebuchadnezzar had not done this. History acquaints us with the fact that the Tyrians, before the destruction of the city had come, had removed their treasures to an island about half a mile from the shore. About 250 years later Alexander came against the island city. The ruins of Tyre which Nebuchadnezzar had left standing were used by Alexander. He constructed out of them with great ingenuity and perseverance a dam from the mainland to the rock city in the sea. Thus literally it was fulfilled, "They shall lay thy stones and thy timber and thy dust in the midst of the water." The sentence pronounced upon that proud city, for so long the powerful mistress of the sea, "Thou shalt be built no more," has been fully carried out.

Of still greater interest are the prophecies which foretell the doom of Egypt. Ezekiel and Nahum mention the Egyptian city No. (Ezek. 30:14-16; Nah. 3:8.) No is Thebes and was the ancient capital of Egypt. The Egyptian name is No-Amon. It had a hundred gates, as we learn from Homer, and was a city of marvelous beauty. It was surrounded by walls twenty-four feet thick, and had a circumference of one mile and three quarters. The Lord announced through Ezekiel that this great city should be rent asunder and that its vast population should be cut off. Five hundred years later Ptolemy Laltyrus, the grandfather of Cleopatra, after besieging the city several years razed to the ground the previously ruined city. Every word given through Ezekiel had come true. One could fill many pages showing the literal fulfillment of Ezekiel's great predictions relating to Egypt. The decline and degradation predicted has come true. The rivers and canals of Egypt have dried up. The land has become desolate. The immense fisheries which yielded such a great income to the rulers of Egypt are no longer in existence. Ezek. 30:7 has found a literal fulfillment. Egypt is a land of ruins and wasted cities. The instruments whom God used in accomplishing this were strangers (Ezek. 30:12) like Cambyses, Amroo, Ochus and others. "There shall be no more a prince of the land of Egypt" (Ezek. 30:13). This too has been literally fulfilled. Ochus subdued rebellious Egypt 350 B. C., and since that time no native prince has ruled in Egypt. It is also written that Egypt should become the basest of the kingdoms, "Neither shall it exalt itself any more above the nations; for I will diminish them that they shall no more rule over the nations." This degradation has fully come to pass. Who would ever have thought that this magnificent country with its vast resources, its wonderful commerce, its great prosperity, its luxuries, the land of marvelous structures, could ever experience such a downfall! Another significant fact is that in spite of the great humiliation and degradation through which Egypt has passed for so many centuries, it is not to experience a total extinction. In this respect her fate differs from that of other nations, "They shall be there a base kingdom" (Ezek. 29:14); this is the condition of Egypt today. And other prophets announce the same fact. One of the earliest prophets is Joel. He prophesied between 860 and 850 B. C. He predicted at that early date, "Egypt shall be a desolation." Isaiah also foretells the awful judgment of this great land of ancient culture. In the light of unfulfilled prophecy we discover the reason why God has not permitted the complete extinction of Egypt. Egypt is yet to be lifted out of the dust and is to receive a place of blessing only second to that of Israel (Isa. 19:22-25). This will be fulfilled when our Lord comes again.

And what more could we say of Idumea, Babylonia, Assyria and other lands. Moab and Ammon, the enemies of Israel, once flourishing nations, have passed away and the numerous judgment predictions have come true. (See Jer. 48-49.) Edom is gone. "O thou that dwellest in the clefts of the rock, that holdest the height of the hill, though thou shouldest make thy nest as high as the eagle, I will bring thee down from thence, saith Jehovah" (Jer. 49:16). "Thou shalt be desolate, O Mount Seir, and all Idumea, even all of it" (Ezek. 35:15). It was an atheist who was first used to report that during a journey of eight days he had found in the territory of Idumea the ruins of thirty cities.

Babylonia and Assyria, once the granaries of Asia, the garden spots of that continent, enjoying a great civilization, are now in desolation and mostly unproductive deserts. The predictions of Isaiah and Jeremiah have been fulfilled. The judgments predicted to come upon Babylon were also fulfilled long ago.*

THE BOOK OF DANIEL

The Book of Daniel, however, supplies the most startling evidences of fulfilled prophecy. No other book has been so much attacked as this great book. For about two thousand years wicked men, heathen philosophers, and infidels have tried to break down its authority. It has proven to be the anvil upon which the critics' hammers have been broken to pieces. The Book of Daniel has survived all attacks. It has been denied that Daniel wrote the book during the Babylonian captivity. The critics claim that it was written during the time of the Maccabees. Kuenen, Wellhausen, Canon Farrar, Driver and others but repeat the statements of the assailant of Christianity of the third century, the heathen Porphyry, who contended that the Book of Daniel was a forgery. Such is the company in which the higher critics are found. The Book of Daniel has been completely vindicated. The prophet wrote the book and its magnificent prophecies in Babylon. All doubt as to that has been forever removed, and men who still repeat the infidel oppositions against the book, oppositions of a past

---

*"How utterly improbable it must have sounded to the contemporaries of Isaiah and Jeremiah, that the great Babylon, this oldest metropolis of the world, founded by Nimrod, planned to be a city on the Euphrates much larger than Paris of today, surrounded by walls four hundred feet high, on the top of which four chariots, each drawn by four horses, could be driven side by side; in the center a large, magnificent park an hour's walk in circumference, watered by machinery; in it the king's twelve palaces, surrounding the great temple of the sun-god with its six hundred-foot tower and its gigantic golden statue—should be converted into a heap of ruins in the midst of a desert! Who today would have any faith in a similar prophecy against Berlin or London or Paris or New York?" (Prof. Bettex.)

generation, must be branded as ignorant, or considered the will-ful enemies of the Bible.

The great dream of Nebuchadnezzar is recorded in the second chapter of the Book of Daniel. Nebuchadnezzar who had been constituted by Jehovah a great monarch over the earth (Jer. 27:5-9) desired to know the future. All his astrologers and soothsayers, his magicians and mediums, could not do that. Their predictions left him still in doubt (Dan. 2:29). God gave him then a dream which contained a most remarkable revelation. The great man-image the king beheld is the symbol of the great world empires which were to follow the Babylonian empire. The image had a head of gold; the chest and arms were of silver; the trunk and the thighs were of brass; the two legs of iron, and the two feet were composed of iron mixed with clay. The Lord made known through the prophet the meaning of this dream.

Nebuchadnezzar and the empire over which he ruled is symbolized by the golden head. An inferior kingdom was to come after the Babylonian Empire; its symbol is silver. This kingdom was to be followed by a third kingdom of brass to bear rule over all the earth. The fourth kingdom was to be strong as iron and was to subdue all things. Exactly three great world powers came after the Babylonian Empire, the Medo-Persian, the Graeco-Macedonian and the Roman. Interesting it is to learn, from the different metals of which the image was composed, the process of deterioration which was to characterize the successive monarchies. The fourth empire, the Roman world power, is seen in its historic division, indicated by the two legs. The empire consisted of two parts, the East and West Roman sections. Then the division of the Empire into kingdoms in which iron (monarchical form of government) and the clay (the rule of the people) should be present is also predicted. How all this has come to pass is too well known to need any further demonstration. These empires have come and gone and the territory of the old Roman Empire presents today the very condition as predicted in Nebuchadnezzar's dream. Monarchies and republics are in existence upon that territory. The final division into ten kingdoms has not yet been accomplished. The unfulfilled portion of this dream we do not follow here. The reader may find this explained in the author's exposition of Daniel.

DANIEL'S GREAT VISION OF THE WORLD POWERS

In the seventh chapter Daniel relates his first great vision. The four beasts he saw rising out of the sea, the type of nations, are symbolical of the same world powers. The lion with eagle's wings is Babylonia. Jeremiah also pictured Nebuchadnezzar as a lion. "The lion has come up from his thicket and the destroyer of the Gentiles is on his way" (Jer. 4:7). Ezekiel speaks of him as a great eagle. (Ezek. 17:3.) The Medo-Persian Empire is seen as a bear raised up on one side and having three ribs in its mouth. The one side appeared stronger because this second world empire had Persia for its stronger element. The three ribs the bear holds as prey predict the conquests of that empire. Medo-Persia conquered exactly three great provinces, Susiana, Lydia and Asia Minor. The leopard with four wings and four heads is the picture of the Graeco-Macedonian Empire. The four wings denote its swiftness and rapid advance so abundantly fulfilled in the conquests of Alexander the Great. The four heads of the leopard predict the partition of this empire into the kingdoms of Syria, Egypt, Macedonia and Asia Minor. The fourth beast, the great nondescript, with its ten horns, and the little horn, still to come, is the Roman Empire. These are wonderful things. Be it remembered that the prophet received the vision when the Babylonian Empire still existed. Here also the character of these empires typified by ferocious beasts is revealed. The great nations of Christendom which occupy the ground of the Roman Empire testify unconsciously to the truth of this great prophecy. The emblems of these nations are not doves, little lambs or other harmless creatures. They have chosen the lion, the bear, the unicorn, the eagle and the double-headed eagle.

ALEXANDER THE GREAT PREDICTED

In the eighth chapter a new prophecy is revealed through Daniel. Once more the Medo-Persian Empire is seen, this time under the figure of a ram with two horns, one higher than the other, and the higher one came up last. It foretells the composition of that empire. It was composed of the Medes and the Persians; the Persians came in last and were the strongest. It conquered in three directions. This corresponds to the bear with the three ribs in the previous chapter.

The he-goat which Daniel sees coming from the west with a great rush is the type of the leopard empire, the Graeco-Macedonian. The same swiftness as revealed in the leopard with four wings is seen here again. The notable horn upon the he-goat, symbolizing the Macedonian Empire, is Alexander the Great. Josephus tells us that Alexander was greatly moved when the Jewish high priest Jaddua acquainted him with the meaning of this prophecy written over two hundred years before. And how was it fulfilled, what is predicted in Dan. 8: 5-8? 334 B. C. the notable horn, Alexander, in goat-like fashion, leaped across the Hellespont and fought successful battles, then pushed on to the banks of the Indus and the Nile and from there to Shushan. The great battles of the Granicus (334 B. C.), Issus (333 B. C.), and Arbella (331 B. C.) were fought, and with irresistible force he stamped the power of Persia and its king, Darius Codomannus, to the ground. He conquered rapidly Syria, Phoenicia, Cyprus, Pyre, Gaza, Egypt, Babylonia, Persia. In 329 he conquered Bactria, crossed the Oxus and Jaxaitis and defeated the Scythians. And thus he stamped upon the ram after having broken its horns. But when the he-goat had waxed very great, the great horn was broken. This predicted the early and sudden death of Alexander the Great. He died after a reign of 12 years and eight months, after a career of drunkenness and debauchery in 323 B. C. He died when he was but 32 years old. Then four notable ones sprang up in the place of the broken horn. This too has been fulfilled, for the empire of Alexander was divided into four parts. Four of the great generals of Alexander made the division, namely, Cassander, Lysimachus, Seleucus and Ptolemy. The four great divisions were Syria, Egypt, Macedonia, and Asia Minor.

ANTIOCHUS EPIPHANES

In verses 19 to 24 of the eighth chapter of Daniel the coming of a wicked leader, to spring out of one of the divisions of the Macedonian Empire and the vile work he was to do, is predicted. He was to work great havoc in the pleasant land, that is, Israel's land.

History does not leave us in doubt about the identity of this wicked king. He is the eighth king of the Seleucid dynasty, who took the Syrian throne and is known by the name of Antiochus Epiphanes, and bore also the name of Epimanes, i. e., "the Madman." He was the tyrant and oppressor of the Jews. His wicked deeds of oppression, blasphemy and sacrilege are fully described in the Book of the Maccabees. Long before he ever appeared Daniel saw him and his wicked work in his vision.

And all this has been fulfilled in Antiochus Epiphanes. When he had conquered Jerusalem he sacrificed a sow upon the altar of burnt offerings and sprinkled its broth over the entire building. He corrupted the youths of Jerusalem by introducing lewd practices; the feast of tabernacles he changed into the feast of Bacchus. He auctioned off the high-priesthood. All kinds of infamies were perpetrated by him and the most awful obscenity permitted and encouraged. All true worship was forbidden, and idol worship introduced, especially that of Jupiter Olympus. The whole city and land was devastated and some 100,000 pious Jews were massacred. Such has been the remarkable fulfillment of this prophecy.

Even the duration of this time of trouble was revealed; and 2,300 days are mentioned. These 2,300 days cover about the period of time during which Antiochus Epiphanes did his wicked deeds. The chronology of these 2,300 days is interesting. Judas Maccabaeus cleansed (lit. justified) the sanctuary from the abomination about December 25, 165 B. C. Antiochus died a miserable death two years later. Going back 2,300 days from the time Judas the Maccabean cleansed the defiled temple, brings us to 171 B. C. when we find the record of Antiochus' interference with the Jews. Menelaus had bribed Antiochus to make him high priest, robbed the temple and instituted the murder of the high priest Onias III. The most wicked deeds in the defilement of the temple were perpetrated by the leading general of Antiochus, Apollonius, in the year 168 B. C. We believe these 2,300 days are therefore literal days and have found their literal fulfillment in the dreadful days of this wicked king from the North. There is no other meaning attached to these days and the foolish speculations that these days are years, etc., lack Scriptural foundation altogether.

THE GREATEST OF ALL

The greatest prophecy in the Book of Daniel is contained in the ninth chapter, the prophecy concerning the 70 weeks, transmitted from heaven through Gabriel. (Dan. 9:24-27.) To many readers of the Book of Daniel it is not quite clear what the expression "seventy weeks" means, and when it is stated that each week represents a period of seven years, many Christians do not know why such is the case. A brief word of explanation may therefore be in order. The literal translation of the term "seventy weeks" is "seventy sevens." Now this word "sevens" translated "weeks" may mean "days" and it may mean "years." What then is meant here, seventy times seven days or seventy times seven years? It is evident that the "sevens" mean year weeks, seven years to each prophetic week. Daniel was occupied in reading the books and in prayer with the seventy years of the Babylonian captivity. And now Gabriel is going to reveal to him something which will take place in "seventy sevens," which means seventy times seven years. The proof that such is the case is furnished by the fulfillment of the prophecy itself.

First we notice in the prophecy that these 70 year-weeks are divided in three parts. Seven times seven (49 years) are to go by till the commanded rebuilding and restoration of Jerusalem should be accomplished. In the twentieth year of Artaxerxes the command was given to rebuild Jerusalem. It was in the year 445 B. C., exactly 49 years after the wall of Jerusalem and the city had been rebuilt. Then 62 weeks are given as the time when Messiah should be cut off and have nothing. This gives us 434 years (62 times 7). Here is a prediction concerning the death of Christ. Has it been fulfilled? Chronology shows that exactly 483 years after Artaxerxes gave the command to restore Jerusalem (445 B. C.), 434 years after the city had been restored, the death of our Lord Jesus Christ took place.

To be more exact, on the day on which our Lord Jesus Christ entered Jerusalem for the last time, the number of years announced by Gabriel expired and the Lord was crucified that week. The proof of it is perfect.

But there is more to be said. As a result of the cutting off of Messiah something else is prophesied. "And the people of the prince that shall come shall destroy the city and the sanctuary." The prince that is to come (and is yet to come) is the little horn of Dan. 7. He arises out of the Roman Empire. The people of the prince that shall come are therefore the Roman people. They have fulfilled this prophecy by destroying the temple and the city.

THE WARS OF THE PTOLEMIES AND SELEUCIDAE

The greater part of the eleventh chapter in Daniel has been historically fulfilled. It is an interesting study. So accurate are the predictions that the enemies of the Bible have tried their very best to show that Daniel did not write these prophecies several hundred years before they occurred. But they have failed in their miserable attempts. We place the startling evidence before our readers.

PROPHECY GIVEN B. C. 534

"And now will I shew thee the truth. Behold, there shall stand up yet three kings in Persia; and the fourth shall be far richer than they all: and by his strength through his riches he shall stir up all against the realm of Grecia." (Verse 2.)

"And a mighty king shall stand up, that shall rule with great dominion, and do according to his will." (Verse 3.)

"And when he shall stand up, his kingdom shall be broken, and shall be divided toward the four winds of heaven; and not to his posterity, nor according to his dominion which he ruled: for his kingdom shall be plucked up even for others besides those." (Verse 4.)

"And the king of the South shall be strong, and one of his

FULFILLMENT

See Ezra 4. 5-24. The three kings were: Ahasuerus, Artaxerxes and Darius, known in history as Cambyses, Pseudo Smerdis, and Darius Hystaspis (not Darius the Mede). The fourth one was Xerxes, who, as history tells us, was immensely rich. The invasion of Greece took place in 480 B. C.

The successors of Xerxes are not mentioned. The mighty king in this verse is the notable horn seen by Daniel on the he-goat in chapter 8, Alexander the Great, 335 B. C.

B. C. 323. Alexander died young. The notable horn was broken. His kingdom was divided into four parts (four winds) after the battle of Ipsus 301 B. C. His posterity did not receive the kingdom, but his four generals, Ptolemy, Lysimachus, Seleucus Nicator and Cassander. Not one of these divisions reached to the glory of Alexander's dominion.

Asia and Greece are not followed but Syria and Egypt become

princes; and he shall be strong above him, and have dominion; his dominion shall be a great dominion." (Verse 5.)

prominent, because the King of the North from Syria, and the King of the South, Egypt, were to come in touch with the Jews. The holy land became involved with both. The King of the South was Ptolemy Lagus. One of his princes was Seleucus Nicator. He established a great dominion, which extended to the Indus.

"And in the end of years they shall join themselves together; for the king's daughter of the South shall come to the King of the North to make an agreement; but she shall not retain the power of the arm; neither shall he stand, nor his arm: but she shall be given up, and they that brought her, and he that begat her, and he that strengthened her in these times." (Verse 6.)

Here is another gap. This verse takes us to 250 B. C. The two who make an alliance are the Kings of the North (Syrian division of the Grecian Empire) and of the South (Egypt). This alliance was effected by the marriage of the daughter of the King of the South, the Egyptian Princess Berenice. daughter of Ptolemy II., to Antiochus Theos, the King of the North. The agreement was that Antiochus had to divorce his wife and make any child of Berenice his heir in the kingdom. The agreement ended in calamity. When Ptolemy died Antiochus Theos in 247 called back his former wife. Berenice and her young son were poisoned and the first wife's son, Callinicus, was put on the throne as Seleucus II.

"But out of a branch of her roots shall one stand up in his estate, which shall come with an army, and shall enter into the fortress of the King of the North, and shall deal against them, and shall prevail." (Verse 7.)

The one out of her roots (Berenice, who had been murdered) was her own brother, Ptolemy Euergetes, who avenged her death. He conquered Syria. He dealt against Seleucus II, King of the North, and slew the wife of Antiochus Theos, who had Berenice poisoned. He seized the fortress, the port of Antioch.

"And shall also carry captives into Egypt their gods, with their princes, and with their precious vessels of silver and gold; and he shall continue more years than the King of the North." (Verse 8.)

Ptolemy Euergetes did exactly as predicted. He returned with 4,000 talents of gold and 40,000 talents of silver and 2,500 idols and idolatrous vessels. Many of these Cambyses had taken to Persia.

"So the King of the South shall come into his kingdom, and shall return into his own land." (Verse 9.)

(*Literal translation*) : "and the same [King of the North] shall come into the realm of the King of the South, but shall return into his own land."

In 240 B. C. Seleucus Callinicus the King of the North invaded Egypt. He had to return defeated. His fleet perished in a storm.

"But his sons shall be stirred up, and shall assemble a multitude of great forces; and one shall certainly come, and overflow, and pass through: then shall he return, and be stirred up, even to his fortress." (Verse 10.)

The sons of Seleucus Callinicus were Seleucus III and Antiochus the Great. Seleucus (Ceraunos) III began war against Egyptian Provinces in Asia Minor. He was unsuccessful. The other son Antioch invaded Egypt and passed through because Ptolemy Philopater did not oppose him. In 218 B. C. Antiochus continued his warfare and took the fortress Gaza.

"And the King of the South shall be moved with choler, and shall come forth and fight with him, even with the King of the North: and he shall set forth a great multitude but the multitude shall be given into his hand." (Verse 11.)

In 217 B. C. Ptolemy aroused himself and fought Antiochus the Great with an immense army. He defeated Antiochus. The multitude was given into the hands of Ptolemy Philopater.

"And when he hath taken away the multitude, his heart shall be lifted up; and he shall cast down many ten thousands: but he shall not be strengthened by it." (Verse 12.)

(*Literal:* "And the multitude shall rise up and his courage increase.")

"For the King of the North shall return, and shall set forth a multitude greater than the former, and shall certainly come after certain years with a great army and with much riches." (Verse 13.)

"And in those times there shall many stand up against the King of the South: also the robbers of thy people shall exalt themselves to establish the vision; but they shall fall." (Verse 14.)

"So the King of the North shall come, and cast up a mount, and take the most fenced cities: and the arms of the South shall not withstand, neither his chosen people, neither shall there be any strength to withstand." (Verse 15.)

"But he that cometh against him shall do according to his own will, and none shall stand before him: and he shall stand in the

The people of Egypt rose up and the weakling Ptolemy became courageous. His victory is again referred to. It was won at Raphia. He might have pressed his victory. But he did not make use of it but gave himself up to a licentious life. Thus "he was not strengthened by it."

About 14 years later, 203 B. C., Antiochus assembled a great army, greater than the army which was defeated at Raphia, and turned against Egypt. Ptolemy Philopater had died and left an infant son Ptolemy Epiphanes.

Antiochus had for his ally Philip, King of Macedon. Also in Egypt many rebels stood up. And then there were, as we read in Josephus, wicked Jews, who helped Antiochus. These "robbers of thy people" established the vision. They helped along the very things which had been predicted, as to trials for them.

All this was fulfilled in the severe struggles, which followed.

The invasion of the glorious land by Antiochus followed. He subjected the whole land unto himself. He also was well dis-

PROPHECY GIVEN B. C. 534   FULFILLMENT

glorious land, which by his hand shall be consumed." (Verse 16.)

posed towards the Jews because they sided with Antiochus the Great against Ptolemy Epiphanes.

"He shall also set his face to enter with the strength of his whole kingdom, and an agreement shall be made with him; thus shall he do: and he shall give him the daughter of women, corrupting her: but she shall not stand on his side, neither be for him." (Verse 17.)

This brings us to the years 198-195 B. C. Antiochus aimed to get full possession of Egypt. An agreement was made. In this treaty between Antiochus and Ptolemy Epiphanes, Cleopatra, daughter of Antiochus was espoused to Ptolemy. Why is Cleopatra called "daughter of women?" Because she was very young and was under the care of her mother and grandmother. The treaty failed.

"After this shall he turn his face unto the isles, and shall take many: but a prince [literally: Captain] for his own behalf shall cause the reproach offered by him to cease; without his own reproach he shall cause it to turn upon him." (Verse 18.)

A few years later Antiochus conquered isles on the coast of Asia Minor.

The captain predicted is Scipio Asiaticus. Antiochus had reproached the Romans by his acts and he was defeated. This defeat took place at Magnesia 190 B. C.

"Then he shall turn his face toward the fort of his own land: but he shall stumble and fall, and not be found." (Verse 19.)

Antiochus returns to his own land. He came to a miserable end trying to plunder the temple of Belus in Elymais.

"Then shall stand up in his estate a raiser of taxes in the glory of the kingdom: but within few days he shall be destroyed, neither in anger, nor in battle." (Verse 20.)

This is Seleucus Philopater B. C. 187-176. He was known as a raiser of taxes. He had an evil reputation with the Jews because he was such an exactor among them. His tax-collector Heliodorus poisoned him and so he was slain "neither in anger, nor in battle."

PROPHECY GIVEN B. C. 534	FULFILLMENT
"And in his estate shall stand up a vile person, to whom they shall not give the honor of the kingdom: but he shall come in peaceably, and obtain the kingdom by flatteries." (Verse 21.)	This vile person is none other than Antiochus Epiphanes. He had no claim on royal dignities, being only a younger son of Antiochus the Great. He seized royal honors by trickery and with flatteries. He is the little horn of chapter 8.
"And with the arms of a flood shall they be overflown from before him, and shall be broken; yea, also the prince of the covenant." (Verse 22.)	He was successful in defeating his enemies. The prince of the covenant may mean his nephew Ptolemy Philometor. He also vanquished Philometor's generals.
"And after the league made with him he shall work deceitfully: for he shall come up, and shall become strong with a small people." (Verse 23.)	He feigned friendship to young Ptolemy but worked deceitfully. To allay suspicion he came against Egypt with a small force but took Egypt as far as Memphis.
"He shall enter peaceably even upon the fattest places of the province; and he shall do that which his fathers have not done, nor his father's father; he shall scatter among them the prey, and spoil, and riches: yea, and he shall forecast his devices against the strongholds, even for a time." (Verse 24.)	He took possession of the fertile places in Egypt under the pretense of peace. He took Pelusium and laid seige to the fortified places Naucratis and Alexandria.
"And he shall stir up his power and his courage against the King of the South with a great army; and the King of the South shall be stirred up to battle with a very great and mighty army; but he shall not stand: for they shall forecast devices against him." (Verse 25.)	This King of the South is Ptolemy Physcon, who was made king after Philometor had fallen into the hands of Antiochus. He had a great army but did not succeed, because treason had broken out in his own camp.

"Yea, they that feed of the portion of his meat shall destroy him, and his army shall overflow: and many shall fall down slain." (Verse 26.)

Additional actions of Antiochus and warfare, in which he was successful, followed.

"And both these kings' hearts shall be to do mischief, and they shall speak lies at one table; but it shall not prosper: for yet the end shall be at the time appointed." (Verse 27.)

The two kings are Antiochus Epiphanes and his associate Philometor. They made an alliance against Ptolemy Euergetes II, also called Physcon. But they spoke lies against each other and did not succeed in their plans.

"Then shall he return into his land with great riches; and his heart shall be against the holy covenant; and he shall do exploits, and return to his own land." (Verse 28.)

In 168 B. C. he returned from his expedition, and had great riches. Then he marched through Judea and did his awful deeds. A report had come to his ears that the Jewish people had reported him dead. In the first and second book of the Maccabees we read of his atrocities. Then he retired to Antioch.

"At the time appointed he shall return, and come toward the South; but it shall not be as the former, or as the latter." (Verse 29.)

He made still another attempt against the South. However, he had not the former success.

"For the ships of Chittim shall come against him; therefore he shall be grieved, and return, and have indignation against the holy covenant: so shall he do; he shall even return, and have intelligence with them that forsake the holy covenant." (Verse 30.)

The ships of Chittim are the Roman fleet. When within a few miles of Alexandria he heard that ships had arrived. He went to salute them. They delivered to him the letters of the senate, in which he was commanded, on pain of the displeasure of the Roman people, to put an end to the war against his nephews. Antiochus said, "he would go and consult his friends;" on which Popilius, one of the legates, took his staff, and instantly drew a circle round Antiochus on the sand, where he stood; and commanded him not to pass that circle, till he had given a definite answer. As a grieved and defeated man he returned and then he fell upon Judea once more to commit additional wickedness. Apostate Jews sided with him.

"And arms shall stand on his part and they shall pollute the sanctuary of strength, and shall take away the daily sacrifice, and they shall place the abomination that maketh desolate." (Verse 31.)

This brings us to the climax of the horrors under Antiochus Epiphanes. The previous record of it is contained in chapter 8. He sent Apollonius with over 20,000 men to destroy Jerusalem. Multitudes were slain, and women and children led away as captives. He issued a command that all people must conform to the idolatry of Greece. A wicked Grecian was sent to enforce the word of Antiochus. All sacrifices ceased and the God-given ceremonials of Judaism came to an end. The temple was polluted by the sacrifices of swine's flesh. The temple was dedicated to Jupiter Olympius. Thus the prediction was fulfilled.

"And such as do wickedly against the covenant shall he corrupt by flatteries: but the people that do know their God shall be strong, and do exploits.
"And they that understand among the people shall instruct

These verses describe the condition among the Jewish people. There were two classes. Those who did wickedly against the covenant, the apostate, and those who knew God, a faithful remnant. The apostates sided with

PROPHECY GIVEN B. C. 534	FULFILLMENT
many: yet they shall fall by the sword, and by flame, by captivity, and by spoil, many days. "Now when they shall fall, they shall be holpen with a little help: but many shall cleave to them with flatteries." (Verses 32-34.)	the enemy, and the people who knew God were strong. This has reference to the noble Maccabees. There was also suffering and persecution.

MANY MORE FULFILLED PROPHECIES

Many other fulfilled prophecies might be quoted. In the last chapter of Daniel an interesting prediction is made concerning the time of the end. "Many shall run to and fro, and knowledge shall be increased." Sir Isaac Newton, the discoverer of the law of gravitation, wrote on Daniel and expressed his belief that some day people would travel at the rate of fifty miles an hour. The French infidel Voltaire many years later laughed at Newton's statement and held it up to ridicule. The time of the end is here and the prophecy of Dan. 12:4 has come true.

In the New Testament are also written prophecies which are now in process of fulfillment. 1 Tim. 4:1, 2; 2 Tim. 3:1-5; 4:1-3; 2 Pet. 2; Jude's Epistle, and other Scriptures predict the present day apostasy.

UNFULFILLED PROPHECY

As stated before, there are many unfulfilled prophecies in the Bible. The literal fulfillment of prophecies in the past vouches for the literal fulfillment of every prophecy in the Word of God. Some of them were uttered several thousand years ago. The world still waits for their fulfillment. May we remember that God does not need to be in a hurry. He knows indeed the end from the beginning. He takes His time in accomplishing His eternal purposes. And may we, His people, who know and love His Word, not neglect prophecy, for the Prophetic Word is the lamp which shineth in a dark place.

CHAPTER VII

LIFE IN THE WORD

BY PHILIP MAURO, ATTORNEY AT LAW, NEW YORK CITY

INTRODUCTION

It must be evident to all who pay close attention to the spiritual conditions of our day that there is being made at this time a very determined and widespread effort to set aside entirely the *authority* of the Bible. Let us note that one of the unique characteristics of that Book is that it claims the right to control the actions of men. It speaks "as one *having* authority." It assumes, and in the most peremptory and uncompromising way, to rebuke men for misconduct, and to tell them what they shall do and what they shall not do. It speaks to men, not as from the human plane, or even from the standpoint of superior human wisdom and morality; but as from a plane far above the highest human level, and as with a wisdom which admits of no question or dispute from men. It demands throughout unqualified submission.

But this assumption of control over men is a direct obstacle to the democratic spirit of the times, which brooks no authority higher than that of "the people," that is to say, of Man himself. To establish and to make universal the principles of pure democracy is the object, whether consciously or unconsciously, of the great thought-movements of our era; and the essence and marrow of democracy is the supreme authority of Man. Hence the conflict with the Bible.

Not only is the Bible, with its peremptory assertion of supremacy and control over mankind, directly counter to the democratic movement, but it is now the *only* real obstacle to the complete independence of humanity. If only the authority of the Scriptures be gotten rid of, mankind will have attained the long-coveted state of absolute independence, which is equivalent to utter lawlessness.

The state of ideal democracy would be accurately described as "lawlessness," since it is manifest that an individual or a society which is under no restraint except such as is self-imposed, is really under no restraint at all. To attain this ideal state is the end and purpose of present day movements; and, in order to promote these movements, that mighty spiritual intelligence who is designated "the spirit that now works in the children of disobedience" (Eph. 2:2) very wisely, and with consummate subtlety, directs the attack, from many different quarters, against the authority of the Bible.

The great mass of men, including the majority of the leaders of the age, are already completely absorbed in the activities of the world and utterly indifferent to the claims of the Bible. As to these, it is only necessary to take care that they are not aroused from their indifference. But the Bible nevertheless, by reason of its hold upon the consciences of the few, exerts, upon society as a whole, a mighty restraining influence, against which the assaults of the enemies of truth are now being directed.

In some quarters the authority of the Bible is directly assailed and its Divine origin disputed in the name of "Science" and of "Scholarship." Much of the learning and theological activity of the day are concentrated upon the attempt to discredit the Bible, and to disseminate views and theories directly at variance with its claims of divine inspiration and authority.

In other quarters the attack takes the form of a pretense of conceding the inspiration of the Bible, coupled with the claim that other writers and other great literary works were equally inspired. "God is not limited," we are told, "and can speak to man, and does speak to man, in our day, in like manner as in the days of Moses, Isaiah, or Paul."

Manifestly it makes practically no difference whether the Bible be dragged down to the level of other books, or other books be exalted to the level of the Bible. The result is the same in both cases; namely, that the unique authority of the Bible is set aside.

But even in quarters where the Divine origin of the Bible is fully recognized, the enemy is actively at work with a view to weakening its influence. There is much teaching abroad (heard usually in connection with certain spiritual manifestations which have become quite common of late) to the effect that those who have the Spirit dwelling in them, and speaking directly to and through them, are independent of the Word of God. This is the form which the idea of a continuing revelation takes in quarters where a direct attack on the authority of Scripture would fail. But the result is the same.

In such a state of things it is manifestly of the very highest importance to insist unceasingly upon the sufficiency, finality and completeness of the Revelation given by God in His Word. With the desire to serve this purpose, even though it be in a very small degree, these pages are written. It would be, however, a task far beyond the capacity of the writer to present all the unique characteristics of the Bible, whereby it is so distinguished from other books that it occupies a class by itself. The writer has, therefore, singled out for consideration one special attribute or characteristic of the Holy Scriptures; namely, that signified by the word "living."

If one is able to apprehend, however feebly, the tremendous fact that the Word of God is a LIVING Word, such knowledge will go far towards affording him protection from what is perhaps the greatest danger of these "perilous times."

I. THE INCARNATE WORD, AND THE WRITTEN WORD: BOTH ARE "LIVING"

Of the many statements which the Bible makes concerning the Word of God, none is more significant, and surely none is of greater importance to dying men, than the statement that the Word of God is a LIVING Word.

In Philippians 2:16 we have the expression, "The Word of Life." The same expression occurs in 1 John 1:1. It is here used of Jesus Christ, the Incarnate Word, whereas in Philippians it is apparently the Written Word that is spoken of. The Written Word and the Incarnate Word are so identified in Scripture that it is not always clear which is referred to. The same things are said of each, and the same characters attributed to each. The fundamental resemblance lies in the fact that each is the revealer or tangible expression of the Invisible God. As the written or spoken word expresses, for the purpose of communicating to another, the invisible and inaccessible thought, so Jesus Christ as the Incarnate Word, and the Holy Scriptures as the Written Word, express and communicate knowledge of the invisible and inaccessible God. "He that hath seen Me hath seen the Father." "Believe Me that I am in the Father, and the Father in Me" (John 14:9,11).

In Hebrews 4:12 we find the statement that "The Word of God is LIVING and powerful, and sharper than any two-edged sword" (R. V.). Clearly this refers to the Written Word. But the very next verse, without any change of subject, directs our attention to the Searcher of hearts (Rev. 2:23), saying, "Neither is there any creature that is not manifest in His sight: but all things are naked and opened unto the eyes of Him with whom we have to do."

Again in 1 Peter 1:23 we read of "the Word of God which liveth," or more literally, "the Word of God living." Here again there might be uncertainty as to whether the Incarnate Word or the Written Word be meant; but it is generally understood that the latter is in view, and the quotation from Isaiah 40:6-8 would confirm this idea.

From these passages we learn that the Word of God is spoken of as a "living" Word. This is a very remarkable statement, and is worthy of our closest examination and most earnest consideration. Why is the Word of God thus spoken of? Why is the extraordinary property of LIFE, or vitality, attributed to it? In what respects can it be said to be a living Word?

But the expression "living," as applied to the Word of God, manifestly means something more than partaking of the kind of life with which we are acquainted from observation. God speaks of Himself as the "Living God." The Lord Jesus is the "Prince of Life." (Acts 3:15.) He announced Himself to John in the vision of Patmos as "He that liveth." Eternal life is in Him. (1 John 5:11.)

It is clear, then, that when we read, "The Word of God is living," we are to understand thereby that it lives with a spiritual, an inexhaustible, an inextinguishable, in a word a divine, life. If the Word of God be indeed living in this sense, then we have here a fact of the most tremendous significance. In the world around us the beings and things which we call "living" may just as appropriately be spoken of as "dying." What we call "the land of the living" might better be described as the land of the dying. Wherever we look we see that death is in possession, and is working according to its invariable method of corruption and decay. Death is the real monarch of this world, and we meet at every turn the gruesome evidence and results of the universal sway of him who has "the power of death, that is, the devil" (Heb. 2:14). "Death reigned" (Rom. 5:17), and still reigns over everything. The mighty and awful power of death has made this earth of ours a great burying ground—a gigantic cemetery.

Can it be that there is an exception to this apparently universal rule? Is there, indeed, in this world of dying beings, where the forces of corruption fasten immediately upon everything into which life has entered, and upon all the works of so-called living creatures, one object which is really LIVING, an object upon which corruption cannot fasten itself, and which resists and defies all the power of death? Such is the assertion of the passages of Scripture which we have quoted. Surely, then, if these statements be true, we have here the most astounding phenomenon in all the accessible universe; and it will be well worth while to investigate an object of which so startling an assertion is seriously, if very unobtrusively, made.

Before we proceed with our inquiry let us note one of many points of resemblance between the Incarnate Word and the Written Word. When "the Word was made flesh and dwelt [tabernacled] among us" (John 1:14), there was nothing in His appearance to manifest His Deity, or to show that "in Him was life" (John 1:4). That fact was demonstrated, not by His blameless and unselfish behavior, nor by His incomparable teachings and discourses, but by His *resurrection from the dead*. The only power which is greater than that of death is the power of life. He had, and exercised, that power, and holds now the keys of death and of hades. (Rev. 1:18, R. V.)

Similarly, there is nothing in the appearance and behavior (so to speak) of the Bible to show that it has a characteristic, even divine life, which other books have not. It bears the same resemblance to other writings that Jesus, the son of Mary, bore to other men. It is given in human language just as He came in human flesh. Yet there is between it and all other books the same difference as between Him and all other men, namely, the difference *between the living and the dying*. "The word of God is living."

It will require, therefore, something more than a hasty glance or a casual inspection to discern this wonderful difference; but the difference is there, and with diligence and attention we may discover some clear indications of it.

II. NO DEFINITIONS OF LIFE

Man's wisdom and learning are incapable of furnishing a definition of life. The attempts of the wisest and most learned to furnish such a definition only serve to exhibit the futility of the attempt.

Herbert Spencer, who has made the most ambitious attempt of modern times to explain the visible universe, gives this as the result of his best efforts to define life: "Life is the continuous adjustment of internal relations to external relations."

This definition manifestly stands as much in need of explanation as that which it purports to explain. But it will serve at least to remind us that the wisdom of men is foolishness with God.

Another eminent man of science defined life as "the twofold internal movement of composition and decomposition, at once general and continuous."

These modern definitions are scarcely an improvement upon that of Aristotle, who defined life as "the assemblage of the operations of nutrition, growth, and destruction."

What a marvellous thing is life, and how far it transcends the comprehension of man, since his best efforts to define it give results so ridiculously inadequate!

The ignorance of scientific men on this subject is frankly confessed by Alfred Russell Wallace, who in one of his latest books, "Man's Place in the Universe," says, "Most people give scientific men credit for much greater knowledge than they possess in these matters." And again: "As to the deeper problems of life, and growth, and reproduction, though our physiologists have learned an infinite amount of curious and instructive facts, they can give us *no intelligible* explanation of them."

But, if none of us can say what life is, we can all distinguish between that which is living (even in the ordinary sense of the word) and that which is not living; and our best idea of the meaning of life is obtained by comparing that which has life (whether animal or vegetable) with that which has not life, as minerals, or any non-living matter. We know that between the two there is a great gulf, which only divine power can span; for it is only the living God who can impart life to that which is lifeless.

We look then at the Written Word of God to see if it manifests characteristics which are found only in living things, and to see if it exhibits, not merely the possession of life of the perishable and corruptible sort with which we are so familiar by observation, and which is in each of us, but life of a different order, imperishable and incorruptible.

III. PERENNIAL FRESHNESS

The Bible differs radically from all other books in its perpetual freshness. This characteristic will be recognized only by those who know the Book in that intimate way which comes from living with it, as with a member of one's family. I mention it first because it was one of the first *unique* properties of the Bible which impressed me after I began to read it as a believer in Christ. It is a very remarkable fact that the Bible never becomes exhausted, never acquires sameness, never diminishes in its power of responsiveness to the quickened soul who comes to it. The most familiar passages yield as much (if not more) refreshment at the thousandth perusal, as at the first. It is indeed as a fountain of living water. The fountain is the same, but the water is always fresh, and always refreshing. We can compare this to nothing but what we find in a living companion, whom we love and to whom we go for help and fellowship. The person is always the same, and yet without sameness. New conditions evoke new responses; and so it is with the Bible. As a living Book it adapts itself to the new phases of our experience and the new conditions in which we find ourselves. From the most familiar passage there comes again and again *a new message;* just as our most familiar friend or companion will have something new to say, as changed conditions and new situations require it from time to time.

This is true of no other book. What man's book has to say we can get the first time; and the exceptions arise merely from lack of clearness on the writer's part, or lack of apprehension on the part of the reader. Man can touch only the surface of things, and he cares only about surface appearances. So, in all his writings, whatever substance they contain lies on the surface, and can be gathered by a capable reader at once. If the Word of God may be compared in this particular to a living person, the books of men may be compared to pictures or statues of living persons. However beautifully or artistically executed, a single view may readily exhaust the latter, and a second and third look will be mere repetitions. The difference is that which exists between the living and the dead. The Word of God is LIVING.

But while the Bible resembles in this important respect a living person, who is our familiar, sympathetic, and responsive companion, it differs from such a human companion in that the counsel, comfort, and support it furnishes are far above and beyond what any human being can supply; and the only explanation of this is that the source of its life and powers is not human, but Divine.

IV. THE BIBLE DOES NOT BECOME OBSOLETE

One of the most prominent characteristics of books written by men for the purpose of imparting information and instruction is that they very quickly become obsolete, and must be cast aside and replaced by others. This is particularly true of books on science, text-books, school-books and the like. Indeed it is a matter of boasting (though it would be hard to explain why) that "progress" is so rapid in all departments of learning as to render the scientific books of one generation almost worthless to the next. Changes in human knowledge, thought and opinion occur so swiftly, that books, which were the standards yesterday, are set aside today for others, which in turn will be discarded for yet other "authorities" tomorrow. In fact, every book which is written for a serious purpose begins to become obsolete before the ink is dry on the page. This may be made the occasion of boasting of the great progess of humanity, and of the wonderful advances of "science;" but the true significance of the fact is that man's books are all, like himself, dying creatures.

The Bible, on the other hand, although it treats of the greatest and most serious of all subjects, such as God, Christ, eternity, life, death, sin, righteousness, judgment, redemption— is always the latest, best, and *only* authority on all these and other weighty matters whereof it treats. Centuries of "progress" and "advancement" have added *absolutely nothing* to the sum of knowledge on any of these subjects. The Bible is always fresh and thoroughly "up to date." Indeed it is far, far ahead of human science. Progress cannot overtake it, or get beyond it. Generation succeeds generation, but each finds the Bible waiting for it with its ever fresh and never failing stores of information touching matters of the highest concern, touching *everything* that affects the welfare of human beings.

V. SCIENCE AND THE BIBLE

Human teachers and teachings have, indeed, frequently set themselves in opposition to some of the statements of the Bible; and it has often been announced, upon human authority, that errors in history and in matters of science have been detected in the Bible. Some, indeed, have endeavored to save the reputation and authority of the Bible by saying that it was not written to teach men "science." In a sense this is true. The Bible was not written to impart that kind of knowledge which "puffeth up," but just the contrary. It was written to impart that kind of information which takes man down by showing him his true position as a ruined, perishing creature, under the condemnation and power of death, and utterly "without strength," that is to say, incapable of doing *anything* to deliver himself out of this deplorable condition. It declares that, "if any man think that he knoweth *anything,* he knoweth *nothing* yet as he ought to know" (1 Cor. 8:2). Such is the plain declaration of Scripture as to the limitations of all human knowledge; and he who knows the most is most conscious of these limitations. But if, by the statement that the Bible was not written to teach "science," it be meant that the Bible is unscientific, that statement is not true. On the contrary, the Bible is the only book in the world that is truly "scientific;" for it is the only book which gives precise, accurate and *absolutely reliable* information upon every subject whereof it treats. It is the only book in the world upon *every* statement of which one may safely put implicit confidence. Countless millions have believed the statements of the Word of God, every one of them to his unspeakable advantage, not one of them to his hurt.

We used to hear a great deal, some thirty years ago, about the many "mistakes of Moses," and the errors which "science," with her keen eye, had detected in the Scriptures. But we hear very little today from scientists themselves about the "conflicts between science and religion." These conflicts have, one by one, ceased, as "science" has revised her hasty conclusions and corrected her blunders. The writer has been a diligent student of the physical sciences and of the philosophies based on them, for upwards of twenty-five years, and a practicing lawyer for a still longer period, and having now acquired a fair knowledge of the text of Scripture, he can say that he is aware of no demonstrated fact of science which is in conflict with a single statement of the Bible. Among all the "assured results of science" there exists not, to his knowledge, evidence sufficient in character and amount to convict the Bible of a single error or misstatement. Of course, such evidence could not exist. The Lord Jesus said of the Word of God, "Thy Word is truth" (John 17:17) ; and of course, true knowledge of God's creation cannot conflict with His Word.

A recent book by Alfred Russel Wallace entitled, "Man's Place in the Universe" (1904), furnishes a striking illustration, on a large scale, of the way in which "science," after leading the thought of cultured and highly educated minds away from the truth revealed by Scripture, sometimes leads it back again.

The reading of Scripture undoubtedly gives, and was clearly intended to give, the impression that the earth is the center of interest in the universe, and the object of the Creator's special care; that it was fitted with elaborate pains to be the habitation of living creatures, and especially of man; and that the sun, moon and stars were created with special reference to their service to the earth. Hence, for many centuries, man believed that the earth was the center of the universe, and (though the Bible does not say so) that the sun and stars were relatively small bodies which moved around and waited upon it.

But these ideas have been completely upset by the discoveries of modern astronomers, who ascertained, at least to their entire satisfaction, that not only is the sun enormously larger than the earth, but that it is attended by other planets, the largest of which is twelve hundred times larger than the earth. Moreover, it has also been learned, so we are told, that our sun itself is but one of an almost infinite number of stars, many of which are immensely greater in size, and which, it may be assumed, are themselves the centers of planetary systems on a much grander scale than our little solar system.

In such a universe as modern astronomy has brought into the view of man our little earth, once thought to be its center of interest and importance, shrinks into utter insignificance. In proportion to the vast universe of which it is a member its size is relatively less than that of a tiny particle of dust in proportion to the mass of the earth itself. How, therefore, can it be supposed that the Creator of so inconceivably great and complex a universe would have a special regard for this insignificant attendant of a fourth-rate sun, and for the still more insignificant creatures who dwell upon it? The earth with all its occupants could drop out of the universe and be no more missed than a single grain of sand from the seashore or a single drop of water from the ocean.

It is inevitable that these teachings of astronomy concerning the universe should have produced impressions directly opposite to those produced by Scripture, and should have placed obstacles in the way of believing the doctrine of redemption by the incarnation and sacrificial death of the Son of God.

But now comes Mr. Wallace, the contemporary of Charles Darwin, and probably at the present day one of the most prominent men of science, and reverses the ideas which have been so widely disseminated in the name of science. Mr. Wallace masses a great body of evidence, derived both from astronomy and physics, to support the propositions, First, that the solar system occupies (and always has occupied) approximately the central portion of this vast universe, getting all the advantages due to such favorable position; Second, that the earth is certainly the only habitable planet in the solar system, and presumably the only habitable spot in the whole universe. Mr. Wallace, by a vast accumulation of facts and inferences, shows that the physical conditions necessary for the maintenance of life depend upon a great variety of complex and delicate adjustments, such as distance from the sun, the mass of the planet, its obliquity to its orbit, the amount of water as compared with land, the surface distribution of land and water, the permanence of this distribution, the density of the earth, the volume and density of the atmosphere, the amount of carbon-dioxide therein, etc. These, and other essential conditions, are met (says Mr. Wallace) only in a planet such as this earth, situated and constructed as it is. From Mr. Wallace's premises, if the universe is assumed to be the work of an intelligent Creator, it would follow that everything in this inconceivably vast and complex universe has been planned and arranged with special reference to making this little earth of ours a place suitable for the habitation of living beings, and especially of mankind.

We give Mr. Wallace's conclusions in his own words. He

says: *"This completes my work as a connected argument, founded wholly upon the facts and principles accumulated by modern science; and it leads, if my facts are substantially correct and my reasoning sound, to one great and definite conclusion,—that man, the culmination of conscious organic life, has been developed HERE ONLY in the whole vast material universe we see around us."*

Thus we have the surprising fact that one of the foremost living exponents of the teachings of science, a man who certainly attaches no importance to the teachings of Scripture, has been at great pains to show that the earth is, after all, the center of, and most important place in, the whole universe; and that, so far as any purpose can be detected in it, the universe may well be supposed to exist for the sole benefit of the earth, and for the sake of producing therein those peculiar conditions necessary for the existence and maintenance of life.

We may say then that, considered merely as a book of instruction, the Bible is, as to every subject whereof it treats, not merely abreast of, but far ahead of, the learning of these and all other times, whether past or future. The impressions it makes upon believing minds are the impressions of *truth,* even though (as in the instance we have just been considering) contemporary science may give, as its settled conclusions, impressions directly to the contrary.

Unlike other books of instruction THE BIBLE DOES NOT BECOME OBSOLETE. This is a fact of immense significance; and its only explanation is that the Bible is a LIVING book, the Word of the living God. All other books partake of the infirmity of their authors, and are either dying or dead. On the other hand, "The Word of God is living."

VI. THE BIBLE IS INDESTRUCTIBLE

The Bible manifests the possession of inherent and imperishable life in that it survives all the attempts that have been made to destroy it.

The Bible is the only book in the world that is truly hated. The hatred it arouses is bitter, persistent, murderous. From generation to generation this hatred has been kept alive. There is doubtless a supernatural explanation for this continuous display of hostility towards the Word of God, for that Word has a supernatural enemy who has personally experienced its power. (Matt. 4:1-10.)

But the natural explanation of this hatred is that the Bible differs notably from other books in that it gives no flattering picture of man and his world, but just the reverse. The Bible does not say that man is a noble being, ever aspiring towards the attainment of exalted ideals. It does not describe the career of humanity as "progress," as the brave and successful struggle of man against the evils of his environment; but quite the contrary, declares it to be a career of disobedience and departure from God, a preference for darkness rather than for light, "because their deeds are evil."

The Bible does not represent man as having come, without any fault of his own, into adverse circumstances, and as being engaged in gradually overcoming these by the development and exercise of his inherent powers. It does not applaud his achievements, and extol his wonderful civilization. Quite the contrary. It records how God saw that the *wickedness* of man was great in the earth, and that every imagination of the thoughts of his heart was only evil continually. (Gen. 6:5.) It speaks of man as "being filled with all unrighteousness, fornication, wickedness, covetousness, maliciousness, full of envy, murder, strife, guile, evil dispositions; whisperers, slanderers, hateful to God, insolent, proud, vaunting, inventors of evil things, disobedient to parents, without understanding, perfidious, without natural affection, implacable, unmerciful" (Rom. 1:29-31 Gr.). It says that "They are *all* under sin," that "There is none righteous, no not one. There is none that understandeth, there is none that seeketh after God. They are all gone out of the way, they are together become unprofitable;

there is none that doeth good, no not one" (Rom. 3:10-12). Man's condition by nature is described as *"dead* in trespasses and sins," "children of disobedience; among whom also we *all* had our conduct in times past in the lusts of our flesh, fulfilling the desires of the flesh and of the mind; and were *by nature* the children of wrath" (Eph. 2:1-3).

The Bible has nothing to say in praise of man or of his natural endowments. On the contrary, it derides his wisdom as "foolishness with God." It declares that God has made foolish the wisdom of this age (1 Cor. 1:20) ; that the natural man is incapable of receiving the things of the Spirit of God (1 Cor. 2:14) ; and that if any man thinks that he knows anything, he knows nothing yet as he ought to know. (1 Cor. 8:2.)

Nor does the Bible predict the ultimate triumph of "civilization." It does not say that the progress of humanity shall bring it eventually to a vastly better state of things. It does not say that human nature shall improve under the influences of education and self-culture, even with that of Christianity added. On the contrary, it declares that evil men "shall wax worse and worse, deceiving, and being deceived" (2 Tim. 3:13).

Even of "this present evil age" (Gal. 1:4), during which the professing church is the most conspicuous object on earth, and during which the world has the enormous benefit resulting from the light of revelation and an open Bible, it is not predicted that man and his world would undergo any improvement, or that the developments of the age would be in the direction of better conditions on earth. On the contrary, the Bible declares that "in the last days perilous [or difficult] times shall come. For men shall be lovers of their own selves, lovers of money, vaunting, proud, evil speakers, disobedient to parents, untruthful, unholy, without natural affection, implacable, slanderers, inconsistent, savage, not lovers of good, betrayers, headstrong, puffed up, lovers of pleasure rather than lovers of God; having a form of piety, but denying the power of it" (2 Tim. 3:1-5 Gr.).

Such is the character of man, and such is to be the result, as Scripture foretells it, of all his schemes of betterment, education, development, self-culture, civilization and character-building. And because of this the Bible is heartily detested. Men have sought nothing more earnestly than they have sought to destroy this appallingly accurate portrait of themselves and their doings. How astonishing it is that any intelligent person should suppose that man drew this picture of himself, and predicted this as the outcome of all his own efforts! No wonder the Bible is hated, and for the simple and sufficient reason that it declares the truth about man and his world. The Lord Jesus set forth clearly both the fact and its explanation when He said to His unbelieving brethren, "The world cannot hate you; but Me it hateth, because I testify of it that *the works thereof are evil"* (John 7:7).

Again, the Bible is hated because it claims the right to exercise, and assumes to exercise, *authority over man.* It speaks as one *having authority.* It issues commands to all. It says, "Thou shalt" and "Thou shalt not." It does not simply advise or commend one course of action rather than another, as one would address an equal, but it directs men imperatively what they shall do, and what they shall not do. In this manner it addresses all ranks and conditions of men—kings and governors, parents and children, husbands and wives, masters and servants, rich and poor, high and low, free and bond. In this, too, we have a characteristic of the Bible which distinguishes it from all other books. It is no respecter of persons. But for this cause also it is hated; for men are becoming more and more impatient of all external authority. The principles of democracy, the essence of which is the supremacy (virtually the *divinity*) of man, has thoroughly leavened all society in the progressive nations of the earth. There is a sentiment abroad, which finds frequent expression and meets always with a sympathetic reception, to the effect that man has been shackled through the ages by narrow theological ideas whereof the Bible is the source, and that the time has arrived for him to throw off this bondage, to arise in his true might and majesty, and to do great things for himself.

It is a most impressive fact that, in all the visible universe, there is nothing that assumes authority over man, or that imposes laws upon him, *except the Bible*. Once thoroughly rid of that troublesome book, and man will be finally rid of all authority, and will have arrived at that state of lawlessness predicted in the New Testament prophecies, wherein society will be ready to accept the leadership of that "lawless one," whose coming is to be after the working of Satan, with all power, and signs, and wonders of falsehood, and with all deceit of unrighteousness in them that perish, because they received not a love of the truth that they might be saved. (2 Thess. 2:7-10.)

This is perhaps the main purpose of the persistent attempts in our day, mostly in the name of scholarship and liberal theology, to break down the authority of Scripture; and we may see with our own eyes that the measure of success of this great apostasy is just what the Bible has foretold.

Other books arouse no hatred. There may be books which men dislike, and such they simply let alone But the Bible is, and always has been, hated to the death. It is the *one book* that has been pursued from century to century, as men pursue a mortal foe. At first its destruction has been sought by violence. All human powers, political and ecclesiastical, have combined to put it out of existence. Death has been the penalty for possessing or reading a copy; and such copies as were found have been turned over to the public executioner to be treated as was the Incarnate Word. No expedient that human ingenuity could devise or human cruelty put into effect, has been omitted in the desperate attempt to put this detested book out of existence. But the concentrated power of man utterly failed in the attempt. Why?

Here is one book among countless millions which is singled out for relentless hatred, and that fact alone is sufficient to provoke astonishment and invite the closest scrutiny to ascertain the explanation of the unique phenomenon. What characteristic is it that distinguishes this Book from all other books in so strange a fashion? Has its influence upon men been corrupting or otherwise evil? Does it teach doctrines dangerous to individuals or communities? Does it promote disorder, vice or crime? On the contrary, it will not be questioned that its influence, wherever it has gone, has been beneficial beyond that of all other books combined, and that the most fruitful human lives are those which have been moulded by its teachings. One explanation alone will account for the astounding fact that such a Book should be the only one now or ever in existence to provoke active and persistent animosity among men who refuse to acknowledge it as from God; namely, that it declares man to be a *fallen* creature, and his whole career to be the mere outworking of his corrupt nature in the path of disobedience; and that it predicts in plain language what the end of that path will be for all who do not accept God's method of deliverance out of it through Jesus Christ.

But, violence having failed to rid man of the Bible, other means have been resorted to in the persistent effort to accomplish that object. To this end the intellect and learning of man have been enlisted. The Book has been assailed from every side by men of the highest intelligence, culture and scholarship. Since the art of printing has been developed there has been in progress a continuous war of books. Many books against THE Book—man's books against God's Book. Its authority has been denied, and its veracity and even its morality have been impugned, its claims upon the consciences of men have been ridiculed; but all to no purpose, except to bring out more conspicuously the fact that the "Word of God is LIVING," and with an indestructible life.

Should any other book incur the hatred of man (which no other book ever has, seeing that all others are man's own productions) it would not be necessary to take measures for its destruction. A book produced by dying men need only be let alone to die of its own accord. The seeds of death are in it from the start. One Book alone has incurred man's hatred, because it is the one Book that is not his own. It is the only thing *in* the whole world that is hostile *to* the whole world-system. One Book only has man attempted to destroy; and yet, in this attempt, though in it all his powers and resources have been employed, he has most conspicuously and ignominiously failed. Why?

A little less than a century and a half ago a book made its appearance which attracted wide attention, particularly in the upper circles of intellect and culture. It was vauntingly entitled the "Age of Reason," and its author, Thomas Paine, was probably without superior in intelligence among his contemporaries. So confident was the author of this book that his reasonings proved the untrustworthiness of Scripture, and destroyed its claim upon the consciences of men as the revelation of the living God, that he predicted that in fifty years the Bible would be practically out of print. But nearly thrice fifty years have passed since this boast was uttered. The boaster and his book have passed away; and their very names are well-nigh forgotten. But the Word of God has maintained its place, and not by human power. They who believe and cherish it are a feeble folk. Not many wise, not many mighty, not many high-born are among them. They have no might of their own to stand against the enemies of the Bible. The situation resembles a scene recorded in 1 Kings 20:27, where the Israelites went out against the Syrians, and we read that "The children of Israel pitched before them like two little flocks of kids; but the Syrians filled the country."

But notwithstanding such great odds, the victory is certain. The enemies of the Bible have indeed filled the country. Yet, they shall all pass away; but the Word of the Lord shall not pass away.

Again, in more recent times, a book of man was put forth, and was hailed as a work which would quickly destroy the credibility of Scripture and put an end to its authority and influence. This was Charles Darwin's "Descent of Man," a book whose influence has been greater, doubtless, than any other that has made its appearance during a century past. The main feature of this work was that it set forth an explanation of the origin of living beings, including man, radically different from that of Genesis, and propounded a theory of propagation of living species directly contrary to the great and immutable law declared nine times over in the first chapter of the Bible in the brief but significant expression, "after his kind."

The delight which Darwin's book caused among the enemies of the Bible, and the spirit in which its appearance was welcomed, are well illustrated by the title bestowed upon it by the eminent naturalist Haeckel, who called it the "Anti-Genesis," declaring that by a single stroke Darwin had annihilated the dogma of Creation. But it was not because of its supposed contribution to truth that Darwin's book was so widely and cordially received, and his utterly unproved hypothesis so readily accepted as an "assured result of science." Its vogue was largely due to the fact that it struck at the very foundation of Scripture. It is useless to pretend that Darwin's theory might be true, and the Bible nevertheless entitled to respect. The Lord Jesus said to a learned man of His day, "If I have told you *earthly things,* and ye believe not, how shall ye believe if I tell you of *heavenly things?*" (John 3:12). If the Bible does not give us a truthful account of the events of the six days recorded in its first chapter, it is not to be trusted as to *any* of its statements.

But we have now the record of about half a century since the publication of Darwin's book; and, though the great movements of unbelief and apostasy are swiftly running their predicted course, there never was a time when the absolute and divine accuracy of Scripture from beginning to end, was more firmly grasped and tenaciously held by those who know it best, and never a time since "science" began to be looked to as an authority and instructor of men when there was less "scientific" basis for the prevalent questioning of the statements of the Bible.

There can be, of course, no real conflict between the Bible and any true discovery of science. Such conflicts as have been supposed to exist arose from hasty and incorrect conclusions, whose chief value in the eyes of many lay in the fact that they contradicted the Bible. As science has been compelled, however reluctantly, to correct her blunders, or to acknowledge that supposedly demonstrated truths were at best but unproved conjectures, the "conflicts" have died out; so that, at the present time, the assured teachings of "science" afford no weapons against the statements of the Bible. On the contrary, the investigations of men, in fields of geology, physics, and palæontology, have brought into view much information recorded ages ago in the Bible, information which, at the time the latter was written, was not in the knowledge of man. As has been already said, there is not a single assertion of the Bible that is in conflict with any demonstrated fact of science. All the investigations, of all the searchers, in all the various fields of search, have not availed to produce evidence sufficient in character and amount to convict Scripture of a single false statement.

But it is time to bring to a close our remarks under this heading, though they might be greatly extended.

We have called attention to the strange fact that, of all the millions of books that have existed, the Bible is the only one that has excited deep and persistent hatred, the only Book which men have sought to get rid of, and that by every conceivable means. We have further called attention to the still stranger fact that, in this attempt to destroy the Bible, the powers of state, of religion, and of learning, have all been enlisted, and that, nevertheless, the number of copies of the Bible goes on steadily increasing. How can these facts be explained except by the statement that "the Word of God is LIVING," and that the source of its life is beyond the reach of man—in the very Being of the Living God?

VII. THE BIBLE IS A DISCERNER OF HEARTS

The power of discernment belongs only to an intelligent living being; and the power of discernment possessed by man does not go beneath the surface of things. Yet the passage in Hebrews, already quoted (4:12), asserts that the Word of God is a "discerner of the thoughts and intents of the heart."

This is a very remarkable statement, yet it is true, and millions of men have felt and recognized the searching and discerning power of the Word of God. We go to it not so much to learn the thoughts of other men, as to learn our own thoughts. We go to other books to find what was in the hearts and minds of their authors; but we go to this Book to find what is in our own hearts and minds. To one who reads it with ever so little spiritual intelligence, there comes a perception of the fact that this Book understands and knows all about him. It lays bare the deepest secrets of his heart, and brings to the surface of his consciousness, out of the unfathomable depths and unexplorable recesses of his own being, "thoughts and intents" whose existence was unsuspected. It reveals man to himself in a way difficult to describe, and absolutely peculiar to itself. It is a faithful mirror which reflects us exactly as we are. It detects our motives, discerns our needs; and having truthfully discovered to us our true selves, it counsels, reproves, exhorts, guides, refreshes, strengthens, and illuminates.

It has been pointed out that the Greek word rendered "discerner" in Hebrews 4:12, means literally "critic" (kritikos), and that this is its only occurrence in Scripture. How very significant is it that the designation "higher critics" has been assumed by that little coterie of men who claim to be able, by their own powers of literary discernment, to assign the dates of production of books and parts of books of Scripture, to detect spurious passages, alleged interpolations, and the like, and to split up books into fragments, assigning bits to one imaginary author and other bits to another; whereas as a matter of fact, it is the Bible itself that is the "Critic" of men.

This is in keeping with the subversive principles of this present evil age, wherein man is seeking to put himself in the place of God. This is "man's day." Man is now the critic of everything, and particularly of God's Word. Of that he is a *"higher* critic."

There is, however, no external evidence to support the higher critical views as to the late origin of the Pentateuch, Daniel, the latter part of Isaiah, etc.; *per contra* every pertinent discovery in the ruins of ancient cities corroborates the statements of Scripture. These theories rest entirely upon the alleged intuitive perceptions of sinful men, compassed about by infirmity, who claim to be able to pass infallibly upon the style and contents of each book of the Bible, to decide when it was written, by whom it could not have been written, and even to divide it up into various portions, assigning each to a different "source."

But high scholarship is not incompatible with belief in the full inspiration and accuracy of Scripture. Dean Burgon, one of the famous scholars of Oxford, says:

"I must be content with repudiating, in the most unqualified way, the notion that a mistake of any kind whatever is consistent with the texture of a narrative inspired by the Holy Spirit of God.

"The Bible is none other but the Word of God, not some part of it more and some part of it less so, but all alike the utterance of Him that sitteth upon the throne, absolute, faultless, unerring, supreme—'The witness of God which He hath testified of His Son.'"

The time is at hand when the haughtiness of man shall be brought low, and the Lord alone shall be exalted in that day. Then the Word of God shall judge the critics.

Meanwhile, the living Word shall continue to be the discerning companion of all who resort to it for the help which is not to be had elsewhere in this world of the dying. In going to the Bible we never think of ourselves as going *back* to a book of the distant past, to a thing of *antiquity;* but we go to it as to a book of the *present*—a living book. And so indeed it is, living in the power of an endless life, and able to build us up and to give us an inheritance among all them that are sanctified. (Acts 20:32.)

VIII.　THE TRANSLATABILITY OF SCRIPTURE

The Word of God manifests itself as a living Word in the very unique property it has of adapting itself and its message to all peoples, and of speaking in all languages, tongues and dialects. The extreme mobility and adaptability of Scripture, as manifested in this way, is comparable only to the power which a living being has of making himself at home in different countries from that in which he was born.

We have here again a characteristic which distinguishes the Bible from all other books, as any one may, with a little attention, clearly perceive. It is a universal rule that a book does not thrive except in the language in which it was written. Men's books will not always bear translation; and the greater the literary value of a book the more it is likely to suffer loss in being translated from one language into another. Change of locality is, to the great majority of books, absolutely destructive.

But to this rule the Bible is a marvellous exception. It seems to run freely into the mould of every language, to adapt itself perfectly thereto, and to speak with equal directness, clearness and authority to all peoples and tribes and nations, in their mother tongue. It does not occur to us that, in reading our common English Bible, we are reading a translation of an Oriental book; and indeed, when an example of the purest and best English is desired, men go with one accord to the Bible.

Considered merely as a poem, there is nothing more exquisite in the English language than the Twenty-third Psalm; and it has been stated that in other languages besides English this Shepherd Psalm is a model of poetical excellence. It never occurs to one reading it that he is reading a translation from another and very different language.

Is not this indeed a very extraordinary fact, and the more so when we consider that the Bible, though a unit, is at the same time highly composite? It comprises specimens of every kind of literature, historical, poetical, biographical, didactic, prophetic, epistolary, etc.

Moreover, it is not the production of a single human being, clothed in a uniform literary style of dress. On the contrary, its several parts were penned by men in widely varying stations in life, from herdsmen and unlearned fishermen, to kings and statesmen; and its styles are as divergent as its writers.

Nor was it the product of one era or period, which would tend to impart some common characteristics, and to prevent wide divergencies. As much as fifteen hundred years elapsed between the writing of its first and its last pages. Yet all parts and styles alike accommodate themselves to the change of language far more readily and perfectly than any human being is able to do when acquiring another tongue.

The property we are now considering is the more remarkable when we consider also the nation from which this unique volume has come. The Jews were anything but a literary people. They were not at all remarkable for culture, learning, art, or philosophy; and they were quite cut off by their peculiar customs, traditions, and religious institutions, from the progressive nations around them. There is no other Jewish literature that is worth talking about. Yet, from such a people has come a volume whose sixty-six books, now that we have them all together, evidently constitute one complete structure, unitary in design, yet which was fifteen centuries in attaining its completed state. This book, after the Jewish people were disintegrated and scattered,—even as that very book had distinctly foretold,—and had become the most despised and persecuted people on earth, has entered into the place of supremacy in every nation which has attained to any degree of civilization, and has held that place without a rival for eighteen centuries, during which period of time every *human* institution has been overturned, not once only, but again and again.

Why is it that the universal Book did not have its origin in the literature of Greece, or of ancient Rome, or in the Elizabéthan epoch of English literature? Why is it that nations which have been famed for their culture and literary genius have produced nothing comparable to the Bible? What collection of sixty-six books from the writings of about thirty authors of any nation could be made that would present any of the characteristics we have been noticing? Yet, it is certain that, it the Bible had a natural, instead of a supernatural origin, it would be far surpassed by the literary product of the literary nations of the earth.

This property of adaptability to all languages and peoples will impress us still more if we compare it in this respect with other Oriental books. The mere fact that it *is* an Oriental book makes its career among the Occidental nations still more miraculous. All attempts to domesticate other Oriental books, particularly sacred books, have been complete failures. Other

Oriental books are sought by scholars only, or by others who have a special interest for inquiring into their contents.

Already the Bible, or portions of it, has been translated into upwards of four hundred languages and dialects; so that it is revealing the grace of God in the gift of His Son, to practically every nation, kindred, tongue and tribe, throughout the world, and is speaking to all peoples *in their own native tongues.*

Like a living person, the Bible has made its way into all lands, has adapted itself to all environments, entered into relations of the most intimate kind with all peoples, and has exerted upon them all its own unique influence. It makes no difference what the people are to whom it goes, how radically different all their customs and institutions from those of that very peculiar people Israel; the Bible makes itself perfectly at home, and takes its own place without delay. Can this, or anything remotely approaching it, be said of any other book? And if not, are we not compelled, if we would have an explanation of this extraordinary difference, to fall back upon the statement that the "Word of God is living"? No other explanation will account for any of the facts we have been considering. This explanation accounts for them all.

The fact we are here considering, that is to say, the career of the Bible among the peoples of the earth, is, indeed, a stupendous and continuing miracle. Why has this particular Book gone to the ends of the earth, and assumed everywhere, and maintained against all opposition, the place of supremacy? What has given to this collection of writings, coming from an insignificant, peculiar, narrow-minded and isolated people, its *universal* character? Why is it that all other books, or collections of books, including the productions of the mightiest intellects and embodying the most superb and lofty specimens of human thought, wisdom, learning and experience, have been narrowly circumscribed in their area of influence, both as to time and space? Why has this particular Book continued ever widening its sphere of influence as the centuries pass, while every other book, after its first vogue, steadily contracts and dwindles? Why does this Book increase while all others decrease?

There is no *natural* explanation for these remarkable facts. In this day, when a natural explanation is sought for all things, the wise men can advance no theory to account for these facts. We sometimes hear, from the enemies of the truth, the admission that the Bible is inspired, but coupled with the statement that other books are equally inspired. For example, a prominent preacher in New York city recently said in an article published in a popular magazine, "God spake to Abraham, and to Samuel and to Isaiah. He has spoken to Henry Ward Beecher, to Tennyson, and to Ruskin." But neither this prominent preacher, nor any other man who is trying in like manner to put the Word of God on the same level as other books, is able to tell us why the writings of these other "inspired" men do not afford some indications of their divine origin similar to those characteristics of the Bible to which we are now calling attention.

The Apostle Paul in the last of his writings (2 Tim. 2: 8, 9) said, "Remember that Jesus Christ of the seed of David was raised from the dead according to my gospel; wherein I suffer as an evil-doer even unto bonds; but the *word of God is not bound.*"

In these words we have the sufficient and the only explanation of the extraordinary and unique career of the Bible. The human custodian of the Word of God may be bound, and may be treated as a malefactor for merely being the bearer of the message; but the living Word of the living God is not, and cannot be, bound. Jehovah Himself has said, "So shall My Word be that goeth forth out of My mouth. It shall not return unto Me void, but it shall accomplish that which I please, and it shall prosper in the thing whereto I sent it" (Isa. 55:11).

But there is more to be noted under this heading. The Bible is the universal Book also in that it not only speaks to all peoples in their own mother tongue, but it addresses itself to all classes of society. Missionaries from every part of the world have reported how the most depraved, ignorant and vicious people will listen at once to the words of Scripture as to no other book, and will recognize them as "good words." Like God Himself His Word is no respecter of persons. Indeed, its sternest denunciations are addressed to persons of rank and of social, ecclesiastical, or political prominence. Its best promises are for the meek and lowly. It has a message for all men, and to the highest as well as the lowest it speaks "with authority," never exhorting from the standpoint merely of superior human wisdom and intelligence, but always as delivering the message of God.

The Bible adapts itself thus to successive generations of men, exhibiting to each individual human being an intimate knowledge of his characteristics, trials and needs. It seems to be waiting for an opportunity to become acquainted with each child of Adam, to direct the steps of his life-journey through this great and terrible wilderness, to warn him of dangers and pitfalls, and to be the man of his counsel to every one who wills not to reject its offer of fellowship. Does not this warrant us in saying that "the Word of God is LIVING"?

IX. THE WORD EXHIBITS THE CHARACTERISTIC OF GROWTH

Growth is one of the characteristics of a living being. The Word of God lodges and grows in human hearts, for there is its real lodgment, rather than in the printed page. The Psalmist says, "Thy Word have I hid in my heart" (Ps. 119:11).

The book of Deuteronomy has much to say about the Word of God. In chapter thirty it declares (verse 14) that "The Word is very nigh unto thee, in thy mouth and in thy heart."

This is repeated in Romans 10:8, with the addition, "that is, the word of faith which we preach."

In 1 Thessalonians 2:13 Paul says to the Thessalonians, "When ye received the Word of God which ye heard of us, ye received it not as the word of men, but as it is in truth, the Word of God, which *effectually worketh also in you* that believe." The believing heart is its lodgment, and there it works to effect some definite results.

In Colossians 3:16 we have the admonition, "Let the word of Christ dwell *in* you richly in all wisdom." It is in the believing heart that the Word dwells richly.

The Lord Jesus, in explaining the parable of the sower, said, "The seed is the Word of God" (Luke 8:11); and again, "The sower soweth *the Word*" (Mark 4:14). (A seed, of course, is worthless except it have life in it.) And He further explained that the seed which fell on good ground "are they which, *in an honest and good heart,* having heard the Word keep it, and bring forth fruit with patience" (Luke 8:15). To the unbelieving Jews the Lord said, "And ye have not His Word *abiding in you;* for whom He hath sent, Him ye believe not" (John 5:38).

In Colossians 1:5, 6, Paul speaks of the "Word of the truth of the Gospel, which is come unto you, as it is in all the world, and bringeth forth fruit."

In these passages we have presented to us the thought of the Word as a living seed or germ, first finding lodgment in the heart of man, and then abiding and growing there.

The growth of the Word of God is specifically mentioned in several striking passages in the Acts of the Apostles. Acts 6:7: *"And the Word of God increased;* and the number of the disciples multiplied in Jerusalem greatly."

Here we are told specifically that the Word of God increased. We learn from this that the mere multiplication of copies of the Scriptures is in itself of no importance. It is of no avail to have the Book in the house, and on the shelf or table, if it be not taken into the heart. But when so received into the heart, the Word of God grows and increases. It is assimilated into the life of him who receives it, and henceforth is a part of himself.

It is important to note what stimulated this recorded increase of the Word of God. The Apostles, who were its custodians or depositories, had found themselves taken up with ministering to the material wants of the flock, and they brought this matter before the body of disciples saying, "It is not reason that we should leave the *Word of God* and serve tables," and they asked that suitable men be appointed for that service while they should give themselves continually "to prayer and the ministry of the Word."

The growth of the Word then, accompanied by a great multiplication of the number of disciples, was the result of faithful ministry of the Word—a ministry which was sustained by prayer.

This method of promoting the growth of the Word of God is highly important. Every believer, having the Word in his heart and in his mouth, may be and should be the means of its propagation; and the extent to which the Word has been spread abroad in this inconspicuous way will not be known until the time when all things shall be manifested. There are great multitudes who would never get the Word from the printed page, or from the spoken sermon or address. Hence the importance of these epistles of Christ written not with ink, but with the SPIRIT of the living God, not in tablets of stone, but in the fleshy tablets of the heart. (2 Cor. 3:3.) Such epistles are read by many who never read the printed page; and the eternal destiny of many souls may depend upon the distinctness and legibility of that writing. May our lives, as believers, be so transparent that the Word written in our hearts may be distinctly seen; and thus, as sons of God we shall shine "as lights in the world holding forth the Word of life" (Phil. 2:15, 16).

The second passage which speaks expressly of the growth of the Word of God is Acts 12:21-24. In this chapter are narrated the last episodes in the life of Herod Antipas. In the first part of the chapter we read how he killed James, the brother of John, with the sword, and finding this course to be popular with the Jews, he apprehended Peter also, and put him in custody, intending after the passover to make this leader of the Apostles the object of a public demonstration, which doubtless would have strengthened Herod still further in the regard of the people. But Peter was delivered from prison by an angel of the Lord who was sent for that purpose.

The closing verses of the chapter tell of a disagreement between Herod and the citizens of Tyre and Sidon, some undescribed incident having occurred which caused the former to be highly displeased with the latter. But they, having gained the favor of King Herod's chamberlain, one Blastus, made overtures of peace and sent a delegation to the king. The reception of this embassy was made an occasion of much pomp and circumstance. Herod put on his royal apparel, sat upon his throne, received the delegation, "and made an oration unto them." This oration was received with extravagant demonstrations. "The people gave a shout, saying, It is the voice of a god, and not of a man."

Herod accepted this tribute, and no doubt was highly pleased therewith. But it is a dangerous thing for mortal and sinful man, however high his station, to accept glory which belongs to God alone. For *immediately* the angel of the Lord smote him, because he gave not God the glory; and he was *eaten of worms* and gave up the ghost. *"But the word of God grew and multipled."*

There is a tremendous lesson here for the many who, in these closing days of the age, are participating in the various movements which, however diverse in appearance, have all the common object of putting man in the place of God, and the word of man in the place of the Word of God. Herod was not stricken down for persecuting the Church, for imprisoning Peter, or for putting James to death, nor yet for his previous murder of John the Baptist. He was smitten for permitting his word to be acclaimed as the Word of God. Herod had often heard the Word of the Lord, for he had listened attentively to the preaching of the Baptist. He had heard of the ministry and miracles of the Lord Jesus, and had even seen Him on that dark betrayal night. He was, therefore, not smitten for something done in ignorance.

The angel of Jehovah had two ministries in that chapter. One was to deliver Peter, who, according to the word of his Lord, was to serve Him to old age (John 21:18). The other was to declare, by smiting the King, the difference between the Word of God and that of the most important man of the country.

Doubtless that was a great oration which Herod delivered on that day. It contained most probably striking utterances, pregnant with wisdom and garbed in the attractions of human eloquence. It was, moreover, the King on his throne who spoke, and we know how the throngs gather to listen on such occasions.

On the other hand, and in striking contrast, the Word of God was in the charge of "unlearned and ignorant men," a despised and persecuted company, whose Leader had but just suffered the ignominious death of a malefactor. What then has become of the words of King Herod? All have utterly perished, centuries ago, from the memory of men. He himself was eaten of worms; "But the Word of God grew and multipled," and has continued so to do from that time to the present.

Not very long ago, at the convening of the American Congress, a message from the President was addressed to that body. Much comment was made on that message because of its great length. Some industrious person counted the words, and found them to be upwards of thirty thousand. They were serious words, too, and weighty, as human utterances go. They dealt with the most important affairs and interests of the nation that regards itself as the greatest on earth. But they were not "the words of eternal life." And for all that the occasion was so recent, and the subject matter so important, it is doubtful if any person can now recall a single sentence of that great message. Few, indeed, would care to do so, or would receive the slightest benefit therefrom, if they could.

The words of kings, and emperors, and presidents, are dying words. From the moment of their utterance they begin to perish; but "the Word of God is living." Being the utterance of the living God that Word can never pass away.

The last of the three passages which speaks of the growth of the Word of God is in Acts 19; and again the context adds greatly to the impressiveness of the lesson taught by the passage.

The scene of the first of the three incidents was in Jerusalem, of the second in Cæsarea, just west of Galilee, and of the third in Ephesus, a Gentile city. Thus there is special mention made of the growth of the Word of God in Judea, in Palestine outside of Judea, and in the Gentile regions beyond. This would seem to signify that the Word of God was not to be limited to territorial boundary, but was to spread and grow in every part of the earth.

The Apostle Paul had spent two years in Ephesus, preaching to such purpose that "all they which dwelt in Asia heard the Word of the Lord Jesus, both Jews and Greeks." And God, moreover, "wrought special miracles by the hands of Paul" (Acts 19:10, 11).

One result of this ministry was that "many of them which used curious arts brought their books together, and burned them before all men; and they counted the price of them and found it fifty thousand pieces of silver. *So mightily grew the word of God and prevailed*" (verses 19, 20).

This is, indeed, a very notable event—a grand demonstration of the power and sufficiency of the Word of God. These books, intrinsically worth so great a sum as fifty thousand pieces of silver, became worse than worthless in the hands of their owners after the latter had received the Word of God. The books thus destroyed had been held in the highest estimation, because they were the manuals of necromancy, or occult arts. They instructed their readers in just such things as are coming into great favor in the present day. But when their owners "believed," they could no longer practice the "curious arts," or even retain the books that described them.

It is very easy to destroy the books of men. Great and mighty as are the powers of darkness which were back of the books burned at Ephesus, those evil powers are not comparable to that which has directed the career of the Word of God. Many have been the attempts to consume it in the flames, but in vain; for the Word of God is living.

This scene at Ephesus has been re-enacted in many a human life. When in quest of help, enlightenment, wisdom, guidance, and knowledge of the unseen, men turn to books; and though disappointed again and again, the inquiring mind, which has felt the need of a source of light external to itself, and has realized that there must be such a source somewhere, never shakes off the habit of seeking it in books. There appears to be a deep-seated consciousness that the desired help is to be found in some book. But men cannot impart to the books written by them what is not in themselves; and so they who gather many books gain little to compensate for their cost and labor. Conjectures and human opinions, philosophies and vain deceits, with all the obscurities and contradictions contained in them, do but leave the mind in perplexity and bewilderment concerning every matter of real importance. And, after all, if one cannot have certainties, but must put up with mere opinions, why should he not prefer his own to another man's, seeing that all are at the best but mere guesses, whereof one is as likely to be true as another? The "wise men" can tell us nothing, for "lo, they have rejected the Word of the Lord; and what wisdom is in them?" (Jer. 8:9).

But when, to one who has undergone this weariness of a vain quest for something sure and satisfying in the books of men, the Word of God comes with the convincing power which it alone possesses, and with the restful assurance which it alone can impart, the books of men become worthless—mere rubbish, fit only to be food for flames. Conjectures are now exchanged for certainties, and profitless speculations for knowledge certified by the sure testimony of Him who knoweth and understandeth all things.

The writer lately heard a servant of Christ relate an incident in his own life which aptly illustrates what we have been saying. Speaking on the injunction of Ephesians 6:10, "Be strong in the Lord," he said, "I well remember a section in my book-case long ago which contained a highly prized set of Emerson's works. One essay in particular I read and re-read, and had marked favorite passages in it. The burden of it was, 'Young man, be strong.' This phrase occurred again and again, and it thrilled and excited me. But it pointed me to no source of strength, for the writer knew of none. He never once said, 'Be strong in the Lord;' and the time came when, realizing the cruel mockery of the words, and the emptiness of this entire system of philosophy, I put the set of well-printed and choicely bound volumes into the flames." He discovered in the Bible the Source of all strength, and the Book displaced the entire set of man's philosophies and empty deceits. "So mightily grew the Word of God and prevailed."

Happy is the man who has "received the Word of God" (Acts 8:14; 11:1, etc.), who has made room for it in his life, and in whose heart and mind it has grown and prevailed.

X. A LIFE-GIVING WORD

We come now to something higher and deeper. The great mystery of a living thing is the power it possesses of propagating its kind. To trace the stream of life to its source is confessedly impossible to man, nor does any philosophic theory account for that stream. The attempt made in recent years to explain life as a mere property of atoms of non-living matter grouped in certain complex combinations, has been confessedly a failure. Professor Huxley, probably the ablest defender of this theory, and who at one time predicted that "protoplasm" (as he named the physical basis of life) might one day be produced in the laboratory, was constrained to admit, before his death, that there was no known link between the living and the non-living.

In the era of great scientific activity which marked the last half of the nineteenth century, many and persistent efforts were made to bring about spontaneous generation; that is to say, to demonstrate that life could be caused by human manipulation to spring up out of non-living matter, and apart from antecedent life. Great was the desire of unbelieving men of science to find a support for this theory, for if established it would flatly contradict the first chapter of the Bible, and thus discredit the statements of the latter upon a subject of the highest importance. In that chapter the first law of biology is enunciated in the words "after his kind;" and this law is applied both to the vegetable kingdom and to the animal—to grass, and herb, and fruit tree, to fowl and fishes, and creeping things, to wild beast and tame beast. Each was commanded to bring forth "after his kind;" and it is needless to say that each has strictly obeyed that Divine command.

The inspired account of Creation does not describe the method whereby God brought into existence the several species of living creatures, and gave to each the distinct characteristics which were to be its perpetual and unvarying endowment. This matter, therefore, belongs to the realm of speculation, into which it is unprofitable to enter. What concerns us is the fact, distinctly stated, and manifestly deemed by the Spirit of God to be of great importance for our instruction in the truth, that

God, in creating the numerous species of living creatures, vegetable and animal, put a permanent difference between them, rigidly confining each species to the reproduction of its own kind.

So important was this law in the mind of the Creator, and so careful was He to impress it upon the mind of man, that the formula is stated nine times in the first chapter of Genesis. There is an emphasis in this which has great significance in view of the theory of organic evolution, which, but a few years ago, was advanced as a "scientific" explanation of the origin of species of living beings, and was accepted as such by nearly all the wise and learned of this world.

After many years' investigation of the philosophy of evolution, an investigation carried on in full sympathy with the widest application of that captivating theory, I have yet to see proof of *a single fact* showing, or tending to show, the operation of the so-called "law" or "principle" of evolution in the world of Nature. No instance has ever been found of a living thing of one species coming from ancestors of another species; and there is not the slightest ground for the belief that such a thing ever happened. On the other hand, every one of the countless billions of reproductions of living creatures—the grass, the herb yielding seed, and the fruit tree yielding fruit—which occur every year, are in accordance with the divine command recorded in the first chapter of Genesis. Oak trees have never betrayed the slightest tendency to produce any fruit but acorns, nor acorns to produce any trees but oaks. The theory of organic evolution, promulgated by Darwin and Wallace, has nothing to commend it except that it offers an alternative to the acceptance of the account of the origin of species given in the Bible.

The attempts made by the empiricists of the last century to bring about, or to demonstrate the possibility of, spontaneous generation of living organisms by human manipulation apart from pre-existing organisms of the same species, were at first thought to have been successful. Infusions of hay were prepared which, after being tightly sealed in suitable flasks, were heated to a temperature sufficiently high (as was supposed) to destroy all life within the flasks. These were then set aside for awhile, and kept under observation; and in the course of time they were found to contain minute livng organisms. These "results of science" were heralded far and wide, and great was the rejoicing occasioned thereby.

But other men of science, among whom the most prominent was Liebig, went over the ground again, repeating the experiments more carefully; and their results showed that, in the earlier experiments, either the flasks had not been tightly sealed, or else the heat to which they were exposed had not been sufficiently great to destroy all the living organisms therein. So conclusive were these later experiments that the theory of spontaneous generation (or "abiogenesis") has had no standing whatever from that time to the present.

The following quotations will accurately inform the reader as to the best scientific opinion on this subject.

Lord Kelvin who, until his recent death, held the leading place among scientific men, used this positive language:

"Inanimate matter cannot become living except under the influence of matter already living. This is a fact in science which seems to me as well ascertained as the law of gravitation."

Again he said: "I am ready to accept as an article of faith in science, valid for all time and in all space, that *life is produced by life and only by life.*"

Professor Huxley, the advocate of the theory of "animal automatism," who at one time contended earnestly that vitality was merely a property of "protoplasm," (that is to say, the property of a particular chemical compound of carbon, oxygen, hydrogen and nitrogen) left this record before his death: "The present state of knowledge furnishes us with no link between the living and the not-living."

Professor Tyndall says: "Every attempt made in our day to generate life independent of antecedent life has utterly broken down."

Such has indeed been, and such must ever be, the result of all human attempts to start the flow of a stream of life, or to divert one which God has started, so as to change the form of manifestation which the Author and Giver of life has given to each species of living creatures.

We wish the reader to understand that we rest nothing whatever upon the outcome of the foregoing scientific controversy, nor upon the above quoted (or any other) statements of human opinion however high their source. Faith has no foundation other than the Word of God.

Men of science may be right or wrong in their deductions from the fragmentary information possessed by them. Generally they are wrong, as is clearly enough shown by the fact that a large part of the work of each generation of men of science consists in overturning or modifying the theories of their predecessors. The foregoing is given as an illustration of the utter futility of setting up the deductions of the human reason against the assertions of the Word of God, and as a caution to the reader, if he be a child of God through faith in Jesus Christ, not to give the slightest credence to any statements made in the name of "science" or "scholarship" which call into question what is written in the inspired Scriptures.

We may ask then, Is the Word of God a living Word in this particular sense? Does it have the mysterious power of imparting life; and if so, is the life it imparts of the same sort as its own? Does it reproduce "after its kind"?

This brings up the great subject of spiritual conception and generation, concerning which the Scripture gives not a little information. Into this highly interesting but difficult subject we will not now enter. Even the beginning and maintenance of physical life in plants and animals (including man) are great and inscrutable mysteries. This is true in all stages of the process, particularly in the initial stage of germination, which is the beginning of a new individual existence by the quickening of a seed derived from a previously existing individual of the same species. How much more mysterious, then, must be the process of spiritual generation! The Lord Jesus, in His conversation with the learned and intellectual Pharisee, Nicodemus, indicated that the subject was a very mysterious one, by the words, "The wind bloweth where it listeth, and thou hearest the sound thereof, but *canst not tell* whence it cometh, and whither it goeth: *so* is every one that is born [or begotten] of the Spirit."

Therefore, even after we have learned all that is given us to know concerning the beginning of physical life in the naturally begotten, and of spiritual life in the supernaturally begotten, the subject remains as mysterious as ever, since the Author of life has reserved it among the "secret things" which "belong unto the Lord our God" (Deut. 29:29).

But the *fact* of natural generation cannot be questioned, though the *process* be involved in unfathomable mystery. The fact of spiritual generation is equally sure to all who believe the Word of God. The Bible plainly declares it, and those who believe on the Christ of God know also by experience the beginning of a new kind of life in their own souls.

For present purposes it is sufficient to point out that spiritual generation is analogous (as might be expected) to natural generation, being effected by means of a seed, which, having been deposited in a prepared place, is quickened by the Spirit of God, and becomes itself "spirit,"—that is to say a new nature which is spiritual in its character; for "that which is born [or begotten] of the Spirit is spirit" (John 3:6).

The fact of spiritual conception, and the nature of the seed whereby it is effected, are plainly declared in 1 Peter 1:23: "Being born [or having been begotten] again, not of corruptible *seed,* but of incorruptible, by THE WORD OF GOD WHICH LIVETH and abideth for ever."

There is an immense amount of truth of the highest importance contained in this passage; but the statement which especially concerns us is that the seed of the new birth is from the living Word ("the Word which LIVETH"). This statement plainly teaches that the Word of God possesses the highest endowment of a living being, namely, that of imparting life. And with this agrees the teaching of the Lord Jesus in the parable of the sower, in the explanation of which He said, "The *seed* is the Word of God" (Luke 8:11).

In consequence of the transgression and fall of the first man, who was the original depository of the life of humanity (Gen. 2:7), the life in him, being "corruptible," became vitiated. Hence, by inexorable law, the seed of his generations also became corrupted. It follows that all men in their natural generation are begotten of corruptible (and corrupted) seed; and have received (and hence must impart to their succeeding generations) a corrupted life. What, therefore, was needed, in order to bring into existence a human family answering to God's purpose in the creation of man (Gen. 1:26), was a new and *incorruptible seed*. This has been supplied in the Word of God. All who believe that Word are begotten again (or from above); not this time of corruptible seed, "but of incorruptible, by the Word of God *which liveth*." It is a living Word.

It is to be noted that this Scripture testifies that the seed of the living Word is not merely uncorrupted, but is "incorruptible." It partakes, therefore, of the nature of the "uncorruptible God" (Rom. 1:23).

This is the guaranty to us that the Word of God is not subject to the corrupting influences of the corrupted and decaying world into which it is come. It is the *only thing* which has not succumbed to the forces of decay and death which reign universally in the earth. Indeed, it has not been affected in the slightest degree by those forces. This has been pointed out at length in the foregoing pages; but the grand truth comes to us with peculiar force in connection with the passage in 1

Peter. We need not be at all concerned as to whether the truth of God, embodied by Him in His word, has been corrupted, for it is incorruptible. And by that Word they who believe are begotten again through the operation of the Holy Spirit. To them "the Spirit is life" (Rom. 8:10).

The same truth is declared in James 1:18, in the words, "Of His own will begat He us with the Word of Truth."

Such is the spiritual conception of the "sons of God." These are born, or begotten. In no other way is a "son" brought into existence save by being begotten of a father. The sons of God must be begotten of God. The Apostle John tells us that they are begotten, "not of the will of the flesh, nor of the will of man" (John 1:13). The Apostle James tells us that "of His own will" they are begotten. Therefore, though the process be inscrutably mysterious, there can be no doubt as to the fact. When the Word of God is truly "heard" and thereby received into a prepared heart, that word becomes truly a seed, spiritual and incorruptible in nature, which, when quickened by the Spirit of God, becomes the life-germ of a new creature—a son of God.

The same truth is very clearly taught in our Lord's explanation of His parable of the sower, to which reference has already been made. Inasmuch as we have His own interpretation of this parable, we need be in no uncertainty as to its meaning. He says, "Those by the wayside are they that hear; then cometh the Devil and taketh away *the Word out of their hearts,* lest they should *believe* and be saved" (Luke 8:12). And again: "But that on the good ground are they which, in *an honest and good heart,* having heard the Word keep it and bring forth fruit with patience."

The method of spiritual conception set forth in these Scriptures, which is effected in a manner quite analogous to natural conception, furnishes the explanation of the connection between "believing" and "life" referred to in many passages of Scripture. One of the most familiar of these is John 5:24

where the Lord Jesus states in the simplest language that the man who hears His Word and believes on Him who sent Him has everlasting life, and is passed out of death into life. Such a man receives the seed in his heart, and the seed is there quickened into life.

Indeed, the great purpose of the Written Word is to impart life—even eternal (that is to say divine) life—to those who are dead through trespasses and sins. The Gospel of John, which is devoted largely to the great subject of eternal life, and from which a large part of our information concerning it is derived, was "written that ye might believe that Jesus is the Christ, the Son of God and that *believing* ye might have *life* through his name" (John 20:31).

The same truth is declared in the familiar passage in Romans 10:9, which sets forth very definitely the special truth which constitutes the substance and marrow of God's revelation in His Word, and which He calls upon men to believe and obey through the preaching of the Gospel, namely that Jesus Christ, who died for sinners, has been *raised from the dead,* and that He is Lord of all, to the glory of God the Father.

The main point to be apprehended in this connection is that a certain state of preparedness of heart is necessary in order that the "good seed" of the Word may germinate and grow there. Such a prepared heart is described in Scripture as a *believing* heart. That prepared state is manifested when a man *believes God,* as Abraham did (Rom. 4:17) ; or, in other words, when a man is ready to receive the Word of God *as* the Word of God, as the Thessalonians did (1 Thess. 2:13).

When a man has been brought, by the operation of the Spirit of God, who is the "Spirit of LIFE in Christ Jesus" (Rom. 8:2, 10), into this state of preparation, then the Word of God, being received into the heart, acts as a seed falling into good soil. Though it be (as we might say) but the tiniest portion of God's truth as revealed in His Word which is thus received by faith, yet it suffices through His power as the means whereby He may quicken a dead soul. For surely the life of the Word is in every part thereof.

Such is the power of the *living* truth to impart life; and herein lies the difference between the truth which God has revealed in His Word, and truth which may be found elsewhere. For there is much truth which is not *living* truth. The multiplication table is truth; but it is not living truth. It has no quickening power. The theorems of geometry are truth; but they are not living truth. Never yet has any man been heard to testify that he had been the wretched and hopeless slave of sin, and had continued in spiritual darkness, fast bound in misery and vice until his eyes were opened by the great truth that two and two make four, or that three angles of a triangle are equal to two right angles; and that thereby his life had been transformed, his soul delivered from bondage, and his heart filled with joy and peace in believing. On the other hand, in the case of a true conversion, it may have been but the shortest and simplest statement of "the Word of the truth of the Gospel" (Col. 1:5) that was heard and believed, such as that "Christ died for the ungodly" (Rom. 5:6), yet it suffices, through the mighty power of Him who raised up Christ from among the dead, to quicken together with Christ a soul that previously was dead in trespasses and sins (Eph. 1:20; 2:5). Thus the Word of truth becomes, in some inscrutable way, the vehicle for imparting that life of which the risen Christ, the Incarnate Word, is the only Source. Eternal life for the individual soul begins through believing "the testimony of God" (1 Cor. 1:2), and the testimony of God which He has in grace given to perishing sinners that they may believe and be saved, is *"concerning His Son"* (Rom. 1:3; 1 John 5:10). "And this is the record [or testimony], that God hath given to us eternal life, and this life is in His Son" (1 John 5:11). Therefore it is written of those who experienced the new birth, "For ye are all the children of God by faith in Christ Jesus" (Gal. 3:26).

The teaching and preaching of the day are largely permeated by a notion to the effect that "science" is in some undefined way supplying to a greater or less extent new foundations for religious faith. We cannot, therefore, insist too strongly upon the *vital* difference (—for it *is* vital—being a difference upon which life depends) between truth revealed by God through His Word, and truth discovered by the investigations of man, and generally spoken of as "scientific" truth. Truth thus obtained has *no relation whatsoever* to faith and eternal life; and the effort to substitute it for, or to oppose it to, the truth revealed in God's Word as the basis of faith, must be ascribed to the activity of the "spirit of error."

Many unspiritual teachers in these last days, and many superficial readers of Scripture, deem it incredible that salvation, which is the beginning of the life of the risen Christ in the soul of a perishing man, should be wrought through an operation so apparently simple as that of receiving God's Word, through faith, into the heart.

The clear declarations of God's Word on this subject are indeed frequently ridiculed in pulpit utterances. But to such minds the germination of a seed by merely casting it into the ground would be equally incredible. These spiritually-blinded ones, wise in their own conceits, miss altogether the teaching of the Bible concerning the wonderful process of spiritual conception and generation, which, in view of the equally mysterious process of natural conception, should not be deemed "a thing incredible." "For the invisible things of Him from the creation of the world are clearly seen, being understood by the things that are made" (Rom. 1:20).

The passage in 1 Peter 1 sets forth, moreover, the fact that spiritual generation through the Word of God conforms to the great biological law stated with such emphatic iteration in the first chapter of Genesis, namely, that the life imparted is the same in kind as that of its source, all the characteristics of the latter being reproduced in it. Emphasis is laid on the fact that the seed is incorruptible, and that the Word, which is its source, is eternal. Moreover, as in John's Gospel, the new, incorruptible, and eternal life, which proceeds from spiritual conception by the Word of God, is put into direct contrast with the natural life or "flesh." "For," continues the Apostle Peter, "all flesh is as grass, and all the glory of *man* as the flower of grass." The prominent characteristic of grass is that it withereth, and of the flower of grass, or of plant life, is that it falleth away. "The grass withereth, and the flower thereof falleth away: but"—in direct contrast with this—"the Word of the Lord endureth for ever." So it does, and so do all they who are begotten of the incorruptible seed of the Word.

The passage closes with the unmistakably plain statement, "And this is the Word which, by the Gospel, is preached unto you."

The result of spiritual generation is, of course, a spiritual infant—a babe. Consequently the next words of the inspired Apostle are in full keeping with, and in confirmation of, the truth we have been considering. "Wherefore, laying aside all malice, and all guile, and hypocrisies, and envies, and all evil speakings" (which are characteristics of the "old man") "*as new-born babes*, desire the sincere milk of the Word, that ye may grow thereby" (1 Peter 2:1, 2). We all know that it is of the first importance that a babe should have appropriate nourishment in order that it may grow; but this belongs to the subject of spiritual nutrition, which will be considered later on.

Other Scriptures testify with equal clearness to the great and glorious truth that those who are begotten of the Spirit, through the incorruptible seed of the Word, receive a nature of the same sort as that of the Divine Source of their life. In the eighth chapter of Romans there is a section devoted to the "sons of God," in whom the Spirit dwells (verses 9-16); and of these it is declared that God predestinated them "to be conformed *to the image of His Son,* that He might be the first-born among many brethren" (verse 30).

Here the truth of likeness with the Son of God is broadly stated. Other passages declare specific features included in this general likeness. Thus 1 John 3:9 states that "whosoever is born of God doth not commit [or practice] sin; for His [God's] seed remaineth in him; and he cannot sin because he is born [begotten] of God. In this the children of God are manifest." The new nature which characterizes the new creature is one that cannot sin; and hence, when this new nature begins to manifest itself in the quickened soul, there is a struggle between its desires and those of the old nature ("the flesh"); for the flesh has desires against the Spirit, and the Spirit has desires against the flesh, and these are directly opposed, the one to the other (Gal. 5:17). Every one who has been begotten from above knows from experience what this struggle means.

Again, in 1 John 3:2, 3, it is stated that now, even at the present time, are we (believers) the sons of God, though we appear so little like it. What we shall be does not yet appear; but we know, upon the clear testimony of Scripture, that "when He shall appear we shall be *like Him;* for we shall see Him as He is."

These statements are so clear that it is not necessary to cite to those who believe the Word of God other passages which declare that spiritual procreation is according to the law repeated nine times in Genesis 1, "after his kind."

In closing this important section of our subject (which might be greatly amplified if our purpose were to treat exhaustively the great truth of spiritual generation) it will be profitable to notice briefly the close relation between the Written Word and the Incarnate Word in the matter of the impartation of spiritual life.

This truth brings before us the Son of God in His wonderful and unique character of the Source of Life to a world and to human beings, which had fallen under the power and dominion of death.

"Through one man [Adam] sin entered the world, and death through sin, and so death passed upon [*lit.* passed through to] all men" (Rom. 5:12). Thus death entered and established its universal sovereignty over all men. Such expressions as "death reigned," "sin reigned unto death" (Rom. 5:14, 17 21), state a fact whereof the evidences meet our eye whichevei way we look.

Therefore, after Adam's transgression and the ruin wrought by it, the most urgent need of the world was LIFE. To this end the Son of God became a partaker of flesh and blood, "that through death He might destroy him who had the power of death, that is the devil" (Heb. 2:14). "I am come," He said, "that they might have *life*" (John 10:10).

In the Gospel by John, the first thing asserted of Him, after setting forth His eternal Deity, and His mighty work as Creator, is the significant statement, "In Him was LIFE" (John 1:4). This is He who "cometh down from heaven and giveth life unto the world" (John 6:33).

We need not cite the many passages of Scripture which witness to Christ as the new Source of life to a world that had fallen under the power of death; but would call attention only to a few of those which connect Him directly with the wonderful process of spiritual generation.

The very first of all prophecies, that concerning the woman's "seed" (Gen. 3:15) is thus fulfilled in Him; and the designation "seed," thus at the very beginning applied to Him as coming in flesh and blood, carries with it the great promise of a new humanity which was to spring up from and out of Himself.

Again, as the "seed" of Abraham, He is the inheritor (for Himself and for His generations) of all the promises made "to Abraham and his seed." That we might not miss the meaning of this truth, so precious to those who, through faith, "are the children of Abraham" (Gal. 3:6), it is expressly stated as follows: "Now to Abraham *and his seed* were the promises made. He saith not, And to seeds, as of many; but as of ONE, And to thy SEED, which is Christ" (Gal. 3:16).

Finally, as David's seed He is the rightful Heir to the kingdom, which he will establish on the earth in the coming age. In promise of this there are many passages such as these: "I will raise up thy seed after thee, which shall be of thy sons; and I will establish his kingdom" (1 Chron. 17:11). "Upon David, and upon his seed and upon his house, and upon his throne, shall there be peace forever from the Lord" (1 Kings 2:33). "I have made a covenant with My chosen, I have sworn unto David My servant, thy seed will I establish forever, and build up thy throne to all generations" (Psa. 89:3, 4). "His seed shall endure forever, and his throne as the sun before Me" (Psa. 89:36).

Thus Christ is set forth as the Seed of the woman, as the Seed of Abraham, and as the Seed of David.

But the great purpose of a seed, and its marvelous inherent power, is to reproduce its kind; and the designation "seed" as applied to the Son of Man has this significance also. He Himself takes up this great lesson when he refers to Himself as the kernel of wheat, saying: "Verily, verily, I say unto you, Except a corn [kernel] of wheat fall into the ground and die, it abideth alone; but if it die, it bringeth forth much fruit" (John 12:24).

Thus the One who alone had a title to live as a man of flesh and blood, laid *that* life down, submitting voluntarily to the power of death, in order that, instead of dwelling forever "alone" (as man) He might bring forth "much fruit." These are His generations, the "many sons" which He brings into glory (Heb. 2:10), the "children" of whom He speaks saying, "Behold I, and the children which God hath given me" (Heb. 2:13).

If we keep in mind the fact that the grains of wheat in the ear are all reproductions of the original seed, we shall see how forcibly and beautifully the parable of the "corn of wheat" teaches the lesson of spiritual generation. The life in those who have been quickened together with Christ (Eph. 2:5) is truly *His* life reproduced in them by the Holy Spirit, who is the Spirit of life in Christ Jesus, and whose law sets us free from the law of sin and death (Rom. 8:2). We may thus say, "Christ who is our life" (Col. 3:4); and as this new life unfolds itself in the being of the believer, and manifests the characteristics of the One who is its source, the former is able also to say, "For me to live is Christ" (Phil. 1:21).

Whether, therefore, we are regarding the Written Word or the Incarnate Word, it is true (as has been well said) that "the Word" is the whole matter or substance of what God has revealed; but it is also true that any portion of that matter or substance which enters into a human heart, and which, as a seed, germinates and performs there the stupendous miracle of reproduction, is also the Word, imparting life "after his kind" —life incorruptible and everlasting as the Word itself.

Thus, in the highest sense of which we can take knowledge, the Word of God is a "Word of Life"—living and reproducing its kind; and thus is being fulfilled the promise to Him who died that we might live, of Whom it was said of old "He shall see *His seed*, He shall prolong his days, and the pleasure of the Lord shall prosper in His hand. He shall see of the travail of His soul and shall be satisfied" (Isa. 53:10, 11).

The believer, too, may say with David, "As for me, I will behold Thy face in righteousness: I shall be satisfied, when I awake, with Thy likeness" (Psa. 17:15). That will be glory for us; but, what is more important, it will be glory also for Him.

XI. THE LIFE-SUSTAINING WORD

The life possessed by human beings is not only a derived life, that is, a life obtained from an external source, but it is a dependent life, requiring continual sustenance. It must be sustained by constant and suitable nutrition, received into the body at short intervals. Man's strength whereof he boasts, and indeed his very existence in the body, are dependent on food, and this food itself must be organic matter, that is to say, matter which has once been living. The fact of this dependence upon food, and upon food which man is utterly unable to make for himself out of inorganic matter, though all the materials are within his reach, should teach him a lesson in humility; but it seems not to have that effect.

We say that man is utterly unable to produce food-stuff though all the materials whereof it is composed are abundantly at hand. This is a pertinent and obvious fact, though one whereof little account is taken. God has imparted to the lowly plant the ministry of supplying food to all the animal creation, and has taught to it, and to it alone, the marvelous secret of converting the minerals of the earth and air—inert, lifeless elements, utterly incapable of furnishing nourishment to animals or man—into living tissue, endowed with the property of nourishing living creatures higher in the scale of life. "He causeth the grass to grow for the cattle, and herb for the service of man; that *he may bring forth food out of the earth*" (Psa. 104:14).

The humble vegetable organism knows how to extract the nitrogen from the earth, and the carbon from the carbon dioxide in the atmosphere, and to combine these, in exactly the proper proportions, with the oxygen and hydrogen in water, and with traces of lime and other elements, forming with the aid of heat and light from the sun, living tissue, suitable and necessary for food. This wonderful operation of chemical synthesis is carried on by the modest vegetable so unostentatiously as to attract little notice; and though it has been under the observation of inquisitive and imitative man for thousands of years he has not the faintest notion of how it is done. All the learning and skill of all the chemists in the world, with the resources of all the laboratories in the world, could not produce an ounce of food, though the elements out of which it is made exist everywhere, and in the greatest abundance.

But God, having imparted physical life to His creatures, has also made ample provision for the maintenance of that life, by supplying through the inscrutable synthesis carried on unceasingly by the vegetable kingdom, abundant food, capable, when taken into the body and properly assimilated, of supplying the waste that is constantly in progress in every part of the body, and of maintaining the strength thereof.

Furthermore, if the conversion of minerals into food-stuff by the members of the vegetable kingdom is a process displaying the marvelous wisdom of God, the process of digestion and nutrition is not less so. Nothing could be more improbable than that food, taken into the body by way of the mouth, should, without any attention or supervision from the tenant of that body, be digested, the valuable parts separated from the worthless, the latter discharged from the body, the former converted into tissue, muscle, bone, sinew, nerve-cell, blood-corpuscle, hair, nails, etc., and distributed automatically throughout the body, each to the place requiring it, and all in due proportion.

In this we have again a process far transcending the comprehension of the most learned men, who must eat and be nourished like other men, and who are equally ignorant of the process whereby their lives are sustained, and whereby they gain the strength which they use to deny God and glorify man.

Men boast in these days of their "independence," and make much of "self-reliance." But this is the height of presumptuous folly; for man is a most helplessly dependent creature, not even able, like the plant, to prepare his own food from the mineral elements, but dependent daily upon living creatures much lower than himself in the scale of being. And so far from having a basis for self-reliance, he does not know how to conduct the simplest of the vital processes of his own body. If his Creator, of whom principally man loves to fancy himself independent, should turn over to him the operation of the least of those essential processes for the briefest time, the poor creature would miserably perish.

As with the physical life, so is it with the spiritual life of those who have been begotten again of the incorruptible seed of the Word. These spiritual beings require appropriate food; and God has abundantly provided for this need. In studying the important subject of spiritual nutrition we shall learn again the relation between Christ, the Incarnate Word, and the Written Word. Both are spoken of repeatedly as food for the children of God.

The third, fourth and fifth chapters of the Gospel by John treat of the imparting of eternal life as the free gift of God through Jesus Christ, the Son of God, to all who believe on Him; and the sixth chapter treats of spiritual nutrition. Therein, after feeding the multitude miraculously, thus showing Himself as the one by whose power food is multiplied in the earth, He reveals Himself as "the Bread of Life." Twice He says, "I am that bread of life" (verses 35 and 48) and in verse 33, "For the bread of God is He which cometh down from heaven, and giveth life unto the world." He Who gives the life is the One who also sustains it. Again He says, "I am the living bread which came down from heaven" (verse 51). And of His words He says, "It is the spirit that quickeneth; the flesh profiteth nothing; *the words* that I speak unto you, they are spirit, and they are life" (verse 63).

These sayings to the natural mind are, of course, meaningless; but they are addressed to faith. "How can this man give us His flesh to eat?" is the question which the unbelieving heart asks. How Christ can impart Himself to sustain the "inner man" is a question to which no answer can now be had. The process is incomprehensible to man. But we have seen that the process of physical nutrition is equally beyond human comprehension and contrary to all *a priori* probabilities.

Looking more particularly at what is said in this connection concerning the written or spoken Word of God we find that the Word of God is "living" in the sense that, like other living substance, it has the property of furnishing nutrition, and thereby sustaining life. It is a life-sustaining Word. But here a notable difference attracts our attention. Physical food comes up out of the earth (Psa. 104:14), while spiritual food comes down out of heaven. (John 6:50.)

Reference has already been made to the fact that, after setting forth the great truth of spiritual conception and generation through the incorruptible seed of the Word of God, the Apostle Peter enjoins attention to spiritual nutrition. "Wherefore," he says, "as new-born babes desire the sincere milk of the word that ye may grow thereby" (1 Peter 2:1, 2). Evidently his Lord's threefold injunction, "Feed My sheep," "Feed My lambs," had impressed upon him the importance of spiritual nutrition. But proper feeding requires appetite for wholesome food, and so he seeks to excite a desire in young Christians for that whereby they may grow. And he immediately connects the Word with Christ saying, "If so be ye have tasted that the Lord is gracious."

The importance of nourishing and sustaining the new life received upon coming to Christ, and the unhappy consequences which always result from neglect of the appropriate diet, have been so often and so forcibly stated by the servants of Christ that it seems hardly necessary to dwell upon this matter. What our subject specially calls for is to note the correspondence between God's way of sustaining man's physical life by food derived from a living source, and His way of sustaining the believer's spiritual life by food from a living source, that is to say from the living Word.

The passages which present the Word of God as the food for His children are very familiar; and in bringing them to mind again we would impress it upon our readers that these statements are not to be taken as if they were poetical or figurative, but as very literal, practical and immensely important. In making man it was not God's plan that he should live by bread, or physical food alone, but "by every word that proceedeth out of the mouth of the Lord" (Deut. 8:3). The manna was given to His people in the wilderness to teach them this lesson, and that they might learn their dependence upon God. Hence this passage was used by the Second Man in His combat with the devil in the wilderness, it being the purpose of the latter to inculcate in man the idea of independence of God. Thus did the Man Jesus Christ, with the Sword of the Spirit, strike sure and true at the central purpose of His great adversary.

It is by *every* word of God that man is to be fed. No part of the Bible can be neglected without loss and detriment; and it will be observed that there is, in the Bible, a variety of spiritual nutriment analogous to the variety of physical food which God has provided for the needs of the physical man. If there be milk for babes, there is also strong food for those who are mature. And there is the penalty of arrested growth paid by those who remain content with the relatively weak diet suitable for infants, who know, perhaps, only that their sins are forgiven; as the Apostle John says: "I write unto you, little children, because your sins are forgiven you" (1 John 2:12). But those who have to be fed on a milk diet, that is to say, the simplest elementary truths of the Gospel, are unskillful in the word of righteousness. Infants cannot do anything for themselves, much less can they prepare food, or render any service to others. Hence the Apostle Paul, writing to the Hebrews, upbraids some of them because, at a time when they ought to have been teachers, they had need to be taught again the first principles, and were become "such as have need of milk and not of strong food. For every one that useth milk is unskillful in the word of righteousness: for he is a babe. But strong food belongeth to them that are of full age" (Heb. 5:12-14).

Jeremiah says, "Thy words were found and I did eat them" (Jer. 15:16). Thereby he found spiritual strength to sustain him in his most difficult and trying ministry, from which, because of his timid and sensitive disposition, he shrank back in agony of soul. To be a good and effective minister of Christ it is necessary that one be well nourished through partaking largely of the abundant spiritual food which the living Word supplies. Thus Paul admonished his child in the faith, Timothy, to whom he wrote, "If thou put the brethren in remembrance of these things, thou shalt be a good minister of Jesus Christ, *nourished up in the words of faith and of good doctrine*" (1 Tim. 4:6).

One practical point with reference to the process of nutrition should be noted. While the living creature cannot comprehend the process, and has no part whatever in supervising it, or carrying it on, and while he is therefore not responsible for the results, the process cannot be carried on unless he takes the food into his being and properly masticates it. Therefore, up to the point of swallowing the food, the living being is responsible, and his volition is exercised. After that the process passes beyond his knowledge and control. Food may be of the best quality, and may be in greatest abundance, but it imparts no nourishment while it remains in the pantry, or on the table.

In like manner the responsibility is with the child of God to partake of the spiritual food so plentifully provided, and to meditate therein day and night (Psa. 1:2). Meditation upon what is read is to spiritual nutrition what mastication is to physical nutrition; and it takes time. The result, however, is ample compensation for time so occupied, for we read of him who observes this simple rule of spiritual dietation that "He shall be like a tree planted by rivers of water, that bringeth forth his fruit in his season, his leaf also shall not wither; and whatsoever he doeth shall prosper" (Psa. 1:3). It means a fruitful life, a vigorous and healthful life, and a prosperous life.

These results are just as sure to follow obedience to the laws of spiritual diet as physical nutrition is to follow attention to the proper reception of material food; and the contrary results are just as sure to follow neglect of those laws in the one case as in the other. The natural mind would be likely to demand an explanation; but faith does not require to know the process, it being sufficient to hear the command. If one refused to partake of his natural food until instructed as to the process of digestion he would starve. In each case the process is inscrutable, but the fact is certain.

XII. THE LIFE-TRANSFORMING WORD

FEEDING upon the Word of God, the bread of life, must necessarily be beneficial to the whole man, including his intellectual and physical being as well as his spiritual.

Much deference is paid in these days to the "powers of the mind." Intellectual prowess is what wins the victories in the fierce commercial struggle of the times. Business men are, of course, keen to take advantage of this condition, as may be seen by the many and costly advertisements of "brain foods;" and many millions of dollars are annually acquired by the shrewd exploiters of these preparations. This, of course, could not be unless there were multitudes who give heed to the assurance that, by the use of the advertised article, it is possible to produce "a new set of brains."

The Bible does not speak of a new set of brains, but it does say to believers, "Be renewed in the spirit of your mind" (Eph. 4:23), and, "Be not conformed to this world [or age], but be ye transformed by the renewing of your mind" (Rom. 12:2). The new man requires a new mind, and provision is made to that end. The old mind, with all its habits of self-occupation (a sure breeder of unhappiness and discontent), its morbid tendencies, its craving for excitement and sensation, its imaginations, appetites, tastes, inclinations and desires, and every high thing that exalteth itself against the knowledge of

God, is to be displaced, and a new mind substituted; for godliness has the promise of the vigor of the life that now is, as well as of that which is to come.

How, then, is this injunction to be carried out? It is of importance to millions of anxious souls to have a clear answer to this question. And it may be had. The every-day incidents and the atmosphere amid which the average man and woman spend their time are such as to produce mental disturbances and disorders to an extent which, if understood, and if anything could impress this thoughtless and excited age, would create wide-spread alarm. It was stated recently that there were twenty-eight thousand inmates of the insane asylums of New York State (a single state of the Union) prior to October, 1907, and that in six months following the industrial convulsion of that month the number of inmates was increased by three thousand. The startling increase in the number of sucides adds its forcible testimony; and the frequency with which one encounters cases of mental depression, insomnia, melancholia, and other nervous disorders, tells of wide-spread and insidious foes which attack the seat of reason, and which call for methods and means of defense and repair which are beyond the resources of medicine.

The writer knows by experience the indescribable horrors of depressed and morbid mental states, and knows, too, what a transformation is effected by the "renewing of the mind" according to the Biblical injunction. Full provision is made for this marvelous transformation, and the conditions wherein it is effected are plainly set forth and are accessible to every believer.

In this case the study of the word used in the command ("be transformed") will make us acquainted with the conditions essential to the transformation. The word in question seems to have been set apart by the Holy Spirit for the purpose of teaching the important and wonderful secret of the transformation of the believer, during his existence in the body, into the likeness of Christ; so that all believers might be able to say with Paul, "We have the mind of Christ."

It will, therefore, surely repay the reader to note carefully the usages of this particular word. Its first occurrence is in the Gospel narratives of the Transfiguration of Jesus Christ, and is in fact the very word there translated "transfigured" (Matt. 17:2; Mark 9:2). The word is literally "metamorphosed." "His face did shine as the sun, and His raiment was white as the light." This may well serve to teach the nature of the change contemplated. It is one that brings the radiance of heaven into the mind and tinges even the commonplace things with a glow of heavenly light.

The next occurrence of the word is, as we have already seen, in Romans 12:2, where believers are enjoined to be not cut out on the pattern of this age, but to be metamorphosed or transfigured by the renewing of their minds.

The third and last occurrence of the word tells us plainly *how* this great transformation is brought about. For the Bible is a very practical book. It comes, moreover, from One Who understands perfectly the limitations of man, Who knows and declares that the latter is, in his natural state, "without strength," that is to say, utterly impotent (Rom. 5:6). We may be sure, therefore, that when God calls upon the quickened soul to do a thing, He puts the means required for it within His reach. And so, in these plain words we read the conditions requisite for effecting the desired transformation: "We all, with unveiled face, beholding as in a mirror the glory of the Lord, *are changed* into the same image from glory to glory, even as by the Spirit of the Lord" (2 Cor. 3:18).

The word here translated "are changed" is the same word (metamorphosed or transfigured) used in the other passages cited; and these are the only occurrences of that word in the Bible.

The teaching is very clear. When the Jews read the Word of God a veil is over their hearts, their minds being blinded (verse 14). Or, as stated in Romans 11:25, "blindness in part is happened to Israel, until the fullness of the Gentiles be come in." Hence, they do not behold there Him of whom the Scriptures testify. But, for us who believe, the veil is done away in Christ, and consequently, all we beholding are transfigured into the same image by the Divine and irresistible operation of the Holy Spirit.

If, when we look into the Word of God. *we do not see Christ there,* we look to no purpose, for He is everywhere in the Book.

Let it be carefully noted that this transformation is not the work of the man who beholds Christ in the Word; for the process is carried on while the former is not occupied with himself at all, or with his transformation, but is absorbed in the contemplation of the glory of the Lord. The transformation is effected by the power of the Spirit of God; and we may learn from this passage the important lesson that occupation with, and concern about, the work of the Spirit in us can only hinder that work. Let it suffice us that He Who has begun a good work *in us* will perform it until the day of Christ. (Phil. 1:6.) Our part, and it should be also our delight, is to be continually beholding or contemplating the glory of the Lord; and while so doing we *"are* changed" into the same image, and all the faster if we are unconscious of ourselves.

Let it be also noted that the transformation is a gradual operation, calling for steadfastness in contemplating the Object placed before us by the Holy Spirit. Little by little, as our gaze is fixed upon Him, the old traits and dispositions which are unlike Him are replaced by His own characteristics. Thus the work proceeds "from glory to glory." The conformation to His image, which is God's purpose for all the sons of God (Rom. 8:29), is not accomplished, as some would have it, by an instantaneous transfiguration, a convulsive upheaval and displacement of the old nature, brought about by working one's emotions into an ecstatic state; but is accomplished gradually while the believer is continually occupied with Christ ("beholding"). There is no hysterical short-cut to the desired result. For Christ must be known from the Written Word under the tuition of the Holy Spirit; and the process should continue during the whole term of the believer's existence in the body.

Thus the living Word becomes the regulator and transformer of the minds of those who diligently seek it. Under its potent influence confusion of thought, perplexities, depressed mental states, and other hurtful conditions are dissipated, and the serene tranquillity and repose of the mind of Christ are reproduced in those who are redeemed by His precious blood.

We are passing through the domain of death, the country of the last enemy that is to be destroyed, and who has put all things in this scene under his feet (1 Cor. 15:26, 27). On every hand our eyes meet the unmistakable evidences of the supreme sovereignty of death. But in this domain of death there is a Living Word—a Living Word in a dying world. The forces of corruption and decay cannot fasten upon it, and it laughs at the attacks of its enemies.

But that Word is here, not merely to manifest life, but rather to impart life to those who are perishing, and to bring them into vital contact with the new Life-Source of humanity, the Son of God, the Second Man, the Lord from Heaven, Who liveth and was dead, and behold He is alive forevermore, and has the keys of death and of Hades (1 Cor. 15:47; Rev. 1:18). He, as Man, has crossed the gulf between the realm of death and that of life. To that end He became "a partaker of flesh and blood," not to improve flesh and blood, but in order that "through death He might destroy him that had the power of death, that is, the devil; and deliver them who through fear of death were all their lifetime subject to bondage" (Heb. 2:14, 15). Having Himself crossed that gulf

He is the Way of life to all who believe on Him, who, having heard His Word—the Word of life—have likewise passed out of death into life (John 5:24).

This is the wonderful provision of God for the deliverance of dying men. In order that they might not die, and because God wills not that any should perish (2 Peter 3:9), He has sent into this dying world a Word of Life. For God is not the God of the dead, but of the living (Matt. 22:32).

In comparison with the provision of divine wisdom, power and grace, from the God who quickeneth the dead (Rom. 4:17), how pitifully foolish and vain are all human schemes for the betterment, reform and cultivation of that old man who has fallen under the sovereignty of death! Men are very ingenious, but none has yet brought forward a scheme for abolishing or escaping death, or for raising the dead. Without that, of what avail are plans of improvement? And what end do they serve but to blind men's minds to the truth that they are dead, and so are beyond all but the power of a God who raises the dead? Surely these schemes are the most successful devices of "the god of this age."

What men need is not morality, but life; not to make death respectable, but to receive the gift of eternal life; not decent interment, but a pathway out of the realm of death. Many men have brought forward their schemes for the "uplift of humanity" (though the results thereof are not yet discernible); but there is only One Man who makes, or ever made, the offer of eternal life. None other has ever said, "I am the resurrection and the life; he that believeth on Me though he were dead yet shall he live. And whosoever liveth and believeth on Me shall never die" (John 11:25, 26). He only claims to be the "Fountain of Living Waters" (Jer. 2:13; John 4:14; 7:37), and says to all who are suffering the thirst of death, "Come unto Me and drink" (John 7:37).

Therefore, in concluding these reflections upon the Living Word, we obey the command, "Let him that heareth say,

Come," and would lovingly repeat the last invitation of grace recorded in the Word of Life:

> "LET HIM THAT IS ATHIRST COME.
> AND WHOSOEVER WILL,
> LET HIM TAKE
> THE WATER OF LIFE
> FREELY."

(Rev. 22:17.)

CHAPTER VIII

IS THERE A GOD?

BY REV. THOMAS WHITELAW, M. A., D. D.,
KILMARNOCK, SCOTLAND

Whether or not there is a supreme personal intelligence, infinite and eternal, omnipotent, omniscient and omnipresent, the Creator, upholder and ruler of the universe, immanent in and yet transcending all things, gracious and merciful, the Father and Redeemer of mankind, is surely the profoundest problem that can agitate the human mind. Lying as it does at the foundation of all man's religious beliefs—as to responsibility and duty, sin and salvation, immortality and future blessedness, as to the possibility of a revelation, of an incarnation, of a resurrection, as to the value of prayer, the credibility of miracle, the reality of providence,—with the reply given to it are bound up not alone the temporal and eternal happiness of the individual, but also the welfare and progress of the race. Nevertheless, to it have been returned the most varied responses.

The Atheist, for example, asserts that there is no God. The Agnostic professes that he cannot tell whether there is a God or not. The Materialist boasts that he does not need a God, that he can run the universe without one. The (Bible) Fool wishes there was no God. The Christian answers that he cannot do without a God.

I. THE ANSWER OF THE ATHEIST

"THERE IS NO GOD"

In these days it will hardly do to pass by this bold and confident negation by simply saying that the theoretical atheist is an altogether exceptional specimen of humanity, and that his audacious utterance is as much the outcome of ignorance as of impiety. When one meets in the "Hibbert Journal" from the pen of its editor such a statement as this: "Society abounds with earnest and educated persons who have lost faith in a living personal God, and see their fellows and foresee themselves passing out of life entirely without hope," and when Blatchford in the English "Clarion" writes: "There is no Heavenly Father watching tenderly over us, His creatures, He is the baseless shadow of a wistful dream," it becomes apparent that theoretical atheism is not extinct, even in cultured circles, and that some observations with regard to it may still be needful. Let these observations be the following:

1. *Belief that there is no God does not amount to a demonstration that no God is.* Neither, it is true, does belief that God is prove the truth of the proposition except to the individual in whose heart that belief has been awakened by the Divine Spirit. To another than him it is destitute of weight as an argument in support of the theistic position. At the same time it is of importance, while conceding this, to emphasize the fact that disbelief in the existence of a Divine Being is not equivalent to a demonstration that there is no God.

2. *Such a demonstration is from the nature of the case impossible.* Here again it may be true as Kant contends that reason cannot demonstrate (that is, by logic) the existence of God; but it is equally true, as the same philosopher admits, that reason can just as little disprove the existence of God. It was well observed by the late Prof. Calderwood of the Edinburgh University that "the divine existence is a truth so plain that it needs no proof, as it is a truth so high that it admits of none." But the situation is altered when it comes to a positive denial of that existence. The idea of God once formed in the mind, whether as an intuition or as a deduction, cannot be laid aside without convincing evidence that it is delusive and unreal. And such evidence cannot be produced. As Dr. Chalmers long ago observed, before one can positively assert

that there is no God, he must arrogate to himself the wisdom and ubiquity of God. He must explore the entire circuit of the universe to be sure that no God is there. He must have interrogated all the generations of mankind and all the hierarchies of heaven to be certain they had never heard of a God.

In short, as Chalmers puts it, "For man not to know God, he has only to sink beneath the level of our common nature. But to deny God he must be God himself."

3. *Denial of the divine existence is not warranted by inability to discern traces of God's presence in the universe.* Prof. Huxley, who once described himself in a letter to Charles Kingsley as "exactly what the Christian world called, and, so far as he could judge, was justified in calling him, an atheist and infidel," appeared to think it was. "I cannot see," he wrote, "one shadow or tittle of evidence that the Great Unknown underlying the phenomena of the universe stands to us in the relation of a Father, loves us and cares for us as Christianity asserts." Blatchford also with equal emphasis affirms: "I cannot believe that God is a personal God who interferes in human affairs. I cannot see in science, or in experience, or in history, any signs of such a God or of such intervention." Neither of these writers, however, it may be presumed, would on reflection advance their incapacity to perceive the footprints or hear the voices of the Creator as proof that no Creator existed, any more than a blind man would maintain there was no sun because he could not see it, or a deaf man would contend there was no sound because he never heard it. The incapacity of Huxley and Blatchford to either see or hear God may, and no doubt does, serve as an explanation of their atheistical creed, but assuredly it is no justification of the same, since a profounder reasoner than either has said: "The invisible things of God since the creation of the world are clearly seen, being perceived through the things that are made, even His everlasting power and divinity; so that they [who believe not] are without excuse."

4. *The majority of mankind, not in Christian countries only, but also in heathen lands, from the beginning of the world onward, have believed in the existence of a Supreme Being.* They may frequently, as Paul says, have "changed the glory of the incorruptible God into an image made like to corruptible man, and to birds and four-footed beasts and creeping things;" but deeply seated in their natures, debased though these were by sin, lay the conception of a Superhuman Power to whom they owed allegiance and whose favor was indispensable to their happiness. It was a saying of Plutarch that in his day a man might travel the world over without finding a city without temples and gods; in our day isolated cases have been cited of tribes—the Andaman Islanders by Sir John Lubbock, and the Fuegians, by Admiral Fitzroy—who have exhibited no signs that they possessed a knowledge either of God or of religion. But it is at least open to question whether the investigators on whose testimony such instances are advanced did not fail to discover traces of what they sought either through want of familiarity with the language of the natives, or through starting with the presupposition that the religious conceptions of the natives must be equally exalted with their own. In any case, on the principle that exceptions prove the rule, it may be set down as incontrovertible that the vast majority of mankind have possessed some idea of a Supreme Being; so that if the truth or falsehood of the proposition, "There is no God," is to be determined by the counting of votes, the question is settled in the negative, that is, against the atheist's creed.

II. THE CONFESSION OF THE AGNOSTIC

"I CANNOT TELL WHETHER THERE IS A GOD OR NOT"

Without dogmatically affirming that there is no God, the Agnostic practically insinuates that whether there is a God or not, nobody can tell and it does not much matter—that man with his loftiest powers of thought and reason and with his best appliances of research, cannot come to speech with God or obtain reliable information concerning Him, can only build up an imaginary picture, like an exaggerated or overgrown man, and call that God—in other words, can only make a God after his own image and in his own likeness without being sure whether any corresponding reality stands behind it, or even if there is, whether that reality can be said to come up to the measure of a Divine Being or be entitled to be designated God. The agnostic does not deny that behind the phenomena of the universe there may be a Power, but whether there is or not, and if there is, whether that Power is a Force or a Person, are among the things unknown and unknowable, so that practically, God being outside and beyond the sphere of man's knowledge, it can never be of consequence whether there be a God or not— it can never be more than a subject of curious speculation, like that which engages the leisure time of some astronomers, whether there be inhabitants in the planet Mars or not.

As thus expounded, the creed of the agnostic is open to serious objections.

1. *It entirely ignores the spiritual factor in man's nature,* —either denying the soul's existence altogether, or viewing it as merely a function of the body; or, if regarding it as a separate entity distinct from the body, and using its faculties to apprehend and reason about external objects, yet denying its ability to discern spiritual realities. On either alternative, it is contradicted by both Scripture and experience. From Genesis to Revelation the Bible proceeds upon the assumption that man is more than "six feet of clay," "curiously carved and wondrously articulated," that "there is a spirit in man," and that this spirit has power not only to apprehend things unseen but to come into touch with God and to be touched by Him, or, in Scripture phrase, to see and know God and to be seen and known by Him. Nor can it be denied that man is conscious of being more than animated matter, and of having power to apprehend more than comes within the range of his senses, for

he can and does entertain ideas and cherish feelings that have at least no direct connection with the senses, and can originate thoughts, emotions and volitions that have not been excited by external objects. And as to knowing God, Christian experience attests the truth of Scripture when it says that this knowledge is no figure of speech or illusion of the mind, but a sober reality. It is as certain as language can make it that Abraham and Jacob, Moses and Joshua, Samuel and David, Isaiah and Jeremiah, had no doubt whatever that they knew God and were known of Him; and multitudes of Christians exist to-day whom it would not be easy to convince that they could not and did not know God, although not through the medium of the senses or even of the pure reason.

2. *It takes for granted that things cannot be adequately known unless they are fully known.* This proposition, however, cannot be sustained in either Science or Philosophy, in ordinary life or in religious experience. Science knows there are such things as life (vegetable and animal), and force (electricity and magnetism for example), but confesses its ignorance of what life and force are as to their essence—all that is understood about them being their properties and effects. Philosophy can expound the laws of thought, but is baffled to unriddle the secret of thought itself, how it is excited in the soul by nerve-movements caused by impressions from without, and how it can express itself by originating counter movements in the body. In ordinary life human beings know each other adequately for all practical purposes while aware that in each there are depths which the other cannot fathom, each being shut off from the other by what Prof. Dods calls "the limitations of personality." Nor is the case different in religious experience. The Christian, like Paul, may have no difficulty in saying, "Christ liveth in me," but he cannot explain to himself or others, how. Hence the inference must be rejected that because the finite mind cannot fully comprehend the infinite, therefore it cannot know the

infinite at all, and must remain forever uncertain whether there is a God or not. Scripture, it should be noted, does not say that any finite mind can fully find out God; but it does say that men may know God from the things which He has made, and more especially from the Image of Himself which has been furnished in Jesus Christ, so that if they fail to know Him, they are without excuse.

3. *It virtually undermines the foundations of morality.* For if one cannot tell whether there is a God or not, how can one be sure that there is any such thing as morality? The distinctions between right and wrong which one makes in the regulation of his conduct may be altogether baseless. It is true a struggle may be made to keep them up out of a prudential regard for future safety, out of a desire to be on the winning side in case there should be a God. But it is doubtful if the imperative "ought" would long resound within one's soul, were the conclusion once reached that no one could tell whether behind the phenomena of nature or of consciousness there was a God or not. Morality no more than religion can rest on uncertainties.

III. THE BOAST OF THE MATERIALIST

"I DO NOT NEED A GOD, I CAN RUN THE UNIVERSE WITHOUT ONE"

Only grant him to begin with an ocean of atoms and a force to set them in motion and he will forthwith explain the mystery of creation. If we have what he calls a scientific imagination, he will let us see the whole process,—the molecules or atoms circling and whirling, dancing and skipping, combining and dividing, advancing and retiring, selecting partners and forming groups, closing in their ranks and opening them out again, building up space-filling masses, growing hotter and hotter as they wheel through space, whirling swifter and swifter, till through sheer velocity they swell and burst, after which they break up into fragments and cool down into a complete planetary system.

Inviting us to light upon this globe, the materialist will show us how through long centuries, mounting up to millions of years, the various rocks which form the earth's crust were deposited. Nay, if we will dive with him to the bottom of the ocean he will point out the first speck of dead matter that sprang into life, protoplasm, though he cannot tell when or how. Having startled us with this, he will lead us up the Great Staircase of Nature with its 26 or 27 steps, and tell us how on this step the vegetable grew into an animal, and how after many more steps the animal became a man, and thus the whole evolutionary drama will be unrolled.

Concerning this theory of the universe, however, it is pertinent to make these remarks:

1. Taken at its full value, with unquestioning admission of the alleged scientific facts on which it is based, *it is at best only an inference or working hypothesis, which may or may not be true and which certainly cannot claim to be beyond dispute.*

2. So far from securing universal acceptance, *it has been repudiated by scientists of the highest repute.* "The Kant-Laplace theory of the origin of the solar system by the whirling masses of nebulous matter, till rings flew off and became the worlds we see," says a German writer, "can no more be defended by any scientist" (Neue Kirchliche Zeitschrift, 1905, p. 957). The attempt to explain in this way the origin of the universe, says Merz, can be described as "belonging to the romance of science" (European Thought in the 19th Cent., p. 285). Indeed Laplace himself put it forward "with great reserve, and only as a likely suggestion" (ibid., p. 285). As regards the derivation of man from the lower animals, it is enough to remember that the late Prof. Virchow maintained that "we cannot designate it as a revelation of science, that man descends from the ape or from any other animal" (Nature, Dec. 8, 1877); that Prof. Paulsen, speaking of Haeckel, says "he belongs already to a dead generation," and calls his theory

of materialistic evolution "an example of incredible frivolity in the treatment of serious problems" (see Princeton Review, Oct., 1906, p. 443); that Prof. Von E. Pfenningsdorf declares "the materialistic explanation of the world to be untenable" (see Theologische Rundschau, 1905, p. 85); that Fleischman in his book, "Die Desendenz Theorie," denies evolution altogether; that Dr. Rudolph Otto admits that "popular Darwinism (Darwinisms Vulgaris)," by which he means "that man is really descended from monkeys," is "theoretically worthless" (Naturalism and Religion, p. 94); and that Prof. Pettigrew of St. Andrew's University writes: "There is, it appears to me, no proof that man is directly descended from the ape, and indirectly from the mollusc or monad" (Design in Nature, Vol. III, p. 1324).

3. *Conceding all that evolutionists demand,* that from matter and force the present cosmos has been developed, *the question remains, whether this excludes or renders unnecessary the intervention of God as the prime mover in the process.* If it does, one would like to know whence matter and force came. For the atoms or molecules, formerly supposed to be ultimates and indivisible, have now been proved by science to be manufactured and capable of being analyzed into myriads of electrons; and it is hardly supposable that they manufactured themselves. Moreover, one would like to know how these atoms or electrons came to attract and repel one another and form combinations, if there was no original cause behind them and no aim before them? If even matter be construed as a form of energy, or force, the difficulty is not removed, since force in its last analysis is the output of will and will implies intelligence or conscious personality.

From this conclusion escape is impossible, except by assuming that matter and force existed from eternity; in which case they must have contained in themselves the germs of life and intelligence—in other words must themselves have been God—in *posse,* if not in *esse,* in potentiality if not in reality.

But against this pantheistical assumption must ever lie the difficulty of explaining how or why the God that was latent in matter or force was so long in arriving at consciousness in man, and how before man appeared, the latent God being unconscious could have directed the evolutionary process which fashioned the cosmos. Till these inquiries are satisfactorily answered, it will not be possible to accept the materialistic solution of the universe.

IV. THE DESIRE OF THE (BIBLE) FOOL

"I WISH THERE WAS NO GOD"

Only a few words need be given to this rejoinder, as the fool does not say in his intellect, but only in his heart, there is no God. In his case the wish is father to the thought. Secretly persuaded in his mind that there is a God, he would much rather there had been none. It would suit him better. But the fact that he cannot advance to a categorical denial of the Divine Existence is an indirect witness to the innate conviction which the human heart possesses, that there is a God in whom man lives and moves and has his being.

V. THE DECLARATION OF THE CHRISTIAN

"I CANNOT DO WITHOUT A GOD, WITHOUT A GOD I CAN NEITHER ACCOUNT FOR THE UNIVERSE AROUND ME, NOR EXPLAIN JESUS CHRIST ABOVE ME, NOR UNDERSTAND THE SPIRITUAL EXPERIENCES WITHIN ME"

1. *Without a God the material universe around the Christian is and remains a perplexing enigma.*

When he surveys that portion of the universe which lies open to his gaze, he sees marks of wisdom, power and goodness that irresistibly suggest the idea of a God. When he looks upon the stellar firmament with its innumerable orbs, and considers their disposition and order, their balancing and circling, he instinctively argues that these shining suns and systems must have been created, arranged and upheld by a Divine Mind. When, restricting his attention to the earth on which he stands, he notes the indications of design or of adaptation of means to end which are everywhere visible, as witnessed, for example, in the constancy of nature's laws and forces, in the endless variety of nature's forms, inanimate and animate, as well as in their wonderful gradation not only in their kinds but also in the times of their appearing, and in the marvelous adjustment of organs to environment, he feels constrained to reason that these things are not the result of chance which is blind or the spontaneous output of matter, which in itself, so far as known to him, is powerless, lifeless and unintelligent, but can only be the handiwork of a Creative Mind. When further he reflects that in the whole round of human experience, effects have never been known to be produced without causes; that designs have never been known to be conceived or worked out without designers and artificers; that dead matter has never been known to spring into life either spontaneously or by the application of means; that one kind of life has never been known to transmute itself spontaneously or to be transmuted artificially into another, neither a vegetable into an animal, nor an animal into a man; and when lastly, accepting the guidance of science, he perceives that in the upward ascent or evolution of nature dead matter was, after an interval, perhaps of millions of years, followed by vegetable life, and this again by animal existence, and this by man precisely as Scripture asserts, he once more feels himself shut up to the conclusion that the whole cosmos must be the production of mind, even of a Supreme Intelligence infinitely powerful, wise and good. Like the Hebrew psalmist he feels impelled to say, "O Lord! how manifold are Thy works: in wisdom hast Thou made them all!"

Should the philosopher interject, that this argument does not necessarily require an Infinite Intelligence but only an artificer capable of constructing such a universe as the present, the answer is that if such an artificer existed he himself would require to be accounted for, since beings that are finite must have begun to be, and therefore must have been caused.

Accordingly this artificer must have been preceded by another greater than himself, and that by another still greater, and so on travelling backwards forever. Hence it was argued by Kant that pure reason could not demonstrate the existence of God, but only of a competent demiurge or world-builder. But this reasoning is fallacious. The human mind cannot rest in an endless succession of effects without a First Cause, like a chain depending from nothing. Kant himself seemed to recognize the unsatisfactory character of his logic, since, after casting out God from the universe as Creator, he sought to bring Him in again as Supreme Moral Governor.

But if man's moral nature cannot be explained without a Supreme Moral Lawgiver, on what principle can it be reasoned that man's intellectual nature demands less than a Supreme Intelligence?

2. *Without a God the Christian cannot explain to himself the Person of Jesus.*

Leaving out of view what the Gospels report about His virgin birth (though we do not regard the narratives as unhistorical or the fact recorded as incredible), and fixing attention solely on the four records, the Christian discerns a personality that cannot be accounted for on ordinary principles. It is not merely that Jesus performed works such as none other man did, and spoke words such as never fell from mortal lips; it is that in addition His life was one of incomparable goodness—of unwearied philanthropy, self-sacrificing love, lowly humility, patient meekness and spotless purity—such as never before had been witnessed on earth, and never since has been exhibited by any of His followers. It is that Jesus, being such a personality as described by those who beheld His glory to be that of an only-begotten from a Father, full of grace and truth, put forth such pretensions and claims as were wholly unfitting in the lips of a mere man, and much more of a sinful man, declaring Himself to be the Light of the World and the Bread of Life: giving out that He had power to forgive sins and to raise the dead; that He had pre-existed before He came to earth and would return to that pre-existent state when His work was done, which work was to die for men's sins; that He would rise from the dead and ascend up into heaven, both of which He actually did; and asserting that He was the Son of God, the equal of the Father and the future Judge of mankind. The Christian studying this picture perceives that, while to it belong the lineaments of a man, it also wears the likeness of a God, and he reasons that if that picture was drawn from the life (and how otherwise could it have been drawn?) then a God must once have walked this earth in the person of Jesus. For the Christian no other conclusion is possible. Certainly not that of the New Theology, which makes of Jesus a sinful man, distinguishing Him from Christ, the so-called ideal figure of the creeds, and calling Him divine only in the sense that other men are divine though in a lesser degree than He. But even the New Theology cannot escape from the implication of its own creed. For if Jesus was the divinest man that ever lived on earth, then naturally His Word should carry more weight than that of any other, and He taught emphatically, not only that there was a personal God whose Son He was, but that men should pray: "Our Father which art in Heaven."

3. *Without a God the Christian cannot understand the facts of his own consciousness.*

Take first the idea of God of which he finds himself possessed on arriving at the age of intelligence and responsibility. How it comes to pass that this great idea should arise within him if no such being as God exists, is something he cannot understand. To say that he has simply inherited it from his parents or absorbed it from his contemporaries is not to solve the problem, but only to put it back from generation to gen-

eration. The question remains, How did this idea first originate in the soul? To answer that it gradually grew up out of
totemism and animism as practiced by the low-grade races
who, impelled by superstitious fears, conceived material objects to be inhabited by ghosts or spirits, is equally an evasion
of the problem. Because again the question arises, How did
these low-grade races arrive at the conception of spirits as
distinguished from bodies or material objects in general?
Should it be responded that veneration for deceased ancestors
begat the conception of a God, one must further demand by
what process of reasoning they were conducted from the conception of as many gods as there were deceased ancestors to
that of one Supreme Deity or Lord of all. The only satisfactory explanation of the latent consciousness of God which
man in all ages and lands has shown himself to be possessed
of is, that it is one of the soul's intuitions, a part of the intellectual and moral furniture with which it comes into the world;
that at first this idea or intuition lies within the soul as a
seed corn which gradually opens out as the soul rises into full
possession of its powers and is appealed to by external nature;
that had sin not entered into the world this idea or intuition
would have everywhere expanded into full bloom, filling the
soul with a clear and radiant conception of the Divine Being,
in whose image it has been made; but that now in consequence
of the blighting influence of sin this idea or intuition has been
everywhere more or less dimmed and weakened and in heathen nations corrupted and debased.

Then rising to the distinctly religious experience of conversion, the Christian encounters a whole series or group
of phenomena which to him are inexplicable, if there is no
God. Conscious of a change partly intellectual but mainly
moral and spiritual, a change so complete as to amount to an
inward revolution, what Scripture calls a new birth or a new
creation, he cannot trace it to education or to environment,
to philosophical reflection or to prudential considerations.

The only reasonable account he can furnish of it is that he has been laid hold of by an unseen but Superhuman Power, so that he feels constrained to say like Paul: "By the grace of God I am what I am." And not only so, but as the result of this inward change upon his nature, he realizes that he stands in a new relation to that Supreme Power which has quickened and renewed him, that he can and does enter into personal communion with Him through Jesus Christ, addressing to Him prayers and receiving from Him benefits and blessings in answer to those prayers.

These experiences of which the Christian is conscious may be characterized by the non-Christian as illusions, but to the Christian they are realities; and being realities they make it simply impossible for him to believe there is no God. Rather they inspire him with confidence that God is, and is the Rewarder of them that diligently seek Him, and that of Him and through Him and to Him are all things; to whom be glory for ever. Amen.

CHAPTER IX

GOD IN CHRIST THE ONLY REVELATION OF THE FATHERHOOD OF GOD

BY ROBERT E. SPEER

"They shall put you out of the synagogues: yea, the hour cometh, that whosoever killeth you shall think that he offereth service unto God. And these things will they do, because they have not known the Father nor me." (John 16:2, 3.)

These words suggest to us that it is not enough for a man just to believe in God. Everything depends on what kind of a god it is in whom he believes. It is a rather striking and surprising comparison at first that our Lord institutes here between a mere belief in God and the possibly horrible moral consequences, on the one hand, and a knowledge of God in Christ and its sure moral effects, on the other. And the lesson would seem to be the inadequacy of any religious faith that does not recognize the revelation of the Father in Jesus Christ and that does not know Jesus Christ as God. It is a little hard for us to take such a great thought as this into our lives, and yet our Lord puts it in unmistakable clearness: on the one hand, the moral inadequacy of a mere belief in God; on the other hand, the moral and spiritual adequacy of a recognition of God as Father exposed in Christ as God.

THEISM NOT SUFFICIENT

In the former of these two verses our Lord makes the first of these two points unmistakably clear. He saw no adequate guarantee of moral rectitude and justice in a mere theistic faith. He suffered in His own death the possibly bitter fruits of a mere theistic faith. The men who put Him to death were ardent believers in God, and they thought they were doing a fine thing for God when they crucified the Son of God. And He told His disciples that the day would come when conscientious men would take out service of God in executing them, and that those who would put them to death would not be bad men, but men who thought that by killing them they were doing God's will.

We see exactly the same great error in our own day. It is no sufficient protection to a man to believe in one God. There are no more rigid monotheists in the world than Mohammedans, and there are some who tell us that in India the moral conditions of the Mohammedans are even worse than the moral conditions of the polytheistic Hindus around about them. It is not so much a matter of how many gods you believe in. I would rather believe in three good gods than in one bad one. One religion is superior to another religion, not because it has less or more gods than that other religion, but because the character of its gods is superior to the character of the gods of that other religion. Our Lord understood completely that a mere faith in God was not going to make a good man, that a man might believe in God and be a murderer, or an adulterer, he might believe in God and put the very apostles of Jesus Christ to death and think that thus he was doing God a great service.

CONSCIENTIOUSNESS NOT SUFFICIENT

It seems to me that it is worth while to stop here for a moment incidentally to note how easy a thing it is for a man to be guilty of conscientious error and crime. It is no defense of a man's conduct to say that he is conscientiously satisfied with what he did. I suppose that most bad things have been done in all good conscience, and that most of the sins that we commit today we commit with a perfectly clean conscience. There is such a thing as a moral color-blindness that is just as real as a physical color-blindness. I was visiting a little while ago one of our well-known girls' schools, and had a discussion with one of the teachers, who said that she thought it did not make so much difference what a pupil believed or did, provided only she was conscientious in her belief and conduct. I told her that it must be quite easy to go to school to her if it did not matter whether you answered right or not, if only you were conscientiously honest in what you said. She might get two absolutely contrary answers to a question and mark each one of them perfect. The whole foundations of the moral universe fall out from beneath the man or the woman who will take that view of it, that there is not really any objective standard of right or wrong at all, that everything hinges on just how a person feels about it, and if they only feel comfortable over the thing it is all right. These men who were going to put the disciples of Jesus Christ to death had no qualms of conscience about it. They would think in doing it that they were doing God a service. The idea that our Lord means to bring out is this, that the standards of a man are dependent upon his conception of God, and He saw no guarantee of moral rectitude and justice in a man's life except as that man grasped the revelation of God as Father that had been made in Jesus Christ, and himself knew Jesus Christ as God.

CHRIST'S MENTION OF "FATHER"

There is no room here to trace this great thought through all the teaching of our Lord, but it would be a good and helpful thing if many of us would take the four Gospels and sit down with two sheets of paper, and write down on one sheet everything that Jesus had to say about *the Father,* and on the other every mention in Christ's teaching of the name of *God.* Lately, I read through the last discourses of Jesus in John with this in mind. Only four times does Jesus so much as mention the name of God, while He speaks of the Father at least forty times. Evidently our Lord conceived that His great message to men was a message of God as Father revealed in

His own life, and He conceived this to be a great practical moral truth, that was to save men from those errors of judgment, of act and of character about which a man has no sure guarantee under a mere monotheistic faith.

IN RELATION TO OUR RELIGIOUS FAITH

1. I think we might just as well now go right to the heart of the thing by considering, first of all, THE RELATIONSHIP OF THIS REVELATION THAT JESUS CHRIST MADE OF THE FATHER-CHARACTER OF GOD IN HIMSELF TO OUR OWN RELIGIOUS FAITH. We begin our Christian creed with the declaration, "I believe in God the Father Almighty." I believe that no man can say those words sincerely and honestly, with an intellectual understanding of what he is saying, who is not saying them with his feet solidly resting on the evangelical conviction; for we know practically nothing about God *as* Father except what we learn from the revelation of God as Father in Jesus Christ. Men say sometimes that the idea of God as Father was in the Old Testament, and there is a sense doubtless in which we can find it there: a patriotic sense for one thing, a poetic sense for another thing. The Hebrews thought of God as the Father, the national Father of Israel.

Now and then there is some splendid burst in the prophets that contains that idea, as when Jeremiah, crying out for God, says, "I am a Father to Israel, and Ephraim is my first-born." Or when Israel is itself crying out through Isaiah, "Jehovah is our Father. He is the potter and we are the clay." But in each sense it is a sort of nationalistic conception of God as the Father of the whole people Israel. And even when the note comes out poetically, it is patriotic still. Turn some time to the 103rd Psalm, where there is the best expression of it, "Like as a father pitieth his children, so the Lord pitieth them that fear him," and even there it is the national cry. Or turn to the 89th Psalm, and there, too, it is national and patriotic: "And he shall cry unto me, Jehovah,

thou art my Father, my God; and the rock of my salvation."
And if in all the great body of the religious poetry of Israel
there are only two or three distinct notes of the fatherhood of
God, we cannot believe that that idea filled any very large
place in the heart of Israel. And in the very last of all the
Old Testament prophecies, the complaint of God is just this,
that the Israelites would not conceive of Him as their Father,
and that even the political conception of God as the Father of
the nation was no reality in the experience of the people.

A NEW CONCEPTION

The revelation of God as the Father of men was a practically new conception exposed in the teaching and in the life
of our Lord Jesus Christ—not in His teaching alone. We
should never have known God as Father by the message of
Jesus Christ only; we should never have been able to conceive
what Christ's idea of God was if we had not seen that idea
worked out in the very person of Jesus Christ Himself. It
was not alone that He told us what God was. He said that
when He walked before men, He was Himself one with the
Father on Whom the eyes of men might gaze: "I am the
way, and the truth, and the life: no one cometh unto the
Father, but by me. If ye had known me, ye would have known
my Father also; from henceforth ye have known Him and
have seen Him. Philip saith unto Him, Lord show us the
Father, and it sufficeth us. Jesus said unto him, Have I been
so long time with you, and dost thou not know me, Philip?
He that hath seen me hath seen the Father; how sayest thou,
Show us the Father? Believest thou not that I am in the
Father, and the Father in me? The words that I say unto
you I speak not from myself: but the Father abiding in me
doeth His works."

JOHN AND MATTHEW

We cannot separate the Christological elements of the
Gospel from the Gospel. The effort is made by throwing the

Gospel of John out of court, and then we are told that with the Gospel of John gone the real work of Christ was just in His message, making known the Father to men, and that the Christological character that we impose upon the Gospel was something foisted upon it later, and not something lying in the mind and thought of Jesus Christ Himself. But I do not see how men can take that view of it until they cut out also the 11th chapter of Matthew. Christ sets forth there the essentially Christological character of His gospel just as unmistakably as it is set forth anywhere in the Gospel of John: "No man knoweth the Son save the Father; and no man knoweth the Father save the Son, and he to whomsoever the Son willeth to reveal him." What I mean is just this, that the only defense of the Unitarian position is a ripping of the Gospel apart so that you cannot recognize it as the Gospel any more. You cannot tear Christ's revelation of the fatherhood of God away from the person of Christ. He did not expose the fatherhood of God by what He said; He exposed the fatherhood of God by what He was; and it is a species of intellectual misconception to take certain words of His and say those words entitle us to believe in God as our Father, while we reject Jesus Christ as His Divine Son, and think that it is possible to hold to the first article of our Christian creed without going on to the second article of it, "And I believe in Jesus Christ, His only Son, our Lord."

CHRIST IS ALL

If you and I subtract from our conception of God what we owe to the person of Jesus Christ, we have practically nothing left. The disciples knew that they would have little left. When it was proposed that they should separate themselves from Christ and the revelation that He was making, these men stood absolutely dumbfounded. "Why, Lord," they said, "what is to become of us? We have no place to go. Thou hast the words of eternal life. There is nothing for us in

Judaism any more." Monotheism was in Judaism; the revelation of God was in Judaism; but that was nothing to the disciples now that they had seen that glorious vision of His Father made known to men in Jesus Christ His Son. It would seem to follow that our attitude towards Jesus Christ is determinative of our life in the Father, and that the imagination that we have a life in the Father that rests on a rejection of the claims of Jesus Christ is an imagination with no foundations under it at all. Take those great words of our Lord: "He that loveth me not keepeth not my words; and the word which ye hear is not mine, but the Father's who sent me. If a man love me, he will keep my word: and my Father will love him, and we will come unto him and make our abode with him." All through these last discourses of Jesus you come upon the two terms, "word" and "words." In the Greek they are not just the singular and the plural of the same word. The word that is translated "word" here is the same word that in the beginning of this Gospel is translated "word," *logos,* which does not mean the utterances of Jesus, which does not mean the things that Jesus said, which does not mean the ideals of life that Jesus erected. We are not complying with that condition when we try to be kind and unselfish and to obey the Golden Rule. What Jesus is setting forth there as the condition of a right attitude toward God is a man's acceptance of the inner secret of His own life, a man's deliberate committing of himself to the great principles that underlie the character and the person of Jesus, a sympathetic union with Himself. And He summed it all up in those words to Philip, "He that hath seen me hath seen the Father." It is in this sense, I say, that you and I cannot honestly declare that we "believe in God the Father" unless we go right on to say, "And in Jesus Christ, His only Son, our Lord," for we know practically nothing about God as Father except what was revealed of God as Father in Him Who said, "I and the Father are one." Do we believe in the fatherhood of God in that sense?

PRACTICAL APPLICATION

2. Perhaps we can answer that question better by going on to ask, in the second place, whether we are REALIZING IN OUR LIVES ALL THE PRACTICAL IMPLICATIONS OF THIS REVELATION OF THE FATHER-CHARACTER OF GOD IN JESUS CHRIST. For one thing, think how it *interprets the mystery and the testing of life*. Now life is simply an enigma on the merely theistic hypothesis. We get absolutely no comfort, no light, no illumination upon what we know to be the great problem of life from a simple belief in God. It only becomes intelligible to us as we understand God to be our Father in the sense in which Jesus Christ revealed Him. Dr. Babcock used to put it in the simple phrase: "You have got to take one of two interpretations of it. You have got to read your life in the terms of fate, or you have got to read it in the terms of fatherhood." Once I accept the revelation of God made in Jesus Christ, my life is still a hard problem to me. There are many things in it that are terribly confused and difficult still; but I begin to get a little light on its deep and impenetrable mysteries. It was just in this point of view that the writer of the great epistle to the Hebrews thought he had some clue to the mystery of his own life, to the chastening of it, to the hard and burning discipline through which he sees we are all passing. It was only when he conceived of himself as being a son of the great Potter Who was shaping the clay Himself that the mystery began to clear a little from his pathway. And it was just so, you remember, that Christ got light on the mystery of His life: "Father, not my will, but thine be done." Only as He remembered and rested deeply upon the character of God as His Father did those great experiences through which He was passing have full intelligibility to Him. After all, it was no fancy that connected the two great ideas of Isaiah, the living idea of the fatherhood of God and the metaphorical idea of God as the Potter shaping his clay. It is only

so that we understand both aspects of our human life. We turn to Rabbi Ben Ezra and see the mystery wrought out there:

> "He fixed thee mid this dance
> Of plastic circumstance,
>   This Present, thou, forsooth, wouldst fain arrest:
> Machinery just meant
> To give thy soul its bent.
>   Try thee and turn thee forth, sufficiently impressed."

When the wheel moves fast, and the hand of the Potter seems cruel upon the clay, and the friction is full of terrible heat, we begin to understand something of it all in realizing that the Potter's hand is the hand of a Father shaping in fatherly discipline the life of His son. "If ye endure chastening, God dealeth with you as sons."

OUR IDEALS

Or think, in the second place, how this conception of God *inspires and rectifies the ideals of our lives.* It was this that suggested the idea to Jesus here. He saw that there was absolutely no guarantee of right standards of life in a mere theistic faith, and there are none. We cannot morally trust Unitarianism if we take it away from living contact with the evangelical tradition. There is too much loose, subjective caprice in it; there is not enough firm and unassailable anchorage in the objective realities of a revelation of the character of God made known to us in His divine Son. We have no guarantee whatever of just and perfect moral ideals that we do not get from the exposure of the father-character of God in the person of Jesus Christ and from personal union with God in Him.

As a simple matter of fact the best ideals of our life we all owe to just that revelation. The ideal of purity—the Jews never had it. They had an ideal of ritual cleanliness, but they had no Christian ideal of moral purity. You cannot find the ideal of purity anywhere in the world where the conception of the father-revelation of God in Christ has not gone. Explain it as you will, it is a simple fact of comparative religion. Can any man find the full ideal of moral purity anywhere in this world where it has not been created by the revelation of the father-character of God in Christ? We owe it to that, and we can not be sure of its perpetuation save where the conviction of that great revelation abides in the faith of man.

Or take our ideal of work. Where did Christ get His ideal of work? "My Father worketh hitherto, and I work." On what ground did He rest His claim upon men to work? "Son, go work today in my vineyard." Our whole ideal of a workingman's life, of a man's using his life to the fullness of its power in an unselfish service is an ideal born of the revelation of the father-character of God in Christ. And forgiveness is an ideal of the same kind. We owe all the highest and noblest ideals of our life to that revelation. And it seems to us something less than fair for a man to take those ideals and then deny their origin, trampling under foot the claims of Him from Whom those ideals came into our lives.

SWEETENS OBEDIENCE

And think *how rational and sweet this conception of God makes obedience.* There is something rational but hardly sweet in the thought of obedience to Him under the simple theistic conception. All the joy of obedience comes when I think of myself as my Father's son and sent to do my Father's will. Our Lord thought of His life just so. "Simon," He said—that last night that Simon tried to defend Him by force—"put up thy sword into its sheath. The cup which my Father hath given me, shall I not drink it?" We get our ideals of obedience and the joy and the delight of obedience from the thought that after all we are simply to obey our Father. In the 14th chapter of the Gospel of John, we get a little vision of what Christ conceives to be the sweetness and the tenderness and the beauty that can come into life from a real acceptance of this revealing of His. "In that day," He says, "ye shall know that I am in my Father, and ye in me, and I in you. He that hath my commandments and keepeth them, he it is that loveth me; and he that loveth me shall be loved of my Father, and I will love him and will manifest myself unto him. If a man love me, he will keep my word; and my Father will love him, and we will come unto him and make our abode with him."

I remember an interview I had some years ago at Asheville. As we sat under the trees, the man with whom I was talking told me he had had a home; he was sure it was the sweetest home that could be found in all the Southern States; and he did not have it any more. The eye that had marked his coming and brightened when he came watched for him no more, and little arms that had been thrown around his neck, and that made his home-coming in the evening a very taste of heaven to him, were no longer there to greet him, nor any little voice to call to him as he came. And he told me that when first that great eclipse fell upon his life it seemed to him that the whole thing was done and that a man was not warranted in trying to live any more. But he found here in this 14th chapter of John these great assurances of which I have just been speaking, that there was another eye that could take the place of that eye that had waited in the years that had passed, other arms that could take the place of those little arms that were now busy with the other children round about the throne of God in heaven. There had come back into life the tenderness—and mark you, that too is a thought that came when Jesus Christ revealed the Father in Himself— there had come back into his life the tenderness and the joy and the gentleness that he had known before, simply because now he had come a little more fully to realize what it was that Jesus Christ by His life and teachings had exposed for the life of man.

COURAGE AND HOPE

And what *new courage and hope* it brings into a man's life. You say to me, "Man, you have got to be like God," and I reply, "Take your preposterous blasphemy away. To be like God?" But you say to me, "He is your own Father, and you are His son. We are not asking you to become like that to which you are essentially unlike; we are simply asking you to become like your Father. It is His own nature in you that He will develop until restored to its full relationship to Him from Whom it came." You talk to us that way about our duty as men in the world, and it makes all the difference between death and life to us. If God the Father did not come near to men in Jesus Christ, I do not know what I am going to do; I do not know where to find the help that I know I need. Nowhere else in the world has any voice arisen to offer it to men. But if God came near men in Jesus Christ and thereby guaranteed our own kinship to Him, I may believe that I can become like Him Whose son I am. It is on just this ground that St. Paul makes his appeal: "Be ye therefore imitators of God *as dear children.*"

RELATION TO PRAYER LIFE

3. And, last of all, think on THE LIGHT THAT THIS CONCEPTION OF GOD THROWS UPON OUR LIFE OF PRAYER. I suspect that prayer has been just a sham to many of us, or a thing that we have done because other people told us it was the thing to do. We never got anything out of it; it never meant anything to us. We might just as well have talked to stone walls as to pray the way we have prayed. We went out and said, "God," and we might just as well have said, "hills," or "mountains," or "trees," or anything else. Why have we not gone into the school of Christ and learned there, alike from His practice and His doctrine, what real prayer is and how a man can do it. You cannot find a single prayer of Christ addressed to God, not one; nor can you find a single

prayer of Christ's in which He so much as mentions God. The third verse of the 17th chapter of John, which says, "And this is eternal life, that they might believe in thee, the only true God, and Jesus Christ, whom thou hast sent," may be an exception, but you will find that Westcott, and others of the best New Testament commentators, regard that phrase as a parenthesis of John the Evangelist, and not part of our Lord's great prayer.

I hope I am not misunderstood. I am meaning only that Christ's conception of God and His practice of prayer did not rest merely on the theistic interpretation of the universe and the nature of its Creator in His majesty and almightiness. They rested on the father conception which He revealed in Himself. Just run over in your thought His prayers: the prayer that He taught us to pray, "Our Father, who art in heaven;" the prayer He offered Himself when the disciples of John the Baptist came to Him: "I thank thee, Father, lord of heaven and earth, that thou hast hidden these things from the wise and the understanding, and hast revealed them unto babes. Even so, Father, for it seemeth good in thy sight;" the prayer that He offered in the temple, when Philip and Andrew came to Him with the message about the Greeks who were seeking to see Him: "Now is my soul troubled, and what shall I say? Father, save me from this hour? But for this cause came I unto this hour;" the prayer that He offered before the grave of Lazarus, "Father, I thank thee that thou hearest me, and I know that thou hearest me always;" the prayer that He put up in Gethsemane, "My Father, if this cup cannot pass from me except I drink it, thy will be done;" and the last prayer of all, when, as a tired little child, He lay down in His Father's arms and fell asleep: "Father, into thy hands I commend my spirit." He never pushed God off into His almightiness; not once in all His life of supplication can you find Him dealing with God in this way. He never smote the heart with the chill of the divine attributes. You may be recalling, perhaps, that one cry of His from the cross, "My God, my God, why hast thou forsaken me?"—a quotation from one of the Psalms and a shout of victory. I think that could be demonstrated to be a shout of victory and not a cry of isolation; but that alone would be your exception. All the other times it was, "Father," "my Father," "holy Father," "righteous Father"—sometimes, we may believe, in the quiet intimacy of His secret consciousness, "my dear Father." What a reality this conception of prayer gives to it. We are not praying to any cold theistic God alone; we are praying to our Father made real to us, warm with the warmth of a great tenderness for us, living with a great consciousness of all our human suffering and struggle and conflict and need.

It makes prayer, for one thing, a rational thing. I can go to my Father and ask Him for the things that I need. There is an exquisite passage in Andrew Bonar's journals in which he speaks of sitting one day in his study and looking out of his window and seeing two of his children pass through the fields. He said as he saw those little children making their way across the fields, the love in his heart overcame him, and he pushed his books away from him on the table, and went to the door and called out across the field to them, and they came running eagerly in response to their father's loving call. And when they had come, and he had caressed them, he said he gave each one of them something simply because the ecstasy of his fatherly love made it impossible that he should not do something then for those two children who were so dear to his heart. Do you suppose that God is an inferior sort of a father? Do you suppose that there are impulses in us toward our children, or in our fathers toward us, that are not simply just the dim and the faded suggestion of nobler and diviner impulses of the father heart of God? Prayer in the sense of supplication for real things becomes a rational reality to men who believe in God in Jesus Christ.

FELLOWSHIP

And how sweet it makes prayer in the sense of living fellowship. Do you suppose that we are nobler characters than that great Father after Whom these human fatherhoods of ours are named? Do you suppose that if it is sweet to us to have our little children come creeping to us in the dark, it is not sweet to our heavenly Father here, everywhere, to have men, His sons, come stealing to His side and His love? This is no excessive way of putting it. Is it not guaranteed to us by those words which our Lord spoke that Easter morning as He stood there by His open grave, and the woman who adored Him was about to clasp His feet, "Mary, go and tell my disciples that I ascend unto my Father, and your Father, my God and your God." Yes, that is the right way to put it today. No God for us, nowhere through the whole universe a real and satisfying God for us, except the God Who is discovered to us in Jesus Christ, and Who is calling to us today by the lips of Christ, "My son, O my son," and Who would have us call back to Him, if we be true men, "My Father, O my Father."

CHAPTER X

THE DEITY OF CHRIST.

BY PROF. BENJAMIN B. WARFIELD, D. D., LL. D.,
PRINCETON THEOLOGICAL SEMINARY.

A recent writer has remarked that our assured conviction of the deity of Christ rests, not upon "proof-texts or passages, nor upon old arguments drawn from these, but upon the general fact of the whole manifestation of Jesus Christ, and of the whole impression left by Him upon the world." The antithesis is too absolute, and possibly betrays an unwarranted distrust of the evidence of Scripture. To make it just, we should read the statement rather thus: Our conviction of the deity of Christ rests not alone on the scriptural passages which assert it, but also on His entire impression on the world; or perhaps thus: Our conviction rests not more on the scriptural assertions than upon His entire manifestation. Both lines of evidence are valid; and when twisted together form an unbreakable cord. The proof-texts and passages do prove that Jesus was esteemed divine by those who companied with Him; that He esteemed Himself divine; that He was recognized as divine by those who were taught by the Spirit; that, in fine, He was divine. But over and above this Biblical evidence the impression Jesus has left upon the world bears independent testimony to His deity, and it may well be that to many minds this will seem the most conclusive of all its evidences. It certainly is very cogent and impressive.

EXPERIENCE AS PROOF.

The justification which the author we have just quoted gives of his neglecting the scriptural evidence in favor of that borne by Jesus' impression on the world is also open to criticism. "Jesus Christ," he tells us, "is one of those essential truths which are too great to be proved, like God, or freedom, or immortality." Such things rest, it seems, not on proofs but on experience. We need not stop to point out that this experience is itself a proof. We wish rather to point out that some confusion seems to have been fallen into here between our ability to marshal the proof by which we are convinced and our accessibility to its force. It is quite true that "the most essential conclusions of the human mind are much wider and stronger than the arguments by which they are supported;" that the proofs "are always changing but the beliefs persist." But this is not because the conclusions in question rest on no sound proofs; but because we have not had the skill to adduce, in our argumentative presentations of them, the really fundamental proofs on which they rest.

UNCONSCIOUS RATIONALITY.

A man recognizes on sight the face of his friend, or his own handwriting. Ask him how he knows this face to be that of his friend, or this handwriting to be his own, and he is dumb, or, seeking to reply, babbles nonsense. Yet his recognition rests on solid grounds, though he lacks analytical skill to isolate and state these solid grounds. We believe in God and freedom and immortality on good grounds, though we may not be able satisfactorily to analyse these grounds. No true conviction exists without adequate rational grounding in evidence. So, if we are solidly assured of the deity of Christ, it will be on adequate grounds, appealing to the reason. But it may well be on grounds not analysed, perhaps not analysable, by us, so as to exhibit themselves in the forms of formal logic.

We do not need to wait to analyse the grounds of our convictions before they operate to produce convictions, any more than we need to wait to analyse our food before it nourishes us; and we can soundly believe on evidence much mixed with error, just as we can thrive on food far from pure. The alchemy of the mind, as of the digestive tract, knows how to separate out from the mass what it requires for its support; and as we may live without any knowledge of chemistry, so we may possess earnest convictions, solidly founded in right reason, without the slightest knowledge of logic. The Christian's conviction of the deity of his Lord does not depend for its soundness on the Christian's ability convincingly to state the grounds of his conviction. The evidence he offers for it may be wholly inadequate, while the evidence on which it rests may be absolutely compelling.

TESTIMONY IN SOLUTION.

The very abundance and persuasiveness of the evidence of the deity of Christ greatly increases the difficulty of adequately stating it. This is true even of the scriptural evidence, as precise and definite as much of it is. For it is a true remark of Dr. Dale's that the particular texts in which it is definitely asserted are far from the whole, or even the most impressive, proofs which the Scriptures supply of our Lord's deity. He compares these texts to the salt-crystals which appear on the sand of the sea-beach after the tide has receded. "These are not," he remarks, "the strongest, though they may be the most apparent, proofs that the sea is salt; the salt is present in solution in every bucket of sea-water." The deity of Christ is in solution in every page of the New Testament. Every word that is spoken of Him, every word which He is reported to have spoken of Himself, is spoken on the assumption that He is God. And that is the reason why the "criticism" which addresses itself to eliminating the testimony of the New Testament to the deity of our Lord has set itself a hopeless task. The New Testament itself would have to be eliminated. Nor can we get behind this testimony. Because the deity of Christ is the presupposition of every word of the New Testament, it is impossible to select words out of the New Testament from which to construct earlier documents in which the deity of Christ shall not be assumed. The assured conviction of the deity of Christ is coëval with Christianity itself. There never was a Christianity, neither in the times of the Apostles nor since, of which this was not a prime tenet.

A SATURATED GOSPEL.

Let us observe in an example or two how thoroughly saturated the Gospel narrative is with the assumption of the deity of Christ, so that it crops out in the most unexpected ways and places.

In three passages of Matthew, reporting words of Jesus, He is represented as speaking familiarly and in the most natural manner in the world, of *"His* angels" (13:41; 16:27; 24:31). In all three He designates Himself as the "Son of man"; and in all three there are additional suggestions of His majesty. "The Son of man shall send forth *His* angels, and they shall gather out of *His* kingdom all things that cause stumbling and those that do iniquity, and shall cast them into the furnace of fire."

Who is this Son of man who has angels, by whose instrumentality the final judgment is executed at His command? "The Son of man shall come in the glory of His Father with *His* angels; and then shall *He* reward every man according to his deeds." Who is this Son of man surrounded by His angels, in whose hands are the issues of life? The Son of man "shall send forth *His* angels with a great sound of a trumpet, and they shall gather together *His* elect from the four winds, from one end of heaven to the other." Who is this Son of man at whose behest His angels winnow men? A scrutiny of the passages will show that it is not a peculiar body of angels which is meant by the Son of man's angels, but just the angels as a body, who are His to serve Him as He commands. In a word, Jesus Christ is above angels (Mark 13:32) —as is argued at explicit length at the beginning of the Epistle to the Hebrews. "To which of the angels said he at any time, Sit on my right hand, etc." (Heb. 1:13).

HEAVEN COME TO EARTH.

There are three parables recorded in the fifteenth chapter of Luke as spoken by our Lord in His defence against the murmurs of the Pharisees at His receiving sinners and eating with them. The essence of the defence which our Lord offers for Himself is, that there is joy *in heaven* over repentant sinners! Why "in heaven," "before the throne of God"? Is He merely setting the judgment of heaven over against that of earth, or pointing forward to His future vindication? By no means. He is representing His action in receiving sinners, in seeking the lost, as His proper action, because it is the normal conduct of heaven, manifested in Him. He is heaven come to earth. His defence is thus simply the unveiling of what the real nature of the transaction is. The lost when they come to Him are received because this is heaven's way; and *He* cannot act otherwise than in heaven's way. He tacitly assumes the good Shepherd's part as His own.

THE UNIQUE POSITION.

All the great designations are not so much asserted as assumed by Him for Himself. He does not call Himself a prophet, though He accepts this designation from others: He places Himself above all the prophets, even above John the greatest of the prophets, as Him to whom all the prophets look forward. If He calls Himself Messiah, He fills that term, by doing so, with a deeper significance, dwelling ever on the unique relation of Messiah to God as His representative and His Son. Nor is He satisfied to represent Himself merely as standing in a unique relation to God: He proclaims Himself to be the recipient of the divine fullness, the sharer in all that God has (Matt. 11:28). He speaks freely of Himself indeed as God's Other, the manifestation of God on earth, whom to have seen was to have seen the Father also, and who does the work of God on earth. He openly claims divine prerogatives—

the reading of the heart of man, the forgiveness of sins, the exercise of all authority in heaven and earth. Indeed, all that God has and is He asserts Himself to have and be; omnipotence, omniscience, perfection belong as to the one so to the other. Not only does He perform all divine acts; His self-consciousness coalesces with the divine consciousness. If His followers lagged in recognizing His deity, this was not because He was not God or did not sufficiently manifest His deity. It was because they were foolish and slow of heart to believe what lay patently before their eyes.

THE GREAT PROOF.

The Scriptures give us evidence enough, then, that Christ is God. But the Scriptures are far from giving us all the evidence we have. There is, for example, the revolution which Christ has wrought in the world. If, indeed, it were asked what the most convincing proof of the deity of Christ is, perhaps the best answer would be, just Christianity. The new life He has brought into the world; the new creation which He has produced by His life and work in the world; here are at least His most palpable credentials.

Take it objectively. Read such a book as Harnack's "The Expansion of Christianity," or such an one as Von Dobschütz's "Christian Life in the Primitive Church"—neither of which allows the deity of Christ—and then ask, Could these things have been wrought by power less than divine? And then remember that these things were not only wrought in that heathen world two thousand years ago, but have been wrought over again every generation since; for Christianity has reconquered the world to itself each generation. Think of how the Christian proclamation spread, eating its way over the world like fire in the grass of a prairie. Think how, as it spread, it transformed lives. The thing, whether in its objective or in its subjective aspect, were incredible, had it not actually occurred. "Should a voyager," says Charles Darwin, "chance to be on the point of shipwreck on some unknown coast, he will most devoutly pray that the lesson of the missionary may have reached thus far. The lesson of the missionary is the enchanter's wand." Could this transforming influence, undiminished after two millenniums, have proceeded from a mere man? It is historically impossible that the great movement which we call Christianity, which remains unspent after all these years, could have originated in a merely human impulse; or could represent today the working of a merely human force.

THE PROOF WITHIN.

Or take it subjectively. Every Christian has within himself the proof of the transforming power of Christ, and can repeat the blind man's syllogism: Why herein is the marvel that ye know not whence He is, and yet He opened my eyes. "Spirits are not touched to fine issues who are not finely touched." "Shall we trust," demands an eloquent reasoner, "the touch of our fingers, the sight of our eyes, the hearing of our ears, and not trust our deepest consciousness of our higher nature—the answer of conscience, the flower of spiritual gladness, the glow of spiritual love? To deny that spiritual experience is as real as physical experience is to slander the noblest faculties of our nature. It is to say that one half of our nature tells the truth, and the other half utters lies. The proposition that facts in the spiritual region are less real than facts in the physical realm contradicts all philosophy." The transformed hearts of Christians, registering themselves "in gentle tempers, in noble motives, in lives visibly lived under the empire of great aspirations"—these are the ever-present proofs of the divinity of the Person from whom their inspiration is drawn.

The supreme proof to every Christian of the deity of his Lord is then his own inner experience of the transforming power of his Lord upon the heart and life. Not more surely does he who feels the present warmth of the sun know that the sun exists, than he who has experienced the re-creative power of the Lord know Him to be his Lord and his God. Here is, perhaps we may say the proper, certainly we must say the most convincing, proof to every Christian of the deity of Christ; a proof which he cannot escape, and to which, whether he is capable of analysing it or drawing it out in logical statement or not, he cannot fail to yield his sincere and unassailable conviction. Whatever else he may or may not be assured of, he knows that his Redeemer lives. Because He lives, we shall live also—that was the Lord's own assurance. Because we live, He lives also—that is the ineradicable conviction of every Christian heart.

CHAPTER XI

THE VIRGIN BIRTH OF CHRIST.

BY THE REV. PROF. JAMES ORR, D. D.,
UNITED FREE CHURCH COLLEGE, GLASGOW, SCOTLAND.

It is well known that the last ten or twenty years have been marked by a determined assault upon the truth of the Virgin birth of Christ. In the year 1892 a great controversy broke out in Germany, owing to the refusal of a pastor named Schrempf to use the Apostles' Creed in baptism because of disbelief in this and other articles. Schrempf was deposed, and an agitation commenced against the doctrine of the Virgin birth which has grown in volume ever since. Other tendencies, especially the rise of an extremely radical school of historical criticism, added force to the negative movement. The attack is not confined, indeed, to the article of the Virgin birth. It affects the whole supernatural estimate of Christ—His life, His claims, His sinlessness, His miracles, His resurrection from the dead. But the Virgin birth is assailed with special vehemence, because it is supposed that the evidence for this miracle is more easily got rid of than the evidence for public facts, such as the resurrection. The result is that in very many quarters the Virgin birth of Christ is openly treated as a fable. Belief in it is scouted as unworthy of the twentieth century intelligence. The methods of the oldest opponents of Christianity are revived, and it is likened to the Greek and Roman stories, coarse and vile, of heroes who had gods for their fathers. A special point is made of the silence of Paul, and of the other writings of the New Testament, on this alleged wonder.

THE UNHAPPIEST FEATURE.

It is not only, however, in the circles of unbelief that the Virgin birth is discredited; in the church itself the habit is spreading of casting doubt upon the fact, or at least of regarding it as no essential part of Christian faith. This is the unhappiest feature in this unhappy controversy. Till recently no one dreamed of denying that, in the sincere profession of Christianity, this article, which has stood from the beginning in the forefront of all the great creeds of Christendom, was included. Now it is different. The truth and value of the article of the Virgin birth are challenged. The article, it is affirmed, did not belong to the earliest Christian tradition, and the evidence for it is not strong. Therefore, let it drop.

THE COMPANY IT KEEPS.

From the side of criticism, science, mythology, history and comparative religion, assault is thus made on the article long so dear to the hearts of Christians and rightly deemed by them so vital to their faith. For loud as is the voice of denial, one fact must strike every careful observer of the conflict. Among those who reject the Virgin birth of the Lord few will be found—I do not know any—who take in other respects an adequate view of the Person and work of the Saviour. It is surprising how clearly the line of division here reveals itself. My statement publicly made and printed has never been confuted, that those who accept a full doctrine of the incarnation —that is, of a true entrance of the eternal Son of God into our nature for the purposes of man's salvation—with hardly an exception accept with it the doctrine of the Virgin birth of Christ, while those who repudiate or deny this article of faith either hold a lowered view of Christ's Person, or, more commonly, reject His supernatural claims altogether. It will not be questioned, at any rate, that the great bulk of the opponents of the Virgin birth—those who are conspicuous by writing against it—are in the latter class.

A CAVIL ANSWERED.

This really is an answer to the cavil often heard that, whether true or not, the Virgin birth is not of essential importance. It is not essential, it is urged, to Christ's sinlessness, for that would have been secured equally though Christ had been born of two parents. And it is not essential to the incarnation. A hazardous thing, surely, for erring mortals to judge of what was and was not essential in so stupendous an event as the bringing in of the "first-begotten" into the world! But the Christian instinct has ever penetrated deeper. Rejection of the Virgin birth seldom, if ever, goes by itself. As the late Prof. A. B. Bruce said, with denial of the Virgin birth is apt to go denial of the virgin life. The incarnation is felt by those who think seriously to involve a miracle in Christ's earthly origin. This will become clearer as we advance.

THE CASE STATED.

It is the object of this paper to show that those who take the lines of denial on the Virgin birth just sketched do great injustice to the evidence and importance of the doctrine they reject. The evidence, if not of the same public kind as that for the resurrection, is far stronger than the objector allows, and the fact denied enters far more vitally into the essence of the Christian faith than he supposes. Placed in its right setting among the other truths of the Christian religion, it is not only no stumbling-block to faith, but is felt to fit in with self-evidencing power into the connection of these other truths, and to furnish the very explanation that is needed of Christ's holy and supernatural Person. The ordinary Christian is a witness here. In reading the Gospels, he feels no incongruity in passing from the narratives of the Virgin birth to the wonderful story of Christ's life in the chapters that follow, then from these to the pictures of Christ's divine dignity given in John and Paul. The whole is of one piece: the Virgin birth is as natural at the beginning of the life of such an One—the divine Son—as the resurrection is at the end. And the more closely the matter is considered, the stronger does this impression grow. It is only when the scriptural conception of Christ is parted with that various difficulties and doubts come in.

A SUPERFICIAL VIEW.

It is, in truth, a *very superficial* way of speaking or think-ing of the Virgin birth to say that nothing depends on this be-lief for our estimate of Christ. Who that reflects on the subject carefully can fail to see that if Christ was virgin born—if He was truly "conceived," as the creed says, "by the Holy Ghost, born of the Virgin Mary"—there must of necessity enter a supernatural element into His Person; while, if Christ was sin-less, much more, if He was the very Word of God incarnate, there must have been a miracle—the most stupendous miracle in the universe—in His origin? If Christ was, as John and Paul affirm and His church has ever believed, the Son of God made flesh, the second Adam, the new redeeming Head of the race, a miracle was to be expected in His earthly origin; with-out a miracle such a Person could never have been. Why then cavil at the narratives which declare the fact of such a miracle? Who does not see that the Gospel history would have been in-complete without them? Inspiration here only gives to faith what faith on its own grounds imperatively demands for its perfect satisfaction.

THE HISTORICAL SETTING.

It is time now to come to *the Scripture itself,* and to look at the fact of the Virgin birth in its historical setting, and its relation with other truths of the Gospel. As preceding the examination of the historical evidence, a little may be said, first, on the *Old Testament preparation.* Was there any such preparation? Some would say there was not, but this is not God's way, and we may look with confidence for at least some indications which point in the direction of the New Testament event.

THE FIRST PROMISE.

One's mind turns first to that *oldest of all evangelical promises,* that the seed of the woman would bruise the head of the serpent. "I will put enmity," says Jehovah to the serpent-tempter, "between thee and the woman, and between thy seed and her seed; he shall bruise thy head, and thou shalt bruise his heel" (Genesis 3:15. R. V.). It is a forceless weakening of this first word of Gospel in the Bible to explain it of a lasting feud between the race of men and the brood of serpents. The serpent, as even Dr. Driver attests, is "the representative of the power of evil"—in later Scripture, "he that is called the Devil and Satan" (Rev. 12:9)—and the defeat he sustains from the woman's seed is a moral and spiritual victory. The "seed" who should destroy him is described emphatically as the *woman's* seed. It was the woman through whom sin had entered the race; by the seed of the woman would salvation come. The early church writers often pressed this analogy between Eve and the Virgin Mary. We may reject any element of over-exaltation of Mary they connected with it, but it remains significant that this peculiar phrase should be chosen to designate the future deliverer. I cannot believe the choice to be of accident. The promise to Abraham was that in *his* seed the families of the earth would be blessed; there the *male* is emphasized, but here it is the *woman*—the woman distinctively. There is, perhaps, as good scholars have thought, an allusion to this promise in 1 Timothy 2:15, where, with allusion to Adam and Eve, it is said, "But she shall be saved through her (or the) child-bearing" (R. V.).

THE IMMANUEL PROPHECY.

The idea of the Messiah, gradually gathering to itself the attributes of a divine King, reaches one of its clearest expressions in *the great Immanuel prophecy,* extending from Isaiah 7 to 9:7, and centering in the declaration: "The Lord Himself will give you [the unbelieving Ahaz] a sign; behold, a virgin shall conceive, and bear a son, and shall call his name Immanuel" (Isa. 7:14; Cf. 8:8, 10). This is none other than the child of wonder extolled in chapter 9:6, 7: "For unto us a child is born, unto us a son is given; and the government shall be upon his shoulder; and his name shall be called Wonderful, Counsellor, The mighty God, The everlasting Father, [Father of Eternity], The Prince of Peace. Of the increase of his government and peace there shall be no end, upon the throne of David, and upon his kingdom," etc. This is the prophecy quoted as fulfilled in Christ's birth in Matt. 1:23, and it seems also alluded to in the glowing promises to Mary in Luke 1:32, 33. It is pointed out in objection that the term rendered "virgin" in Isaiah does not necessarily bear this meaning; it denotes properly only a young unmarried woman. The context, howeyer, seems clearly to lay an emphasis on the unmarried state, and the translators of the Greek version of the Old Testament (the Septuagint) plainly so understood it when they rendered it by *parthenos,* a word which *does* mean "virgin." The tendency in many quarters now is to admit this (Dr. Cheyne, etc.), and even to seek an explanation of it in alleged Babylonian beliefs in a virgin-birth. This last, however, is quite illusory.[1] It is, on the other hand, singular that the Jews themselves do not seem to have applied this prophecy at any time to the Messiah—a fact which disproves the theory that it was this text which suggested the story of a Virgin birth to the early disciples.

[1]For the evidence, see my volume on "The Virgin Birth," Lecture VII.

ECHOES IN OTHER SCRIPTURES.

It was, indeed, when one thinks of it, only on the supposition that there was to be something exceptional and extraordinary in the birth of this child called Immanuel that it could have afforded to Ahaz a sign of the perpetuity of the throne of David on the scale of magnitude proposed ("Ask it either in the depth, or in the height above." Ver. 10). We look, therefore, with interest to see if there are any *echoes* or *suggestions* of the idea of this passage in other prophetic scriptures. They are naturally not many, but they do not seem to be altogether wanting. There is, first, the remarkable Bethlehem prophecy in Micah 5:2, 3—also quoted as fulfilled in the nativity (Matt. 2:5, 6)—connected with the saying: "Therefore will he give them up, until the time that she who travaileth hath brought forth" ("The King from Bethlehem," says Delitzsch, "who has a nameless one as mother, and of whose father there is no mention"). Micah was Isaiah's contemporary, and when the close relation between the two is considered (Cf. Isa. 2:2-4, with Micah 4:1-3), it is difficult not to recognize in his oracle an expansion of Isaiah's. In the same line would seem to lie the enigmatic utterance in Jer. 31:22: "For Jehovah hath created a new thing in the earth: a woman shall encompass a man" (thus Delitzsch, etc.).

TESTIMONY OF THE GOSPEL.

The germs now indicated in phophetic scriptures had apparently borne no fruit in Jewish expectations of the Messiah, when *the event took place* which to Christian minds made them luminous with predictive import. In Bethlehem of Judea, as Micah had foretold, was born of a virgin mother He whose "goings forth" were "from of old, from everlasting" (Micah 5:2; Matt. 2:6). Matthew, who quotes the first part of the verse, can hardly have been ignorant of the hint of pre-existence it contained. This brings us to the testimony to the miraculous birth of Christ in our first and third Gospels—the only Gospels which record the circumstances of Christ's birth at all. By general consent the narratives in Matthew (chapters 1, 2) and in Luke (chapters 1, 2) are independent—that is, they are not derived one from the other—yet they both affirm, in detailed story, that Jesus, conceived by the power of the Holy Spirit, was born of a pure virgin, Mary of Nazareth, espoused to Joseph, whose wife she afterwards became. The birth took place at Bethlehem, whither Joseph and Mary had gone for enrollment in a census that was being taken. The announcement was made to Mary beforehand by an angel, and the birth was preceded, attended, and followed by remarkable events that are narrated (birth of the Baptist, with annunciations, angelic vision to the shepherds, visit of wise men from the east, etc.). The narratives should be carefully read at length to understand the comments that follow.

THE TESTIMONY TESTED.

There is no doubt, therefore, about the testimony to the Virgin birth, and the question which now arises is—What is the *value* of these parts of the Gospels as evidence? Are they genuine parts of the Gospels? Or are they late and untrustworthy additions? From what sources may they be presumed to be derived? It is on the truth of the narratives that our belief in the Virgin birth depends. Can they be trusted? Or are they mere fables, inventions, legends, to which no credit can be attached?

The answer to several of these questions can be given in very brief form. The narratives of the nativity in Matthew and Luke are undoubtedly *genuine parts* of their respective Gospels. They have been there since ever the Gospels themselves had an existence. The proof of this is convincing. The chapters in question are found in every manuscript and version of the Gospels known to exist. There are hundreds of manuscripts, some of them very old, belonging to different parts of the world, and many versions in different languages (Latin, Syriac,

Egyptian, etc.), but these narratives of the Virgin birth are found in all. We know, indeed, that a section of the early Jewish Christians—the Ebionites, as they are commonly called —possessed a Gospel based on Matthew from which the chapters on the nativity were absent. But this was not the real Gospel of Matthew: it was at best a mutilated and corrupted form of it. The genuine Gospel, as the manuscripts attest, always had these chapters.

Next, as to the Gospels themselves, they were not of late and non-apostolic origin; but were *written by apostolic men,* and were from the first accepted and circulated in the church as trustworthy embodiments of sound apostolic tradition. Luke's Gospel was from Luke's own pen—its genuineness has recently received a powerful vindication from Prof. Harnack, of Berlin—and Matthew's Gospel, while some dubiety still rests on its original language (Aramaic or Greek), passed without challenge in the early church as the genuine Gospel of the Apostle Matthew. Criticism has more recently raised the question whether it is only the "groundwork" of the discourses (the "Logia") that comes directly from, Matthew. However this may be settled, it is certain that the Gospel in its Greek form always passed as Matthew's. It must, therefore, if not written by him, have had his immediate authority. The narratives come to us, accordingly, with high apostolic sanction.

SOURCES OF THE NARRATIVES.

As to the *sources* of the narratives, not a little can be gleaned from the study of their internal character. Here two facts reveal themselves. The first is that the narrative of Luke is based on some old, archaic, highly original Aramaic writing. Its Aramaic character gleams through its every part. In style, tone, conception, it is highly primitive—emanates, apparently, from that circle of devout people in Jerusalem to whom its own pages introduce us (Luke 2:25, 36-38). It has, therefore, the highest claim to credit. The second fact is even more important. A perusal of the narratives shows clearly— what might have been expected—that the information they convey was derived from no lower source than Joseph and Mary themselves. This is a marked feature of contrast in the narratives—that Matthew's narrative is all told from Joseph's point of view, and Luke's is all told from Mary's. The signs of this are unmistakable. Matthew tells about Joseph's difficulties and action, and says little or nothing about Mary's thoughts and feelings. Luke tells much about Mary—even her inmost thoughts—but says next to nothing directly about Joseph. The narratives, in short, are not, as some would have it, contradictory, but are independent and complementary. The one supplements and completes the other. Both together are needed to give the whole story. They bear in themselves the stamp of truth, honesty, and purity, and are worthy of all acceptation, as they were evidently held to be in the early church.

UNFOUNDED OBJECTIONS.

Against the acceptance of these early, well-attested narratives, what, now, have the objectors to allege? I pass by the attempts to show, by critical elimination (expurging Luke 1:35, and some other clauses), that Luke's narrative was not a narrative of a Virgin birth at all. This is a vain attempt in face of the testimony of manuscript authorities. Neither need I dwell on the alleged "discrepancies" in the genealogies and narratives. These are not serious, when the independence and different standpoints of the narratives are acknowledged. The genealogies, tracing the descent of Christ from David along different lines, present problems which exercise the minds of scholars, but they do not touch the central fact of the belief of both Evangelists in the birth of Jesus from a virgin. Even in a Syriac manuscript which contains the certainly wrong reading, "Joseph begat Jesus," the narrative goes on, as usual, to recount the Virgin birth. It is not a contradiction, if Matthew is silent on the earlier residence in Nazareth, which Luke's object led him fully to describe.

SILENCE OF MARK AND JOHN.

The objection on which most stress is laid (apart from what is called the evidently "mythical" character of the narratives) is the *silence* on the Virgin birth in the remaining Gospels, and other parts of the New Testament. This, it is held, conclusively proves that the Virgin birth was not known in the earliest Christian circles, and was a legend of later origin. As respects the Gospels—Mark and John—the objection would only apply if it was the design of these Gospels to narrate, as the others do, the circumstances of the nativity. But this was evidently not their design. Both Mark and John knew that Jesus had a human birth—an infancy and early life—and that His mother was called Mary, but of deliberate purpose they tell us nothing about it. Mark begins his Gospel with Christ's entrance on His public ministry, and says nothing of the period before, especially of how Jesus came to be called "the Son of God" (Mark 1:1). John traces the divine descent of Jesus, and tells us that the "Word became flesh" (John 1:14); but how this miracle of becoming flesh was wrought he does not say. It did not lie within his plan. He knew the church tradition on the subject: he had the Gospels narrating the birth of Jesus from the Virgin in his hands: and he takes the knowledge of their teaching for granted. To speak of contradiction in a case like this is out of the question.

SILENCE OF PAUL.

How far Paul was acquainted with the facts of Christ's earthly origin it is not easy to say. To a certain extent these facts would always be regarded as among the privacies of the innermost Christian circles—so long at least as Mary lived—and the details may not have been fully known till the Gospels were published. Paul admittedly did not base his preaching of his Gospel on these private, interior matters, but on the broad, public facts of Christ's ministry, death, and resurrection. It would be going too far, however, to infer from this that Paul had no knowledge of the miracle of Christ's birth. Luke was Paul's companion, and doubtless shared with Paul all the knowledge which he himself had gathered on this and other subjects. One thing certain is, that Paul could not have believed in the divine dignity, the pre-existence, the sinless perfection, and redeeming headship, of Jesus as he did, and not have been convinced that His entrance into humanity was no ordinary event of nature, but implied an unparalleled miracle of some kind. This Son of God, who "emptied" Himself, who was "born of a woman, born under the law," who "knew no sin" (Phil. 2:7, 8; Gal. 4:4; 2 Cor. 5:21), was not, and could not be, a simple product of nature. God must have wrought creatively in His human origin. The Virgin birth would be to Paul the most reasonable and credible of events. So also to John, who held the same high view of Christ's dignity and holiness.

CHRIST'S SINLESSNESS A PROOF.

It is sometimes argued that a Virgin birth is no aid to the explanation of Christ's *sinlessness*. Mary being herself sinful in nature, it is held the taint of corruption would be conveyed by one parent as really as by two. It is overlooked that the whole fact is not expressed by saying that Jesus was born of a virgin mother. There is the other factor—"conceived by the Holy Ghost." What happened was a divine, creative miracle wrought in the production of this new humanity which secured, from its earliest germinal beginnings, freedom from the slightest taint of sin. Paternal generation in such an origin is superfluous. The birth of Jesus was not, as in ordinary births, the creation of a new personality. It was a divine Person—already existing—entering on this new mode of existence. Miracle could alone effect such a wonder. *Because* His human nature had this miraculous origin Christ was the "holy" One from the commencement (Luke 1:35). Sinless He was, as His whole life demonstrated; but when, in all time, did natural generation give birth to a sinless personality?

THE EARLY CHURCH A WITNESS.

The history of the early church is occasionally appealed to in witness that the doctrine of the Virgin birth was not primitive. No assertion could be more futile. The early church, so far as we can trace it back, in all its branches, held this doctrine. No Christian sect is known that denied it, save the Jewish Ebionites formerly alluded to. The general body of the Jewish Christians—the Nazarenes as they are called—accepted it. Even the greater Gnostic sects in their own way admitted it. Those Gnostics who denied it were repelled with all the force of the church's greatest teachers. The Apostle John is related to have vehemently opposed Cerinthus, the earliest teacher with whom this denial is connected.

DISCREDITED VAGARIES.

What more remains to be said? It would be waste of space to follow the objectors into their various theories of a *mythical* origin of this belief. One by one the speculations advanced have broken down, and given place to others—all equally baseless. The newest of the theories seeks an origin of the belief in ancient Babylonia, and supposes the Jews to have possessed the notion in pre-Christian times. This is not only opposed to all real evidence, but is the giving up of the contention that the idea had its origin in *late* Christian circles, and was unknown to earlier apostles.

THE REAL CHRIST.

Doctrinally, it must be repeated that the belief in the Virgin birth of Christ is of the highest value for the right apprehension of Christ's unique and sinless personality. Here is

One, as Paul brings out in Romans 5:12 ff., who, free from sin Himself, and not involved in the Adamic liabilities of the race, reverses the curse of sin and death brought in by the first Adam, and establishes the reign of righteousness and life. Had Christ been naturally born, not one of these things could be affirmed of Him. As one of Adam's race, not an entrant from a higher sphere, He would have shared in Adam's corruption and doom—would Himself have required to be redeemed. Through God's infinite mercy, He came from above, inherited no guilt, needed no regeneration or sanctification, but became Himself the Redeemer, Regenerator, Sanctifier, for all who receive Him. "Thanks be unto God for His unspeakable gift" (2 Cor. 9:15).

CHAPTER XII

THE GOD-MAN*

BY THE LATE JOHN STOCK

Jesus of Nazareth was not mere man, excelling others in purity of life and conduct and in sincerity of purpose, simply distinguished from other teachers by the fullness of His knowledge. *He is the God-man.* Such view of the person of Messiah is the assured foundation of the entire Scriptural testimony to Him, and it is to be irresistibly inferred from the style and strain in which He habitually spake of Himself. Of this inferential argument of the Saviour we can give here the salient points only in briefest presentation.

1. *Jesus claimed to be the Son of God.* We meet with this title in the Book of Daniel. It was used by Nebuchadnezzar to describe that fourth wonderful personage who walked with the three Hebrew confessors in the fire (3:25), and who was, doubtless, the Lord Jesus Christ revealing Himself in an assumed bodily form to His heroic servants. This majestic title is repeatedly appropriated to Himself by our Master. (See John 5:25; 9:35; 11:4, etc.) In His interview with Nicodemus He designated Himself, *"The Only Begotten Son of God"* (John 3:18).

When confronted with the Sanhedrim, Jesus was closely questioned about His use of this title; and He pleaded guilty to the indictment. (See Matt. 26:63, 64, and 27:43; cf. Luke 22:70, 71, and John 19:7.) It is clear from the narrative that the Jews understood this glorious name in the lips of Jesus to be a blasphemous assertion of divine attributes for Himself.

They understood Jesus to thus claim *equality with God*

*Abbreviated and published by permission of the American Baptist Publication Society.

(see John 5:18); and to *make Himself God.* (See John 10:33.) Did they understand Him? Did they overestimate the significance of this title as claimed by our Lord? How easy it would have been for Him to set them right. How imperative were His obligations to do so, not merely to Himself, but to these unhappy men who were thirsting for His blood under a misapprehension. Did not every principle of philanthropy require Him to save them from the perpetration of the terrible murder which He knew they were contemplating? Yes, if they were mistaken, it was a heinous crime in our Lord not to undeceive them. But not a word did He say to soften down the offensiveness of His claim. He allowed it to stand in all its repulsiveness to the Jewish mind, and died without making any sign that He had been misapprehended. He thus accepted the Jewish interpretation of His meaning, and sealed that sense of the title, *Son of God,* with His heart's blood. Nothing can be clearer, then, than the fact that Jesus died without a protest for claiming equality with God, and thus making Himself God. We dare not trust ourselves to write what we must think of Him under such circumstances, if He were a mere man.

2. *Jesus, on several occasions, claimed a divine supremacy in both worlds.* Take for example His description of the final judgment: "The Son of man shall send forth His angels, and they shall gather out of His kingdom all things that offend, and them which do iniquity: and shall cast them into the furnace of fire: there shall be wailing and gnashing of teeth" (Matt. 13:41). The kingdom is His, and all the angels of God are His obedient servants.

He declared in the plainest terms that He will preside as the Universal Judge at the last great day, and that His wisdom and authority will award to every man his appropriate doom. "When the Son of man shall come in His glory, and all the holy angels with Him, then shall He sit upon the throne of His glory; and before Him shall be gathered all nations; and He shall separate them one from another, as a shepherd divideth his sheep from the goats; and He shall set the sheep on His right hand, but the goats on the left" (Matt. 25:31-33). His voice will utter the cheering words, "Come, ye blessed," and the awful sentence, "Depart, ye cursed" (Matt. 25:31-46). Without hesitation, equivocation, or compromise Jesus of Nazareth repeatedly assumed the right and the ability to discriminate the moral character and desserts of all mankind from Adam to the day of doom. His sublime consciousness of universal supremacy relieved the claim of everything like audacity, and only made it the natural sequence of His incarnate Godhead. "All power," He said, "is given unto Me in heaven and in earth" (Matt. 28:18).

This idea germinated in the minds of His followers and apostles. The vivid picture recorded in the twenty-fifth chapter of Matthew gave a coloring to all their subsequent thoughts about their divine Master. They ever after spake of Him as "ordained to be the Judge of the quick and the dead" (Acts 10:42; 17:31). They testified that "We must all appear before the judgment seat of Christ; that every one may receive the things done in his body, according to that he hath done, whether it be good or bad" (2 Cor. 5:10; Rom. 14:10).

Thus the mind of John the Apostle was prepared for the subsequent revelations of Patmos, when he heard his glorified Lord claim to "have the keys of hell and of death" (Rev. 1:18), and saw the vision of the "great white throne, and Him that sat on it, from whose face the earth and the heaven fled away" (Rev. 20:11).

But who is this that claims to grasp and wield the thunderbolts of eternal retribution; who professes to be able to scrutinize the secret purposes and motives, as well as the words and deeds, of every man that has been born, from the first dawn of personal responsibility to the day of death? Can anything short of indwelling omniscience qualify Him for such an intricate and complicated and vast investigation? If He could not search *"the reins and the hearts"* (to use His own words to John), how could He give to every one of us according to his works? (Rev. 2:23.) The brain reels when we think of the tremendous transactions of the last day, and the momentous interests then to be decided forever and ever; and reason tells us, that if the Judge who is to preside over these solemnities be a man, He must be a God-man. If Jesus is to be the universal and absolute Judge of our race—a Judge from whose decisions there will be no appeal, He must be "God manifest in the flesh." But what can we think of Him, if in setting up this claim He mislead us?

3. *Jesus always claimed absolute and indisputable power in dealing with every question of moral duty and destiny.* To quote Mr. Newman, the mere deist, "I find Jesus Himself to set up oracular claims. I find an assumption of pre-eminence and unapproachable moral wisdom to pervade every discourse from end to end of the Gospels. If I may not believe that Jesus assumed an oracular manner, I do not know what moral peculiarity in Him I am permitted to believe."* There is no possibility of denying the truth of these words. Jesus claimed to be absolute Lord in the whole region of morals. He settled the meaning and force of old laws, and instituted new ones by His own authority. Take the Sermon on the Mount as an illustration. With what a self-possessed peremptoriness does He define the existing legislation of God, and enlarge its limits! With what conscious dignity does He decide every question in the whole range of human duty with the simple—"But I say unto you!" Seven times in one chapter does he use this formula. (See Matt. 5:20, 22, 28, 32, 34, 39, 44.) And in the application of the sermon He declared Him only to be the wise man and built upon solid rock, who hears His sayings and does them. (Matt. 7:24.) Well might the people be aston-

---

*In "Phases of Faith," by Francis William Newman, M. A., page 150.

ished at His doctrine; for verily "He taught them as one having authority, and not as the scribes" (Matt. 7:28, 29). But
the tone which pervades the Sermon on the Mount runs
through the whole of the teaching of Jesus of Nazareth. He
ever speaks as if He were the Author and Giver of the law;
as if He had the power to modify any of its provisions according to His own ideas of fitness; and as if He were the Supreme
Lord of human consciences. His style is utterly unlike that of
any inspired teacher before or after Him. They appealed to
the law and to the testimony. (See Isa. 8:20.) But Jesus
claimed an inherent power to modify and to alter both.

The Sabbath was the symbol of the entire covenant made by
God with Israel through the ministry of Moses. (See Exod.
31:12-17.) But Jesus asserted His complete supremacy over
this divine institution. These were His emphatic words: *"For
the Son of man is Lord also of the Sabbath day"* (Matt. 12:8;
Mark 2:28; Luke 6:5). He could, of His own will, relax
the terrors of the Jewish Sabbath, and even supersede it altogether by the Christian "Lord's Day." He was Lord of all
divine institutions.

And in the Church He claims the right to regulate her doctrines and her ordinances according to His will. The apostles
He commissioned to baptize in His name, and charged them to
teach their converts to observe all things whatsoever He had
commanded them. (Matt. 28:19-20.) Thus John was prepared for the sublime vision of the Son of man as "He that
holdeth the seven stars in His right hand, who walketh in the
midst of the seven golden candlesticks" (Rev. 2:1); and as "He
that hath the key of David, He that openeth, and no man
shutteth; and shutteth, and no man openeth" (Rev. 3:7).

And the authority which Jesus claimed extends into heaven,
and to the final state of things. He affirmed that He would
ascend to share His Father's dominion, and to sit in the throne
of His glory. (See Matt. 19:28.) The counterpart to which
announcement is found in His declaration to John in Patmos:

"to him that overcometh will I grant to sit with Me in My throne, even as I also overcame, and am set down with My Father in His throne" (Rev. 3:21). The manner in which the Lord spake of Himself in connection with the heavenly state bore much fruit in the hearts and sentiments of His disciples. To them this life was being "absent from the Lord" as to His visible presence: and their one beautiful idea of heaven was that it was being "present with the Lord" (2 Cor. 5:6, 8). He had taught them to regard Him as their "all in all," even in their eternal state; and with unquestioning faith they cherished the one blessed hope of being forever with the Lord. All other ideas of the celestial world were lost sight of in comparison with this absorbing anticipation.

The very mansions which they were to occupy in the Eternal Father's house, Jesus said, He would assign to them (John 14:2). He asserted His right to give away the crowns and glories of immortal blessedness as if they were His by indisputable right. He wills it, and it is done. He constantly reminded His disciples of rewards which He would give to every servant whom, at His coming, He found to be faithful. (Compare Matt. 24:44 with 45, 46, 47; 25:14-46, etc.)

It is true Jesus will give these honors only to those for whom they are prepared by His Father; for, in their designs of mercy, the Father, the Son, and the Holy Spirit are *one*. Still He will, of right, dispense the blessing to all who receive it. For these were our Lord's true words: "To sit on My right hand, and on My left, is not Mine to give, but [or, except] it shall be given to them for whom it is prepared of My Father" (Matt. 20:23). The language logically implies our Lord's absolute right to give the crowns; but only to such as are appointed to these honors by the Father.

These ideas are repeated in vision to John. Jesus gives "right to the tree of life" (Rev. 2:7). In the praises of the redeemed host, as described in that marvelous Apocalypse, they ever ascribe their salvation and glory to Jesus, and the sinless angels swell the chorus of Immanuel's praises, while the universe, from its myriad worlds, echoes the strain. (Rev. 5:8-14.)

In the description of the final state of things—a state which shall be subsequent to the millennium (whatever that may be)—(Rev. 20:1-10), and also to the final judgment of both righteous and wicked (Rev. 20:11-15), and to the act of homage and fealty described in 1 Cor. 15:24-28, we find the Lamb still and forever on the throne. The Church is still "the bride, the Lamb's wife" (Rev. 21:9). In that consummated state of all things, "The Lord God Almighty and the Lamb are the temple of it" (Rev. 21:22), the glory of God lightens it, "and the Lamb is the light thereof" (Rev. 21:23), the pure river of water of life still flows from beneath the throne of God and of the Lamb (Rev. 22:1), "the throne of God and of the Lamb shall be in it; and His servants shall serve Him: and they shall see His face; and His name shall be in their foreheads" (Rev. 22:3, 4). Throughout the Apocalypse we never find Jesus among the worshippers. He is there the worshipped One on the throne, and with that picture the majestic vision closes.

The inspired apostles had imbibed these ideas from the personal teaching of their Lord, and subsequent revelations did but expand in their minds the seed-thoughts which He had dropped there from His own sacred lips. Paul nobly expressed the sentiments of all his brethren when he wrote, "Henceforth there is laid up for me a crown of righteousness, which the Lord, the righteous judge, shall give me at that day; and not to me only, but unto all them also that love His appearing" (2 Tim. 4:8). But surely He who claims supremacy, absolute and indisputable, in morals, in divine institutions, in the Church on earth, in heaven, and in a consummated universe forever, must be Lord of all, manifest in human form. If he were not, *what* must He have been to advance such assumptions, and what must the book be which enforces them?

4. *Jesus asserted His full possession of the power to forgive sins*. The moral instincts of the Jews were right when they put the question, "Who can forgive sins but God only?" (Mark 2:7.) We do not wonder that, with their ideas of Christ, they asked in amazement, "Who is this that forgiveth sins also?" (Luke 7:49), or that they exclaimed, in reference to such a claim, from such a quarter, "This man blasphemeth" (Matt. 9:3).

And yet Christ declared most emphatically, on more than one occasion, His possession of this divine prerogative, and healed the palsied man in professed attestation of the fact. (Luke 5:24.) Those who would eliminate the miraculous element from the second narrative altogether, must admit that Matthew, Mark, and Luke all relate most circumstantially that Jesus did at least profess to work a miracle in support of His claim to possess power to forgive sins. If He wrought the miracle, His claim is established; and if He did not work it, but cheated the people, then away with Him forever as an arrant impostor! But if He wrought it, and proved His claim, He must be equal with His Father; for the Jews were right, and no one "can forgive sins but God only." Could a mere man cancel with a word the sin of a creature against his Maker? The very thought is a blasphemy.

5. *Jesus claimed the power to raise His own body from the grave, to quicken the souls of men into spiritual life, and to raise all the dead at the last great day*. Jesus likened His body to a temple which the Jews should destroy, and which He would raise up again in three days. (John 2:19-21.) He affirmed that He had power to lay down His life, and power to take it up again. (John 10:18.) He decleared that the *spiritually* dead—for the physical resurrection is spoken of afterward as a distinct topic—should hear His voice and live. (John 5:25.) And then He tells us not to wonder at this, for the day is coming when, by His omnific fiat, all the generations of the dead "shall come forth; they that have done good, unto

the resurrection of life; and they that have done evil, unto the resurrection of damnation" (John 5:28, 29).

But if Jesus were not, in some mysterious sense, the Lord of His own life, what power had He to dispose of it as He pleased? And how could He recall it when gone? And how could he communicate spiritual life, if He were not its Divine Fountain? And how could He raise the dead from their graves, if He were not the Almighty Creator? All these claims, if genuine, necessitate faith in the Godhead of Jesus.

6. *Jesus declared that He had the ability to do all His Father's works.* The Saviour had healed the impotent man at the pool of Bethesda on the Sabbath day. When accused by the Jews of sin for this act, our Lord justified Himself by the ever-memorable words, "My Father worketh hitherto [that is, on the Sabbath day in sustaining and blessing the worlds], and I work"—on the same day, *therefore,* in healing the sick,— thus indirectly asserting His right to do all that His Father did, and, as the Jews put it, claiming *such* a Sonship as made Him "equal with God." But our Lord did not abate one iota of His claim. True, He admitted that, *as the Incarnate Mediator,* He had received His authority from the Father, but He declared that "What things soever the Father doeth, these also doeth the Son likewise" (John 5:17-19). Now, no language can overestimate the sublimity of this claim. Christ affirmed that He possessed full right and ability to do all that the Eternal Father had the right and ability to do. Was such language ever used by the most inspired or the most daring of mere mortals? We do not forget that our Lord was careful to declare that the Father had committed all judgment to Him (John 5:22), but had He not Himself been a partaker of the Godhead how could He, as the Incarnate One, have been qualified to be armed with the prerogative so vast? He who can do all the works of God must be God!

7. *Jesus spake of Himself as the greatest gift of infinite mercy even.* In His conversation with Nicodemus, Christ

spake of Himself in these terms: "God so loved the world, that He gave His only begotten Son, that whosoever believeth in Him, should not perish, but have everlasting life" (John 3:16), by which our Lord evidently meant to convey the idea that the gift of the Son was the richest gift of divine love.

And this idea proved powerfully germinant in the minds of the apostles. They elaborated the argument. By the gift of Christ above all others, they taught us: "God commended His love towards us" (Rom. 5:8; see, too, John 4:10). They reasoned thus, having learned their logic from the lips of their Lord, "He that spared not His own Son, but delivered Him up for us all, how shall He not with Him also freely give us all things?" (Rom. 8:32). The argument of the apostle is *from the greater to the less*. It assumes that Christ Jesus is greater than all things. It would have no force on any other principle. More than this, it assumes that Christ is *infinitely* greater than all things, so that all the other expressions of divine goodness to our race dwindle into insignificance when compared with the gift of Christ. But can such representations as these be harmonized with the notion that Christ is merely a gifted man? Would they not deserve to be called *hyperbole run mad* on such an hypothesis? And imagine a mere man to stand forward and proclaim himself the choicest gift of God's love to our race. What a monstrous exaggeration and egotism! If Christ be greater than all other divine gifts combined, must He not be the God-man? On the evangelical hypothesis such representations are seen to be neither bombast nor rhetorical exaggeration, but sober, solid truth; and we can say with the seraphic Paul, without reserve: "Thanks be unto God for His *unspeakable* gift" (2 Cor. 9:15).

8. *Jesus announced Himself as the center of rest for the human soul.* Who has not thrilled under the mighty spell of those mighty words: "Come unto Me, all ye that labor and are heavy laden, and *I* will give you rest. Take My yoke upon you, and learn of Me; for I am meek and lowly in heart; and

ye shall find rest unto your souls. For My yoke is easy and My burden is light" (Matt. 11:28-30). In this invitation our Lord proclaims Himself to be everything to the soul. We are to come to Him, to take His yoke upon us, and to learn of Him. In receiving *Him* we shall find rest unto our souls, for *He* will give us rest.

Now, God alone is the resting-place of the human spirit. In Him, and in Him only, can we find assured peace. But Jesus claims to be our rest. Must He not, then, be God Incarnate? And very noticeable is the fact that, in the same breath in which He speaks of Himself in these august terms, He says: "I am meek and lowly in heart." But where were His meekness and lowliness in making such a claim, if He were simply a man like ourselves?

In the same spirit are those memorable passages in which this wonderful personage speaks of Himself as our peace. "Peace I leave with you, My peace I give unto you; not as the world giveth, give I unto you" (John 14:27). "These words have I spoken unto you, that in *Me* ye might have peace" (John 16:33). Thus ever does the Lord concentrate our thoughts upon *Himself*. But what must He be to be worthy of such supreme attention?

9. *Jesus permitted Thomas to adore Him as his Lord and his God, and pronounced an eulogium upon the faith thus displayed.* (John 20:28.) On this fact we quote the admirable comment of Dean Alford: "The Socinian view, that these words, '*my Lord and my God,*' are merely an exclamation, is refuted, (1) By the fact that no such exclamations were in use among the Jews. (2) By the εἶπεν αὐτῷ (he said to *Him,* that is, Christ). (3) By the impossibility of referring ὁ κύριός μου, my Lord, to another than Jesus. (See verse 13.) (4) By the New Testament usage of expressing the vocative by the nominative with an article. (5) By the utter psychological absurdity of such a supposition; that one just convinced of the presence of Him whom he deeply

loved, should, instead of addressing Him, break out into an irrelevant cry. (6) By the further absurdity of supposing that if such were the case, the Apostle John, who, of all the sacred writers, most constantly keeps in mind the object for which he is writing, should have recorded anything so beside that object. (7) By the intimate connection of πεπίστευκας, *thou hast believed.* (See next verse.)

"Dismissing it, therefore, we observe that this is *the highest confession* of faith which has yet been made; and that it shows that (though not yet fully) the meaning of the previous confessions of His being '*the Son of God*' was understood. Thus John, in the very close of his Gospel iterates the testimony with which he began it—to the Godhead of the Word who became flesh, and, by this closing confession, shows how *the testimony of Jesus to Himself* had gradually deepened and exalted the apostles' conviction, from the time when they knew Him only as ὁ υἱὸς τοῦ Ἰωσήφ (1:46), 'the son of Joseph,' till now, when He is acknowledged as their Lord and their God." (Alford's Greek New Testament, on the passage.)

These judicious remarks leave nothing to be added as to the real application of the words, "my Lord and my God." But how did the Saviour *receive* this act of adoration? He commended it, and held it up for the imitation of the coming ages. "Jesus saith unto him, Thomas, because thou hast seen Me, thou hast believed: blessed are they that have not seen, and yet have believed" (29). He thus most emphatically declared His Lordship and Godhead. But how fearful was His crime in so doing, if He was only a Socinian Christ!

This conversation produced a deep impression upon the apostolical mind, and upon the early Church. Stephen invoked Jesus in prayer with his dying breath. (Acts 7:59.) Paul thrice besought the Lord (Jesus) in supplication, that this thorn in the flesh might be taken from him, and received an answer from the Lord. (2 Cor. 12:8, compared with the *next* verse, the 9th.) The prayer was offered to Jesus, and was responded to by Jesus, as the context demonstrates.

The primitive disciples are thus described: "All that in every place call upon the name of Jesus Christ our Lord, both theirs and ours" (1 Cor. 1:2).

Every convert was, by Christ's orders, baptized in His name conjointly with that of the Father and the Holy Spirit; and thus the whole Church was taught to adore Him as equal with God at the solemn hour of religious profession. (Matt. 28:19.)

The apostolical benediction invokes Jesus in prayer with God and the Holy Ghost (2 Cor. 13:14), and the entire sacred record closes with a solemn litany to the Son: "The grace of our Lord Jesus Christ be with you all. Amen" (Rev. 22:21). Again we ask, Who is this if He be not the God-man?

10. *Jesus indirectly compared Himself with God.* He did so in these words: "No man knoweth the Son [Luke gives it, "Who the Son is"], but the Father; neither knoweth any man the Father [Luke gives it, "Who the Father is"], save the Son, and he to whomsoever the Son will reveal Him" (See Matt. 11:27 and Luke 10:22). These statements are, perhaps, the most remarkable that fell even from the lips of Jesus. In them He asserted the Son to be as great a mystery as the Father, and consequently as difficult to know. This was in effect claiming equality with God. Nothing less can be made of it. Then, too, the Lord professed such a knowledge of God as can only be possessed by God. He indeed asserted that He knew the Father as well as the Father knew Him. Altogether, no language can well be more shockingly familiar and profane than these words of the Saviour were, if He were no more than a man. Let the reader well ponder them in the version both of Matthew and Luke.

On one occasion our Lord declared, "My Father is greater than all" (John 10:29); and on another, "My Father is greater than I" (John 14:28). But if our Lord was *only* a man, what need was there that He should tell us *this*? What should we think of any mere mortal who should stand up in our midst, and deliberately tell us that the Eternal Father is greater than he? Should we not question his sanity? Or should we not look upon the very comparison as a blasphemy? For what can justify a creature in such a virtual likening of himself to God? We are compelled to the conclusion that there must have been some other element in our Lord's nature, besides the human, which warranted Him in making so remarkable a statement. What danger was there that we should fail to recognize the superiority of the Eternal Father to the man Christ Jesus, if the latter was *no more than* a man? These words, generally supposed to be a stronghold of Unitarianism, are, in truth, an indirect testimony to the orthodox faith. For what comparison can there be between the Creator and a mere creature, between Infinity and one who is "less than nothing and vanity"?

11. *Jesus demands of us an unhesitating and unlimited faith in Himself; such faith, in short, as we should only exercise in God.* We are to believe in Him for the salvation of our entire being; not merely as pointing out to us the way to heaven, but as being *Himself* the way. He puts faith in Him in the same category as faith in the Father. (John 14:1.) The spirit of His teaching about the faith to be reposed in Him is given in His words to the woman of Samaria: "If thou knewest the gift of God, and who it is that saith unto thee, Give me to drink, thou wouldest have asked of Him, and He would have given thee living water." "Whosoever drinketh of the water that I shall give him shall never thirst; but the water that I shall give him shall be in him a well of water springing up into everlasting life" (John 4:10-14). Unless we exercise faith in His person and work,

figuratively called eating His flesh and drinking His blood, we have no life in us (John 6:53); but if any man eat of this bread, he shall live forever (51). Those who have given themselves up into the arms of Christ by faith receive eternal life from Him, and shall never perish. (John 10:28.) They are as much in the arms of Jesus as in the arms of the Father; and their safety is as much secured by one as by the other (compare 28, 29, 30). In fact, in this gracious transaction the Son and the Father are one (30). Well might the Jews, with their views of His origin, take up stones to stone Him for these claims, saying as they did it, "We stone Thee for blasphemy, because that Thou, being a man, makest Thyself God" (33). Our Lord's vindication of Himself, by a reference to the language of Psalm 82:6, is an illustration of the *argument from the less to the greater.* If in *any* sense the Jewish rulers might be called gods, how much more properly might *He,* the only begotten Son of the Father, be so designated? "Without Me ye can do nothing," is in short the essence of the Saviour's teaching about Himself. (See John 15:1-5.)

This is the sum of the Gospel message: Believe in the Lord Jesus Christ and ye shall be saved. It was a demand repeatedly and earnestly pressed by the Saviour, and inculcated by His apostles; and we say deliberately, that to exercise such a faith in Jesus as He required and the Gospel enforces, would, *with Socinian views,* be to expose ourselves to the terrible anathema: "Cursed is the man that trusteth in man, and that maketh flesh in his arm" (Jer. 17:5). How could my soul be safe in the arms of a mere man? How dare I trust my eternal redemption to the care of such a Christ? And on what principle did Paul say: "I can do all things through Christ who strengtheneth me" (Phil 4:13). And how can Jesus be "All in all" to true believers of every nation? (Col. 3:11.)

12. *The affection and devotion to His glory, which Jesus demands, are such as can be properly yielded only to God.* As we are to trust Christ for everything, so we are to give up everything for Him, should He demand the sacrifice. This was a doctrine which the Lord repeatedly taught. Let our readers study Matt. 10:37-39, and the parallel passage, Luke 14:26, 27, and they will see at once how uncompromising is the Saviour's demand. Father, mother, son, daughter, wife, and even life itself are all to be sacrificed, if devotion to Christ necessitates the surrender. All creatures, and all things, and our very lives are to be to us as nothing when compared with Christ. God Himself demands no less of us, and no more. What more *could* the Eternal Creator require? The moral law says: "Thou shalt love the Lord thy God with all thy soul, and with all thy strength, and Him only shalt thou serve." But Christ bids us love *Him* thus, and demands of us the homage and sacrifice of our whole being; now, if He be not the *Author* of our being, what right has He to urge such a demand upon us? I could not love Christ as He requires to be loved, if I did not believe in Him as the Incarnate God. To do so with Socinian views would be idolatry. Yet the motives which reigned in the hearts of inspired apostles are summed up in this one: "The love of Christ constraineth us," and they laid down the law, that all men are henceforth to live "not to themselves, but to Him who died for them and rose again" (2 Cor. 5:14, 15). And Jesus declared that our eternal destiny will take its character from our compliance or non-compliance with His demands: "Whosoever therefore shall confess Me before men, him will I confess also before My Father who is in heaven. But whosoever shall deny me before men, him will I also deny before My Father who is in heaven" (Matt. 10:32, 33, 38-42, cf. Matt. 25:45, 46), and the sentiment is echoed in apostolic teaching, the language of which is, "If any man love not the Lord Jesus Christ, let him be Anathema Maranatha" (1 Cor. 16:22). But clearly the suspension of such tremendous issues on the decree of our love for the person of a mere creature, is an idea utterly revolting to our moral sense. He must be the God-man.

13. *Jesus set Himself forth as the appropriate end of our lives and of all divine providences.* He requires us to live for Him, and for His glory. As we have seen, life is to be sacrificed, if fidelity to Him shall so require. The sickness of Lazarus, He taught, was ordered, "that the Son of God might be glorified thereby" (John 11:4). He expounded the scope of the Holy Spirit's mission in one pregnant sentence: *"He shall glorify Me"* (John 16:14; John 15:26).

This Messianic reading of all things proved wonderfully suggestive. It is amplified in the apostolical Epistles. Thus, Christ is "Lord both of the dead and the living" (Rom. 14:9). The great object of apostolic desire was, that Christ might be magnified in their bodies, whether by life or by death. (Phil. 1:20.) The early Church's one idea of the present state was: "For to me to live is Christ" (Phil. 1:21). And they looked forward to the final Epiphany, because Christ would then "come to be glorified in His saints, and to be admired in all them that believe," and because His name will then be "glorified in you" (2 Thess. 1:10-12).

Under Him, as the Universal Head, all things are finally to be gathered, and towards this consummation all things are now working. (See Eph. 1:10.)

Now, such a presentation of Christ by Christ, and by His apostles inspired by Himself and His Spirit, we cannot harmonize with Socinian views. For surely He, *for whose glory* we are to live, and the whole universe exists, must be the Lord of all, God over all, blessed for evermore. What right has our Lord to be the supreme End of life, if He be not its Source, its Preserver, in short, its God?

14. *Very suggestive, too, are those passages in which Jesus promised His continued presence to His disciples after His ascension.* Beautiful are the words: "Where two or three

are gathered together in My name, there am I in the midst of them" (Matt. 18:20). One of the last promises of our Lord was, "Lo, I am with you alway, even unto the end of the world" (Matt. 28:20). No perverse criticism can explain away these assurances; they guarantee the perpetual, personal presence of Jesus with all His disciples to the end of time.

And this idea had a wonderful influence over the thoughts and actions of the men whom Jesus inspired. They lived as those who were perpetually under their Lord's eye. Thus one speaks in the name of all: "Wherefore we labor, that, whether present or absent [from Christ as to his bodily presence, see 6 and 8], we may be accepted of Him [Christ]" (2 Cor. 5:9). Though denied His bodily presence, His divine they knew to be ever with them; hence they labored to please Him, and the best wish they could breathe for each other was, "The Lord Jesus Christ be with thy spirit" (2 Tim. 4:22).

And John saw Him in vision ever holding the ministerial stars in His right hand, and walking in the midst of the golden lamps—the churches. (Rev. 2:1.)

But how can we explain such representations as these, if Messiah be possessed of but one nature—the human, which must of necessity be local and limited as to its presence? Who is this that is always with His disciples in all countries at the same moment, but the Infinite One in a human form? We feel His presence; we know He is with us; and in this fact we have evidence that He is more than a man.

The line of argument we have been pursuing is by no means exhausted, but our space is filled. Every time we read the New Testament through, we detect new illustrations of the force of the testimony illustrated in this paper. Let the reader re-peruse for himself the sacred record with an eye to the hints which we have thrown out. Let him weigh again the old familiar phrases in which the Lord speaks, or is spoken of, and ask himself how he can explain them on any other principle than the orthodox view of our Lord's person and work, and he will be astonished to find how this view is woven into the very texture of the whole Gospel. Jesus Christ was neither the Holy One, nor the Just One, if He were not the God-man. (See Acts 3:14; Acts 2:27; Acts 7:52.) In short, we must tear up our Bibles and wait for a new Christ, if He of Nazareth be not what all His teachings compel us to believe He was, God Incarnate.

A Socinian may well ask: "Whence hath this man this wisdom, and these mighty works?" (Matt. 13:54); but to us that question is forever answered by the assurance that "The Word was made flesh and dwelt among us (and we beheld His glory, the glory as of the only begotten of the Father,) full of grace and truth" (John 1:14).

The argument is *cumulative,* and must be looked at as a whole as well as in detail. To us it appears irresistible.

Let no Unitarian seek to evade its force by taking refuge in those passages which affirm Christ's inferiority, as man and mediator, to His Father; such as Mark 13:32; John 10:29, and John 14:28. Such passages as these are not to the purpose. No one denies that, as man and mediator, our Lord was inferior to His Father. But to prove that He was inferior in one sense, does not disprove that He was equal in another sense. When you have demonstrated that He was a man, you have not shaken, or even touched, the evidence that He was God. The Saviour had a human soul with its natural limitation of knowledge, and a human body with exposure to death. This is admitted on all sides. The orthodox believe it as truly as their Unitarian friends. But the Gospel testimony teaches us something more. It reveals the Godhood of Jesus of Nazareth, and tells us that He thought it no robbery to claim equality with His Father. It is, therefore, disingenuous, or, at least, illogical, to quote testimonies to the humanity of the Christ in reply to the proof of His possession of a divine nature as well. The two questions are quite distinct. It is a *non sequitur* to affirm that Jesus is not God because He was a man. The point to be demonstrated is *that He was not both*.

There are two classes of Scriptures relating to our Lord: the first, affirming His possession of a human nature, with all its innocent frailties and limitations; the second, ascribing to Him a divine nature, possessed of the attributes of Godhood, performing divine works, and worthy of supreme honor and worship. Unitarians can only fairly explain one of these classes of Scriptures, the former; but Trinitarians can accept both classes, and expound them in their integrity and fullness. We are not stumbled by evidences that Jesus was "bone of our bone, and flesh of our flesh." We rejoice in Him as in one "touched with a feeling of our infirmities;" but we have no need to refine away, by a subtle and unfair criticism, the ascription to His person of divine perfections and works.

We gladly recognize the learning and the talents of many of the prominent Unitarian divines. We know that by the side of some of them we are but babes in intellect and attainment. But we remember that there was a time when "Jesus answered and said, I thank thee, O Father, Lord of heaven and earth, because Thou hast hid these things from the wise and prudent, and hast revealed them unto babes" (Matt. 11:25).

The times demand of us a vigorous re-assertion of the old truths, which are the very foundations of the Gospel system. *Humanity needs a Christ whom all can worship and adore.* The mythical account of Strauss' "Leben Jesu"; the unreal and romantic Christ of Renan's "Vie de Jesus"; and even the merely human Christ of "Ecce Homo," can never work any deliverance in the earth. Such a Messiah does not meet the yearnings of fallen human nature. It does not answer the pressing query, "How shall man be just with God?" It supplies no effective or sufficient agency for the regeneration of man's moral powers. It does not bring God down to us in our nature. Such a Christ we may criticise and admire, as we would Socrates, or Plato, or Milton, or Shakespeare; but we cannot trust Him with our salvation; we cannot love Him with all our hearts; we cannot pour forth at His feet the homage of our whole being; for to do so would be idolatry.

A so-called Saviour, whose only power to save lies in the excellent moral precepts that He gave, and the pure life that He lived; who is no longer the God-man, but the mere man; whose blood had no sacrificial atoning or propitiatory power in the moral government of Jehovah, but was simply a martyr's witness to a superior system of ethics—is not the Saviour of the four Gospels, or of Paul, or Peter, or John. It is not under the banners of such a Messiah that the Church of God has achieved its triumphs. The Christ of the New Testament, of the early Church, of universal Christendom; the Christ, the power of whose name has revolutionized the world and raised it to its present level, and under whose guidance the sacramental host of God's redeemed are advancing and shall advance to yet greater victories over superstition and sin, is Immanuel, God with us, in our nature, whose blood "cleanseth us from all sin," and who is "able to save, even to the uttermost, all that come unto God through Him."

CHAPTER XIII

THE PERSON AND WORK OF JESUS CHRIST

FROM "SOME RECENT PHASES OF GERMAN THEOLOGY,"*

BY BISHOP JOHN L. NUELSEN, D. D., M. E. CHURCH, OMAHA, NEB.

Every Old Testament problem becomes in course of time a New Testament question. Every Biblical question places us after a while face to face with Him who is the center of the whole Bible, with Jesus Christ. In the present discussion over the person and Gospel of Jesus Christ, I shall confine myself to pointing out briefly some of the most interesting and important features of this subject.

WAS JESUS A REAL, HISTORICAL PERSON?

In the closing years of the eighteenth century the thought was advanced by a number of rationalistic theologians that the doctrines held by the Church and formulated in her creeds were the joint product of New Testament religion and Greek philosophy. This thought was taken up by Professor Harnack of Berlin, and in his great work, "History of the Christian Doctrine," he disclosed the complicated process by which the Church in developing her doctrines became Hellenized; thus it was made incumbent upon the student of Church history to extricate, by a process of careful analysis and comparison, the genuinely Christian elements from the meshes of foreign thought. Harnack, it is true, applied this principle only to post-apostolic times, but since the appearance of his book investigation has proceeded along the same lines and is now covering the Biblical writings as well.

---

*Copyright by Jennings & Graham, and published by permission.

Old Testament scholars and Semitists—as Gunkel, Meyer, Meinhold, Gressmann, Winckler, Simmern, Jensen—followed the traces of Babylonian influences down through the period of later Judaism to New Testament times; New Testament scholars—as Schurer, Baldensperger, Bousset, Pfleiderer, Schmiedel, Holtzman, Weinel, Wernle, Wrede—studied Greek and Jewish thought in its influence upon the early Christian writings. They deemed it necessary to eliminate first the whole of Johannine theology as a foreign substance; then they threw overboard the Apostle Paul as the great perverter of the simple teachings of Christ; next they cleared the Synoptical Gospels of all Babylonian, Egyptian, Phrygian, Jewish, Greek and other foreign matter. They have just about finished this arduous work of purifying and simplifying the Gospels by this double process of "religionsgeschichtliche" analysis and comparison, in order to discover the real, historical Christ; they meet at the feet of this Christ, to see Him as He really is; but behold, He is no more! Not a trace of Him is left. Trait after trait, feature after feature, has been analyzed and compared, until neither manger nor cross nor grave, not even His garments, are left. A few years ago we had, by the grace of the most advanced scholarship, at least a plain Galilean peasant with a very good heart. Even if His mind was rather too simple, we were allowed to believe in a kind-hearted carpenter's son, who went about doing good, and to whom at least eight rather inoffensive sayings could be historically traced; as, for example, the saying; "It is more blessed to give than to receive;" but even this peasant has evaporated, or rather, the great Babylonian flood which the mighty Bel caused to drown all mankind has completely swallowed up the little that was left of Jesus of Nazareth.

I beg pardon for this tone of levity. The whole matter would be very serious if it were not so utterly absurd. But the fact is that German theology is just now confronted with the question, was Jesus Christ a real, historical person, or is He nothing but a literary hero?

From two very different quarters the question as to the historicity of Jesus of Nazareth has been raised. At first blush we may think it is ridiculous to raise the question at all. And so it is. But the very fact that scholars do raise the question and mean to be taken seriously, is the necessary result of tendencies in theology which have been fostered until they have reached this culmination point. This fact will, I trust, open the eyes of many in Germany, and in America as well, who are in the habit of intrusting themselves to the guidance of brilliant and charming leaders without realizing at the start whither they were going.

WAS CHRIST A PRODUCT OF BABYLONIAN MYTHOLOGY?

The first avenue which led to the negation of the historicity of Jesus Christ is the "religionsgeschichtliche" comparison. The religionsgeschichtliche study of the New Testament aims, as Professor Bousett puts it, "to understand the origin and development of Christianity by means of an investigation of the whole environment of primitive Christianity." Applying this principle to the person and work of Christ, Professor Pfleiderer of Berlin, in his "Early Conceptions of Christ," finds that the Christ of the Church has been formed out of those myths and legends which are the common property of religion all over the world.

The elements of the figure are roughly separable into five groups. There is Christ, the Son of God; Christ the Conqueror; Christ the Wonder-worker; Christ the Conqueror of death and the Lifegiver; Christ the King of kings and Lord of lords. The materials for each of these conceptions were taken from various sources. They came from Judaism, from Hellenism, from Mithraism, and the Graeco-Egyptian religion, from Zoroastrianism, and even from Buddhism. They came gradually, and gradually the conception took shape.

The specific contribution of Babylonian mythology to the picture of Christ, as depicted in the Gospels, consists, according to Professor Zimmern, of the following points: (1) "The conception of Christ as a pre-mundane, heavenly, Divine being, who is at the same time the Creator of the world; (2) The accounts of the miraculous birth of Christ, of the homage offered to the new-born child, and of the persecutions; (3) The conception of Christ as the Saviour of the world, and as ushering in a new period of time, appearing as He does in the fullness of time; (4) The conception of Christ as being sent into the world by the Father; (5) The doctrinal aspects of the suffering and death of Christ, apart from the historic facts; (6) The doctrine of the descent of Christ into Hades; (7) The doctrine of the resurrection of Christ on the third day after His death; (8) The doctrine of His ascension after forty days; (9) The doctrine of Christ's glory, sitting at the right hand of God and reigning with the Father; (10) The belief in the coming again of Christ at the end of days in kingly glory, and also of the last conflict with the powers of evil; (11) The idea of the marriage of Christ with His Bride at the beginning of the new time, of the new heaven, and the new earth."

While Professor Zimmern advances these thoughts very carefully and guardedly, Professor Jensen, of the University of Marburg, affirms most positively that the whole life of Christ is essentially a Jewish version of the Babylonian Gilgamesh Epos. His book appeared February, 1907, is a large volume of over one thousand pages, and bears the title, "The Epos of Gilgamesh in the World Literature. The Origins of the Old Testament Patriarch, Prophet, and Redeemer Legends, and of the New Testament Jesus Legend."

The main contention of the book is stated by the author himself in the following words: "That practically all of the Gospel narrative is purely legendary, and that there is no reason at all to consider anything that is told of Jesus as historical. The Jesus legend is an Israelitish Gilgamesh legend. —As a Gilgamesh legend the Jesus legend is a sister legend to numerous, particularly to most of the Old Testament, legends." In his concluding chapter Professor Jensen writes: "Jesus of Nazareth, in whom, as in the Son of God and the Saviour of the world, Christianity has believed for nearly two thousands years, and who is regarded, even by the most advanced scholarship of our own day, as a good and great man who lived and died the sublime pattern of the ideal ethical life—this Jesus has never lived upon earth; neither has He died, because He is nothing but an Israelitish Gilgamesh. We, the children of a much lauded time of progress and achievements, we who look down upon the superstitions of the past with a forbearing smile, we worship in our cathedrals and churches, in our meetinghouses and schools, in palaces and shanties, a Babylonian deity." There was a time when critical analysis of the Biblical texts ran wild. Professor Jensen's book is comparison run mad.

I should not have taken the time to quote from Jensen, but should have dismissed his book wth a forbearing smile, if he were not taken seriously by a number of scholars. To my amazement I noticed that as careful and sane a scholar as Professor Zimmern wrote an extended review of the book approving it almost without qualification, and saying: "Jensen will hardly succeed at once in seeing his ideas accepted. But truth is not depending upon immediate success, and will in this case, even as in others, be victorious, though not without great trouble, and only slowly. The weight of facts which this book adduces is too immense."

The other reason why I referred to this book is to show that the logical and unavoidable result of explaining everything distinctively Christian in the Bible by applying the principle of comparison, or, in other words, that the strict and unhampered following of the "religionsgeschichtliche" method, as it is in vogue at present, must lead to absurdities.

THE MYTH OF THEODORE ROOSEVELT

Allow me a digression. I wish to apply these same principles of analysis and comparison to a modern personality, following strictly the methods of Professor Jensen. Suppose Lord Macaulay's famous New Zealander, whom he pictures as standing upon a broken arch of London Bridge, in the midst of a vast solitude, to sketch the ruins of St. Paul's should come over to America and dig in the sand-hills covering the Congressional Library in Washington. He finds a great pile of literature which originated in the first few years of the twentieth century. In the very learned book which our New Zealand scholar publishes he refers to the fact that at the beginning of the twentieth century the head of the great American nation was supposed to be a strong and influential man by the name of Theodore Roosevelt. His name has gone down in history, but our scholar proves that Theodore Roosevelt was no historical person at all. He never lived; he is merely the personification of tendencies and mythological traits then dominant in the American nation.

For instance, this legendary hero is commonly pictured with a big stick. Now, this is plainly a mythological trait, borrowed from the Greeks and Romans, and represents really the thunderbolt of Jupiter. He is pictured as wearing a broad brimmed hat and large eye-glasses. This mythological feature is borrowed from old Norse mythology, and represents Woden endeavoring to pierce through the heavy clouds of fog covering his head. A great many pictures show the legendary hero smiling and displaying his teeth. This is a very interesting feature, showing the strong African influences in American civilization. Many contradictory legends are told about this man. He was a great hunter; he was a rough rider; but he was also a scholar and author of a number of learned books. He lived in the mountains, on the prairie, and in a large city. He was a leader in war, but also a peacemaker. It is said that he was appealed to by antagonizing factions, even by warring nations, to arbitrate. It is self-evident that we have here simply the personification of prominent character traits of the American people at various stages of their historical development. They loved to hunt, to ride, to war; reaching a higher stage of civilization, they turned to studying, writing books, making peace; and all these contradictory traits were, in course of time, used to draw the picture of this legendary national hero. Some mythological features have not yet been fully cleared up; for instance, that he is often represented in the shape of a bear or accompanied by bears. For a while these "Teddy Bears" were in nearly every house, and it seems as if they even were worshipped, at least by the children. There is no doubt that some remote astral conception lies at the root of this rather puzzling feature.

But two reasons are conclusive to establish the legendary thesis: (1) The American nation, at the beginning of the twentieth century, had hardly emerged from the crudity of fetichism and witchcraft. Many traces of fortune-telling, charms, sorcery, and other forms of superstition can be found by studying the daily papers. Even this hero Roosevelt was given to some such superstition. Whenever he desired to bring any one under his spell and charm him, he took him by the hand and pronounced a certain magical word. As far as I can discover it spells something like "dee-lighted." (2) The other conclusive proof is the name. Theodore is taken from the language of a people representing the southern part of Europe and means "Gift of God;" Roosevelt is taken from the language of a people representing the northern part of Europe, and means "Field of Roses." The idea is evident. This hero personifies the union of the two European races which laid the foundations of early American civilization—the Romanic and the Teutonic races; and the Americans imagined that a man who united in himself all those wonderful traits of character must necessarily be a miraculous "Gift of God," and furthermore they thought that if a man personifying their ideals really had full sway, their country would be changed to a "Field of Roses."

This explanation is strictly scientific. No doubt a good many machine politicians and heads of trusts would be delighted to awake some morning and find out that Theodore Roosevelt is nothing but a mythological figure. But, he is not. He is a living fact and tremendous power in the life of our nation. And so is Jesus Christ.

THE CHRIST OF LIBERAL THEOLOGY

The other avenue which led to the negation of the historicity of Jesus Christ is the well-known modernization and reduction of the life and work of Jesus which liberal theologians have accomplished by means of literary and historical criticism. The history of the critical investigation of the life of Jesus during the last hundred and fifty years is an intensely interesting and instructive study. It has recently been summarized by Dr. A. Schweitzer in his book, "From Reimarus to Wrede." (Reimarus, the contemporary of Lessing, whose "Wolfenbuttler Fragmente" mark the beginning of modern critical research in the life of Christ; Professor William Wrede, who died in November, 1906, was one of the most prominent liberal theologians.) A more popular presentation of the subject, covering the latest phases, is given by Professor Grutzmacher in his booklet, "Is the Liberal Picture of Jesus Modern?"

Without going into the history of this investigation, I merely state that the life of Christ as it is presented now by all liberal theologians—like Harnack, Bousset, Weinel, Wrede, Holtzmann, Julicher, Wernle—as the established result of critical scientific research, is gained, not from an examination of the whole New Testament material, but by means of a complicated process of finding the alleged true sources from which this life may be construed. The oldest portions of the New Testament literature, the Pauline writings, are not to be considered as genuine sources, because, as Professor Wernle states, "Jesus knew nothing of that which to St. Paul is everything. That Jesus regarded Himself as an object of worship must be doubted; that He ascribed any meritorious atonement to His death is altogether improbable. Paul is not a disciple of Jesus. He is a new phenomenon. Paul is much further removed from Jesus in his teaching than he would seem to be when regarded only chronologically."

We turn now to the four Gospels, but of these "the Gospel of John can in no wise be considered a historical source," says Harnack; and he is seconded in this assertion by all liberals. Says Wernle: "St. John must retire in favor of the Synoptic Gospels as source of the life of Christ. Jesus was as the Synoptics represent Him, not as St. John depicts Him." And again: "In the first Gospels there is nothing taught concerning redemption, atonement, regeneration, reception of the Holy Spirit. An altogether different picture is presented by the greater part of the other New Testament writings, especially by the writings of Paul and John."

But even the Synoptic Gospels have to be critically analyzed in order to find the true portrait of Christ. The Gospels of Matthew and Luke, especially in their accounts of the infancy and of the death of Jesus and of the events that took place after His death, and in many other instances as well, are rather a portraiture of the crude beliefs of the early Christian churches than a historically trustworthy account of the real facts. Even in the Gospel of Mark, which is considered the oldest and purest, we find, according to Professor Wernle, that "the historic portrait of Jesus is quite obscured; His person is placed in a grotesquely fantastic light."

Thus analytical criticism is compelled to search for the sources of the Gospels, and it claims to have found principally two of them; namely, the older Mark document, the source of the present Gospel of St. Mark, and the Logia, or collection of sayings of Jesus, the supposed source of the Gospel of St. Matthew. It is probably true that our present Gospels are based upon previous sources; but, in the absence of fixed data, it is impossible to determine with any degree of certainty just what those sources contained. But critical acumen cannot rest satisfied even with those sources. Says Wernle: "They are not free from the possibility of modification and adulteration. They represent the belief of the Christians as it developed in the course of four decades." It is therefore needful to distinguish between genuine elements and later additions in those sources. This is an exceedingly difficult and delicate task, especially since we do not know, for a certainty, the form nor the substance of those sources. How is it accomplished? We have noted an "inner consciousness" of many textual critics. I am reminded of this when I hear Harnack blandly say: "Whoever has a good eye for the vital and a true sense of the really great must be able to see it, and distinguish between the kernel and the transitory husk;" or when I hear Professor Pfleiderer speak of "healthy eyes;" or see how Bousset finds the proofs of genuineness in the fact that "it is psychologically comprehensible," or Mehlhorn in the fact that "it could not have been invented." It is with a sense of relief that we read Professor Bousset's refreshingly naive concession that where we find the sources too meager "we may occasionally make use of our imagination."

Unfortunately our imagination is not a safer guide in historical and scientific matters than is our inner consciousness, and the eyesight of no two men is exactly alike. A few years ago there was in Berlin an exhibition of paintings representing scenes from the life of Christ. Hundreds of paintings were exhibited; they were very interesting to look at, but they did not contribute anything to our knowledge of the real appearance of Jesus Christ. They were nothing but the portraitures of the conceptions which the various artists entertained as to the features of Christ. Each artist portrayed his own ideal of Jesus. Some of the portraits looked so strange that no one would have thought it a picture of Jesus Christ if it had not been labeled as such.

This is precisely the case with all these modern attempts to write a life of Jesus Christ minus St. Paul, minus St. John, minus Matthew, Luke and Mark. If you examine the character of this Jesus closely, you will find that He is really a portraiture of what the author considers his ideal of a pure and holy life, clothed in the garb of an Oriental peasant two thousands years ago.

We cannot here reproduce the details of this twentieth-century ideal in its strange and ancient environments; it is a picture of a man from whom every supernatural, miraculous, mysterious trait has been erased. "Jesus has nowhere overstepped the limits of the purely human," says Bousset; and again: We do no longer start with the thought that Jesus was absolutely different from us; that He was from above, we from below. And consequently we do no longer speak of the divinity of Christ."

Doubts and fears, joys and griefs, moments of ecstasy and of utter dejection, all the changing moods of a poor human heart, may be found in His life. "He was a poor, disquieted man, at times shouting with joy, at times woefully despondent," writes Gustave Frenssen, and adds: "Sometimes He was treading upon the very borderland of exalted insanity."

On the whole, Jesus was the personification of faith in God, brotherly love, and faith in immortality; at times He seems to have taken Himself as the Messiah of His people; in everything He was subject to the limitations of mankind. There is only one difference between this modern view and the old rationalistic view. While the old rationalists, by all sorts of exegetical jugglery, vainly attempted to show that their human and purely naturalistic view of Jesus was really contained in the New Testament records, the modern rationalists are outspoken in their assertion that their own view is radically different from that of the New Testament writers. They do not in the least try to bridge over this chasm, but state emphatically as Julicher does: "Where even the first apostles have totally misunderstood Jesus we must try to understand Him better."

This is the picture of Christ which the leading liberal theologians of today have scattered broadcast in tens of thousands of copies of cheap pamphlets, which is described Sunday after Sunday in thousands of pulpits both in Germany, and, somewhat modified and as yet retouched, also in America. But again a reaction has set in, the sweep of which can not as yet be wholly comprehended.

THE VERDICT OF INFIDELITY

A pupil of modern liberal theologians, the former pastor Gustav Frenssen, who is a novel-writer of great force, wrote a novel, "Hilligenlei" (Holy Land), of which hundreds of thousands of copies were sold. The hero of this novel, Kai Jans, is, as is generally admitted, a true reproduction of the picture of Christ as painted by the liberal theologians. This book, as well as some other recent publications, gave rise to a number of reviews of the "modern Christ" by eminent literary men and by philosophers who do not claim to be Christians, but are known and desire to be known as leaders of free thought. Some of them were formerly theologians, but have lost their faith in the fundamental truths of Christianity. Of these writers I mention Adolf Bartels, editor of the "Kunstwart," Leo Berg, Eduard von Hartmann, A. Drews, W. Von Schnehen, C. A. Bernoulli, Dr. Kalthoff, the President of the League of Monists, and also two physicians, Doctors De Loosten and E. Rasmussen.

What do these men say? The two physicians claim that the only rational explanation of this Christ is to consider Him as one of the great pathological figures in the world's history; that means, in other words, that He was partially insane. The others say exactly what conservative theologians—as B. Weiss, Ihmels, Kahler, Zahm, Haussleiter, Grutzmacher, Lemme, and others—always have said against this naturalistic representation of Jesus, and what was ignored by liberal theologians. But here are men who were trained in the methods of Pfleiderer, Bousset, and their kin; men who possess as much critical acumen and philosophic penetration as do the liberal leaders; men whose thinking is in no wise fettered by dogmatic prejudices,—and their almost unanimous verdict is really remarkable.

All of them say that this picture of Christ is both unscientific and unhistorical. It is unscientific, because the methods applied are purely subjective. Says Dr. Kalthoff, after analyzing the Jesus of a number of modern theologians: "Every scholar leaves of the words of Christ only what he can make use of according to his preconceived notions of what is historically possible. Lacking every historical definiteness, the name of Jesus has become an empty vessel into which every theologian pours his own thoughts and ideas."

Eduard von Hartmann shows that the only results which this method of analytical criticism has arrived at are negative results. "The historic Christ remains a problematical figure which is of no religious value at all." W. von Schnehen quotes the liberal Professor Steck, who says: "A strict application of these principles of research will show that there is not one solitary word of Jesus of which we know for certain that it was spoken thus and not otherwise by Jesus," and uses this assertion to prove that all pictures of Christ are admittedly uncertain, and consequently unscientific.

But another argument which is of much greater import is advanced. Kalthoff, von Schnehen, and von Hartmann reason thus: If the liberal theologians admit that their picture of Christ is different from that which was believed by the Church during all the centuries of her existence—different from that of St. Paul, of St. John, of the Synoptic Gospels, of the sources of the Synoptic Gospels; if, as Professor Pfleiderer says, "Jewish phophecy, rabbinical teachings, Oriental gnosis, and Greek philosophy had already put the colors on the palette from which the picture of Christ was painted in the New Testament writings;" if, as is admitted, the Church was built from the very beginning, not upon the Galilean peasant Jesus, but upon the Christ, the Son of God; and if this Christ is nothing but the creation of speculative theologians, as Paul and John—then there is no need at all of a historic Christ. It is not necessary at all that a man Jesus of Nazareth should ever have lived in order to explain the fact of Christianity.

Even from the point of view of present religious needs of human nature this Jesus of liberal theology is unnecessary. Orthodox theology is Christ-centric; liberal theology is God-centric. "Back to Christ," exclaims Professor Wernle, "but only as a means to return to God the Father. God the Father is to regain that supremacy over our lives which Jesus had intended to give Him, but of which theological dogma has deprived Him." The modern thinkers mentioned above can not see the need of any human mediator between God and man. They want a living, present God, and a constant present communion with Him, if they want a God at all. Neither a Catholic saint nor a dead Jew is to stand between their own lives and God. Says Professor Drews: "The belief in the personal grandeur and the beauty of character of the man Jesus has nothing to do with religion." W. von Schnehen writes still more explicitly: "Even if God should have revealed Himself in the personality of the man Jesus of Nazareth, it is utterly useless to me, unless God reveals Himself to me likewise. If He does reveal Himself to me, then His revelation to Jesus is of no more import to me than is His revelation to any good man or His revelation in nature. The exemplary moral and religious perfection of Jesus is of no benefit whatever to any one except he has in his being the same moral and religious forces which were in Jesus. But if these powers are inherent in him and can be developed in his life, then it makes no difference by whom they become energized, by Jesus or by some one else."

Quite pathetic are the words of Professor Drews, showing, as they do, the restlessness of an honest but irreligious mind and the dissatisfaction with substitutes in religion: "We are consumed by a burning desire for salvation and we should be satisfied with this fabric of the theologians, this picture of the historic Christ, who changes His features under the hands of every professor of theology who works at it. We need the presence of God, and not His past." And Dr. Kalthoff writes quite correctly: "A God in whom we must believe because scholars say that two thousand years ago the son of a Jewish carpenter believed in Him, is not worth the printer's ink that is being squandered about Him."

THE CHRIST OF THE NEW TESTAMENT THE ONLY CHRIST

I will come to a close. Why have I asked you to read all these quotations? For two reasons: In the first place, I desired to show that the modern method of subjective analysis of the sources and of the "religionsgeschichtliche" comparison leads, and as a matter of fact did lead, to a complete negation of the historicity of the person of Christ. In the second place, I wished to point out that the modern, liberal conception of Christ, which strips Him of all distinctively divine elements and makes a pure man of Him, be He ever so good and holy, be He ever so sublime a pattern of a perfect life, be He ever so trustworthy a guide to God, does not and can not satisfy the modern man. He repudiates this man-made Jesus, and even accuses his makers of lack of scientific spirit and of dishonesty. Says von Schnehen: "Christianity is not belief in the man Jesus, but faith in Christ the Saviour and Son of God. Not the man Jesus, the lovable preacher and teacher of morals, who did not shrink back from death in obedience to what was His conviction, has conquered the world, but Christ the Son of God, who died upon the cross in order to redeem a lost world. This is the Christ of the Gospels and of the Church. It is dishonest to call this modern view of Jesus and of His religion Christian or evangelical."

It has ever been the mistake of rationalism to try to make Christianity acceptable to the average man by taking off the edges of its supranaturalism. It has ever been a failure, and ever will be so. The testimonies of these modern men show that the portrait of Christ painted by liberal theologians of our own day is an utter failure. They prove that the modern man, as well as man centuries ago, needs and wants exactly the Christ of the Church and the Gospels or no Christ at all.

The only true, historically and scientifically true, picture of the life and work and Gospel of Christ is the one which is given in the New Testament as a whole. The modern historians and philosophers tell the modern liberal theologians in very plain language to be honest and quit calling themselves preachers of the Gospel of Christ if they do not believe in the Christ of the Gospels, and quit calling their congregations churches of Christ if they do not believe in the Christ of the Church. Modern man is opposed to all shams and insincerities. He has no patience with men who, while using the old phraseology, cleverly substitute their self-made Jesus for the God-given Christ. The Christ can not be changed. He is the same yesterday, today and forevermore.

THE CERTAINTY AND IMPORTANCE OF THE BODILY RESURRECTION OF JESUS CHRIST FROM THE DEAD

BY REV. R. A. TORREY, D. D.

The resurrection of Jesus Christ from the dead is the corner-stone of Christian doctrine. It is mentioned directly one hundred and four or more times in the New Testament. It was the most prominent and cardinal point in the apostolic testimony. When the apostolic company, after the apostasy of Judas Iscariot, felt it necessary to complete their number again by the addition of one to take the place of Judas Iscariot, it was in order that he might "be a witness with us of His resurrection" (Acts 1:21, 22). The resurrection of Jesus Christ was the one point that Peter emphasized in his great sermon on the Day of Pentecost. His whole sermon centered in that fact. Its key-note was, "This Jesus hath God raised up, whereof we all are witnesses" (Acts 2:32, cf. vs. 24-31). When the Apostles were filled again with the Holy Spirit some days later, the one central result was that "with great power gave the Apostles *witness of the resurrection of the Lord Jesus.*" The central doctrine that the Apostle Paul preached to the Epicurean and Stoic philosophers on Mars Hill was Jesus *and the resurrection.* (Acts 17:18, cf. Acts 23:6; 1 Cor. 15:15.) The resurrection of Jesus Christ is one of the two fundamental truths of the Gospel, the other being His atoning death. Paul says in 1 Cor. 15:1, 3, 4, "Moreover, brethren, I declare unto you the Gospel which I preached unto you, which also ye have received, and wherein ye stand; For I delivered unto you first of all that which I also received, how that Christ died for our sins according to the Scriptures; And that He was buried, and *that He rose again* the third day according to the Scriptures." This was the glad tidings, first, that Christ died for our sins and made atonement; and second, that He rose again. The crucifixion loses its meaning without the resurrection. Without the resurrection, the death of Christ was only the heroic death of a noble martyr. With the resurrection, it is the atoning death of the Son of God. It shows that death to be of sufficient value to cover all our sins, for it was the sacrifice of the Son of God. In it we have an all-sufficient ground for knowing that the blackest sin is atoned for. Disprove the resurrection of Jesus Christ and Christian faith is vain. "If Christ be not risen," cries Paul, "then is our preaching vain and your faith is also vain" (1 Cor. 15:14). And later he adds, "If Christ be not risen, your faith is vain. You are yet in your sins." Paul, as the context clearly shows, is talking about the bodily resurrection of Jesus Christ. The doctrine of the resurrection of Jesus Christ is the one doctrine that has power to save any one who believes it with the heart. As we read in Rom. 10:9, "If thou shalt confess with thy mouth the Lord Jesus, and shalt believe in thine heart that *God hath raised Him from the dead,* thou shalt be saved." To know the power of Christ's resurrection is one of the highest ambitions of the intelligent believer, to attain which he sacrifices all things and counts them but refuse (Phil. 3:8-10 R. V.).

While the literal bodily resurrection of Jesus Christ is the corner-stone of Christian doctrine, it is also the Gibraltar of Christian evidence, and the Waterloo of infidelity and rationalism. If the Scriptural assertions of Christ's resurrection can be established as historic certainties, the claims and doctrines of Christianity rest upon an impregnable foundation. On the other hand, if the resurrection of Jesus Christ from the dead cannot be established, Christianity must go. It was a true instinct that led a leading and brilliant agnostic in England to say, that there is no use wasting time discussing the other miracles. The essential question is, Did Jesus Christ rise from the dead? adding, that if He did, it was easy enough to believe the other miracles; but, if not, the other miracles must go.

Are the statements contained in the four Gospels regarding the resurrection of Jesus Christ statements of fact or are they fiction, fables, myths? There are three separate lines of proof that the statements contained in the four Gospels regarding the resurrection of Jesus Christ are exact statements of historic fact.

I. THE EXTERNAL EVIDENCE OF THE AUTHENTICITY AND TRUTHFULNESS OF THE GOSPEL NARRATIVES

This is an altogether satisfactory argument. The external proofs of the authenticity and truthfulness of the Gospel narratives are overwhelming, but the argument is long and intricate and it would take a volume to discuss it satisfactorily. The other arguments are so completely sufficient and overwhelming and convincing to a candid mind that we can do without this, good as it is in its place.

The next argument is from—

II. THE INTERNAL PROOFS OF THE TRUTHFULNESS OF THE GOSPEL RECORDS

This argument is thoroughly conclusive, and we shall state it briefly in the pages which follow. We shall not assume anything whatever. We shall not assume that the four Gospel records are true history; we shall not assume that the four Gospels were written by the men whose names they bear, though it could be easily proven that they were; we shall not even assume that they were written in the century in which Jesus is alleged to have lived and died and risen again, nor in the next century, nor in the next. We will assume absolutely nothing. We will start out with a fact which we all know to be a fact, namely, that we have the four Gospels today, whoever wrote them and whenever they were written. We shall place these four Gospels side by side, and see if we can discern in them the marks of truth or of fiction.

1. The first thing that strikes us as we compare these Gospels one with another is that they are *four separate and independent accounts*. This appears plainly from the apparent discrepancies in the four different accounts. These apparent discrepancies are marked and many. It would have been impossible for these four accounts to have been made up in collusion with one another, or to have been derived from one another and so many and so marked discrepancies to be found in them. There is harmony between the four accounts, but the harmony does not lie upon the surface; it comes out only by protracted and thorough study. It is precisely such a harmony as would exist between accounts written or related by several different persons, each looking at the events recorded from his own standpoint. It is precisely such a harmony as would not exist in four accounts manufactured in collusion, or derived one from the other. In four accounts manufactured in collusion, whatever of harmony there might be would appear on the surface. Whatever discrepancy there might be would only come out by minute and careful study. But with the four Gospels the case is just the opposite. Harmony comes out by minute and careful study, and the apparent discrepancy lies upon the surface. Whether true or false, these four accounts are separate and independent from one another. (The four accounts also supplement one another, the third account sometimes reconciling apparent discrepancies between two.)

These accounts must be either a record of facts that actually occurred or else fictions. If fictions, they must have been fabricated in one of two ways—either independently of one another, or in collusion with one another. They cannot have been fabricated independently of one another; the agreements are too marked and too many. It is absolutely incredible that four persons sitting down to write an account of what never occurred independently of one another should have made their stories agree to the extent that these do. On the other hand, they cannot have been made up, as we have already seen, in collusion with one another; the apparent discrepancies are too numerous and too noticeable. It is proven they were not made up independently of one another; it is proven they were not made up in collusion with one another, so we are driven to the conclusion that they were not made up at all, that they are a true relation of facts as they actually occurred. We might rest the argument here and reasonably call the case settled, but we will go on still further:

2. The next thing we notice is that *each of these accounts bears striking indications of having been derived from eye witnesses*

The account of an eye witness is readily distinguishable from the account of one who is merely retailing what others have told him. Any one who is accustomed to weigh evidence in court or in historical study soon learns how to distinguish the report of an eye witness from mere heresay evidence. Any careful student of the Gospel records of the resurrection will readily detect many marks of the eye witness. Some years ago when lecturing at an American university, a gentleman was introduced to me as being a skeptic. I asked him, "What line of study are you pursuing?" He replied that he was pursuing a post graduate course in history with a view to a professorship in history. I said, "Then you know that the account of an eye witness differs in marked respects from the account of one who is simply telling what he has heard from others?" "Yes," he replied. I next asked, "Have you carefully read the four Gospel accounts of the resurrection of Christ?" He replied, "I have." "Tell me, have you not noticed clear indications that they were derived from eye witnesses?" "Yes," he replied, "I have been greatly struck by this in reading the accounts." Any one who carefully and intelligently reads them will be struck with the same fact.

3. The third thing that we notice about these Gospel narratives is *their naturalness, straightforwardness, artlessness and simplicity.*

The accounts, it is true, have to do with the supernatural, but the accounts themselves are most natural. There is a remarkable absence of all attempt at coloring and effect. There is nothing but the simple, straightforward telling of facts as they actually occurred. It frequently happens that when a witness is on the witness stand, the story he tells is so artless, so straightforward, so natural, there is such an entire absence of any attempt at coloring or effect that his testimony bears weight independently of anything we may know of the character or previous history of the witness. As we listen to his story, we say to ourselves, "This man is telling the truth." The weight of this kind of evidence is greatly increased and reaches practical certainty when we have several independent witnesses of this sort, all bearing testimony to the same essential facts, but with varieties of detail, one omitting what another tells, and the third unconsciously reconciling apparent discrepancies between the two. This is the precise case with the four Gospel narratives of the resurrection of Christ. The Gospel writers do not seem to have reflected at all upon the meaning or bearing of many of the facts which they relate. They simply tell right out what they saw in all simplicity and straightforwardness, leaving the philosophizing to others. Dr. William Furness, the great Unitarian scholar and critic, who certainly was not over-much disposed in favor of the supernatural, says, "Nothing can exceed in artlessness and simplicity the four accounts of the first appearance of Jesus after His crucifixion. If these qualities are not discernible here, we must despair of ever being able to discern them anywhere."

Suppose we should find four accounts of the battle of Monmouth. Suppose, furthermore, that nothing decisive was known as to the authorship of these four accounts, but, when we laid them side by side, we found that they were manifestly independent accounts. We found, furthermore, striking indications that they were from eye witnesses. We found them all marked by that artlessness, straightforwardness and simplicity that always carries conviction; we found that, while apparently disagreeing in minor details, they agreed substantially in their account of the battle—even though we had no knowledge of the authorship or date of these accounts, would we not, in the absence of any other accounts, say, "Here is a true account of the battle of Monmouth?" Now this is exactly the case with the four Gospel narratives. Manifestly separate and independent from one another, bearing the clear marks of having been derived from eye witnesses, characterized by an unparalleled artlessness, simplicity and straightforwardness, apparently disagreeing in minor details, but in perfect agreement as to the great central facts related. If we are fair and honest, if we follow the canons of evidence followed in court, if we follow any sound and sane law of literary and historical criticism, are we not logically driven to say, "Here is a true account of the resurrection of Jesus." Here again we might rest our case and call the resurrection of Jesus from the dead proven, but we go on still further:

4. The next thing we notice is the *unintentional evidence of words, phrases, and accidental details.*

It oftentimes happens that when a witness is on the stand, the unintentional evidence that he bears by words and phrases which he uses, and by accidental details which he introduces, is more convincing than his direct testimony, because it is not the testimony of the witness, but a testimony of the truth to itself. The Gospel accounts abound in evidence of this sort.

Take, as the first instance, the fact that in all the Gospel records of the resurrection, we are given to understand that Jesus was not at first recognized by His disciples when He appeared to them after His resurrection, e. g., Luke 24:16; John 21:4. We are not told why this was so, but if we will think awhile over it, we will soon discover why it was so. But the Gospel narratives simply record the fact without attempting to explain it. If the stories were fictitious, they certainly would never have been made up in this way, for the writer would have seen at once the objection that would arise in the minds of those who did not wish to believe in His resurrection, that is, that it was not really Jesus Whom the disciples saw. Why, then, is the story told in this way? For the self-evident reason that the evangelists were not making up a story for effect, but simply recording events precisely as they occurred. This is the way in which it occurred, therefore this is the way in which they told it. It is not a fabrication of imaginary incidents, but an exact record of facts carefully observed and accurately recorded.

Take a second instance: In all the Gospel records of the appearances of Jesus after His resurrection, there is not a single recorded appearance to an enemy or opponent of Christ. All His appearances were to those who were already believers. Why this was so we can easily see by a little thought, but nowhere in the Gospels are we told why it was so. If the stories had been fabricated, they certainly would never have been made up in this way. If the Gospels were, as some would have us believe, fabrications constructed one hundred, two hundred, or three hundred years after the alleged events recorded, when all the actors were dead and gone and no one could gainsay any lies told, Jesus would have been represented as appearing to Caiaphas, and Annas, and Pilate, and Herod, and confounding them by His re-appearance from the dead. But there is no suggestion even of anything of this kind in the Gospel stories. Every appearance is to one who is already a believer. Why is this so? For the self-evident reason that this was the way that things occurred, and the Gospel narratives are not concerned with producing a story for effect, but simply with recording events precisely as they occurred and as they were observed.

We find still another instance in the fact that the recorded appearances of Jesus after His resurrection were only occasional. He would appear in the midst of His disciples and disappear, and not be seen again perhaps for several days. Why this was so, we can easily think out for ourselves––He was evidently seeking to wean His disciples from their old-time communion with Him in the body, and to prepare them for the communion with Himself in the Spirit that was to follow in the days that were to come. We are not, however, told this in the Gospel narratives. We are left to discover it for ourselves, and this is all the more significant for that reason. It is doubtful if the disciples themselves realized the meaning of the facts. If they had been making up the story to produce effect, they would have represented Jesus as being with them constantly, as living with them, eating and drinking with them, day after day. Why then is the story told as recorded in the four Gospels? Because this is the way in which it had all occurred. The Gospel writers are simply concerned with giving the exact representation of the facts as witnessed by themselves and others.

We find another very striking instance in what is recorded concerning the words of Jesus to Mary at their first meeting. (John 20:17.) Jesus is recorded as saying to Mary, "Touch me not, for I am not yet ascended to My Father." We are not told why Jesus said this to Mary. We are left to discover the reason for it if we can, and the commentators have had a great deal of trouble in discovering it. Their explanations vary widely one from another. I have a reason of my own which I have never seen in any commentary, but which I am persuaded is the true reason, but it would probably be difficult to persuade others that it was the true reason. Why then is this little utterance of Jesus put in the Gospel record without a word of explanation, and which it has taken eighteen centuries to explain, and which is not altogether satisfactorily explained yet? Certainly a writer making up a story would not put in a little detail like that without apparent meaning and without an attempt at an explanation of it. Stories that are made up are made up for a purpose; details that are inserted are inserted for a purpose, a purpose more or less evident, but eighteen centuries of study have not been able to find out the purpose why this was inserted. Why then do we find it here? Because this is exactly what happened. This is what Jesus said; this is what Mary heard Jesus say; this is what Mary told, and therefore this is what John recorded. We cannot have a fiction here, but an accurate record of words spoken by Jesus after His resurrection.

We find still another instance in John 20:4-6: "So they ran both together; and the other disciple did outrun Peter, and came first to the sepulchre. And he, stooping down and looking in, saw the linen clothes lying; yet went he not in. Then cometh Simon Peter following him, and went into the sepulchre, and seeth the linen clothes lie." This is all in striking keeping with what we know of the men from other sources. Mary, returning hurriedly from the tomb, bursts in upon the two disciples and cries, "They have taken away the Lord out of the sepulchre, and we know not where they have laid Him." John and Peter sprang to their feet and ran at the top of their speed to the tomb. John, the younger of the two disciples (it is all the more striking that the narrative does not tell us here that he was the younger of the two disciples), was fleeter of foot and outran Peter and reached the tomb first, but man of retiring and reverent disposition that he was (we are not told this here but we know it from a study of his personality as revealed elsewhere) he did not enter the tomb, but simply stooped down and looked in. Impetuous but older Peter comes lumbering on behind as fast as he can, but when once he reaches the tomb, he never waits a moment outside but plunges headlong in. Is this made up, or, is it life? He was indeed a literary artist of consummate ability who had the skill to make this up if it did not occur just so. There is incidentally a touch of local coloring in the report. When one visits today the tomb which scholars now accept as the real burial place of Jesus, he will find himself unconsciously obliged to stoop down in order to look in.

Still another instance is found in John 21:7: "Therefore, that disciple whom Jesus loved saith to Peter, It is the Lord. Now when Simon Peter heard that it was the Lord, he girt his fisher's coat unto him, (for he was naked,) and did cast himself into the sea." Here again we have the unmistakable marks of truth and life. The Apostles had gone at Jesus' command into Galilee to meet Him there, but Jesus does not at once appear. Simon Peter, with the fisherman's passion still stirring in his bosom says, "I go a-fishing." The others replied, "We also go with thee." They fished all night, and, with characteristic fishermen's luck, caught nothing. In the early dawn Jesus stands upon the shore, but the disciples did not recognize Him in the dim light. Jesus calls to them, "Children, have ye any meat?" And they answer, "No." He bids them cast the net on the right side of the ship and they will find. When the cast was made, they were not able to draw it for the multitude of fishes. In an instant, John, the man of quick spiritual perception, says, "It is the Lord." No sooner does Peter, the man of impulsive action, hear it than he grasps his fisher's coat, casts it about his naked form and throws himself overboard and strikes out for shore to reach his Lord. Is this made up, or, is it life? This is not fiction. If some unknown author of the fourth Gospel made this up, he is the master literary artist of the ages, and we should take down every other name from our literary pantheon and place him above them all.

We find a still more touching instance in John 20:15: "Jesus saith unto her, Woman, why weepest thou? whom seekest thou? She, supposing Him to be the gardener, saith unto Him, Sir, if thou hast borne Him hence, tell me where thou hast laid Him, and I will take Him away." Here is surely a touch that surpasses the art of any man of that day or any other day. Mary had gone into the city and notified John and Peter that she had found the sepulchre empty. They start on a run for the sepulchre. As Mary has already made the journey twice, they easily far outstrip her, but with heavy heart and slow and weary feet, she makes her way back to the tomb. Peter and John have long gone when she reaches it, broken-hearted, thinking that not only has her beloved Lord been slain, but that His tomb has been desecrated. She stands without weeping. There are two angels sitting in the tomb, one at the head and the other at the feet where the body of Jesus had lain. But the grief-stricken woman has no eye for angels. They say unto her, "Woman, why weepest thou?" She replies, "Because they have taken away my Lord, and I know not where they have laid Him." A rustle in the leaves at her back and she turns around to see who is coming. She sees Jesus standing there, but, blinded by tears and despair, she does not recognize her Lord. Jesus also says to her, "Why weepest thou? Whom seekest thou?" She, supposing it to be the gardener who is talking to her, says, "Sir, if thou hast borne Him hence, tell me where thou hast laid Him and I will take Him away." Now remember who it is that makes the offer, and what she offers to do; a weak woman offers to carry a full grown man away. Of course, she could not do it, but how true to a woman's love that always forgets its weakness and never stops at impossibilities. There is something to be done and she says, "I will do it," "Tell me where thou hast laid Him, and I will take Him away." Is this made up? Never! This is life; this is reality; this is truth.

We find another instance in Mark 16:7: "But go your way, tell His disciples *and Peter* that He goeth before you into Galilee: there shall ye see Him, as He said unto you." What I would have you notice here are the two words, *"and Peter."* Why *"and Peter?"* Was not Peter one of the disciples? Surely he was, the very head of the apostolic company. Why then, "and Peter?" No explanation is given in the text, but reflection shows it was the utterance of love toward the despondent, despairing disciple who had thrice denied his Lord. If the message had been simply to the disciples Peter would have said, "Yes, I was once a disciple, but I can no longer be counted such. I thrice denied my Lord on that awful night with oaths and curses. It does not mean me." But our tender compassionate Lord through His angelic messenger sends the message, "Go tell His disciples, and whoever you tell, be sure you tell poor, weak, faltering, backslidden, broken-hearted Peter." Is this made up, or is this a real picture of our Lord? I pity the man who is so dull that he can imagine this is fiction. Incidentally let it be noted that this is recorded only in the Gospel of Mark, which, as is well known, is Peter's Gospel. As Peter dictated to Mark one day what he should record, with tearful eyes and grateful heart he would turn to him and say, "Mark, be sure you put that in, 'Tell His disciples *and Peter.* "

Take still another instance in John 20:27-29: "Then saith He to Thomas, Reach hither thy finger, and behold My hands; and reach hither thy hand, and thrust it into My side; and be not faithless but believing. And Thomas answered and said unto Him, My Lord and my God. Jesus saith unto him, Thomas, because thou hast seen Me, thou hast believed: blessed are they that have not seen, and yet have believed." Note here two things; the action of Thomas and the rebuke of Jesus. Each is too characteristic to be attributed to the art of some master of fiction. Thomas had not been with the disciples at the first appearance of our Lord. A week had passed by. Another Lord's Day had come. This time Thomas makes sure of being present; if the Lord is to appear, he will be there. If he had been like some of our modern doubters, he would have taken pains to be away, but, doubter though he was, he was an honest doubter and wanted to know. Suddenly Jesus stands in the midst. He says to Thomas, "Reach hither thy finger, and behold My hands, and reach thither thy hand, and thrust it into My side: and be not faithless but believing." At last Thomas' eyes are opened. His faith long dammed back bursts every barrier and sweeping onward carries Thomas to a higher height than any other disciple had as yet reached—exultingly and adoringly he cries, as he looks up into the face of Jesus, "My Lord and My God!" Then Jesus tenderly, but searchingly, rebukes him. "Thomas," He says, "because thou hast seen Me, thou hast believed. Blessed are they [who are so eager to find and so quick to see, and so ready to accept the truth, that they do not wait for actual visible demonstration but are ready to take truth on sufficient testimony] that have not seen and yet have believed." Is this made up, or is this life? Is it a record of facts as they occurred, or a fictitious production of some master artist?

Take still another instance: In John 21:15-17 we read: "So when they had dined, Jesus saith to Simon Peter, Simon, son of Jonas, lovest thou me more than these? He saith unto Him, Yea, Lord; Thou knowest that I love Thee. He saith unto him, Feed My lambs. He saith unto him again the second time, Simon, son of Jonas, lovest thou Me? He saith unto Him, Yea, Lord, Thou knowest that I love Thee. He saith unto him, Feed My sheep. He saith unto him *the third time,* Simon, son of Jonas, lovest thou Me? Peter *was grieved because He said unto him the third time,* Lovest thou Me? And he said unto Him, Lord, Thou knowest all things;

Thou knowest that I love Thee. Jesus saith unto him, Feed My sheep." Note especially here the words, "Peter was grieved because He said unto him *the third time, Lovest thou Me?*" Why did Jesus ask Peter three times, "Lovest thou Me?" And why was Peter grieved because Jesus did ask him three times? We are not told in the text, but, if we read it in the light of Peter's thrice repeated denial of his Lord, we will understand it. As Peter had denied his Lord thrice, Jesus three times gave Peter an opportunity to reassert his love. But this, tender as it was, brings back to Peter that awful night when in the courtyard of Annas and Caiaphas, he thrice denied his Lord, and "Peter was grieved because He said unto him the third time, Lovest thou Me." Is this made up? Did the writer make it up with this fact in view? If he did, he surely would have mentioned it. It cannot have been made up. It is not fiction. It is simply reporting what actually occurred. The accurate truthfulness of the record comes out even more strikingly in the Greek than in the English version. Two different words are used for "love." Jesus, in asking Peter, "Lovest thou Me?" uses a strong word denoting the higher form of love. Peter, replying, "Lord, Thou knowest that I love Thee," uses a weaker word, but one denoting a more tender form of love. Jesus, the second time uses the stronger word, and the second time in his reply Peter uses the weaker word. In His third question, Jesus comes down to Peter's level and uses the weaker word that Peter had used from the beginning. Then Peter replies, "Lord, Thou knowest all things, Thou knowest that I love Thee," using the same weaker word. This cannot be fiction. It is accurately reported fact.

Take still another instance: In John 20:16 we read, "Jesus saith unto her, Mary. She turned herself and saith unto Him, Rabboni; which is to say, Master." What a delicate touch of nature we have here! Mary is standing outside the tomb overcome with grief. She has not recognized her

Lord, though He has spoken to her. She has mistaken Him for the gardener. She has said, "Sir, if thou hast borne Him hence, tell me where thou hast laid Him, and I will take Him away." Then Jesus utters just one word. He says, "Mary." As that name came trembling on the morning air, uttered with the old familiar tone, spoken as no one else had ever spoken it but He, in an instant her eyes were opened. She falls at His feet and tries to clasp them, and looks up into His face, and cries, "Rabboni, my Master." Is this made up? Impossible! This is life. This is Jesus, and this is the woman who loved Him. No unknown author of the second, third, or fourth century, could have produced such a masterpiece as this. We stand here unquestionably face to face with reality, with life, with Jesus and Mary as they actually were.

One more important illustration: In John 20:7 we read, "And the napkin, that was about His head, not lying with the linen clothes, but wrapped together in a place by itself." How strange that such a little detail as this should be added to the story with absolutely no attempt at explaining. But how deeply significant this little unexplained detail is. Recall the circumstances. Jesus is dead. For three days and three nights his body is lying cold and silent in the sepulchre, as truly dead as any body was ever dead, but at last the appointed hour has come, the breath of God sweeps through the sleeping and silent clay, and in that supreme moment of His own earthly life, that supreme moment of human history, when Jesus rises triumphant over death and grave and Satan, there is no excitement upon His part, but with that same majestic self-composure and serenity that marked His whole career, that same Divine calm that He displayed upon storm-tossed Galilee, when His affrighted disciples shook Him from His slumbers and said, "Lord, carest thou not that we perish?" and He arose serenely on the deck of the tossing vessel and said to the wild, tempestuous waves and winds, "Be still," and there was a great calm: so now again in this sublime, this awful moment, He does not excitedly tear the napkin from His face and fling it aside, but absolutely without human haste or flurry, or disorder, He unties it calmly from His head, rolls it up and lays it away in an orderly manner in a place by itself. Was that made up? Never! We do not behold here an exquisite masterpiece of the romancer's art; we read here the simple narrative of a matchless detail in a unique life that was actually lived here upon earth, a life so beautiful that one cannot read it with an honest and open mind without feeling the tears coming into his eyes.

But some one will say, all these are little things. True, and it is from that very fact that they gain much of their significance. It is just in such little things that fiction would disclose itself. Fiction displays itself different from fact in the minute; in the great outstanding outlines you can make fiction look like truth, but when you come to examine it minutely and microscopically, you will soon detect that it is not reality but fabrication. But the more miscroscopically we examine the Gospel narratives, the more we become impressed with their truthfulness. There is an artlessness and naturalness and self-evident truthfulness in the narratives, down to the minutest detail, that surpasses all the possibilities of art.

The third line of proof that the statements contained in the four Gospels regarding the resurrection of Jesus Christ are exact statements of historic fact, is

III. THE CIRCUMSTANTIAL EVIDENCE FOR THE RESURRECTION OF CHRIST

There are certain proven and admitted facts that demand the resurrection of Christ to account for them.

1. Beyond a question, the foundation truth preached in the early years of the Church's history was the resurrection. This was the one doctrine upon which the Apostles were ever

ringing the changes. Whether Jesus did actually rise from the dead or not, it is certain that the one thing that the Apostles constantly proclaimed was that He had risen. Why should the Apostles use this as the very corner-stone of their creed, if not well attested and firmly believed?

But this is not all: They laid down their lives for this doctrine. Men never lay down their lives for a doctrine which they do not firmly believe. They stated that they had seen Jesus after His resurrection, and rather than give up their statement, they laid down their lives for it. Of course, men may die for error and often have, but it was for error that they firmly believed. In this case they would have known whether they had seen Jesus or not, and they would not merely have been dying for error but dying for a statement which they knew to be false. This is not only incredible but impossible. Furthermore, if the Apostles really firmly believed, as is admitted, that Jesus rose from the dead, they had some facts upon which they founded their belief. These would have been the facts that they would have related in recounting the story. They certainly would not have made up a story out of imaginary incidents when they had real facts upon which they founded their belief. But if the facts were as recounted in the Gospels, there is no possible escaping the conclusion that Jesus actually arose. Still further, if Jesus had not arisen, there would have been evidence that He had not. His enemies would have sought and found this evidence, but the Apostles went up and down the very city where He had been crucified and proclaimed right to the faces of His slayers that He had been raised and no one could produce evidence to the contrary. The very best they could do was to say the guards went to sleep and the disciples stole the body while the guards slept. Men who bear evidence of what happens while they are asleep are not usually regarded as credible witnesses. Further still, if the Apostles had stolen the body, they would have known it themselves and would not have been ready to die for what they knew to be a fraud.

2. Another known fact is the change in the day of rest. The early church came from among the Jews. From time immemorial the Jews had celebrated the seventh day of the week as their day of rest and worship, but we find the early Christians in the Acts of the Apostles, and also in early Christian writings, assembling on the first day of the week. Nothing is more difficult of accomplishment than the change in a holy day that has been celebrated for centuries and is one of the most cherished customs of the people. What is especially significant about the change is that it was changed by no express decree but by general consent. Something tremendous must have occurred that led to this change. The Apostles asserted that what had occurred on that day was the resurrection of Christ from the dead, and that is the most rational explanation. In fact it is the only reasonable explanation of the change.

3. But the most significant fact of all is the change in the disciples themselves, the moral transformation. At the time of the crucifixion of Christ, we find the whole apostolic company filled with blank and utter despair. We see Peter, the leader of the apostolic company, denying his Lord three times with oaths and cursings, but a few days later we see this same man, filled with a courage that nothing could shake. We see him standing before the council that had condemned Jesus to death and saying to them, "Be it known unto you all, and to all the people of Israel, that by the name of Jesus Christ of Nazareth, whom ye crucified, whom God raised from the dead, even by Him doth this man stand before you whole" (Acts 4:10). A little further on when commanded by the council not to speak at all nor teach in the name of Jesus, we hear Peter and John answering, "Whether it be right in the sight of God to hearken unto you more than unto God, judge ye. For we cannot but speak the

things which we have seen and heard" (Acts 4:19, 20). A little later still after arrest and imprisonment, in peril of death, when sternly arraigned by the council, we hear Peter and the Apostles answering their demand that they should be silent regarding Jesus, with the words, "We ought to obey God rather than man. *The God of our fathers raised up Jesus whom ye slew and hanged* on a tree. Him hath God exalted with His right hand to be a Prince and a Saviour, for to give repentance to Israel, and forgiveness of sins. And we are His witnesses of these things" (Acts 5:29-32). Something tremendous must have occurred to account for such a radical and astounding moral transformation as this. Nothing short of the fact of the resurrection and of their having seen the risen Lord will explain it.

These unquestionable facts are so impressive and so conclusive that even infidel and Jewish scholars now admit that the Apostles believed that Jesus rose from the dead. Even Ferdinand Baur, father of the Tübigen School, admitted this. Even David Strauss, who wrote the most masterly "Life of Jesus" from the rationalistic standpoint that was ever written, said, "Cnly this much need be acknowledged that the Apostles firmly believed that Jesus had arisen." Strauss evidently did not wish to admit any more than he had to but he felt compelled to admit this much. Schenkel went even further and said, "It is an indisputable fact that in the early morning of the first day of the week following the crucifixion, the grave of Jesus was found empty. It is a second fact that the disciples and other members of the apostolic communion were convinced that Jesus was seen after the crucifixion." These admissions are fatal to the rationalists who make them. The question at once arises, "Whence these convictions and belief?" Renan attempted an answer by saying that "the passion of a hallucinated woman (Mary) gives to the world a resurrected God." (Renan's "Life of Jesus," page 357.) By this, Renan means that Mary was in love with Jesus; that after His crucifixion, brooding over it, in the passion of her love, she dreamed herself into a condition where she had a hallucination that she had seen Jesus risen from the dead. She reported her dream as a fact, and thus the passion of a hallucinated woman gave to the world a resurrected God. But the reply to all this is self-evident, namely, the passion of a hallucinated woman was not competent to this task. Remember the make-up of the apostolic company; in the apostolic company were a Matthew and a Thomas to be convinced, outside was a Saul of Tarsus to be converted. The passion of a hallucinated woman will not convince a stubborn unbeliever like Thomas, nor a Jewish tax-gatherer like Matthew. Whoever heard of a tax-gatherer, and most of all of a Jewish tax-gatherer, who could be imposed upon by the passion of a hallucinated woman? Neither will the passion of a hallucinated woman convince a fierce and conscientious enemy like Saul of Tarsus. We must look for some saner explanation than this. Strauss tried to account for it by inquiring whether the appearance might not have been visionary. Strauss has had, and still has, many followers in this theory. But to this we reply, first of all, there was no subjective starting point for such visions. The Apostles, so far from expecting to see the Lord, would scarcely believe their own eyes when they did see Him. Furthermore, whoever heard of eleven men having the same vision at the same time, to say nothing of five hundred men (1 Cor. 15:6) having the same vision at the same time. Strauss demands of us that we give up one reasonable miracle and substitute five hundred impossible miracles in its place. Nothing can surpass the credulity of unbelief.

The third attempt at an explanation is that Jesus was not really dead when they took Him from the cross, that His friends worked over Him and brought Him back to life, and what was supposed to be the appearance of the raised Lord was the appearance of one who never had been really dead and was now merely resuscitated. This theory of Paulus has been brought forward and revamped by various rationalistic writers in our own time and seems to be a favorite theory of those who today would deny the reality of our Lord's resurrection. To sustain this view, appeal has been made to the short time Jesus hung upon the cross and to the fact that history tells us of one in the time of Josephus taken down from the cross and nursed back to life. But to this we answer: (1). Remember the events preceding the crucifixion; the agony in the garden of Gethsemane; the awful ordeal of the four trials; the scourging and the consequent physical condition in which all this left Jesus. Remember too the water and the blood that poured from His pierced side. (2). In the second place, we reply, His enemies would have taken, and did take, all necessary precautions against such a thing as this happening. (John 19:34.) (3). We reply, in the third place, if Jesus had been merely resuscitated, He would have been so weak, such an utter physical wreck, that His re-appearance would have been measured at its real value, and the moral transformation in the disciples, for which we are trying to account, would still remain unaccounted for. The officer in the time of Josephus, who is cited in proof, though brought back to life, was an utter physical wreck. (4). We reply in the fourth place, if brought back to life, the Apostles and friends of Jesus, who are the ones who are supposed to have brought Him back to life, would have known how they brought Him back to life, and that it was not a case of resurrection but of resuscitation, and the main fact to be accounted for, namely, the change in themselves would remain unaccounted for. The attempted explanation is an explanation that does not explain. (5). In the fifth place, we reply, that the moral difficulty is the greatest of all, for if it was really a case of resuscitation, then Jesus tried to palm Himself off as one risen from the dead, when in reality He was nothing of the sort. In that case, He would be an arch-impostor, and the whole Christian system rests on a fraud as its ultimate foundation. Is it possible to believe that such a system of religion as that of Jesus Christ, embodying such exalted principles and precepts of truth, purity and love, "originated in a deliberately planned fraud"? No one whose own heart is not cankered by fraud and trickery can believe Jesus to have been an impostor, and His religion to have been founded upon fraud. A leader of the rationalistic forces in England has recently tried to prove the theory that Jesus was only apparently dead by appealing to the fact that when the side of Jesus was pierced blood came forth and asks, "Can a dead man bleed?" To this the sufficient reply is that when a man dies of what is called in popular language, a broken heart, the blood escapes into the pericardium, and after standing there for a short time it separates into serum (the water) and clot (the red corpuscles, blood), and thus if a man were dead, if his side were pierced by a spear, and the point of the spear entered the pericardium, "blood and water" would flow out just as the record states it did, and what is brought forth as a proof that Jesus was not really dead, is in reality a proof that He was, and an illustration of the minute accuracy of the story. It could not have been made up in this way, if it were not actual fact.

We have eliminated all other possible suppositions. We have but one left, namely, Jesus really was raised from the dead the third day as recorded in the four Gospels. The desperate straits to which those who attempt to deny it are driven are themselves proof of the fact.

We have then several independent lines of argument pointing decisively and conclusively to the resurrection of Christ from the dead. Some of them taken separately prove the fact, but taken together they constitute an argument that makes doubt of the resurrection of Christ impossible to the candid mind. Of course, if one is determined not to believe, no amount of proof will convince him. Such a man must be left to his own deliberate choice of error and falsehood; but any man who really desires to know the truth and is willing to obey it at any cost must accept the resurrection of Christ as an historically proven fact.

A brilliant lawyer in New York City some time ago spoke to a prominent minister of that city asking him if he really believed that Christ rose from the dead. The minister replied that he did, and asked the privilege of presenting the proof to the lawyer. The lawyer took the material offered in proof away and studied it. He returned to the minister, and said, "I am convinced that Jesus really did rise from the dead. But," he then added, "I am no nearer being a Christian than I was before. I thought that the difficulty was with my head. I find that it is really with my heart."

There is really but one weighty objection to the doctrine that Jesus arose from the dead, and that is, "There is no conclusive evidence that any other ever arose." To this a sufficient answer would be, even if it were certain that no other ever arose, it would not at all prove that Jesus did not arise, for the life of Jesus was unique, His nature was unique, His character was unique, His mission was unique, His history was unique, and it is not to be wondered at, but rather to be expected, that the issue of such a life should also be unique. However, all this objection is simply David Hume's exploded argument against the possibility of the miraculous revamped. According to this argument, no amount of evidence can prove a miracle, because miracles are contrary to all experience. But are miracles contrary to all experience? To start out by saying that they are is to beg the very question at issue. They may be outside of your experience and mine, they may be outside the experience of this entire generation, but your experience and mine and the experience of this entire generation is not "all experience." Every student of geology and astronomy knows that things have occurred in the past which are entirely outside of the experience of the present generation. Things have occurred within the last ten years that are entirely outside of the experience of the fifty years preceding it. True science does not start with an *a priori* hypothesis that certain things are impossible, but simply examines the evidence to find out what has actually occurred. It does not twist its observed facts to make them accord with *a priori* theories, but seeks to make its theories accord with the facts as observed. To say that miracles are impossible, and that no amount of evidence can prove a miracle, is to be supremely unscientific. Within the past few years, in the domain of chemistry for example, discoveries have been made regarding radium which seemed to run counter to all previous observations regarding chemical elements and to well established chemical theories. But the scientist has not therefore said that these discoveries about radium cannot be true; he has rather gone to work to find out where the trouble was in his previous theories. The observed and recorded facts in the case before us prove to a demonstration that Jesus rose from the dead, and true science must accept this conclusion and conform its theories to this observed fact. The fact of the actual and literal resurrection of Jesus Christ from the dead cannot be denied by any man who will study the evidence in the case with a candid desire to find what the fact is, and not merely to support an *a priori* theory.

CHAPTER XV

THE PERSONALITY AND DEITY OF THE HOLY SPIRIT.

BY REV. R. A. TORREY, D. D.

IMPORTANCE OF THE DOCTRINE.

One of the most characteristic and distinctive doctrines of the Christian faith is that of the personality and deity of the Holy Spirit. The doctrine of the personality of the Holy Spirit is of the highest importance from the standpoint of worship. If the Holy Spirit is a divine person, worthy to receive our adoration, our faith and our love, and we do not know and recognize Him as such, then we are robbing a divine Being of the adoration and love and confidence which are His due.

The doctrine of the personality of the Holy Spirit is also of the highest importance from the practical standpoint. If we think of the Holy Spirit only as an impersonal power or influence, then our thought will constantly be, how can I get hold of and use the Holy Spirit; but if we think of Him in the Biblical way as a divine Person, infinitely wise, infinitely holy, infinitely tender, then our thought will constantly be, "How can the Holy Spirit get hold of and use me?" Is there no difference between the thought of the worm using God to thrash the mountain, or God using the worm to thrash the mountain? The former conception is low and heathenish, not differing essentially from the thought of the African fetich worshipper who uses his god to do his will. The latter conception is lofty and Christian. If we think of the Holy Spirit merely as a power or influence, our thought will be, "How can I get more of the Holy Spirit?"; but if we think of Him as a divine Person, our thought will be, "How can the Holy Spirit get more of me?" The former conception leads to self-exaltation; the latter conception to self-humiliation, self-emptying, and self-renunciation. If we think of the Holy Spirit merely as a Divine power or influence and then imagine that we have received the Holy Spirit, there will be the temptation to feel as if we belonged to a superior order of Christians. A woman once came to me to ask a question and began by saying, "Before I ask the question, I want you to understand that I am a Holy Ghost woman." The words and the manner of uttering them made me shudder. I could not believe that they were true. But if we think of the Holy Spirit in the Biblical way as a divine Being of infinite majesty, condescending to dwell in our hearts and take possession of our lives, it will put us in the dust, and make us walk very softly before God.

It is of the highest importance from an experimental standpoint that we know the Holy Spirit as a person. Many can testify of the blessing that has come into their own lives from coming to know the Holy Spirit, as an ever-present, living, divine Friend and Helper.

There are four lines of proof in the Bible that the Holy Spirit is a person.

CHARACTERISTICS OF THE HOLY SPIRIT.

1. *All the distinctive characteristics of personality are ascribed to the Holy Spirit in the Bible.*

What are the distinctive characteristics or marks of personality? Knowledge, feeling and will. Any being who knows and feels and wills is a person. When you say that the Holy Spirit is a person, some understand you to mean that the Holy Spirit has hands and feet and eyes and nose, and so on, but these are the marks, not of personality, but of corporeity. When we say that the Holy Spirit is a person, we mean that He is not a mere influence or power that God sends into our lives but that He is a Being who knows and feels and wills. These three characteristics of personality, knowledge, feeling and will, are ascribed to the Holy Spirit over and over again in the Scriptures.

KNOWLEDGE.

In 1 Cor. 2:10, 11 we read, "But God hath revealed them unto us by His Spirit: for the Spirit searcheth all things, yea, the deep things of God. For what man knoweth the things of a man, save the spirit of man which is in him? Even so the things of God knoweth no man, but the Spirit of God." Here "knowledge" is ascribed to the Holy Spirit. The Holy Spirit is not merely an illumination that comes into our minds, but He is a Being who Himself knows the deep things of God and who teaches us what He Himself knows.

WILL.

We read again in 1 Cor. 12:11, R. V., "But all these worketh the one and the same Spirit, dividing to each one severally as He will." Here "will" is ascribed to the Holy Spirit. The Holy Spirit is not a mere influence or power which we are to use according to our wills, but a Divine Person who uses us according to His will. This is a thought of fundamental importance in getting into right relations with the Holy Spirit. Many a Christian misses entirely the fullness of blessing that there is for him because he is trying to get the Holy Spirit to use Him according to his own foolish will, instead of surrendering himself to the Holy Spirit to be used according to His infinitely wise will. I rejoice that there is no divine power that I can get hold of and use according to my ignorant will. But how greatly do I rejoice that there is a Being of infinite wisdom who is willing to come into my heart and take possession of my life and use me according to His infinitely wise will.

MIND.

We read in Romans 8:27, "And He that searcheth the hearts knoweth what is the mind of the Spirit, because He maketh intercession for the saints according to the will of

God.[v] Here "mind" is ascribed to the Holy Spirit. The word here translated "mind" is a comprehensive word, including the ideas of thought, feeling and purpose. It is the same word used in Romans 8:7, where we read, "The carnal mind is enmity against God: for it is not subject to the law of God, neither indeed can be." So then, in the passage quoted we have personality in the fullest sense ascribed to the Holy Spirit.

LOVE.

We read still further in Romans 15:30, "Now I beseech you, brethren, for the Lord Jesus Christ's sake and for the *love of the Spirit,* that ye strive together with me in your prayers to God for me." Here "love" is ascribed to the Holy Spirit. The Holy Spirit is not a mere blind, unfeeling influence or power that comes into our lives. The Holy Spirit is a person who loves as tenderly as God, the Father, or Jesus Christ, the Son. Very few of us meditate as we ought upon the love of the Spirit. Every day of our lives we think of the love of God, the Father, and the love of Christ, the Son, but weeks and months go by, with some of us, without our thinking of the love of the Holy Spirit. Every day of our lives we kneel down and look up into the face of God, the Father and say, "I thank Thee, Father, for Thy great love that led Thee to send Thy only begotten Son down into this world to die an atoning sacrifice upon the cross of Calvary for me." Every day of our lives we kneel down and look up into the face of our Lord and Saviour, Jesus Christ, and say, "I thank Thee, Thou blessed Son of God, for that great love of Thine that led Thee to turn Thy back upon all the glory of heaven and to come down to all the shame and suffering of earth to bear my sins in Thine own body upon the cross." But how often do we kneel down and say to the Spirit, "I thank Thee, Thou infinite and eternal Spirit of God for Thy great love that led Thee in obedience to the Father and the Son to come into this world and seek me out in my lost estate, and to follow me day after day and week after week and year after year until Thou hadst brought me to see my need of a Saviour, and hadst revealed to me Jesus Christ as just the Saviour I needed, and hadst brought me to a saving knowledge of Him." Yet we owe our salvation just as truly to the love of the Spirit as we do to the love of the Father and the love of the Son.

If it had not been for the love of God, the Father, looking down upon me in my lost condition, yes, anticipating my fall and ruin, and sending His only begotten Son to make full atonement for my sin, I should have been a lost man today. If it had not been for the love of the eternal Word of God, coming down into this world in obedience to the Father's commandment and laying down His life as an atoning sacrifice for my sin on the cross of Calvary, I should have been a lost man today. But just as truly, if it had not been for the love of the Holy Spirit, coming into this world in obedience to the Father and the Son and seeking me out in all my ruin and following me with never-wearying patience and love day after day and week after week and month after month and year after year, following me into places that it must have been agony for Him to go, wooing me though I resisted Him and insulted Him and persistently turned my back upon Him, following me and never giving me up until at last He had opened my eyes to see that I was utterly lost and then revealed Jesus Christ to me as an all-sufficient Saviour, and then imparted to me power to make this Saviour mine; if it had not been for this long-suffering, patient, never-wearying, yearning and unspeakably tender love of the Spirit to me, I should have been a lost man today.

INTELLIGENCE AND GOODNESS.

Again we read in Neh. 9:20, R. V., "Thou gavest also Thy good Spirit to instruct them, and withheldest not Thy manna from their mouth, and gavest them water for their thirst." Here "intelligence" and "goodness" are ascribed to the Holy

Spirit. This does not add any new thought to the passages already considered, but we bring it in here because it is from the Old Testament. There are those who tell us that the personality of the Holy Spirit is not found in the Old Testament. This passage of itself, to say nothing of others, shows us that this is a mistake. While the truth of the personality of the Holy Spirit naturally is not as fully developed in the Old Testament as in the New, none the less the thought is there and distinctly there.

GRIEF.

We read again in Ephesians 4:30, "And grieve not the Holy Spirit of God, whereby ye are sealed unto the day of redemption." In this passage "grief" is ascribed to the Holy Spirit. The Holy Spirit is not a mere impersonal influence or power that God sends into our lives. He is a person who comes to dwell in our hearts, observing all that we do and say and think. And if there is anything in act or word or thought, or fleeting imagination that is impure, unkind, selfish, or evil in any way, He is deeply grieved by it.

This thought once fully comprehended becomes one of the mightiest motives to a holy life and a careful walk. How many a young man, who has gone from a holy, Christian home to the great city with its many temptations, has been kept back from doing things that he would otherwise do by the thought that if he did them his mother might hear of it and that it would grieve her beyond description. But there is One who dwells in our hearts, if we are believers in Christ, who goes with us wherever we go, sees everything that we do, hears everything that we say, observes every thought, even the most fleeting fancy, and this One is purer than the holiest mother that ever lived, more sensitive against sin, One who recoils from the slightest sin as the purest woman who ever lived upon this earth never recoiled from sin in its most hideous forms; and, if there is anything in act, or word, or thought, that has the slighest taint of evil in it, He is grieved beyond description. How often some evil thought is suggested to us and we are about to give entertainment to it and then the thought, "The Holy Spirit sees that and is deeply grieved by it," leads us to banish it forever from our mind.

THE ACTS OF THE SPIRIT.

2. The second line of proof in the Bible of the personality of the Holy Spirit is that *many acts that only a person can perform are ascribed to the Holy Spirit.*

SEARCHING, SPEAKING AND PRAYING.

For example, we read in 1 Cor. 2:10 that the Holy Spirit searcheth the deep things of God. Here He is represented not merely as an illumination that enables us to understand the deep things of God, but a person who Himself searches into the deep things of God and reveals to us the things which He discovers. In Rev. 2:7 and many other passages, the Holy Spirit is represented as speaking. In Gal. 4:6, He is represented as crying out. In Romans 8:26, R. V., we read, "And in like manner the Spirit also helpeth our infirmity: for we know not how to pray as we ought; but the Spirit Himself maketh intercession for us with groanings which cannot be uttered." Here the Holy Spirit is represented to us as praying, not merely as an influence that leads us to pray, or an illumination that teaches us how to pray, but as a Person Who Himself prays in and through us. There is immeasurable comfort in the thought that every regenerate man or woman has two Divine Persons praying for him, Jesus Christ, the Son of God at the right hand of the Father praying for us (Heb. 7:25; 1 John 2:1); and the Holy Spirit praying through us down here. How secure and how blessed is the position of the believer with these two Divine Persons, whom the Father always hears, praying for him.

TEACHING AND GUIDING.

In John 15:26, 27, we read, "But when the Comforter is come, whom I will send unto you from the Father, even the Spirit of truth, which proceedeth from the Father, He shall testify of me: And ye also shall bear witness, because ye have been with me from the beginning." Here the Holy Spirit is very definitely set forth as a Person giving testimony, and a clear distinction is drawn between His testimony and the testimony which those in whom He dwells give. Again in John 14:26 we read, "But the Comforter, which is the Holy Ghost, whom the Father will send in my name, He shall teach you all things, and bring all things to your remembrance whatsoever I have said unto you." And again in John 16:12-14, "I have yet many things to say unto you, but ye cannot bear them now. Howbeit when He, the Spirit of truth, is come, He will guide you into all truth: for He shall not speak of Himself; but whatsoever He shall hear, that shall He speak: and He will show you things to come. He shall glorify me: for He shall receive of mine, and shall shew it unto you." (cf. also Neh. 9:20.) In these passages, the Holy Spirit is set forth as a teacher of the truth, not merely an illumination that enables our mind to see the truth, but One who personally comes to us and teaches us the truth. It is the privilege of the humblest believer to have a divine person as his daily teacher of the truth of God. (cf. 1 John 2:20, 27.)

In Romans 8:14 ("For as many as are led by the Spirit of God, they are the sons of God") the Holy Spirit is represented as our personal guide, directing us what to do, taking us by the hand, as it were, and leading us into that line of action that is well-pleasing to God. In Acts 16:6, 7 we read these deeply significant words, "Now when they had gone throughout Phrygia and the region of Galatia, and were *forbidden of the Holy Ghost* to preach the word in Asia, after they were come to Mysia, they assayed to go into Bithynia: but *the Spirit suffered them not."* Here the Holy Spirit is represented as taking command of the life and conduct of a servant of Jesus Christ. In Acts 13:2 and Acts 20:28, we see the Holy Spirit calling men to work and appointing them to office. Over and over again in the Scriptures actions are ascribed to the Holy Spirit which only a person could perform.

THE OFFICE OF THE SPIRIT.

3. The third line of proof of the personality of the Holy Spirit is that *an office is predicated to the Holy Spirit that could only be predicated of a person.*

"ANOTHER COMFORTER."

We read in John 14:16, 17, "And I will pray the Father, and he shall give you another Comforter, that He may abide with you forever; even the Spirit of truth; whom the world cannot receive, because it seeth Him not, neither knoweth Him: but ye know Him; for He dwelleth with you, and shall be in you." Here we are told it is the office of the Holy Spirit to be "another Comforter" to take the place of our absent Saviour. Our Lord Jesus was about to leave His disciples. When He announced His departure to them, sorrow had filled their hearts (John 16:6). Jesus spoke words to comfort them. He told them that in the world to which He was going there was plenty of room for them also (John 14:2). He told them further that He was going to prepare that place for them (John 14:3) and that when He had thus prepared it, He was coming back for them; but He told them further that even during His absence, while He was preparing heaven for them, He would not leave them orphaned (John 14:18), but that He would pray the Father and the Father would send to them another Comforter to take His place. Is it possible that Jesus should have said this if that One Who was going to take His place after all was not a person, but only an influence or power, no matter how beneficent and divine? Still further, is it conceivable that He should have said what He does say in John 16:7, "Nevertheless I tell you the truth; *It is expedient for you* that I go away; for if I go not away, the Comforter will not come unto you; but, if I depart, I will send Him unto you," if this other Comforter that was coming to take His place was only an influence or power?

ONE AT OUR SIDE.

This becomes clearer still when we bear in mind that the word translated "Comforter" means comforter plus a great deal more beside. The revisers found a great deal of difficulty in translating the Greek word. They have suggested "advocate," "helper" and a mere transference of the Greek word "Paraclete" into the English. The word so translated is *Parakleetos,* the same word that is translated "advocate" in 1 John 2:1; but "advocate" does not give the full force and significance of the word etymologically. Advocate means about the same as *Parakleetos,* but the word in usage has obtained restricted sense. "Advocate" is Latin; *Parakleetos* is Greek. The exact Latin word is *"advocatus,"* which means one called to another. (That is, to help him or take his part or represent him.) *Parakleetos* means one called alongside, that is, one who constantly stands by your side as your helper, counsellor, comforter, friend. It is very nearly the thought expressed in the familiar hymn, "Ever present, truest friend." Up to the time that Jesus had uttered these words, He Himself had been the *Parakleetos* to the disciples, the Friend at hand, the Friend who stood by their side. When they got into any trouble, they turned to Him. On one occasion they desired to know how to pray and they turned to Jesus and said, "Lord, teach us to pray" (Luke 11:1). On another occasion Peter was sinking in the waves of Galilee and he cried, saying, "Lord, save me. And immediately Jesus stretched forth His hand, and caught him," and saved him (Matt. 14:30, 31). In every extremity they turned to Him. Just so now that Jesus has gone to be with the Father, while we are awaiting His return, we have another Person just as divine as He, just as wise, just as strong, just as able to help, just as loving, always by our side and ready at any moment that we look to Him, to counsel us, to teach us, to help us, to give us victory, to take the entire control of our lives.

CURE FOR LONELINESS.

This is one of the most comforting thoughts in the New Testament for the present dispensation. Many of us, as we have read the story of how Jesus walked and talked with His disciples, have wished that we might have been there; but to-day we have a Person just as divine as Jesus, just as worthy of our confidence and our trust, right by our side to supply every need of our life. If this wonderful truth of the Bible once gets into our hearts and remains there, it will save us from all anxiety and worry. It is a cure for loneliness. Why need we ever be lonely, even though separated from the best of earthly friends, if we realize that a divine Friend is always by our side? It is a cure for breaking hearts. Many of us have been called upon to part with those earthly ones whom we most loved, and their going has left an aching void that it seemed no one and no thing could ever fill; but there is a divine Friend dwelling in the heart of the believer, who can, and who, if we look to Him to do it, will fill every nook and corner and every aching place in our hearts. It is a cure from the fear of darkness and of danger. No matter how dark the night and how many foes we may fear are lurking on every hand, there is a divine One who walks by our side and who can and will protect us from every danger. He can make the darkest night bright by the glory of His presence.

But it is in our service for Christ that this thought of the Holy Spirit comes to us with greatest helpfulness. Many of us do what service we do for the Master with fear and trembling. We are always afraid that we may say or do the wrong thing;

and so we have no joy or liberty in our service. When we stand up to preach, there is an awful sense of responsibility upon us. We tremble with the thought that we are not competent to do the work that we are called to do, and there is the constant fear that we shall not do it as it ought to be done. But if we can only remember that the responsibility is not really upon us but upon another, the Holy Spirit, and that He knows just what ought to be done and just what ought to be said, and then if we will get just as far back out of sight as possible and let Him do the work which He is so perfectly competent to do, our fears and our cares will vanish. All sense of constraint will go and the proclamation of God's truth will become a joy unspeakable, not a worrying care.

PERSONAL TESTIMONY.

Perhaps a word of personal testimony would be pardonable at this point. I entered the ministry because I was obliged to. My conversion turned upon my preaching. For years I refused to be a Christian because I was determined that I would not preach. The night I was converted, I did not say, "I will accept Christ," or anything of that sort. I said, "I will preach." But if any man was never fitted by natural temperament to preach, it was I. I was abnormally timid. I never even spoke in a public prayer meeting until after I had entered the theological seminary. My first attempt to do so was an agonizing experience. In my early ministry I wrote my sermons out and committed them to memory, and when the evening service would close and I had uttered the last word of the sermon, I would sink back with a sense of great relief that that was over for another week. Preaching was torture. But the glad day came when I got hold of the thought, and the thought got hold of me, that when I stood up to preach another stood by my side, and though the audience saw me, the responsibility was really upon Him and that He was perfectly competent to bear it, and all I had to do was to stand back and get as far out of sight as possible and let Him do the work which the Father sent Him to do. From that day preaching has not been a burden nor a duty but a glad privilege. I have no anxiety nor care. I know that He is conducting the service and doing it just as it ought to be done, and even though things sometimes may not seem to go just as I think they ought, I know they have gone right. Often times when I get up to preach and the thought takes possession of me that He is there to do it all, such a joy fills my heart that I feel like shouting for very ecstasy.

TREATMENT OF THE HOLY SPIRIT.

4. The fourth line of proof of the personality of the Holy Spirit is: *a treatment is predicated of the Holy Spirit that could only be predicated of a person.*

We read in Isa. 63:10, R. V., "But they rebelled and grieved His Holy Spirit: therefore he was turned to be their enemy, and Himself fought against them." Here we see that the Holy Spirit is rebelled against and grieved. (Cf. Eph. 4:30.) You cannot rebel against a mere influence or power. You can only rebel against and grieve a person. Still further we read in Heb. 10:29, "Of how much sorer punishment, suppose ye, shall he be thought worthy, who hath trodden under foot the Son of God, and hath counted the blood of the covenant wherewith He was sanctified, an unholy thing, and hath done despite unto the Spirit of grace?" Here we are told that the Holy Spirit is "done despite unto," that is "treated with contumely." (Thayer's Greek-English Lexicon of the New Testament.) You cannot "treat with contumely" an influence or power, only a person. Whenever a truth is presented to our thought, it is the Holy Spirit who presents it. If we refuse to listen to that truth, then we turn our backs deliberately upon that divine Person who presents it; we insult Him.

Perhaps, at this present time, the Holy Spirit is trying to bring to the mind of the reader of these lines some truth that the reader is unwilling to accept and you are refusing to listen. Perhaps you are treating that truth, which in the bottom of your heart you know to be true, with contempt, speaking scornfully of it. If so, you are not merely treating abstract truth with contempt, you are scorning and insulting a Person, a divine Person.

LYING TO THE HOLY SPIRIT.

In Acts 5:3, we read, "But Peter said, Ananias, why hath Satan filled thine heart to lie to the Holy Ghost, and to keep back part of the price of the land?" Here we are taught that the Holy Spirit can be lied to. You cannot tell lies to a blind, impersonal influence or power, only to a person. Not every lie is a lie to the Holy Spirit. It was a peculiar kind of lie that Ananias told. From the context we see that Ananias was making a profession of an entire consecration of everything. (See ch. 4:36 to 5:11.) As Barnabas had laid all at the apostles' feet for the use of Christ and His cause, so Ananias pretended to do the same, but in reality he kept back part; the pretended full consecration was only partial. Real consecration is under the guidance of the Holy Spirit. The profession of full consecration was to Him and the profession was false. Ananias lied to the Holy Spirit. How often in our consecration meetings today we profess a full consecration, when in reality there is something that we have held back. In doing this, we lie to the Holy Spirit.

BLASPHEMY AGAINST THE HOLY SPIRIT.

In Matt. 12:31, 32, we read, "Wherefore I say unto you, All manner of sin and blasphemy shall be forgiven unto men: but the blasphemy against the Holy Ghost shall not be forgiven unto men. And whosoever speaketh a word against the Son of man, it shall be forgiven him; but whosoever speaketh against the Holy Ghost, it shall not be forgiven him, neither in this world, neither in the world to come." Here we are told that the Holy Spirit may be blasphemed. It is impossible to blaspheme an influence or power; only a Person can be blasphemed. We are still further told that the blasphemy of the Holy Spirit is a more serious and decisive sin than even the blasphemy of the Son of Man Himself. Could anything make more clear that the Holy Spirit is a person and a divine person?

SUMMARY.

To sum it all up, THE HOLY SPIRIT IS A PERSON. The Scriptures make this plain beyond a question to any one who candidly goes to the Scriptures to find out what they really teach. Theoretically, most of us believe this, but do we in our real thought of Him, in our practical attitude toward Him, treat Him as a Person? Do we regard Him as indeed as real a Person as Jesus Christ, as loving, as wise, as strong, as worthy of our confidence and love and surrender as He? The Holy Spirit came into this world to be to the disciples and to us what Jesus Christ had been to them during the days of His personal companionship with them. (John 14:16, 17.) Is He that to us? Do we walk in conscious fellowship with Him? Do we realize that He walks by our side every day and hour? Yes, and better than that, that He dwells in our hearts and is ready to fill them and take complete possession of our lives? Do we know the "communion of the Holy Ghost?" (2 Cor. 13:14.) Communion means fellowship, partnership, comradeship. Do we know this personal fellowship, this partnership, this comradeship, this intimate friendship of the Holy Spirit? Herein lies the secret of a real Christian life, a life of liberty and joy and power and fullness. To have as one's ever-present Friend, and to be conscious that one has as his ever-present Friend, the Holy Spirit, and to surrender one's life in all its departments entirely to His control, this is true Christian living.

CHAPTER XVI

THE HOLY SPIRIT AND THE SONS OF GOD

BY REV. W. J. ERDMAN, D. D.,

GERMANTOWN, PENNSYLVANIA

It is evident from many tracts and treatises on the Baptism of the Holy Spirit that due importance has not been given to the *peculiar characteristic* of the Pentecost gift in its relation to *the sonship of believers.*

Before considering this theme a few brief statements may be made concerning the personality and deity of the Holy Spirit and His relation to the people of God in the dispensations and times preceding the Day of Pentecost.

1. *The Holy Spirit, the Comforter, another Person, but not a different Being.*

In general it may be said, He is not an "influence" or a sum and series of "influences," but a personal Being with names and affections, words and acts, interchanged with those of God.

He is God as Creator. (Gen. 1:2; Psa. 104:30; Job 26:13; Luke 1:35.) He is one with God as Jehovah (Lord) in providential leading and care, and susceptible of grief on account of the unholiness of His chosen people. We cannot grieve an "influence," but only a person, and a person, too, who *loves us.* (Psa. 78:40; Eph. 4:30.) He is one with God as Adonai (Lord), whose glory Isaiah beheld and John rehearses, who commissioned the prophet and sent forth the apostle. (Isa. 6:1-10; John 12:37-41; Acts 13:2; 20:15-18.) In these Scriptures one and the same act is that of Jehovah and of Jesus and of the Holy Spirit.

Besides the clear evidence of personality and equality in the baptismal words and in the benediction (Matt. 28:19;

2 Cor. 13:14), the promise of Jesus affirms the presence and the abiding of the Spirit to be one with His own and with the Father's in this Word. "If a man love Me he will keep My words, and My Father will love him, and we will come unto him and make our abode with him" (John 16:23). Above all, the name "another Comforter" (Paraclete) suggests a Person who would do for the disciples what Jesus the other Comforter (Luke 2:25) had been doing for them. He speaks, testifies, teaches, reminds, reproves, convicts, warns, commands, loves, consoles, beseeches, prays, intercedes, (often the word is "paracletes"); in brief, all these and other acts and dealings are not those of an impersonal medium or influence, but of a person, and One who in the nature of the case cannot be less than God in wisdom, love and power, and who is one with the Father and the Son; *another Person indeed, but not a different Being.*

2. *The spiritual, Divine life in the people of God is the same in kind in every age and dispensation,* but *the relation* to God in which *the life was developed of old* was *different* from that which now exists between believers as sons and God as Father, and in accordance with that relationship the Holy Spirit acted.

He was of old the Author and Nourisher of all spiritual life and power in righteous men and women of past ages, in patriarch and friend of God, in Israelites as minors and servants, in pious kings and adoring psalmists, in consecrated priests and faithful prophets; and whatever truth had been revealed, He employed to develop the Divine life He had imparted. From the beginning, He used promise and precept, law and type, Psalm and ritual to instruct, quicken, convince, teach, lead, warn, comfort and to do all for the growth and establishment of the people of God.

The Psalms run through the gamut of the spiritual experience possible for those, who while waiting for the consolation of Israel and the future out-pouring of the Holy Spirit, were "apart from us" not to be "made perfect" as sons and as "worshipers." More than one prayed, "Teach me to do Thy will, for Thou art my God; let Thy good Spirit lead me into the land of uprightness" (Psa. 143:10). But there was then still lacking among men the consummate Reality and perfect Illustration of a Son of God.

When at last, all righteousness and holy virtues appeared in a Life of filial love and obedience, even in Christ "the first-born of many brethren," then the Mold and Image of the spiritual life of the saints of the old covenant, who were waiting for sonship, was seen perfect and complete.

It was pre-eminently the life of a Son of God and not only of a righteous man; of a Son ever rejoicing before the Father, His whole being filled with filial love and obedience, peace and joy. In ways Godward and manward, in self-denial and in full surrender to His Father's will, in hatred of sin and in grace to sinners, in purity of heart and forgiveness of injuries, in gentleness and all condescension, in restful yet ceaseless service, in unity of purpose and faultless obedience—in a word, in all excellencies and graces, in all virtues and beauties of the Spirit, in light and in love, the Lord Jesus set forth the mold and substance of the life spiritual, divine, eternal.

3. *Redemption must precede both the sonship and the gift of the Spirit.*

This is very clearly seen in the Apostle's argument on the great subject: "God sent forth His Son, born of a woman, born under the law, that He might redeem them that were under the law, that we might receive the adoption of sons. And because ye are sons God sent forth the Spirit of His Son into our hearts, crying, Abba, Father" (Gal. 4:4-6). The word "adoption" signifies the placing in the state and relation of a son. It is found in Romans 9:4; 13:15, 23; Gal. 4:5; Eph. 1:5.

In the writings of John believers are never called sons, but "children" ("born ones"), a word indicating nature, kinship.

Sonship relates not to nature, but to legal standing; it comes not through regeneration, but by redemption. The disciples of Jesus had to wait until the Son of God had redeemed them; and then on the redeemed disciples the Spirit of God was poured at Pentecost, not to make believers sons, but because they had become sons through redemption. In brief, sonship, though ever since redemption inseparable from justification, does in the order of salvation succeed justification. Justification in Rom. 5:1 precedes the "grace" of sonship in 5:2. This "access" or "introduction" is of the justified into the presence of God as Father; and it is through Christ and by the Spirit. (Eph. 2:18; 3:12.)

We were "predestined" to be sons of God, and to be "conformed to the image of His Son" (Eph. 1:5; Rom. 8:29). In Eph. 1:5 the "sonship" is rather corporate; all believers are viewed as one "son," one "body," just as Jehovah said of Israel, "My son," "My first born." This corporateness is really to be understood in Gal. 3:28, which may read, "Ye are all one son in Christ Jesus," instead of "one man." (See also Eph. 4:13; 1 Cor. 12:12.)

And this image is His as glorified, so that until we have been conformed to His body of glory, our "adoption" or sonship is not complete nor our experience of redemption finished. (Rom. 8:23.)

And special emphasis should be laid upon the truth that sins were before God only *pretermitted* until the atonement was made; "propitiation for the pretermission [passing over] of sins that are past" (Rom. 3:25); "for the redemption of the transgressions that were under the first testament" (Heb. 9:15).

Remission came through the great offering for sin, just as sonship came through this redemption; and as the Spirit was given because believers had become sons, so also He could be given because believers had received the remission of their sins. This is the invariable order; faith in Christ, remission of sins, gift of the Holy Spirit.

Yea, more, as without the gracious power of the Spirit of God *the new birth* would be impossible, so without the redeeming blood of Christ the estate of sonship would have been unattainable; the Spirit and the blood are equally necessary to the full accomplishment of the eternal purpose of God.

In brief, through redemption the new dignity of sonship was conferred, the new name "sons" was given to them as a new name "Father" had been declared of Him; a new name was given to the life in this new relation, "the life eternal," and a new name, "Spirit of His Son," was given to the Holy Spirit, who henceforth, with new truth and a new commandment, would nourish and develop this life and illumine and lead believers into all the privileges and duties of the sons of God.

These facts are then all related to and dependent upon each other; Jesus must first lay the ground of the forgiveness of sins of past and future times in His work of redemption and reconciliation; as risen and glorified, not before, He is "the first-born of many brethren," to whose image they are predestined to be conformed; as the Son, He declared to them the name of God as Father, the crowning name of God corresponding to their highest name, sons of God. As His "brethren" in this high and peculiar sense, He did not call them until He had first suffered, died, and risen again from the dead, but that name is the first word He spoke of them on the morning of resurrection, as if it were the chiefest joy of His soul to name and greet them as His brethren, and sons of God, being in and with Him "sons of the resurrection;" and because they were sons, the Father, through the Son, sent forth the Spirit of His Son into their hearts, crying, "Abba, Father!"

It is the marvelous dignity of a sonship in glory, like that of our Lord Jesus, with all its attendant blessings and privileges, service and rewards, suffering and glories, to which the gift of the Holy Spirit is related in this present dispensation.

Accordingly when the disciples were baptized with the Spirit on the Day of Pentecost they were not only endued with ministering power, but they also then entered into the experience of sonship. Then they knew as they could not have known before, though the Book of the Acts records but little of their inner life, that through the heaven-descended Spirit the sons of God are forever united with the heaven-ascended, glorified Son of God. Whether they at first fully realized this fact or not, it is seen as in the Gospel of John, they were in Him and He in them. Was Jesus begotten of the Spirit, so were they; was He not of the world as to origin and nature, neither were they; was He loved of the Father, so were they, and with the same love; was He sanctified and sent into the world to bear witness to the truth, so likewise He sent them; did He receive the Spirit as the seal of God to His Sonship, so were they sealed; was He anointed with power and light to serve, so they received the unction from Him; did He begin to serve when there came the attesting Spirit and confirming word of the Father, so they began to serve when the Spirit of the Son, the Witness, was sent forth into their hearts, saying Abba, Father; was He, after service and suffering, received up in glory, so shall they obtain His glory when He comes again to receive them unto Himself. Verily, "we are as He is in this world." (1 John 4:17; John 10:36; 17:1-26; Rom. 5:5.)

In view of these truths of Divine revelation how foolish the wisdom of the natural man and how sadly misleading the doctrine which makes the "fatherhood of God and the brotherhood of man," which are by nature and creation, identical and co-extensive with that which is by grace and redemption; for not only does the imperative word, "Ye must be born again," sweep away all the merit and glory of man as he is by the first birth, but also, the predestination to a sonship like that of the Son of God in glory lifts the "twice-born" to a height and dignity never conceived of by the natural man.

4. In the *gift of the Holy Spirit on the Day of Pentecost all gifts* · for believers in Christ were contained and were *related* to them as *Sons of God* both individually and cor-poratively as the Church the Body of Christ.

In kind, as can be seen on comparison, there was no dif-ference in His gifts and acts before and after that day, but the new Gift was now to dwell in the hearts of men as sons of God and with more abundant life and varied manifesta-tions of power and wisdom.

But by the Spirit the one Body was formed and all gifts are due to His perpetual presence. (1 Cor. 12: 14.) Also, it is to be understood that such a word of Jesus, "If ye then being evil know how to give good gifts unto your children, how much more shall your Heavenly Father give the Holy Spirit to them that ask Him," could not have been fulfilled until a later hour, for repeating His promise at another time it is said of Jesus, "But this spake He of the Spirit which they that believed on Him should receive, for the Holy Ghost was not yet given, because Jesus was not yet glorified" (John 3: 7-39). These are some of the *anticipative sayings* of our Lord, not to be made good until He had died and risen again. The good things could not be given until "transgression had been forgiven and sin covered." The water could not pour forth until the Rock had been smitten. And as to the use of the words, "baptize" and "pour," they afterwards, in later Scriptures, imply the original incorporating act.

It is significant that after Pentecost only the words, "filled with the Spirit," are used. Nothing is said of an individual receiving a new or fresh "baptism of the Spirit." It would imply that the baptism is one for the whole Body until all the members are incorporated; one the outpouring, many the fillings; one fountain, many the hearts to drink, to have in turn a well of water springing up within them.

The disciples were indeed endued with power for service according to promise; on *that* especially their eyes and hearts had been fixed; that was the chief thing for them; but in the light of later Scriptures it is seen that the chief thing with God was not only to attest the glory of Jesus by the gift of the Spirit, but also *"in one Spirit to baptize into one body"* the "children of God," who until then were looked upon as "scattered abroad," as unincorporated members. (1 Cor. 12: 13; John 11: 52; Gal. 3: 27, 28.) And the Gift, whether to the Body or to the individual member, is once for all. As the Christian is once for all in Christ, so the Holy Spirit is once for all in the Christian; but the intent of the presence of the Spirit is often but feebly met by the believer, just as his knowledge of what it is to be "in Christ" is often most defective.

5. *The Holy Spirit is given at once on the remission of sins* to them that believe in Christ Jesus as their Lord and Saviour.

It is, however, to be observed that as the Spirit acts according to the truth known, or believed and obeyed, *an interval* unspiritual or unfruitful *may come* between the remission of sins and the *marked manifestation* of the Spirit, either in relation to holiness of life, or to power for service, or to patience in trials. It certainly is the divine ideal of a holy life, that the presence of the Spirit should at once be *made manifest* on the forgiveness of sins, and continue in increasing light and power to the end. (Rom. 5: 1-5; Titus 3: 4-7.)

And this steady onward progress more and more unto the perfect day has been and is true of many, who from early childhood, or from the day of conversion, in the case of adults, were led continuously by the Spirit and never came to one great crisis. With others it is not so, for it is the confession of a large number of men and women, afterward eminent for holiness, devotion, endurance, that their life previous to such crisis had been hardly worth the name of Christian. Whatever explanation or "philosophy" of such experience may be given, the following is true of the majority.

The full truth of the sonship and salvation of believers may not have been taught them when they first believed; the life may have begun under a yoke of legal bondage; the freedom of filial access may have been doubted, even though their hearts often burned within them because of the presence of the unknown Spirit; and thus weary, ineffective years passed, attended with but little growth in grace or fruitful service, or patient resignation, until a point was reached in various ways, and through providences often unexpected and most marvelous, when at last the Holy Spirit made Himself manifest in the fulness of His love and power.

That there is *with God* an interval between justification and the giving of the Spirit (an interval such as certain theories contend for), cannot be proved. The unsatisfactory experience of the ignorant Christian may lead him to think he never had the Spirit.

There are, however, certain intervals recorded in the New Testament which should be considered. The one between the ascension and Pentecost was for a peculiar preparation through prayer and waiting on the Lord; that of the forty days between the resurrection and the ascension was a continuation of the presence of Jesus the other Comforter, and of whom it is written, "He opened their understanding that they understand the Scriptures," so doing what His Holy Spirit was to do when He came; and during the previous days of His public ministry not only did Jesus teach, but as attested at the confession of Peter, also the Father was revealing truth to men: "Flesh and blood hath not revealed it unto thee, but My Father who is in heaven."

In the light of this word to Peter it may be said that up to Pentecost the Spirit of God was at work in the world in the modes of the old dispensation, but that when the Day of

Pentecost came His peculiar work began in relation to believers as sons of God. Even the breathing of Christ upon the disciples on the evening of the day of His resurrection was, in accordance with the many symbolic acts and sayings recorded in the Gospel of John, symbolic of the Mighty Breath of Pentecost, for both the symbol and the reality were associated with the enduement of power for the service which began at Pentecost. Besides, they were told forty days later to tarry in Jerusalem for such enduement. They could not already have received it and yet be told to wait for it. And Thomas was not present on the evening of that breathing.

As to other intervals; that in case of the converts on the Day of Pentecost was doubtless for the confirmation of the apostolic authority; that of the Samaritans when Philip preached may be accounted for by remembering the religious feud between Jew and Samaritan which now must be settled for all time and the unity of the Church established. Also seeing "salvation is from the Jews," the authority of Jewish apostles must be affirmed, for to them Christ had committed the founding of the Church. (Acts 8: 14-17.)

In regard to Paul, it is evident from the narrative, he knew not the full import of the appearing of Jesus, until Ananias came. The recovery of sight, the forgiveness of sins, the filling of the Holy Spirit, all took place during this interview. He received the Spirit, as was befitting the Apostle to the Gentiles, in a Gentile city, far away from the other apostles, for his apostleship was to be "not from men, neither through a man" (Acts 9: 10-19; 22: 6-16).

But the case of Cornelius proves that *no interval at all need exist,* for the moment Peter spoke this word, received by faith by Cornelius and those present, the Holy Spirit who knew their hearts fell on them: "To Him give all the prophets witness that through His name whosoever believeth in Him shall receive *the remission of sins.*" Peter intended to say more, but God showed by the sudden outpouring of the Spirit that Peter had said enough, for from Peter's report to the church in Jerusalem we learn that he intended to say more, and not only say more but probably do more, so making an interval even as in the case of the Samaritans through baptism, prayer and laying on of his hands that they might receive the Holy Ghost. (Acts 8: 14-17; 10: 43-44; 11: 15, 16.)

It is especially to be noted in this connection that the text of Eph. 1: 13, so often quoted as proving a long interval between faith in Christ and "the sealing of the Spirit," "In whom also *after* that ye believed, ye were sealed with that Holy Spirit of promise," lends no authority for such long interval of time, for the word "after" implies more than the Greek participle warrants, and accordingly the Revision reads, "In whom having also believed, ye were sealed with the Holy Spirit of promise;" *but the very same participle,* "having believed," used by Paul in Ephesians, is used by Peter in the Acts in rehearsing the interview with Cornelius, who received the Spirit *immediately.* (Acts 2: 17.)

Neither does the remaining instance of the twelve disciples of John the Baptist whom Paul found in Ephesus, prove that such an interval is necessary or inevitable today; for they had not even heard that Jesus had come, and that redemption had been accomplished, and the Spirit given; but as soon as remission of sins in the name of Jesus was preached to them, they believed, were baptized, and through prayer and the laying on of Paul's hands, received the Holy Spirit. (Acts 19: 1-6.)

The question Paul addressed to them, "Have ye received the Holy Ghost since ye believed?" (or in the Revision, "Did ye receive the Holy Ghost when ye believed?") has been most strangely applied in these days to Christians, whereas it was pertinent to these disciples of John only. *To address it to Christians now is to deny a finished redemption, the sonship of believers and the once-for-all out-pouring of the Holy Spirit.*

And it is implied in the case of Cornelius* with which the Apostle Peter had nothing to do except to preach the word, that when the apostles had passed away *the mold of experience* common for all succeeding centuries would be *that of these Gentile converts* wherever in Christendom or heathendom the Gospel of Christ might be preached.

6. The *conditions of the manifestation* of the presence and power of the Spirit are *the same,* at conversion or at any later, deeper experience of the believer, whether in relation to fuller knowledge of Christ, or to more effective service, or to more patient endurance of ill, or to growth in likeness to Christ.

The experience, in each case, is run in the same mold; *each part, each word or fact of Christ, must be received in the same attitude and condition of mind as the first,* when He was seen as the Bearer of our sins, even *by faith alone.*

Negatively, it may be said that the conditions are confessed weakness and inability to help oneself; the end of nature's wisdom, power, righteousness has been reached; utter despair of there being any good thing *"in the flesh"* settles over the soul, a willingness to look to God alone for help begins to stir in the heart. Convictions of unfaithfulness and self-seeking mingle with a hunger and thirst for righteousness and a life worthy of the name of Christian.

It is not, however, as consciously sinless in themselves that the Spirit is given to them who "seek the blessing," but to them as sinless "in Christ." Believers in Christ begin their life in the very standing of the Son of God Himself. Neither do the Scriptures teach, as implied or expressed in certain theories, that there is an interval between the remission of sins and "the sealing of the Spirit," and that "justified" believers may die during such interval having never been "sealed," and so never been "in Christ," and never been attested sons of God.

---

*Acts 10.

Such belief contradicts the very grace of God and implies that sonship depends upon the gift of the Spirit and not upon redemption and the remission of sins, and would read, "Because ye have the Spirit ye are sons," instead of, "And because ye are sons, God sent forth the Spirit of His Son into your hearts, crying, Abba, Father." It also follows that such justified ones devoid of the Spirit are not Christ's nor Christians, for it is plainly written, "But if any man hath not the Spirit of Christ, he is none of His;" and also, "No man can say, Jesus is Lord, but in the Holy Spirit." And as to the proof of the presence of the Spirit at such times, whatever emotions or high raptures may attend the discoveries of the love and power of God in the case of some, they are not to be the tests and measures for all. Conversions are not alike in all, neither are the manifestations of the Spirit. He may come like the sun at high noon through rifted clouds or like a slowly deepening dawn; like a shower or like the dew; like a great tide of air or like a gentle breathing; but "all these worketh the one and self-same Spirit." But more than all, the proof is seen in growth in holiness, in self-denials for Christ's sake, in the manifold graces and abiding fruit of the Spirit.

As in the apostolic day so now the desire exists for the manifestation of the Spirit in marvelous ways; but a life sober, righteous, holy, lived in the hope of the glory to come, is the more excellent way of the Spirit's manifestation and undeniable proof of His indwelling.

Positively, the requirements or inseparable accompaniments of the manifestation of the indwelling Spirit, whether for holy living or faithful service, must be drawn from the example of the Son of God our Lord Jesus. And they are *prayer, obedience, faith,* and above all *a desire and purpose to glorify Christ.* All, indeed, may be summed up in one condition, and that is, *to let God have His own will and way with us.*

If, then, it is to believers as sons of God, to whom and in whom and through whom the Holy Spirit manifests His presence and power, it would follow that whatever Jesus did in order to fulfil His mission in the power of the Spirit, believers must do; and we find His life to have been a life of *prayer* for all the gifts and helps of God, a life of *obedience,* always doing the things that pleased the Father; and so, never left alone, a life of *faith* in the present power of God, a life of *devotion* to the glory of God, so that at its close He, through the eternal Spirit, offered Himself without blemish unto God.

But the chief and all-including condition and proof is the desire and purpose to glorify Christ.

The prayer should not be so much for this or that gift, or this or that result, as for Christ Himself to be made manifest to us and through us. The Apostle who was most filled with the Spirit sums all up in that one great word, "For me to live is Christ." As Jesus the Son of God glorified the Father, so the sons of God are to glorify Christ.

The Spirit cannot be where Christ is denied as Redeemer, Life and Lord of all. Christ is "the Truth," and the Spirit is "the Spirit of the Truth;" all is personal, not ideal, for the sum and substance of material wherewith the Spirit works is Christ. The Spirit cannot be teaching if Christ is not seen in "the law of Moses, and in the prophets, and in the Psalms," as well as in the Gospels, or if Christ is not acknowledged to have continued "to do and to teach" in the Acts and in the Epistles what He began in the Gospels.

If Christ is indeed the wisdom of God unto salvation, the Holy Spirit alone can demonstrate it unto the minds and hearts of men; and He has *no mission* in the world separable from Christ and His work of redemption. The outer work of Christ and the inner work of the Spirit go together. The work *for* us by Christ is through the *blood,* the work *in* us by the Spirit is through the *truth;* the latter rests upon the former; and without the Spirit, substitutes for the Spirit and

His work will be accompanied by substitutes for Christ and His work. The importance, therefore, of the presence and work of the Holy Spirit should be estimated according to that far-reaching and all-touching word of Christ, "He shall glorify Me" (John 16:13-15).

To glorify Christ is to manifest Him as supremely excellent; to blind the eyes of men to that glory is the purpose of the god of this world; therefore, which spirit is at work in a man or in a church can easily be told.

7. In conclusion, the sum of all *His mission is to perfect in saints the good work He began, and He molds it all according to this reality of a high and holy sonship:* He establishes the saints in and for Christ. (2 Cor. 1:21.) According to this reality their life and walk partake of thoughts and desires, hopes and objects, unworldly and heavenly. Born of God and from above, knowing whence they came and whither they are going, they live and move and have their being in a world not realized by flesh and blood.

Their life is hid with Christ in God; their work of faith is wrought out in the unseen abode of the Spirit; their labor of love is prompted by a loyal obedience to their Lord, who is absent in "a far country" to which both He and they belong; their sufferings are not their own but His, who, from out of the Glory could ask, "Why persecutest thou Me?" Their worship is of the Father "in spirit and in truth" before the mercy seat, "in the light which no man can approach unto;" their peace is "the peace of God," which can never be disturbed by any fear or trouble which eternal ages might disclose; their joy is "joy in the Lord," its spring is in God and ever deepening in its perpetual flow; their hope is the coming of the Son of God from heaven and the vision of the King in His beauty amidst the unspeakable splendors of His Father's house; and through all the way, "thorn and flower," by which they are journeying to the heavenly country; it is the good Spirit who is leading them. (Isa. 63:7-14.)

CHAPTER XVII

OBSERVATIONS ON THE CONVERSION AND APOSTLESHIP OF ST. PAUL

BY LORD LYTTELTON

ANALYZED AND CONDENSED BY REV. J. L. CAMPBELL, D. D.,
CAMBRIDGE, MASS.

The object of this paper is to present in an abbreviated form the famous argument of Lord Lyttelton in defense of Christianity based on the conversion of the Apostle Paul. A few words about the man himself and about the interesting circumstances in which this treatise was written will properly introduce the subject.

George Lyttelton was born at Hagley, Worcestershire, England, January 17, 1709, and died on Tuesday morning, August 22, 1773, aged sixty-four years. He belonged to a distinguished "family of long descent and gentle blood, dwelling for centuries on the same spot." Educated at Eton and Oxford, he soon afterwards entered Parliament, "and for many years the name of George Lyttelton was seen in every account of every debate in the House of Commons." From this, he advanced successively to the position of lord commissioner of the treasury, and of chancellor of the exchequer, after which he was raised to the peerage. He was also a man of letters and his closing years were devoted almost wholly to literary pursuits. He was a writer of verse as well as prose and Dr. Samuel Johnson has furnished us with his biography in his "Lives of the Poets." Outside of his books, which comprise nine octavo volumes, his Memoirs and Correspondence make two additional volumes that were compiled and edited by Robert Phillimore in 1845.

The eighteenth century was the darkest period religiously in the history of England since the time of the Reformation. It was the age of the great deists, agnostics, rationalists and unbelievers, when "all men of rank are [were] thought to be infidels." Like so many of the literary men of his time, George Lyttelton and his friend Gilbert West were led at first to reject the Christian religion. On the Sabbath forenoon before he died, in an interview with Dr. Johnson, Lyttelton said, "When I first set out in the world I had friends who endeavored to shake my belief in the Christian religion. I saw difficulties which staggered me," etc. In his biography of Lord Lyttelton, Dr. Johnson adds, "He had, in the pride of juvenile confidence, with the help of corrupt conversation, entertained doubts of the truth of Christianity." His intimacy with Bolingbroke, Chesterfield, Pope and others of the same kind had no doubt influenced him in this direction. Rev. T. T. Biddolph tells us that both Lyttelton and West, "men of acknowledged talents, had imbibed the principles of infidelity. * * * Fully persuaded that the Bible was an imposture, they were determined to expose the cheat. Lord Lyttelton chose the Conversion of Paul and Mr. West the Resurrection of Christ for the subject of hostile criticism. Both sat down to their respective tasks full of prejudice; but the result of their separate attempts was, that they were both converted by their efforts to overthrow the truth of Christianity. They came together, not as they expected, to exult over an imposture exposed to ridicule, but to lament over their own folly and to felicitate each other on their joint conviction that the Bible was the word of God. Their able inquiries have furnished two of the most valuable treatises in favor of revelation, one entitled 'Observations on the Conversion of St. Paul' and the other 'Observations on the Resurrection of Christ.'" West's book was the first published. Lyttelton's work appeared at first anonymously in 1747, when he was thirty-eight years of age. The edition which lies before me contains seventy-eight compact pages. It is addressed in the form of a letter to Gilbert West. In the opening paragraph he says, "The conversion and apostleship of St. Paul alone, duly considered, was of itself a demonstration sufficient to prove Christianity to be a divine revelation." Dr. Johnson remarked that it is a treatise "to which infidelity had never been able to fabricate a specious answer." Dr. Philip Doddridge, who became Lyttelton's most intimate religious friend, speaks of it as "masterly," and, "as perfect in its kind as any our age has produced." Testimonials of this kind might be multiplied indefinitely.

Let us now turn to an examination of the book itself. Lyttelton naturally begins by bringing before us all the facts that we have in the New Testament regarding the conversion of St. Paul; the three accounts given in the Acts; what we have in Galatians, Philippians, Timothy, Corinthians, Colossians and in other places. (Acts 9:22-26; Gal. 1:11-16; Phil. 3:4-8; 1 Tim. 1:12, 13; 1 Cor. 15:8; 2 Cor. 1:1; Col. 1:1, etc.) Then he lays down four propositions which he considers exhaust all the possibilities in the case.

1.   Either Paul was "an impostor who said what he knew to be false, with an intent to deceive;" or

2.   He was an enthusiast who imposed on himself by the force of "an overheated imagination;" or

3.   He was "deceived by the fraud of others;" or, finally,

4.   What he declared to be the cause of his conversion did all really happen; "and, therefore the Christian religion is a divine revelation."

I.   PAUL NOT AN IMPOSTOR

More than half his argument (about forty pages) is devoted to the first of these propositions, which is really the key to the whole situation. Is this story of Paul's conversion so often repeated in Acts and Epistles a fabrication, put forth by a designing man with the deliberate purpose and intention of deceiving?

Lyttelton at once raises the question of motive. What could have induced him while on his way to Damascus, filled with implacable hatred against this whole sect, to turn around and become a disciple of Christ?

1. Was it wealth?

No, all the wealth was in the keeping of those whom he had forsaken; the poverty was on the side of those with whom he now identified himself. So poor had they been, that those among them possessed of any little property sold whatever belonged to them in order to provide for the dire necessities of the rest. Indeed, one of the burdens afterwards laid upon Paul was to collect means for those who were threatened with starvation. Such was the humble condition of these early Christians, that he often refused to take anything from them even for the bare necessities of life, but labored himself to provide for his scanty needs. To the Corinthians, he writes, "Even unto this present hour we both hunger, and thirst, and are naked, and are buffeted, and have no certain dwelling place; and we toil working with our hands." (1 Cor. 4:11, 12. See also 2 Cor. 12:14; 1 Thess. 2:4-9; 2 Thess. 3:8, etc.) In his farewell to the elders of Ephesus, he appeals to them as knowing it to be true that, "I coveted no man's silver or gold or apparel. Ye yourselves know that these hands ministered unto my necessities, and to them that were with me" (Acts 20:33, 34). He forsook the great Jewish hierarchy with its gorgeous temple and its overflowing treasuries, where his zeal in putting down the hated sect of the Nazarene would have been almost certainly rewarded with a fortune. He cast in his lot among the poverty-stricken disciples of Jesus Christ, among whom it was his ambition to be poor. Near the end of his life he presents to us the picture of an old man shivering in a Roman dungeon and pathetically asking for a cloak to be sent him to cover his naked and suffering limbs during the severity of an Italian winter.

2. *Was it reputation?*

No; those with whom he united were held in universal contempt; their Leader had been put to death as a criminal among thieves; the chiefs of the cause that he had espoused were illiterate men. On the other hand, the wisest and the greatest men in all the land indignantly rejected the teachings of this new sect. The preaching of Christ crucified was to the Jew a stumbling block and to the Greeks foolishness. There was no reputation for the great disciple of Gamaliel in parting with his splendid honors and identifying himself with a lot of ignorant fishermen. He would only be execrated as a deserter and betrayer of the Jewish cause, and he might rest assured that the same bloody knife that slew the Shepherd of the scattered flock would soon be unsheathed against himself. All the reputation that he had so zealously built up was gone the hour that he went over to the new religion, and from that day on contempt was his portion. He was accounted as the filth of the world and the offscouring of all things. (1 Cor. 4:13.)

3. *Was it power he was after?*

We know what men have done to get into positions of prominence and dominion over their fellows. Mahomet, the popes, and many others, put forth spiritual claims so as to promote thereby their own temporal ends. How was it with Paul? His whole career was marked by a complete absence of all self-seeking. He had no eye to worldly ambitions. He interfered with nothing, "in government or civil affairs; he meddled not with legislation; he formed no commonwealths; he raised no seditions; he affected no temporal power." He assumed no pre-eminence over other Christians. He regarded himself as not worthy to be called an apostle, as less than the least of all saints, as the chief of sinners. Those engaged in like work he called "fellow-laborers" and "fellow-servants." Even if the truth was spread by those hostile to him, through "envy and strife," so long as Christ was proclaimed, "therein

I rejoice, yea, and will rejoice" (Phil. 1:18). He did not lord it over the churches, even over those that he himself had founded. To the Pauline party in Corinth he exclaims, "Was Paul crucified for you? or were ye baptized in the name of Paul?" (1 Cor. 1:13). "We preach not ourselves, but Christ Jesus as Lord, and ourselves as *your servants* for Jesus' sake" (2 Cor. 4:5). Those who, from selfish motives seek for influence over people pander to them and flatter them [as, e. g. did Absalom]. There was nothing of this with Paul. He rebuked the churches unsparingly for their sins, and did not hesitate, if need be, to incur their displeasure. Disclaiming all pre-eminence and position and power, he preached Christ and Him crucified as the head, and hid and buried self behind the cross. Earth to him was nothing. His eye was fixed on "the recompense of reward" (Heb. 11:26).

4. *Was his motive the gratification of any other passion?*

Impostors have pretended to receive divine revelations as a pretext in order that they might indulge in loose conduct. Was it so here? No; for all Paul's teachings were in the most absolute antagonism to any such purpose. "His writings breathe nothing but the strictest morality, obedience to magistrates, order, and government, with the utmost abhorrence of all licentiousness, idleness, or loose behavior under the cloak of religion." Writing to the Thessalonians, he utters the challenge, "Ye are witnesses, and God also, how holily and righteously and unblameably we behaved ourselves toward you that believe" (1 Thess. 2:10). "We wronged no man, we corrupted no man, we took advantage of no man" (2 Cor. 7:2). The whole teaching of the Apostle is in the sternest and most uncompromising hostility to everything but the highest and holiest ideals.

5. *Was it a pious fraud?*

That is to say, did Paul pretend to receive a divine revelation in order to give him prestige in advancing the teachings of Christianity? But Christianity was the one thing he had set out to destroy. To become a Christian was to incur the hatred, the contempt, the torments and the violent deaths suffered by Christians in that day. Why then this sudden change in Paul's own views regarding the unpopular teachings of the Nazarene? Would he have endured "the loss of all things" and exulted over it, for what he knew was a fraud? Would he have spent a life of the most arduous toil to induce others to make every earthly sacrifice while he knew that behind it all he was practising a delusion? It would be an imposture as unprofitable as it was perilous, both to himself the deceiver and to the others whom he deceived. The theory confutes itself. Only the sternest conviction that he had received a divine revelation could have induced Paul to pass through what he himself had suffered, or to have asked others to do the same. "If we have only hoped in Christ in this life, we are of all men most pitiable" (1 Cor. 15:19).

But had he practiced a deception, he could not have successfully carried it out. Men sometimes act capriciously. Suppose that Paul "just did it" without any motive that can be imagined; then he must have ignominiously failed in his attempt to perpetuate such a fraud. How could he, e. g., have become such an adept in the mysteries and secrets of the new religion as to be an authority and an apostle of it, if he had to depend for his special knowledge on information received from men who knew well by bitter experience that he was their capital enemy? It must have come in another way, and his own account makes it plain. "For neither did I receive it [the Gospel] from man, nor was I taught it, but it came to me through revelation of Jesus Christ" (Gal. 1:12). Had he fabricated the story of his conversion he would certainly have located it in a place so remote or hidden that there could be no witnesses to refute. [Joe Smith, e. g., and the golden plates of the Book of Mormon.] Instead of that the miracle of Paul's conversion, with its great light from heaven exceeding the brightness of the sun, is placed in the public highway near Damascus; at noonday, when their senses could not be deceived, and when all the accompanying soldiers and commissioners were with him on the spot. Had there been a shadow of disproof, how promptly the Jews in Damascus would have nipped the falsehood in the bud by the testimony of the witnesses who were present with Paul at the time. Or, when the Apostle stood on the castle stairs in Jerusalem and told the whole story, why did not the Jewish authorities silence him at once and forever by showing that nothing of the kind had ever taken place, and proved it by the abundant evidence of the competent witnesses who were with him—if it were not true? It was an event that took place before the eyes of the world, and would be made at once a matter of the strictest scrutiny. And the truth of the fact was so incontestably established that it had become a matter of common knowledge. The Jews said the utmost they could against Paul before the Roman court, and yet Paul appealed directly to King Agrippa in presence of Festus as to his own personal knowledge of the truth of the story. "For the king knoweth of these things, unto whom also I speak freely; for I am persuaded that none of these things is hidden from him; for this hath not been done in a corner" (Acts 26:26)—"a very remarkable proof both of the notoriety of the fact, and the integrity of the man, who, with so fearless a confidence, could call upon a *king* to give testimony for him, even while he was sitting in judgment upon him." Moreover, how came it that Ananias went to meet such an enemy in Damascus, if the story of his conversion was made up? If Paul was an impostor, then all his miracles were simply tricks or sleight-of-hand. Nevertheless, he, a despised and hated Jew, set himself to the appalling task of converting the Gentile world—teaching doctrines that shocked every prejudice and at which they were wont to mock in derision. Arrayed against him were the magistrates with their policy and power, the priests with their interests and craft, the people with their prejudice and passions, the philosophers with their pride and wisdom. Could he by feats of jugglery in presence of a shrewd, hostile people strike Elymas the sorcerer, blind; heal a cripple at Lystra; restore the pythoness at Philippi; shake open with a prayer the doors of a prison; raise the dead to life, etc., so that thousands were converted and great pure churches renouncing all sin and dishonesty, established throughout the Roman world? Our author shows that this would be impossible without divine help and therefore he concludes that he has proven (1) that Paul was not a cheat telling a trumped-up story about his conversion, and (2) if he were, he could not have succeeded.

II. PAUL NOT AN ENTHUSIAST WHO IMPOSED ON HIMSELF

This second argument covers twenty pages. Was Paul a deluded enthusiast whose overheated imagination imposed on him so that he imagined to be true that which had never really taken place? Lord Lyttelton makes an analysis of the elements that enter into the make-up of a man of this type. He finds these to be five.

(*1*) *Great heat of temper.*

While Paul had intense fervor, like all great men, yet it was everywhere governed by discretion and reason. His zeal was his servant, not the master of his judgment. He possessed consummate tact which proves self-control. In indifferent matters he became "all things to all men;" to the Jews he became a Jew, to them that are without law as without law, to the weak he became weak—all, that he might gain some. (1 Cor. 9:19-23.) "His zeal was eager and warm, but tempered with prudence, and even with the civilities and decorums of life, as appears by his behavior to Agrippa, Festus and Felix; not the blind, inconsiderate, indecent zeal of an enthusiast."

(*2*) *Melancholy.*

He regards this as a prominent mark of misguided zeal. He finds nothing of it in Paul. There is great sorrow over his former ignorant persecution of the church, but there are no gloomy self-imposed penances such as melancholy fanatics inflict upon themselves. He had a desire to depart and be with Christ, but there was nothing morbid about it. It was all based on the revelation that he already had of the rewards that awaited him in the life to come. He tactfully met the Athenians adroitly claiming to be the interpreter of "The unknown god" whose altar they themselves had erected. He never hesitated to avert injustice by claiming his privileges as a Roman citizen He was the very antithesis of gloominess. In whatever state he was, he had learned to be content. Neither his actions, nor his writings, nor his interested greeting and salutations, show the slightest tincture of melancholia.

(*3*) *Ignorance.*

This charge could not be laid up against the Apostle. Brought up at the feet of the great Gamaliel, he appeared to be master not only of Jewish, but also of Greek (and Roman) learning

(*4*) *Credulity.*

As a resident of Jerusalem, Paul could not be a stranger to the fame of the miracles wrought by Jesus. He had the facts of the resurrection of our Lord, of Pentecost and all the miracles wrought by the Apostles up till the death of Stephen. Far from being credulous, he had barred his mind against every proof and refused to believe. "Nothing less than the irresistible evidence of *his own senses,* clear from all possibility of doubt, could have overcome his unbelief."

(*5*) *Vanity or self-conceit.*

Vanity and fanaticism usually go together. Men of this type flatter themselves that on account of their superior worth they are the recipients of extraordinary favors and gifts from God, and of these they make their boast. There is not one word in his Epistles, nor one act recorded in his life, in which the slightest mark of this appears. When compelled to vindicate his apostolic claim from wanton attack he does it effectively, but in the briefest way and with many apologies for being compelled to speak thus of himself. (2 Cor. 11:1-30.) When he had a vision of heaven, he modestly withheld his own name and covered it up in the third person. For fourteen years he observed absolute silence in regard to this special mark of the divine favor. (2 Cor. 12:1-12.) Would this be the way a vain man would act? Neither is Paul that planteth, nor Apollos that watereth, anything, but God who gives the increase. (1 Cor. 3:4-7.) Instead of self-conceit, he writes of himself in terms of the most complete abnegation. Everywhere it is "not I, but the grace of God that was with me." (1 Cor. 15:10.) His modesty appears on every page.

(6) But now suppose that in some way wholly unaccountable, Paul had actually been swept away by enthusiasm at the time, and imposed on himself, by imagining the events that took place. Lyttelton's reply is that such a thing was impossible. He here uses the argument that has since been employed so effectively to dispose of Renan's vision theory of the resurrection of our Lord. In such circumstances men always see what they expect to see. An imagined vision will be in accord with the opinions already imprinted on one's mind. Paul's purpose was clearly fixed. At his own request he had been clothed with authority to persecute the Christians, and he was now on his way from Jerusalem to Damascus on this very errand. He looked upon Christ as an impostor and a blasphemer who had justly been put to death. All his passions were inflamed to the highest degree against His followers. He started on his northward journey "breathing out threatenings and slaughter against the disciples of the Lord" (Acts 9:1). "And being exceedingly mad against them, I persecuted them even unto foreign cities" (Acts 26:11) "There was the pride of supporting a part he had voluntarily engaged in, and the credit he found it procured him among the chief priests and rulers, whose commission he bore." In these circumstances

a wild enthusiast might indeed imagine he saw a vision, but it would be one urging him onward to do the thing which he had started out to accomplish. With nothing having happened to change his opinions or alter the bent of his mind, it would be as impossible for him, in a moment, to have imagined the complete revolution that is recorded in the New Testament as it would be for a rapid river to "carry a boat against the current of its own stream." We might add, as well expect the mighty rushing river itself, without any cause to stop in its course and rush violently backward up a steep mountain side, as to expect the whole current of Paul's thought and feeling and imagination and purpose to be instantly reversed without any cause. It could not take place. And it would have been just as impossible for all those who were with him to have experienced the same delusion, for they also saw the light above the brightness of the noonday sun and they heard the voice from heaven, although they understood not the words. But suppose it were a meteor that burst upon them? How then account for the words that Paul heard speaking in the Hebrew tongue and the dialogue which followed? How account for his going to a certain spot in Damascus, in accordance with instructions here received? How account for the knowledge that Ananias had, and that led to their interview? How account for the miracle after three days whereby Paul's blindness was healed? And how account for the mighty works and wonders afterward wrought by Paul, all consequent on this first revelation? [Following the suggestion of, perhaps, Krenkel, a New England professor is credited with teaching that at his conversion Paul had simply an epileptic attack. But, had all the company that were with him a like attack at the same instant, for they all saw something? And, moreover, no disorder of this or any other kind can account for the facts in the case. Paul's marvelous lifework revolutionized the history of his age, and his influence is powerfully felt yet, after nearly two thousand years, all over the world. One is almost tempted to say that if such is the result of an attack of epilepsy, what a pity that such a professor as this had not a similar attack. Then possibly he, too, might yet be heard from in the world.]

III. PAUL WAS NOT DECEIVED BY OTHERS

This third possible solution Lyttelton dismisses with a single page. The fraud of others could not have deceived him; for, (1) It was morally impossible that the disciples of Christ could have thought of such a fraud at the instant of Paul's greatest fury against them.

(2) It was physically impossible for them to do it. Could they produce a light brighter than the midday sun; cause him to hear a voice speaking out of that light; make him blind for three days and then return his sight at a word, etc.? There were no Christians around when the miracle of his conversion took place.

(3) No fraud could have produced those subsequent miracles which he himself actively wrought and to which he so confidently appealed in proof of his divine mission.

IV. CHRISTIANITY A DIVINE REVELATION

Our author considers that he has furnished sufficient evidence to show (1) that Paul was not an impostor deliberately proclaiming what he knew to be false with intent to deceive; (2) that he was not imposed upon by an overheated imagination, and (3) that he was not deceived by the fraud of others. Unless, therefore, we are prepared to lay aside the use of our understanding and all the rules of evidence by which facts are determined, we must accept the whole story of Paul's conversion as literally and historically true. We have therefore the supernatural, and the Christian religion is proved to be a revelation from God.

Endeavoring as closely as possible to follow the original and yet considerably in my own language, I have sought to give the essence of Lord Lyttelton's matchless argument which has been blessed to thousands of doubting souls. May this outline lead to candid examination, as such an examination should inevitably lead to Him whom Paul saw in the midst of the glory near the gate of Damascus.

CHAPTER XVIII

CHRISTIANITY, NO FABLE

BY REV. THOMAS WHITELAW, M. A., D. D.,
KILMARNOCK, SCOTLAND

I. The first mark of the truthfulness of Christianity is to be found in

ITS SUPREME EXCELLENCE

as a Religious System. The unapproachable beauty and resistless charm of its conception, and the unique character of the means by which it seeks to carry out its aims, are not reconcilable with the notion of Fable.

If, however, notwithstanding, Christianity is a Fable, then it is the Divinest Fable ever clothed in human speech. Nothing like it can be found in the literature of the world. Paul only spoke the unvarnished truth when he declared that eye had not seen nor ear heard, neither had the mind of man conceived the things which God had revealed to men in the Gospel.

NOT OF HUMAN ORIGIN

1. The very conception of the Gospel as a scheme for rescuing a lost world from the guilt and power of Sin, for transforming men into servants of righteousness, followers of Christ, and children of God, each one resembling Himself and partaking of His nature, and for eventually lifting them up into a state of holy and blessed immortality like that in which He Himself dwells—that conception never took its rise in the brains of a human fable monger, and least of all in that of a crafty priest or political deceiver—no, not even in that of the best and most brilliantly endowed thinker, poet, prophet or philosopher that ever lived. Men do not write novels and compose fictions in order to redeem their fellows from guilt and

sin, to comfort and support them in death, and to prepare them for immortality. Even those who regard Christianity as being based on delusions and deceptions do not assert that the object of its instructors was anything so lofty and spiritual, but rather that its fabricators sought thereby to enrich themselves by imposing on their credulous fellows, blinding them to the truth by setting before them fictions as if they were facts, frightening them with ghostly terrors and so securing a hold upon their services or their means. The latest sensation provided by German speculation as to the origin of Christianity is that it was manufactured in Rome in the time of Trajan, i. e., about the beginning of the second century, in order to help on a great liberation movement amongst the Jewish slave proletariat against their tyrannical masters, and that in fact it was an imaginary compound of Roman Socialism, Greek Philosophy and Jewish Messiahism. Neither of these, however, is the account furnished by Christianity itself in its accredited documents, of its aim, which, as already stated, is to deliver men from sin and death. The very grandeur of this aim proves that Christianity has not emanated from the mind of man, but must have proceeded from the heart of God. And it may be safely contended that Infinite Wisdom and Love makes no use of fables and deceptions, legends and fictions to further its purposes and realize its aims.

2. If, in addition, the details of the Christian Scheme be considered, that is to say, the particular means by which it proposes to effect its aim, it will further appear that the idea of fiction and fable must be laid aside and that of reality and truth set in its place. It will not be seriously questioned that the details of the Christian Scheme are substantially and briefly these: (1) that God in infinite love and out of pure grace, from eternity purposed to provide salvation for the fallen race of man; (2) that in order to carry out that purpose He sent His own Son, only begotten and well-beloved, the

brightness of His Glory and the express image of His Person, into this world in the likeness of sinful flesh, to die for men's sins, thereby rendering satisfaction for the same, and to rise again from the dead, thereby showing that God had accepted the Sacrifice and could on the ground of it be just and the justifier of the ungodly, as well as bringing life and immortality to light; and (3) that on the ground of this atoning work Salvation is offered to all on the sole condition of faith. This being so, can any one for a moment believe that forgers and fable-mongers would or could have invented so divine a tale? All experience certifies the contrary.

Whensoever men have attempted to construct schemes of Salvation, they have not sought the origin of these schemes in God but in themselves. Human schemes have always been plans by which men might be able to save themselves, with such salvation as they have supposed themselves to need—not always a Salvation from sin and death; more frequently a salvation from material poverty, bodily discomfort, mental ignorance and generally temporal needs. Nor have they ever dreamt of a salvation that should come to them through the mediation of another, and certainly not of God Himself in the Person of His Son; but always of a salvation through their own efforts. Never of a Salvation by grace through faith and therefore free; but always of a Salvation by works and through merit and therefore as a debt—a Salvation by outward forms and magical rites, or by education and culture.

WHO INVENTED IT?

3. Then, it may be added: If the Christian Scheme is a fable, who invented the idea of an Incarnation? For to Jewish minds at any rate such an idea was foreign, being forbidden by their strong monotheism. Who put together the picture of Jesus as it appears in the Gospels? Who conceived the notion of making it that of a sinless man, and doing it so successfully that all subsequent generations of beholders, with a

few exceptions at most, have regarded Him as sinless? Yet a sinless man had never been seen before nor has ever been beheld since His appearance. Who supplied this Jesus with the superhuman power that performed works only possible to God, and with the superhuman wisdom that fell from His lips, if such wisdom was never spoken but only imagined? It is universally allowed that the power and wisdom of Jesus have never been surpassed or even equalled. Whose was the daring genius that struck out the notion not merely of making atonement for Sin, but of doing this by Christ's giving His life a ransom for many and demonstrating its reality through His rising from the dead? These conceptions were so incredible to His followers at the first and have been so unacceptable to natural man since that it is hard to believe any fable-monger would have selected them for his work, even though they had occurred to him. And who suggested the doctrine of a general resurrection at the end of time?—a doctrine to which unaided human science or philosophy has never been able to attain.

The impartial reasoner must perceive that in all these themes we are dealing not with purely human thoughts but with thoughts that are divine and that it is idle to talk of them as fabulous or untrue. "God is not a man that He should lie." He is neither a tyrant that He should seek to oppress men, nor a false priest that He should want to cheat men, nor a novelwriter that He should study to amuse men, but a Father whose dearest interest is to save men, who is Light and in Him is no darkness at all, and whose words are like Himself, the same yesterday, today and forever.

II. The second mark of truthfulness in the Christian Scheme is

ITS PERFECT ADAPTATION

to the end for which it was designed.

1. Assuming for the moment that the Christian System is entirely a product of the human mind, or a pure fabrication,

the question to be considered is, Whether it is at all likely that it would perfectly answer the end for which it was intended. If that end was to deceive men in order to enslave and degrade them, then its concocters have signally outwitted themselves; for no sooner does a man accept Christianity than he finds that if he is deceived thereby, it is a blessed deception which makes it impossible to keep him in subjection or degradation since it illuminates his understanding, purifies his heart, cleanses his imagination, quickens his conscience, strengthens his will and ennobles his whole nature. "Ye shall know the truth and the truth shall make you free," said Christ. On the other hand if its end was to do this very thing, then undoubtedly its end has been reached; but the mere fact that it has been reached shows that the Scheme has not proceeded from the human mind as a work of fiction, but from the heart of God as a Scripture of truth.

2. If there be one thing more characteristic of man's works than another, it is imperfection. Magnificent as some of man's inventions have been, few of them are absolutely free from defects, and those that are freest have been brought to their present state of excellence only by slow and short stages and after repeated modifications and improvements— witness the printing press, the steam engine, telegraphy, electrical power and lighting, musical instruments, aeroplanes, etc. And what is more, however perfect any human invention may appear to be at the present moment, there is no guarantee that it will not be in time superseded by something more adapted to the end it has in view.

The case, however, is different with God's works which, like Himself, are all perfect; and if it shall turn out on examination that the Christian System is perfectly adapted to the end it has in view, viz., Salvation, and has never needed to be changed, modified or improved, then the inference will be unavoidable that it is God's work and not man's, and as a consequence not a fiction but a fact, not fable but truth.

I am aware that at the present moment there are those who declare that Christianity is played out, that it has served its day, that it has lost its hold on men's minds and will require to give place to some other panacea for the ills of life. But for the most part that is the cry of those who have not themselves tried Christianity and hardly understand what it means. And in any case no effective substitute for Christianity has ever been put forward by its opponents or critics. Nor has any attempt to modify or improve Christianity as a system of religious doctrine ever been successful. Perhaps one of the most strenuous efforts in this direction has been that of so-called liberal (alias rationalistic) theology which seeks to divest Christianity of all its supernatural elements, and in particular of its divine-human Jesus by reducing Him to the dimensions of an ordinary man—in which case it is obvious, the whole superstructure of Christianity would fall to the ground. Yet a contributor to the Hibbart Journal (Jan. 1910) who himself does not accept orthodox Christianity writes of "The Collapse of Liberal Christianity," and frankly confesses that "the simple Jesus of Liberal Christianity cannot be found," which amounts to an admission that the picture of Jesus in the Gospels as a Divine Man, a supernatural Christ, is no fiction but a sublime truth.

3. A detailed examination of the Christian Scheme shows that means better fitted to secure its ends could not have been devised.

a. It will not be denied that part of the aim of Christianity is to restore mankind in general and individuals in particular to the favor and fellowship of God, out of which they have been cast by sin. Whether the Bible is right in its explanation of the origin of sin need not now be argued. Common observation as well as individual conscience testifies to the fact of sin; and the disastrous condition of the race induced by sin Christianity proposes to remedy—not by telling men that sin is only a figment of the imagination (which men know better than believe); or, if a reality, so trifling a matter that God will overlook it (which men in their best moments doubt); and certainly not by asking men to save themselves (which they soon discover they cannot do); but by first setting forth sin in all its moral loathsomeness and legal guiltiness, and then announcing that God Himself had provided a lamb for a burnt-offering, even His own Son, upon whom He has laid the iniquity of us all, and that now He is in Christ reconciling the world unto Himself, not imputing unto men their trespasses.

b. A second thing proposed by Christianity is to make men holy, to free them from the love and practice of sin, to conform them in the love and practice of truth and righteousness; and this it seeks to do by giving man a new heart and a right spirit, by changing his nature, implanting in it holy principles and putting it under the government of the divine and eternal spirit.

That the means are adequate has been proved by the experience of the past nineteen centuries, in which millions of human souls have been translated out of darkness into light and turned from the service of Satan to the service of the Living God. And what is more, other methods have been tried without effecting any permanent transformation of either hearts or lives. Magical incantations, meaningless mummeries, laborious ceremonies, painful penances, legislations, education, philanthropy, have in turn been resorted to, but in vain. Never once has the Gospel method been fairly tried and proved inefficient.

c. A third thing Christianity engages to do, is to confer on those who accept it a blessed immortality—to support them when they come to die, to cheer them with the prospect of a happy existence while their bodies are in the grave, to bring those bodies forth again and in the end to bestow on their whole personality a glorious unending life beneath a new heaven and a new earth wherein dwelleth righteousness.

And Christianity does this by first securing its adherents a title to eternal life through the obedience unto death of Christ, next by making them meet for the inheritance through the indwelling and operation of Christ's spirit, then by opening for them the gates of immortality through Christ's resurrection, and finally by Christ's coming for them at the end of the age.

Now can anything more complete be thought of as a Scheme of Salvation? Is there any part of it that is not exactly fitted to its place and suited to its end? So far is this from being the case that not a single pin can be removed from the building without bringing down the whole superstructure. Abstract from Christianity the Incarnation, or the Atonement, or the Resurrection, or the Exaltation, or the Future coming, and its framework is shattered. Take away Pardon or Purity or Peace or Sonship or Heaven, and its value as a system of religion is gone. But these are not assertions that will hold good of fables and fictions, myths and legends, which might all be tampered with, taken from or added to, without endangering their worth. Hence, it is fair to argue, that a scheme so admirably adjusted in all its parts, so complete in its provisions and so exquisitely adapted to its design, could only have emanated from the mind of Him who is wonderful in counsel and excellent in working, who is the true God and the Eternal Life.

III. A third mark of truthfulness in the Christian system is

ITS CONSPICUOUS SUCCESS

in effecting the end for which it was designed.

Had Christianity been a baseless imagination, or a superstitious legend, is there reason to suppose either that it would have lived so long or that it would have achieved the wonders it has done during the past nineteen centuries—either upon individuals or upon the world at large? It is true that mere length of time in which a religion has prevailed when considered by itself, is no sufficient guarantee of the truth of that religion, else Buddhism would possess a higher certificate of truthfulness than Christianity; but when viewed in connection with the beneficial results in elevating mankind, both individually and collectively, which have followed from a religion, the length of time during which it has continued is no small testimony to its truth. Still the practical effects of a religion upon individuals and upon the world at large, as has been said, forms an argument in its favor which cannot easily be set aside.

1. As to the INDIVIDUAL. Had the facts upon which Christianity is based been purely fictitious, had the story of the Incarnation, Death and Resurrection of Jesus been only a legend, and had the promise of pardon, purity and peace, of everlasting life and glory which Christianity holds out to men been a deception instead of a verity, does any one imagine it would have effected the transformations it has wrought on individual hearts and lives? I remember that the first lie told by the devil in Eden plunged the whole race of mankind into spiritual death. I have yet to learn that a lie hatched by even good people can save men from perdition and lift them to heaven, can bless them with inward happiness and assure them of divine favor, can comfort them in sorrow, strengthen them in weakness, sustain them in death and fit them for eternity. And yet that is what Christianity can do—has done in past ages to millions who have tried it, and is doing to-day to thousands who are trying it. It will take more than has been said by critics and scoffers to persuade me that these things have been done by a fable. I have heard of fables and fictions, legends and superstitions amusing men and women, diverting them when wearied, occupying them when idle, taking their thoughts off serious matters, and even helping them to shut their eyes against death's approach; I never heard of their bringing souls to God, assuring them of His favor,

cleansing them from sin, blessing them with peace, preparing them for eternity. But these again are what Christianity can do and does; and so I reason it is not a fable, but a fact, not a legend but a history, not an imaginary tale, but a solid truth.

2. And when to this I add what it has done on the BROAD THEATRE OF THE WORLD, my faith in its truth is confirmed. Nineteen centuries ago Christianity started out on its conquering career. It had neither wealth nor power, nor learning, nor social influence, nor imperial patronage upon its side. It was despised by the great ones of the earth as a superstition. It was looked upon by Jew and Gentile as subversive of religion and morals. Its adherents were collected from the dregs of the population, from the poor and the ignorant (at least in the world's estimation); and its apostles were a humble band, mostly of fishermen—though they soon had their ranks enlarged by the accession of one (Paul) whose mental force and religious earnestness were worth to Christianity whole battalions of common disciples or of average preachers. But what was one, even though he was an intellectual and spiritual giant, to the mighty task set before it of conquering the world and making all nations obedient to the Faith? Yet that task was immediately taken in hand and with what success the annals of the past centuries declare.

In the first century, which may be called the Apostolic Age, it practically defeated Judaism, by establishing itself as an organized religion, not in Palestine alone, but in Asia Minor, and in some of the chief cities of Europe. To this it was no doubt helped by the destruction of Jerusalem in the year 70 by the armies of Titus; but the undermining of Judaism was being gradually brought about by the spread of the Christian Faith.

In the next two centuries, which may be called the Age of the Fathers, it overcame paganism, substituting in wide circles the worship of Jesus for the worship of heathen divinities and of the Roman Emperor. Not without passing through fierce tribulation in the long succession of persecutions with which it was assailed did it achieve the victory, but in its experience was repeated the experience of Israel in Egypt—"the more it was afflicted the more it multiplied and grew," so that by the end of the third and the beginning of the fourth century it had within its pale about a fifth of the Roman Empire.

From that time on Christianity applied itself to the task of making nominal Christians into real ones; and but for the mercy of God at the Reformation it might have been defeated But God's Spirit brooded upon the moral and spiritual waste as erst He did upon the material in the beginning, and God's Word said—"Let there be light!" and there was light. Luther in Germany, Calvin in Geneva, and Knox in Scotland, with others in different parts arose as champions of the Truth and recalled men's thoughts to the simplicities and certainties of the Gospel; and a great awakening overspread the nominally Christian world.

Thereafter Christianity took a forward step among the nations; and is now doing for the world what no other religion has done or can do—neither Buddhism, nor Confucianism, nor Mohammedanism—what no modern substitute for Christianity can do—whether materialism, or agnosticism, or spiritism, or socialism; and just because of this we may rest assured that Christianity is no cunningly devised fable but a divinely revealed truth—that it alone contains hope for the world, as a whole, and for generation after generation as it passes, and that the day will yet come when it will fill the globe.

In short, when one remembers that Christianity has built up the Christian church and that the Christian church has been the most powerful factor in creating modern civilization, it becomes an impossibility to credit the allegation or even to harbor the suspicion, that it is founded on a lie. By its fruits it may be tested. Notwithstanding the imperfections that adhere to the Christian church, so far as it is a human institution, few will deny that its existence in the world has been productive of preponderatingly good results; and on that certificate alone it may be claimed that the Christianity of which the church is a concrete and living embodiment is no "cunningly devised fable" but a "Scripture of Truth."